Designing Embedded Internet Devices

Designing Embedded Internet Devices

by Dan Eisenreich
Brian DeMuth

Newnes
An imprint of Elsevier Science

Amsterdam   Boston   London   New York   Oxford   Paris
San Diego   San Francisco   Singapore   Sydney   Tokyo

Newnes is an imprint of Elsevier Science.

 Recognizing the importance of preserving what has been written, Elsevier
Science prints its books on acid-free paper whenever possible.

Library of Congress Cataloging-in-Publication Data

ISBN: 1-878707-98-1

British Library Cataloguing-in-Publication Data
A catalogue record for this book is available from the British Library.

The publisher offers special discounts on bulk orders of this book.
For information, please contact:

Manager of Special Sales
Elsevier Science
200 Wheeler Road
Burlington, MA 01803
Tel: 781-313-4700
Fax: 781-313-4882

For information on all Newnes publications available, contact our World Wide
Web home page at: http://www.newnespress.com

10 9 8 7 6 5 4 3 2 1

Printed in the United States of America

Acknowledgments

We would like to gratefully acknowledge

... the fine folks at Dallas Semiconductor for squeezing such a capable JVM on an 8-bit microcontroller.

... all of the hard work proofreading and organizing the draft for the book by the folks at Newnes (Kelly, Carol, Harry).

Dedication

Dan
To Keisha and Emily

Brian
To Linda, whose love and support made this possible.

Contents

What's on the CD-ROM?

Included on the accompanying CD-ROM:

- A directory containing all of the example programs in the book organized by chapter.
- A full searchable eBook version of the text in Adobe pdf format.
- Appendix A, providing information on TINI components and pinout
- Appendix B, a listing of `ByteUtils.java`, which is used in a number of the example programs.
- Appendix C, a compilation of simple input/output circuits that can be easily connected to various types of I/O for sensing or controlling external devices.

Each example from the book is in a separate folder that is named according to the program name and the corresponding listing number from each chapter, so the proper listing ought to be very easy to find.

To compile these listings using the supplied makefile (for linux) or build.bat (for Windows) you will need to set your environment variable as instructed in Chapter 3 of the book. Specifically, `TINI_HOME` must be set to point to the TINI API installation directory and `OW_HOME` must be set to point to the 1-wire API installation directory.

The build.bat and Makefiles included with the compile instructions for each listing assume that you are using API 1.02d or e.

On Windows/DOS, if you get an "Out of environment space" error, then you will need to increase the default environment space available for MS-DOS programs. To do this, add this line to your `config.sys` and then reboot your system:

```
SHELL=C:\COMMAND.COM C:\ /E:2048 /P
```

See http://support.microsoft.com/default.aspx?scid=kb;EN-US;q230205 for more information.

This is how we are setting the `CLASSPATH` for Windows (95/98/2000/NT/XP):

```
SET  CLASSPATH=c:\jdk1.3.1\lib\;c:\jdk1.3.1\lib\comm.jar;.
SET  OW_HOME=c:\opt\1wire
SET  CLASSPATH=%CLASSPATH%;%OW_HOME%\lib\OneWireAPI.jar
SET  TINI_HOME=c:\opt\tini1.02d
SET  CLASSPATH=%CLASSPATH%;%TINI_HOME%\bin\tini.jar;
     %TINI_HOME%\bin\tiniclasses.jar
```

This is how we are setting the CLASSPATH for Linux:

```
CLASSPATH=/usr/java/jdk1.3/lib/:
   /usr/java/jdk1.3/commapi/comm.jar OW_HOME=/opt/onewire
CLASSPATH=$CLASSPATH:$OW_HOME/lib/OneWireAPI.jar.
TINI_HOME=/opt/tini
CLASSPATH=$CLASSPATH:$TINI_HOME/bin/tini.jar:
    $TINI_HOME/bin/tiniclasses.jar
export TINI_HOME OW_HOME CLASSPATH
```

## CHAPTER 1

Introduction

Why should you read this book?

The target audience of this book is anyone interested in merging practical electronic devices with the Internet: students, teachers, home automation enthusiasts, hobbyists, and small businesses. Computer programmers looking for a gentle introduction to the world of hardware will benefit, as will hardware designers looking to expand their skills into the realm of JAVA programming. College engineering and computer science departments will find in this book a wealth of possibilities for lab projects that expose students to cutting-edge technology with minimal expense. Why should you read this book? The best reason of all: fun. This book will provide anyone interested in tinkering with hardware on the net hours of fun. Another reason: the future. Even if you're not interested in making hardware, this book will give you a practical glimpse into what the real future and potential of the Internet is.

The first Internet wave connected people via computer, popularizing things such as email, search engines, and online shopping. The next wave is going to be Internet appliances: electronic devices connected to the Internet. Ever wondered how those "live internet cams" work? They're probably the most recognizable example of hardware connected to the web. In the past they were tremendously expensive and tended to be supported by engineering departments as an experimental thing. The future is going to see a tremendous expansion of low-cost, practical devices, connected to the Internet for home use.

A good example might be a future VCR. Have you ever found yourself at work, wishing you had set the VCR to program your favorite show? A VCR that was an Internet appliance would give you the capability of programming your VCR from a web page, wherever you may be. Another good example of an Internet appliance might be a piece of hardware that allows you to control your thermostat, your lights, and your water heater from a web site. Cheap Internet appliance technology will make controlling devices in your home from a web page commonplace. Will everything in your house be "on the web" in the future? Probably not. But the growing number of people with Internet on their desk and the proliferation of cell phones and PDAs that can interact with web pages represents a growing market. That market is raising the attention of countless companies both large and small, looking to make products to put into every home. This book will examine commercial technology, discussing in great detail an inexpensive web-enabled microcontroller that can be used to connect a variety of devices to the web.

Why should you read this book? So when the next big Internet wave happens, you'll be in front of it! (And, there is that fun thing, too.)

What this book will do for you

This book is a complete introduction to Internet-enabled devices. We provide all of the information you need to inexpensively build your own web-enabled hardware. Specifically, we'll show you:

1. The basic terms and concepts required to understand the technology of web-enabled devices. This includes detailed sections on networking and Java programming.

2. A quick overview of commercially available, web-enabled, microcontrollers, comparing their price and availability.

3. A step-by-step examination of TINI[1], the Tiny InterNet Interface, a commercially available hardware/software package designed for use as a web interface to hardware. We'll examine the hardware, software, and available enhancements in detail.

How this book is laid out

The information in this book is divided into 14 chapters.

Chapters 1 through 4 provide basic technical definitions with respect to networking and Internet clients and servers. We're going to go into some detail on Java, the modern object-oriented, internet-ready, programming language rapidly becoming the language of choice for network applications. We're not going to teach you Java, but we are going to cover some of the key features of the language that are very relevant to our topic, and are frequently not taught in the average Java course.

---

[1] TINI is a registered trademark of Dallas Semiconductor. TINI can be purchased on the iButton website, http://www.ibutton.com/TINI/

Chapters 5 through 8 discuss, in great detail, the hardware and software behind TINI, Dallas Semiconductor's commercially available, web-enabled microcontroller. This will include a high-level discussion of how the system works and an explanation of how to obtain and set up the hardware and software on your own Windows or Linux PC. Following that, we'll present an indepth discussion of the TINI hardware. We're going to explain what it is and how it works. Then, in a similar fashion, we're going to take apart the TINI software. Finally, with detailed technical discussions of the TINI hardware and software as background, we'll present detailed sections on how to upgrade the TINI hardware.

Chapters 9 through 12 consist of detailed technical discussions of the various I/O busses provided by TINI. These include 1-Wire, CAN, I²C, and standard serial and parallel ports. Every topic is profusely illustrated, and filled with examples.

Chapter 13 discusses how to connect TINI to a network, including how to attach a modem to TINI. This allows you to dial-in to TINI and have it act as a PPP server, or dial-out to an Internet service provider (ISP) allowing PPP clients to run on TINI.

Finally, Chapter 14 provides a summary.

How to get the most out of this book

Our book is not a novel, requiring cover-to-cover reading; rather, it's a combination technology intro, how-to guide, and reference manual. What one needs to read, and how to get the most out of that reading, depends on who you are and what your goals are.

1. For those who are simply curious about how web-enabled devices might be implemented, chapters 1, 2, 4, and 5 should be read. They will give the necessary background and technical depth. Chapters 10, 11, and 12 can be skimmed to provide additional information on the breadth of devices that can be connected to a web-enabled device.

2. For those who are unfamiliar with microcontrollers but plan on implementing a web-enabled device of some sort, chapters 1 through 7 should be read. There's enough information there to get you up and running. The remaining chapters can be skimmed to provide technical ideas, and serve as an excellent reference.

3. For those who are familiar with TINI, chapters 6 through 13 are an excellent reference.

What you should already know

While you don't have to be an engineer or computer scientist to have a lot of fun with this book, there are a few prerequisites. First, we assume that you understand basic electronics such as how to read circuit diagrams and how to use a soldering iron to build simple electronic circuits. Lastly, but most importantly, we assume basic knowledge of the Java programming language. We're going to provide detailed explanations of how to get and install the Java language for your Windows or Linux computer, as well as how to obtain the appropriate technology-specific software and class libraries. We do this to provide a solid foundation on which to build our later examples. We're going to explain in detail the Java examples we provide. But our book isn't going to teach you Java. If you're unfamiliar with Java, you may want to consider the following references.

1. Java 2 Platform, Standard Edition, v 1.3 API Specification.
   http://java.sun.com/j2se/1.3/docs/api/index.html

2. Campione, Mary and Walrath, Kathy.
   The Java Tutorial Second Edition: Object-Oriented Programming for the Internet,
   http://web2.java.sun.com/docs/books/tutorial/.
   Addison-Wesley, 1998.

3. Flanagan, David.
   Java in a Nutshell: A Desktop Quick Reference,
   O'Reilly & Associates, 1999.

4. Flanagan, David.
   Java Examples in a Nutshell,
   O'Reilly & Associates, 1999.

5. Wu, C. Thomas.
   An Introduction to Object Oriented Programming with Java,
   McGraw Hill College Div, 1998.

We hope you enjoy this book.

## CHAPTER 2

Computer Networks

Since this book is about designing network-enabled devices, it probably makes some sense to start with a little discussion about networks. This is not a substitute for a complete lesson in building computer networks, but just enough to establish some terms and common ground to get you through this book. Throughout this book we'll be talking primarily about 10base-T Ethernet networks using the TCP/IP protocols (there are many other ways to network computers together that are far beyond the scope of this book; see the reference section at the end of the chapter).

Network Hardware

So what is a computer network? A network is a collection (two or more) of computers that are connected together for sharing data and resources. Networks are commonly categorized by their geographical size. A **local area network** (a LAN) is a group of computers and associated devices that share a common communication line and are typically located within a small geographic area, such as in your home or in an office building, or even a single department in a company. A local area network may connect as few as two or three users, as in a home network, or as many as several hundred users, as in a business. A **metropolitan area network** (a MAN) is a bit more diverse, incorporating computers and LANs that are distributed over a few miles of area, as you would find between corporate buildings or on a college campus. A **wide area network** (a WAN) is a widely geographically dispersed computer network that is composed of multiple LANs and MANs and can be spread across a country or around the globe. The **Internet** (sometimes simply referred to as "the Net") is a worldwide network of many computer networks (LANs, MANs, and WANs) that is accessible to hundreds of millions of people worldwide.

A really simple network

Connecting two computers together forms the simplest computer network, as shown in Figure 2-1. The computers, often referred to as **hosts** or **nodes** on a network, are connected to the network through a **network interface card** (NIC). The network interface is a computer circuit board or card (or sometimes a single integrated circuit) that provides the logic for sending and receiving data from and to the host computer. There are a number of ways to connect these computers but by far the most common way is by using an Ethernet connection.

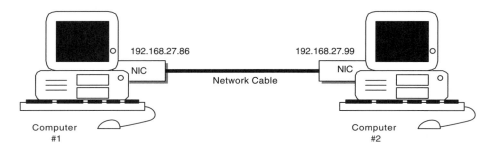

Figure 2-1: A really simple computer network

Ethernet is the most widely used local area network technology these days, particularly for home networks and small offices. It is fully described and specified in IEEE standard 802.3 (if knowing that sort of thing is important to you). The most commonly installed Ethernet system is called 10BASE-T and provides transmission speeds up to 10 Mbps. The designation **10BASE-T** is a shorthand identifier: The "10" in the media type designation refers to the transmission speed of 10 Mbps, the "BASE" refers to baseband signaling (not broadband), which simply means that only a single Ethernet signal set is carried on the cable, and the "T" represents twisted-pair. The reason we even mention this is because other types of Ethernet are becoming more popular like 100BASE-T (100 mbps) and 100BASE-F ("F" for fiber) but for this book we are only really concerned with 10Base-T and 100 Base-T (often printed as 10/100Base-T).

Another thing we need to note about this simple network of two computers is the cable directly connecting the two computers, commonly called a **crossover cable**. A crossover cable is a special type of Ethernet cable that is used to interconnect two computers by "crossing over" (reversing) their respective pin contacts for transmitted and received data. It allows the data transmitted by one computer to be connected to the receiving pin on the other and vice-versa. While this may seem like a trivial point, it is important to know that this is a crossover cable and what it does.

One last thing: each node in the network has a unique address, its network address. This is not a big deal with a simple network of two computers but as the networks expand and LANs are connected to other LANs and WANs, this is increasingly important. We will talk more about this address in a subsequent section.

A small office and home network

Connecting multiple computers together to form a home or small office network is almost as simple as the previous two-computer network, just involving a few more components. Refer to Figure 2-2 for a slightly more complex network configuration.

The first thing you will notice is the use of a **network hub**, usually simply called a

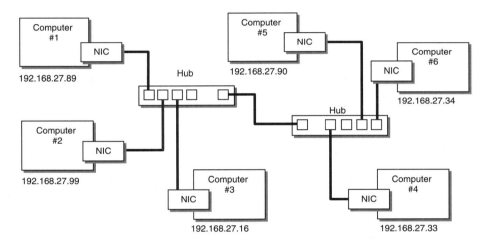

Figure 2-2: A complex network

hub. A hub is a connector where network data arrives from one or more directions and is forwarded out in all of the other directions. Each of the computers in our network is connected to the network through a hub. Internal to the hub, the transmit wires from one computer are connected to the receive wires of the others; in others words the hub also performs the crossover function that the crossover cable did in the two-computer network. So this network is connected with network cables that are "straight through." The wires on pin 1 through 8 are connected to pins 1 through 8 on the opposite end, with no crossover. Hubs are connected to each other through an uplink port. The **uplink port** is similar to an ordinary port but the wires have not internally been reversed so it can be connected to another hub to increase the number of nodes in your network. If the hub does not have an uplink port then hubs can be connected to each other with a crossover cable.

Again, notice that each node in the network has a unique address, its network address. We will talk more about this address in a subsequent section.

Connecting a LAN to the Internet (or a LAN, MAN, WAN)

Broadband connection

Now that we have our local area network as discussed above, how would we then connect this to other networks, either another LAN or a WAN or even the Internet? This is done with a wide variety of network devices. Some of these are:

- Hub – A hub is the generic name for a device where several nodes are connected to a network. A hub may be a repeater, switch, or a router. A hub may perform the function of several of these components.

- Gateway – A gateway is a generic name for a device that is used to connect multiple networks together. A gateway may be a repeater, bridge or router.

- Repeater – A repeater is a network hub that serves as a connection between 2 segments of a network. Repeaters only amplify all information they receive and pass it through to all of its ports.

- Router – A router is a smart hub, which can connect segments of different networks that use a different protocol.

- Switch – A switch is a network hub that acts like a repeater but instead of passing information on to all of its ports, it establishes a direct connection to the destination port.

- Bridge – A bridge is a device for connecting segments of a network or multiple networks that use the same protocol.

All of these devices are somewhat similar—in fact, the functions of several are often combined in one device. We will connect our LAN to the Internet with one of these generic network gateway devices. There are several types of gateways: repeaters, bridges, and routers. The technical distinction between these components is based on which layer of the Internet Protocol they operate on and that is really beyond the scope of this chapter. We will then connect our gateway to a modem. A modem (and there are many types of modems) can also act as a gateway from a LAN to a WAN but are usually separate devices. The modem modulates outgoing digital signals from a computer or other digital device to analog signals suitable for transmission on conventional telephone lines, cable TV coax, Digital Subscriber Line (DSL) or fiber and then demodulates the incoming analog signal and converts it to a digital signal. This is the type of gateway shown in the following network, Figure 2-3.

This LAN could also be connected to another LAN or WAN with a simple hub or gateway without the modem. But if we opt for the hub, then this would not keep this

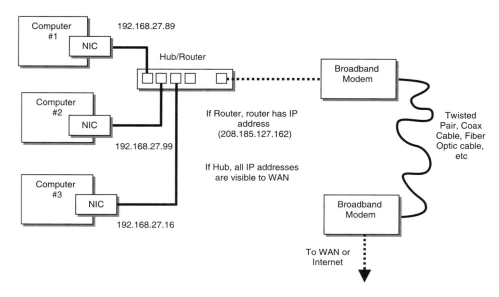

Figure 2-3: Broadband network

local area network as a separate network. This network would then be a part of the larger WAN. The hub passes all data from its input to all of the lines on the network. This is one of the reasons for creating smaller networks or sub-networks—to isolate data transmission between computers.

Alternate broadband connection

An alternate way to connect a simple network is to use a computer with two network interface cards as shown in Figure 2-4. In essence, this computer (and appropriate software) acts as the gateway and router for your local area network. It is important to note that one NIC has a network address that is known only to the WAN or Internet and the other NIC has a network address that is known only to the LAN. These addresses can be either static or dynamically allocated. This would allow you to use static IP addresses on your LAN and connect to your ISP with static or dynamic addresses. Windows 98 Second Edition directly supports multiple NICs and Internet sharing, and there are numerous software packages that can add this function to either Windows or Linux.

Dial up connection

A final alternative for connecting your LAN to a WAN or Internet is the use of a PPP connection through a dial-up modem. This is shown in Figure 2-5. **Point-to-Point Protocol** (PPP) is a protocol for communication between two computers using a serial interface, typically a personal computer connected by phone line to a service provider. But this can be as simple as a serial line with no modem. Essentially, it packages your computer's TCP/IP packets and forwards them to the server.

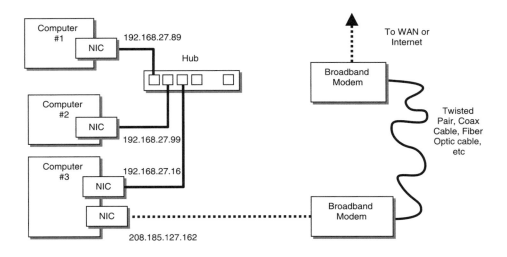

Figure 2-4: Alternate broadband network

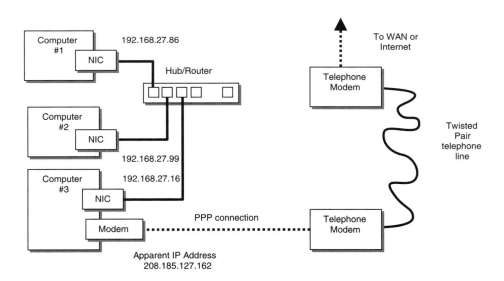

Figure 2-5: PPP network connection

The 10/100 Base-T cable

Ethernet uses a special type of cable called twisted pair. **Twisted pair** cable is made of four pairs (in this case) of insulated copper wires that are twisted around each other in pairs to reduce electromagnetic induction between pairs of wires. The combination of these four sets of twisted wires forms a network cable that is commonly referred to as **Category-5** or **CAT 5** cable. It derives that name from the American National Standards Institute/Electronic Industries Association (ANSI/EIA) Standard 568, in which this cable is specified. That same specification lists several standards that specify categories of twisted pair cabling systems (wires and connectors) in terms of the maximum data rates that they can reliably sustain. This specification describes the cable material as well as the types of connectors and junction blocks to be used in order to conform to a particular category. CAT5 cable is different from the wire you buy at your local hardware store for connecting your phone or computer modems to a wall jack, which is not twisted pair, but is a side-by-side wire also known as *silver satin*.

The two most popular specifications are CAT 3 and CAT 5. While the two cables may look identical, CAT 3 is intended for a lower data rate and can cause transmission errors if used for faster speeds. CAT 3 cabling is for signals that are 16 MHz or less and is suitable for 10base-T networks, while CAT 5 cable must pass a 100-MHz test to be suitable for 100base-T networks.

The connector on a 10/100 BASE-T cable is an RJ45, which is short for Registered Jack-45. This is an eight-pin connector that is commonly used for network cables, especially Ethernet. The RJ-45 connectors look very much like the modular connectors

Table 2-1: Network cable wire categories

Category	Maximum Data Rate	Typical Applications
CAT 1	< 1 Mbps	Voice telephone service Integrated Services Digital Network (ISDN)
CAT 2	4 Mbps	
CAT 3	16 Mbps	10Base-T Ethernet
CAT 4	20 Mbps	
CAT 5	100 Mbps	100Base-T Ethernet
CAT5e	100 Mbps	100Base-T Ethernet with improved transmission
CAT6	250 Mbps	Proposed Standard
CAT7	600 Mbps	Proposed Standard

on modern telephones (RJ-11), but they are somewhat wider as they have eight wires in them. There are many, many types of RJ style connectors and they vary widely.

Since we have talked about twisted pair cable and all that, perhaps it would make sense if we also discussed the detail of the Ethernet cable (the wire colors/order) and crossover cable so you can wire up your network. Essentially, the difference between 10Base-T and 100Base-T is the data rate. In Table 2-1 we can see that 10base-T needs at least a CAT3 cable to support the 10 mbps data rate error free and 100Base-T needs CAT5 wire. If you are wiring up a new network it is probably better to make it with CAT5 and wire it for 100 mbps, even if you are going to use it for 10Base-T communications. It will work just fine for 10 mbps and it's ready to upgrade to 100Base-T. It's also easier to find CAT5 cable and it is not noticeably more expensive. If you use CAT3 cable for a 10Base-T, when you upgrade you will need new wires and you run the risk of getting all of your 10-mbps wiring confused with 100-mbps wire—and you'll just have a great big mess on your hands.

Shown in Figure 2-6 is the wiring for a straight-through (not a crossover) cable that is more typical for network connections. The wire color order is the same for both ends of the cable.

Figure 2-6: 10/100Base-T Straight-through cable

Shown in Figure 2-7 is the wiring for the crossover cable that we used for our simple two-node network above. You will notice that the wire color order is not the same for both ends of this cable. You should carefully label or mark your crossover cables so that they are not easily confused with straight-through cables. I make mine from a different color cable so that they are immediately obvious.

Figure 2-7: 10/100Base-T Crossover cable

Table 2-2 lists the wire colors and pin numbers for both straight-through and cross-over cables. You may find reference to that fact that only pins 1, 2, 3 and 6 are used in 10/100 Base-T network cables. This is generally true but there are some networks like 100Base-T4 that use the remaining wires, and faster networks like 1000Base-T also use all four pairs and are capable of supporting error-free transmission using CAT5e cable ("e" means "enhanced" for lower crosstalk between the conductors of the neighboring twisted pairs in the same cable). If you completely wire the connector, you will maximize the usefulness of your cables by allowing them to be used in many possible network configurations.

Table 2-2: 10/100 Base-T cable wire color code

Straight-through Cable (Both Ends)	Crossover Cable (One End)
1 – White/Orange	1 – White/Green
2 – Orange	2 – Green
3 – White/Green	3 – White/Orange
4 – Blue	4 – Blue
5 – White/Blue	5 – White/Blue
6 – Green	6 – Orange
7 – White/Brown	7 – White/Brown
8 – Brown	8 – Brown

Network Addresses

Each computer or node in a network really has two addresses. Actually, each interface in a computer or node has two addresses, as a single computer (or any network device) can have multiple network interfaces. These addresses are the **Internet Address** and the **Ethernet address**. The Ethernet address is a hardware address that identifies this specific network interface. The Internet address is a logical address that provides routing information so other computers on the network can find it.

Ethernet address

An Ethernet hardware address is also known as the Media Access Control (MAC) Address. This is a 12-digit hexadecimal (0-9, A-F) number that uniquely identifies your (and every other) Ethernet adapter. Manufacturers are assigned Ethernet address blocks to use, and they are used to identify each machine on the network. Ethernet addresses are usually shown as bytes separated by a colon or a dash, like this:

```
00:06:35:00:6B:BF    or    00-06-35-00-6B-BF
```

The Ethernet address is always exactly 12 hexadecimal digits, so all leading zeroes are significant and must be entered. Since this address is a physical address it is programmed into the network interface card and generally cannot be changed, while the Internet Address is a logical address and can be reassigned as needed. Also, there is no direct correlation between the Ethernet and Internet address and one cannot be calculated based on the other. Ethernet addresses are unique and never reused, unlike an Internet address that can be used on sub-networks and isolated networks. For the scope of this book it is not necessary to know more detail about the Ethernet address.

Internet addresses

The Internet Address is also called an **IP address** or **Host Address**. It is a logical address assigned to the network interface card in your computer. An IP address (where IP means Internet Protocol) is how one computer can find another computer on a network. Each node must know its own address on the network and that of any other computer with which it will communicate. The IP address is a 32-bit binary number that identifies each packet of information sent across the network. The IP address is usually expressed as four decimal numbers, each representing eight bits, separated by periods. This is sometimes known as the "dot address" or as "dotted quad notation." For instance, in the example network shown in Figure 2-2, address 192.168.27.16 is the IP address of one of the machines. This is internally stored and used as the integer 3,232,242,448 which is 11000000.10101000.00011011.00010000. This can be represented in decimal numbers as shown:

```
1100 0000 . 1010 1000 . 0001 1011 . 0001 0000
   192    .    168    .     27    .     16
```

Domain names

The numerical version of the IP address is usually represented by a name or series of names called the **domain name**—for instance, www.someplace.com or ftp. filearchive.edu, which is mapped into a static IP address using the **Domain Name System** (**DNS**). The DNS is a hierarchical database used for translating the domain name to an IP address. When your computer needs to translate a domain name into a numerical IP address, it asks a domain name server to provide this information.

Network classes

The original Internet Protocol defines IP addresses in five major classes of address structure, Classes A through E. This has been named **classful routing** (probably in hindsight considering some of the improvements made to IP addressing that we will get to in a minute). Each of these classes allocates one portion of the 32-bit Internet address format to a network address and the remaining portion to the specific host machines within the network specified by the address. Class E is reserved for experimental use. Class D addresses are used for multicasting. Multicasting is data transmission between a single sender and multiple receivers on a network.

Class A networks use the 8 leftmost bits (the leftmost of the dotted quads) to designate the network number. The leftmost bit of these 8 bits is always 0, so Class A IP addresses range from 0.x.x.x to 127.x.x.x, except that address 0.x.x.x and 127.x.x.x are reserved for special use so this means there are 126 possible Class A networks. The rest of the dotted quads refer to the specific hosts or nodes on a large network. Since there are 24 bits in the remaining address, this means there can be 2^{24} possible hosts in each class A network, except that the all 0's case is reserved and means "this network" and the all 1's case is used for broadcasting, which leaves 16,777,214 possible hosts. So, a portion of the IP address represents the network number or address and a portion represents the local machine address.

Class B networks use the 16 leftmost bits (the leftmost two dotted quads) to designate the network number. The leftmost two of these 16 bits are always 10 so Class B addresses range from 128.0.x.x to 191.255.x.x, which means there are 16,384 possible Class B networks. The remaining two dotted quads (16 bits) refer to specific hosts or nodes on these networks. These 16 bits means there are 2^{16} possible hosts in each Class B network, except that the all 0's case is reserved and means "this network" and the all 1's case is used for broadcasting, which leaves 65,534 possible hosts. Using the above example, here's how the IP address is divided:

```
155.185 . 127.162
Network   Host
Address   Address
```

Class C networks use the 24 leftmost bits (the leftmost three dotted quads) to designate the network number. The leftmost three of these 24 bits are always 110 so Class C addresses range from 192.0.0.x to 223.255.255.x, which means there are 2,097,152 possible Class C networks. The remaining 8 bits (the right most dotted quad) refers to the specific hosts or nodes on each of these networks. These 8 bits means that there are 2^8 possible hosts in each class C network or 254 possible hosts (256 minus the all 0's and all 1's case as in the Class A and B networks). In the class C network the addresses from 192.168.0.0 to 192.168.255.0 are reserved for networks not directly connected to the Internet.

If you are really curious, you can look up the addresses in the different classes and see who they are assigned to on the "IP Network Index"[1] web page.

Not considering all of the reserved addresses in class A, B and C, there are 2^{23} or 4,294,967,296 possible IP addresses. While this might seem like a lot of addresses, many were not being used by the Class A address owners and with the rapid growth of broadband users and dedicated network devices, it turns out this is not enough addresses to support the future growth of the Internet. To overcome this limited

---

[1] IP Network Index, http://ipindex.dragonstar.net/

address space, a number of fixes have been devised, such as Subnetworking and Classless Inter-Domain Routing.

Subnetworks

A **subnetwork** is a logically separate portion of a larger network. It is a way of taking a single network address and splitting it so that a single network address can be used on several local networks. While not 100% technically accurate, it is kind of like splitting a class A or B network into smaller networks (or subnetworks). If you wanted to a add subnet to the sample address above, then some portion of the host address could be used for a subnet address. A company with a Class B address who needed more than 254 host machines, but far fewer than the 65,533 host addresses possible, would essentially be "wasting" most of the block of addresses allocated. That company could use several subnets and the remaining could be allocated to another company. A class A network address could be subnetted by allocating the second and maybe even the third dotted quad for a subnet address. A class B network address could be subnetted by allocating the third dotted quad for the subnet address as shown in this example:

```
        155.185   .   127   .   162
        Network       Subnet     Host
        Address       Address    Address
```

To determine which part of the IP address was the host address and which was the subnet address, the IP address was paired with a subnet mask. This mask was used to separate the extended-network prefix (the network address and the subnet address) from the host address (logically ANDing the address and the subnet mask returns just the extended network prefix). With this technique, each of the quads of the subnet mask was either all binary 1's or all 0's (255 or 0).

```
IP address    155.185.127.162      10011011.10111001.11111111.10100010
Subnet mask   255.255.255.0        11111111.11111111.11111111.00000000
                                   Extended Network Prefix     Host
                                                               Number
```

Classless Inter-Domain Routing (CIDR) was developed to effectively solve some of the problems with classful routing and some of the limitations of subnetting and extended network prefix by providing a new and more flexible way to specify network addresses in routers.

CIDR uses a variable-length subnet mask that does not necessarily have to be divided on any of the whole byte boundaries of the dotted quads. CIDR essentially eliminates classful routing (class A, B, D networks) by allowing the subnet mask to be any size. With CIDR a network address might look like this:

```
IP address    155.185.127.162    10011011.10111001.11111111.10100010
Subnet mask   255.255.248.0      11111111.11111111.11111000.00000000
                                 Extended Network Prefix   Host
                                                           Number
```

This could also be specified by simply saying how many bits were 1's. In the example above, this is 21. So a CIDR address is also shown like this.

```
155.185.127.162/21
```

The "155.185.127.162" is the network address and the "21" means that the first 21 bits are the network part of the address, leaving the last 11 bits for the host addresses.

There are also a number of other benefits of CIDR supporting route aggregation, which greatly simplifies network router routing tables.

DHCP

So far, our IP address discussion above assumes that IP addresses are assigned on a static basis, that you get a specific address for each node in your network and things stay that way. **Dynamic Host Configuration Protocol (DHCP)** is a protocol that lets a network automatically assign an IP address to each node in a network as it is connected to the network. With the growing number of Internet users these days, many IP addresses are assigned dynamically from a pool of allocated address. This lets many corporate networks and online services economize on the number of IP addresses they use by sharing the pool of IP addresses with a large number of users. This is very often the case if you use a dial-up TCP/IP connection. Here your IP address will vary from one login session to the next because it is assigned to you from a pool that is much smaller than the total number of users. DHCP lets a network administrator supervise and distribute IP addresses from a central point and automatically sends a new IP address when a computer is plugged into a different place in the network.

Understanding IP addressing thoroughly could certainly take up this entire book and that's not the point of this book. If you need to know more about IP addressing you are encouraged to read some of the material listed in the reference section of the chapter.

Network Communication

We now turn our attention to the inner workings of TCP/IP, mostly because we will need it when we talk about sockets and some of the different protocols later on in the book. TCP/IP is named after the most commonly used protocols in the Internet Protocol set:

- TCP = Transmission Control Protocol
- IP = Internet Protocol

TCP/IP is the basic communication language or protocol of the Internet. It can also be used as a communications protocol in a private network (either an intranet or an extranet). TCP/IP is a two-layer protocol. The higher layer, Transmission Control Protocol, manages the assembling of a message or file into smaller packets (see packet) that are transmitted over the Internet and received by a TCP layer that reassembles the packets into the original message. The lower layer, Internet Protocol, handles the address part of each packet so that it gets to the right destination. Each gateway computer on the network checks this address to see where to forward the message. Even though some packets from the same message are routed differently than others, they'll be reassembled at the destination.

Protocols

Discussions of network communications often center on what is known as a **protocol stack**. A **protocol** is the set of rules that computers (or other network devices) in a network use when they communicate. In essence, a protocol is the language the network devices use to talk to each other. A protocol stack is an abstract model that divides the network up into layers, based on functions and communication protocols used in those functions. Each layer in the stack only talks to the layer above or below it, using the protocols defined in those layers. As information is passed down the stack, it is encapsulated. **Encapsulation** is basically a process of adding a protocol specific header to the information received from the layer above. As information is passed up the stack, the header specific to the current layer is stripped off and the data is sent to the layer above. By adhering to this protocol stack concept, software and hardware can be designed without worrying about the details of what's going on in all the layers, just the neighboring layers. Things become reusable, transportable, device independent.

The **OSI** (Open Systems Interconnection) **reference model** is an ideal protocol stack of sorts. You will see this model in most discussions and textbooks on network protocols. Its purpose is to guide software developers and hardware designers so that their products will consistently work with other products. The reference model defines seven layers of functions that take place at each end of a communication. Although OSI is not always strictly adhered to in terms of keeping related functions together in a well-defined layer, many if not most products involved in telecommunications make an attempt to describe them in relation to the OSI model. The software and hardware that furnishes these seven layers of functions are usually a combination of the computer operating system, applications (such as your Web browser), TCP/IP or alternative transport and network protocols, and the software and hardware that enable you to put a signal on one of the lines attached to your computer. The OSI reference model is shown in Figure 2-8 and each layer is described below.

- **The application layer** is where common services of the operating system are offered to all applications. This layer is *not* the application itself, although some applications may perform application layer functions.)

- **The presentation layer** is usually the part of an operating system that converts incoming and outgoing data from one format to another (for example, from a text stream into a popup window with the newly arrived text). This is sometimes called the syntax layer. Compression/decompression and encryption/decryption are performed in this layer.

- **The session layer** initiates, coordinates, synchronizes and terminates conversations and exchanges between the applications at each end. It deals with session and connection coordination.

- **The transport layer** manages the transmission of messages, determining whether all packets have arrived, and checks for errors.

- **The network layer** handles the routing and forwarding of the data on the network.

- **The data-link layer** is the layer that provides synchronization for the physical level. It provides data transmission protocol knowledge and management.

- **The physical layer** conveys the data stream through the network at the electrical and mechanical level.

What is essential about TCP/IP is that it is a layered protocol that loosely follows this OSI Reference model. Each layer adds information onto the previous layers without modifying the contents of the previous layer. TCP/IP is actually (some will argue this point) implemented in four layers as shown in Figure 2-8.

At the top of this stack is the application layer. It is so named because it is at this highest level where we run user applications such as web browsers, Telnet, and FTP programs. The communications protocols associated with the application layer are the related HTTP, Telnet and FTP protocols specific to those applications. At the bottom of the stack is hardware, requiring vendor-specific device drivers. In between are the transport, network and link layers. Each is designed to introduce another level of modularity from top to bottom. Our discussion is going to focus on the transport layer.

The transport layer uses communication protocols such as TCP (transport control protocol) and UDP (user datagram protocol) to encapsulate data in the various application layer protocols and forward it to the Internet layer for encapsulation into the Internet Protocol. TCP is considered a connection based protocol, because when two entities communicate using TCP, there is guaranteed receipt of the information, or errors are reported. UDP is not a connection-based protocol. Packets of data are sent and there is no acknowledgement of receipt of data.

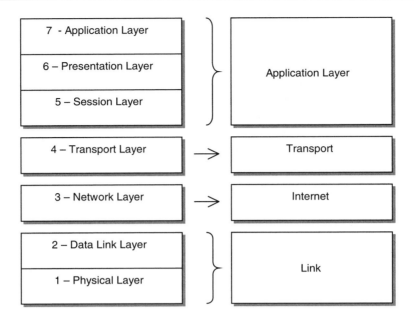

Figure 2-8: TCP/IP protocols

Part of the application layer has some very useful functions that we will make extensive use of throughout this book: Telnet, HTTP, FTP and SMTP.

- **Telnet** is the way to access another computer on a network. Telnet is both a user application and an underlying TCP/IP protocol for accessing remote computers.

- **Hypertext Transfer Protocol** (HTTP) is the set of rules for exchanging multimedia files (text, graphic images, sound, video) on the World Wide Web. A web server delivers files to your web browser using the HTTP protocol.

- **Simple Mail Transfer Protocol** (SMTP) is a TCP/IP protocol used for sending and receiving e-mail messages.

- **File Transfer Protocol** (FTP) is the simple protocol for exchanging files between computers on a network.

Client/server

All of the above listed protocols (Telnet, FTP, HTTP, SMTP) are used in a client/ server relationship.

In the computing sense, a **client** is a program or computer that is requesting information (data) or a service from another program or another computer. A web browser is the most commonly recognized client these days. A **server** is a computer or program (the term can apply to either) that provides information or services to other computer programs on the same computer or to another computer in a network. A web server is a common example. The client/server relationship describes the relationship between two computer programs in which one program, the client, makes a service request from another program, the server, which fulfills the request. There are many, many types of clients and servers, each specializing in receiving and processing or storing and distributing a certain king of information.

Ports and Sockets

The means by which these client/server computers communicate over the network is through **sockets**, and the language they speak are **protocols** (more on those in the next section).

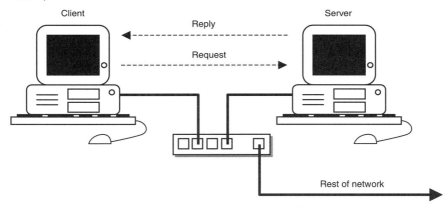

Figure 2-9: Client/server

A socket is a *logical* connection for computer applications to pass information back and forth between networked computers. In a similar fashion, a serial port is a *physical* connection for passing information between a computer and a peripheral device. A socket is one endpoint of a two-way communication link between two programs running on the network. Two-way communication over the Internet is typically performed by client-server pairs. A server creates a socket that can listen for connection requests from clients. When a client creates a socket, a connection request is made. The mechanism that associates a specific client socket to a specific server socket is a port. A **port** is a 16-bit number typically associated with a particular application layer service such as web browsing (the HTTP protocol), Telnet, or FTP.

Client/server communication proceeds as follows. A server creates a special server socket that is associated with, or *binds*, to a specific port number. It then listens for client requests for connections to that port. When a client wants to communicate with the service offered the server, it creates a socket to that port. The server accepts the connection and responds with information.

Port numbers 1-1023 are reserved and correspond to pre-defined services such as email, web pages, Telnet, FTP, ping, finger, time, etc. Table 2-3 lists port numbers and services for some well-known ports. Use these port numbers with caution! Unless you are trying to write programs to communicate with these predefined services, choose a port number 1024 or higher.

Table 2-3: Some common ports

Port	Service
7	Echo
13	Daytime
20	FTP Data
21	FTP Control
23	Telnet
25	SNMP
53	DNS
70	Gopher
79	Finger
80	http
119	NNTP

A very detailed (and long) list of port assignments can be found on the "Assigned Port Numbers"[2] page and also in RFC1700. Port numbers 1024 –65,535 are available for use in your own programs to form custom services.

Summary

So now you have a nice quick overview of networks. This really was not intended to be a complete lesson in building computer networks; in fact, we have just barely scraped the surface. Hopefully, however, you now have enough information to successfully complete the projects in the rest of this book and the background to understand them. We would encourage you to examine some of the references listed next if you need more information or are just curious.

References

1.   Charles Spurgeon's Ethernet Web Site.
     http://wwwhost.ots.utexas.edu/ethernet/

---

[2] Assigned Numbers, http://www.isi.edu/in-notes/iana/assignments/port-numbers

2. Configuring the DNS Service.
   http://www.cisco.com/univercd/cc/td/doc/product/iaabu/cddm/cddm111/
   adguide/dns.htm

3. TechFest Ethernet Technical Summary.
   http://www.techfest.com/networking/lan/ethernet.htm

4. Bennett, Geoff.
   Designing TCP/IP Networks.
   Van Nostrand Reinhold, 1995

5. Semeria, Chuck.
   Understanding IP Addresses: Everything You Ever Wanted To Know.
   3Com Corporation, April 26, 1996.
   http://www.3com.com/nsc/501302.html

6. A Request for Comments (RFC) is a document written by the Internet
   Engineering Task Force. These are the result of a committee drafting and
   subsequently reviewed by interested parties. Some become Internet standards, however, through subsequent RFCs that supercede an existing RFC.
   You can view the RFCs online in a number of places; one of the more
   complete is "Internet RFC/STD/FYI/BCP Archives,"
   http://www.faqs.org/rfcs/

   These are some common RFCs that you might want to know about if you are
   working on a project that uses a specific protocol for communication:

   - 791 = IP
   - 1700 = Assigned numbers
   - 1920 = Telnet
   - 959 = FTP
   - 977 = NNTP

## CHAPTER 3

Java Essentials for Embedded Networked Devices

Throughout this book, we will be using Java[1] as the language of choice for controlling our network-enabled devices. In this chapter, we will discuss getting the Java Development Kit (JDK version 1.3) and the Java runtime environment up and running on your computer, for both Microsoft Windows[2] and Linux. If you already have Java installed, and are familiar with programming in Java, then you can probably skip this chapter (or just skim through it so you know what's here).

The Java Development Kit

Java is distributed by Sun Microsystems in the form of the Software Development Kit (SDK). The SDK includes the Java compiler, Java debugger, a number of development tools, and the Java Runtime Environment (JRE). The JRE consists of the Java virtual machine, the Java platform core classes, and supporting files. Along with the base Java classes, we will be using a number of the Application Programming Interfaces (API). An API is the interface through which an application program accesses the operating system and other services. In other words, an API is like a library of subroutine packages for a specific purpose. An example would be the class libraries used for accessing a computer's serial ports. The API provides a level of abstraction between the application and the lower-level software, hardware, or privileged utilities to ensure the portability of the code.

You will need to download the current version of the Java Software Development Kit from Sun's "Java Products & API's" web page[3]. This is also called the J2SE for "Java 2 Platform, Standard Edition." This book is based on the Java 2 Software Development Kit (SDK) version 1.3 for your platform (Windows or Linux). The

---

[1] Java is a registered trademark of Sun Microsystems.
[2] Windows 95, Windows 98, Windows XP, Windows 2000 and Windows NT are registered trademarks of Microsoft Corporation.
[3] Java Products & API's, http://java.sun.com/products/

basic installation steps are listed here but if you run into difficulties, you should follow the more detailed installation instructions listed on the Sun web page.

For Windows

Remove any older version of the Java Development Kit you may have installed on your computer. (Click on the START button and select Settings, Control Panel, Add/ Remove Programs and examine this list of installed applications.)

Go to the "Java Products & API's" web page and click on the link for "Java 2 SDK, Standard Edition." Download Java 2 SDK, saving the file (j2sdk1_3_0-win.exe) in a temporary directory.

Using Windows Explorer, double-click on the file you just downloaded to execute the Java SDK installer. This will install Java on your computer. Follow the instructions. This will create a directory hierarchy on your disk starting in C:\JDK1.3 (or a different disk if your disks are labeled differently). If you download and install a newer version, then some of the filenames and path names will change to reflect the version number.

Windows 95/98

On Windows 95/98 you must edit your Autoexec.bat file and add a folder to your PATH environment variable. Using Notepad (or some other ASCII editor), open your c:\autoexec.bat file. If you already have a PATH environment variable set, then you will need to add the location of the Java binaries. After the PATH environment variable, insert a new line that will append the c:\jdk1.3\bin\ directory to the existing path.

```
SET PATH=c:\jdk1.3\bin\;%PATH%
```

If you don't have a PATH environment variable, add one by inserting a line at the bottom of the autoexec.bat file like this:

```
SET PATH=c:\jdk1.3\bin\;c:\windows
```

Save the file and exit the editor. This PATH environment variable tells the operating system where to find the Java programs when you need them.

Windows 2000, Windows NT, Windows XP

For Windows 2000 and Windows NT you will have to use the "System" tool in the "Control Panel." Select the "Environment" tab and look for "Path" in the User Variables and System Variables. If a path variable exists, add the location of the Java binaries (c:\jdk1.3\bin\, unless you installed Java someplace else). If you don't have a path variable, create one.

For Windows XP, use the "System" tool in the "Control Panel." Select the "Advanced" tab and click on the "Environment" button (under "startup and recovery"). Modify or create the path variable as above.

At this point, you don't need to have the CLASSPATH variable set. We will cover that in a later section.

To test out your installation of the Java SDK you need to restart your computer. Do that and then create a simple test program to verify that all is well so far. A simple "HelloWorld" program like the following should work just fine.

Listing 3-1: HelloWorld.java

```
public class HelloWorld {
    // Simple program to make sure compiler is installed ok
    public static void main( String args[] ) {
        System.out.println( "Hello, World!" );
    }
}
```

Open a DOS command window.

```
c:\> notepad HelloWorld.java
```

Enter the Java program above into the text editor. Save the file and exit the editor. Then compile and run the program:

```
c:\> javac HelloWorld.java
c:\> java HelloWorld
```

If there were no errors from either of the last two commands above, then you are all set to move on to installing the serial port API for Java. If you saw any errors when compiling or running the program, then you should carefully check the program you entered to see that you typed it correctly. Also check to see that you installed the Java Software Development Kit properly. While these instructions are for J2SE version 1.3, by the time you read this book Sun will probably have released a newer version. It is likely that the installation procedures will be slightly different.

These are some common errors and their solutions:

```
C:\> javac HelloWorld.java
Bad command or file name
```

- c:\jdk1.3\bin is not in your PATH environment variable. Or you added it but you didn't restart your computer. Check your current PATH with this DOS command: echo %PATH%

```
C:\chapter03> java HelloWorld
Exception in thread "main" java.lang.NoClassDefFoundError:
HelloWorld
```

- Didn't compile HelloWorld.java (javac HelloWorld.java).

- HelloWorld.java had errors so the compiler didn't write the class file.

- You have a CLASSPATH environment variables set and "." (current folder) is not in the CLASSPATH or there are errors in your CLASSPATH (like not separating folders with a semicolon). Check your current CLASSPATH with this DOS command: echo %CLASSPATH%

For Linux

Go to Sun's "Java Products & API's" web page[4] and click on the link for "Java 2 SDK, Standard Edition." Download the Java 2 SDK tar file (j2sdk-1_3_0-linux-rpm.bin) to a temporary directory. Be sure to select the Linux (for Intel x86) version. In these instructions we will be using the RPM file but you can just as easily download the **GNUZIP Tar shell script** (but many of these instructions will not apply).

Change to the temporary directory you saved this file in. Change the permissions of the file so it is now executable (chmod +x j2sdk-1_3_0-linux-rpm.bin) and then execute it (./j2sdk-1_3_0-linux-rpm.bin). This will unpack and verify the RPM file. You will have the file j2sdk-1_3_0-linux.rpm placed in the current directory. If you download and install a newer version then some of the filenames and path names will change to reflect the version number.

You will need to be root to complete the installation. Install the RPM file (rpm -iv j2sdk-1_3_0-linux.rpm). This will install Java in /usr/java subdirectory.

On Linux you will need to edit your shell startup file and add the directory of the Java binaries to your PATH environment variable. Using vi (or some other ASCII editor), edit your $HOME/.cshrc (for C shell, or $HOME/.profile for ksh, sh or bash). You should already have a PATH environment variable set so you will need to add the location of the Java binaries to it. After the PATH environment variable, insert a new line that will append the /opt/jdk/bin/ directory to the existing path.

For C shell:

```
set path = ($path /usr/java/jdk1.3/bin)
```

For ksh, sh and bash shells:

```
PATH=$PATH:/usr/java/jdk1.3/bin
```

Save the file and exit the editor. This PATH environment variable tells the operating system where to find the Java programs when you need them.

At this point, you don't need to have the CLASSPATH variable set. We will do that in a following section.

To test out your installation of the Java SDK, you will need to logout and log in again to load your new startup file. Do that and then create a simple test program to verify that all is well so far. We will use the "HelloWorld" program from listing 3-1.

---

[4] Java Products & API's web page, http://java.sun.com/products/

Create a subdirectory and create a test Java program:

```
% vi HelloWorld.java
```

Enter the Java program above into the text editor. Save the file and exit the editor. Then compile and run the program:

```
% javac HelloWorld.java
% java HelloWorld
```

If there were no errors from either of the last two commands, then you are all set to move on to installing the serial port API for Java. If there were error messages, then read the installation instructions above and on the Sun web pages and try to figure out what went wrong and fix it. Most likely you overlooked a step or mistyped something. Some common mistakes are: Not properly editing the PATH environment variable, or not rebooting the computer after editing the PATH.

If you saw any errors when compiling or running the program then you should carefully check the program you entered to see that you typed it correctly. Also check to see that you installed the Java Software Development Kit properly. While these instructions are for J2SE version 1.3, by the time you read this book Sun may have released a newer version. It is likely that the installation procedures will be slightly different.

These are some common errors and their solutions:

```
% javac HelloWorld.java
javac: Command not found
```

- /usr/java/jdk1.3/bin is not in your PATH environment variable. Or you added it but you didn't restart your computer. Check your current PATH with this command: echo $PATH

```
% java HelloWorld
Exception in thread "main" java.lang.NoClassDefFoundError:
HelloWorld
```

- Didn't compile HelloWorld.java (javac HelloWorld.java)

- HelloWorld.java had errors so the compiler didn't write the class file.

- You have a CLASSPATH environment variable set and "." (the current folder) is not in the CLASSPATH or there are errors in your CLASSPATH (like not separating the directories with a colon). Check your current CLASSPATH with this command: echo $CLASSPATH

Now that we have the Java compiler and runtime environment going, it may interest you to know about the various options you can use when compiling programs with javac and running programs with Java. Typing javac -help or java -help will display the command options you can use.

```
% javac -help
Usage: javac <options> <source files>
where possible options include:
   -g                       Generate all debugging info
   -g:none                  Generate no debugging info
   -g:{lines,vars,source}   Generate only some debugging info
   -O                       Optimize; may hinder debugging or
                            enlarge class file

  -nowarn                   Generate no warnings
  -verbose                  Output messages about what the compiler
                            is doing
  -deprecation              Output source locations where deprecated
                            APIs are used
  -classpath <path>         Specify where to find user class files
  -sourcepath <path>        Specify where to find input source files
  -bootclasspath <path>     Override location of bootstrap class
                            files
  -extdirs <dirs>           Override location of installed extensions
  -d <directory>            Specify where to place generated class
                            files
  -encoding <encoding>      Specify character encoding used by
                            source files
  -target <release>         Generate class files for specific VM
                            version

% java -help
Usage: java [-options] class [args...]
        (to execute a class)
   or  java -jar [-options] jarfile [args...]
        (to execute a jar file)

where options include:
   -cp -classpath <directories and zip/jar files separated by :>
                   set search path for application classes and
                        resources
   -D<name>=<value>
                   set a system property
   -verbose[:class|gc|jni]
                   enable verbose output
   -version        print product version and exit
   -showversion    print product version and continue
   -? -help        print this help message
   -X              print help on non-standard options
```

Serial Port Communications

Once the Java Software Development Kit is working smoothly, we need to add support for accessing the serial ports on our computer. This will be important for the rest of this book, so we need to get this ironed out now. Sun has developed a set of Java low-level classes for reading from and writing to serial ports.

There are three levels of classes in the Java communications API:

- High-level classes that manage access and ownership of communication ports.

- Low-level classes that provide an interface to physical communications ports.

- Driver-level classes that provide an interface between the low-level classes and the underlying operating system. Driver-level classes are part of the implementation but not the Java communications API.

All three levels are provided by SUN for the `javax.comm` API for Win32 and Solaris. The driver level classes are not provided by SUN for Linux. They are available from a different source. This makes the Linux installation of `javax.comm` a little more difficult (just a little).

For Windows

To install the `javax.comm` serial port classes for Windows 98/95/NT, go to the Sun "Java Communications API" web page[5] and download the current release of the Java Communications API. Save the ZIP file in a temporary directory. In the ZIP file is a readme.html and a file named PlatformSpecific.html that gives more detailed installation instructions. The general installation is summarized here but if you have problems or if you are installing a newer version, then you should consult these files for details.

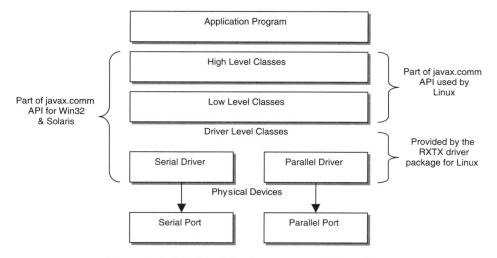

Figure 3-1: Model of the javax.comm API package

---

[5] Java Communications API, http://java.sun.com/products/javacomm/

Unzip the `javacommxx-win32.zip` file into C:\jdk1.3\. It will unzip into a folder named commapi. You will need to copy three files from this folder to the jdk\bin, jdk\jre\bin, jdk\jre and jdk\lib folders. Copy win32comm.dll to the jdk\bin and jdk\jre\bin folders, comm.jar to the jdk\lib folder and `javax.comm.properties` to the jdk\lib and jdk\jre\lib folders. From a DOS command prompt:

```
c:\> cd \jdk1.3
c:\jdk1.3\> copy jdk\commapi\win32com.dll jdk\bin
c:\jdk1.3\> copy jdk\commapi\win32com.dll jdk\jre\bin
c:\jdk1.3\> copy jdk\commapi\comm.jar jdk\lib
c:\jdk1.3\> copy jdk\commapi\javax.comm.properties jdk\lib
c:\jdk1.3\> copy jdk\commapi\javax.comm.properties jdk\jre\lib
```

Now you will need to create a CLASSPATH environment variable so javac and Java programs can find these classes and drivers.

Windows 95/98

For Windows 95/98 you must edit your c:\autoexec.bat file again. Using Notepad (or some other ASCII editor), open your c:\autoexec.bat file. If you already have a CLASSPATH environment variable set, you will need to add the location of comm.jar to it by adding a line similar to the following, just after the CLASSPATH line you already have.

```
SET CLASSPATH=%CLASSPATH%;c:\jdk1.3\lib\comm.jar;.
```

If you don't have a CLASSPATH environment variable, add one by inserting a line at the bottom of the autoexec.bat file like this:

```
SET CLASSPATH=c:\jdk1.3\lib\comm.jar;.
```

Notice that we are also adding the current working directory to the CLASSPATH environment variable as specified by the single dot ("."). You can add other directories for other classes by separating them with the semicolon (";"). Note that this is one of the few differences between the Windows version of the JDK and the Linux version, where you will use the colon (":") to separate directories in your CLASSPATH environment variable. Save your autoexec.bat file and exit the editor. Now you will need to reboot your computer for these changes to be effective. Do that now.

Windows 2000, Windows NT, Windows XP

For Windows 2000 and Windows NT you will need to edit your environment variables in the usual way. Use the "System" tool in the "Control Panel." Select the "Environment" tab and look for CLASSPATH in the user variables and system variables. If it already exists, select it and edit its value in the text box. Add to the value; be sure to separate the multiple paths with a semicolon(";").

```
c:\jdk1.3\lib\comm.jar;.
```

If it does not exist, click the "Variable" text box and enter the variable name, CLASSPATH, then click in the "value" text box and enter the CLASSPATH value as above.

For Windows XP, use the "System" tool in the "Control Panel." Select the "Advanced" tab and click on the "Environment" button (under "startup and recovery"). Modify or create the CLASSPATH variable as above.

If it does not exist, click in the "Variable" text box and enter the variable name, CLASSPATH, then click in the "value" text box and enter the CLASSPATH value as above.

Now let's test your installation of the Java Communications API to verify that everything is installed properly. We will use the same folder named "test" that we used in verifying the JDK was installed. Here is a simple Java program that finds all known ports on your computer and lists them by name. These will be known ports—some may not actually exist. This program doesn't really do anything all that useful, but when it compiles, runs and spits out some output (without any errors), then you will know that the Java Communications API was installed properly.

Listing 3:2: PortLister.java

```java
import javax.comm.*;
import java.util.*;

// List all of the ports on my computer.

public class PortLister {

    public static void main(String[] args) {

        // e = All PortIdentifiers on the computer (parallel, serial, etc)
        Enumeration e = CommPortIdentifier.getPortIdentifiers();

        while (e.hasMoreElements()) {
            CommPortIdentifier PortID = (CommPortIdentifier) e.nextElement();
            System.out.print( PortID + " is " + PortID.getName() );

            switch( PortID.getPortType() ) {
                case CommPortIdentifier.PORT_SERIAL:
                    System.out.print( ", serial port" );
                    break;
                case CommPortIdentifier.PORT_PARALLEL:
                    System.out.print( ", parallel port" );
                    break;
                default:
                    System.out.print( ", unknown port type" );
                    break;
            }
            System.out.println();
        }
    }
}
```

Open a DOS command window.

```
c:\> notepad PortLister.java
```

Enter the Java program above into the text editor. Save the file and exit the editor. Then compile and run the program:

```
c:\> javac PortLister.java
c:\> java PortLister
```

This is what the output from Windows looks like:

```
C:\> java PortLister
javax.comm.CommPortIdentifier@25ab41 is COM1, serial port
javax.comm.CommPortIdentifier@e3e60 is COM2, serial port
javax.comm.CommPortIdentifier@2125f0 is COM3, serial port
javax.comm.CommPortIdentifier@41cd1f is COM4, serial port
javax.comm.CommPortIdentifier@1afa3 is LPT1, parallel port
javax.comm.CommPortIdentifier@31f71a is LPT2, parallel port
```

If you saw any errors when compiling or running the program, then you should carefully check the program you entered to see that you typed it correctly. Also check to see that you installed the javax.comm API properly.

These are some common errors and their solutions:

```
C:\> javac PortLister.java
PortLister.java:4: package javax.comm does not exist
import javax.comm.*;
```

- Your CLASSPATH environment variable does not contain the folder for the javax.comm libraries (\jdk1.3\lib\comm.jar), the javax.comm API was not installed properly, or you did not restart your computer since modifying your CLASSPATH.

For Linux

To install the javax.comm serial port classes for Linux, go to the Sun "Java Communications API" web page[6] and download the current release of the Java Communications API for Solaris/x86. Save the tar file in a temporary directory. In the tar file is a readme.html and a file named PlatformSpecific.html that provides more detailed installation instructions. The general installation is summarized here, but if you have problems or if you are installing a newer version then you should consult these files for details.

Decompress and untar the javacommxx-x86.tar.Z file into /opt/jdk. It will create a directory named commapi.

```
$ cd /usr/java/jdk1.3/
$ cp $HOME/download/javacomm20-x86.tar.gz .
```

---

[6] Java Communications API, http://java.sun.com/products/javacomm/

```
$ gunzip javacomm20-x86.tar.gz
$ tar -xf javacomm2-x86.tar
```

Now you will need to create a CLASSPATH environment variable so javac and Java programs can find these classes and drivers. Put the `commapi.jar` file in the CLASSPATH. Using vi (or some other ASCII editor), edit your $HOME/.cshrc (for C shell, or $HOME/.profile for ksh, sh or bash). If you have been using Java, you might already have a CLASSPATH environment variable set, so you will need to add the location of the javax.comm libraries to it.

For C shell:

```
set CLASSPATH=/usr/java/jdk1.3/commapi/comm.jar:.
set PATH=$PATH:/usr/java/jdk1.3/bin
export CLASSPATH PATH
```

For ksh, sh and bash shells:

```
CLASSPATH=/usr/java/jdk1.3/commapi/comm.jar:.
PATH=$PATH:/usr/java/jdk1.3/bin
export CLASSPATH PATH
```

Save the file and exit the editor. This CLASSPATH environment variable tells the java compiler and run time system where to find the java class libraries when you need them.

Also you need to get `rxtx`. Remember the figure above for the `javax.comm` API? Recall that Linux low-level drivers are not part of the package. Sun has implemented drivers for Windows and Solaris operating systems only (so far). You will need to get the low-level serial port drivers from the RXTX Web Site[7]. Download the latest version (in this case `rxtx-1.4-5.tar.gz`) and save this in your /opt directory. Decompress and untar the file. Run "make jcl" and then "make install." Refer to the INSTALL files for detailed installation instructions.

```
% gunzip rxtx-1.4-5.tar.gz
% tar -xf rxtx-1.4-5.tar
% cd rxtx-1.4-5
% ./configure
% make jcl
% make install
```

If all went well and there were no errors, you can proceed to testing the installation of the javax.comm libraries. Use the same program for Windows as provided above. This is the type of output you should get for Linux:

```
% javac PortLister.java
% java PortLister
```

---

[7] RXTX Web Site, http://www.rxtx.org/

```
javax.comm.CommPortIdentifier@9df52312 is /dev/ttyS0, serial port
javax.comm.CommPortIdentifier@9e212312 is /dev/ttyS1, serial port
javax.comm.CommPortIdentifier@9dd52312 is /dev/ttyS2, serial port
javax.comm.CommPortIdentifier@9d4d2312 is /dev/ttyS3, serial port
javax.comm.CommPortIdentifier@9d752312 is /dev/lp0, parallel port
javax.comm.CommPortIdentifier@9da12312 is /dev/lp1, parallel port
javax.comm.CommPortIdentifier@9c852312 is /dev/lp2, parallel port
```

Note that not all of these ports are actual ports. The program simply verifies that the `javax.comm` API and RXTX were installed and that they function correctly (no compile or runtime errors). This simple test only prints the names of the ports it finds. It does not test them to see if they are real and if they work.

If you saw any errors when compiling or running the program, then you should carefully check the program you entered to see that you typed it correctly. Also check to see that you installed the `javax.comm` API properly.

These are some common errors and their solutions:

```
% javac PortLister.java
PortLister.java:4: package javax.comm does not exist
import javax.comm.*;
```

- Your CLASSPATH environment variable does not contain the folder for the `javax.comm` libraries (/usr/java/jdk1.3/lib/comm.jar or /usr/java/jdk1.3/commapi/comm..jar), the `javax.comm` API was not installed properly, rxtx was not installed properly, or you did not restart your computer since modifying your CLASSPATH.

Here is a simple test you can perform to determine if a particular class you need is included in any of the entries in your classpath environment variable or if you have installed javax.comm correctly. Use the java class file disassembler, javap, that is included with the Sun JDK. This will search the entries in your `classpath` looking for the specified class. If it can't find it, then either your `classpath` is incorrect or you have installed the javax.comm. incorrectly.

From a DOS or Linux command line type:

```
C:\> javap javax.comm.CommPort
```

Javap will print out a list of the public fields and methods in the javax.comm.CommPart class. Something like this:

```
public abstract class javax.comm.CommPort extends java.lang.Object {
    protected java.lang.String name;
    javax.comm.CommPort();
    public java.lang.String getName();
    ...
    public abstract int getOutputBufferSize();
}
```

If you see a message like Class 'javax.comm.CommPort' not found, then the CommAPI files are either not in the correct place or you have not properly included them in the classpath.

Significant Topics for Review in the Java Language

The previous section discussed how to obtain and set up Java for both Windows and Linux personal computers. Now, we're going to talk briefly about the Java language itself. Again, we're not trying to *teach* you Java—rather, we're going to cover aspects of the language that are especially relevant to our main topic of web-enabled devices. In addition, we're going to review some basic elements of the language that are key to understanding the examples that will be sprinkled throughout the book. The example programs in this introductory portion of the book will be presented in somewhat tedious detail, being first presented in their entirety and then explained code block by code block. We hope that by explaining these more fundamental examples in great detail, we'll be laying a strong foundation for our later, more complicated examples, which will be explained on a somewhat higher level. There are a number of excellent, free, online references for Java. If you need more detail than what is presented in this quick review, check these references. They are listed in the references section at the end of this chapter.

Classes, objects, methods, constructors

Java, in many ways is very similar to C, C++, and other languages: it uses the familiar curly braces {} to denote code blocks, it has all the usual conditional statements (if/then/else, etc.) and loop control statements (for, while, etc.). It distinguishes itself from the other languages in that it is designed from the ground up to be an object-oriented language. You can't program in Java without using object-oriented techniques and that requires understanding classes, objects, and methods (among other things).

- A software **object** is an entity that contains information on both state and behavior. State is contained in variables and behavior is manifested through what are called *methods*.

- **Methods** are code blocks that perform operations on an object's variables.

- A **class** is a template for the creation of objects, an object's methods, and its variables.

- A **constructor** is the Java program element that creates an object.

- An object is an **instance** of a class.

While the terminology and definitions are always important to understand, the only way to really make any sense of this is to write some code. Let's look at a simple example.

Listing 3-3: Fruit.java

```java
public class Fruit {
    String fruitType;
    boolean isTart;
    int calories;

    public Fruit(String ft, boolean it, int cal) {
        this.fruitType = ft;
        this.isTart = it;
        this.calories = cal;
    }
    public void printData(String str) {
        System.out.print(str + " is a type of " + this.fruitType);
        if (this.isTart) {
            System.out.print(" that is tart and ");
        } else {
            System.out.print(" that is not tart and ");
        }
        System.out.println(" has about " + this.calories + " calories");
    }

    public static void main(String[] args) {
        Fruit grannySmith = new Fruit("apple", true, 80);
        Fruit bartlet = new Fruit("pear", false, 100);
        Fruit cavendish = new Fruit("banana", false, 110);
        grannySmith.printData("grannySmith");
        bartlet.printData("bartlet");
        cavendish.printData("cavendish");
    }
}
```

All Java programs are essentially class definitions. In the program above, we have defined a class called Fruit that provides a template for the creation of Fruit objects. Let's take a closer look at the Fruit class. The beginning few lines of our class definition

```java
public class Fruit {
    String fruitType;
    boolean isTart;
    int calories;
```

define the class name and variables. According to this template, each time we create a fruit object, it will have three variables: a string, a Boolean flag, and an integer. The next few lines of our program are the constructor for the fruit object:

```java
public Fruit(String ft, boolean it, int cal) {
    this.fruitType = ft;
    this.isTart = it;
    this.calories = cal;
}
```

When called, the constructor is passed values for the three variables and it uses them to initialize the object. The next program block is a method that, when called, prints out the object's variables:

```
public void printData(String str) {
    System.out.print(str + " is a type of " + this.fruitType);
    if (this.isTart) {
        System.out.print(" that is tart and ");
    } else {
        System.out.print(" that is not tart and ");
    }
    System.out.println(" has about " + this.calories + " calories");
}
```

Finally, there is the `main()` method. This is a program block that is executed when this Java class is run. The first three lines declare different instances of the fruit object and call the `fruit` constructor. The next three lines invoke the `printData()` method for each of the objects.

```
public static void main(String[] args) {
    Fruit grannySmith = new Fruit("apple", true, 80);
    Fruit bartlet = new Fruit("pear", false, 100);
    Fruit cavendish = new Fruit("banana", false, 110);
    grannySmith.printData("grannySmith");
    bartlet.printData("bartlet");
    cavendish.printData("cavendish");
}
}
```

Compile and run this program; the output should look like this:

```
C:\> javac Fruit.java
C:\> java Fruit
grannySmith is a type of apple that is tart and has about 80 calories
bartlet is a type of pear that is not tart and has about 100 calories
cavendish is a type of banana that is not tart and has about 110 calories
```

OOP diagrams

OOP, for those of you who don't speak nerd, stands for Object-Oriented Programming. OOP diagrams are a graphical way of representing programs written using object-oriented languages. Different symbols are used for classes, objects, class variables, instance variables, and methods. The OOP diagram is just a drawing of these symbols in the proper relationship to one another. We will make occasional use of OOP diagrams throughout this book. OOP diagrams perform two useful functions:

1. In order to make the diagrams, you have to understand what your objects are, what your variables are, and what your methods are. So, in that sense, they force you to think OOP.

2. A picture is worth a thousand words. It's much easier to quickly grasp what a program is trying to do by looking at a diagram.

Figure 3-2 illustrates the basic components in the scheme we will use for making OOP diagrams. This is not an all-inclusive list of the symbols. Constructors, overloaded methods, overridden methods, and other aspects of Java can also be illustrated on OOP diagrams but have not been shown on the diagram to keep it simple. We'll explain additional, advanced features in OOP diagrams along the way.

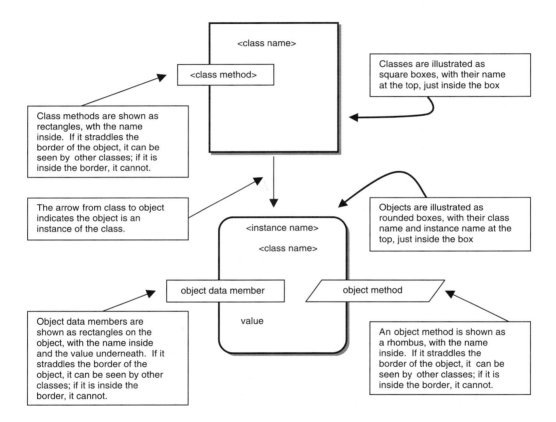

Figure 3-2: A diagram showing the symbols used in OOP diagrams

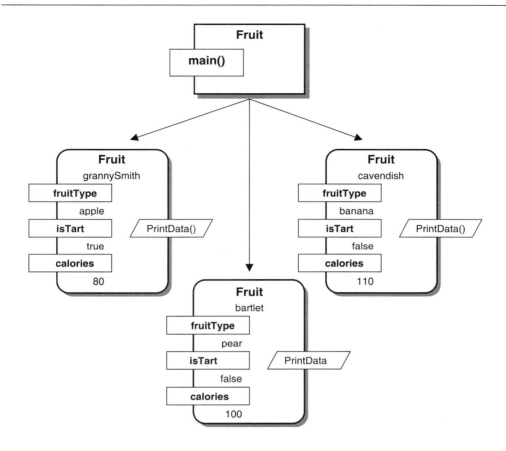

Figure 3-3: The OOP diagram for the Fruit Class

Inheritance

We've seen that Java is an object-oriented language. Java programs are classes that represent templates for the creation of objects. These objects contain variables and methods that operate on the variables. Another important concept contained within this is that these classes form a hierarchy. A class can extend another class and in doing so inherit some of its objects. By inheriting a class's objects, that object's methods and variables are also inherited.

The inheritance in this hierarchy doesn't just apply to adjacent classes; by inheriting from a class you inherit whatever it may have inherited, and so on. The following is a concise summary of important concepts with respect to inheritance.

- **Subclass** is the term used to describe the class that is extending, or inheriting from, a higher class. **Superclass** is the term used to describe the class that is being extended or inherited from. One can think of the superclass as the ancestor and the subclass as the descendent.

- Java.lang.Object is the Java class at the very top of the Java class hierarchy. All classes extend it either directly or indirectly.

- To inherit from a class other than Object, you use the `extends` clause. Without that, a class will extend the Object class by default.

- You can only directly extend one class at a time. That is to say, Java doesn't support multiple inheritance.

- Constructors are not inherited.

- There are ways of controlling what can and cannot be inherited from a class. For instance, declaring a class, its objects, methods or variables as `private` prevents them from being inherited.

- If a subclass declares a method that has the same name as a method in the superclass, that method is said to be overridden. If the superclass had declared that method as final, this would not be allowed. Overridden methods can be accessed with the `super` keyword.

- If a subclass declares a variable that has the same name as a variable in the superclass, that variable is said to be hidden. If the superclass had declared that variable as final, this would not be allowed. Hidden variables can be accessed with the super keyword.

Inheritance is dependent on visibility modifiers and the location of subclasses with respect to superclasses. The following is a table that summarizes various inheritance configurations.

Table 3-1: Table of visibility modifiers and what they mean

Methods and Data Members	public	protected	default	private
Accessible from the same class?	x	x	x	x
Accessible to classes and subclasses from the same package?	x	x	x	
Accessible to classes and subclasses from a different package?	x			
Inherited by subclasses in the same package?	x	x	x	
Inherited by subclasses in a different package?	x	x		

Reading about inheritance is all well and good, but the best way to understand it is to experiment with it. Consider the following Java program.

Listing 3-4: Tree.java

```
public class Tree {
    String location;
    int yearsOld;
    int heightInFeet;

    public Tree() {
        this.location = "Unknown";
        this.yearsOld = 0;
        this.heightInFeet = 0;
    }

    public Tree(String loc, int yrsOld, int ht) {
        this.location = loc;
        this.yearsOld = yrsOld;
        this.heightInFeet = ht;
    }

    public void printTreeData() {
        System.out.println("Location: " + this.location);
        System.out.println("Age: " + this.yearsOld + " years old");
        System.out.println("Height: " + this.heightInFeet + " feet high");
    }

    public static void main(String[] args) {
        Tree juniper = new Tree("north forty", 10, 30);
        Tree walnut = new Tree("back forty", 80, 60);
        System.out.println("Juniper tree data:");
        juniper.printTreeData();
        System.out.println("\n" + "walnut tree data:");
        walnut.printTreeData();
    }
}
```

The structure of this Java class is very much like the previous example, `Fruit.java`. The beginning few lines of our class definition,

```
public class Tree {
    String location;
    int yearsOld;
    int heightInFeet;
```

define the class name and variables. According to this template, each time we create a tree object, it will have three variables: a string, and two integers. The next few lines of our program are the constructors for the `Tree` object. In this case there are two constructors. Which constructor to be executed depends on the number of arguments provided. If all three arguments are provided, the three-argument constructor will be executed, and if none are provided, the no-argument constructor will be executed.

```java
public Tree() {
    this.location = "Unknown";
    this.yearsOld = 0;
    this.heightInFeet = 0;
}
public Tree(String loc, int yrsOld, int ht) {
    this.location = loc;
    this.yearsOld = yrsOld;
    this.heightInFeet = ht;
}
```

Next is a method that prints out the variables along with some text.

```java
public void printTreeData() {
    System.out.println("Location: " + this.location);
    System.out.println("Age: " + this.yearsOld + " years old");
    System.out.println("Height: " + this.heightInFeet + " feet high");
}
```

Finally, there is the `main()` method. This is the program block that is executed when this Java class is run. The first two lines declare different instances of the `Tree` object and call the constructor. Since the constructor has three arguments, it will be the second constructor in the class definition that gets executed. The next few lines call the `printTreeData()` method and print some text to the screen.

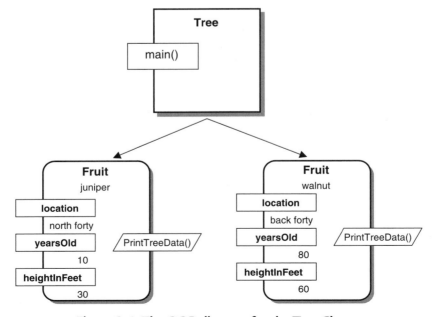

Figure 3-4: The OOP diagram for the Tree Class

```
public static void main(String[] args) {
    Tree juniper = new Tree("north forty", 10, 30);
    Tree walnut = new Tree("back forty", 80, 60);
    System.out.println("Juniper tree data:");
    juniper.printTreeData();
    System.out.println("\n" + "walnut tree data:");
    walnut.printTreeData();
}
```

The output of this program looks like this:

```
C:\> javac Tree.java
C:\> java Tree
Juniper Tree Data:
Location: north forty
Age: 10 years old
Height: 30 feet high

walnut tree data:
Locaton: back forty
Age: 80 years old
Height: 60 feet high
```

It's a straightforward example very much like `Fruit.java`. What if we wanted to make a class that was related to the `Tree` class, but much more specific? What if we wanted to make a class that described fruit trees? Since fruit trees are a subset of trees, they would have the same characteristics as trees but would also contain information specific to fruit trees. To do this, we will make a class that `extends` the `Tree` class. Consider the following program.

Listing 3-5: FruitTree.java

```
public class FruitTree extends Tree {
    String harvestDate;
    String harvestMethod;

    public FruitTree() {
        this.harvestDate = "unknown";
        this.harvestMethod = "unknown";
    }
    public FruitTree(String hd, String hm) {
        this.harvestDate = hd;
        this.harvestMethod = hm;
    }
    public FruitTree(String loc, int yrsOld, int ht, String hd, String hm) {
        super(loc, yrsOld, ht);
        this.harvestDate = hd;
        this.harvestMethod = hm;
    }
```

```
    public void printFruitTreeData() {
        System.out.println("Harvest Method: " + this.harvestMethod);
        System.out.println("Harvest Date: " + this.harvestDate);
    }

    public static void main(String[] args) {
        FruitTree crabApple = new FruitTree("late July", "hand picking");
        FruitTree bingCherry = new FruitTree("Front Yard", 7, 25,
                                    "late July", "cherry picker");
        System.out.println("Bing Cherry Tree Information:");
        bingCherry.printFruitTreeData();
        bingCherry.printTreeData();
        System.out.println("\n" + "Crab Apple Tree Information:");
        crabApple.printFruitTreeData();
    }
}
```

The beginning few lines of our program

```
public class FruitTree extends Tree {
    String harvestDate;
    String harvestMethod;
```

define the class name and variables. According to this template, each time we create a
FruitTree object, it will have two string variables. But note the use of the extends
keyword. By declaring that the FruitTree class extends the Tree class, the
FruitTree objects will inherit the methods and variables that our Tree objects have
and therefore actually have five variables associated with each object. The next
several code blocks are all constructors. In this case, we are providing three
constructors with different numbers of arguments. The number of arguments in the
constructor call will determine which gets executed.

There is another interesting point to be mentioned. When the FruitTree constructor
is called, the first thing it does is attempt to execute a Tree constructor, because the
inherited variables also need to be initialized upon object creation. If there is no
reference to the Tree constructor in the Fruit Tree constructor, it will call the no-
argument Tree constructor. The five argument constructor explicitly references the
Tree constructor through the use of the super() keyword, which refers to the
constructor of the superclass. Since it is used, and three arguments are placed into it,
it will cause the three argument Tree constructor to be called, as opposed to the no
argument Tree constructor. We could have left the no argument constructor out of the
Tree class and the Tree class alone would have compiled and run properly.

```
public FruitTree() {
    this.harvestDate = "unknown";
    this.harvestMethod = "unknown";
}
public FruitTree(String hd, String hm) {
```

```
        this.harvestDate = hd;
        this.harvestMethod = hm;
}
public FruitTree(String loc, int yrsOld, int ht, String hd, String hm) {
        super(loc, yrsOld, ht);
        this.harvestDate = hd;
        this.harvestMethod = hm;
}
```

The next code block is a method that prints out the two variables that are declared in the `FruitTree` class. We're not going to have it print out the variables inherited from the `Tree` class, because we're inheriting the specific method that does that from the `Tree` class as well as the variables.

```
    public void printFruitTreeData() {
        System.out.println("Harvest Method: " + this.harvestMethod);
        System.out.println("Harvest Date: " + this.harvestDate);
    }
```

Finally, there is the `main()` method. This is the program block that is executed when this Java class is run. The first two lines declare different instances of the `FruitTree` object and call the constructor. Since the first constructor call has only two arguments, the two-argument `FruitTree` constructor gets executed. The second `FruitTree` constructor call has five arguments, which causes the five-argument constructor to be executed.

The next few lines after that call the `printTreeData()` method and print some text to the screen. Here, we are supplying different numbers of arguments to the `FruitTree` constructor and in the case of the `bingCherry` object, we are accessing the inherited method `printTreeData`.

```
public static void main(String[] args) {
    FruitTree crabApple = new FruitTree("late July", "hand picking");
    FruitTree bingCherry = new FruitTree("Front Yard", 7, 25,
                                    "late July", "cherry picker");
    System.out.println("Bing Cherry Tree Information:");
        bingCherry.printFruitTreeData();
        bingCherry.printTreeData();
        System.out.println("\n" + "Crab Apple Tree Information:");
        crabApple.printFruitTreeData();
}
```

The output of this program looks like this:

```
C:\> javac FruitTree.java
C:\> java FruitTree
Big Cherry Tree Information:
Harvest Method: cherry picker
Harvest Date: late July
Location: Front Yard
```

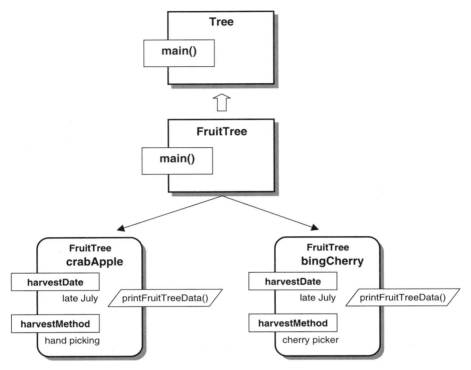

Figure 3-5: The OOP diagram for the FruitTree Class

```
Age: 7 years old
Height: 25 feet high

Crab Apple Tree Information:
Harvest Method: hand picking
Harvest Date: late July
```

Before leaving our discussion of inheritance, we are going to take a quick look at overridden methods and hidden variables. Consider the following simple program.

Listing 3-6: Ancestor.java

```
class  Ancestor {
String stringVariable;
    public void printStuff() {
        System.out.println("This is the ancestor's method");
        stringVariable = "Ancestor";
    }
}
```

```
public class Descendant extends Ancestor {
    String stringVariable;

    public void printStuff() {
        super.printStuff();
        System.out.println("stringVariable = " + super.stringVariable);
        System.out.println("This is the descendant's method");
        stringVariable = "Descendant";
        System.out.println("stringVariable = " + stringVariable);
    }

    public static void main(String[] args) {
        Descendant chld = new Descendant();
        chld.printStuff();
    }
}
```

In this example, our superclass is called `Ancestor`. It has one variable, one method, and we've provided no constructors. We are instead relying on the default, no-argument, constructor which Java provides when we don't define a constructor. The subclass in this example is called `Descendant`. It has one variable, one method, and no constructors. The interesting thing about this example is that the subclass and superclass each have a method and variable with the *same* name. The `printStuff()` method in the subclass is said to have overridden the `printStuff()` method in the superclass. The variable `stringVariable` in the subclass is said to be hiding the variable of the same name in the superclass. Each can still be accessed, however, through the use of the `super` keyword. When we used `super` in the previous example, we were referring to the superclass constructor. Now, we are using it to refer to an instance of the superclass, giving us a mechanism of accessing its methods and variables. The output of this program looks like this:

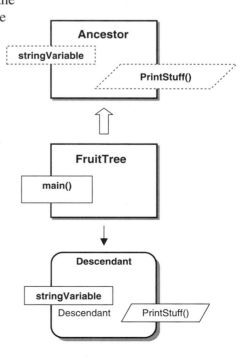

```
C:\> Java Descendant
This is the ancestor's method
stringVariable = Ancestor
This is the descendant's method
stringVariable = Descendant
```

Figure 3-6: The OOP diagram for the Ancestor Class

Having looked at method overriding in `Descendant.java`, are you ready for something really scary? Consider the following program, `OverRidden.java`.

Listing 3-7: OverRidden.java

```java
public class OverRidden extends Tree {
    String harvestDate;
    String harvestMethod;

    public OverRidden() {
        this.harvestDate = "unknown";
        this.harvestMethod = "unknown";
    }

    public OverRidden(String hd, String hm) {
        this.harvestDate = hd;
        this.harvestMethod = hm;
    }

    public OverRidden(String loc, int yrsOld, int ht, String hd,
                                                String hm) {
        super(loc, yrsOld, ht);
        this.location = loc;
        this.yearsOld = yrsOld;
        this.heightInFeet = ht;
        this.harvestDate = hd;
        this.harvestMethod = hm;
    }

    public String toString() {
        return(
            "Harvest Method: " + this.harvestMethod + "\n"
                    + "Harvest Date: "
                    + this.harvestDate);
    }


    public static void main(String[] args) {
        OverRidden crabApple = new OverRidden("late July", "hand picking");
        OverRidden bingCherry = new OverRidden("Front Yard", 7, 25,
                                    "late July", "cherry picker");
        System.out.println("Bing Cherry Tree Information:");
        System.out.println(bingCherry);
        bingCherry.printTreeData();
        System.out.println("\n" + "Crab Apple Tree Information:");
        System.out.println(crabApple);
    }
}
```

The output of this program is exactly like that of `FruitTree.java`. But this program has one twist. Instead of a `printFruitTreeData()` method as we had before, we now have a method called `toString()`, that we never explicitly call.

```
public String toString() {
    return(
        "Harvest Method: " + this.harvestMethod + "\n"
                    + "Harvest Date: "
                    + this.harvestDate);
}
```

This is another example of method overriding. What are we overriding? By naming our own `toString()` method, we are overriding the `Object.toString()` method. We are inheriting the `toString()` method from the `Object` class, because every class ultimately `extends` the `object` class. We never have to explicitly call it in this case, because the `System.out.println()` method calls the appropriate `toString()` method for us based on the type of object passed in its argument.

In this section we've taken a brief look at the hierarchical nature of Java provided by inheritance. This has by no means been a complete discussion but rather a refresher of some of the more salient and critical characteristics of inheritance.

Errors, exceptions, and exception handling

Nothing is worse than software that crashes. Java provides a method for handling software errors through what is known as **exception handling**. This section will briefly discuss exceptions and exception handling, including:

- Definition of exceptions and exception handling

- Different types of exceptions

- Exception examples: a specified exception, our very own exception

An **exception**, simply put, is something going wrong during the course of program execution. **Exception handling** is the term used to describe how the program will deal with these exceptions. When an unexpected condition occurs, an exception object is created and the method or class that experienced the error condition is said to **throw** the exception. The exception object can then be passed throughout the program and handled where it's most appropriate to do so. The basic mechanism in Java for handling these exception objects is the `try/catch` block. Consider a simple example.

Listing 3-8: CheckedException.java

```
import java.io.*;
// This program will NOT compile
```

```
public class CheckedException {

    public static void main(String[] args) {
        String inputLines;
        BufferedReader myFile = new BufferedReader(
            new FileReader(args[0]));
        while ((inputLines=myFile.readLine()) != null) {
            System.out.println(inputLines);
        }
    }
}
```

The program example above tries to open a text file, read in the text, and print that text to the screen. The code block responsible for doing that work is enclosed in a try/catch block. That indicates that the program will try to perform the operations inside the block, and if it is unable to because of an exception, it will catch the exception and execute the code in the catch code block. If we tried to compile the above program without the try/catch statements, we would receive a compiler error.

`C:\> javac CheckedException.Java`

```
CheckedException.Java:5: Exception Java.io.FileNotFoundException must
be caught, or it must be declared in the throws clause of this method.
    BufferedReader myFile = new BufferedReader(new
FileReader(args[0]));
                                                        ^
CheckedException.Java:6: Exception Java.io.IOException must be caught,
or it must be declared in the throws clause of this method.
    while ((inputLines=myFile.readLine()) != null) {
                                           ^
2 errors
```

The reason for this is that several of the methods used in the program *throw* exceptions, which requires provisions to check for, or *catch* them. The Java API shows which methods throw exceptions and precisely which exceptions they throw. In our example, close() and readLine() are methods of the BufferedReader class, which both throw an exception called IOException. IOException is a class that extends the Exception class and is superclass to a host of more specific classes such as the FileNotFoundException. The FileReader constructor throws the FileNotFoundException, which can be caught separately, or as an IOException because it's a subclass of that exception. The following revised version compiles without errors.

Listing 3-9: FixedCheckedException.java

```
import java.io.*;
// This one will compile
```

```
public class FixedCheckedException {
    public static void main(String[] args) {
        String inputLines;
        try {
            BufferedReader myFile = new BufferedReader(
                                   new FileReader(args[0]));
            while ((inputLines=myFile.readLine()) != null) {
                System.out.println(inputLines);
            }
        } catch(IOException e) {
            System.out.println("There was an IOException");
        }
    }
}
```

As already noted, there are numerous different types of exceptions, but since exceptions are themselves objects, they form an inheritance hierarchy.

Errors are nonrecoverable conditions that should not be caught. They usually indicate serious flaws in the logic of the program.

Exceptions are abnormal conditions that should be caught and dealt with. Exceptions can further be broken down into different types:

- Checked Exceptions are exceptions that are checked by the Java compiler. The compiler is looking to see that your program is either performing exception handling through a try/catch block or specifying that the method throws an exception, thereby passing any exception on and forcing other calling methods to perform exception handling. This is commonly referred to as the "catch or specify" requirement. The IOException from the example above is a checked exception. Checked exceptions are not runtime exceptions—that is, they don't occur during program operation.

- Runtime Exceptions are exceptions that occur during program operation. Rules governing runtime exceptions and checked exceptions are different. Methods that throw runtime exceptions do not have to be enclosed in try/catch blocks, which is to say the "check or specify" requirement does not apply to them. The rules are different because runtime exceptions can occur in very numerous and unpredictable ways. It can be too difficult for the compiler to check for them and too difficult for the programmer to "catch or specify" them all. Good examples of runtime exceptions are division by zero and ArrayIndexOutOfBoundsException. They can be caught by try/catch blocks just like any other exception, but methods at risk for throwing these exceptions don't have to be enclosed in try/catch blocks to get the program to compile.

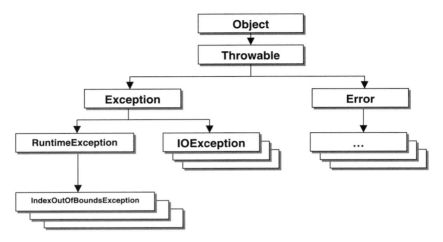

Figure 3-7: Error diagram

We've seen an example of a checked exception in which we caught the exception in a `try/catch` block. Let's now look at the same example, but now instead of catching the exception, let's specify it.

Listing 3-10: SpecifiedException.java

```
import java.io.*;
public class SpecifiedException {
    public static void main(String[] args) throws IOException {
        String inputLines;
        BufferedReader myFile = new BufferedReader(
                                 new FileReader(args[0]));
        while ((inputLines=myFile.readLine()) != null) {
            System.out.println(inputLines);
        }
    }
}
```

The program, `SpecifiedException.java`, will compile and run even though we are no longer catching the checked exceptions. This is because we are specifying them through the use of the `throws` keyword and we are meeting the "catch or specify" requirement.

Since exceptions are essentially a class hierarchy descending from the `Throwable` class, there's nothing preventing us from extending the `Exception` class ourselves and writing our own exceptions. Consider the following:

Listing 3-11: CustomException.java

```java
import java.io.*;
//  This program will NOT compile

public class CustomException {
    public static class FileIsTooShortException extends Exception {
        public FileIsTooShortException(String str) {
            super(str);
        }
    }

    public void readFile(String fileName) throws
                                    FileIsTooShortException {
        String inputLines;
        int index = 0;
        try {
            BufferedReader myFile = new BufferedReader(
                                new FileReader(fileName));
            while ((inputLines=myFile.readLine()) != null) {
                System.out.println(inputLines);
                index++;
            }
        } catch(IOException e) {
            System.out.println("There was an IOException");
        }
        if (index < 200) {
            throw new FileIsTooShortException("That file is too small");
        }
    }

    public static void main(String[] args) {
        CustomException dummy = new CustomException();
        dummy.readFile(args[0]);
    }
}
```

This program contains a class definition for a new exception, a
`FileIsTooShortException`. The definition consists of nothing more than a
constructor that calls the superclass constructor, which in this case will be the
`Exception` constructor.

```java
    public static class FileIsTooShortException extends Exception {
        public FileIsTooShortException(String str) {
        super(str);
        }
    }
```

Exactly what a `FileIsTooShortException` is supposed to mean isn't clear from the constructor. It becomes clear in the method below. Here, we have defined a method, `printFile()`, that accepts a file name as an argument, opens the file and then prints out the lines to the screen. Since several of the methods used throw `IOExceptions`, there is a `try/catch` block for exception handling. But, we have also specified that this method throws an exception, a `FileIsTooShortException`. In conjunction with this, the method counts the number of lines. If the number of lines is less than 200, it uses the `FileIsTooShortException` constructor to create an `Exception` object and `throws` that object.

```
public void readFile(String fileName) throws
                              FileIsTooShortException {
   String inputLines;
   int index = 0;
   try {
      BufferedReader myFile = new BufferedReader(
            new FileReader(fileName));
      while ((inputLines=myFile.readLine()) != null) {
         System.out.println(inputLines);
         index++;
      }
   } catch(IOException e) {
   System.out.println("There was an IOException");
   }
   if (index < 200) {
      throw new FileIsTooShortException("That file is too small");
   }
}
```

Finally, there is the `main()` method. This simply creates a dummy `CustomException` object and invokes the `printFile()` method.

```
public static void main(String[] args) {
   CustomException dummy = new CustomException();
   dummy.readFile(args[0]);
}
```

If you try to compile this program, you will see the following:

```
c:\> javac CheckedException.java
CustomException.Java:28: Exception CustomException.
FileIsTooShortException must be caught, or it must be declared
in the throws clause of this method.
   dummy.readFile(args[0]);
             ^
1 error
```

This is actually a good thing! It means that we have succeeded in making our own custom exception. The program as written has a custom checked exception built into it, `FileIsTooShortException`. The method that throws that exception is `printFile()`. Since it's a checked exception, we have to either "catch or specify" the exception. To `catch` it, we would embed the `printfile()` method in a `try/catch` block. To specify it, we would have to declare that the method calling `printFile()` throws the `FileIsTooShortException` (thereby passing the buck). Since the program above does neither of these, we should see exactly the error we are seeing. Both fixes are illustrated below. The catch method of fixing it:

Listing 3-12: CatchCustomException.java

```java
import java.io.*;
public class CatchCustomException {
    public static class FileIsTooShortException extends Exception {
        public FileIsTooShortException(String str) {
            super(str);
        }
    }

public void readFile(String fileName) throws FileIsTooShortException {
        String inputLines;
        int index = 0;
        try {
            BufferedReader myFile = new BufferedReader(
            new FileReader(fileName));
            while ((inputLines=myFile.readLine()) != null) {
                System.out.println(inputLines);
                index++;
            }
        } catch(IOException e) {
            System.out.println("There was an IOException");
        }

        if (index < 200) {
            throw new FileIsTooShortException("That file is too small");
        }
    }

    public static void main(String[] args) {
        CatchCustomException dummy = new CatchCustomException();
        try {
            dummy.readFile(args[0]);
        } catch(FileIsTooShortException e) {
            System.out.println("We are experiencing a strange new exception");
        }
    }
}
```

The specify way of fixing this:

Listing 3-13: SpecifyCustomException.java

```java
import java.io.*;
public class SpecifyCustomException {
    public static class FileIsTooShortException extends Exception {
        public FileIsTooShortException(String str) {
            super(str);
        }
    }

    public void readFile(String fileName) throws
                                    FileIsTooShortException {
        String inputLines;
        int index = 0;
        try {
            BufferedReader myFile = new BufferedReader(
                                    new FileReader(fileName));
            while ((inputLines=myFile.readLine()) != null) {
                System.out.println(inputLines);
                index++;
            }
        } catch(IOException e) {
            System.out.println("There was an IOException");
        }
        if (index < 200) {
            throw new FileIsTooShortException("That file is too small");
        }
    }

    public static void main(String[] args) throws
                                    FileIsTooShortException {
        SpecifyCustomException dummy = new SpecifyCustomException();
        dummy.readFile(args[0]);
    }
}
```

Before leaving this section, there is one more brief topic to address: the `finally` keyword. In addition to the `catch` portion of the `try/catch` block, Java provides a mechanism for cleaning up after exception handling. This is the `finally` keyword. Code located within the `finally` block gets executed no matter what happens inside the `try/catch` block. It's a good place to close any open files or devices.

Listing 3-14: FinallyExample.java

```java
import java.io.*;
public class FinallyExample {
    public static void main(String[] args) {
```

```
        String inputLines;
        BufferedReader myFile = null;
        try {
           myFile = new BufferedReader(new FileReader(args[0]));
           while ((inputLines=myFile.readLine()) != null) {
              System.out.println(inputLines);
           }
        } catch(IOException e) {
           System.out.println("There was an IOException");
        } finally {
           try {
              myFile.close();
           } catch (IOException e2) {
              System.out.println(
                   "There was an IOException in closing the file");
           }
        }
     }
}
```

The `finally` block in the code above will always be executed after the first `try` block. So no matter what kind of exception happens in the first `try`/`catch` block, the program will at least attempt to close the `BufferedReader`.

Network Programming

One of the strong points of Java is that the language has networking capabilities built in. This section will briefly highlight some of the capabilities that are most relevant to the hardware projects we'll be considering later, particularly sockets, ports and URLs.

In the previous chapter on networks we discussed the TCP/IP protocol stack. The programs that follow are written at the application layer of this protocol stack, using `Java.net` classes to communicate over the Internet using the connection-based TCP. Classes exist in the `Java.net` library that allow for the use of UDP (user datagram protocol) to communicate over the Internet, but we won't be considering them here. TCP is a connection-based protocol and as a connection-based protocol it uses sockets and ports as the basis for these connections.

Two-way communication over the Internet typically is performed by client/server pairs. Client/server communication with sockets proceeds as follows:

1. A server creates a special socket, called a server socket, that can listen for connection requests from clients. This server socket is associated with, or **binds**, to a specific port number. That port number will be a well-known port number associated with the specific service the server offers. It then listens for client requests for connections to that port.

2. When a client wants to communicate with the service offered by the server, the client creates a client socket. Usually we let the operating system randomly pick an unused port to bind to the socket, but we can specify it if we want to. A communication request is then sent to the server socket, informing it of the client socket's address and desire to communicate.

3. The server is listening for connections on the server's well-known port and when it receives a client request, it creates another socket, using a randomly chosen unused port (1024 or higher) and responds back to the client. The server only uses the well-known port to listen for client connection requests. Upon receiving them, it passes the request onto a different local port to be handle to actual data transfers.

Java provides capabilities for reading and writing to sockets through the Java.net class library classes. The most relevant classes for our discussion are the `InetAddress`, `Socket`, and `ServerSocket` classes. While a socket refers to one endpoint of a network communication, Java `Socket` objects contain information on both endpoints of a connection. Let's consider some examples.

Reading and writing to a socket (a simple client)

The following program is a very simple HTTP client. Given an Internet address such as www.java.sun.com and a web page such as index.html, it initiates a socket communication to the well-known port 80 (HTTP services) and requests a web page. The web page is printed to the screen in raw HTML format.

Listing 3-15: HttpSocketClient.java

```
import java.net.*;
import java.io.*;

public class HttpSocketClient {
    public static void main(String[] args) {
        try {
            InetAddress addr = InetAddress.getByName(args[0]);
            Socket webSocket = new Socket(addr, 80);
            BufferedWriter clientRequest = new BufferedWriter(
                new OutputStreamWriter(webSocket.getOutputStream()));
            BufferedReader serverResponse = new BufferedReader(
                new InputStreamReader(webSocket.getInputStream()));
            clientRequest.write("GET /" + args[1] + " HTTP/1.1\n");
            clientRequest.write("Host: " + args[0] + ":80\n\n");
            clientRequest.flush();
            while(serverResponse.readLine() != null) {
                System.out.println(serverResponse.readLine());
            }
        }
```

```
            serverResponse.close();
            clientRequest.close();
            webSocket.close();
        } catch(Exception e){e.printStackTrace();}
    }
}
```

The program consists of only one method, `main()`, that takes two string arguments: an Internet domain name and a web page. We take the first of those arguments, the domain name, and pass it to the `InetAddress` constructor, creating an `InetAddress` object called `addr`. The `getByName()` method will accept a host name or an IP address. This is one way of passing host information to the `Socket` constructor. There are eight versions of the `Socket` constructor, taking different types of arguments. We could have passed the domain name string `args[0]` directly to the constructor without having first gone through the process of creating the `InetAddress`. But this way gave us a context to show one more networking related class, `InetAddress`. The `InetAddress` object `addr` is passed to the socket constructor along with the port number, 80. This means we will be trying to contact the service running at port 80 on the host machine we specify. Port 80 corresponds to the predefined service of web browsing using HTTP. Locally, our `Socket` object `webSocket`, is not open on port 80. Java is choosing, at random, an unused port, above 1023. The socket address, made up of our host machine and the client port number, is passed to the server during this socket creation.

```
public class HttpSocketClient {
    public static void main(String[] args) {
        try {
            InetAddress addr = InetAddress.getByName(args[0]);
            Socket webSocket = new Socket(addr, 80);
```

Having created a `Socket` object called `webSocket`, we are going to use two of its methods to establish IO streams to the socket. It's a good idea to use a buffered stream, so for writing to the socket, we will use a `BufferedWriter` stream. Its constructor needs to be given an `OutputStreamWriter` as an argument, so we need to create an `OuputStreamWriter`. The `OutputStreamWriter` constructor takes an `OutputStream` as its argument, so we need to get an `OutputStream`. The `getOutputStream()` method of the `Socket` library will provide that output stream. Instead of declaring named objects for the `OutputStream` and the `OutputStreamWriter`, we just use their creation as arguments to the required constructor and cascade them all together. This avoids a lot of naming objects that will never be referred to again. To read from the socket, we use an `InputStreamReader`. Its creation follows a similar process as the `OutputStreamWriter`. We now have an `InputStreamReader`, `serverResponse`, that corresponds to what we are reading from the socket and we have an `OutputStreamWriter`, `clientRequest`, that corresponds to what we are sending to the socket.

```
BufferedWriter clientRequest = new BufferedWriter(
        new OutputStreamWriter(webSocket.getOutputStream()));
BufferedReader serverResponse = new BufferedReader(
        new InputStreamReader(webSocket.getInputStream()));
```

The next few lines write an HTTP client request to the socket using the `write()` method of the `BufferedWriter` class. The data isn't actually sent until the `flush()` method is called. It's very important to note that the specific syntax of the text sent to the HTTP server is very exacting. While HTTP1.1 is a well-defined protocol, vendors differ in how tolerant they are of deviation from the protocol. We could omit the second line,. the "`Host: `" + args[0] + "`:80\n\n`" line, and this program would still work for most servers we would try. But it wouldn't work for all of them. And it's critical that the line ends with two new lines (\n) as opposed to just one.

```
clientRequest.write("GET /" + args[1] + " HTTP/1.1\n");
clientRequest.write("Host: " + args[0] + ":80\n\n");
clientRequest.flush();
```

After sending the HTTP GET request to the server through our socket, we use the `readLine()` method of the `BufferedReader` class to read back the response from the server through the socket. When there are no more lines, we close the `Buffered Reader`, the `BufferedWriter`, and the socket. Since many of these methods throw exceptions, we have a `catch()` block at the end.

```
                while(serverResponse.readLine() != null) {
                    System.out.println(serverResponse.readLine());
                }
                serverResponse.close();
                clientRequest.close();
                webSocket.close();
            } catch(Exception e){e.printStackTrace();}
    }
}
```

To execute the program, try the following:

```
c:\> javac HttpSocketClient.java
c:\> java HttpSocketClient www.rhubarbinfo.com index.html
Date: Mon, 15 Jan 2001 13:45:20 GMT
Filter-Revision: 1.90
Content-length: 14580

    "http://www.w3.org/TR/REC-html40/loose.dtd">

<link rel="STYLESHEET" TYPE="text/css" HREF="styles.css">

[lots of html spews forth, omitted for brevity]
</td></tr><!—msnavigation—></table></body>
null
```

The program we just described represents about the simplest client we could construct. In creating a socket connection to port 80 on a remote machine, it asks to be connected to the service provided at port 80. That service is an HTTP web server. Next we will construct the corresponding server.

Reading and writing to a socket (a simple server)

The program below represents a very simple server. It listens on port 80 for clients requesting connections. When it detects a client connection request, it creates a socket to communicate with the client, creates a BufferedWriter, and then writes a simple web page to that socket. It doesn't actually read anything from the client.

Listing 3-16: HttpSocketServer.java

```
import java.util.*;
import java.io.*;
import java.net.*;

public class HttpSocketServer {
    public static void main(String[] args) {
        int port = 80;
        try {
            ServerSocket srv = new ServerSocket(port);
            Date currentDate;
            String currentTime;
            while (true) {
                currentDate = new Date();
                currentTime = currentDate.toString();
                Socket mySocket = srv.accept();
                System.out.println("Connection Accepted @" +
                                        currentTime);
                BufferedWriter serverResponse = new BufferedWriter(
                    new OutputStreamWriter(mySocket.getOutputStream()));

                writePage(serverResponse, currentTime);
                mySocket.close();
            }
        } catch (IOException e) {
            e.printStackTrace();
            System.out.println("There is an IOException in
                                        HttpSocketServer");
        }
    }

    public static void writePage(BufferedWriter wr, String ct) {
        try {
            wr.write("HTTP/1.0 200 OK\n");
            wr.write("Content-type: text/html\n\n");
            wr.write("<HTML><HEAD>\n");
```

```
            wr.write("<TITLE>Hello Web Client!</TITLE>\n");
            wr.write("<H3><CENTER>Hello Web Client!</CENTER></H3>\n");
            wr.write("</HEAD>\n");
            wr.write("<BODY><CENTER>\n");
            wr.write("The current time is " + ct);
            wr.write("</CENTER></BODY></HTML>\n");
            wr.flush();
            wr.close();
        } catch (IOException e) {
            e.printStackTrace();
            System.out.println("There is an IOException in writePage");
        }
    }
}
```

The program begins with importing several necessary Java libraries. The class name and the `main()` method are declared. The `SocketServer` constructor is called to create a `SocketServer` object called `srv`, at port 80. The `srv` object, while not a `Socket` object itself, has methods that will allow us to create a `Socket` object when a client tries to connect to the port on which it was created, in this case port 80. That new socket is not located on port 80, but is located on a non-well-known port, randomly chosen by Java. This frees the server port to continue to listen for more client requests.

```
import java.util.*;
import java.io.*;
import java.net.*;

public class HttpSocketServer {
    public static void main(String[] args) {
        int port = 80;
        try {
        ServerSocket srv = new ServerSocket(port);
        Date currentDate;
        String currentTime;
```

Following the basic declarations in the `main()` method, the program contains a loop that will run forever. Not exactly elegant programming, but it allows us to create a fairly uncluttered example. Each loop, a new `Date` object is created, and from that a string that contains the current time. Then, the `SocketServer` object `srv` is now used with the `accept()` method. This method waits until a client tries to connect to port 80. The loop will thus wait at this point until something tries to connect to our server. When something does, the `accept()` method will return a `Socket` object. We've called this object, `mySocket`, and it has information about both the local socket and remote socket. Locally, it is not bound to port 80, but a randomly selected port above 1023. A string containing the current time is printed to the screen from which we invoked the server. As in the example above, we create a `BufferedWriter` stream to write to the socket and call that stream `serverResponse`. The `serverResponse` `BufferedWriter` object and the string containing the current time are sent as arguments to a method that will print HTML to the client.

```
while (true) {
    currentDate = new Date();
    currentTime = currentDate.toString();
    Socket mySocket = srv.accept();
    System.out.println("Connection Accepted @" + currentTime);
    BufferedWriter serverResponse = new BufferedWriter(
            new OutputStreamWriter(mySocket.getOutputStream()));

    writePage(serverResponse, currentTime);
```

Finally, the socket is closed and we `catch()` any `IOException` that may have occurred.

```
    mySocket.close();
    }
} catch (IOException e) {
    e.printStackTrace();
    System.out.println("There is an IOException in HttpSocketServer");
}
}
```

The method `writePage()` takes a `BufferedWriter` and a string containing the time as arguments. The `write()` method of the `BufferedWriter` class is used to send text to the socket. The text sent by this message is in HTTP protocol format. You can think of this as our server response to a client request. This is again a case where great care has to be given to follow the protocol specification closely. Many web browsers will correctly print server responses that don't strictly follow the HTTP standard, but some do not. Note the two new line characters (`\n`) in the `Content-type` line of the server response. Without the second new line character, the web browser client will generally not recognize the response.

The text isn't actually written to the stream until the `flush()` method is invoked. The stream is closed and we `catch` any `IOException` that might have occurred.

```
public static void writePage(BufferedWriter wr, String ct) {
    try {
        wr.write("HTTP/1.0 200 OK\n");
        wr.write("Content-type: text/html\n\n");
        wr.write("<HTML><HEAD>\n");
        wr.write("<TITLE>Hello Web Client!</TITLE>\n");
        wr.write("<H3><CENTER>Hello Web Client!</CENTER></H3>\n");
        wr.write("</HEAD>\n");
        wr.write("<BODY><CENTER>\n");
```

```
            wr.write("The current time is " + ct);
            wr.write("</CENTER></BODY></HTML>\n");
            wr.flush();
            wr.close();
        } catch (IOException e) {
            e.printStackTrace();
            System.out.println("There is an IOException in writePage");
        }
    }
}
```

To try this program out, invoke the HttpSocketServer program from the command line and then open up a web browser and type in the URL http://127.0.0.1/ Both the command line window and the browser should respond as shown below. Since web browsers frequently cache web pages, sometimes when you hit refresh, the web page may not update. The IP address 127.0.0.1 is what is known as the loop-back address. It refers to the machine you are running on (the localhost).

```
c:\> javac HttpSocketServer.java
c:\> java HttpSocketServer
connection Accepted @Fri Jan 12 22:36:25 PST 2001
```

Figure 3-8: Web browser image

Reading and writing to a socket (a slightly less simple server)

The server we looked at in the previous example was very simple. It suffered from the fact that the server contained a loop that would never end, forcing you to shut the window down to kill the program. Let's look at a similar example in which the server now examines client requests to look for a command to shut down.

The program below creates a `ServerSocket` object binding to port 80. It uses that `ServerSocket` object to listen for client requests for connection to port 80. When it sees one, it creates a separate `Socket` object, on a different port, to the client. Buffered IO streams are created to read and write from the socket. Each time the client requests a connection to the server, a count is incremented and that count is sent back to the client in the form of text that will be viewed by a browser as a web page. The text is passed through the streams via HTTP protocol. This is an example of data encapsulation: HTML text is being passed to a web browser via HTTP. The web page has HTML FORM elements in it that can be used by the browser to send back a command to either increment the counter, or quit. Client requests are examined to see whether or not they contain the QUIT command. If so, the streams and socket are closed and the server is shut down.

Listing 3-17: HttpImporvedServer.java

```java
import java.util.*;
import java.io.*;
import java.net.*;

public class HttpImprovedServer {
    public static void main(String[] args) {
        int port = 80;
            int count=0;
            boolean serverFlag = true;
        try {
            ServerSocket srv = new ServerSocket(port);
            while (serverFlag) {
                Socket mySocket = srv.accept();
                BufferedWriter serverResponse = new BufferedWriter(
                    new OutputStreamWriter(mySocket.getOutputStream()));

                BufferedReader clientRequest = new BufferedReader(
                    new InputStreamReader(mySocket.getInputStream()));

                String str;
                str= clientRequest.readLine();
                System.out.println(str);
                if (str.startsWith("GET /?QUIT")) {
                    serverFlag = false;
                    sayGoodbye(serverResponse, count);
```

```
            } else {
               count++;
               writePage(serverResponse, count);
            }
            clientRequest.close();
            mySocket.close();
                }
    } catch (IOException e) {
        e.printStackTrace();
        System.out.println("Problem with main");
    }
}

public static void writePage(BufferedWriter wr, int df) {
    String str=String.valueOf(df);
    try {
        wr.write("HTTP/1.0 200 OK\n");
        wr.write("Content-type: text/html\n\n");
        wr.write("<HEAD>\n");
        wr.write("<TITLE>This is a counting test web page</TITLE>\n");
        wr.write("<H3><CENTER>An HTTP counter</CENTER></H3>\n");
        wr.write("</HEAD>\n");
        wr.write("<BODY><CENTER>\n");
        wr.write("Push the Button to Update the Count\n");
        wr.write("<FORM>");
        wr.write("<INPUT TYPE=SUBMIT NAME='Increment' VALUE='Increment'>");
        wr.write("<INPUT TYPE=SUBMIT NAME='QUIT' VALUE='QUIT'>");
        wr.write("</FORM>");
        wr.write("The current count = " + str);
        wr.write("</CENTER></BODY>\n");
        wr.flush();
    } catch (IOException e) {
        e.printStackTrace();
        System.out.println("There is an IOException in writePage");
    }
}

public static void sayGoodbye(BufferedWriter wr, int df) {
    String str=String.valueOf(df);
    try {
        wr.write("HTTP/1.0 200 OK\n");
        wr.write("Content-type: text/html\n\n");
        wr.write("<HEAD>\n");
        wr.write("<TITLE>Goodbye!</TITLE>\n");
        wr.write("<H3><CENTER>Goodbye</CENTER></H3>\n");
        wr.write("</HEAD>\n");
        wr.write("<BODY><CENTER>\n");
        wr.write("The final count = " + str);
        wr.write("</CENTER></BODY>\n");
        wr.flush();
```

CHAPTER **1**

Introduction

Why should you read this book?

The target audience of this book is anyone interested in merging practical electronic devices with the Internet: students, teachers, home automation enthusiasts, hobbyists, and small businesses. Computer programmers looking for a gentle introduction to the world of hardware will benefit, as will hardware designers looking to expand their skills into the realm of JAVA programming. College engineering and computer science departments will find in this book a wealth of possibilities for lab projects that expose students to cutting-edge technology with minimal expense. Why should you read this book? The best reason of all: fun. This book will provide anyone interested in tinkering with hardware on the net hours of fun. Another reason: the future. Even if you're not interested in making hardware, this book will give you a practical glimpse into what the real future and potential of the Internet is.

The first Internet wave connected people via computer, popularizing things such as email, search engines, and online shopping. The next wave is going to be Internet appliances: electronic devices connected to the Internet. Ever wondered how those "live internet cams" work? They're probably the most recognizable example of hardware connected to the web. In the past they were tremendously expensive and tended to be supported by engineering departments as an experimental thing. The future is going to see a tremendous expansion of low-cost, practical devices, connected to the Internet for home use.

A good example might be a future VCR. Have you ever found yourself at work, wishing you had set the VCR to program your favorite show? A VCR that was an Internet appliance would give you the capability of programming your VCR from a web page, wherever you may be. Another good example of an Internet appliance might be a piece of hardware that allows you to control your thermostat, your lights, and your water heater from a web site. Cheap Internet appliance technology will make controlling devices in your home from a web page commonplace. Will everything in your house be "on the web" in the future? Probably not. But the growing number of people with Internet on their desk and the proliferation of cell phones and PDAs that can interact with web pages represents a growing market. That market is raising the attention of countless companies both large and small, looking to make products to put into every home. This book will examine commercial technology, discussing in great detail an inexpensive web-enabled microcontroller that can be used to connect a variety of devices to the web.

Why should you read this book? So when the next big Internet wave happens, you'll be in front of it! (And, there is that fun thing, too.)

What this book will do for you

This book is a complete introduction to Internet-enabled devices. We provide all of the information you need to inexpensively build your own web-enabled hardware. Specifically, we'll show you:

1. The basic terms and concepts required to understand the technology of web-enabled devices. This includes detailed sections on networking and Java programming.

2. A quick overview of commercially available, web-enabled, microcontrollers, comparing their price and availability.

3. A step-by-step examination of TINI[1], the Tiny InterNet Interface, a commercially available hardware/software package designed for use as a web interface to hardware. We'll examine the hardware, software, and available enhancements in detail.

How this book is laid out

The information in this book is divided into 14 chapters.

Chapters 1 through 4 provide basic technical definitions with respect to networking and Internet clients and servers. We're going to go into some detail on Java, the modern object-oriented, internet-ready, programming language rapidly becoming the language of choice for network applications. We're not going to teach you Java, but we are going to cover some of the key features of the language that are very relevant to our topic, and are frequently not taught in the average Java course.

---

[1] TINI is a registered trademark of Dallas Semiconductor. TINI can be purchased on the iButton website, http://www.ibutton.com/TINI/

```
        } catch (IOException e) {
            e.printStackTrace();
        System.out.println("There is an IOException in sayGoodbye");
        }
    }
}
```

The program starts with the usual import statements to access the necessary libraries and the class declaration. The main method begins by declaring a port variable, an integer count variable, and a boolean flag. The flag, serverFlag, is used to identify whether or not the program should continue to look for client requests in a loop. A ServerSocket object binding to port 80 is created that will allow it to wait for client connection requests to port 80 via the accept() method.

```
import java.util.*;
import java.io.*;
import java.net.*;

public class HttpSocketServer {
public static void main(String[] args) {
    int port = 80;
  int count=0;
  boolean serverFlag = true;
    try {
        ServerSocket srv = new ServerSocket(port);
```

A loop based on our flag, serverFlag, begins. We start by waiting for the client connection request to port 80. When it occurs, a Socket object is created on a different port, to provide communication to the client. IO streams are created for reading and writing to this socket, clientRequest and serverResponse. Again, we used BufferedWriter and Bufferedreader objects as our streams.

```
while (serverFlag) {
    Socket mySocket = srv.accept();
    BufferedWriter serverResponse = new BufferedWriter(
            new OutputStreamWriter(mySocket.getOutputStream()));
    BufferedReader clientRequest = new BufferedReader(
            new InputStreamReader(mySocket.getInputStream()));
```

A String object is declared and it is used to hold the text that the client is sending to the server via the socket. It's read from the socket via the readLine() method. The string is printed to the screen in which the server was invoked. It is then scanned for the text that would result if the QUIT form element on the web page being served by our server has been depressed. If it finds it, we set our flag so that our continuous loop is stopped and the server is shutdown. A goodbye/final count web page is served to the client before the shutdown. If the input from the client does not indicate a QUIT, it increments our count variable and serves the web page right back to the client with the revised count. All of the web page serving is done via one of two methods. Once the client has been served either a goodbye page or a revised count page, the `clientRequest` stream and the `mySocket Socket` object is closed.

```
        String str;
            str= clientRequest.readLine();
            System.out.println(str);
            if (str.startsWith("GET /?QUIT")) {
                serverFlag = false;
                sayGoodbye(serverResponse, count);
            } else {
                count++;
                writePage(serverResponse, count);
            }
            clientRequest.close();
            mySocket.close();
                }
    } catch (IOException e) {
        e.printStackTrace();
        System.out.println("Problem with main");
    }
}
```

This method, `writePage()`, writes an HTML web page using the HTTP protocol to the client via the socket. It takes a `BufferedWriter` and an integer as arguments. The first two lines written represent the HTTP protocol sever response header. The rest is HTML text. The web page is actually a very simple page that features a count, representing the number of times the page has been served The HTML also contains a form having two buttons. One button is pressed if you want to increment the count, the other is pressed if you want to shut down the server. After writing the text to the socket, we catch any `IOException` that may have occurred. All writing to the socket is done via the `BufferedWriter.write()` method.

```
public static void writePage(BufferedWriter wr, int df) {
        String str=String.valueOf(df);
        try {
            wr.write("HTTP/1.0 200 OK\n");
            wr.write("Content-type: text/html\n\n");
            wr.write("<HEAD>\n");
            wr.write("<TITLE>This is a counting test web page</TITLE>\n");
            wr.write("<H3><CENTER>An HTTP counter</CENTER></H3>\n");
            wr.write("</HEAD>\n");
            wr.write("<BODY><CENTER>\n");
            wr.write("Push the Button to Update the Count\n");
            wr.write("<FORM>");
            wr.write("<INPUT TYPE=SUBMIT NAME='Increment' VALUE='Increment'>");
            wr.write("<INPUT TYPE=SUBMIT NAME='QUIT' VALUE='QUIT'>");
            wr.write("</FORM>");
            wr.write("The current count = " + str);
            wr.write("</CENTER></BODY>\n");
```

```
        wr.flush();
    } catch (IOException e) {
        e.printStackTrace();
        System.out.println("There is an IOException in writePage");
    }
}
```

This method, `sayGoodBye()` also writes an HTML web page using the HTTP protocol to the client via the socket. Like the `writePage()` method, it takes a `BufferedWriter` and an integer as arguments. The first two lines written represent the HTTP protocol server response header. The rest is HTML text. This web page prints the final count and some text saying "goodbye." After writing the text to the socket, we catch any `IOException` that may have occurred. All writing to the socket is done via the `BufferedWriter.write()` method.

```
public static void sayGoodbye(BufferedWriter wr, int df) {
    String str=String.valueOf(df);
    try {
        wr.write("HTTP/1.0 200 OK\n");
        wr.write("Content-type: text/html\n\n");
        wr.write("<HEAD>\n");
        wr.write("<TITLE>Goodbye!</TITLE>\n");
        wr.write("<H3><CENTER>Goodbye</CENTER></H3>\n");
        wr.write("</HEAD>\n");
        wr.write("<BODY><CENTER>\n");
        wr.write("The final count = " + str);
        wr.write("</CENTER></BODY>\n");
        wr.flush();
    } catch (IOException e) {
        e.printStackTrace();
        System.out.println("There is an IOException in sayGoodbye");
    }
}
```

To try this program out, invoke the `HttpImprovedServer` program from the command line and then open up a web browser and type in the URL http://127.0.0.1/ Both the command line window and the browser should respond as shown below. The IP address 127.0.0.1 is what is known as the loop-back address. It refers to the machine you are running on (the localhost). The command line looks like this:

```
c:\> javac HttpImprovedServer.java
c:\> java HttpImprovedServer
GET / HTTP/1.1
GET /?Increment=Increment HTTP/1.1
GET /?Increment=Increment HTTP/1.1
GET /?Increment=Increment HTTP/1.1
GET /?Increment=Increment HTTP/1.1
GET /?Increment=Increment HTTP/1.1
GET /?Increment=Increment HTTP/1.1
GET /?QUIT=QUIT HTTP/1.1
```

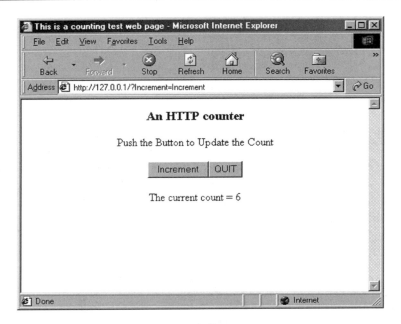

Figure 3-9: Web browser image #2

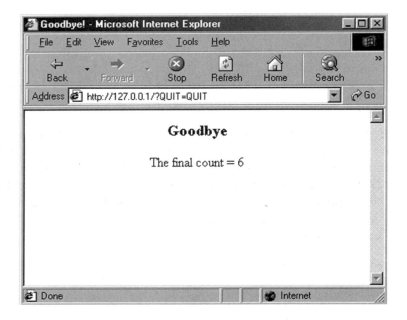

Figure 3-10: Web browser image #3

Programming with URLs

All of the previous examples of networking involved the use of the `Socket` and `ServerSocket` classes. Before leaving our discussion of network programming, there's one more topic to be touched upon, the topic of `URL` objects.

A **URL**, or Uniform Resource Locator, typically refers to an Internet address such as http://java.sun.com. But in the `java.net` class library, there is a `URL` class. The `URL` class provides a variety of useful methods for getting network information and for parsing information out of a provided URL. The `URL` class also provides ways for us to read directly from a URL or form connections. Below is a simple example.

This program is a simple HTTP web client, very much like our first socket example. It takes a string URL as a command line argument, then creates a `URL` object, `webURL`, from that argument. An IO stream is created using the `openStream()` method of the `webURL` object, which will allow us to read directly from the URL we gave as an argument. We create a `BufferedReader`, `webReader`, to read from the `URL` object, `webURL`. The `readLine()` method of the `webReader` object returns lines of text of the web page we entered as an argument. We stop reading when there are no more lines, and then close the IO stream. Finally, we use various methods of the `webURL` object to parse out information about the URL we just read from.

One interesting thing to note about this process is that we didn't have to write any HTTP client request information to the server, as we did when we made the simple HTTP client using sockets. This is because the URL class acts as a protocol handler for us. It takes care of issuing those commands in its methods, transparent to us.

Listing 3-18: HttpURLClient.java

```java
import java.net.*;
import java.io.*;

public class HttpURLClient {
    public static void main(String[] args) {
        try {
            URL webURL = new URL(args[0]);
            BufferedReader webReader = new BufferedReader(
                    new InputStreamReader(
                    webURL.openStream()));
            String singleLine;
            while ((singleLine = webReader.readLine()) != null) {
                System.out.println(singleLine);
            }
            webReader.close();
            System.out.println("Protocol = " + webURL.getProtocol());
```

```
            System.out.println("Path = " + webURL.getPath());
            System.out.println("Port = " + webURL.getPort());
            System.out.println("File = " + webURL.getFile());
            System.out.println("Host = " + webURL.getHost());
        } catch(Exception e) {e.printStackTrace();}
    }
}
```

To test this program, we'll run it in conjunction with our HttpImprovedServer example.

```
c:\> java HttpURLClient http://127.0.0.1:80/
<HEAD>
<TITLE>This is a counting test web page</TITLE>
<H3><CENTER>An HTTP counter</CENTER></H3>
</HEAD>
<BODY><CENTER>
Push the Button to Update the Count
<FORM>
<INPUT TYPE=SUBMIT NAME='Increment' VALUE='Increment'>
<INPUT TYPE=SUBMIT NAME='QUIT' VALUE='QUIT'>
</FORM>
The current count = 1<CENTER><BODY>
Protocol = http
Path = /
Port = 80
File = /
Host = 127.0.0.1
```

Meanwhile, the window we run the server from looks like this:

```
c:\> javac HttpImprovedServer.java
c:\> java HttpImprovedServer
GET / HTTP/1.1
```

Nowhere in our example HttpURLClient are we explicitly writing the GET command to the stream. It's taken care of for us by the URL class. The URL class has many applications; we will be using it primarily for the parsing methods.

This section has been a quick look at network programming. Many of the concepts, especially that of reading and writing to sockets, will be used and expanded on in later sections of this book.

Threads

The simple HTTP servers in the previous sections raise an interesting issue: while functional, they were not very useful because they only talked to *one* client at a time. That's not really the true spirit of networking. Networking is all about connecting many clients to a single server. That requires the server to be multitasking, or doing more than one thing at a time. Java has a multitasking capability called threads.

A thread, in Java, refers to a single sequential flow of control within a program. Java programs can be multi-threaded. Many different sequential flows can be operating in parallel, independently. We could be doing completely different things at the same time in different threads, or we could be doing multiple copies of the same activity in different threads. As with `Exceptions`, and `Sockets`, and `URLs`, `Threads` are also a Java class.

There are two basic ways to implement threads in a Java program.

1. Make your own Java class that extends the Thread class.

2. Make your own Java class that implements the runnable interface.

Implementing threads by extending the thread class

This is the method of choice when your threads might be used by other classes. We will start by looking at a simple example.

Listing 3-19: CountingThread.java

```java
class CountingThread extends Thread {
    String threadName;
    int waitTime;
    public CountingThread(String tName, int wTime) {
        this.threadName = tName;
        this.waitTime = wTime;
    }

    public void run() {
        int count = 0;
        while(count < 25) {
            count++;
            System.out.println(this.threadName + " " + count);
            try {
                sleep((long)this.waitTime);
            } catch(Exception e) {System.out.println("Couldn't Sleep");}
        }
    }
}

public class ExtFourThreads {
    public static void main(String[] args) {
        int one = Integer.parseInt(args[0]);
        int two = Integer.parseInt(args[1]);
        int three = Integer.parseInt(args[2]);
        int four = Integer.parseInt(args[3]);
        new CountingThread("One", one).start();
        new CountingThread("Two", two).start();
        new CountingThread("Three", three).start();
```

```
        new CountingThread("Four", four).start();
    }
}
```

This example implements four threads, each counting to 25 and printing the count out as it goes. Each thread has its own delay between increments that is set when the program is invoked. The first few lines,

```
class CountingThread extends Thread {
    String threadName;
    int waitTime;
    public CountingThread(String tName, int wTime) {
        this.threadName = tName;
        this.waitTime = wTime;
    }
```

represent the constructor for our threads. Note that we are extending the thread through the use of the `extends` keyword. Each of our threads has two variables, a name and a delay time. Next comes the `run()` method.

```
public void run() {
    int count = 0;
    while(count < 25) {
        count++;
        System.out.println(this.threadName + " " + count);
        try {
            sleep((long)this.waitTime);
        } catch(Exception e) {System.out.println("Couldn't Sleep");}
    }
}
```

The `run()` method is a pre-existing method of the `Thread` superclass. It is executed when we invoke the `Thread.start()` command, since `CountingThread` is a subclass of `Thread`, and they both have a method named `run()`. We are overriding the `run()` method in the `Thread` class. Lastly, we have a second class in the same file as our `CountingThread` class, called `FourThreads`. This class is actually the program we will run from the command line. The `ExtFourThreads` class makes use of the `CountingThread` class. This is often the case when you implement threads by extending the `Thread` class: they get used by other classes.

```
public class ExtFourThreads {
    public static void main(String[] args) {
        int one = Integer.parseInt(args[0]);
        int two = Integer.parseInt(args[1]);
        int three = Integer.parseInt(args[2]);
        int four = Integer.parseInt(args[3]);
        new CountingThread("One", one).start();
        new CountingThread("Two", two).start();
        new CountingThread("Three", three).start();
```

```
        new CountingThread("Four", four).start();
    }
}
```

`ExtFourThreads` reads in four strings from the command line (spaces between them) and converts them to long values for use as the sleep values for the different threads. The constructor is called four times, generating four new threads and at the same time the `start()` method is invoked. This causes our overridden version of the `run()` method to execute. Four separate counting processes proceed, each with user-defined delays between increments. The program output looks like this (much abbreviated):

```
c:\> javac ExtFourThreads.java
c:\> java ExtFourThreads 1000 200 500 5000
....

three 25
one 14
one 15
four 4
....
```

That's a very simple example illustrating one form of the thread concept. The same concept can be applied to the HTTP servers we looked at in the previous section on networking. The example below is a threaded HTTP server that serves a simple web page that shows the current time. The time can be updated by pushing an HTML form button on the page. There is also a QUIT button on the form. It doesn't really cause the program to "quit," but it takes you to a different page. It's included in the program because it illustrates reading from the socket as well as writing. This program is closely modeled after the nonthreaded incrementing page we saw earlier in the section on networking.

Listing 3-20: HttpThread.java

```java
import java.util.*;
import java.io.*;
import java.net.*;

class HttpThread extends Thread {
    Socket threadSocket;
    HttpThread(Socket thrdSock) {
        this.threadSocket = thrdSock;
    }

    public void run() {
        try {
            BufferedWriter serverResponse = new BufferedWriter(
                    new OutputStreamWriter(this.threadSocket.getOutputStream()));
```

```
            BufferedReader clientRequest = new BufferedReader(
                    new InputStreamReader(this.threadSocket.getInputStream()));
            String str;
            str=clientRequest.readLine();
            System.out.println(str);
            Date currentDate = new Date();
            String currentTime = currentDate.toString();

            if (str.startsWith("GET /?QUIT")) {
                sayGoodbye(serverResponse);
                clientRequest.close();
                this.threadSocket.close();
                System.exit(0);
            } else {
                writePage(serverResponse, currentTime);

            }
            clientRequest.close();
            this.threadSocket.close();
        } catch (IOException e) {
            e.printStackTrace();
            System.out.println("Problem with run");
        }
    }

    public static void writePage(BufferedWriter wr, String str) {
        try {
            wr.write("HTTP/1.0 200 OK\r\n");
            wr.write("Content-type: text/html\n\n");
            wr.write("<HEAD>\r\n");
            wr.write("<TITLE>Java Http Time Server</TITLE>\r\n");
            wr.write("<H3><CENTER>Java HTTP Time Server</CENTER>< H3>\r\n");
            wr.write("</HEAD>\r\n");
            wr.write("<BODY><CENTER>\r\n");
            wr.write("Push the Button to Update the Time\r\n");
            wr.write("<FORM>");
            wr.write("<INPUT TYPE=SUBMIT NAME='UPDATE' VALUE='UPDATE'>");
            wr.write("<INPUT TYPE=SUBMIT NAME='QUIT' VALUE='QUIT'>");
            wr.write("</FORM>");
            wr.write("The current time = " + str);
            wr.write("</CENTER></BODY>\r\n");
            wr.flush();
        } catch (IOException e) {
            e.printStackTrace();
            System.out.println("Problem with writePage");
        }
    }

    public static void sayGoodbye(BufferedWriter wr) {
        try {
```

```
            wr.write("HTTP/1.0 200 OK\r\n");
            wr.write("Content-type: text/html\n\n");
            wr.write("<HEAD>\r\n");
            wr.write("<TITLE>Goodbye!</TITLE>\r\n");
            wr.write("<H3><CENTER>Goodbye</CENTER></H3>\r\n");
            wr.write("</HEAD>\r\n");
            wr.write("<BODY><CENTER>\r\n");
            wr.write("</CENTER></BODY>\r\n");
            wr.flush();
        } catch (IOException e) {
            e.printStackTrace();
            System.out.println("Problem with sayGoodbye");
        }
    }
}

public class HttpThreadServer {
    public static void main(String[] args) {
        int port = 80;
        try {
            ServerSocket srv = new ServerSocket(port);
            while(true) {
                Socket mySocket = srv.accept();
                new HttpThread(mySocket).start();
            }
        } catch(Exception e) {System.out.println("Problem with main()");}
    }
}
```

The program begins with a simple constructor. The argument for the constructor is a socket. As in our simple example, we are extending the thread class and overriding the run() method.

```
    class HttpThread extends Thread {
        Socket threadSocket;
        HttpThread(Socket thrdSock) {
            this.threadSocket = thrdSock;
        }
```

The run() method contains the bulk of the code. A BufferedReader and BufferedWriter is formed using the socket as an instance variable of the thread object. The input stream is scanned to see if the "GET /?QUIT" is in the input stream. If it is, that means the HTTP request was the result of the "QUIT" form button being pressed. If not, it calls a method that prints a web page to the socket client showing the current time.

```
public void run() {
    try {
        BufferedWrigter serverResponse = new BufferedWriter(
            new OutputStreamWriter(this.threadSocket.getOutputStream()));
```

```
        BufferedReader clientRequest = new BufferedReader(
            new InputStreamReader(this.threadSocket.getInputStream())));
        String str;
        str=clientRequest.readLine();
        System.out.println(str);
        Date currentDate = new Date();
        String currentTime = currentDate.toString();
        if (str.startsWith("GET /?QUIT")) {
            sayGoodbye(serverResponse);
            clientRequest.close();
            this.threadSocket.close();
            System.exit(0);
        } else {
            writePage(serverResponse, currentTime);

        }
            clientRequest.close();
            this.threadSocket.close();
        } catch (IOException e) {
            e.printStackTrace();
            System.out.println("Problem with run");
        }
    }
}
```

The methods `writePage()` and `sayGoodbye()` print web information to the socket connection. They are only slight modifications of the methods of the same name we used in Listing 3-17, so we won't go into them further. Finally, we have a short class that contains the `main()` method. This is the class that we will execute from the command line. It creates a server socket and then listens on port 80 for connections. When connections are being requested from clients, a socket is created and given as an argument to the thread constructor. The `Thread.start()` method is called, which executes the `run()` method. The thread then services the http request and `main()` is free to continue listening for more clients.

```
public class HttpThreadServer {
    public static void main(String[] args) {
        int port = 80;
        try {
            ServerSocket srv = new ServerSocket(port);
            while(true) {
                Socket mySocket = srv.accept();
                new HttpThread(mySocket).start();
            }
        } catch(Exception e) {System.out.println("Problem with main()");}
    }
}
```

To try this program out, invoke the `HttpThreadServer` program from the command line and then open up a web browser and type in the URL http://127.0.0.1/ Both the command line window and the browser should respond as shown below. The IP address 127.0.0.1 is what as known as the loop-back address. It refers to the machine you are running on (the localhost).

```
c:\> javac HttpThreadServer.java
c:\> java HttpThreadServer
GET /?UPDATE=UPDATE HTTP/1.1
GET /?UPDATE=UPDATE HTTP/1.1
GET /?UPDATE=UPDATE HTTP/1.1
GET /?UPDATE=UPDATE HTTP/1.1
GET /?UPDATE=UPDATE HTTP/1.1
GET /?UPDATE=UPDATE HTTP/1.1
GET /?QUIT=QUIT HTTP/1.1
```

The previous two examples have shown the first way of implementing threads. That method is to extend the thread class and override the `run()` method. In both examples, we had a separate class that made use of our thread subclass. The second way of implementing threads is to `implement` the `Runnable` interface.

Figure 3-11: Web browser image #3

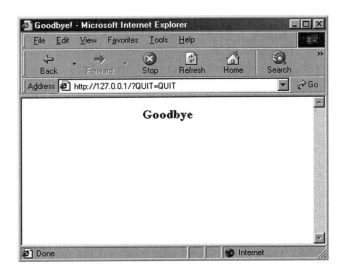

Figure 3-12: Web browser image #4

Implementing threads by implementing the runnable interface

While we're not going to go into detail about interfaces, simply put, an **Interface** in Java is a named collection of method definitions, without implementations. They are instead filled with abstract method declarations. By implementing an interface, you are essentially establishing a contract to implement all of the abstract classes declared in the interface.

Our first thread example, the four threaded counting program, can easily be made to implement the Runnable interface.

Listing 3-21: IndependentCounting.java

```
public class IndependentCounting implements Runnable {
    String threadName;
    int waitTime;
    Thread actualThread;

    public IndependentCounting(String tName, int wTime) {
        this.threadName = tName;
        this.waitTime = wTime;
        actualThread = new Thread(this);
        actualThread.start();
    }

    public static void main(String[] args) {
```

```
        int one = Integer.parseInt(args[0]);
        int two = Integer.parseInt(args[1]);
        int three = Integer.parseInt(args[2]);
        int four = Integer.parseInt(args[3]);
        new IndependentCounting("Thread One Count = ", one);
        new IndependentCounting("Thread Two Count =", two);
        new IndependentCounting("Thread Three Count = ", three);
        new IndependentCounting("Thread Four Count =", four);
    }

    public void run() {
        int count = 0;
        while(count < 25) {
            count++;
            System.out.println(this.threadName + " " + count);
            try {
                Thread.sleep((long)waitTime);
            } catch(Exception e) {System.out.println("Couldn't Sleep");}
        }
    }
}
```

The significant thing to note about this program is that it is implemented inside a single class, whereas our other example had the threads implemented in one class and used in another. Let's take a closer look.

The program begins with a class definition statement, declares three variables, and defines a constructor. Note the use of the keywords implements runnable, which states that it is implementing the Runnable interface. As in the CountingThread example, we have a string variable representing the thread name and an integer representing the user-defined wait time for each thread. We now have an additional variable, actualThread, associated with each IndependentThread object. The constructor initializes the string and the integer as before, but this time it also calls the Thread constructor and calls the start() method of the Thread class. This causes the run() method to be executed.

```
    public class IndependentCounting implements Runnable {
        String threadName;
        int waitTime;
        Thread actualThread;

        public IndependentCounting(String tName, int wTime) {
            this.threadName = tName;
            this.waitTime = wTime;
            actualThread = new Thread(this);
            actualThread.start();
        }
```

The `main()` method is executed when the Java program is executed from the command line. It accepts four command line parameters (the integer wait times) and passes them to the `IndependentCounting` constructor, which is invoked four times. Each time it is invoked, the constructor causes the `run()` method to be executed.

```java
public static void main(String[] args) {
    int one = Integer.parseInt(args[0]);
    int two = Integer.parseInt(args[1]);
    int three = Integer.parseInt(args[2]);
    int four = Integer.parseInt(args[3]);
    new IndependentCounting("Thread One Count = ", one);
    new IndependentCounting("Thread Two Count =", two);
    new IndependentCounting("Thread Three Count = ", three);
    new IndependentCounting("Thread Four Count =", four);
}
```

The `run()` method is almost identical to the `run()` method used in the `CountingThread` example with one exception. When we invoke the `sleep()` method in this example, we need to use a fully qualified path to ensure the Java compiler understands what class we want the sleep method to be taken from. To do this, we precede it with the class name, `Thread`.

```java
public void run() {
    int count = 0;
    while(count < 25) {
        count++;
        System.out.println(this.threadName + " " + count);
        try {
            Thread.sleep((long)waitTime);
        } catch(Exception e) {System.out.println("Couldn't Sleep");}
    }
}
```

The program output looks like this:

```
c:\> javac IndependentCounting.java
c:\> java IndependentCounting 1000 200 500 5000
....

Thread Three Count =  25
Thread One Count =    14
Thread One Count =    15
Thread Four Count =   4

....
```

Serial ports

We are now going to examine how to access your computer's serial ports. In order to do this, we need some sort of serial device to talk to. A serial port loopback plug is probably the simplest. These are very cheap and easy to make using the proper female connector for your serial port. The necessary connections are shown in the figures below for both 9-pin and 25-pin serial ports. Note that the dotted line is an optional wire that some loopback plugs have. This is not necessary for the examples in the book (but it won't hurt either). Once your loopback plug is installed on your serial port, compile and run the program `SerialLoopTest.java` in the listing below. Don't forget that you need `comm.jar` on your `CLASSPATH` environment variable for this to compile and run.

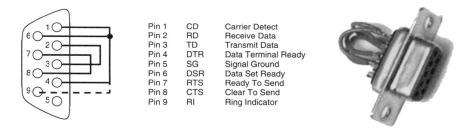

Pin 1	CD	Carrier Detect
Pin 2	RD	Receive Data
Pin 3	TD	Transmit Data
Pin 4	DTR	Data Terminal Ready
Pin 5	SG	Signal Ground
Pin 6	DSR	Data Set Ready
Pin 7	RTS	Ready To Send
Pin 8	CTS	Clear To Send
Pin 9	RI	Ring Indicator

Figure 3-13: Serial loopback 9-pin plug

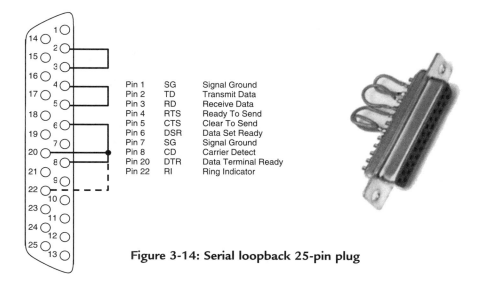

Pin 1	SG	Signal Ground
Pin 2	TD	Transmit Data
Pin 3	RD	Receive Data
Pin 4	RTS	Ready To Send
Pin 5	CTS	Clear To Send
Pin 6	DSR	Data Set Ready
Pin 7	SG	Signal Ground
Pin 8	CD	Carrier Detect
Pin 20	DTR	Data Terminal Ready
Pin 22	RI	Ring Indicator

Figure 3-14: Serial loopback 25-pin plug

Listing 3-22: SerialLoopTest.java

```java
import java.io.*;
import java.util.*;
import javax.comm.*;

public class SerialLoopTest implements Runnable,
                                       SerialPortEventListener {

    static CommPortIdentifier portId;
    static Enumeration portList;

    static InputStream inputStream;
    static OutputStream outputStream;

    static SerialPort serialPort;
    Thread readThread;

    static String message2send = "Hello Port!";
    static String messagereceived;

    static byte[] inbuf = new byte[20];
    int i = 0;
    static String portname;

    public static void main(String[] args) {

        // check out the command line args
        if (args.length < 1) {
            System.out.println( "Specify a port! (COM1 or /dev/ ttyS0)." );
            return;
        } else {
            portname = args[0];
            System.out.println( "Testing port: " + portname );
        }

        try {
            // Get the ID of this port
            portId =
            CommPortIdentifier.getPortIdentifier(portname);
            // Is it a serial port?
            if (portId.getPortType() !=
            CommPortIdentifier.PORT_SERIAL) {
                System.out.println( "Port is not a serial port");
                return;
            }
        }
        catch(NoSuchPortException e) {
            System.out.println("No Such Port!");
            return;
```

```
    }
    catch (Exception e) { System.out.println(e); }
    SerialLoopTest tester = new SerialLoopTest();
}

public SerialLoopTest() {
    try {
        serialPort = (SerialPort) portId.open("Serial Loop Test", 2000);
    }
    catch(PortInUseException e) {
        System.out.println("Port In Use.");
        return;
    }
    catch (Exception e) {
        System.out.println(e);
        return;
    }

    try {
        serialPort.addEventListener(this);
    }
    catch (TooManyListenersException e) {
                            System.out.println(e); }

    // Turn on some notifiers so we can catch them with an event listener.
    serialPort.notifyOnDataAvailable(true);
    serialPort.notifyOnCTS(true);
    serialPort.notifyOnDSR(true);

    // We don't really need to set the port parameters for a loop back test
    // but if you did, this is how you would.
    try {
        serialPort.setSerialPortParams(19200,
            SerialPort.DATABITS_8,
            SerialPort.STOPBITS_1,
            SerialPort.PARITY_NONE);
        serialPort.setFlowControlMode(SerialPort.FLOWCONTROL_NONE);
    }
    catch (UnsupportedCommOperationException e) {
        System.out.println(e);
    }

    try {
        inputStream = serialPort.getInputStream();
        outputStream = serialPort.getOutputStream();
    }
    catch (IOException e) { System.out.println(e); }

    readThread = new Thread(this);
    readThread.start();
```

```
    }

    public void run() {
        // send characters out the port
        try {
            outputStream.write( message2send.getBytes() );
        }
        catch (IOException e){ System.out.println(e); }

        System.out.println("Flipping RTS...");
        serialPort.setRTS( ! serialPort.isRTS() );

        System.out.println("Flipping DTR...");
        serialPort.setDTR( ! serialPort.isDTR() );
        try { Thread.sleep(1000); } catch (Exception e) { }

        serialPort.removeEventListener();
        serialPort.close();

        System.out.print( i + " bytes read from port " + portname
                            + ". " );
        if (i<1) {
            System.out.println( "Maybe something is not working." );
        }
        else { System.out.println();   }
    }

    public void serialEvent(SerialPortEvent event) {
        // determine whuch event has happened
        switch(event.getEventType()) {
        case SerialPortEvent.BI:
        case SerialPortEvent.OE:
        case SerialPortEvent.FE:
        case SerialPortEvent.PE:
            System.out.println("Some status line changed.");
            break;
         case SerialPortEvent.CD:
            System.out.println("Status line CD changed.");
            break;
        case SerialPortEvent.CTS:
            System.out.println("Status line CTS changed.");
            break;
        case SerialPortEvent.DSR:
            System.out.println("Status line DSR changed.");
            break;
        case SerialPortEvent.RI:
            System.out.println("Status line RI changed.");
            break;
        case SerialPortEvent.OUTPUT_BUFFER_EMPTY:
            System.out.println("Buffer Empty");
```

```
            break;
        case SerialPortEvent.DATA_AVAILABLE:
            byte[] readBuffer = new byte[20];
            try {
                while (inputStream.available() > 0) {
                    int numBytes = inputStream.read(readBuffer);
                    i += numBytes;
                    messagereceived = new String(readBuffer);
                    System.out.println("Read: " + messagereceived);
                }
            }
            catch (IOException e) { System.out.println(e); }
            break;
        }
    }
}
```

The output looks like this:

```
C:\> javac SerialLoopTest
C:\> java SerialLoopTest COM1
Testing port: COM1
Read: Hello Po
Read: rt!
Flipping RTS...
Status line CTS changed.
Flipping DTR...
Status line DSR changed.
11 bytes read from port COM1.
```

Notice that the "Hello Port!" is split between two reads. This will vary depending on the capability of your computer and what other applications are running. For Linux machines you would use `/dev/ttyS0` (or the name of your serial port) and you will get the same output.

The line `portId = CommPortIdentifier.getPortIdentifier(portname);` finds the port named by `portname` and assigns its identifier to `portId`. Once you have the port identifier you can then determine the type of port (`getPortType()`), its name (`getName()`), and if it is already owned by another process (`isCurrentlyOwned();` and `getCurrentOwner()`). This port identifier is the internal Java name for the port that you might call COM1 or /dev/ttyS0. The `getPortIdentifier()` method can throw the `NoSuchPortException` exception if this port does not exist. This is not always accurate. Many PC motherboards are configured to support two serial ports but with only one port having the necessary driver chips installed (to save money). Java will not throw the `NoSuchPortException` exception for this; it thinks the port is really there. Also, on Linux, if you have a real serial port that you don't have permission to read or write to, Java will throw the `NoSuchPortException` exception. This method will catch clearly wrong port names (such as `/dev/hda1` or `CON1`).

The line `serialPort = (SerialPort) portId.open("Serial Loop Test",
2000);` opens the serial port and assigns an owner to it. The number 2000 is a
timeout value. The open method will wait this many milliseconds for the port to open
before timing out. If the port is owned by another Java application then this method
will throw a `PortInUseException` exception. If the port is owned by another, non-
Java, application then this exception will not be thrown. We have found this does not
work reliably, tending not to notice if any application (Java or not) is using a serial
port.

We then set up an event listener, `serialPort.addEventListener(this);` so we can
watch the activity on the serial port. The event listener, further down in the listing,
will tell us what activity is going on for that port. We tell the event listener that we are
particularly interested in the following events:

```
serialPort.notifyOnDataAvailable(true);
serialPort.notifyOnCTS(true);
serialPort.notifyOnDSR(true);
```

We want to be notified when there is data available, when the **Clear-To-Send** line has
changed, and when the **Data Set Ready** line has changed. We need to specifically tell
the event listener what we are interested in, as there are many things we can monitor
and we don't want the event listener being called for things we don't care about. We
chose these because they make a good example and because we can check for them
with the loop-back connector. You can also take this opportunity to set the
communication parameters for the serial port. Notice the lines:

```
serialPort.setSerialPortParams(19200,
    SerialPort.DATABITS_8,
    SerialPort.STOPBITS_1,
    SerialPort.PARITY_NONE);
serialPort.setFlowControlMode(SerialPort.FLOWCONTROL_NONE);
```

In this case, setting these parameters has no effect on the workings of this program. I
show these here as examples only. Once the port is open and configured, we can start
reading from and writing to it. The lines:

```
inputStream = serialPort.getInputStream();
outputStream = serialPort.getOutputStream();
```

get the input and output streams for this port so we can read and write to it. We then
start a thread running to talk to the port.

```
readThread = new Thread(this);
readThread.start();
```

This doesn't need to be in a thread, but this is a common way to do this. The rest of
the communication with the serial port takes place in the `run` method and in the
`serialEvent` method. This is where the loopback testing begins; the `run` method

writes data and changes status lines while the `serialEvent` method reads the data and watches the status lines. The run method does three things. We write a message to the serial port using the `outputStream.write` method, we then check the RTS and DTR status lines, and invert them.

```
outputStream.write( message2send.getBytes() );
serialPort.setRTS( ! serialPort.isRTS() );
serialPort.setDTR( ! serialPort.isDTR() );
```

Originally we tried setting the status lines to either `true` or `false` but we discovered that they are left in an arbitrary state and this technique didn't work very satisfactorily. Besides, this gives us a chance to try using some of the methods to examine the state of the status lines (like `isDTR()`, `isRTS()`). We are pretty much done with sending data to the port. The sleep is necessary so the program won't exit before the event listener has a chance to catch the activity and report on it. Don't forget to remove the event listener and close the port. While this may not seem like an important thing to do for this little simple program, we found that on some Windows machines the Java program won't exit and return to the shell until these are done.

```
try { Thread.sleep(1000); } catch (Exception e) { }
serialPort.removeEventListener();
serialPort.close();
```

As soon as the data is sent, the `SerialEvent` event listener is triggered. The `serialEvent` listener is a simple switch that examines the event type and reports that. In the case of the event being `SerialPortEvent.DATA_AVAILABLE` we then read from the serial port's input stream.

```
while (inputStream.available() > 0) {
    int numBytes = inputStream.read(readBuffer);
    i += numBytes;
    messagereceived = new String(readBuffer);
    System.out.println("Read: " + messagereceived);
}
```

Once again, we want to call your attention to the output from this program. Notice that not all of the data is read in at the same time. This could be the result of many different things, such as the process being interrupted by another event or the data being sent slower than it is being read. In either case, this is probably typical for an event listener: you will not get everything you are expecting in one event. This can be dealt with by simply implementing a buffer in your program and each read appends the data to the buffer.

Summary

While some of these examples have been fairly detailed, they are a far cry from a full tutorial on each topic. We hope to have shown you a wide sampling of the methods and techniques you will need to assist you in developing robust programs for communicating with your network-enabled devices. There are a number of excellent references for Java. If you need more detail than what is presented in this quick review, then you should check the references listed at the end of this chapter.

References

1. *Java 2 Platform, Standard Edition, v 1.3 API Specification*, http:// java.sun.com/j2se/1.3/docs/api/index.html

2. Campione, Mary and Walrath, Kathy, *The Java Tutorial Second Edition: Object-Oriented Programming for the Internet*, http:// web2.java.sun.com/docs/books/tutorial/, Addison-Wesley, 1998.

3. Chan, Patrick and Lee, Rosanna, *The Java Developers Almanac 2000*, Addison-Wesley, 2000.

4. Harold, Elliotte Rusty, *Java Network Programming*, O'Reilly & Associates, 2000.

5. *The Java Language Specification*, http://java.sun.com/docs/books/jls/ second_edition/html/j.title.doc.html.

6. *Interfacing the Serial/RS232 Port*, http://www.senet.com.au/~cpeacock (one of the many available loopback plug pinout diagrams).

CHAPTER 4

Overview of Embedded Networked Devices

Cheap Internet appliance technology will make controlling devices in your home, business or factory from a web page commonplace in the near future. This book will examine some of the available commercial technology you can apply to making just about any device network-enabled. We will take you step by step through the process of connecting several simple devices to the web. The first step in the process will be selecting a capable microcontroller. There are many microcontroller boards that claim to be web-enabled on the market now, and there are many more that you can build from a schematic and a few components. The tables below list and compare a number of commercially available network-enabled microcontroller boards (Table 4-1) and some of the "free" schematics available for constructing your own devices (Table 4-2).

Table 4-1: Commercially available network-enabled microcontrollers

EtherNut[1]	Processor:	Atmel Atmega103
	Ethernet Controller:	Realtek RTL8019AS
$125	Ports:	RS-232
+ power supply and	Network:	10base-T
cables	PIO:	24
	Memory:	128K Flash, 4K EEPROM, 32K RAM
	Protocols:	TCP/IP, HTTP
	Preferred Language:	C

EtherNut uses the Licorice[2] open source real-time kernel. Schematics and PCB layout files are available from the web page. Expansion boards are available.

[1] Ethernet – http://www.egnite.de/ethernut/
[2] Licorice kernel – http://liquorice.sourceforge.net/

Net186[3]	Processor:	AMD Am186-EX
	Ethernet Controller:	AMD Am79C961A
$420	Ports:	2 RS-232
	Network:	10base-T
	PIO:	32
	Memory:	512K Flash, 512K RAM
	Protocols:	TCP/IP, HTTP
	Preferred Language:	C, Assembly

This is an AMD evaluation board. Online information says this retails for $230 but both retailers referenced list the price as $420 (US dollars).

Orlin Technology	Processor:	PIC16F877 20Mhz microcontroller
OT731[4]	Ethernet Controller:	n/a
	Ports:	2 RS232, RJ11 telephone, RJ11 MPLAB-ICD
$299	Network:	2400 baud "plain old telephone system" modem
	Memory	128K serial flash EEPROM
	Protocols:	TCP/IP, UDP, PPP
	Preferred Language:	PIC Assembly

Other features include an LCD display, pushbutton switches, and a thermometer.

Picoweb[5]	Processor:	Atmel AT90S8515
	Ethernet Controller:	Realtek RTL8019AS
$149	Ports:	RS-232
	Network:	10base-T
	PIO:	16
	Memory:	8K Flash, 512K EEPROM, 512K RAM
	Protocols:	TCP/IP, HTTP
	Preferred Language:	Assembly

Schematic is available on the web site.

Rabbit TCP/IP[6]	Processor:	Rabbit Microprocessor
	Ethernet Controller:	Realtek RTL8019AS
$199 development	Ports:	RS-232, RS485
kit	Network:	10base-T
	PIO:	4 digital inputs
	Memory:	512K Flash, 128K RAM
	Protocols:	TCP/IP, HTTP, SMTP, FTP
	Preferred Language:	C

TCP/IP source code is included in development kit.

---

[3] Net186 – http://www.amd.com/products/epd/desiging/evalboards/4.net186eva/
[4] Orlin Technology OT731 – http://www.orlin.com
[5] Picoweb – http://www.picoweb.net/prodpw1.html
[6] Rabbit – http://www.rabbitsemiconductor.com/products/rab20_tcpip/rab20_tcpip_devkit.html

Siteplayer[7]

$99

Processor:	Unknown (seems to be based on a Philips 8051)
Ethernet Controller:	Unknown
Ports:	none
Network:	10base-T
PIO:	8 (output), 4 PWM
Memory:	48K Flash, 768 bytes RAM
Protocols:	TCP/IP, HTTP
Preferred Language:	SiteObjects

Siteplayer needs to be embedded into some larger appliance or you need the development kit to provide the connectors and support.

Snijder EJC[8]

$ (?)

Processor:	ARM7TDMI
Ethernet Controller:	unknown
Ports:	RS232, RS485, TTL, I²C, 8bit DI/DO, VGA, LCD
Network:	10base-T
Memory:	8MB flash, 8MB DRAM
Protocols:	TCP/IP, HTTP, SMTP, FTP, TELNET, POP3
Preferred Language:	Java

They also offer a development board for use with the EJC Embedded Java Controller

---

SX Evak Kit[9]

$199

Processor:	Scenix SX52BD
Ethernet Controller:	Realtek RTL8019AS
Ports:	2 RS-232
Network:	10base-T
Memory:	32K EEPROM
Protocols:	TCP/IP, HTTP, SMTP, DHCP
Preferred Language:	C

This is an evaluation board.

TINI[10]

$85
+ power supply
and cables

Processor:	Dallas Semiconductor 80C390
Ethernet Controller:	SMSC LAN91C96
Ports:	RS-232, **1-wire**
Socket card expandable:	2 more RS-232 ports, CAN, I²C
PIO:	16 on socket card
Network:	10base-T
Memory:	512K Flash, 512K RAM (each expandable to 1 Mbyte)
Protocols:	TCP/IP, FTP, Telnet, DHCP (can add HTTP, SMTP)
Preferred Language:	**Java**

This information is valid for the TINI simm and e20 socket card combination. Other socket cards provide different ports and memory expansion. TINI includes a multitasking, Unix-like, operating system. Schematic is available on the web site.

---

[7] Siteplayer – www.siteplayer.com
[8] Snijder EJC – http://www.snijder.com
[9] SX Eval Kit – http://www.ubicom.com/ethernet/ethernet_sx_stack_eval.html
[10] TINI – http://www.ibutton.com/TINI/

μCsimm[11]	Processor:	Motorola 68ex328
	Ethernet Controller:	Cirrus Logic CS8900A
$300	Ports:	RS-232
	Network:	10base-T
	PIO:	21
	Memory:	2 Mbyte Flash, 8 Mbyte RAM
	Protocols:	TCP/IP
	Preferred Language:	C

This thing runs a Linux derivative, so it's closer to a microcomputer than a microprocessor.

Xecom AWC86[12]	Processor:	AMD Am186
$159 + , connectors,	Ethernet Controller:	Unknown
cables, power	Ports:	2 RS-232
supply	Network:	10base-T
	PIO:	34 (22 and 8 analog in and 2 analog out on the AWC86A)
	Memory:	512K Flash, 512K RAM
	Protocols:	TCP/IP, HTTP, SMTP, FTP
	Preferred Language:	C

Includes a real-time operating system. Requires a development board or other host board to provide connectors and power.

X-traWeb X-node[13]	Processor:	8 bit microcontroller, details unknown
	Ethernet Controller:	n/a
$ (?)	Ports:	RS232, RS485, I²C, "pulse" inputs, wireless, analog I/O
	Network:	via RS232 modem (?)
	Memory:	8 K flash, 512 bytes RAM
	Protocols:	TCP/IP, HTTP, PPP, PAP, CHAP, SLIP, UDP
	Preferred Language:	unknown

Works in conjunction with another product, the X-gate.

---

[11] mCsimm – http://www.uclinux.org/ucsimm/
[12] Xecom – http://xecom.com/
[13] X-traWeb – http://www.x-traweb.com

**Table 4-2: "Free" schematics available for constructing
your own microcontroller board**

Ipic[14]		
	Processor:	MicroChip PIC12C509A
	Ethernet Controller:	none (done on PIC)
< $25	Ports:	None
	Network:	Slip connection
	Memory:	1K ROM, 256K RAM
	Protocols:	TCP/IP, HTTP, Telnet, SLIP
	Preferred Language:	Assembly

A minimal implementation of a network-enabled device. Schematics and TCP source are **not** provided at the web site.

webACE[15]		
	Processor:	Fairchild ACE1101MT8
	Ethernet Controller:	None (done on ACE)
< $10	Ports:	I²C
	Network:	Slip connection
	Memory:	1K EEPROM, 256K RAM
	Protocols:	TCP/IP, HTTP, Telnet, SLIP
	Preferred Language:	Assembly

Schematic on web site. TCP/IP source is not.

Uwebserver[16]		
	Processor:	MicroChip PIC16F84
	Ethernet Controller:	Seiko S-7600A (iChip)
< $35	Ports:	RS-232, I²C
	Memory:	1K Flash, 68 bytes RAM
	Protocols:	TCP/IP, HTTP
	Preferred Language:	Assembly

Includes schematics, source code, PCB layout files.

MicroChip AN724[17]		
	Processor:	MicroChip PIC16C63A
	Ethernet Controller:	CH1786LC (really a modem)
	Ports:	PPP, I²C
	PIO:	22
	Memory:	4K EPROM, 192 bytes RAM
	Protocols:	PPP
	Preferred Language:	C, Assembly

This is from a Microchip application note. Application note includes schematic and PIC assembly source code.

---

[14] iPic – http://www-ccs.cs.umass.edu/shri/iPic.htm

[15] WebAce – http://world.std.com/~fwhite/ace/

[16] uWebserver – http://www.mycal.net/wsweb/design/

[17] Using PICmicro® MCUs to Connect to Internet via PPP
http://www.microchip.com/10/appnote/category/internet/index.htm

MicroChip AN731[18]	Processor:	MicroChip PIC16F877
	Ethernet Controller:	Seiko S-7600A (iChip)
	Ports:	RS-485, I²C
	PIO:	22
	Memory:	8K Flash, 368 bytes RAM
	Protocols:	TCP/IP
	Preferred Language:	C, Assembly

This is from a Microchip application note. Application note includes schematic and PIC assembly source code.

In reviewing these tables and by visiting the web sites of these manufacturers, you will see a wide variety of microcontroller board capabilities and costs. While many of these devices are simply embedded web page servers, we are looking for a microcontroller that has the potential for a wide range of applications as well as being programmed in a straightforward manner (read "high level language" here). We have selected the TINI[19] microcontroller from Dallas Semiconductor as the platform for most of the projects in the book. While many of the microcontroller boards could do the job, this is the only one with the combination of low-cost, high-level language (Java), and variety of ports and interfaces.

In the remainder of this book, we're going to be examining the hardware and software behind the TINI microcontroller. Here is a brief overview of what we will be examining in detail over the next few chapters

Figure 4-1: The TINI microcontroller board

---

[18] Embedding PICmicro Microcontrollers in the Internet
http://www.microchip.com/10/appnote/listing/index12.htm
[19] TINI is a registered trademark of Dallas Semiconductor.

- Chapter 5 – Starting up TINI for the first time
- Chapter 6 – TINI hardware
- Chapter 7 – TINI software
- Chapter 8 – Enhancing your TINI board's capabilities
- Chapter 9 – The TINI ports (serial and parallel)
- Chapter 10 – The TINI 1 wire port
- Chapter 11 – The TINI I²C interface
- Chapter 12 – The TINI CAN interface
- Chapter 13 – Connecting your TINI to a network

Getting Started with TINI

This chapter will get you started with your TINI without overwhelming you with detail (we save that for the next 8 chapters). It focuses on installing the TINI classes and libraries, getting TINI up and running, and then getting the 1-Wire libraries installed (so you can control things with your desktop or laptop computer as well) and verified, so that everything is working properly.

What Is TINI?

The TINI microcontroller is a small computer that executes Java bytecode and has built-in Ethernet networking and interfaces for connecting many different types of hardware. The name TINI stands for "Tiny InterNet Interface" and refers to both the TINI Chip Set and the TINI Board.

The TINI CPU is the Dallas Semiconductor DS80C390[1]. TINI has built-in serial, parallel, 1-Wire, I²C and Controller Area Network (CAN) ports, with extra pins for controlling optional devices. It can address up to 1Mb of RAM and 1 Mb of Flash ROM. The TINI board also contains an RS232 interface, a real-time clock, a unique Ethernet MAC address, and a battery backup for the RAM. The Ethernet controller supports 10-Base-T networking and allows you to Internet-enable many applications. The Flash ROM contains the TINI firmware, Java Virtual Machine, and Java class libraries. It also has space to store a bootstrap program.

TINI is a 1-¼″ x 4″ form factor, the footprint of a typical memory SIMM (Single Inline Memory Module), so that a TINI microcontroller can fit almost anywhere. With TINI you can Web-enable just about any piece of electrical equipment. You can develop Java applications for TINI quickly and easily to provide an Internet or intranet interface for your equipment.

---

[1] DS80C390 datasheet – http://www.dalsemi.com/datasheets/pdfs/80c390.pdf

The 1-Wire Net, sometimes known as a MicroLAN, is a low-cost network based on a PC or microcontroller communicating digitally over twisted-pair cable with 1-Wire components. A 1-Wire Net-based system consists of three main elements: a bus master (such as a TINI microcontroller or a microprocessor) with controlling software, the wiring and associated connectors, and 1-Wire devices. An economical DS9097 COM Port Adapter is available to interface a personal computer's RS-232 interface to a 1-Wire network.

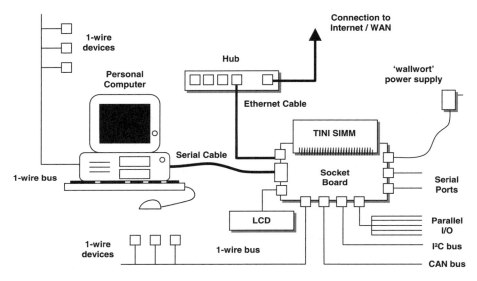

Figure 5-1: The TINI and 1-Wire connections

Getting Started

This is a practical discussion of how to get started, obtain and set up all of the pieces.

The TINI SIMM

TINI is available in two forms, the 512-kbyte SRAM version and the 1-Mbyte SRAM version. In fact, they are both the same but with the 512-kbyte version, only one of the two SRAM chips has been soldered to the SIMM, while the other is empty. In Chapter 6 we will discuss the details of this memory (512k and 1 Mbyte) and in Chapter 8 we will show you how to add memory to the 512-kbyte version. Both of these are available from the Dallas Semiconductor iButton Store[2].

---

[2] iButton Store – http://www.ibutton.com/TINI/hardware/index.html

Figure 5-2: The TINI SIMM
(The components will be identified in Chapter 6.)

The socket board

As TINI is a SIMM, it has no sockets on it for connecting to external devices, just a single edge connector. To connect TINI to various devices like the serial port and a network, it needs to be plugged into a host or motherboard that either provides the needed connections or offers sockets and connectors for the various connections. Why is it like this? TINI is intended to be a plug-in "brain" on an appliance. The appliance should provide the necessary connection directly to the TINI SIMM. For development and testing purposes (and for small-scale applications where a custom motherboard is too costly) it is possible to use one of the many prototype sockets available that provides the needed connectors for TINI and various interfaces. Table 5-1 below lists and compares some of these available socket boards for TINI.

Unless noted otherwise, all socket boards include:

- 72-pin SIMM connector
- RJ45 Ethernet connector
- Power connector
- RJ11 1-Wire network connector

Table 5-1: TINI socket boards

Dallas Semiconductor E10 socket[3]	100 mm X 160 mm DB9 (DTE RS-232) connector iButton clip
$20.00	Expansion space (not populated with components) for: • Second 72-pin SIMM connector • 512K Flash ROM expansion • Dual RS232 port with hardware handshake • Parallel I/O lines (16 inputs, 16 outputs) • LCD display connector • CAN bus interface • Output-only RS232 (RJ11) diagnostic port • On board 5VDC reculator

[3] E10 socket – http://www.ibutton.com/TINI/developers/index.html

Dallas Semiconductor **E20 socket**[4] $35	Same as the E10 socket with but the onboard +5V regulator is populated (for a 8 to 20V AC/DC supply).
E50 socket[5] $200	Same as the E10 but it is fully populated will all optional connectors, jacks and components (but no LCD display, just the connector).
TILT socket[6] $39-$43	100 mm X 100 mm DB9 (DTE RS-232) connector iButton clip Reset button CAN transceiver and CAN connector Power regulator (6-9 VDC supply) Optional CAN net with 82C25X twisted pair driver
STEP socket[7] $89-$129	100 mm X 100 mm Second 72-pin SIMM connector DB9 (DTE RS-232) connector DB9 for serial 1 Pushbuttons and LEDs Prototype area Socket for boot flash CAN connector Power regulator (8-24 VDC/AC supply) SBX expansion connector Optional components • DS1820 temperatures sensor • DS2450 for a analog inputs • IrDA in place of serial port
Proto adapter[8] $28.50	All SIMM pins are brought out to labeled headers for breadboard development (0.100" prototyping board) Available with 68 or 72 pin SIMM socket

---

[4] Dallas Semiconductor's E10 socket – http://www.ibutton.com/TINI/developers/index.html

[5] Systronix E50 socket – http://www.systronix.com/tini/sp.htm

[6] Systronix TILT socket – http://www.systronix.com/tini/tilt.htm

[7] Systronix STEP socket – http://www.systronix.com/tini/step.htm

[8] Viniculum's proto adapter – http://www.vinculum.com/1001.php

Nexus[9]

This is an expansion board for the proto adapter (above)
Accepts 68 and 72 pin TINI protoAdapters

$30

Provies space for:
- Reset switch
- Second SIMM socket
- Pads for the addition of two DB9's, one RJ11 and an iButton clip for use as the developer sees fit

Includes a protoModule (protoModule provides a marix of 0.1" spaced plated through holes for prototyping circuitry).

TINITutor[10]

£80 (about $130)

108 x 175 mm board
8 dip switches for input (or connector for 8 bit input)
8 leds for digital output (or connector for 8 bit output)
Pushbutton for interrupt generation
External interrupt connector
8bit DAC and connector
8bit ADC and connector
2 Line LCD display
connectors for the 1-wire bus, I2C bus, can bus,
Can interface with bus driver
2 serial ports
On board regulator

TiniTutor comes with real time experiments already configured on the board, so you can get straight down to writing real time Java with TINI. The experiments use all the peripherals including the ADC, DAC, LCD, 8bit Digital IO, interrupt generator.

Get your TINI running

For the devices that we will build in the remainder of this book, you need a TINI SIMM, a TINI socket board, a 9-pin RS-232 cable, an Ethernet cable, and a power supply. To complete this chapter you will also need a 1-Wire device, a serial port 1-Wire adapter and a short length of CAT3 or better cable with a RJ11 on one end (to connect to the 1-Wire device).

- The TINI SIMM can be either the 512-kbyte version or the 1-Mbyte version.

- The TINI socket board needs to support the serial, 1-Wire and network connectors.

- The RS-232 cable (serial cable) should have a 9-pin male connector on one end and a 9-pin female connector on the other and have wires 1,2,3,4 (minimum, all 9 is good too) connected in a straight-through fashion (not a null modem cable).

[9] Viniculum's NEXUS socket – http://www.vinculum.com/1004.php
[10] TayLec Ltd's TINITutor board – http://www.taylec.co.uk/

- The Ethernet cable is a standard 10base-T CAT5 cabled with RJ45 connectors on both ends. Whether you use a straight-through cable or a crossover cable depends on whether or not you're connecting your TINI to your computer's network card or your LAN hub.

- The TINI board requires 5 volts. The type of power supply you use depends on the socket board you use. If your socket board has an on-board regulator, then you need to pick a supply that is compatible with that (such as a 9–12-volt AC or DC supply, 250-mA (minimum) in the case of the E20). If your choice of socket board does not have a regulator, then you will need to use a 5-volt, DC, 250-mA (minimum), regulated power supply.

Now, let's connect this all together. Connect your TINI to your personal computer using the serial cable. Connect your TINI Ethernet connector to either your LAN hub with a straight-through CAT5 cable or directly to the network interface card in your personal computer with a crossover cable (you don't need a network to use TINI). Plug in the power supply and connect that to the TINI power connector. Your TINI should indicate it is on by lighting the "D1" LED (marked on the circuit board) on the TINI SIMM. After a few seconds the "D4" LED will light up, indicating that it has a network connection.

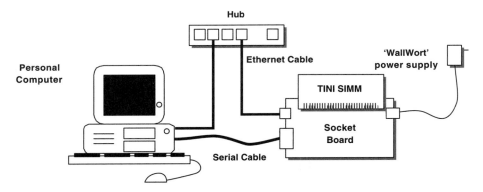

Figure 5-3: A simple TINI connection

The next step is loading the various pieces of software on your personal computer. Several Java class libraries are necessary to get your TINI development system working. This includes the base TINI Java virtual machine, TINI development libraries, and 1-Wire development libraries for both TINI and your personal computer. These are schematically shown in Figure 5-4:

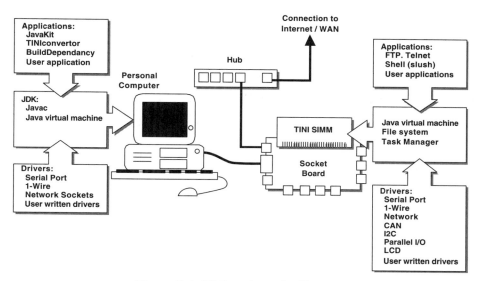

Figure 5-4: TINI and 1-Wire libraries

TINI libraries, utilities, TINI 1-Wire libraries

The main software library and utilities for TINI are supplied by Dallas Semiconductor. To install and verify them, follow these simple steps. Instructions are provided for both Windows and Linux systems.

For Windows

Download the TINI SDK[11] (`tini1_02.tgz` or the current version) to a temporary directory.

Using Winzip or other archive program, open this archive and extract all of the files to the folder of your choice. This will create a folder named `tini1.02` (or a similar name, depending on the current version) in that folder and a number of files and folders under that. In our case we extracted these files to the root folder of our c: drive so the TINI API files are in `c:\tini1.02\`. We will call this the TINI_HOME directory.

Windows 95/98

Edit your `autoexec.bat` file and add an environment variable that indicates the TINI_HOME directory and also add the location of `tini.jar` to your `CLASSPATH` environment variable.

```
C:\>notepad autoexec.bat
```

---

[11] TINI SDK – http://www.ibutton.com/TINI/software/index.html

Create a TINI_HOME environment variable.

```
SET TINI_HOME c:\tini1.02
```

You set your CLASSPATH with a line similar to this:

```
SET CLASSPATH=c:\jdk1.3\lib\;c:\jdk1.3\lib\comm.jar;%TINI_HOME%\bin\tini.jar;.
```

Windows 2000, Windows NT, Windows XP

For Windows 2000 and Windows NT you will have to use the "System" tool in the "Control Panel." Select the "Environment" tab and create a new system variable called TINI_HOME. Set its value to be c:\tini1.02. Edit the CLASSPATH system variable and change its value to be:

```
c:\jdk1.3\lib\;c:\jdk1.3\lib\comm.jar;%TINI_HOME%\bin\tini.jar;.
```

For Windows XP, use the "System" tool in the "Control Panel." Select the "Advanced" tab and click on the "Environment" button (under "startup and recovery"). Create a TINI_HOME system variable and edit the CLASSPATH variable as for NT.

In the next section we will run JavaKit to talk to your TINI (you can skip the next part if you don't use Linux).

Linux

Download the TINI SDK[12] (`tini1_02.tgz` or the current version) to a temporary directory.

Uncompress the file and then untar it in the /opt directory (or any other directory you choose).

```
% cd downloads
% mv tini1_02.tgz /opt
% cd /opt
% uncompress tini1_02.tgz
% tar -xf tini1_02.tar
```

This will create a folder `/opt/tini1.02/` (or a similar name depending on the current version) and a number of files and folders under that. You can install any of these files just about anyplace you like but you need to keep track of where you do and adjust the installation instructions in the book accordingly.

Next, we need to add `tini.jar` to your CLASSPATH environment variable and add an environment variable that indicates the TINI_HOME directory. Using your favorite ASCII editor, edit your shell startup file as we did in Chapter 3.

---

[12] TINI SDK – http://www.ibutton.com/TINI/software/index.html

For C shell:

```
set TINI_HOME /opt/tini1.02
set CLASSPATH=
/jdk1.3/lib/:/usr/java/jdk1.3/commapi/comm.jar:$TINI_HOME/bin/
tini.jar:.
```

For ksh, sh and bash shells:

```
set TINI_HOME /opt/tini1.02
export TINI_HOME
CLASSPATH=/jdk1.3/lib/:/usr/java/jdk1.3/commapi/comm.jar:$TINI_HOME/
bin/tini.jar:.
export CLASSPATH
```

Save the file. For these changes to be current, you need to start a new shell. The easiest way to do this is to logout and login again so all shells will use the new CLASSPATH definition.

Running JavaKit

JavaKit is an application that uses the serial port on your computer to connect to your TINI board's serial port. We will use JavaKit for configuring your TINI's firmware. A full discussion of JavaKit is provided in Chapter 7. This chapter is just enough to get you started. To run JavaKit from Windows, you need to open a DOS window. This DOS command should run Javakit:

```
C:\>java -cp \jdk1.3\lib\comm.jar;%TINI_HOME%\bin\tini.jar JavaKit
```

Note that if \jdk1.3\lib\comm.jar and %TINI_HOME%\bin\tini.jar are in your CLASSPATH then this DOS command should work as well:

```
C:\>java JavaKit
```

The Linux commands are almost the same:

```
% java -cp /usr/java/
jdk1.3/lib/:/usr/java/
jdk1.2/commapi/
comm.jar:$TINI_HOME/bin/
tini.jar JavaKit
```

or

```
% java JavaKit
```

An alternative, handy way of starting JavaKit is to create a JavaKit.bat file and put this in any folder that is listed in your PATH environment variable (like C:\WINDOWS\). The file should contain the following script (which should be a single line with no returns or new lines):

```
java -cp
\opt\jdk\lib\comm.jar;%TINI_HOME%\bin\tini.jar
JavaKit -port COM1 %1 %2 %3 %4 %5 %6 %7 %8 %9
```

This will allow you to treat JavaKit as if it is a new DOS command. You will need the %1..%9 in the batch file because from time to time you will need to pass command line arguments to JavaKit. For Linux we can simply create an alias for JavaKit. In our shell startup file.

For bash:

```
alias javakit='java -cp /usr/java/jdk1.3/lib/:/
usr/java/jdk1.3/commapi/comm.jar: $TINI_HOME/
bin/tini.jar JavaKit &'
```

For c-shell:

```
alias javakit 'java -cp /usr/java/jdk1.3/lib/:/
usr/java/jdk1.3/commapi/comm.jar: $TINI_HOME/
bin/tini.jar JavaKit &'
```

What this means: You need the `comm.jar` (to access your PC's serial port) and you need the `tini.jar` (the class library for TINI) to run JavaKit. `JavaKit` is a class in the tini.jar file. If you are not familiar with jar files and to satisfy any curiosity about what one looks like, you can view the contents of `tini.jar` (or any other jar file by specifying the appropriate pate and filename) use this DOS command:

```
C:\>jar -tf \opt\tini\bin\tini.jar
META-INF/
META-INF/MANIFEST.MF
BuildTINIROM$BryanInt.class
BuildTINIROM.class
TINIConvertor.class
...
JavaKit$1.class
JavaKit$2.class
JavaKit$ChoiceListener.class
JavaKit$CloseHandler.class
JavaKit$InputHandler.class
JavaKit$LoadFile.class
JavaKit$MacroRunner.class
JavaKit$MListener.class
JavaKit$SerialEventListener.class
JavaKit$SpecialKeyListener.class
JavaKit.class
BuildDependency.class
WatchDog.class
```

If you have installed everything correctly you should see the JavaKit GUI.

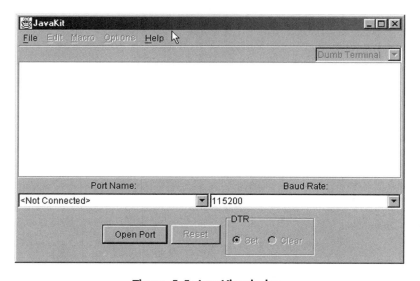

Figure 5-5: JavaKit window

If you don't see this, check the error messages carefully.

Possible errors:

- ```
  Exception in thread
  "main"
  java.lang.NoClassDefFound
  Error: Javakit
  ```

As far as this book is concerned, most of the differences between Windows and Linux can be summarized as follows:

- For separating directories in a path, use "/" for Linux and "\" for Windows.
- For separating elements in the CLASSPATH use ":" for Linux and ";" for Windows.
- For referring to environment variables use %var_name% for Windows and $var_name for Linux.
- Windows calls the serial ports COM1, COM2, etc. Linux uses /dev/ttyS0, /dev/ttyS1, etc.

Probably means you have incorrectly specifed the location of the tini.jar in the classpath.

- ```
  Exception in thread "main" java.lang.NoClassDefFoundError:
  javax/comm/UnsupportedCommOperationException
  ```

Probably means you have incorrectly specified the location of the comm.jar in your classpath.

Now let's connect to TINI. Change the "Port Name" selection box to your serial port that you have connected to TINI, in this case COM1 (Linux folks should use the proper name for Linux such as /dev/ttyS0; the selection box will show the names of the available ports). If the port you have connected to TINI is not listed, there is a problem with the serial port. Exit JavaKit and check that serial ports are properly installed and configured. After selecting the proper serial port, leave the "Baud Rate" set to 115200 and press the "Open Port" button. You should now see a screen similar to this:

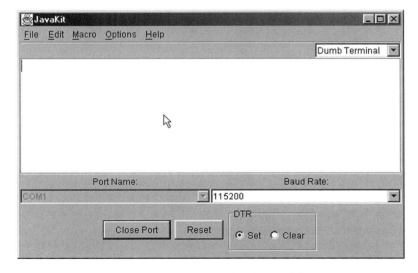

Figure 5-6: JavaKit after selecting serial port

If you are using a properly wired socket board from Dallas Semiconductor and a serial cable that is fully wired, you can press the "Reset" button on the JavaKit GUI. If you are using another socket board, this reset button may not work for a variety of reasons.

- Your serial cable does not have pin 4 connected.

- Your socket board does not support reset through the serial cable.

- Your socket board needs a jumper connected to enable this feature.

- Your socket board has a hardware reset button.

Either way, reset your board. You should see the start of the TINI loader:

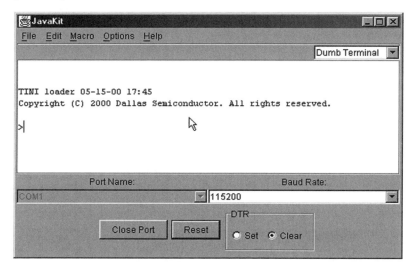

Figure 5-7: JavaKit after "reset"

At this point you can either boot your TINI (start the Java virtual machine and TINI shell) or you can load a new version of the TINI virtual machine. We will load a new virtual machine in Chapter 7; for now we are just getting started. At the > prompt in the JavaKit window, type an "e" and press Enter. This will boot your TINI. A whole bunch of stuff will scroll by in this window—you can use the scroll bars to read through this if you are interested.

At this point you are ready to login to your TINI. Press any key to get the login prompt and login. Initially, your TINI has a user called "root" and root's password is set to "tini". Try this.

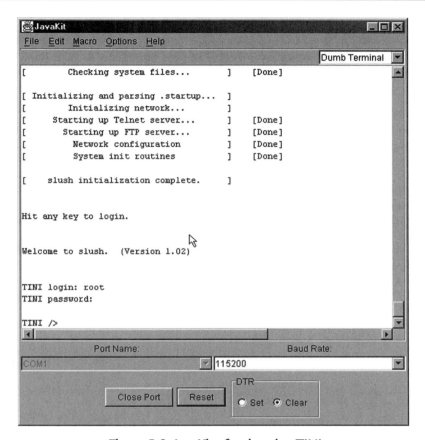

Figure 5-8: JavaKit after booting TINI

You are now logged into the TINI shell called *slush*. We are not quite done. You have successfully connected to your TINI through the serial port of the PC. We now need to configure the TINI network settings so you can connect to it through your LAN. We will use the `ipconfig` command to set your network addresses. Type `ipconfig -help` for all of the available options. You will need to know what IP address you want to assign to your TINI, your gateway address, and your subnet mask. These all need to be consistent with your LAN addresses. A much more thorough and detailed discussion on network connection is to be found in Chapter 13. An example of this command would be this:

```
ipconfig -a 192.168.1.85 -m 255.255.255.0
```

In this case this TINI has the IP address 192.168.1.85 and an IP mask of 255.255.255.0. Set an IP address for your TINI using an address that is consistent with your network. At this point you should be able to connect to your TINI through a Telnet session from any computer in your network. From a DOS command window (or the Windows RUN command prompt):

```
C:\>telnet 192.168.1.85
```

and you will get a Telnet window connected to your TINI. Login using the same username and password that you did through JavaKit. If you have gotten this far, then you are now ready to try your hand at compiling and running your first TINI Java program.

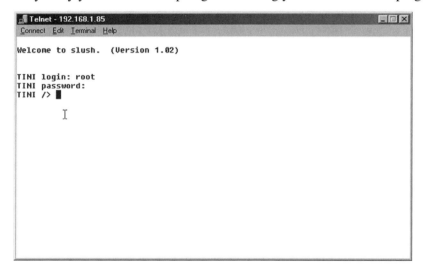

Figure 5-9: Telnet to TINI

Your first TINI program

In this section we will be checking to see that your TINI libraries and classes are properly installed by writing your first TINI program (Windows or Linux, it's all the same). We will be writing the traditional HelloWorld program, compiling it, porting it to TINI and running it. Use your favorite text editor to create HelloWorld.java; enter the program exactly as listed here. This is the exact same HelloWorld.java as used earlier in Chapter 3.

Listing 5-1: HelloWorld.java

```
public class HelloWorld {
    public static void main( String args[] ) {
        System.out.println( "Hello, World!" );
    }
}
```

Save the file. From a command window compile the program:

```
C:> javac HelloWorld.java
```

Now we need to convert the Java class file to a format that is recognized by the TINI virtual machine. To do that we will be using the TINIConvertor that is supplied in the tini.jar class archive. Notice that we need to add the `tiniclasses.jar` to our CLASSPATH so we will use the –cp command line parameter to tell the Java runtime system to use the supplied CLASSPATH rather than the environment variable (it's also convenient that we don't need most of what is already specified in the CLASSPATH that is defined in your autoexec.bat file). The following command should be entered as a single command (it's long and won't fit on a single line in a DOS window or in this book).

```
C:\>java -cp
%TINI_HOME%\bin\tini.jar;%TINI_HOME%\bin\tiniclasses.jar;.
TINIConvertor -f HelloWorld.class -o HelloWorld.tini -d
%TINI_HOME%\bin\tini.db
```

If all went well, you should have seen some output from TINIConvertor like this:

```
TINIConvertor + ZIP
Version 0.73 for TINI
built on or around January 24, 2001
Disassembler/Builder Version 0.15 TINI, October 30, 2000
JiBDB 0.60 for TINI, November 10, 2000
Copyright (C) 1996 - 2001 Dallas Semiconductor Corporation.
MainStartClass: First available.
Target address: 0x70100
Changed tag to 8000
Adding file: HelloWorld.class
Set mainClassIndex to: 0
Using ROM API Version: 8009
Writing Class Offsets
Writing Application: HelloWorld
Writing: HelloWorld
Total Application length: 125
Writing Application Entry point
Main offset for class with main: 32
class num: 0
main class index: 0
main class tag: 8000
Finished with build.
```

If you got any error messages, check your CLASSPATH and make sure that you specified the directories properly and that you included the -d `%TINI_HOME%\bin\tini.db`, as this tells the TINIConvertor how to convert .class files to .tini format. Also, if you are using Linux, remember that it is case sensitive.

Now we need to get the `HelloWorld.tini` file on to your TINI. To do this we will use FTP.

```
C:\>ftp 192.168.1.85
Connected to 192.168.1.85.
220 Welcome to slush.  (Version 1.02)  Ready for user login.
User (192.168.1.85:(none)): root
331 root login allowed. Password required.
Password: tini
230 User root logged in.
ftp> send HelloWorld.tini
200 PORT Command successful.
150 ASCII connection open, putting HelloWorld.tini
226 Closing data connection.
ftp: 173 bytes sent in 0.00Seconds 173000.00Kbytes/sec.
ftp> quit
221 Goodbye.
```

Login to your TINI either through JavaKit or Telnet. We prefer Telnet because by now we have disconnected the serial cable from our TINI. Also, since TINI is a network-capable device, you can place it anywhere you have a network connection (but not necessarily a serial port) so this is a good thing to get used to doing.

```
C:\>telnet 192.168.1.85
Trying 192.168.1.85...
Connected to 192.168.1.85.
Escape character is '^]'.

Welcome to slush.  (Version 1.02)

TINI login: root
TINI password: tini
TINI /> ls
HelloWorld.tini
etc
TINI /> java HelloWorld.tini
Hello, World!
TINI />
```

There are a few possible problems that might sneak in if you are not careful.

- ```
  TINI /> java HelloWorld.tini
  Could not execute file: java.lang.RuntimeException: Could not
  execute file. Bad API version = 8009
  ```

  The version of the TINI API you used to compile your Java program and the TINI virtual machine on the TINI SIMM must match. This error means you have loaded a newer version of the TINI API on your computer than there is in your TINI SIMM. To correct this, skip ahead to Chapter 7 to find out how to update the TINI virtual machine.

- ```
  TINI /> java HelloWorld
  HelloWorld does not exist.
  ```

  You need to type the full filename on TINI. This would be *HelloWorld.tini*.

- If your TINI hangs (no response), odds are you are trying to run a program that is not in the proper HEX file format. In other words, check that you are not trying to execute the .java or .class file.

OK, now you have completed your first TINI java program and ported it to your TINI and it ran successfully. Notice that we used the `ls` command to list the files on TINI (slush is a Linux-like shell). We then ran the HelloWorld program in a similar manner to how we would run it on a PC, except that you will notice that we specified the .tini file extension. Also notice that the TINI shell is case sensitive.

1-Wire Libraries

Remember that we mentioned that a 1-Wire network is a simple, low-cost network for communicating digitally over twisted-pair cable with 1-Wire components? Well, we will be using a number of 1-Wire devices in later chapters so now we are going to install the classes and libraries for 1-Wire. The TINI libraries include the classes for 1-Wire communication. To make life a little easier, we will also install the 1-Wire API on your PC so you can communicate with 1-Wire devices through the serial port of your personal computer as well. As before, we'll provide both Windows and Linux instructions.

Windows

For Windows, there are two ways we can talk to 1-Wire devices: With a Java API, and with a native library. We will install and use both. Download the "1-Wire API for Java"[13] and the "iButton-TMEX Windows 32-Bit Install 3.12" (or the current version if 3.12 is not the current version) from the "iButton-TMEX and Developers' Tool Kit"[14] web page. The current version (as of this writing) of the 1-Wire API is `owapi0_01.tgz` and the current version of the TMEX driver package is `tm312_32.exe`. The 1-Wire API is a package of Java classes for communicating with 1-Wire devices connected to your computer's serial or parallel port. The TMEX package (at least the part that we are concerned with) is a native Windows driver for communicating with the 1-Wire devices. You don't need this native driver package for most applications, but it makes 1-Wire communication a little faster. It does, however, give you a little more flexibility in terms of which hardware adapters you can use.

To install the 1-Wire Java API, create a subfolder in your C:\opt\ folder called onewire (or you can place the 1-Wire API files in any folder of your choice). Using Winzip or other archive program, open the `owapi0_01.tgz` archive and extract all of

---

[13] 1-Wire API for Java – http://www.ibutton.com/software/1wire/1wire_api.html

[14] iButton TMEX and Developers' Tool Kit – http://www.ibutton.com/software/tmex/index.html

the files to your \opt\onewire folder (or the folder of your choice). This will create a number of files and folders under that which contain the 1-Wire API classes, documentation and examples. You can install any of these files just about any place that you like, but keep track of where you do and adjust the installation instructions in the book. While it is not required for the 1-Wire API, it is convenient to add an environment variable, OW_HOME, by editing your autoexec.bat file. This environment variable should be defined as the location that you chose to install the 1-Wire API. We will use this environment variable to reference to the 1-Wire libraries when we need to include them in the CLASSPATH for compiling Java programs. It is also helpful to put the 1-Wire API libraries in your CLASSPATH.

Windows 95/98

In your autoexec.bat file, someplace after you have set your CLASSPATH, add the following line:

```
SET OW_HOME=c:\opt\onewire
SET CLASSPATH=%CLASSPATH%;%OW_HOME%\lib\OneWireAPI.jar
```

Windows 2000, Windows NT, Windows XP

For Windows 2000 and Windows NT you will have to use the "System" tool in the "Control Panel." Select the "Environment" tab and create a new system variable called OW_HOME. Set its value to be c:\opt\onewire. Edit the CLASSPATH system variable and change its value to be:

```
%CLASSPATH%;%OW_HOME%\lib\OneWireAPI.jar
```

For Windows XP, use the "System" tool in the "Control Panel." Select the "Advanced" tab and click on the "Environment" button (under "startup and recovery"). Create a OW_HOME system variable and edit the CLASSPATH variable as for NT.

To install the TMEX native drivers, tm312_32.exe, simply double click on the file name from Windows Explorer and follow the install script instructions. This will install the 1-Wire API in "C:\Program Files\Dallas Semiconductor\iButton-TMEX (32-Bit) V3.12" or a similar folder depending on the current version. There are two programs in there that we will use later on, but we mention them now while we are discussing these files.

- iBView32.exe – This is an iButton viewer. The iButton Viewer is a Windows program for communicating with iButtons and other 1-Wire Net compatible 1-Wire devices.

- SetPrt32.exe – This is a tool for selecting the default iButton port. We will use this in Chapter 10.

Linux

Download the "1-Wire API for Java". Note that there are no native drivers for 1-Wire on Linux as there are for Windows. This is OK; the Java 1-Wire API will work just fine. The current version (as of this writing) of the 1-Wire API is `owapi0_01.tgz`. The 1-Wire API is a package of Java classes for communicating with 1-Wire devices connected to your computer's serial or parallel port.

Create a subdirectory in your /opt directory called `onewire` (or you can install this API in any other directory of your choice). Uncompress and untar the `owapi0_01.tgz` archive and extract all of the files to your /opt/onewire directory (or the directory of your choice). This will create a number of files and folders under that which contain the 1-Wire API classes, documentation and example.

```
% cd downloads
% mv owapi0_01.tgz /opt
% cd /opt
% gunzip owapi0_01.tgz
% tar -xf owapi0_01.tar
% rm owapi0_01.tar
```

While it is not required for the 1-Wire API, it is convenient to add an environment variable, `OW_HOME`, by editing your shell initialization file (`.bash_profile` or `.cshrc` depending on the shell you use). This environment variable should be defined as the location that you chose to install the 1-Wire API. We will use this environment variable to reference to the 1-Wire libraries when we need to include them in the `CLASSPATH` for compiling Java programs. It is also helpful to put the 1-Wire API libraries in your `CLASSPATH`. In your shell initialization file, someplace after you have set your `CLASSPATH`. In your `autoexec.bat` file, add the following line:

For C shell:

```
set OW_HOME=c:\opt\onewire
set CLASSPATH = ${CLASSPATH}:${OW_HOME}/lib/OneWireAPI.jar
```

For ksh, sh and bash shells:

```
set OW_HOME=c:\opt\onewire
set CLASSPATH=$CLASSPATH:$OW_HOME/lib/OneWireAPI.jar
export OW_HOME CLASSPATH
```

Hardware

You will need some sort of 1-Wire port adapter (these things will be discussed in detail in Chapter 10), like the DS9097U. This adapter connects to a serial port on your computer and allows you to connect 1-Wire devices to it through a RJ11 connector. Figure 5-10 shows both a Serial 1-Wire adapter and a Parallel iButton holder. Both of these are available from Dallas Semiconductor in their iButton web page[15]. We will be using the serial adapter for this section. The parallel iButton holder will require the use of the native drivers from the TMEX package.

---

[15] iButton – http://www.ibutton.com/

Figure 5-10:
A serial port 1-Wire adapter

First 1-Wire program

We will check that both the PC and the TINI 1-Wire libraries are properly installed by writing a very simple program. You will need some sort of 1-Wire device. The schematic shown in Figure 5-11 includes a single 1-Wire device, the DS2401 (the DS2401 1-Wire component is the same as is in the DC1990A iButton only the package is different), which is a Silicon Serial Number. This device returns the 64-bit serial number of the device. While a rather simple schematic, this will illustrate the basic method for communicating on the 1-Wire bus and querying a device for information. Details of the 1-Wire bus will be discussed in Chapter 10. The sole point of the little sample is to verify that you have installed the TINI 1-Wire libraries correctly so that you are ready for more complex applications in future chapters.

Use your favorite text editor to enter the following program (or better yet, copy from the accompanying CD). The 1-Wire software and the details of 1-Wire devices will be discussed in Chapter 10.

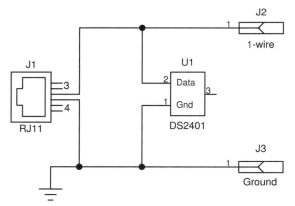

Figure 5-11:
Simple 1-Wire schematic

Listing 5-2: FindDevices.java

```
import java.util.*;
import com.dalsemi.onewire.*;
import com.dalsemi.onewire.adapter.*;
import com.dalsemi.onewire.container.*;
```

```
// Finds 1-wire devices and lists the type and serial number.
class FindDevices {

    public static void main(String[] args) {

    DSPortAdapter adapter = null;
        try {
            // Get the default adapter
            adapter = OneWireAccessProvider.getDefaultAdapter();
            // Let me override the default adapter if I choose
            if (args.length > 0)
                adapter.selectPort( args[0] );
        }
        catch (Exception e) {
            System.out.println(e);
        }
        try {
            // If there is a 1-wire adapter on the specified port, use it
            if (adapter.adapterDetected()) {
                // Tell the 1-wire adapter to look for all devices
                adapter.setSearchAllDevices();
                adapter.targetAllFamilies();
                // Get a list of all Devices on the 1-wire net on this adapter
                Enumeration ibutton_enum = adapter.getAllDeviceContainers();
                // For each device, tell me something about it
                while( ibutton_enum.hasMoreElements() ) {
                    OneWireContainer node =
                        (OneWireContainer) ibutton_enum.nextElement();
                    System.out.print( "    Container: " + node.getName());
                    System.out.print( " " + node.getAddressAsString());
                    System.out.println();
                }
            }
            adapter.freePort();
        }
        catch (Exception e) {
        }
    }
}
```

This program will compile on both Windows and Linux computers. You need to compile this with different classes in your CLASSPATH if you are compiling this for TINI. You will also need to convert the class file to a special format for TINI. In these examples, we show you how to compile and run this program for both Linux and Windows and also how to compile this on both Windows and Linux and then run it on TINI. Note that if you set your environment CLASSPATH for either Windows or Linux, it will need to be different depending on whether you are compiling for your personal computer or for porting to TINI. We will show how to use the javac and java command line options to override the environment CLASSPATH so you can see exactly which classes are needed for each instance (it does get a bit confusing at times). Also notice that we show the command on multiple lines. This is for clarity only, since it is hard to fit a long command line clearly on a printed page.

Compile from Windows, run from Windows

```
C:\>java FindDevices.java
```

If this doesn't work (the compiler complains about missing classes) then you need to add some things to your CLASSPATH as described previously, or perhaps there was a typo. We can also specify the libraries we need on the command line like this:

```
C:\>javac -classpath c:\jdk1.3\lib\;c:\jdk1.3\lib\comm.jar;.;
%OW_HOME%\lib\OneWireAPI.jar FindDevices.java
```

```
C:\>java FindDevices
```

```
        Container: DS1920 700000004B8F1010
        Container: DS2406 CB00000017006112
        Container: DS1990A 21000007997D9F01
```

In this example you can see several devices. In the schematic, we only used a single Silicon Serial Number, a DS2401. You may notice that there is no DS2401 listed. This is because the 1-Wire API chooses to list it using its iButton name of DS1990A. These are the same device, just in a different package. iButtons are packaged in metal cans about the diameter of a nickel. You will also notice the DS2406 and the DS1920 devices are other 1-Wire devices that we added to this circuit that will not show up when you run your program. We will be using these other devices later on in the book.

Compile from Windows, run from TINI

```
C:\>javac -classpath %TINI_HOME%\bin\tiniclasses.jar;
  %TINI_HOME%\bin\owapi_dependencies_TINI_001.jar;.
  FindDevices.java
```

Now we need to convert the FindDevices.class file to a format for TINI. To do this we use TINIConvertor (TINIConvertor is in the tini.jar file).

```
C:\>java -cp %TINI_HOME%\bin\tini.jar TINIConvertor -f FindDevices.class
        -d %TINI_HOME%\bin\tini.db -o FindDevices.tini
```

```
TINIConvertor + ZIP
Version 0.73 for TINI
built on or around January 24, 2001
Disassembler/Builder Version 0.15 TINI, October 30, 2000
JiBDB 0.60 for TINI, November 10, 2000
Copyright (C) 1996 - 2001 Dallas Semiconductor Corporation.
```

```
MainStartClass: First available.
Target address: 0x70100
Changed tag to 8000
Adding file: FindDevices.class
Set mainClassIndex to: 0
Using ROM API Version: 8009
Writing Class Offsets
Writing Application: FindDevices
Writing: FindDevices
Total Application length: 382
Writing Application Entry point
Main offset for class with main: 127
class num: 0
main class index: 0
main class tag: 8000
Finished with build.
```

Notice there are no errors. If you saw any errors, check carefully to see that you specified all the file names properly. Now we need to get the `FindDevices.tini` file to our TINI.

```
C:\>ftp 192.168.1.85

Connected to 192.168.1.85.
220 Welcome to slush.  (Version 1.02)  Ready for user login.
User (192.168.1.85:(none)): root
331 root login allowed. Password required.
Password: tini
230 User root logged in.
ftp> send FindDevices.tini
ftp> quit
```

We need to connect to our TINI to run the program. We will use Telnet, but you can just as easily use JavaKit to connect through the serial port.

```
C:\>telnet 192.168.1.85
Trying 192.168.1.85...
Connected to 192.168.1.85.
Escape character is '^]'.
Welcome to slush.  (Version 1.02)
TINI login: root
TINI password: tini


TINI /> java FindDevices.tini
        Container: Device type: 10 700000004B8F1010
        Container: Device type: 18 1C00000002795818
        Container: Device type: 12 CB00000017006112
        Container: Device type: 01 21000007997D9F01
```

Notice that there are no container names, just "device type" followed by a number. Why? Because TINIConvertor didn't build in the dependencies from the 1-Wire

Container classes so TINI doesn't know the names of these devices. To do this, use BuildDependency and include the 1-Wire API.

```
C:>java -cp %TINI_HOME%\bin\tini.jar BuildDependency -f
FindDevices.class -d %TINI_HOME%\bin\tini.db -o FindDevices.tini -x
%TINI_HOME%\bin\owapi_dep.txt -p %OW_HOME%\lib\onewireAPI.jar -add
OneWireContainer10;OneWireContainer18
```

Now use FTP to copy your `FindDevices.tini` to your TINI stick (refer to the first section of Chapter 6 if you don't know what this is) and then open a Telnet session like we did in the previous steps. Run the new version of the program:

```
TINI /> java FindDevices.tini
        Container: DS1920 700000004B8F1010
        Container: DS1963S 1C00000002795818
        Container: Device type: 12 CB00000017006112
        Container: Device type: 01 21000007997D9F01
```

Notice that we only included the OneWireContainer10 and OneWireContainer18 so these names are now known and that containers 01 and 12 are not. We could have added them to the list for BuildDependency also. Also notice that there is another 1-Wire device, device type 18. This is a DS1963S (Secure Hash Algorithm iButton) that we had stuck in the iButton socket on our TINI socket board. If you have an iButton on your TINI socket, you may also see a different device.

Compile from Linux, run from Linux

```
% javac -classpath /usr/java/jdk1.3/lib/:.:$OW_HOME/lib/OneWireAPI.jar
FindDevices.java

% java -cp /usr/java/jdk1.3/lib/:.:$OW_HOME/lib/OneWireAPI.jar
FindDevices
        Container: DS1920 700000004B8F1010
        Container: DS2406 CB00000017006112
        Container: DS1990A 21000007997D9F01
```

Compile from Linux, run from TINI

```
% javac -classpath $TINI_HOME/bin/tiniclasses.jar:
.:$TINI_HOME/bin/owapi_dependencies_TINI_001.jar FindDevices.java
% java -cp $TINI_HOME/bin/tini.jar TINIConvertor -
f FindDevices.class -d $TINI_HOME/bin/tini.db -o FindDevices.tini

TINIConvertor + ZIP
Version 0.73 for TINI
built on or around January 24, 2001
Disassembler/Builder Version 0.15 TINI, October 30, 2000
JiBDB 0.60 for TINI, November 10, 2000
Copyright (C) 1996 - 2001 Dallas Semiconductor Corporation.
```

```
MainStartClass: First available.
Target address: 0x70100
Changed tag to 8000
Adding file: FindDevices.class
Set mainClassIndex to: 0
Using ROM API Version: 8009
Writing Class Offsets
Writing Application: FindDevices
Writing: FindDevices
Total Application length: 382
Writing Application Entry point
Main offset for class with main: 127
class num: 0
main class index: 0
main class tag: 8000
Finished with build.


C:\>ftp 192.168.1.85

Connected to 192.168.1.85.
220 Welcome to slush.  (Version 1.02)  Ready for user login.
User (192.168.1.85:(none)): root
331 root login allowed. Password required.
Password: tini
230 User root logged in.
ftp> send FindDevices.tini
ftp> quit


C:\>telnet 192.168.1.85
Trying 192.168.1.85...
Connected to 192.168.1.85.
Escape character is '^]'.
Welcome to slush.  (Version 1.02)
TINI login: root
TINI password: tini


TINI /> java FindDevices.tini
        Container: Device type: 10 700000004B8F1010
        Container: Device type: 18 1C00000002795818
        Container: Device type: 12 CB00000017006112
        Container: Device type: 01 21000007997D9F01
```

Again, as with Windows compilation, you will notice that there are no Container names. Why? Because TINIConvertor didn't build in the dependencies from the container classes. To do this use BuildDependency and include the 1-Wire API.

```
% java -cp $TINI_HOME/bin/tini.jar BuildDependency
 -f FindDevices.class -d $TINI_HOME/bin/tini.db -o FindDevices.tini -x
 /opt/tini/bin/owapi_dep.txt -p $OW_HOME/lib/OneWireAPI.jar   -add
OneWireContainer10,OneWireContainer18
```

The FTP and Telnet session are skipped for this, since it's the same as in the previous steps.

```
TINI /> java FindDevices.tini
        Container: DS1920 700000004B8F1010
        Container: DS1963S 1C00000002795818
        Container: Device type: 12 CB00000017006112
        Container: Device type: 01 21000007997D9F01
```

OK, this was a quick tour by example of the different ways to compile and run Java 1-Wire programs on both your PC and on TINI from either Windows or Linux. If you had any problems you should check out the differences between Windows and Linux. Note that with Linux we used commas, not a semicolon to separate the added classes in BuildDependency (we could have used commas in the Windows version but you can't use semicolons in the Linux version). Also, always remember that Linux is case sensitive.

Summary

So, what we have done here is install and verify all of the TINI and 1-Wire APIs and classes and necessary drivers on your computer. We have written a few simple programs and exercised most of the tools we will be using

> The important things to remember from this chapter:
>
> TINI_HOME – Where the TINI API is installed
>
> OW_HOME – Where the 1-Wire API is installed
>
> CLASSPATH – Should include comm.jar, tiniclasses.jar, OneWireAPI.jar and possibly tini.jar

throughout the rest of this book. Remember, this chapter was meant to be *just* enough to get you started; we will be discussing 1-Wire in detail in Chapter 10 and most of the software programs we used here we will discuss in detail in Chapter 7.

References

1. *The Tiny InterNet Interface FAQ,*
    http://www.jguru.com/jguru/faq/faqpage.jsp?name=TINI

2. *Introducing TINI: Tiny InterNet Interface,*
    http://www.ibutton.com/TINI/

3. *What Is The 1-Wire Net?*
    http://www.dalsemi.com/products/autoinfo/1wirenet.html

4. *Application Note 132, Quick Guide to 1-wire Net using PCs and Microcontrollers,*
    http://www.dalsemi.com/datasheets/pdfs/app132.pdf

5. *Tech Brief No1, 1-Wire Net Design Guide,*
    http://www.dalsemi.com/techbriefs/tb1.html

## CHAPTER 6

The TINI Hardware

This chapter examines the TINI hardware and some of the associated interface boards that allow you to connect to it. We will begin by systematically reviewing each component on the TINI schematic. We will also present useful programs that demonstrate some of the features of the TINI API as they relate to the hardware and provide tables and charts that will be used in the remainder of this book.

What is TINI?

The term TINI can actually refer to more than one thing. With respect to hardware, TINI is a design concept that consists of an embeddable chipset that you can incorporate into your own products to make them Java-powered and web-enabled. That chipset consists of a DS80C390 microprocessor, a flash ROM, and a static RAM. The term TINI can also be applied to the "TINI stick," which is a specific, pre-manufactured design implementation using the TINI chipset. The "stick" consists of the TINI chip set, along with a host of interface devices mounted on a 72-pin SIMM. It runs on 5V DC, (+/- 5%, 250mA) and utilizes an 18.432-MHz clock, which is frequency doubled to 36.864 MHz after the initial portions of the booting process. Dallas Semiconductor has created this as a reference design to give people an easy way to get up to speed using the TINI chipset. You can use the TINI stick in your products, by simply embedding it as is. Alternatively, you can use it as a debugging platform to develop your design, then later build the chip set into your application. When we discuss TINI in this chapter, we will be referring to the pre-made reference design, the "TINI stick."

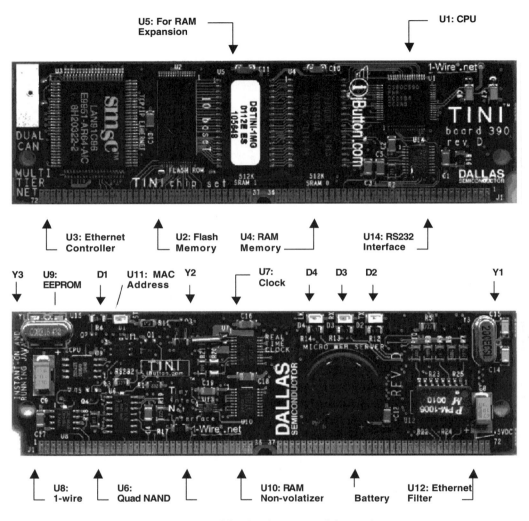

Figure 6-1: Front and back of a TINI Stick, Design Rev D

Versions

There have already been a variety of different versions of the TINI stick. The original design used a 68-pin SIMM instead of the 72-pin SIMM used now. Current versions now come with a choice of either 512k or 1Mb of RAM. Unless otherwise noted, we will be discussing the 512k version of the device as shown in schematic version D, dated Oct 12, 2000 (both memory versions are the same design and board—the 512Mb version simply has half the memory).

A high-level look at TINI

Included with this book is the complete schematic for the TINI stick. Before we delve into it in detail, let's take a high-level look at the design of the TINI stick[1].

What's in a TINI stick?

- A Dallas Semiconductor microcontroller, the DS80C390, which is a descendent of the 8051. It has six 8-bit ports that can be used for a variety of functions (more on that later).

- An 18.432-MHz oscillator for the microcontroller.

- A 512k x 8 static RAM, with space on the circuit board for an additional 512K x 8 static RAM. The design uses a 19-bit address space and has separate chip selects for the two RAM devices. This gives TINI a theoretical on-board RAM potential of 2Mb (by using 1Mb x 8 RAMs instead of 512k). The RAM devices are for user program storage.

- A 512k x 8 FLASH ROM. This is divided into 8 banks, and it houses the bootstrap loader, the runtime environment, and the primary Java application (frequently slush).

- A Dallas Semiconductor real-time clock, so that applications have access to true "time."

- A battery, which provides power to the real-time clock and the static RAM devices when the board isn't powered up.

- A RAM nonvolatizer subsystem that works with the battery so that user programs remain in the RAMs even when the stick is powered down.

- A DS2480 iButton interface, so that TINI can talk to external 1-Wire devices. There is also an internal 1-Wire bus on the stick, used for communicating with on-board 1-Wire devices.

- An RS232 interface that provides level shifting to the serial interface of the microprocessor.

- A 10-Base-T Ethernet interface.

- Miscellaneous decoupling capacitors, resistors, status LEDs, and jumpers.

The TINI stick has additional capabilities, such as I^2C and CAN interfaces, that are an integral feature of the DS80C390 microprocessor.

---

[1] TINI Datasheet – http://www.ibutton.com/TINI/dstini2.pdf

A quick look at how it works

When TINI is powered up, the CPU first copies the *bootstrap loader* from the flash memory to a 4k SRAM located inside the CPU itself. Then it transfers control to the runtime environment (tini.tbin), which ultimately will start the primary Java application. The primary Java application can be the slush operating system (slush.tbin), or some other Java program that has been installed as a .tbin file. The loader, runtime environment, and primary Java application reside in the flash memory. Other applications that are executed later, by the primary Java application, reside in RAM as .tini files. The flash memory is nonvolatile by virtue of its technology. The RAM is made nonvolatile through the use of a battery backup. Additionally, you can change the contents of the flash, by loading in a different .tbin file (such as an updated tini.tbin or slush.tbin) and the contents of the RAM will remain unchanged.

The boot process on TINI occurs as the result of a reset and there are a couple of different ways the reset can occur. First, it can reset as the result of the power being turned off and on. This is called a power-on reset (POR). Second, the TINI CPU can be reset with the power already on, by having its CPURST line pulled high. This is referred to as an external reset. External resets and PORs behave somewhat differently. During a POR, the bootstrap loader is loaded into the CPU and then immediately allows the runtime environment to take over. During external resets, the device reboots, but during the booting process the bootstrap loader will wait to receive a special pattern of characters before turning control over to the runtime environment. If it receives this pattern of characters within three seconds of the reset, the loader will execute a mini command shell that can be controlled via the serial0 port. That shell can be used to load new software into the flash. If the loader doesn't see this pattern within 3 seconds, it will continue the normal booting process, and transfer control to the runtime environment and primary application[2]. This is how the bootstrap loader gets its name—it is the bit of firmware we use to load a new runtime environment or a new primary Java application into the TINI flash.

The Various Components of the TINI Stick

Having introduced the basic TINI system, let's take a more detailed look at each of these components.

The SIMM (Single Inline Memory Module) edge connector

The TINI stick connects to the outside world through a 72-pin SIMM edge connector, mechanically identical to the ones used on PC memory modules. To make use of the TINI stick, you must mate with this connector in some fashion. The E10/E20 socket board, or the Vinculum proto-board are two examples of products that mate with the TINI edge connector and provide interfaces to its signals.

---

[2] *The TINI Specification and Developer's Guide*, Don Loomis, Addison-Wesley, 2001, pages 19 and 20.

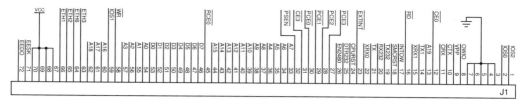

Figure 6-2: Detail of the TINI SIMM connector
(All TINI schematics and portions of TINI schematics have been used with permission,
Copyright 2001 Dallas Semiconductor.)

Table 6-1: SIMM connector signal names and explanations

68 PIN TINI	72 PIN TINI	Signal Name	Signal Description
—	1	IOS2	Used with the EEPROM inside the LAN91C96
—	2	IOS1	Used with the EEPROM inside the LAN91C96
1-3	3-7	GND	Digital Circuit Ground.
4-5	—	USB	Future USB connection
6	8	OWIO	1-Wire Input/Output Pin[1]
7	9	VPP	+12V supply input for EPROM programming [2]
8	10	CTX	CAN bus TX line or bi-directional port pin
9	11	CRX	CAN bus RX line or bi-directional port pin
10	12	CE0	CPU chip enable 0 [3]
11	13	A19	Address line A19 [4]
12	14	TX1	Serial Port 1 output TTL
13	15	XRX1	Serial Port 1 input TTL [5]
14	16	RD	CPU read strobe [5]
15	17	INTOW	Internal 1-Wire bus [6]
16	18	SMCRST	Peripheral reset from CPU
17	19	TX232	Serial Port 0 output
18	20	RX232	Serial Port 0 input
19	21	TX	Serial Port 0 output TTL
20	22	XRX0	Serial Port 0 input TTL [6]
21	23	EXTINT	CPU interrupt input
22	24	CPURST	CPU reset input [7]
23	25	DTR232	RS232 CPU reset input [8]
24	26	EN2480	On-board DS2480 enable
25-28	27-30	PCE3-0	Peripheral chip enables from CPU [5]
29	31	CE3	Chip Enable 3 from CPU [5]
30	32	PSEN	Program Store enable from CPU [5]
31-34	33–36	A7–A4	Address lines A7 – A4 [5]
35-42	37–44	A8–A15	Address lines A8 – A15 [5]
43	45	RCE0	CE0 return to on-board Flash ROM [4]

44-51	46-53	D7-D0	Data lines [5]
52-55	54–57	A0–A3	Address lines A0 – A3 [5]
56	58	WR	CPU Write Strobe [5]
57	—	NC	No Connect
—	59	IOS1	Used with the EEPROM inside the LAN91C96
58-60	60–62	A16-A18	Address lines A16 – A18 [5]
61,62	63,64	ETH3,ETH6	10Base-T differential inputs.
63,64	65,66	ETH2,ETH1	10Base-T differential outputs.
65-68	67-70	Vcc	+5V DC +/- 5% @ 250mA max [9]
	71	EESK	Used with the EEPROM inside the LAN91C96
	72	EEDO	Used with the EEPROM inside the LAN91C96

[1] 1-Wire bus with slew-rate-controlled pull-down, active pull-up, ability to switch in Vpp to program EPROM, and ability to switch in Vdd through a low-impedance path to program EEPROM or to perform a temperature conversion.

[2] Vpp may be connected to +12V DC to allow EPROM programming with the on-board DS2480. If Vpp is not used in this manner, it must be connected to Vcc.

[3] To execute from the on-board Flash ROM, connect CE0 to RCE0. If an external boot-up memory is provided, RCE0 must be pulled high (Vcc) to disable the on-board Flash ROM or data bus interference could occur. Logic in the CE0 to RCE0 path must take care to present minimal delay (< 6 ns) to the CE0 signal.

[4] Address bus, data bus and strobe lines are subject to strict loading limitations. Exceeding these limits can cause erratic system operation with on-board as well as off-board resources. Be sure to buffer any signals that will be heavily loaded off-board. Always adhere to the design specifications to assure reliable system operation.

[5] Must be pulled high (Vcc) if not used.

[6] The internal 1-Wire bus (INTOW) is a micro-controller port pin that drives the CPU status LED and links to the board's 1-Wire EPROM memory chip that contains the DSTINI1's Ethernet MAC address. Other 1-Wire devices may be connected to this bus in the future to convey configuration DSTINI1 data to the DSTINI. If this bus is shorted to ground (low) during system boot-up, a Master Clear will be invoked. This forces the contents of the SRAM to be reinitialized.

[7] CPURST must be taken high (Vcc) and then released to cause a reset of the DSTINI1. An active state on the DTR232 will also take this line high. This line is pulled down through a 22k Ω pull-down on-board.

[8] The RS232 level DTR control line is used to invoke a DSTINI1 reset when asserted. This is to facilitate loaders and diagnostic equipment that must invoke a reset of the board to gain control of the system. This line is pulled to –8 V via 22K ohms and has a 0.01 µF capacitor filter to prevent cross talk on an open DTR conductor from causing spurious resets of the DSTINI if this function is not used.

[9] TINI board power consumption is rated at no more than 250 mA.

The processor and oscillator module

The CPU on TINI, the DS80C390, is technically called a Dual CAN high-speed microprocessor. It's compatible with the 8051 instruction set. It has six 8-bit ports. Under software control, most have one or more functions. The DS80C390 has two integrated CAN controllers, and it has an integrated UART, capable of controlling two serial ports. This processor is extremely flexible and there are a number of ways it can be used. We will concern ourselves with how it is used on the TINI stick. We'll start by looking at its pin-out and examining what all of its signals do for us.

Figure 6-3 shows a close up of the CPU on the TINI schematic. Notice that there are numerous labels for each pin. Let's make some sense of this, by taking a closer look at a couple of the pins.

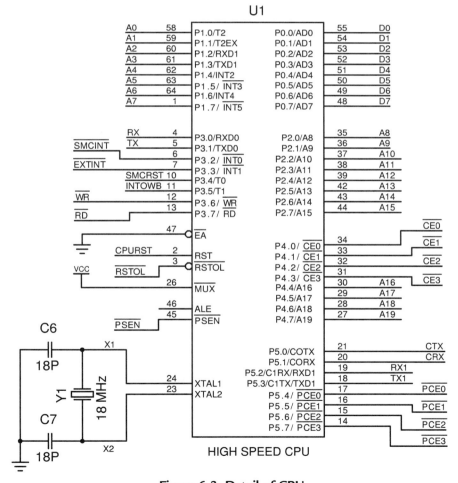

Figure 6-3: Detail of CPU

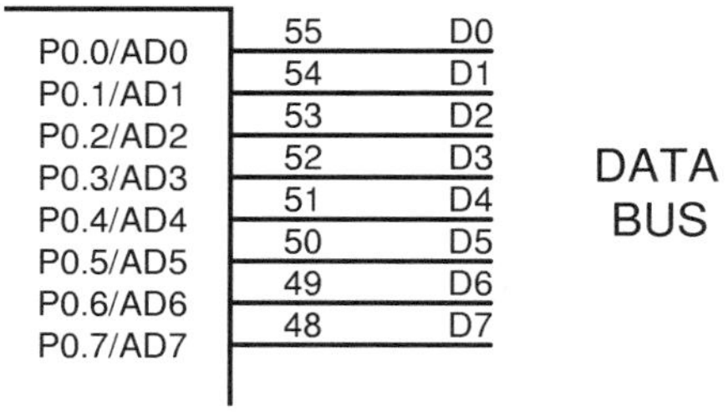

P0.0/AD0	55	D0
P0.1/AD1	54	D1
P0.2/AD2	53	D2
P0.3/AD3	52	D3
P0.4/AD4	51	D4
P0.5/AD5	50	D5
P0.6/AD6	49	D6
P0.7/AD7	48	D7

DATA
BUS

**Figure 6-4: Detail of Port 0,
Illustrating port labeling conventions**

Referring to the figure, the label P0 refers to port 0 of the CPU's six 8-bit ports. P0.0 is the least significant bit in that port, P0.1 the next bit, etc. The label AD0 accompanying the P0.0 label is an indication of that pin's function as described in the general DS80C390 data sheet (AD0 indicates that it is an 8-bit bus that can be either an address or data bus, and it is the least significant bit). The label 55 is the pin number on the package, and the label D0 is the net name assigned to this pin on the TINI schematic. It's an indication of how this pin is being used by TINI. Unless otherwise noted, we will make use of the port/bit designator (P0.0), and the TINI schematic net name. Let's go around the CPU and examine what all these signals do.

Port0, P0.0 to P0.7, is the data bus and consists of TINI signals D0 to D7.

Port1, P1.0 to P1.7, is part of the address bus and makes up TINI signals A0 to A7.

Port2, P2.0 to P2.7, is more of the address bus and makes up TINI signals A8 to A15.

Port3, P3.0 to P3.7, provides a variety of different functions:

- P3.0 is the RX signal, the receive input for the CPU's serial port.

- P3.1 is the TX signal, the transmit output for the CPU's serial port.

- P3.2 is the /SMCINT signal. This is an interrupt input, coming from the Ethernet controller device.

- P3.3 is the /EXTINT signal. This is an interrupt input, coming from a user-defined external hardware source. A simple demo program describing how to use this hardware interrupt is included in Chapter 9 (ExtIntDemo.java).

- P3.4 is the SMCRST signal. This is an output that serves to reset the Ethernet controller. The SMCRST signal is used to disable the outputs of various peripherals during power-up. This signal starts out high and goes low only after TINI has completed its reset sequence and the firmware is ready to put the peripheral drivers into a known state (like the network IC and parallel I/O). Because this signal goes low only after the TINI firmware is up and running, it is a good signal to use to prevent I/O activity during start-up.

- P3.5 is the INTOWB signal. This is the internal 1-Wire bus and is bi-directional.

- P3.6 is the /WR signal. This is the active low write enable for memories and is associated with the data and address buses.

- P3.7 is the /RD signal. This is the active low read enable for the memories and is also associated with the data and address buses.

Port 4, P4.0 to P4.7, provides the remaining address signals and chip enable signals:

- P4.0 is the /CE0 signal. This is the chip enable output for the flash memory. It's routed off stick and doesn't actually go to the on-board flash. The on-board flash, U2, has a signal named /RCE0 as its chip enable, instead. /RCE0 comes from the TINI edge card connector. For many applications, such as when using an E20 socket board or the Vinculum proto-board, you are probably going to route the /CE0 output on the SIMM edge connector right back into the /RCE0 input signal on the SIMM. The reason they didn't just hardwire the /CE0 signal from the CPU directly to the flash memory has to do with flexibility. By not hardwiring it, we can use the /CE0 externally to select a different, external flash, should we desire it.

- P4.1 is the /CE1 signal. This is the chip enable output for U4, the 512k static ram, which is SRAM0. It doesn't go directly to SRAM0, but is gated through U13. The U13 device is effectively an or gate controlled by U10, the RAM nonvolatizer. /CE1 does not go off stick.

- P4.2 is the /CE2 signal. This is the chip enable output for U5, the second 512k static ram, which is SRAM1. Depending on the stick version you have, this component is most likely not installed. Like /CE1, this signal is not routed directly to the ram, but rather, it is gated through the or gate U13, which is controlled by the ram nonvolatizer U10. /CE2 is also not routed off stick.

- P4.3 is the /CE3 signal. This a chip enable output that serves a variety of functions. It serves as the address enable for the Ethernet controller, chip enable for the real-time clock, and it's routed off stick for use decoding addresses for memory reads and writes to peripheral devices.

- P4.4 to P4.7 are the remaining address bus signals, A16 to A19.

Port 5 represents a variety of functions.

- P5.0 is the CTX signal. This is the CAN transmit output signal for the CAN0 CAN controller. It is routed off the stick. This pin is also used for the SCL line for I²C communication.

- P5.1 is the CRX signal. This is the CAN receive input signal for the CAN0 CAN controller. It is routed off the stick. This pin is also used for the SDA line for I²C communication.

- P5.2 is the RX1 signal. This is the input representing the received data from the external 1-Wire bus data coming from the iButton interface circuitry. This signal is not routed off stick. This pin can also be used for either the CTX signal (CAN transmit) for the CAN1 CAN controller or the RX signal for the serial1 port.

- P5.3 is the TX1 signal. This is an output representing the data to be transmitted out the external 1-Wire bus via the iButton interface circuitry. This signal is routed off stick. This pin can also be used for either the CRX signal (CAN receive) for the CAN1 CAN controller, or the TX signal for the Serial1 port.

- P5.4 to P5.7 are the /PCE0, /PCE1, /PCE2, and /PCE3 signals. These are peripheral chip enable outputs and can be used as chip enables to perform memory reads and writes to peripheral devices. They are routed off chip.

You have program control of some of these through ports (port 3 and port 5) using the BitPort class of the TINI API. You can access Port5 through the BytePort class as well. Refer to the TINI API documentation for more information on these classes.

Beyond the six 8-bit ports, there are a handful of additional CPU signals that are used by TINI. We'll refer to them by the net name on the TINI schematic.

CPURST is the CPU reset input. When this signal is pulled high, the CPU resets. This signal comes from a small circuit that converts the DTR signal into the CPURST signal. CPURST is routed off stick. It can be used by off-stick devices that need to reset the CPU, or, as a way to reset off-stick devices, when the CPU resets.

/RSTOL is the reset output low signal. It is an active low output signal that goes low whenever the CPU is resetting, the watchdog timer has expired, during the crystal warm-up phase, or whenever the CPU VCC drops below the value on CPURST. /RSTOL controls the reset on the real time clock, U7. It is not routed off-stick.

XTAL1 and XTAL2 are the crystal inputs the CPU.

/PSEN is the program store enable output signal. This is an active low CPU output that is low whenever the CPU is accessing memory. It acts as an output enable for the flash ROM (U2), SRAM0 and SRAM1 (U4 and U5), the real-time clock (U7), and the Ethernet controller (U3).

Programming example: the watchdog timer

The CPU has an interesting feature known as a *watchdog timer*, that we can utilize in our Java applications. The watchdog timer is a clock, internal to the CPU, that keeps track of the passage of time since the last time it was *fed*. If the watchdog timer doesn't get fed within a certain interval, it resets the CPU. You can set this interval. Below is a very simple program that demonstrates the use of the watchdog timer.

You pass the program one command line parameter, the timer interval, in milliseconds. The watchdog will start counting down, and if your interval of time passes, TINI will reboot. You can *feed* the timer, restarting the timer, and temporarily preventing the reboot by hitting any key. We'll first present the code in its entirety, then we'll go through it bit by bit.

Listing 6-1: WatchDogDemo.java

```
import java.io.*;
import com.dalsemi.system.*;

public class WatchDogDemo {
  public static void main(String[] args) {
    int feedInterval;
    if (args.length == 0) {
      feedInterval = 10000;
    } else {
      feedInterval = Integer.parseInt(args[0]);
    }
    TINIOS.setWatchdogTimeout(feedInterval);
    System.out.println("Hit any key to feed the dog!");
    while(true) {
      try {
        int keyBoardInput = System.in.read();
      } catch(Exception e) {System.out.println(e);}
      TINIOS.feedWatchdog();
      System.out.println("You have just fed the watchdog!");
    }
  }
}
```

We need to import two libraries, `java.io` because we print to the screen, and `com.dalsemi.system`, because that's where the watchdog class lives. Our class will be called WatchDogDemo.

```
import java.io.*;
import com.dalsemi.system.*;

public class WatchDogDemo {
```

Our program has one method, `main()`. We begin by doing some simple checking to make sure we have been given a command line parameter. If not, we will use a default of 10 seconds, which is 10000 milliseconds. The integer, `feedInterval`, is the time interval for our watchdog timer.

```
public static void main(String[] args) {
    int feedInterval;
    if (args.length == 0) {
        feedInterval = 10000;
    } else {
        feedInterval = Integer.parseInt(args[0]);
    }
```

Next, we set the watchdog timer interval, by using the `TINIOS.setWatchdogTimeout()` method. We also print a line to the screen, giving instructions.

```
    TINIOS.setWatchdogTimeout(feedInterval);
    System.out.println("Hit any key to feed the dog!");
```

We create a loop, which will wait for a key to be pressed. Whenever a key is pressed, we'll exit the loop, and feed the dog with the `TINIOS.feedWatchdog()` method, and print a phrase to the screen. If we don't exit the loop by the time the timer expires, the TINI will reboot.

```
    while(true) {
        try {
            int keyBoardInput = System.in.read();
        } catch(Exception e) {System.out.println(e);}
        TINIOS.feedWatchdog();
        System.out.println("You have just fed the watchdog!");
    }
  }
}
```

The following are the commands that can be used to compile the program. We are assuming that the WatchDogDemo.java file is in its own folder, and the commands below are being executed in that folder. Again, the Javac and Java commands are shown with their command line parameters on separate lines, only for readability. They all need to be on the same line for each command.

```
C:\> javac -classpath %TINI_HOME%\bin\tiniclasses.jar
          -d tini WatchDogDemo.java
C:\> java -classpath %TINI_HOME%\bin\tini.jar TINIConvertor
          -f tini
          -o tini\WatchDogDemo.tini
          -d %TINI_HOME%\bin\tini.db
```

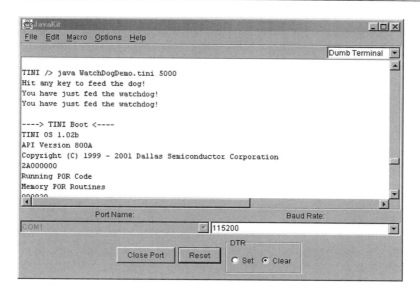

Figure 6-5: Sample output of the WatchDogDemo program

Figure 6-5 shows a screen capture of the WatchDogDemo program in action. We could execute the program from a Telnet session through Ethernet, but we won't see exactly when the reboot happens, as nothing will be printed back to us (we'll simply lose the connection). So, we've used JavaKit to demonstrate it, because this will allow us to see exactly when the watchdog reboots, as the system messages will be echoed back to us during the reboot. In the example, we've moved the program over to TINI via ftp (Ethernet), then logged onto the stick via JavaKit. Upon running the program, we've selected a 5-second delay between "feedings." We hit a key a couple of times, at less than 5-second intervals, to feed the dog, then let the watchdog reboot.

The Memory

A few words about the TINI address space

The term *address space* refers to the range of addresses that the TINI operating system can make use of. This address space bears some examination.

The TINI address space is broken up into two four-megabyte blocks: 0–0x3FFFFF and 0x800000–0xBFFFFF. This immediately leads to an interesting question. The TINI schematic shows a 20-bit address bus, which implies our address space should be 1 Mbyte. If our address bus is only 20 bits, how can we address 8 Mbytes? The answer is through the use of the chip enable signals, /CE0–/CE03, and /PCE0–/PCE3. Each of these chip enables refers to 1 Mbyte of our 8-Mbyte space.

Table 6-2: Mapping chip enable signals to the address regions they select

Chip Enable	Memory Range Selected
/CE0	0x000000 - 0x0FFFFF
/CE1	0x100000 - 0x1FFFFF
/CE2	0x200000 - 0x2FFFFF
/CE3	0x300000 - 0x3FFFFF
/PCE0	0x800000 - 0x8FFFFF
/PCE1	0x900000 - 0x9FFFFF
/PCE2	0xA00000 - 0xAFFFFF
/PCE3	0xB00000 - 0xBFFFFF

So, on the TINI stick, we'll see a 20-bit address whose placement within the 8-Mbyte space is determined by which one (and only one) of the chip enables is pulled low (Table 6-2). Even though we only have those 20 address lines on the stick, in software, we will proceed as if we have a 24-bit address bus. For example, the `Dataport` class makes use of addresses 0x00000000 – 0x003FFFFF, and 0x00800000 – 0x00BFFFFF. The TINI Firmware will look at the lower 20 bits of that and send it out TINI stick signal lines A0 – A19, while it uses the upper four bits to select which of the eight chip select signals is to be driven low. Many examples using the `Dataport` class are included in Chapter 9, when we discuss memory-mapped I/O.

The TINI memory map

In the previous section, we looked at the address space of TINI. A related concept is the memory map. The memory map defines where the TINI OS thinks devices reside within the address space. A general memory map for TINI has been documented in several places by the manufacturer, but a more detailed memory map has only been discussed in the TINI interest group message archive[3]. Below, we're going to present the memory map as described in the interest group. In doing so, we're also incorporating corrections that were presented in the message archive.

Table 6-3: TINI stick memory map

Address (hex)	Chip Enable	Contents
0x000000 – 0x07FFFF	/CE0	Flash ROM 1 (On Board, 512K)
0x080000 – 0x0FFFFF	/CE0	Flash ROM 2 (image or off-board)[1]
0x100000 – 0x17FFFF	/CE1	Image of SRAM0 (512K)[2]
0x180000 – 0x1FFFFF	/CE1	SRAM0 (512K)
0x200000 – 0x27FFFF	/CE2	SRAM1 (512K)

[3] TINI Interest Group Archives – http://lists.dalsemi.com/maillists/tini/

0x280000 – 0x2FFFFF	/CE2	Image of SRAM1 (512K)[3]
0x300000 – 0x307FFF	/CE3	SMC Ethernet Controller[4]
0x308000 – 0x30FFFF	/CE3	Available Peripheral CODE & DATA space (32K)
0x310000 – 0x31FFFF	/CE3	Real Time Clock[5]
0x320000 – 0x3FFFFF	/CE3	Available Peripheral CODE & DATA space (896K)[6]
0x800000 – 0x8FFFFF	/PCE0	Off Board RAM or peripheral space (1Mbyte)
0x900000 – 0x9FFFFF	/PCE1	Off Board RAM or peripheral space (1Mbyte)
0xA00000 – 0xAFFFFF	/PCE2	Off Board RAM or peripheral space (1Mbyte)
0xB00000 – 0xBFFFFF	/PCE3	Off Board RAM or peripheral space (1Mbyte)

[1] The 512K memory has an 18 bit address bus, but is residing in a 1Mbyte region in memory. This means that two addresses refer to the same spot in memory, which results in the lower half of this 1Mbyte memory space looking exactly like the upper half (an *image* of itself).

[2] See note 1.

[3] See note 1.

[4] If we just look at the address bits involved on the LAN91C96 device, it would appear that it could reside in a larger space. It's place in the memory map as presented here has been taken on faith from discussions on the TINI interest group message.

[5] While the Real Time Clock has been given a 64K block in memory, it only uses one specific location within that block. The rest is room for future expansion.

[6] The memory map as posted to the TINI interest group message list had this region as being 0x320000 – 0x38FFFF. We believe that was a typo.

In our map, again, we see 24-bit addresses. The lower 20 bits map directly to A0–A19 on the stick, and the upper four bits imply one of eight chip enables going to logic '0'. There are a couple of items to note about the map. The first deals with the concept of *images*. Our memory parts are 512k each, and as such, they only use a 19-bit address bus. But they are residing in their own 1-Mbyte memory space within the map. This means that there is a redundancy in our addressing: two memory map addresses map to a single physical memory location. So, one-half of the 1-Mbyte region will look exactly like the other half, hence the term *image*.

The second thing to note about this map is that there are subtleties involved with respect to how the firmware and hardware interact, making it difficult to see why the map is defined the way it is sometimes. As we go through the individual portions of the design, we'll discuss what we know about why this map is defined the way it is.

Flash ROM

The flash ROM on TINI, U2, is an Advanced Micro Devices AM29F040B, 512k x 8 device. It is an Electrically Erasable Programmable Read-Only Memory, or EEPROM[4]. It is nonvolatile. The TINI flash ROM houses the bootstrap loader, the runtime environment, and the primary Java application.

[4] AM29F040B datasheet – http://www.amd.com/us-en/assets/content_type/ white_papers_and_tech_docs/21445.pdf

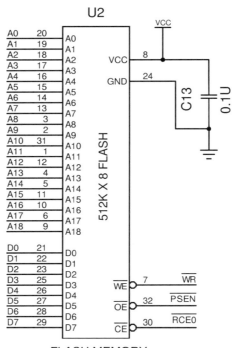

Figure 6-6:
Detail of the flash ROM

FLASH MEMORY
AM29F040B 55 NS

Table 6-4: The function of the various banks inside the flash ROM.

Bank (Each 64K)	Description of Contents
0	Boot Loader
1, 2	Firmware (tini.hex) } Runtime
3, 4, 5, 6	API (tiniapi.hex) } Environment
7	Primary Java application started by the runtime environment (TINI OS). Usually slush, but it can be a user created application as long as it's less than 64K.

The term "flash" is used to describe a type of electrically erasable, programmable, read-only memory that doesn't have to be erased or reprogrammed one bit at a time. Rather, it does this in large sectors or blocks, via internal control circuitry. The flash ROM is nonvolatile and retains its contents even when powered down. The flash ROM on the TINI stick is divided up into eight 64k sectors, or banks.

The flash ROM uses the /WR and /PSEN signals for write enabling and output enabling, as do the static RAMs SRAM0 and SRAM1. The chip enable on the FLASH, however, is handled a little differently. The flash chip enable is the /RCE0 signal, or remote chip enable, coming from the SIMM edge connector. This means that if we want to use this on-board flash as the source of our firmware, as described in Table 6-4, we need to generate the /RCE0 signal externally and feed it back onto the TINI. The flash memory uses 20 address bits, A0 through A18. As shown on the memory map, the on-board flash lives at 0x000000 – 0x07FFFF in our address space and is selected by chip enable 0, /CE0. The position of the flash in the memory map follows by simply looking at the range of possible addresses achievable on A0-A18. There's nothing subtle going on there.

The simplest way to generate the remote chip enable, /RCE0, is to simply loop the /CE0 signal right back into /RCE0. That works fine as long as you aren't trying to make use of an alternate, off-stick flash ROM. If you are trying to make use of off-stick ROM, then the signal /RCE0 needs to be disabled (set to "1") when you want to access the off-stick flash, through some simple decoding circuitry.

Static RAM

The random access memory, or RAM, used on the TINI stick is the SAMSUNG KM684000BLI-5L 512k x 8 static ram device[5]. There are other manufacturers making equivalent devices. These devices are volatile memories, and would normally lose their contents upon losing power. They are made nonvolatile on TINI through the use of a lithium battery and a special battery controller. A version of the stick with U4 populated with a 1-Mbyte memory is also available. The TINI static RAM is where all Java applications other than the primary Java application (frequently slush) are stored.

The RAMs, like the flash ROM, use /WR as the write enable and /PSEN as the output enable. The RAM chip enables, however, are the RAM chip enable signals /RAMCE1 and /RAMCE2. They are signals that derived from their corresponding CPU chip enable signals /CE1 and /CE2. The CPU chip enables are gated with the /CEO1 output of the DS1321 RAM nonvolatizer. If /CEO1 goes to logic "1", the U13 outputs /RAMCE1 and /RAMCE2 will go to logic "1" and the RAMs will be disabled. This is essentially a write-protect feature. /CEO1 will go high 1.5 µs after a power failure is detected, disabling the RAMs.

The SRAMs are not powered from VCC. Instead, they are powered by MVCC, which is a signal generated by the RAM nonvolatizer circuitry. The MVCC signal remains powered up by the lithium battery when the off-board VCC powers down. The

---

[5] KM684000BLI-5L datasheet – http://www.samsungelectronics.com/semiconductors/ SRAM/Low_Power/Low_Power_5V/4M_bit/KM684000BLG/KM684000B.htm

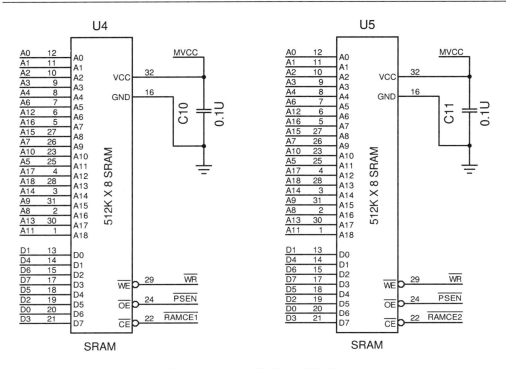

Figure 6-7: Detail of the SRAMs

switching of MVCC from the external VCC power supply to the lithium battery supply, VBAT, is the primary function of the RAM nonvolatizer.

The SRAM's place in the memory map also follows directly from the range of possible addresses achievable on A0–A18. The fact that SRAM0 is selected by /CE1 and SRAM1 is selected by /CE2 is a result of an arbitrary design decision: that's simply how they defined it to be. Another curious feature of the RAM devices is the address ordering. The address lines attach to the component out of order—i.e., signal A13 goes to A17 on the device, and so forth. We believe this merely had to do with circuit board routing convenience. Since there's a one-to-one mapping from an 18-bit address to a single memory location, it doesn't really make any difference whether or not the signals are in order.

The RAM nonvolatizer

The RAM nonvolatizer manages the crossover from external power to battery backup whenever the stick is powered down. It keeps the contents of the RAM safe and allows the real-time clock to maintain current time when the power is shut off. The RAM nonvolatizer circuitry has at its heart U10, a DS1321, flexible nonvolatile controller with lithium battery monitor.

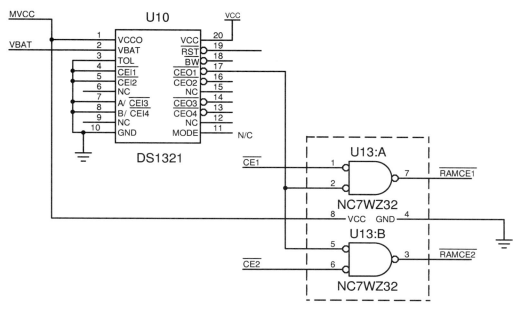

Figure 6-8: Detail of the RAM nonvolatizer circuitry

The DS1321, U10, watches the VCC coming from an off-stick source and uses that to power the RAM supply, MVCC, until it senses the VCC dropping, or powering down. Then it switches over to the supply from the lithium battery, VBAT, to power MVCC. The point at which power failure detection is "triggered" is determined by what the TOL signal on the DS1321 is set to. Since TOL is set to ground, according to the data sheet, any time VCC enters the region between 4.75V and 4.5V, power failure protection will be initiated.

U13, a Fairchild NC7WZ32[6] logic IC, is a dual OR gate. This OR gate combines the /CEO1 signal from the DS1321 and the /CE1 and /CE2 signals from the CPU to generate /RAMCE1 and /RAMCE2. The /CEO1 signal is governed by the /CEI1 signal on the DS1321. With the /CEI1 signal tied low, according to the data sheet, /CEO1 will always be low unless there is a power failure. During a power failure, the DS1321 will wait 1.5 μs and then drive the /CEO1 high, thus forcing the /RAMCE1 and /RAMCE2 signals high, disabling the SRAM devices. As mentioned in the RAM section, this basically acts as a write-protect feature during events in which the power is fluctuating, failing, or powering down. The write-protect feature will allow enough time for a write in progress to complete, but stop any further write operations. This is described more fully in the DS1321 data sheet.

---

[6] NC7WZ32 datasheet – http://www.fairchildsemi.com/pf/NC/NC7WZ32.html

The RAM nonvolatizer in this version of the schematic is somewhat different than that of previous versions. Rev B, for instance, did not utilize U13, and fed the /CE1 and /CE2 chip enables from the CPU directly into the DS1321 and took the /RAMCE1 and /RAMCE2 signals directly from it. This implemented a similar write-protect concept to the one described above. That method has since been modified to the current scheme.

The RAM nonvolatizer also has an active low reset output, /RST, that is an input signal to the CPU reset circuitry. We'll discuss that next.

The CPU Reset circuitry

We noted before that TINI can be reset in a couple of different ways: a power-on reset, and an external reset. The CPU reset portion of the circuit handles the external reset, which provides JavaKit with a way to access the bootstrap loader so that we can update the contents of the flash memory. It uses a logical AND gate to combine the DTR signal from the RS232 interface, and an active low Reset output from the DS1321 to generate the signal CPURST, which resets the CPU.

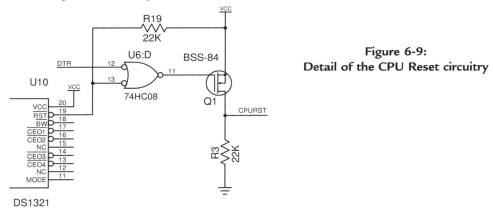

Figure 6-9:
Detail of the CPU Reset circuitry

U6, which is a 74HC08 quad AND gate, has two inputs that under normal conditions will be at logic "1", the active low reset of the DS1321 battery monitor and DTR, the data terminal ready output of the RS232 interface. If either of those signals goes low, the output of the AND will go to logic "0," and that will turn on Q1, which is a BSS-84, p channel field effect transistor (FET)[7]. When Q1 is turned on, current will flow through R3, driving CPURST high, which resets the entire TINI stick. Using the DTR signal as a mechanism to reset TINI has pros and cons. On the plus side, it gives you a surefire way of resetting the device through the serial port. The JavaKit software relies on this. The down side is that you have to work around this if you intend to use the serial port yourself for things such as talking to a modem. If your

---

[7] BSS-84 datasheet – http://www.fairchildsemi.com/ds/BS/BSS84.pdf

application pulls DTR low, or upsets it in any way, the TINI stick will immediately reboot. The work-around is usually in the form of a jumper that can be used to connect or disconnect a signal to the DTR232 signal. This signal comes onto the TINI stick from the SIMM edge card, and is the input to the RS232 interface that generates the DTR signal that feeds the reset circuitry.

The internal 1-Wire net

The TINI stick has an internal 1-Wire bus that it uses to communicate between the CPU and various on-board system resources.

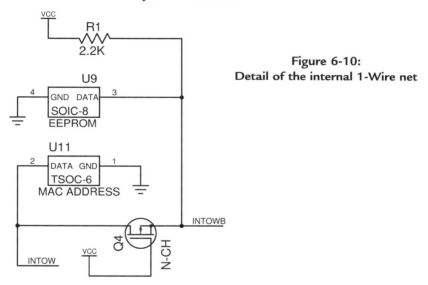

Figure 6-10:
Detail of the internal 1-Wire net

Looking at the figure, INTOWB comes from the CPU and is pulled high by R1. It connects to 1-Wire EEPROM, U9, that's absent on many of the earlier board revisions—it appears to be for some sort of 1-Wire expansion device. The n-channel FET, Q4, acts as a pass transistor that transmits INTOWB onto the signal INOW and to U11. U11 is a DS2502-UNW, Unique ID and Ethernet Address device. It is a 1-Wire device. INTOWB goes to the CPU, but does not get routed off stick. INTOW does get routed off stick. According to information gleaned from the TINI news group, the reason for this is as follows. Apparently there was interest in being able to grab the Ethernet address from the stick even when it wasn't powered up. If the stick isn't powered up, Q4 is shut off and isolates INTOWB from INTOW. Thus, if the stick isn't powered up, U11 looks like an isolated 1-Wire device and you can access it externally using the INTOW signal. If the stick is powered up, Q4 is turned on, and connects INTOWB to INTOW. There are classes within the Java API that allow you to access the internal 1-Wire net, and the components on it. Right now, on the stick, the only use for the internal 1-Wire net is to store the Ethernet address and to control the CPU status LED.

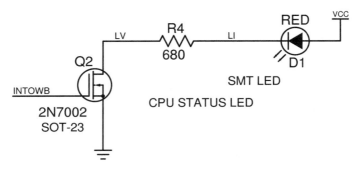

Figure 6-11: Detail of the CPU Status LED

Under normal conditions, the INTOWB signal is being pulled high. This turns on Q2, a 2N7002, n channel, FET[8]. This causes current to flow through R4, which turns on D1, the CPU status LED. During reset conditions and rebooting, the INTOWB signal is pulled low, turning off Q2 and the CPU status LED.

This is probably a convenient place to show an example of using the TINI API BitPort class. With this simple program you can control the CPU status LED, demonstrating how simple it is to control the various CPU Port lines.

Listing 6-2: BitPortTest.java

```
import com.dalsemi.system.*;

public class BitPortTest {

    static void main(String[] args ) {
        BitPort LED = new BitPort( BitPort.Port3Bit5 );

        for( int i=0; i<10; i++) {
            LED.set();
            TINIOS.sleepProcess( 200 );
            LED.clear();
            TINIOS.sleepProcess( 200 );
        }
    }
}
```

Compile and convert this to a .tini file, FTP it to your TINI and then run it. The only output you will see is the CPU status LED blinking on and off ten times. While this program is very short, it shows what you can do with the BitPort class—you can write logic "1" (set) and logic "0" (clear) on selected CPU pins. With the BitPort

---

[8] 2N7002 datasheet – http://www.fairchildsemi.com/ds/2N/2N7002.pdf

class you can access any bit on port 5 and the lower 6 bits of port 3. Other ports control the address bus and data bus and giving API level access to these ports probably would not be wise (or necessary). The ports were shown in Figure 6-4.

The external 1-Wire I/O, or iButton interface

The TINI stick has the 1-Wire bus designed for communicating with remote 1-Wire devices. This is provided by a DS2480 iButton interface. The DS2480 takes byte-oriented commands from the CPU, independent of 1-Wire timing, and converts them into proper 1-Wire timing and protocol. It has separate transmit and receive inputs that get converted into a single 1-Wire bus signal. This is more efficient than the 1-Wire interface on the internal 1-Wire bus, where the timing must be generated by the CPU.

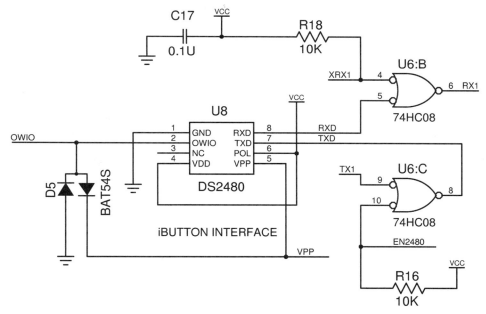

Figure 6-12: Detail of the external 1-Wire interface

The external 1-Wire bus uses the RX1 and TX1 signals from the CPU; these make up the serial1 port. Also used are several signals that get routed off stick. These are EN2480, XRX1, and OWIO. TX1 is also routed off stick. EN2480 and XRX1 can be used to gate, or control the flow of transmitted and received data through the iButton interface circuitry. Both signals are pulled high, and are inputs to U6, which is an AND gate we saw earlier when we looked at the CPU reset circuitry. If they are allowed to just be pulled high, then RX1, the output of AND gate B, will be RXD, the receive output of the DS2480. TX1 will flow through AND gate C, and become TXD, the transmit input to the DS2480. In this configuration, 1-Wire data comes onto the stick externally via the 1-Wire I/O signal, OWIO, and gets converted to byte data that goes to the CPU via the RX1 signal. Byte data comes back from the CPU, gets converted to 1-Wire protocol and gets sent back out the OWIO signal.

What if you wanted to use serial1 port for something other than 1-Wire? You can use the XRX1 and EN2480 signals to essentially disable the iButton interface circuitry. By pulling the signal EN2480 low, externally, TX1 won't make it through U6 gate C, and will no longer drive the external 1-Wire bus. By putting data on XRX1, the external 1-Wire bus won't be driving RX1, XRX1 will. This is just a mechanism for adding a little flexibility into the TINI stick.

Finally, the VPP signal is the EPROM programming voltage input to the DS2480. It provides a means of supplying a higher voltage to the external 1-Wire bus, useful for some of the 1-Wire devices such as EEPROM, that require it for writing. D5 is a BAT54S Schottky Barrier diode[9] that appears to be serving as over-voltage protection on the OWIO and VPP signals.

For more details on 1-Wire, refer to Chapter 10.

The RS232 interface

The TINI stick has a built-in RS232 interface, provided by a DS232A device, U14.

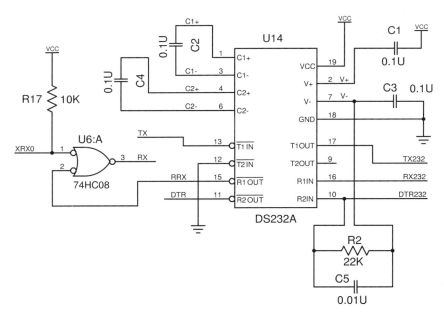

Figure 6-13: Detail of the RS232 serial interface

---

[9] BAT54 datasheet – http://www.fairchildsemi.com/ds/BA/BAT54S.pdf

This interface uses CPU pins RX and TX, which are associated with serial0 on TINI. Signals routed off stick are TX, TX232, RX232, DTR232, and XRX0. TX232 and RX232 are standard RS232 transmit and receive signals. XRX0 serves a function much like XRX1 did on the external 1-Wire interface. If we want to use serial0 for some other purpose than RS232, we can bypass the RS232 interface circuitry. Since TX goes from the CPU to the DS232A and to the edge card connector, we can transmit directly from the CPU off stick, and ignore the TX232 data coming from the DS232A. If we send data onto the stick on the XRX0 signal, it will arrive at U6, an AND gate. As long as the signal RRX going into the other AND gate input is high, our serial0 RX data will now be coming from XRX0. Thus, TX and XRX0 form a basis for using serial0 independent of the RS232 interface circuitry.

The signal DTR232 is of special note. It emerges from the DS232A as the signal DTR. As we mentioned in our discussion of the reset circuitry, if the DTR signal gets pulled low, the CPU will be reset. This is an external reset, as opposed to a power-on reset. During external resets, the device reboots, but during the booting process the bootstrap loader will wait to receive a special pattern of characters before turning control over to the runtime environment. If it receives this pattern of characters within three seconds of the reset, the loader will execute a mini command shell that can be controlled via the serial0 port. If it doesn't see this pattern within 3 seconds, it will continue the normal booting process, and load the runtime environment and primary application. This is how JavaKit works. JavaKit resets TINI by pulling DTR232 low, causing DTR to go low, causing CPURST to go high, causing an external reset. The loader enters this command shell and awaits instructions from JavaKit via Serial0. This is a good way to give us control of TINI, but it has implications. This means that any serial0 application that you intend to use needs to take this into account. If you attach a modem to serial0, and it pulls DTR232 low, you will initiate an external reset. In this sense, the TINI RS232 interface really only implements the send and receive portions of the traditional complement of signals found on a 9-pin or 25-pin RS232 cable.

There are a number of classes that are involved in using the RS232 interface, including `javax.comm.SerialPort`, `TINISerialPort`, `SerialInputStream, and SerialOutputStream`. This is discussed in detail in Chapter 13.

The real-time clock

TINI is capable of maintaining a time reference. It does this via a DS1315 real-time clock chip, U7. This device, as well as the SRAM, is backed up by a 3V lithium battery.

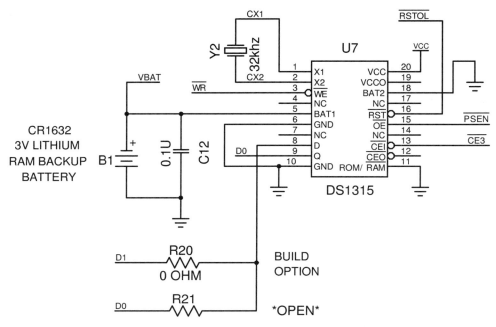

Figure 6-14: Detail of the real-time clock

The DS1315 is called a Phantom Time Chip in the product data sheet. While it's capable of acting as a nonvolatile memory controller, the TINI stick doesn't make use of this feature of the device (it uses a separate DS1321 for that). The key signals are /RSTOL, /PSEN, /CE3, /WR, and D0. Communication is serial, via reading or writing 64-bit data streams to D0, in 8-bit chunks. /PSEN serves as the output enables, /WR the write enable, and /CE3 is the chip enable. It's reset with /RSTOL. What's being read and written? Time. One can set the current time, and the device will then maintain that time, even with the power off. One can later read the time from the device. Reading and writing the time follows a specific format that, fortunately, we don't have to worry about too much. The TINI Java API includes classes for reading and writing to the real-time clock. If you are interested in exactly how the device works, the data sheet explains it in detail. The Java class that we can use to talk to the real-time clock is `com.dalsemi.system.Clock`. Listing 6-3 is an example of how to read and write to the real-time clock. You can actually set and read the clock in units as small as one-hundredth of a second.

The real-time clock's place in the memory map is one of the memory map subtleties we mentioned earlier. Whereas on the memory devices the spot in the map was determined by the range of possible addresses on its bus, in combination with a chip enable, the real-time clock's place in the map is determined by actions behind the scenes in the firmware. A fairly complete discussion of this is found in the TINI interest group message archive. Simply put, the real-time clock is addressed serially, when you supply it with a 64-bit recognition sequence on D0. So, it really only takes up one specific location in the memory map, but the whole region 0x310000-0x31FFFF is allocated to make sure there is plenty of elbow room and for future expansion.

Programming example: using the real-time clock

The code below implements a very simple demo of the real-time clock. It reads the current time from the clock, then changes the settings of the clock based on information you provide on the command line. Finally, it prints the updated time. We'll first present the code in its entirety, then we'll go through it bit by bit.

Listing 6-3: ReadWriteClock.java

```
import java.io.*;
import java.util.*;
import com.dalsemi.system.*;

public class ReadWriteClock {
    public static void main(String[] args) {
        if (args.length == 5)
        {
            com.dalsemi.system.Clock Clk = new com.dalsemi.system.Clock();
            long time = Clk.getTickCount();
            System.out.print("Time Before Writing to Clock: ");
            System.out.println(new java.util.Date(time));
            Integer year = Integer.valueOf(args[0]);
            Integer month = Integer.valueOf(args[1]);
            Integer date = Integer.valueOf(args[2]);
            Integer hour = Integer.valueOf(args[3]);
            Integer minute = Integer.valueOf(args[4]);
            Clk.setYear(year.intValue());
            Clk.setMonth(month.intValue());
            Clk.setDate(date.intValue());
            Clk.setHour(hour.intValue());
            Clk.setMinute(minute.intValue());
            Clk.setPm(true);
            Clk.setRTC();
            System.out.print("Time after Writing to Clock: ");
            System.out.println(new java.util.Date(Clk.getTickCount()));
        }
        else
        {
            System.out.println("Enter year month date hour minute");
            System.out.println("Example: 2001 11 10 7 32");
        }
    }
}
```

We import some class libraries and declare our class, `ReadWriteClock`.

```
import java.io.*;
import java.util.*;
import com.dalsemi.system.*;

public class ReadWriteClock {
```

We only have one method in our program, `main()`. We do some simple error checking, to determine that we have the right number of arguments, and we create a `Clock` object.

```
public static void main(String[] args) {
    if (args.length == 5) {
        com.dalsemi.system.Clock Clk = new com.dalsemi.system.Clock();
```

Here, we grab the current time, and print it to the screen.

```
long time = Clk.getTickCount();
System.out.print("Time Before Writing to Clock: ");
System.out.println(new java.util.Date(time));
```

Now, we take the five command line parameters we used, representing what we want to set our clock to, and convert them to integers.

```
Integer year = Integer.valueOf(args[0]);
Integer month = Integer.valueOf(args[1]);
Integer date = Integer.valueOf(args[2]);
Integer hour = Integer.valueOf(args[3]);
Integer minute = Integer.valueOf(args[4]);
```

We set the clock:

```
Clk.setYear(year.intValue());
Clk.setMonth(month.intValue());
Clk.setDate(date.intValue());
Clk.setHour(hour.intValue());
Clk.setMinute(minute.intValue());
Clk.setPm(true);
Clk.setRTC();
```

Finally, we grab the new time and print it to the screen, demonstrating that we did, in fact, change the clock's settings.

```
    System.out.print("Time after Writing to Clock: ");
    System.out.println(new java.util.Date(Clk.getTickCount()));
        } else {
        System.out.println("Enter year month date hour minute");
        System.out.println("Example: 2001 11 10 7 32");
        }
    }
}
```

The following are the commands that can be used to compile the program. We are assuming that the ReadWriteClock.java file is in its own folder, and the commands below are being executed in that folder. Again, the javac and java commands are shown with their command line parameters on separate lines, only for readability. They all need to be on the same line for each command.

```
C:\> javac -classpath %TINI_HOME%\bin\tiniclasses.jar
        -d tini ReadWriteClock.java
C:\> java -classpath %TINI_HOME%\bin\tini.jar TINIConvertor
        -f tini
        -o tini\ReadWriteClock.tini
        -d %TINI_HOME%\bin\tini.db
```

We execute the program by copying it over to TINI via FTP, then running it from a Telnet session. The output looks like this:

```
TINI />
TINI /> date
Sat Nov 10 04:56:33 GMT 2001
TINI /> java ReadWriteClock.tini 2001 12 9 8 12
Time Before Writing to Clock: Sat Nov 10 04:57:32 GMT 2001
Time after Writing to Clock: Sun Dec 09 08:12:32 GMT 2001
TINI /> date
Sat Dec 9 08:12:36 GMT 2001
TINI />
```

We first checked the date, and noticed that it was completely wrong. We ran ReadWriteClock.tini and set the time to the current time. The program accessed the clock, retrieving the current (incorrect) time, printed it to the screen, then wrote the new (correct) time to the clock. It then retrieved the correct time and printed it to the screen. Finally, we checked the time from the command line.

The Ethernet controller

TINI has an on-board Ethernet interface that allows a 10Base-T Ethernet connection. The complete interface section of TINI has a variety of components. We're going to take a quick look at the main device, the LAN91C96 Ethernet controller. This is produced by Standard Microsystems Corporation, from which a complete datasheet can be obtained[10]. It is listed as a LAN91C96 ISA/PCMCIA Single Chip Full Duplex Ethernet Controller with magic Packet. The schematic shows the Ethernet controller as an SMC91C94/96, but it is really referring to either the LAN91C94 or LAN91C96. Since the LAN91C94 device has been discontinued, most TINI boards will have the LAN91C96.

The actual 10-Base-T signals that are used for the Ethernet communications are ETH1, ETH2, ETH6, and ETH3. Simplified, that boils down to differential transmit

---

[10] SMC91C94 Datasheet – http://www.smsc.com/main/catalog/lan91c96.html

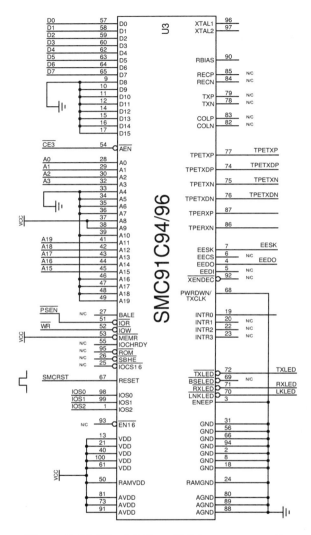

Figure 6-15: The 10-Base-T Ethernet controller

and differential receive, respectively. There are a number of other signals that are routed off stick, specifically EESK, EEDO, IOS0, IOS1, and IOS2. We won't be making use of them. They deal with accessing an EEPROM inside the device. Refer to the LAN91C96 data sheet for further details on those signals. The signal /SMCINT is an interrupt signal being sent to the CPU to tell it needs to deal with activity on the Ethernet controller. It's generated via Q3, which acts to invert the actual signal SMCINT, as it emerges form the LAN91C96 device. The signal SMCRST is an input, arriving from the CPU that resets the Ethernet controller after power-up. /CE3 acts as the address enable. The address bus on the device will only be examined if this is low. /PSEN acts as the read enable for the device, and /WR acts as the write enable. D0 through D7 form a bi-directional data bus on the device; A0 through A3 and A15 through A19 are used to address this device. Essentially, the device acts as a memory. When TINI wants to send data out the Ethernet interface, it writes to it as if it were a memory. When data has arrived at the interface, an interrupt is generated and the CPU reads it from the device again like a memory.

The Ethernet interface circuitry also controls three LEDs, D2, D3, and D4. D2 and D3 are the transmit and receive LEDs respectively; they light up when data is being transmitted or received. The third LED, D4, is the link LED that lights when the Ethernet interface is connected to another Ethernet interface that is powered up.

The TINI memory map states that the Ethernet interface resides from 0x300000 to 0x307FFF. Looking at the addressing of the LAN91C96, it would appear that its place in the memory map would be different from 0x300000 to 0x307FFF. This is most likely another example of subtleties in the memory map. A little discussion of this can be found in the TINI interest group archive. Fortunately, the Ethernet interface is robust and its operation is transparent to the user, so we don't need to pry into its inner workings all that much.

Table 6-5: LEDs on TINI

LED	Function
D1	CPU Status LED
D2	Ethernet Transmit LED
D3	Ethernet Receive LED
D4	Link Status LED

The I²C interface

The TINI stick can communicate via the I²C bus protocol. We will be discussing this in some detail in Chapter 11, but we'll take a very quick introductory look at it here.

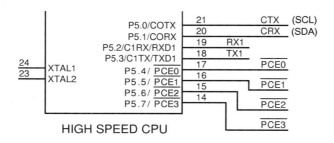

Figure 6-16: Detail of CPU, showing location of I²C bus pins

The I²C capability of TINI is handled entirely by the CPU and is accomplished in software through the I2CPort class using P5.0 for the SCL (clock) and P5.1 as the SDA (data) line. These port pins also serve double duty as CAN interface pins, and have a built-in weak pull-up. The two I²C signals are named CTX and CRX on the schematic, and they get routed off stick through the SIMM connector. The I²C signals are essentially ready to connect up to an appropriate I²C device.

The CAN interface

The TINI CPU has two CAN controllers integrated into it. The resources for one of them overlap with the resources used for I²C (P5.0, and P5.1), and the resources used or the other one overlap with the resources used for serial0 (P5.2 and P5.3). Because of the importance of serial0, P5.0 and P5.1 are the most likely candidates for use with CAN, which is why those signals on the schematic get labeled CTX and CTR (CAN transmit and CAN receive). We have a whole chapter that delves into the wonders of CAN, so we're only going to give it a brief mention here. It should be noted that CTX and CRX aren't necessarily CAN ready. They need to be connected to a CAN controller interface device such as the Phillip's Semiconductor, PCA82C250[11]. There is no such device on the TINI stick, but there is a spot for one of these on the E10/E20 socket board.

The E10/E20 Socket Board

The E10/E20 socket board is an evaluation platform that allows you to connect a TINI stick to a variety of different interfaces. It has many features, some of which come "ready to use," while others are "unpopulated," requiring you to add components to the board yourself.

The product is offered in three versions, E10, E20, and E50, the difference being that the E20 has the components for a regulated power supply populated on the board, while the E10 does not. Both the E10 and E20 have numerous other features that are not populated. The E50 is the E10/E20 with all of the components populated. The product is also being updated frequently, adding or removing certain features. We will be discussing the E20, Rev C. Let's take a look at the main features.

What's in an E20 socket board?

- A 72-pin SIMM socket that accepts the TINI stick. There is unpopulated space for an additional SIMM socket, which could be used to make custom hardware in a 72-pin SIMM format and mate it to TINI.

- A DB-9 serial connector (female) that connects to TINI serial0. We use this with JavaKit. There is also a populated DB-9 serial (male) connector and an

---

[11] PCA82C250 datasheet – http://www.semiconductors.philips.com/pip/PCA82C250U/N4

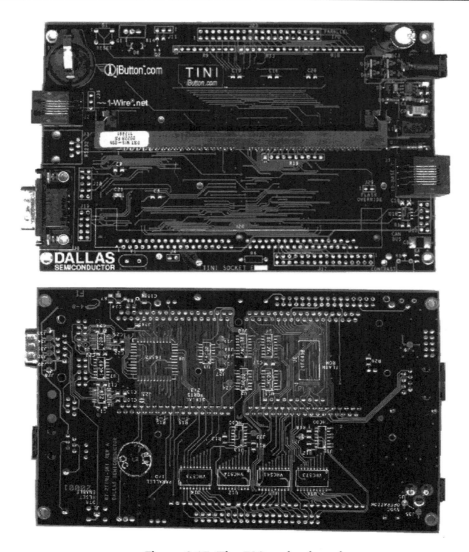

Figure 6-17: The E20 socket board

RS232 line driver that appears to be present in anticipation of a future TINI stick revision. (The current stick doesn't use this feature.) There are unpopulated spaces for a dual UART, two RS232 line driver chips and pinout extensions that allow the addition of two RS232 ports (serial2 and serial3).

- An RJ-11 connector that allows access to the TINI External 1-Wire bus, and an iButton clip, that allows an iButton to be connected to the External 1-Wire bus.

- A DTR Reset Enable jumper that allows you to conveniently connect or disconnect the serial0 DTR232 signal from TINI to your DTR signal on the serial cable. This is very useful when switching back and forth between JavaKit and other applications that use serial0. There is unpopulated space for a rest switch.

- An RJ-45 connector for Ethernet.

- Unpopulated space for a CAN interface chip, and a pinout extension so that you can add a serial cable for use with CAN.

- A 5V regulated power supply that can accept 8–24V AC/DC. This is a really important feature. TINI is exacting in its power requirements and inexpensive 5V DC power supplies (simple adapters for consumer electronics) aren't always accurate and clean enough. The 5V regulated power supply lets you use a cheap DC adapter, as long as it supplies between 8–24V (AC or DC). It provides TINI with a clean, 5V DC. This supply can also be disabled by jumpers, should you want to supply (or test) your own 5V DC supply.

- Unpopulated space for an off-stick flash memory, and associated decode circuitry, so the stick uses it and not the flash on the stick.

- A large, unpopulated, parallel output section.

- Miscellaneous capabilities involving the internal 1-Wire bus, including a diagnostics port, EPROM, and a special "first birthday" jumper.

The E20 in greater detail

Next, we'll take a closer look at some of these capabilities by examining the schematic.

The serial interface and DTR reset enable

Serial0 is accessed on the E20 via a female DB-9 connector (J6). Only two of the traditional RS232 signals are supported, transmit (TX232) and receive (RX232). The Data Transmit Ready signal (DTR232X) is used primarily to reset TINI and access the bootstrap loader. Other signals on the DB-9 can be hardwired to one of two power supply nets (V+ or Vcc). These jumpers are open on the board as shipped.

The DTR reset enable consists of a jumper that can be easily removed and replaced. With the jumper in place, TINI will reset if DTR232X is pulled low. This allows you to configure serial0 for use with JavaKit (jumper in place) or maybe a modem (jumper removed). The switch, S1, is not populated. It's intended to act as a pushbutton reset.

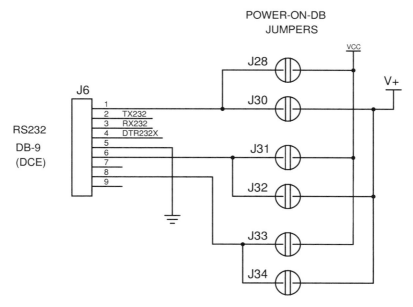

Figure 6-18: Detail of the Serial0 DB-9 connector

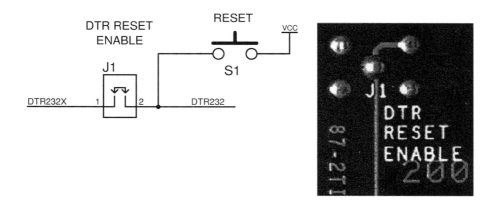

Figure 6-19: Detail of the DTR Reset jumper

The external 1-Wire interface

There are three main components to the external 1-Wire interface on the E20. They are all populated, and shown below.

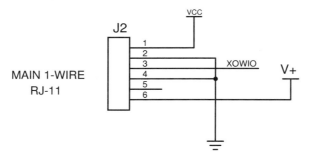

Figure 6-20: Detail of the RJ-11, external 1-Wire interface connector

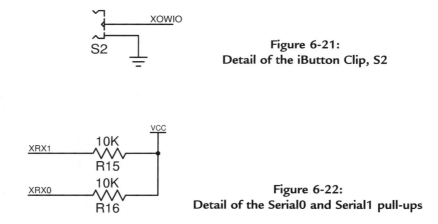

Figure 6-21:
Detail of the iButton Clip, S2

Figure 6-22:
Detail of the Serial0 and Serial1 pull-ups

The pull-up is of special note. XRX1 is a signal that can be used to override the iButton interface on TINI. By pulling it high here, we guarantee that serial1 will use the iButton interface circuitry on the TINI stick. Similarly, XRX0 ensures serial0 will use the RS232 interface on the TINI stick.

The Ethernet interface

The 10-base-T Ethernet interface uses an RJ-45 connector.

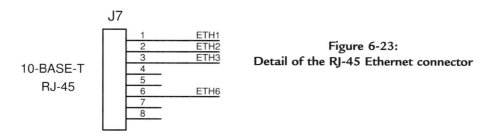

Figure 6-23:
Detail of the RJ-45 Ethernet connector

The CAN interface

CAN is supported via unpopulated board footprints that allow you to connect (via extension cable) to a DB-9 connector. There is also a spot for a CAN interface chip such as a PCA82C250.

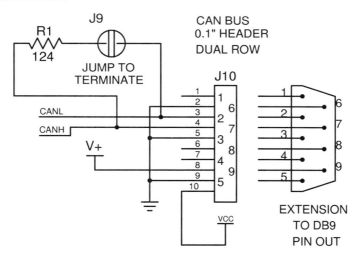

Figure 6-24: Detail of the CAN bus section

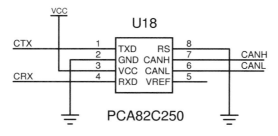

Figure 6-25: CAN interface chip area

The regulated power supply

The regulated power supply circuitry on the E20 is shown in Figure 6-26.

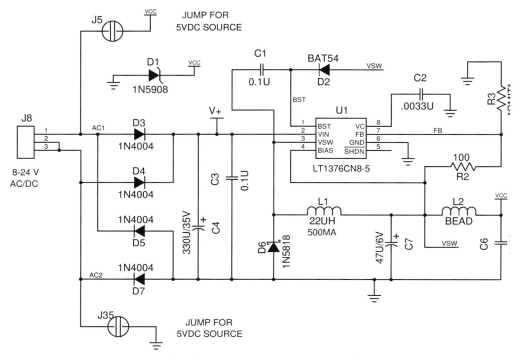

Figure 6-26: Detail of the power supply circuitry

It accepts 8-24V AC/DC but can be bypassed by shorting jumpers J5 and J35. You would use this if you already have a 5V DC power supply you want to use or test with TINI. The connector is male, which mates to many inexpensive multi-voltage AC adapters.

Additional FLASH

The E20 has a variety of components related to using an external flash with TINI. There is space on the board for the FLASH, as well as selection circuitry.

The selection circuitry, shown in Figure 6-28, is unpopulated, with the exception of J27, which is shorted on the board as shipped. The schematic says "default is J13 and J16 closed," but that's assuming we've installed the second flash. Since the E20 ships without the flash, the jumpers aren't shorted either. With J27 shorted, the signal /RCE0 is equal to /CE0, which puts the stick's on-board flash as the default flash.

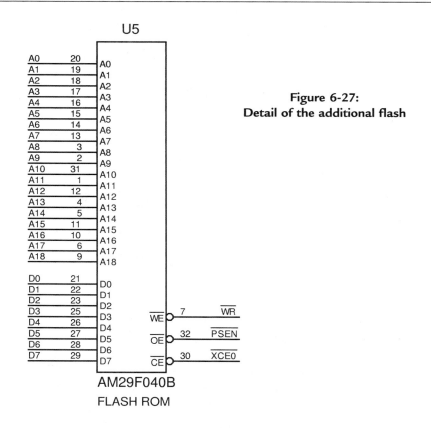

Figure 6-27:
Detail of the additional flash

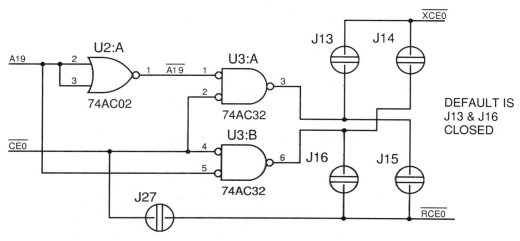

Figure 6-28: Detail of flash selection circuitry

If we did install the flash on the E20, with J13 and J16 closed, our chip enables would become

$$/RCE0 = /CE0 + A19$$

$$/XCE0 = /CE0 + /A19$$

The "+ " is shorthand for logical OR provided by U3. This would change our memory map.

Table 6-6: Memory map for external flash

Address (hex)	Chip Enable	Contents	E20 Jumpers Closed
0x000000 - 0x07FFFF 0x080000 - 0x0FFFFF	/CE0 /CE0	Flash on E20 Flash on TINI Stick	J13 and J16
0x000000 - 0x07FFFF 0x080000 - 0x0FFFFF	/CE0 /CE0	Flash on TINI Stick Flash on E20 St	J14 and J15

Instead of having an onboard flash, and an image of it, we now have our external flash, then our internal flash. The external flash will be the one used by TINI. Closing J14 and J15 instead of J13 and J16 will cause the external flash and the TINI onboard flash to change places. The flash onboard the stick would now be the one used. In either case, if you intend to add the flash to the E20 and utilize jumpers J13, J14, J15, and J16, you will need to open J27.

There is an additional feature on the socket board dealing with the flash: a flash override. This is J29 on the socket board. It is not populated.

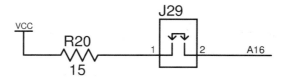

Figure 6-29: Detail of flash override

This is a precautionary device for use in the unlikely event that you should want to upgrade the loader program in your flash. When updating the loader, the old loader first replicates itself in bank 1 of the flash, at 0x10000, then loads the new one at 0. If you short J29, the CPU is forced to execute the loader at 0x10000. So, if during the loader update, something goes wrong before the new loader is completely installed, you can always recover by shorting J29 and forcing the execution to begin with the old loader now residing at 0x10000.

Support for Serial2 and Serial3

The E20 has complete support in the form of unpopulated component footprints for two additional RS232 ports. There isn't space for two additional DB-9 connectors, but they can be connected via cable and the pin extensions on the E20.

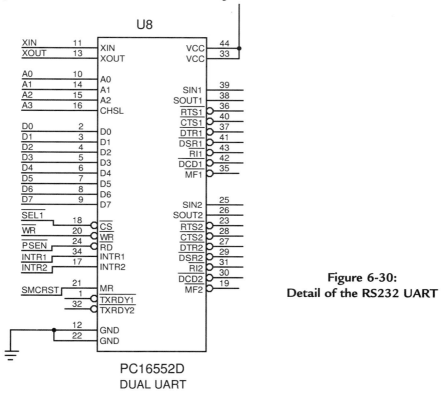

Figure 6-30: Detail of the RS232 UART

The UART that provides serial2 and serial3 has a region allocated for it in the TINI memory map provided by U10, which is a 1-of-8 decoder.

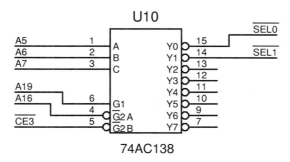

Figure 6-31: Detail of the /SEL0 and /SEL1 generating circuitry

Table 6-7: Memory map for /SEL0 and /SEL1

Signal Selected	Address Range to Select Signal (X=don't care)		
	A23	...	A0
/SEL0	0011 1XX0 XXXX XXXX 000X XXXX		
/SEL1	0011 1XX0 XXXX XXXX 001X XXXX		

External interrupt selection circuitry

The TINI CPU has one external interrupt input, /EXTINT, available for use by off-stick peripherals. If there are multiple peripherals generating interrupts, they have to go through some glue logic.

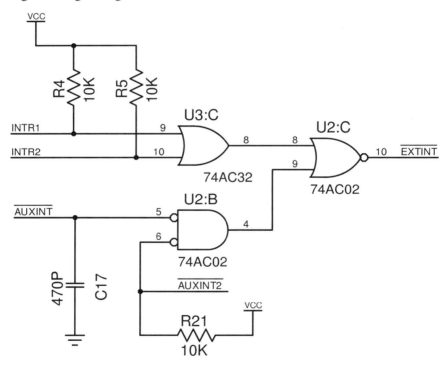

Figure 6-32: Detail of external interrupt circuitry

INT1 and INT2 come from the UART in the RS232 section of the socket board. Since you may want to use the external interrupt selection circuitry without the UART being present, space for pull-ups R4 and R5 are provided. /AUXINT comes from the parallel IO section and /AUXINT2 comes from the expansion SIMM connector. /EXTINT will go low if any of these signals go low.

Internal 1-Wire interface

There are three odds and ends on the socket board that connect to the internal 1-Wire bus in the TINI stick. They are the diagnostic port, the first birthday jumper, and a 1-Wire EPROM. None are populated. The first birthday jumper can be used to clear the heap. The diagnostic port can be used to read debug information. The EPROM can probably be used to house a small amount of ID information, such as a serial number, network address, etc.

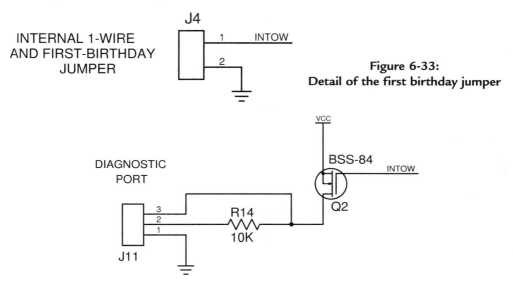

INTERNAL 1-WIRE
AND FIRST-BIRTHDAY
JUMPER

**Figure 6-33:
Detail of the first birthday jumper**

DIAGNOSTIC
PORT

Figure 6-34: Detail of the diagnostics port

U11

**Figure 6-35:
Detail of U11, the 1-Wire
EPROM/EEPROM**

The parallel IO section

The parallel IO section of the E20 socket board takes the 8-bit bidirectional data bus of TINI and turns it into two pairs of 8-bit busses. Each pair consists of an 8-bit bus for writing and an 8-bit bus for reading. Figure 6-36, shows the circuitry for one of the pairs.

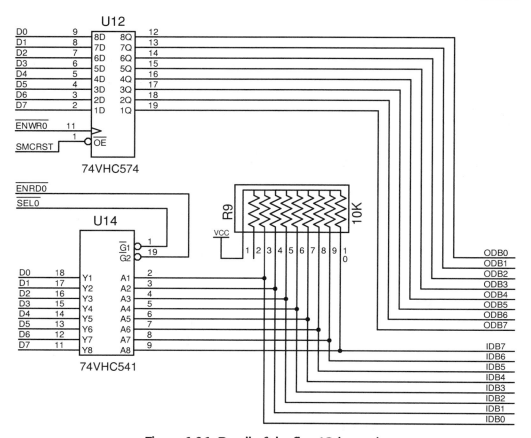

Figure 6-36: Detail of the first IO bus pair

U12 is an octal D type flip-flop with tri-state outputs[12] that latch the data bus from TINI (D0-D7) onto the output lines ODB0-ODB7. That latching occurs when /ENWR0, "enable write 0", goes low. The output enable for this device is SMCRST, the reset input for the Ethernet controller device (although it's used for a number of peripherals on TINI as well). If the TINI board is being reset, SMCRST will go high briefly. During this logic "1" period, U12 will be tri-stated—that is, the outputs will be set to a high impedance state. This keeps random information that may be on the data bus during power-on from inadvertently being written to the output devices. U14 is an octal, tri-state, line driver that is selected by /ENRD0, "enable read 0", and /SEL0. When both /ENRD0 and /SEL0 go low, U14 will pass the 8-bit input bus IDB0–IDB7 through to the TINI data bus D0–D7. The second pair of 8-bit data buses behaves the same way as the first.

---

[12] 74VHC574 datasheet – http://www.fairchildsemi.com/pf/74/74VHC574.html

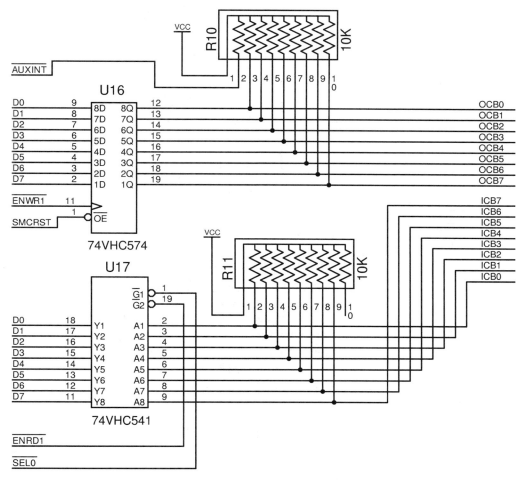

Figure 6-37: Detail of the second IO bus pair

U16 is another octal D type flip-flop with tri-state outputs[13]. It latches the data bus from TINI (D0–D7) onto the output lines OCB0–OCB7. That latching occurs when /ENWR1, "enable write 0," goes low. The output enable for this device is SMCRST and performs the same function as in the other output device. U17 is an octal, tri-state, line driver that is selected by /ENRD1, "enable read 0," and /SEL0. When both /ENRD1 and /SEL0 go low, U17 will pass the 8-bit input bus ICB0–ICB7 through to the TINI data bus D0–D7.

---

[13] 74VHC541 datasheet – http://www.fairchildsemi.com/pf/74/74VHC541.html

The selection circuitry that creates the signals /ENRD0, /ENWR0, /ENRD1, and /ENWR1 is shown in Figure 6-38.

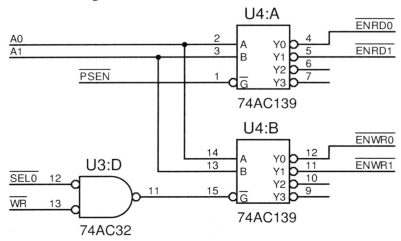

Figure 6-38: Detail of the parallel IO selection circuitry

U4 is a dual 1-of-4 decoder[14]. One of the decoders handles selecting circuitry for reads and one handles selecting circuitry for the writes. U3 is an OR gate whose output will be logic "1" unless both inputs are "0." This means that the second decoder (U4:B) will only be selected if both /SEL0 and /WR are low. Decoder U4:A is selected by /PSEN, which is active during memory reads. Table 6-8 illustrates the memory map for reading and writing to the parallel port on the E20.

Table 6-8: Memory map for the parallel port

Signal Selected	Address Range to Select Signal (X=don't care) A23 ··· A0						Comment
ODB0-ODB7	0011	1XX0	XXXX	XXXX	000X	XX00	Must be Writing
OCB0-OCB7	0011	1XX0	XXXX	XXXX	000X	XX01	Must be Writing
IDB0-IDB7	0011	1XX0	XXXX	XXXX	000X	XX00	Must be Reading
ICB0-ICB7	0011	1XX0	XXXX	XXXX	000X	XX01	Must be Reading

The LCD interface from earlier versions

Earlier versions of the E20 socket board had unpopulated component space for an LCD interface. While this feature has been removed from the current revision of the E20, the concept for the LCD interface still works. You simply have to implement the same circuitry on a breadboard. This is discussed extensively in Chapter 8.

---

[14] 74AC139 datasheet – http://www.fairchildsemi.com/pf/74/74AC139.html

Other TINI socket accessories

A number of companies produce accessories for TINI. Here is a quick summary of some of them.

Vinculum Technologies Group

Vinculum Technologies Group[15] produces several accessories. They have a product called the TINI ProtoAdaptor, which features a SIMM socket, power connector, DTR jumper, DB-9 serial connector, and RJ-45 Ethernet connector on a narrow circuitboard strip that has tall wire wrap pins (connecting to the TINI signals) on the board. This board can be inserted into a solderless breadboard for experimentation, or it can be used in conjunction with another of their products, the TINI Nexus. The TINI Nexus has a connector that mates to the long pins on the TINI Proto Adaptor, as well as an additional SIMM socket, and board footprints for a variety of connectors and components. They also produce a product called the ProtoModule, which is a small SIMM circuit board that has no components on it. What it does have is an array of holes and a labeled SIMM edge card that mates with the SIMM sockets used for TINI. You can use this board to make your own hardware for mating with a TINI.

**Figure 6-39: A Vinculum Technologies ProtoAdaptor with a TINI,
in a solderless breadboard**

[15] Vinculum Technologies Group – http://www.vinculum.com

Figure 6-40: A TINI in a ProtoAdaptor in a solderless breadboard, connected to a ProtoModule

Systronix

A company called Systronix produces several TINI-related products, including the TILT, (TINI Initial Learning Tool), the STEP (Systronix TINI Engineering Platform), and the STEP+. These comprise a tiered family of socket boards, ranging from the basic to the sophisticated. Complete details on all their products can be found on their website[16].

Additional products and vendors

A host of other products are available for TINI, with a variety of companies making them. A good place to keep tabs on new developments is the TINI website partner marketplace, which lists information on products available for the TINI stick[17].

---

[16] Systronix – http://www.systronix.com

[17] TINI Marketplace – http://www.ibutton.com/TINI/marketplace/index.html

Making a custom TINI socket

To either make your own socket or to integrate the TINI SIMM into your own design, you will need to connect a minimum set of wires to the TINI SIMM: power (one of pin 67–70), ground (one of pins 3–7) and tie /RCE0 (pin 45) to /CE0 (pin 12). This will allow you to power up TINI and TINI will boot. You need to tie /RCE0 to /CE0 so TINI can select the on-board FLASH. While this may be a minimum wiring for TINI, it will not allow you to communicate with TINI in any way. Depending on your application, you will need to connect some of the following as well:

- Connect ETH1 (pin 66), ETH2 (pin 65), ETH3 (pin 64), ETH6 (pin63) to an Ethernet connector if you need network connectivity.

- Connect TX232 (pin 19) and RX232 (pin 20) to a serial connector or a serial device if serial0 connection is needed.

- Connect OWIO (pin 8) to the active line of a 1-Wire bus if 1-Wire communication is needed.

  - Also, you might need to connect Vpp (pin 9) to +12 volts if you need to program any 1-Wire EEPROM devices.

- Connect DTR232 to a switch or other device if you need to perform a hardware reset of TINI.

These connections are show in Figure 6-41.

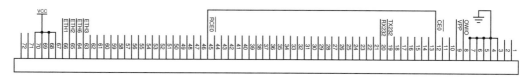

Figure 6-41: Minimum socket configuration

Summary

This chapter has been an overview of TINI hardware, specifically the TINI stick and E20 socketboard. We've made an effort to constantly relate the hardware to the TINI memory map, and explain how address selection is being decoded. Many topics touched upon here are expanded on in other chapters, specifically CAN, 1-Wire, I²C, and enhancing.

References

1. *TINI datasheet,*
    http://www.ibutton.com/TINI/dstini2.pdf

2. *The TINI Specification and Developer's Guide*, Don Loomis,
    Addison-Wesley, 2001, pages 19-20.

3. *TINI Interest Group archives,*
    lists.dalsemi.com/maillists/tini/

4. *TINI SIMM and Socket Schematics,*
    www.ibutton.com/TINI/hardware/

## CHAPTER 7

The TINI Software

In this chapter we are going to examine in detail the various software programs and Application Program Interface (API) packages you will be using to program the TINI microcontroller. To make full use of this chapter you should already have the TINI up and running and be familiar with the TINI hardware. We will discuss all of the software that you can download from Dallas Semiconductor for your TINI and even a few other programs that will help you with program development

JavaKit

We briefly mentioned JavaKit in Chapter 5. JavaKit is a program that is supplied by Dallas Semiconductor for communicating with the TINI over a serial port connection. JavaKit is used to download applications to TINI, run programs on TINI and configure TINI's network and server settings. JavaKit is written in Java and the source can be downloaded from the TINI web site, should you find a reason for studying the source or modifying it.

Because JavaKit communicates with your TINI through a serial port, it requires the Java Communications API that you installed in Chapter 3. JavaKit will run on any platform to which the Communications API has been ported (Windows 95/98/NT/2000/XP, Linux).

You can run JavaKit from Windows with the following command line:

```
java -cp \opt\jdk\lib\comm.jar;\opt\tini\bin\tini.jar JavaKit
```

where \opt\jdk is the installation directory for the Java SDK and \opt\tini is the installation directory for the TINI API.

You can run JavaKit on Linux with the following command:

```
java -cp /opt/jdk/lib/comm.jar:/opt/tini/bin/tini.jar JavaKit
```

For the remainder of this book we will be showing only Windows commands unless there is a significant change for the Linux commands (such as in the case where we make a c-shell script or something that does not translate as easily).

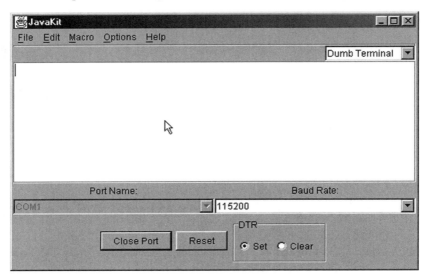

Figure 7-1: JavaKit window

JavaKit will tell you what command line options it will take if you ask. Type `JavaKit -help` (actually any unrecognized option will have JavaKit dump its options). This is shown here:

```
c:> javakit -help

Unknown option: -help

JavaKit           Version 2.1.10

Dallas Semiconductor Corporation
-===============================-

Usage: java JavaKit <-options>
Where basic options include:
-port            Specifies the COM port to auto open.
-baud            Specifies the baud rate to use (default is 115200.)
-macro           Specifies a macro file to auto load.
                    Pass multiple macro files separated by commas.
-exitAfterRun    Specifies that JavaKit should exit after running the
                    macro file(s) specified with "-macro".
-log             Generates a log file called JavaKit.log.
```

```
-advanced          Show advanced options.
-allow             Allow loading files to a bank higher than bank 7.
```

Notice the "-advanced" option. If you run `javakit -advanced` you will see these additional options:

```
-padSize           Specifies the size of the pad string when
                      writing to Hex files to flash ROM (default is 12.)
-binPause          Specifies the number of milliseconds to pause after
                      a binary segment write. (default is 50ms.)
-bankSize          Specifies the size of each memory bank.
                      Default: 65536
-ROMSize           Specifies the total size of the Flash ROM.
                      Default: 524288
-flushWait         Wait time after sending a portion of binary data.
                      Default: 50 ms.
-resetWait         Wait time after sending a DTR toggle.
                      Default: 100 ms.
-debug             Enables debug mode.
-noDTRTest         Instructs JavaKit not to test for DTR connected on
                      File->Load.
```

You can see from these commands and from the menus in JavaKit that it is possible to automate the various tasks for which you might use JavaKit. For the most part we will be using JavaKit for loading the TINI API and then configuring it. All the rest of our work on TINI will be done through network programs such as Telnet and FTP.

JavaKit can record the commands and actions you issue and save them to a macro file so you can rerun the exact session again. This is useful if you are configuring a number of TINI boards with like settings. To do this you will use the macro feature. To enable that, you must switch JavaKit from "Dumb Terminal" to "JavaKit Terminal" using the selection box on the upper right of the JavaKit window. You can start or stop recording a macro using the macro pull-down menu, and you can save or load macros using the file pull-down menu.

JavaKit will leave a JavaKit.tmp file in the directory from which you ran it. This contains the communication settings you used for that session. If you changed them from the defaults, they will be restored from this file the next time you run JavaKit. If you run JavaKit from a number of different directories, then you will have a number of these JavaKit.tmp files hanging around.

Figure 7-2:
JavaKit terminal selection box

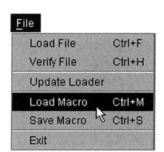

Figure 7-3:
JavaKit macro menu selection

Figure 7-4:
JavaKit file menu selection

Terminal

If you simply need to connect to your TINI to run various programs and you don't have a network connection, you can use any terminal program to connect to your TINI over a serial line instead of JavaKit. In the following figures, you can see a Hyperterm terminal window and a Linux Eterm window (running minicom) with an active TINI connection. Notice the settings dialogs. You will need to configure your terminal emulator for 115,200 bits per seconds, 8 data bits, no parity, 1 stop bit, no hardware or software flow control. Also note that if you are using an E10 or E20 socket from Dallas Semiconductor, you will need to remove the solder bridge on jumper J1 on the back of the socket board. This jumper, when removed, prevents the DTR line on the serial port from resetting your TINI board. This is explained in Chapter 9.

The TINI Loader

When you connect your TINI serial port to your computer's serial port and communicate with it using JavaKit, the first software program on TINI that you meet is the TINI Bootstrap Loader. The loader is a small program that is stored in bank 0 of the flash ROM on TINI. The loader code is executed when the TINI board is powered up or reset. You will send commands to the loader through the serial port using JavaKit. You will need the loader commands to load or upgrade the TINI firmware, to load your own programs into flash ROM, or to clear the Java heap. The loader is essentially permanent in the flash ROM since this is not something that you can easily restore. You should be careful when experimenting with the loader commands so you don't accidentally clobber the loader, which is not easy to do but is possible. If, by some weird chance, the bootstrap loader does get clobbered, then your only option is to send the board back to Dallas Semiconductor to have it reprogrammed.

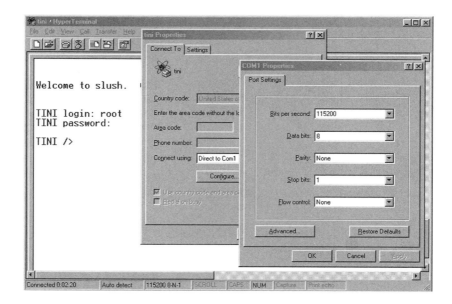

Figure 7-5: Hyperterm window connected to a TINI

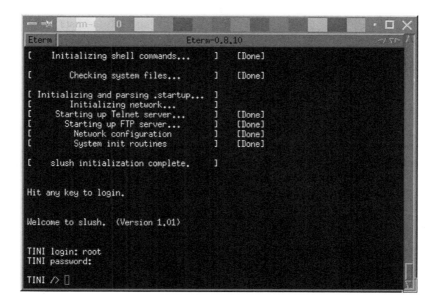

Figure 7-6: Linux minicom connected to a TINI

To view the loader command set, type a "?" at the loader's ">" prompt.

```
>?

TINI loader 05-15-00 17:45
Copyright (C) 2000 Dallas Semiconductor. All rights reserved.
Selected bank = 18. Executing from bank 40

B [bank]      - select Bank
C [range]     - CRC range in selected bank
D [range]     - Dump hex from selected bank
E             - Exit loader
F x [range]   - Fill range in bank with byte x
G             - Goto 0 in selected bank in paged mode.
H or ?        - Help
L             - Load hex
M             - Move loader to selected bank
S             - Set comm Speed to 1/2 present
T             - Tests
V             - Verify hex
X [offset]    - eXecute code at offset in this segment
Z n           - Zap flash sector n (0-F). n=0AAH for all TINI software
```

The loader commands are more completely documented in the file "Commands for TINI Loader"[1] available on the iButton web site and loader source code (in 8051 assembly) can be found in the file "Hex Bootstrap Loader For DS80C390"[2].

The TINI Firmware

It is at this loader prompt that you will use JavaKit to upload a new version of the TINI firmware. The most recent version of the TINI firmware can be downloaded from the Dallas Semiconductors TINI software web page and installed following the instructions provided in Chapter 5. The firmware is in a file named `tini.tbin`. To load your TINI hardware with a new version of the TINI firmware, start JavaKit. From the JavaKit window, select the proper serial port and press the reset (you will need to have the J1 jumper marked "DTR RESET ENABLE" shorted in order for JavaKit to successfully load the firmware). Then, from the "File" menu bar, select "Load File" and navigate through your file system to find the `tini.tbin` file (`c:\opt\tini\bin\` if you followed the installation instructions in Chapter 5). Select the `tini.tbin` file and press the open button. JavaKit will communicate with the loader and start to load the new TINI firmware into the flash ROM. You will see something similar to this in your JavaKit window:

---

[1] Commands for TINI Loader – http://www.ibutton.com/presentations/LDoc.txt
[2] Hex Bootstrap Loader For Ds80c390 – http://www.ibutton.com/presentations/L0515.txt

```
Loading file: C:\Opt\Tini\bin\tini.tbin.

Please wait... (ESC to abort.)
Load complete.
```

Be patient; this can take almost a full minute to complete.

Up to this step there can be several things that might have gone wrong.

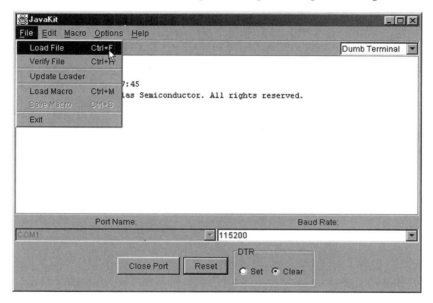

Figure 7-7: Using JavaKit to load the TINI firmware

When you pressed the "Reset" button you may have seen an error message indicating that you do not have the DTR reset enabled on your TINI socket board, as shown in Figure 7-8. Verify that this is or is not correct. Sometimes JavaKit gets confused and issues this error message even though everything is OK. In that case, press the "Reset" button again. It might take several tries. If this message persists, it may mean that even though you have the proper jumper on the socket board, your serial cable does not have this signal connected. You will need to verify this also. Your serial cable needs pins 2, 3, 4 and 5 connected at a minimum.

After you found the `tini.tbin` file and pressed the "Open" button, you may have seen an error message indicating that you do not have the DTR reset enabled on your TINI socket board also as shown in Figure 7-8. If you have followed the steps in the previous error message to verify that you do indeed have this jumper connected, then try the load again. If that does not help, exit JavaKit and run JavaKit again, this time with the `-noDTRtest` command line option.

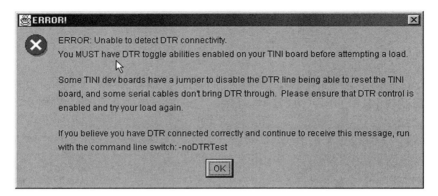

Figure 7-8: JavaKit DTR error message

You may see an error message like the following (Figure 7-9). This means you selected the wrong file (you do NOT want the `tini.db` file).

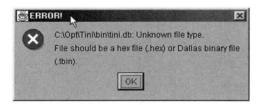

Figure 7-9: JavaKit wrong file type error message

At this point you have loaded the TINI firmware into TINI. For the most part, you will rarely use the loader for anything but booting TINI and possibly clearing the heap.

The heap is an area of reserved memory that programs use to store data. Having a certain amount of heap storage already obtained from the operating system makes it easier for the operating system to manage. If programs don't exit properly (such as when they crash or exit prematurely) the heap is left with inaccessible blocks. This can be common during program development but should not be common for a stable program. Anyway, you may run out of heap space (you will see an error message like *"Insufficient Heap"*) and you may need to clear the heap. This is done by resetting TINI and, from the Loader prompt (>), typing

B18
F0

Clearing the heap will destroy any files you may have stored in RAM and it will destroy any state information saved by slush, so you may have to reset the IP address from JavaKit before you can connect to your TINI via the network.

The TINI firmware includes a JVM (Java Virtual Machine) and Application Program Interface (API). Application programs that we will write in Java will utilize the API to access the capabilities of the underlying hardware resources of TINI. The JVM and API includes full support for threads as well as all primitive Java data types and strings. The JVM provides access to the core Java packages: `java.lang`, `java.io`, `java.net` and `java.util` and also provides access to a number of TINI specific classes that allow access to the TINI hardware layer and resources. Dallas Semiconductor has updated the TINI firmware as the hardware and software develops.

The TINI API[3]

We briefly discussed the TINI API in Chapter 5, and here we will be digging in a little deeper. The TINI API is the set of packages (classes and methods) for interfacing the TINI hardware to the Java Virtual Machine. In other words, these are the set of Java classes you will use to program TINI specific features like the 1-Wire network that are not part of the Java Virtual Machine. Here we will provide a quick overview of the various packages in the current TINI API and include some package diagrams that help map out how the classes fit and interrelate. Some of the packages will be discussed in more detail in other parts of this book (like 1-Wire, CAN, Network, I²C, ports). You will find the TINI API documentation in the `javadocs\firmware` folder of your TINI install folder (`%TINI_HOME%\docs\javadocs\firmware` if you followed the installation method described in the book). Some of the package descriptions have been grouped together because they either work together or the classes in one package directly extend the classes of another package. Figure 7-10 shows the key to the diagrams we will be using.

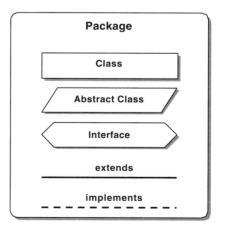

Figure 7-10:
Key to package diagrams

---

[3] TINI Software – http://www.ibutton.com/TINI/software/index.html

`com.dalsemi.comm` – This package provides the basic communication classes and methods for accessing some of the TINI-specific hardware devices. This includes: Serial ports, CAN (Controller Area Network) bus, and the LCD (liquid crystal display).

`com.dalsemi.fs` – This package is an extension to the standard `java.io.File` class. It provides methods for accessing the file permissions and the owner ID of TINI files.

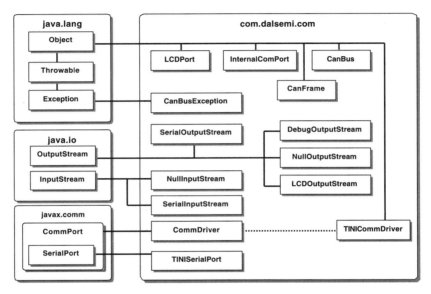

Figure 7-11: Diagram of the com.dalsemi.com package

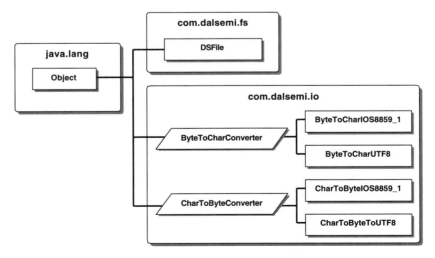

Figure 7-12: Diagram of the com.dalsemi.fs and com.dalsemi.io packages

com.dalsemi.io – This package provides interfaces and implementations for the conversion of bytes to characters and characters to bytes for a particular encoding scheme, like ISO 8859-1 (see "The ISO 8859 Alphabet Soup"[4] and "The ISO8859-1 table"[5]) and UTF8 (see "RFC2253 - UTF-8 String Representation of Distinguished Names"[6]).

com.dalsemi.onewire – Contains the single class OneWireAccessProvider which manages the Dallas Semiconductor 1-Wire adapter class. This enables an application to be adapter independent.

com.dalsemi.onewire.adapter – This package contains the base classes for all 1-Wire port adapter objects.

com.dalsemi.onewire.container – This package includes the classes and methods to manipulate specific 1-Wire devices.

com.dalsemi.onewire.utils – This package contains the utilities necessary to translate and verify 1-Wire Network addresses and perform 8- and 16-bit cyclic redundancy checks.

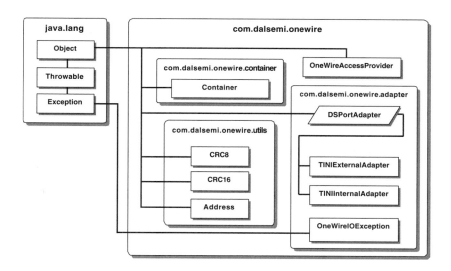

Figure 7-13: Diagram of the com.dalsemi.onewire.* packages

---

[4] The ISO 8859 Alphabet Soup – http://czyborra.com/charsets/iso8859.html
[5] The ISO8859-1 table – http://www.ramsch.org/martin/uni/fmi-hp/iso8859-1.html
[6] UTF-8 String Representation of Distinguished Names – ftp://ftp.isi.edu/in-notes/rfc2253.txt

`com.dalsemi.shell` – This package contains the abstract class and implementation of a system shell for TINI. This shell interacts between a program and the TINI operating system, and provides the current environment and the user ID of the current process. Methods are provided for converting to and from the numerical user ID and its text representation and for determining whether a particular user is an administrator.

`com.dalsemi.shell.server` – This package provides an abstract class for a generic server and a server session. Servers will listen on some system resource for connection requests. When a connection request arrives, the server starts up a session to handle that request. Servers are designed to be multi-threaded, allowing multiple simultaneous connections.

`com.dalsemi.shell.server.ftp` – This package extends `com.dalsemi.shell.server` to implement a simple FTP server as described in RFC 959 (see "File Transfer Protocol"[7]). This server uses a ServerSocket to listen on the specified port (defaults to port 21) for FTP connection requests. For each connection made, an FTP session is created. All command processing is handled by the FTP session, not the server.

`com.dalsemi.shell.server.serial` – This package extends `com.dalsemi.shell.server` to implement a serial port server. This server listens for user connections on TINI port serial0. For each connection made, a Serial session is created. All command processing is handled by the session.

`com.dalsemi.shell.server.telnet` – This package extends `com.dalsemi.shell.server` to implement a Telnet server as described in RFC 854 (see "Telnet Protocol Specification"[8]). This server uses a ServerSocket to listen on the specified port (defaults to port 23) for Telnet connection requests. For each connection made, a Telnet session is created. All command processing is handled by the Telnet session.

`com.dalsemi.system` – This package provides a number of classes for managing TINI memory, accessing the state of the TINI operating system, and classes for accessing TINI hardware such as: the watchdog timer, the clock, the bitport, the byteport, and the dataport, interrupts, I^2C interface and "a collection of hopefully useful debug utilities."

`com.dalsemi.tininet` – This package provides classes for managing the parameters of the TINI network .

`com.dalsemi.tininet.dhcp` – This package provides a class that implements a DHCPClient for dynamically obtaining new IP Addresses.

---

[7] File Transfer Protocol – ftp://ftp.isi.edu/in-notes/rfc959.txt
[8] Telnet Protocol Specification – ftp://ftp.isi.edu/in-notes/rfc854.txt

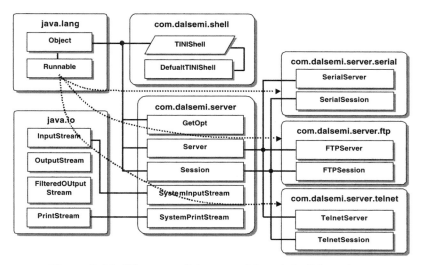

Figure 7-14: Diagram of the com.dalsemi.shell.* package

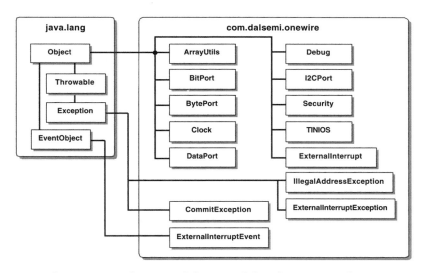

Figure 7-15: Diagram of the com.dalsemi.system package

com.dalsemi.tininet.dns – This package provides a class that implements a DNS (Domain Name System) lookup service according to RFC 1035.

com.dalsemi.tininet.http – This package provides a class that implements a simple HTTP server (see "Hypertext Transfer Protocol"[9]).

---

[9] Hypertext Transfer Protocol – http://www.w3.org/Protocols/

`com.dalsemi.tininet.icmp` – This package provides a class that implements an ICMP (ping) echo request server (see "Internet Control Message Protocol"[10]).

`com.dalsemi.tininet.ppp` – This package provides a class that implements Point-to-Point Protocol (PPP) for providing IP packet transport over a serial link (see "The Point-to-Point Protocol"[11]).

`com.dalsemi.protocol` – This package provides classes for working with server protocols, headers and URLs.

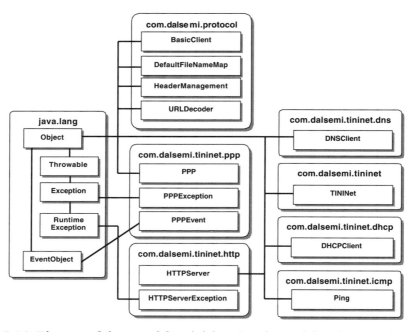

Figure 7-16: Diagram of the com.dalsemi.tininet.* and com.dalsemi.protocol packages

The next thing to do after loading the TINI firmware is to load the TINI shell (slush) into TINI so you can actually log in and configure your network settings. Before we do that, however, we will take a little time to discuss the TINI API.

Slush, the TINI Operating System Shell

Slush is the TINI command-line shell environment provided by Dallas Semiconductor. It is similar to a very simple UNIX-like shell. In the default configuration of TINI, slush is loaded into bank 7 of the flash ROM so it runs as the default program when you power on your TINI.

---

[10] Internet Control Message Protocol – ftp://ftp.isi.edu/in-notes/rfc792.txt
[11] The Point-to-Point Protocol – ftp://ftp.isi.edu/in-notes/rfc1661.txt

Slush provides a handful of commands that interface to the TINI firmware. Slush is used for development and when you need to run interactive sessions on your TINI, but it is not a necessary part of the TINI. Once you have your application developed, you can load that program into bank 7 to run instead of slush (or you can run it as a program from slush if you want).

Starting slush

You load slush onto your TINI in a manner similar to loading the TINI firmware. From the JavaKit "File" menu bar, select "Load File" and navigate through your file system to find the slush.tbin file (same place as the tini.tbin file). Press the "Open" button to load slush to your TINI. This may take 5–10 seconds and you will see the same messages you did when loading the TINI firmware. If you saw any error messages (similar to what you might see when loading the firmware), try again.

To execute the TINI firmware (the Java Virtual Machine) and any Java program you loaded, such as slush, you will need to exit the loader by typing "E" at the loader prompt. Do that now. You will see a long list of messages like the following:

```
—> TINI Boot <—
TINI OS 1.02
API Version 8009
Copyright (C) 1999 - 2001 Dallas Semiconductor Corporation
31000000
Running POR Code
Memory POR Routines
000020
0080,0100,0180,0200,0280,0300,0380,0400,0480,0500,0580,0600,0680,0700,Tran-
sient blocks freed: 074F, size: 024620
CPersistant blocks freed: 0000, size: 000000
KM_Init Passed
Ethernet MAC Address Part Found

TTS Revision: 170 , Date: 1/25/01 2:11p
Thread_Init Passed
External Serial Port Init
External serial ports not enabled
Memory Available: 06FB60
Creating Task:
0100
01
Loading application at 0x070100
Creating Task:
0200
02
Application load complete
```

```
[-=          slush Version 1.02          =-]
[               System coming up.          ]
[          Beginning initialization...     ]
[             Not generating log file.     ]    [Info]
[          Initializing shell commands...  ]    [Done]

[                Checking system files...  ]    [Done]

[ Initializing and parsing .startup...     ]
[                Initializing network...   ]
[             Starting up Telnet server... ]    [Done]
[              Starting up FTP server...   ]    [Done]
[               Network configuration      ]    [Done]
[               System init routines       ]    [Done]

[       slush initialization complete.     ]


Hit any key to login.
```

At this point you can press any key and get the TINI login prompt. The default user for a new TINI is root and the default password is "tini" (you won't see this echoed to the screen as you type it).

```
Welcome to slush.   (Version 1.02)

TINI login: root
TINI password: tini

TINI />
```

If you did not get to the "`Hit any key to login`" prompt, you may have seen an error message similar to the following:

```
——> TINI Boot <——
TINI OS 1.0
API Version 8005
Copyright (C) 1999, 2000 Dallas Semiconductor Corporation
After the OS loads, it will try to bootstrap the program stored in
bank 7 - this is usually the slush command shell. Here is where you
might encounter the problem you described:
Loading application at 0x070000
Bad API Version:8009
Load App Failed!
```

This boot message is saying that you have version 1.0 (API version 8005) of the firmware loaded, while at the same time you are trying to run a version of slush compiled with TINI OS 1.02 (API version 8009). The numbers you see may be different but the point is that the firmware version and the slush version are not the same. That is why you get the "Bad API Version" message. You need to go back a few steps and reload the firmware (perhaps you skipped this) or download the latest TINI API to get the `tini.tbin` and `slush.tbin` files again. This error message typically is seen when one upgrades to a new version of the TINI API and tries to load slush without loading the firmware first (it's easy to forget these things). Table 7-1 shows the various updates to the TINI firmware and how the TINIOS version relates to the API version.

Table 7-1: TINI API versions

TINI OS version	API Version
0.6a	8000
1.0 beta 1	8001
1.0 beta 2	8002
1.0 beta 2.1	8003
1.0 beta 2.2	8004
1.0	8005
1.01	8006
1.02 pre-release 1	8007
1.02 pre-release 3	8008
1.02	8009
1.02b	800A
1.02c	800B
1.02d	800C
1.02e	800D
1.1 beta 1	9000
1.1 beta 2	9001
1.10	9002

Slush commands

You can get an idea of what you can do with slush by typing `help` once you login.

```
TINI /> help
Available Commands:
```

append	arp	cat	cd
chmod	chown	clear	copy
cp	date	del	df
dir	downserver	echo	ftp
gc	genlog	help	history
hostname	ipconfig	java	kill
ls	md	mkdir	move
mv	netstat	nslookup	passwd
ping	ps	pwd	rd
reboot	rm	rmdir	sendmail
setenv	source	startserver	stats
stopserver	su	touch	useradd
userdel	wall	wd	who
whoami			

For more detailed help on any command, type `help` followed by the name of the command. Try this:

```
TINI /> help ls
ls [option] FILE

Returns a listing of the files.
[-l]    Show file attributes
Alias: dir
```

In the TINI installation directory on your computer, (`\opt\tini\docs`), is the file `slush.txt` that fully describes each command, its usage, and provides details you might need to know.

Managing programs and files

Slush provides a rich set of commands for manipulating files, file permissions and the slush directory hierarchy. Slush commands do not understand wildcards like *.tini. Actually * is a valid character in a slush filename, as are a number of other special characters that would not be legal in Windows or Linux (* ? $ # @, to name a few). Remember, in order to keep the memory size of slush small, it is a very small implementation of a Unix/Linux-like shell. All of the commands are implemented in a very minimal way.

Slush allows you to redirect program input/output from commands, as well as running Java programs in the background, very much in the same way as you would with Unix/Linux. Use the "<" symbol to redirect input from a file, the ">" symbol to redirect output to a file, the ">&" symbols to redirect stdout and stderr to a file, and "&" to run a Java program in the background. Running slush commands in the background other than the Java command is not currently supported.

For example, to run the program `myProg.tini` in the background and redirect the output to a file named `runlog.txt`, use the following command:

```
TINI/ > java myProg.tini > runlog.txt &
TINI/ >
```

In addition to redirecting output to a file, you can redirect output to the null device (for example, `java test.tini > null`) if you want to suppress the output from a Java program, or redirect the output to the serial port (`java test.tini > S0`). S0 indicates the TINI serial port named "serial0" and is currently the only port supported for redirection to a port. You must have admin privileges to redirect to the serial0 port, and should not do this if you are already at a serial server prompt (as you are when you log in through JavaKit or a Terminal emulator) because slush will stop the serial server before running the command and then bring it back up after the command is complete.

All of the slush commands are summarized in the following tables. Brackets ("[ ]") around some of the command options means that these parameters are optional.

Table 7-2: Slush file/program commands

Command Name	Command Options	Command Description
append	SRC DEST	Append the contents of the file SRC to the end of file DEST.
cat	FILE	Display the contents of a FILE
cd	DIR	Change directory to DIR (use .. for moving up 1 level). Use pwd to display the name of the current directory.
chmod	[[u|o][+|-][r|w|x]] [##]	Each file has 2 permissions which control the user's and other's ability to access that file. Each of these 2 permissions can have a combination of Read Write or eXecute permission enabled or disabled.
chown	USER FILE	Change the owner of a file to the specified user.
copy	SRC DEST	Alias of cp
cp	SRC DEST	Make a copy file named SRC and call it DEST..
del	FILE	Alias of rm
df		Display the amount of free RAM.
dir		Alias of ls
gc		This commands runs the garbage collector that frees memory that is no longer being used and also reorganizes the available memory space in the heap so that it isn't fragmented.
java	FILE [&]	Execute a Java prrogram. Optionally running it in the background.
kill	PROCESS	Kill the identifed process. Use ps to display all running processes.
ls	[-l] [DIR]	List the contents of the current directory. Use –l list provide a long list which includes more detail: permissions, owner, size, date created. If DIR is specified, list the contents of the specifed directory in the current directory.
md	DIR	Alias of mkdir
mkdir	DIR	Make a directory named DIR.
move	OLD NEW	Alias of mv
mv	OLD NEW	Move (rename) a file from OLD to NEW.
ps		List the running processes.
pwd		Print the name of the current directory.
rd		Alias of rmdir.
rm	FILE	Remove (delete) the named FILE.
rmdir	DIR	Remove the directory DIR in the current directory. DIR must be empty (no files or subdirectories in it) and you must have permission to write to that directory.
source	[-d] FILE	Execute the specified script FILE. Use –d to turn off verification that its an ascii file.
touch	FILE	Update the date on the specified file to whatever the system clock is.

Managing users

Slush offers a minimal set of commands for managing users, but enough to get the job done.

Table 7-3: Slush user management commands

Command Name	Command Options	Command Description
passwd	[USER]	Set the password for the specified user. If the user is not specifed, the current user is assumed. You will be prompted for the new password. You must be an admin (root) to change the password of another user.
useradd	[-n USERNAME] [-p PASSWORD] [-i USERID]	Adds a user to the system. If you don't specify the username, password or userid through the options you will be prompted for them. Valid id's range from 1 to 255: 0 is reserved for guest login 1-127 for normal users 128 is reserved for root 129-255 for super user privileges.
userdel	USER	Delete the specified user from the system. Current user must have admin priveledge (userid > 127).
wall	MESSAGE	Broadcast a message to all users that are logged in.
wd	[-i INT] [-p INT] [-s]	Set or display the slush watchdog timer settings. -i sets the watchdog interval in ms and must be used with –p, -p sets the feed interval in ms and must be less than watchdog interval, -s stops the current watchdog timer. wd with no options, displays the current watchdog settings.
who		Lists all users who are currently logged into slush.
whoami		Display the name and userid of the current user.
su	[USER]	Switch user to either the specified user or if no user is specifed, switch to root. Either way, you will be prompted for a password.

Managing connectivity

Table 7-4: Slush connectivity commands

Command Name	Command Options	Command Description
arp		Display all ARP (address resolution protocol) cache entries.
ftp	[-d][-s FILE][HOST]	Connect to a remote FTP server specified by HOST. –d turns on debug output and –s uses the specified FILE as the command script for FTP.
hostname	[NAME]	Sets the TINI hostname or if no NAME is specified, displays the current hostname.

ipconfig	[-a xx.xx.xx.xx]	Configures or displays the network settings. If no options
	[-n domainname]	are specified then display the current settings.
	[-m xx.xx.xx.xx]	
	[-g xx.xx.xx.xx]	-a sets IP address and must be used with the -m option,
	[-p xx.xx.xx.xx]	-n set domain name, -m sets the subnet mask and must
	[-s xx.xx.xx.xx]	be used with the -a option, -g sets the gateway address,
	[-t dnstimeout]	-p sets the primary DNS address, -s sets the secondary
	[-d]	DNS address, -t sets the DNS timeout (set to 0 for
	[-r]	backoff/retry), -d uses DHCP to lease an IP address, -r
	[-x]	releases the currently held DHCP IP address, -x lists all
	[-h xx.xx.xx.xx]	Interface data, -h sets the mailhost, -C commits the
	[-C]	current network configuration to flash, -D disables
	[-D]	restoration of configuration from flash, and -f indicates
	[-f]	to not prompt for confirmation.
netstat		Displays all TCP connections.
nslookup	[NAME|IP]	Displays the name or IP of the given argument. For
		nslookup to work properly you must have a valid DNS
		server configured through ipconfig.
ping	HOST [number]	Sends ICMP ECHO_REQUEST packets to network the
		specified HOST. An optional number of requests can be
		specified, thius defaults to 1.
sendmail	[-f fromAddr]	Sends a simple email message to designated recipients.
	[recipient(s)]	The recipients (or cc list) is separated by commas.
	[cc's]	
setenv	VARIABLE VALUE	Set the variable to the value in the current environment. If
		no parameters (VARIABLE and VALUE) are specified then
		it displays the current environment. If the VARIABLE is
		specifed but no VALUE is given then the variable is
		defined with no value.
genlog	[-e][-d]	Toggles the system log generation on boot. –e enables log
		generation, -d disables it. When enabled, the boot time
		messages are logged to /etc/.log, when disabled, the .log
		file are deleted.
startserver	[-s][-t][-f]	Starts up the specified server. –s starts the serial server, -t
		starts the Telnet server, -f starts the FTP server.
stopserver	[-s][-d][-t][-f]	Shuts down the specified server. -s stops the serial server,
		-d disables console output when used with –s, -t stops the
		Telnet server, -f stops the FTP Server.
downserver	[-s][-d][-t][-f]	Alias for stopserver.

We will discuss the `ipconfig` command in a bit more detail in Chapter 13.

The slush FTP client supports the following commands:

```
open ARG          : Opens the FTP server at address ARG
user [ARG]        : Logs in as user ARG
bin               : Changes to binary transfer mode
ascii             : Changes to ASCII transfer mode
```

```
list              : Lists the files in the current directory
pwd               : Lists the full path of the current directory
cd ARG            : Changes the current directory to ARG
get ARG           : Gets the file ARG from the server
put ARG           : Puts the file ARG on the server
exit, bye, quit   : Quit
```

Miscellaneous slush commands

This is a list of some of the miscellaneous commands that didn't neatly fit into one of the previous categories.

Table 7-5: Slush miscellaneous commands

Command Name	Command Options	Command Description
clear		Clears the screen. Works only for a VT100 compatible terminal emulator. Does not work for either the Dumb Terminal or JavaKit Terminal using JavaKit.
date	[-t] [MMDDYYYYHHMMSS] [timezone]	Sets the system date and time. If no options are specified then this command displays the currently set date and time. If –t is specified, this command lists the valid timezones.
echo	TEXT	Echos the TEXT to the display. This is useful for displaying progress in slush scripts.
help	[COMMAND]	Displays the usage information for slush commands. If no COMMAND is specified, then help displays a list of all slush commands.
history		Displays the last few slush commands. The number of commands that slush remembers is determined by the environment variable HISTORY.
reboot	[-f][-h][-a]	This command shuts down all servers and then cleanly reboots the system. -f specified to not prompt for confirmation, -h tells slush to clear heap on reboot, -a tells slush to clear heap and system memory on reboot.
stats	[-v]	Display the current status of TINI, slush and the currently running servers. –v turns on verbose mode which gives a little more information.

Optional slush commands

These commands are located in the `src\Optional\SlushCommands` directory of the Slush source code. The next major section in the chapter discusses adding user and optional commands to slush. Because of size restrictions, to use them you might have to remove a current slush command.

Table 7-6: Slush optional commands

Command Name	Command Options	Command Description
diff	FILE1 FILE2	Diff does a byte for byte compare of FILE1 to FILE2. When a difference is found, the offset and the differing bytes are displayed.
pollmemory	[-i interval] [-s] [-p port]	Starts a thread that will send the amount of free RAM to the given port every interval. -i specifies the report interval in milliseconds, -p specifies the port to send to, -s stops the memory reporter.
PPP	[-a xx.xx.xx.xx] [-p password] [-r xx.xx.xx.xx] [-u username] [-x serial port_number] [-s][-d][-c]	Sets the options for PPP connections. -a specifies the local IP address, -c tells slush to close the connection, -p sets the login password, -r sets the remote IP address, -u sets the login username, -x sets the serial port number used by ppp, -s starts the PPP server, -d starts the PPP client.
sled	[FILE]	Edit the specified file using a basic vi like command set. Only works from Telnet sessions using terminal emulators that support VT100 emulation (does not work from JavaKit).
threadstat		Displays information about the number of currently running threads.

See the file `slush.txt` in the docs directory of your TINI installation directory (`\opt\tini\docs\slush.txt`) for a description of the SLED command set.

Slush files and environment

When slush is first started, it creates several default system files, placing them in the `/etc` directory. These files are

- `.tininet`
- `.startup`
- `passwd`

passwd

User login information is kept in the `/etc/passwd` file. The user's name, hash of their password, and user ID are the only things in this file. Slush has two accounts set up by default: **root** with the initial password of "tini" and userid of 128, and **guest** with the initial password "guest" and userid of 0. Valid user IDs range from 0 to 255 and have privileges assigned based on this number according to the Table 7-7:

Table 7-7: Slush UserID privileges

UserID	Privilege
0	Guest
1-127	Normal User
128	Root
129-255	Admin User

You can use `cat` to view the passwd file. Mine looks like this right now:

```
root:f8491b67e91f837c13c3444965281bcee5fca964:128
guest:1bb6e3a2abc20f654fe62fd139790c06394885d3:0
dan:d8721aa38bec040436b459f2a76bbcb8fefaa7ff:007
rosie:ec246b45190ffc78f200c21c2bf6954b9b8e9c11:32
brian:6b4fd9e73f777b1ce2ff2f88d04380c8c09c26af:111
```

You can edit this with a text editor (Sled on TINI) but there is no real need. Use the useradd and userdel commands to add and delete users and the passwd command to change user's passwords. The password is stored as a hash using the `com.dalsemi.system.Security.hashMessage()` method, which is based on the "Federal Information Processing Standards Publication 180-1, Secure Hash Standard."[12]

.startup file

Any user with admin permission can place commands to be run on boot time in the `/etc/.startup` file. These commands will be executed as if they were from a slush prompt. Any .tini program files run with the java command will be forced to run in the background.

The default `.startup` file looks like this:

```
########
#Autogen'd slush startup file
setenv FTPServer enable
setenv TelnetServer enable
setenv SerialServer enable
##
#Add user calls to setenv here:
##
initializeNetwork
########
#Add other user additions here:
```

There are two main uses for this file: to set any necessary environment variables and to start your own program automatically at boot time. You can add your slush commands to the end of this file, to have them run on boot time. If you don't want any of the servers started on boot, you can delete the appropriate lines.

---

[12] FIPS 180-1 Secure Hash Standard – http://www.itl.nist.gov/fipspubs/fip180-1.htm

Sometimes you may add commands to the .startup file but you may occasionally want to login without running them. To skip executing the contents of the `.startup` file, press the "5" key during the slush boot up. Slush will still enable the serial server, but will not execute the `.startup` file.

.tininet file

The `/etc/.tininet` file contains TINI's hostname and domain name. The default hostname is TINI. There is no default domain name. You can change the contents of the file with the `hostname` command.

```
TINI /> hostname TINI.cool.net
TINI /> hostname
TINI.cool.net
TINI /> cat /etc/.tininet
HostName:TINI
DomainName:cool.net
TINI />
```

Also notice that the hostname is used in the Slush prompt. If you change the hostname the prompt will change to that new hostname on your next login.

```
TINI /> hostname astatine.element.e
TINI /> hostname
astatine.element.e
TINI /> logout
Connection Terminated

Welcome to slush. (Version 1.02)

astatine login: root
astatine password:
astatine /> hostname
astatine.element.e
astatine />
```

The domain name (but not the host name) may also be set using `ipconfig` command.

```
astatine /> ipconfig -n new.name
astatine /> hostname
astatine.new.name
```

In addition to these special files, TINI allows for an optional home directory for each user and an optional `.login` file for each user to customize their environment.

User Home

A directory created in the root directory with the same name as a user will become that user's home directory upon logging in. In other words, whatever your username is, if you create a directory in / with the same name, that will be the default login directory.

```
TINI /> whoami
root UID: 128
TINI /> mkdir dan
TINI /> logout
Connection Terminated

Welcome to slush.   (Version 1.02)

TINI login: dan
TINI password:
TINI /dan> pwd
/dan
TINI /dan>
```

.login file

Any user can also place a `.login` file in their home directory. Every line in this file will be executed as it would be from the slush command prompt. This is very much like the `.startup` file but can be unique for each different user. You can comment out lines by inserting a '#' at the beginning of a line.

```
TINI /dan> echo "echo Hi Dan, Welcome back." > .login
TINI /> logout
Connection Terminated

Welcome to slush.   (Version 1.02)

TINI login: dan
TINI password:
Hi Dan, Welcome back. TINI /dan>
```

Obviously this little example is simple, but you can see the possibilities.

Servers in slush

You have already seen from looking at the slush commands and the TINI API that slush supports three servers—an FTP server, a Telnet server and a serial port server.

You can check to see what servers are serving with the `netstat` command, and you can view who these users are with the `who` command.

```
TINI /dan> netstat
Connection count: 13
   Local Port    Remote Port    Remote IP       State
1:      23           ----       ---------       LISTEN
2:      21           ----       ---------       LISTEN
3:      21           4640       192.168.1.18    ESTABLISHED
4:      21           4641       192.168.1.2     ESTABLISHED
5:      21           4642       192.168.1.18    ESTABLISHED
6:      21           4643       192.168.1.18    ESTABLISHED
7:      21           4644       192.168.1.36    ESTABLISHED
8:      23           4645       192.168.1.18    ESTABLISHED
```

```
TINI /dan> who
Serial
======
root

Telnet
======
dan
rosie

 FTP
======
dan
rosie

guest
```

FTP server

The FTP server listens on port 21 for connection requests. Each connection starts a new session to handle that request. You can change the configuration options for the FTP server with the following environment variables:

```
setenv FTP_ALLOW_ROOT [true/false]   - Allow or disallow root to login
                                       to FTP.  Default is true.
setenv FTP_TIMEOUT    [Number of ms] - Inactivity timeout.  0 is
                                       infinite.  Default infinity.
setenv FTP_ALLOW_ANON [true/false]   - Allow or disallow anonymous
                                       login.  Default is true.
setenv FTP_LOG_ANON   [file]         - Log file for anonymous logins.
                                       The directory (and the file if
                                       it exists) must have "other"
                                       write permission.
setenv FTP_WELCOME    [file]         - File to display on successful
                                       login.
setenv FTP_CONNECT    [file]         - File to display on connection.
```

Note that any changes in the environment by changing the value of these variables will not take effect until the FTP server is restarted.

Telnet server

The Telnet server listens on port 23 for connection requests. Each connection starts a new session to handle that request. You can change the configuration options for the Telnet server with the following environment variables:

```
setenv TELNET_ALLOW_ROOT [true/false] - Allow or disallow root to
                                        login to Telnet.  Default is
                                        true.
```

```
setenv TELNET_TIMEOUT [Number of ms]   - Inactivity timeout.  0 is
                                         infinite.  Default infinity.
setenv TELNET_WELCOME [file]           - File to display on successful
                                         login.
```

Note that any changes in the environment by changing the value of these variables will not take effect until the Telnet server is restarted.

Serial server

The Serial Server provides TTY login to the slush system. This server handles connections from JavaKit or a terminal emulator. You can change the config-uration options each serial login with the following environment variables:

```
setenv HISTORY    [size]        - Size of history command buffer.
setenv BROADCASTS [true/false]  - Allow or disallow wall broadcasts.
                                  Default is true.
```

Note that any changes in the environment caused by changing the value of these variables will not take effect until the Serial server is restarted.

Slush is set up by default to use serial0 at 115200 bits per second. If you need to change the port, or set the speed down to 19200, you need to edit `Slush.java`. Change the SERIAL_PORT and SERIAL_SPEED and other variables to your needs, and rebuild. We will be discussing how to go about modifying Slush in a few sections.

That about does it with Slush for now. Next, we will start working with the TINI software development tools.

Programming TINI

In this section we will be working our way through the various software development tools and writing Java specifically for TINI. You have already had a quick overview from Chapter 5. Here we will be digging in deeper. Here is a rough outline of the steps for developing software for the TINI microcontroller:

- Know what parts of Java are not implemented on TINI and what the limitations of TINI are. See "TINI Firmware 1.02 Current Limitations"[13] for a complete list of the limitations of TINI. Also see "TINI Firmware 1.02"[14] for a complete list of which parts of Java TINI does not implement.

- Learn how to develop Java programs for a small microcontroller with limited resources. (See **tips** below.)

- Know the hardware (Chapter 6).

[13] TINI Firmware 1.02 Current Limitations – http://www.ibutton.com/TINI/hardware/limit.html
[14] TINI Firmware 1.02 – http://www.ibutton.com/TINI/hardware/differ.html

- Write your Java program.
- Compile. Make sure to include tini.jar in your CLASSPATH.
- Convert the bytecode (.class file) to TINI format using TINIConvertor or BuildDependency (discussed in subsequent sections).
- Port the program to TINI by using FTP or Javakit (discussed in subsequent sections).
- Run the program.
- Sit back and watch it run or debug it as necessary.

Tips for your programs

TINI is a small microcontroller with a limited amount of memory. As a result, the TINI firmware does not support the full Java API. Additionally, there are a number of things that you can do as a programmer to take advantage of the hardware and things you need know to avoid problems. Make sure you consult the online lists of the limitations mentioned above. Here is a short list of some of the things you need to keep in mind when programming your TINI (as of TINI API version 1.02).

Threads

- All threads run at the same priority. `Thread.setPriority()` will not throw an exception, but will not change the runtime priority of that thread.

- Threads can block on I/O; this increases CPU cycle availability to other threads and processes. Network threads will block on `accept()` until a connection is established. Reads will block until data is received.

- The TINI OS limits the number of processes to 8, with 16 threads per Java process. One process is consumed by the garbage collector. The application (typically slush) is another process.

Memory

- A quick and memory-saving way to print the amount of free RAM is:
  `com.dalsemi.system.Debug.intDump(Control.getFreeRAM())`

  `System.out.println()` consumes lots of memory.

- If you consume large amounts of memory, especially in iteration-based loops, it is a good idea to call the garbage collector periodically yourself with `System.gc()`. The garbage collector will kick off automatically when memory dips below a certain threshold, but major garbage collection during program run will cause the collector to run for long periods of time in the background.

- If you are doing lots of I/O then avoid reading and writing a single byte at a time. Either use a buffered stream or write byte arrays.

- Native modules can't be larger than 64k.

- The maximum size of any array is 64k.

- Avoid doing string concatenation with the "+" operator. If you have to concatenate more then one thing to a string, use StringBuffer and its append function instead. It's faster plus takes less memory.

Networking

- MulticastSocket – Only one local interface can send and receive on a given group.

- TINI does not support IP datagram fragmentation/reassembly.

- TINI has 24 total allowed socket connections.

- TINI does not support IP layer routing.

Good ideas

- Print a banner—make one of the first lines of your program a println of some kind so you know right off if your program is running. If you do not see this line, it is possible your heap is in an unknown state. You may want to clear out the heap.

- Check `com.dalsemi.system.ArrayUtils` for various fast array comparison/fill methods.

Java classes/methods (API 1.02d)

- TINI currently supports only a subset of reflection. `Class.forName()`, `newInstance()`, etc., are supported, but `java.lang.reflect.Array`, Constructor, Field, etc. are not yet supported. See API_Diffs.txt for a full list of nonsupported classes and methods.

- TINI does not currently support serialization.

- `printStackTrace()` is only partially supported. The fully qualified exception name will be printed, but not the method stack list. The full method names do not currently exist in the .tini files.

- PPP Dial on demand is not currently supported and get/setIdleTimeout() is not supported.

- The method `Date.toLocaleString()` returns the same thing as `Date.toString()`. This is because TINI does not support any of the date formatting classes.

- Only the default locale is supported. Others can be added by users in their Java programs.

- Dates representing times before January 1, 1970 will not return correct values for their fields, either through a Calendar object or through a Date object.

- A class file is limited to 255 static fields (including all super classes' static fields) and 255 instance fields (including all super classes' instance fields).

- A class file is limited to 127 methods (including all super classes' methods, excluding native methods). A class file is limited to 255 native methods.

- A method is limited to 63 local variables.

File system

- Each converted class file can't be larger than 64k.

- Directories can only hold 254 files. Attempting to add more will result in an `IOException`.

- An `IOException` will be thrown when attempting to create files with names longer than 247 characters.

A quick technique to determine if TINI supports the classes and methods you are interested in is to use javap (the Java class file disassembler) to examine the TINI API. The following example compares the TINI API to the SUN JDK API for the java.lang.Math class. You will notice that the trigonometric functions have not been included in the TINI API.

```
C:\>javap -bootclasspath
%TINI_HOME%\tiniclasses.jar java.lang.Math


Compiled from Math.java
public final class java.lang.Math extends
java.lang.Object
        /* ACC_SUPER bit NOT set */
{
    public static final double E;
    public static final double PI;
    static final double zero;
    static final double two54;
    public static double abs(double);
    public static float abs(float);
    public static int abs(int);
    public static long abs(long);
    public static double ceil(double);
    public static double floor(double);
    public static double log(double);
    public static double max(double, double);
    public static float max(float, float);
    public static int max(int, int);
    public static long max(long, long);
    public static double min(double, double);
    public static float min(float, float);
    public static int min(int, int);
    public static long min(long, long);
    public static synchronized double random();
    public static double rint(double);
    public static long round(double);
    public static int round(float);
    public static double sqrt(double);
}
```

```
C:\>javap -classpath c:\jdk1.3.1\lib\ java.lang.Math
Compiled from Math.java
public final class java.lang.Math extends java.lang.Object {
    public static final double E;
    public static final double PI;
    public static strictfp double sin(double);
    public static strictfp double cos(double);
    public static strictfp double tan(double);
    public static strictfp double asin(double);
    public static strictfp double acos(double);
    public static strictfp double atan(double);
    public static strictfp double toRadians(double);
    public static strictfp double toDegrees(double);
    public static strictfp double exp(double);
    public static strictfp double log(double);
    public static strictfp double sqrt(double);
    public static strictfp double IEEEremainder(double, double);
    public static strictfp double ceil(double);
    public static strictfp double floor(double);
    public static strictfp double rint(double);
    public static strictfp double atan2(double, double);
    public static strictfp double pow(double, double);
    public static strictfp int round(float);
    public static strictfp long round(double);
    public static strictfp double random();
    public static strictfp int abs(int);
    public static strictfp long abs(long);
    public static strictfp float abs(float);
    public static strictfp double abs(double);
    public static strictfp int max(int, int);
    public static strictfp long max(long, long);
    public static strictfp float max(float, float);
    public static strictfp double max(double, double);
    public static strictfp int min(int, int);
    public static strictfp long min(long, long);
    public static strictfp float min(float, float);
    public static strictfp double min(double, double);
    static {};
}
```

TINIConvertor

Once your Java program is written and it compiles error free, you will need to convert the .class files to a format that the TINI Java Virtual Machine likes. The tool to use is TINIConvertor, which is supplied by Dallas Semiconductor in the tini.jar package. TINIConvertor combines and converts normal class files into a single file that can be directly ported to TINI. The following example shows how to run TINIConvertor and have it list the possible command line options.

One important thing to note is that TINIConvertor can generate two different kinds of files for the TINI Java Virtual Machine: .tini files and .tbin files. A .tini file is a converted Java class file that's intended to be executed from inside the Slush operating system. You generate the .tini file on your PC, move it over to your TINI via FTP, then Telnet onto the TINI and execute your .tini program under Slush. A .tbin file is designed to be loaded into the TINI boot sector and will execute when the TINI is rebooted (instead of Slush). You generate a .tbin file on your PC, move it to your TINI via the JavaKit program, then reboot TINI to watch it execute. TINIConvertor will generate either one for you, based on a command line parameter. When developing a program, it's often smart to generate .tini files and test them under Slush, which provides a certain amount of control. Then, when the program works just the way you want it, you can turn it into a .tbin file and make it a bootable program.

```
C:>java -cp %TINI_HOME%\bin\tini.jar TINIConvertor

TINIConvertor + ZIP
Version 0.73 for TINI
built on or around January 24, 2001
Disassembler/Builder Version 0.15 TINI, October 30, 2000
JiBDB 0.60 for TINI, November 10, 2000
Copyright (C) 1996 - 2001 Dallas Semiconductor Corporation.
MainStartClass: First available.
Target address: 0x70100
USAGE: TINIConvertor -f <classfile/ZIPfile/directory> -o <outfile> -d
<JiBDB>
Other options
-v (verbose output)
-m <class containing the static void main() to execute>
-n <native file>
-l (use flash file format)
-t <target address> (starting address, defaults to 0x70100)
```

      -d   Tells TINIConvertor where the database is that it will need to convert the .class files into .tini files. You will always need to specify this. This should be %TINI_HOME%\bin\tini.db

-f   Specifies the class file or directory to convert. If you specify a directory then TINIConvertor will convert all of the .class files it finds and then write out one converted file.

-o   Specifies the name of the output file. Typically this is a .tini file.

-l   Tells TINIConvertor to use the flash file format. This file format allows you to load your program in the flash boot sector instead of Slush.

BuildDependency

BuildDependency is essentially TINIConvertor with a front-end added for finding and including Java class file dependencies. These dependencies may be other parts of the TINI API that are not included in the firmware, like the 1-Wire containers in com.dalsemi.onewire.container.*. You can view the command line options and usage information for BuildDependency by running it without any parameters:

```
C:>java -cp %TINI_HOME%\bin\tini.jar BuildDependency

Dallas Semiconductor TINI Program Building Tool
BuildDependency 1.03, January 24, 2001 (KLA)
_____


This program is meant to be used to build applications for TINI
where building one class into a TINI application means that many
other classes (dependency classes) must be built in, such as programs
that use the 1-Wire API.  See the BuildDependency_README for more
information on using this program.
Usage:
    java BuildDependency [options]

options:-add NAMES  - The names of the dependencies to add to this
                      project. This is a semi-colon or comma separated
                      list of dependency names.
        -p PATH     - Path to your dependency classes.  This is a
                      semi-colon or comma separated list that can
                      include multiple jar files and directories.
        -x DEP_FILE - A semi-colon or comma separated list of
                      filenames of dependency text database files—
                      multiple files can now be specified, although
                      note that if a key is redefined, only the last
                      definition found will be used by
                      BuildDependency—the keys won't be added.
                      BuildDependency has a default set of
                      dependencies used for 1-Wire programs.  See the
                      readme for more on this file's format.
```

```
    -debug      — See the entire output of TINIConvertor
    -dep        — See the entire dependency list using the
                  specified depdendency file or the default.
    -depNAME    — See the depdendency list for dependency named
                  NAME.
-Any TINIConvertor Option
                — BuildDependency supports all TINIConvertor
                  options by directly passing any other options to
                  TINIConvertor.

For example, for a program that uses 1-Wire Containers for the DS1920,
DS1921, and the DS1996, I might try running: (EOLN's added for clarity)
    java BuildDependency -f ReadTemp.class -o readtemp.tini
        -d d:\tini1.01\bin\tini.db -p OneWire.jar
        -add OneWireContainer10;OneWireContainer21;OneWireContainer0C

************************************************************************
* NOTE: 1. Dependency classes must already be compiled.               *
************************************************************************
```

BuildDependency takes all of the TINIConvertor options and a few additional ones.

-x   Is a list of filenames that your program is dependent on. This can also be a file that is a list of file names. One such file, owapi_dep.txt (`%TINI_HOME%\bin\owapi_dep.txt`), is included with TINI; it lists all of the 1-Wire container dependencies.

-p   Specifies the path to use for finding the dependency files. If your program is dependent on the 1-Wire containers, then this option probably should be set to `%TINI_HOME%\bin\owapi_dependencies_TINI_001.jar` (API versions 1.02 and 1.02b used this name, 1.02c and later used the name `owapi_dependencies_TINI.jar`. While this difference may seem minor, it will break any scripts that you might use to compile and convert your TINI programs).

-add Specifies a list of dependencies to be added to the .tini file that is created. For example, if your program uses a Dallas Semiconductor DS1820 temperature sensor that has a family code of 10, then you would need to `-add OneWireContainer10`.

Getting complex builds to work properly with `BuildDependency` is sometimes difficult and often appears to be impossible. Persistence, patience and exploring all possibilities (no matter how wrong you might think they are) often pays off. Sometimes things that you think should work, don't. But there are several ways to do the same thing, so try the alternatives.

A TINI example

Now that we have discussed the tools needed to convert Java class files to a format that TINI recognizes, we will demonstrate the use of these programs on a Java program of our own. We will be examining a threaded web server (based on the threaded web server developed in Chapter 3) that prints out some TINI statuses like current time, uptime, API version, amount of free memory, all connected 1-Wire devices, etc. The point of this is to show you a complex TINI program example and to show more about `TINIConvertor` or `BuildDependency` tools. Then we will add our threaded web server to the .startup so it starts up automatically on boot and then we'll install it on TINI in place of Slush. The program listing is shown below, `TiniWebStat.java`:

Listing 7-1: TiniWebStat.java

```java
import java.util.*;
import java.io.*;
import java.net.*;
import com.dalsemi.system.*;
import com.dalsemi.tininet.*;
import com.dalsemi.onewire.*;
import com.dalsemi.onewire.adapter.*;
import com.dalsemi.onewire.container.*;
import com.dalsemi.onewire.container.OneWireContainer.*;

/*
  This program implements an HTTP server on TINI that
  prints out the last time TINI rebooted and a whole bunch
  of stats on your TINI.
*/

public class TiniWebStat implements Runnable {
    protected Socket mySocket;
    String who;

    public TiniWebStat(Socket mySocket) {
        this.mySocket = mySocket;
    }

    public static void main(String[] args) throws IOException {
        int port = 80;

        ServerSocket srv = new ServerSocket(port);

        // listen forever and start new threads as requests come in
        while (true) {
            Socket mySocket = srv.accept();
```

```
            TiniWebStat f2 = new TiniWebStat(mySocket);
            Thread myThread = new Thread(f2);
            myThread.start();
        }
    }

    // This is the content of each thread
    public void run() {
        float upT;
        try {
            OutputStreamWriter osr =
                new OutputStreamWriter(mySocket.getOutputStream());
            BufferedWriter bwtr = new BufferedWriter(osr);
            InputStreamReader isr =
                new InputStreamReader(mySocket.getInputStream());
            BufferedReader rd = new BufferedReader(isr);


            // write out the one and only page and then clean up
            writePage(bwtr);
            rd.close();
            mySocket.close();
        }
        catch (IOException e) {
            e.printStackTrace();
        }
    }

    //
    public static void writePage(BufferedWriter wr) {

        Date now  = new Date(System.currentTimeMillis());

        // import form com.dalsemi.system
        long uptm = TINIOS.uptimeMillis()/1000; // convert ms to secs
        int ram   = TINIOS.getFreeRAM();
        int tsk   = TINIOS.getTaskID();
        String hw = TINIOS.getTINIHWVersion();
        String sr = TINIOS.getTINISerialNumber();
        String fr = TINIOS.getTINIOSFirmwareVersion();
        String sh = TINIOS.getShellName();

        // import from com.dalsemi.tininet
        String dn = TININet.getDomainname();
        String en = TININet.getEthernetAddress();
        String hn = TININet.getHostname();
        String ip = TININet.getIPAddress();

        // figure out uptime in days, hours, minutes, seconds
        int h = (int)(uptm/3600);
```

```
int m = (int)((uptm % 3600)/60);
int s = (int)(uptm % 60);
int d = h/24;
h = h % 24;

try {
    wr.write("HTTP/1.0 200 OK\r\n");
    wr.write("Content-type: text/html\r\n");
    wr.write("<HTML><HEAD>\r\n");
    wr.write("<TITLE>TINI Stats</TITLE>\r\n");
    wr.write("</HEAD>\r\n");
    wr.write("<H1>TINI Stats</H1>\r\n");
    wr.write("<BODY><BLOCKQUOTE><PRE>\r\n");
    wr.write("The current time:      " + now + "<br>" );
    wr.write("TINI has been up for:  " + d + " days, " );
    wr.write(h + " hours, " + m + " minutes, " + s + "
            seconds.<br>");
    wr.write("Hardware version:      " + hw  + "<br>" );
    wr.write("Firmware version:      " + fr  + "<br>" );
    wr.write("Serial Number:         " + sr  + "<br>" );
    wr.write("Free RAM:              " + ram + "<br>" );
    wr.write("Current Shell:         " + sh  + "<br>" );
    wr.write("Task ID:               " + tsk + "<br>" );
    wr.write("Hostname:              " + hn  + "<br>" );
    wr.write("Domainname:            " + dn  + "<br>" );
    wr.write("Ethernet(MAC) address: " + en  + "<br>" );
    wr.write("IP adddress:           " + ip  + "<br>" );
    wr.write("<br>");
    wr.write("One wire devcies connected:<br>");

    Enumeration adapter_enum =
            OneWireAccessProvider.enumerateAllAdapters();

    while( adapter_enum.hasMoreElements() ) {
       DSPortAdapter adapter=(DSPortAdapter)
                adapter_enum.nextElement();
       wr.write( "Adapter: " + adapter.getAdapterName() +
                "<br>" );

       adapter.setSearchAllDevices();
       adapter.targetAllFamilies();
       Enumeration ibutton_enum =
                adapter.getAllDeviceContainers();

       while( ibutton_enum.hasMoreElements() ) {
          OneWireContainer node =
             (OneWireContainer) ibutton_enum.nextElement();
          wr.write(" - " + node.getName() + " - " +
             node.getAddressAsString() + "<br>");
       }
```

```
        }

        wr.write("</PRE></BLOCKQUOTE></BODY></HTML>\r\n");
        wr.flush();
    }
    catch (IOException e) {
    }
    catch (Exception e) {
    }
  }
}
```

As you examine the preceding Java program, you will notice the use of a number of the packages we discussed in the TINI API section (above). For instance, we import several of the `com.dalsemi.*` packages:

```
import com.dalsemi.system.*;
import com.dalsemi.tininet.*;
import com.dalsemi.onewire.*;
```

From the `com.dalsemi.system.TINIOS` package, we use a number of methods to get the status of TINI (uptime, amount of free RAM, and Task ID), and some of the TINI hardware and software versions. From the `com.dalsemi.tininet.TININet` package, we get a number of pieces of information on the network settings, and from the `com.dalsemi.onewire.*` package, we get the 1-Wire adapters and a list of all the 1-Wire devices attached to each adapter.

Compile this program with the following command line

```
C:\>javac -classpath %TINI_HOME%\bin\tiniclasses.jar;. TiniWebStat.java
```

Once this is compiled, we need to convert the .class file to a file that is compatible with the TINI firmware. Run TINIConvertor:

```
C:\>java  -cp %TINI_HOME%\bin\tini.jar TINIConvertor
         -d %TINI_HOME%\bin\tini.db
         -f TiniWebStat.class
         -o TiniWebStat.tini
```

We've generated a .tini file, so we will be running it under slush. With no errors, you can copy the file to your TINI with FTP and use Telnet to login and run the program. If you found any errors, check that you have typed all of the compile and `TINIConvertor` commands properly and that the program has been typed in accurately.

> The Java command line has been shown with newlines added for clarity. We will continue to show them this way throughout the book. Since the command lines are often longer than can fit on a single line of printed text, this is much easier to see the various parameters than if we show the commands like this:
>
> ```
> C:\>java -cp %TINI_HOME%\bin\tini.jar
> TINIConvertor -d %TINI_HOME%\bin\tini.db
> -f TiniWebStat.class -o TiniWebStat.tini
> ```

```
C:\>ftp 192.168.1.85
Connected to 192.168.1.85.
220 Welcome to slush.  (Version 1.02)   Ready for user login.
User (192.168.1.85:(none)): root
331 root login allowed. Password required.
Password: tini
230 User root logged in.
ftp> send TiniWebStat.tini
200 PORT Command successful.
150 ASCII connection open, putting TiniWebStat.tini
226 Closing data connection.
ftp: 2135 bytes sent in 0.00Seconds 2135000.00Kbytes/sec.
ftp> quit
221 Goodbye.

C:\> telnet 192.168.1.85
Trying 192.168.1.85...
Connected to TINI.
Escape character is '^]'.

Welcome to slush.  (Version 1.02)

TINI login: root
TINI password: tini
TINI /> java TiniWebStat.tini &
TINI />
```

Note that the "&" at the end of `java TiniWebStat.tini &` runs the TiniWebStat server as a background thread. Now start up a web browser on your desktop computer and browse to your TINI. We wrote the server to listen to port 80. You need to enter http:// followed by the IP address of your TINI followed by a :80. In this case, my TINI board's IP address is 192.168.1.85. You need to replace that with your TINI board's IP address.

Notice that 1-Wire devices are listed as "`Device Type: 01`" rather than the specific Dallas Semiconductor device name.

```
One wire devcies connected:
Adapter: TINIExternalAdapter
 - Device type: 10 - 700000004B8F1010
 - Device type: 18 - 1C00000002795818
 - Device type: 12 - CB00000017006112
 - Device type: 01 - 21000007997D9F01
Adapter: TINIInternalAdapter
 - Device type: 89 - 9F5E70005C8D1089
```

This is because the device name returned by `OneWireContainer.getName()` is using the default name as supplied by `com.dalsemi.onewire.container` and not by the specific container type (there is a container type for each type of device). To get the

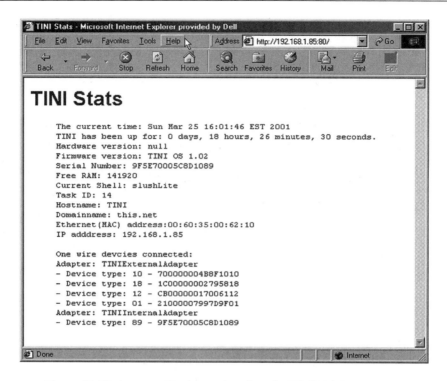

Figure 7-17: Internet Explorer showing the TiniWebStat output

device name from these containers it is necessary to combine the dependencies into the .tini class file using `BuildDependency`. The following will do this:

```
C:\> java -cp %TINI_HOME%\bin\tini.jar BuildDependency
        -f TiniWebStat.class
        -o TiniWebStat.tini
        -d %TINI_HOME%\bin\tini.db
        -p %TINI_HOME%\bin\owapi_dependencies_TINI.jar
        -x %TINI_HOME%\bin\owapi_dep.txt
        -add OneWireContainer01;OneWireContainer10;OneWireContainer12;
            OneWireContainer18
        -debug
```

This command may exceed the DOS command line size so you may have to create a batch file and put this command in the file and then execute the file, which is a good thing because you don't want to type a command this long more than once anyway.

So run `BuildDependency` on `TiniWebStat.class` and then FTP the `TiniWebStat.tini` file to your TINI. Before you run this new version, make sure you kill the old one—it's still running (unless you have rebooted the TINI).

```
TINI /> ps
3 processes
1: Java GC (Owner root)
2: init (Owner root)
3: TiniWebStat.tini (Owner root)
TINI /> kill 3
TINI /> java TiniWebStat.tini &
```

Now browse the TiniWebStat server again and examine the output. Notice that the "Device Type" has now changed to the actual Dallas Semiconductor device name (in the cases where there is a named container—not all containers have named containers, as you can see in the following output).

```
One wire devices connected:
Adapter: TINIExternalAdapter
 - DS1920 - 700000004B8F1010
 - DS1963S - 1C00000002795818
 - DS2406 - CB00000017006112
 - DS1990A - 21000007997D9F01
Adapter: TINIInternalAdapter
 - Device type: 89 - 9F5E70005C8D1089
```

One drawback to this is that building in the device names also builds in a whole pile of other methods. Examine the last few lines of TINIConvertor and the last few lines of BuildDependency to look at the final file byte size. With TINIConvertor the Total Application Length is 2084 bytes; with BuildDependency the Total Application Length is 28575 bytes. Quite a big difference. This is because some of the containers we have included here have long dependency lists (lots of methods).

Now that we have our server running, how can we make this server start automatically whenever the TINI is rebooted? There are two ways: 1. Add the java TiniWebStat.tini command to the .startup file; or 2. Replace slush with TiniWebStat.tbin (which requires running BuildDependency with the -l flag). First, let's try adding this to the .startup file. Using FTP, get the /etc/.startup file.

```
C:\>ftp 192.168.1.85
Connected to 192.168.1.85.
220 Welcome to slush.  (Version 1.02)  Ready for user login.
User (192.168.1.85:(none)): root
331 root login allowed. Password required.
Password:
230 User root logged in.
ftp> cd etc
250 CWD command successful.
ftp> get .startup
200 PORT Command successful.
150 ASCII connection open, getting .startup
226 Closing data connection.
ftp: 225 bytes received in 0.16Seconds 1.41Kbytes/sec.
```

```
ftp> quit
221 Goodbye.
C:\>
```

Now edit the .startup file using your favorite text editor (such as Notepad). Change the file, adding a single line `java TiniWebStat.tini` to the end of the file. Save the file. Your .startup will now look like this:

```
########
#Autogen'd slush startup file
setenv FTPServer enable
setenv TelnetServer enable
setenv SerialServer enable
##
#Add user calls to setenv here:
##
initializeNetwork
########
#Add other user additions here:
java /TiniWebStat.tini
```

Now FTP the file back to your TINI:

```
C:\>ftp 192.168.1.85
Connected to 192.168.1.85.
220 Welcome to slush.  (Version 1.02)  Ready for user login.
User (192.168.1.85:(none)): root
331 root login allowed. Password required.
Password:
230 User root logged in.
ftp> cd etc
250 CWD command successful.
ftp> send .startup
200 PORT Command successful.
150 ASCII connection open, putting .startup
226 Closing data connection.
ftp: 247 bytes sent in 0.00Seconds 247000.00Kbytes/sec.
ftp> quit
221 Goodbye.
```

Through a Telnet session you can verify the file is there (use `cat`). Now reboot your TINI.

```
TINI /> reboot
```

Give your TINI a few seconds to reboot and then, using your web browser, check to see that the server is running again. You can also login to TINI and use the `ps` command to check the running processes:

```
TINI /> ps
3 processes
1: Java GC (Owner root)
2: init (Owner root)
3: /TiniWebStat.tini (Owner root)
```

That was fairly easy, no? Now let's try running the server in place of Slush.

Recompile the server into the .tbin format with BuildDependency, like this:

```
C:\> java  -cp %TINI_HOME%\bin\tini.jar BuildDependency
           -l
           -f TiniWebStat.class
           -o TiniWebStat.tbin
           -d %TINI_HOME%\bin\tini.db
           -p %TINI_HOME%\bin\owapi_dependencies_TINI.jar
           -x %TINI_HOME%\bin\owapi_dep.txt
           -add OneWireContainer01;OneWireContainer10;OneWireContainer12;
                OneWireContainer18
           -debug
```

Using JavaKit, load the `TiniWebStat.tbin` file. After loading the file, don't forget to press "E" at the loader prompt to exit the loader and start executing the `TiniWebStat.tbin` program. You will notice in the JavaKit window that the last line you see is "Application load complete." At that point you can browse your web server. Remember, at this point we have replaced Slush with TiniWebStat so you cannot FTP or Telnet into your TINI. To login to your TINI you will need to use JavaKit to re-load `Slush.tbin`. Play with your new web server for a little while and than re-load Slush, as we are going to continue on with more new things.

Modifying slush

Now that you have seen how easy it is to replace slush with your own program, we are going to start some simple modifications to slush itself. Slush is fitted with a variety of commands for development of TINI applications but it doesn't have to end there. We can add some new commands to slush and remove a few of the ones we don't need or want. We are going to discuss three ways to modify slush: recompiling slush, deleting commands from slush, and adding new commands to slush.

Recompiling Slush

Before we start to add and delete commands, let's first determine that we can properly recompile slush and transfer it to a TINI and verify that we are actually running our new version of slush. We need to start by creating a directory in which we can unpack the slush source files and recompile them. For this section we are using the directory `c:\projects\modslush`. You can use this or create a directory of your choosing.

```
C:\> mkdir projects
C:\> cd projects
C:\> mkdir modslush
C:\> cd modslush
```

Note that you need to find the Slush source jar file; it should be in `%TINI_HOME%\src\`. Look for the file SlushSrc.jar. You will need to use the Java jar program to unpack the jar and create the slush directory hierarchy in `\projects\modslush\`.

```
C:\> jar -xf %TINI_HOME%\src\SlushSrc.jar
```

Now change directory to `\projects\modslush\com\dalsemi\slush\` and look around.

```
C:\> cd com\dalsemi\slush
C:\> dir
.                  <DIR>              03-18-01   3:32p  .
..                 <DIR>              03-18-01   3:32p  ..
COMMAND            <DIR>              03-18-01   3:32p  command
COMMAN~1  JAV            17,117      03-19-01   6:54a  CommandInterpreter.java
SLUSH~1   JAV            49,776      03-25-01   4:40p  Slush.java

C:\> cd command
C:\> dir
.                  <DIR>              03-18-01   3:32p  .
..                 <DIR>              03-18-01   3:32p  ..
ADDUSE~1  JAV             6,226      03-19-01   6:54a  AddUserCommand.java
APPEND~1  JAV             4,562      03-19-01   6:54a  AppendCommand.java
ARPCOM~1  JAV             5,823      03-19-01   6:54a  ARPCommand.java
CATCOM~1  JAV             3,536      03-19-01   6:54a  CatCommand.java
CDCOMM~1  JAV             3,421      03-19-01   6:54a  CdCommand.java
CHMODC~1  JAV             6,385      03-19-01   6:54a  ChmodCommand.java
CHOWNC~1  JAV             3,244      03-19-01   6:54a  ChownCommand.java
...
FTPCOM~1  CLA             7,559      03-19-01   7:17a  FTPCommand.class
NETSTA~1  CLA             2,485      03-19-01   7:17a  NetStatCommand.class
STATSC~2  JAV             8,588      03-18-01   4:11p  StatsCommand.java
WHOAMI~1  CLA             1,153      03-19-01   7:17a  WhoamiCommand.class
WALLCO~1  CLA             1,254      03-19-01   7:17a  WallCommand.class
```

Notice where `Slush.java` is located (`\projects\modslush\com\dalsemi\slush\`). View this in your favorite text editor. Notice around line 418 the method `initializeShellCommands()`. This is where commands are added to the slush shell command list. For each of the commands in the `initializeShellCommands()` method notice that in `\projects\modslush\com\dalsemi\slush\command\` is a separate Java class that implements this command. We will make a simple change to slush so we know for sure that the newly compiled version is indeed what we are running on TINI when we do finally succeed in loading it there.

- Edit StatsCommand.java (in
  `\projects\modslush\com\dalsemi\slush\command\`)

- Somewhere around line 60, after the `static find byte[]` declarations, we are going to add a greeting message so that we know we are using our new version of Slush. Insert these lines:

  ```
  // Added for verification
  static final byte[] greeting = "Greetings from SLUSH!".getBytes();
  ```

- Then around line 135, find the code that looks like this:

```
try
{
    // Display system version info (add API version)
    out.write(slushVer);
    out.write(osVer);
```

- Modify this to print out the greeting message by adding a line, like this:

```
try
{
    // Display system version info (add API version)
    out.write(greeting);
    out.write(slushVer);
    out.write(osVer);
```

These changes simply make the `stats` command in slush print out the greeting as the first line of output. This way, after slush has been ported to our TINI we can verify that we are actually running the version of slush that we just compiled and not the real slush. Save the modified StatCommand.java file if you have not done so already and exit the editor.

Compile slush. Do this by compiling slush.java. All of the commands will be compiled also.

```
C:\> set SMUSH=C:\projects\modslush
C:\> cd \projects\modslush\com\dalsemi\slush\
C:\> javac -classpath %TINI_HOME%\bin\tiniclasses.jar;%SMUSH%;.
Slush.java
```

Notice how we have the CLASSPATH set for finding both the `tiniclasses.jar` **and** the slush classes by specifying the path to the top level of the slush source files and using the SMUSH environment variable. If you place your slush source files somewhere else on your disk, you need to set the SMUSH environment variable appropriately. We do not specify the path all the way to where the slush.java lives; these are included in slush.java through the import statements:

```
import com.dalsemi.slush.command.*;
```

The `com.dalsemi.slush.command` is specified in the import statement and provides the path to `com\dalsemi\slush\command` so we only include in the CLASSPATH where to find the start of this path.

When you compile slush you will see this message:

```
Note: Slush.java uses or overrides a deprecated API.
Note: Recompile with -deprecation for details.
```

If you want to see what has been deprecated[15] (usage is no longer recommended) add the -deprecation option to the compile command and then you will see four warnings like this:

```
Slush.java:1081: warning: readLine() in java.io.DataInputStream
    has been deprecated while ((line = input.readLine()) != null)
```

If you saw any errors when compiling slush, be sure you included the proper path to tiniclasses.jar and the top level of the slush source in your CLASSPATH. Also check that you have correctly made the modifications to StatCommand.java (including the semicolon at the end of the two lines that you added).

Next we need to run TINIConvertor to make the .class files into a .tbin file.

```
C:\> java -cp %TINI_HOME%\bin\tini.jar TINIConvertor
        -o Slush.tbin
        -l
        -d %TINI_HOME%\bin\tini.db
        -f .
```

We have included some new command line options to TINIConvertor

-l   Tells TINIConvertor to use the flash file format. We do this because we are going to load slush into the beginning of the flash as the boot program.

-f   Specifies to TINIConvertor the class file to convert. A "." will use the current directory (and included subdirectories and files).

-o   Specifies the name of the output file, Slush.tbin.

-d   Specifies the path to the TINIConvertor database, tini.bd.

You should not have seen any errors but, if you did, likely possibilities include either not properly specifying the path to tini.jar (so Java can't find the TINIConvertor), not properly specifying the path to tini.db, and not specifying the "." for the input file/directory.

When TINIConvertor runs, you will see some output lines like the following (where you see ... , many of the similar messages were deleted to shorten the output printed here):

```
TINIConvertor + ZIP
Version 0.73 for TINI
built on or around January 24, 2001
Disassembler/Builder Version 0.15 TINI, October 30, 2000
JiBDB 0.60 for TINI, November 10, 2000
Copyright (C) 1996 - 2001 Dallas Semiconductor Corporation.
MainStartClass: First available.
```

---

[15] How and When To Deprecate APIs – http://java.sun.com/products/jdk/1.2/docs/guide/misc/deprecation/deprecation.html

```
Target address: 0x70100
Changed tag to 8000
Recursing directory: .
directory: /home/dan/Projects/book/newslush/com/dalsemi/slush/./command
Adding file: /home/dan/Projects/book/newslush/com/dalsemi/slush/./
command/StatsCommand.class
...
Adding file: /home/dan/Projects/book/newslush/com/dalsemi/slush/./
Slush.class
Adding file: /home/dan/Projects/book/newslush/com/dalsemi/slush/./
CommandInterpreter.class
Set mainClassIndex to: 51
Using ROM API Version: 8009
Writing Class Offsets
Writing: com/dalsemi/slush/command/StatsCommand
...
Writing: com/dalsemi/slush/command/NetStatCommand
Writing: com/dalsemi/slush/Slush$SlushDHCPListener
Writing: com/dalsemi/slush/Slush$1
Writing Application: com/dalsemi/slush/Slush
Writing: com/dalsemi/slush/Slush
Writing: com/dalsemi/slush/CommandInterpreter
Total Application length: 56931
Writing Application Entry point
Main offset for class with main: 6965
class num: 51
main class index: 51
main class tag: 8033
Converting to flash format. (56979 bytes)
Segment start address: 70100, length: 56979, CRC: dbda
Flash file size: 56986
Finished with build.
```

The first important thing to notice here is the "Finished with build" line, which means TINIConvertor successfully converted the class files. Note the "Flash file size: 56990". Yours may differ slightly depending on what you personalized. Recall from a previous section in this chapter that each converted class file can't be larger than 64k. This will be more important when we start adding new commands to Slush.

The last thing we need to do is to get this new slush.tbin file to your TINI using JavaKit and try running it.

```
C:\> javakit -port COM1 -noDTRtest
```

Use the –noDTRtest command line switch if you previously found you needed it. When JavaKit starts up, press the reset button and then use the file/load menu command. Find the slush.tbin file you just created, select it and press OK. If you received an error, try loading the new slush again. When loading is complete and you see the loader prompt ">" press E enter to exit the loader and start executing slush. Once slush completes booting you can log in.

Now let's test our new slush. Try the stats command and see what happens.

```
TINI /> stats
Greetings from SLUSH!
TINI slush null
TINI OS 1.02

System up time:
     Days: 0
    Hours: 0
  Minutes: 0
  Seconds: 12

Free RAM: 355264

FTP Server    :active
Telnet Server:active
Serial Server:active
```

If this didn't work, go back to verify that you did all the steps properly. Also be sure to check that you loaded the new slush and not the original slush.tbin.

We have verified that we can successfully recompile slush and get it to our TINI board, so we can move on to more complex modifications to slush with confidence.

Modifying the slush command set

Now that you have shown you can recompile slush relatively easily, let's actually do some real, beneficial modifications to slush. Modifying an existing slush command is as simple as editing the `command` class, as we did with `StatsCommand.java`. Deleting commands from slush is as simple as removing the reference from the `initializeShellCommands()` method in `slush.java`. Adding new commands to Slush consists of writing a new command implementation and adding that command to the `initializeShellCommands()` method.

We can remove commands we don't need or don't want. For instance, we can improve the security of our TINI by removing all commands that allow us to add new users or delete files, or we can simply remove the commands we don't need and increase the available memory for other purposes. We can add new aliases for commands in an effort to make slush easier to use. And we can even add new commands. In the slush source directory hierarchy Dallas Semiconductor has included several additional commands for slush that are not part of the base compilation (because they take up more memory).

First things first. Open `slush.java` in a text editor and examine the source code. Notice how slush works (sort of). Skip down to around line 418, to the method `initializeShellCommands`. You will see a number of lines like this one:

```
CommandInterpreter.addCommand("arp", new ARPCommand());
```

There should be a line like this for each command in slush. This is where slush commands are added to the command interpreter. In this case `arp` is the command that is added to slush and `ARPCommand` is the name of the corresponding class that implements this command (we will look at that part in a bit). To remove commands from slush, you could simply delete the lines like this for the commands you don't want. Similarly, to add new commands, you could add lines like this for the new classes that contain new slush commands. Also, scroll down a little and examine the copy command:

```
SlushCommand copy = new CopyCommand();
CommandInterpreter.addCommand("copy", copy);
CommandInterpreter.addCommand("cp", copy);
```

This is essentially the same as the previous single line for adding a command to slush, except that we first define a new "SlushCommand" object and then we add it to the command interpreter twice, with different names, `cp` and `copy`. This is how aliases for commands are added to slush.

Edit Slush.java

Around line 417, look for the method

```
private void initializeShellCommands()
```

In here, comment out the commands you don't want buy putting // at the beginning of the line. I commented out the `chown`, `arp`, `useradd`, `userdel`, `sendmail`, `append`, `who`, `whoami`, `clear`, `wd` and `wall` commands.

```
// CommandInterpreter.addCommand("chown", new ChownCommand());
```

Also, since we are making some changes, I find that I want to use `more` rather than `cat` to view a text file, so we are going to add that as an alias to Slush. Change:

```
CommandInterpreter.addCommand("cat", new CatCommand());
```

To:

```
SlushCommand    cat = new CatCommand();
CommandInterpreter.addCommand("cat", cat);
CommandInterpreter.addCommand("more", cat);
```

Recompile slush as we did in the previous step. Notice the final file size.

```
...
Converting to flash format. (56585 bytes)
Segment start address: 70100, length: 56585, CRC: a7a9
Flash file size: 56592
Finished with build.
```

Not much smaller, is it? What happened? We commented out the commands *but* they are still added to the `slush.tbin` by TINIConvertor because the .class files are still in the command directory. We need to go back in and delete the .class files for these commands, as they are still there from our previous compiles. Notice that the class for useradd is `AddUserCommand.class` and userdel is `RemoveUserCommand.class`.

You don't need to recompile—you simply need to rerun TINIConvertor after these class files have been removed. Examine the final file size.

```
...
Converting to flash format. (49159 bytes)
Segment start address: 70100, length: 49159, CRC: b65b
Flash file size: 49166
Finished with build.
```

OK, that's much better. Now load the new version of slush to the TINI and test it out. It should work just fine. You can verify these commands are not in Slush. Try a few:

```
TINI /> whoami
ERROR: Unknown Command: whoami

TINI /> who
ERROR: Unknown Command: who
```

Also notice that "help" does not list the commands you deleted.

Adding optional commands to slush

Now that you have deleted some commands from slush, you have room to add some new commands. Some commands come with slush but are not in the initial version to save space (if they were included slush would exceed 64kbytes). You can add these if you want to use them. These commands are: `PPPCommand.class`, `SledCommand.class`, `PollMemoryCommand.class`, `ThreadStatCommand.class`, and `DiffCommand.class`. These are found in `%TINI_HOME%\src\OptionalSlushCommandsSrc.jar`. The command lines options and function of these commands were discussed near the beginning of this chapter. To add these commands:

```
C:\> cd \projects\slush
C:\> jar -xf %TINI_HOME%\src\OptionalSlushCommandsSrc.jar
```

This will unjar the optional slush commands into `com\dalsemi\slush\command`, so be sure to change directory to `\projects\slush` so these new optional commands will be placed in the existing slush hierarchy.

Edit slush.java and add some of these lines to the `initializeShellCommands()` method:

```
CommandInterpreter.addCommand("PPP", new PPPCommand());
CommandInterpreter.addCommand("sled", new SledCommand());
CommandInterpreter.addCommand("pollmemory", new PollMemoryCommand());
CommandInterpreter.addCommand("threadstat", new ThreadStatCommand());
CommandInterpreter.addCommand("diff", new DiffCommand());
```

You probably can't get away with adding all of these commands at once, unless you remove a number of existing commands, because you will exceed the 64kbyte limit for the flash file format.

Compile slush and run TINIConvertor. If you see output of TINIConvertor similar to the following, then you have exceeded the 64kbyte limit and you need to remove some slush commands (and don't forget to delete *all* of the class files for the commands you deleted).

```
Converting to flash format. (76497 bytes)
Segment start address: 70100, length: 65280, CRC: 39fc
*****************************************************************************
*****************************************************************************
Warning, address exceeds normal TINI flash memory boundaries!
(0x80000)
*****************************************************************************
*****************************************************************************
Segment start address: 80000, length: 11217, CRC: e9b0
Flash file size: 76511
Finished with build.
```

Adding new commands to slush

But it doesn't end there. We can just as easily create our own commands and add them to slush. For this, we are putting back in the commands we deleted or commented out in the previous steps and removing the optional commands that we added, as they are going to take memory space. We will be then be adding a new command, `owr`, (for 1-Wire report), which will list all 1-Wire devices by type and serial number on all 1-Wire busses. This is the source for `OwrCommand.java` that implements the `owr` command. Copy the file to the slush\command directory.

Listing 7-2: OwrCommand.java

```java
package com.dalsemi.slush.command;

import com.dalsemi.shell.server.*;
import java.io.*;
import java.util.*;
import com.dalsemi.system.*;
import com.dalsemi.slush.*;
import com.dalsemi.onewire.*;
import com.dalsemi.onewire.adapter.*;
import com.dalsemi.onewire.container.*;

public class OwrCommand implements SlushCommand
{
    public String getUsageString()
    {
        return "owr\r\n\r\nDisplay current 1-wire devlice list.";
    }

    public void execute(SystemInputStream in, SystemPrintStream out,
                        SystemPrintStream err, String[] args,
```

```
                        Hashtable env) throws Exception
{
    boolean verbose = false;
    for(int i = 0; i < args.length; i++) {
        if(args[i].equals("-v")) {
            verbose = true;
        }
        else {
            out.println(getUsageString());
            return;
        }
    }

    Slush slush = (Slush)TINIOS.getShell();

    try
    {
        Enumeration adapter_enum =
                OneWireAccessProvider.enumerateAllAdapters();

        while( adapter_enum.hasMoreElements() ) {
            DSPortAdapter adapter=(DSPortAdapter)
                            adapter_enum.nextElement();
            out.println( "Adapter: " + adapter.getAdapterName() );

            adapter.setSearchAllDevices();
            adapter.targetAllFamilies();
            Enumeration ibutton_enum =
                adapter.getAllDeviceContainers();

            while( ibutton_enum.hasMoreElements() ) {
                OneWireContainer node =
                    (OneWireContainer) ibutton_enum.nextElement();
                out.println(node.getName() + " - " +
                    node.getAddressAsString());
            }
        }
    }
    catch (Exception e)
    {
        out.println("Error displaying stats");
        out.println(e);
    }
  }
}
```

You may notice that this is essentially an extension of the FindDevices.java
program we developed in Chapter 5 to verify we installed the 1-Wire libraries
properly. If you are curious how this works, you can compare this program to any of
the other slush commands. We have only implemented two methods:

`getUsageString()` and `execute()`. The `getUsageString()` method is called from slush whenever the user asks for help on this command (`help owr`). The `execute()` method is called from `slush` whenever the user types the `owr` command by the slush command interpreter. This command then asks the TINI firmware for a list of all 1-Wire adapters:

```
Enumeration adapter_enum =
OneWireAccessProvider.enumerateAllAdapters();
        while( adapter_enum.hasMoreElements() ) {
            DSPortAdapter  adapter=(DSPortAdapter)
                            adapter_enum.nextElement();
            out.println( "Adapter: " + adapter.getAdapterName() );
            . . .
```

We then ask each adapter it finds for a list of all 1-Wire devices connected to that adapter:

```
            adapter.setSearchAllDevices();
            adapter.targetAllFamilies();
            Enumeration ibutton_enum =
                            adapter.getAllDeviceContainers();
            while( ibutton_enum.hasMoreElements() ) {
                . . .
```

We then print out a little information on each 1-Wire device.

```
            OneWireContainer node =
                (OneWireContainer) ibutton_enum.nextElement();
            out.println(node.getName() + " - " +
                            node.getAddressAsString());
```

We will be getting deeper into the 1-Wire API and the details of 1-Wire in Chapter 10.

To add this new command to slush, edit `Slush.java` and in the `initializeShellCommands()` method, add a line like the following to add the `owr` command to the command interpreter:

```
    CommandInterpreter.addCommand("owr", new OwrCommand());
```

Save `slush.java`, recompile slush and run `TINIConvertor` exactly as we did in the previous examples.

```
C:\>set SMUSH=\projects\modslush
C:\>javac -classpath %TINI_HOME%\bin\tiniclasses.jar;%SMUSH%
Slush.java
C:\>java  -cp %TINI_HOME%\bin\tini.jar TINIConvertor
        -o Slush.tbin -l
        -d %TINI_HOME%\bin\tini.db
        -f .
```

. . .

```
Converting to flash format. (57585 bytes)
Segment start address: 70100, length: 57585, CRC: 78da
Flash file size: 57592
Finished with build.
```

Use JavaKit to send the slush.tbin file to TINI and then test it.

```
TINI /> owr
Adapter: TINIExternalAdapter
Device type: 10 - 700000004B8F1010
Device type: 18 - 1C00000002795818
Device type: 12 - CB00000017006112
Device type: 01 - 21000007997D9F01
Adapter: TINIInternalAdapter
Device type: 89 - 9F5E70005C8D1089
```

Wow, it works! Notice the "`Device type:`" for the container name. That's because we didn't use `BuildDependency` to build in the container classes that contain the actual names of the 1-Wire devices. Now this is where `BuildDependency` gets tricky (or just plain odd). We would think this command would work (due to DOS command line limits you may need to put the following into a batch file and execute that):

```
C:\> java  -cp %TINI_HOME%\bin\tini.jar BuildDependency
           -f .
           -o slush.tbin
           -l
           -d %TINI_HOME%\bin\tini.db
           -x %TINI_HOME%\bin\owapi_dep.txt
           -p %TINI_HOME%\bin\owapi_dependencies_TINI.jar
           -add OneWireContainer01;OneWireContainer10
           -debug
```

Notice that we included the `-add OneWireContainer01;OneWireContainer10` which tells `BuildDependency` to include the class files for these classes by looking them up in the `owapi_dep.txt` file, which tells `BuildDependency` which .class files to include from `owapi_dependencies_TINI.jar`.

But it doesn't work.

```
Could not create the application: Could not Add class com/dalsemi/
onewire/container/OneWireContainer01 JiBDB Error: Attempted addition
of duplicate class "com/dalsemi/onewire/container/OneWireContainer01"
BuildDependency clean-up complete.
The program did not successfully terminate.
Try running with the '-debug' option to determine the cause.
```

This is really odd. Why does it think we are adding a duplicate class of `OneWireContainer01`? It has to do with the way BuildDependency looks for included files. It's possible to get BuildDependency to work with something like the following:

```
C:\>java  -cp %TINI_HOME%\bin\tini.jar BuildDependency
          -f slush.class
          -f commandinterpreter.class
          -f command\
          -f Slush$SlushDHCPListener.class
          -o slush.tbin
          -l
          -d %TINI_HOME%\bin\tini.db
          -x %TINI_HOME%\bin\owapi_dep.txt
          -p %TINI_HOME%\bin\owapi_dependencies_TINI.jar
          -add OneWireContainer01;OneWireContainer10
          -debug
```

However, this gets rather unmanageable. For one thing, javac will split up large class files into several smaller pieces. (Look at the directory in which we are compiling Slush right now. You will see Slush$1.class as well as Slush.class.) We will need to include all of these intermediate class files using the –f directive to BuildDependency. A simpler way to deal with this is to compile Slush from one level higher in the directory hierarchy and let the –f directive include the whole subdirectory we are using.

```
C:\> cd ..
C:\> notepad build.bat
```

Enter the following into Notepad (or your favorite text editor) but as a single line of text:

```
java  -cp %TINI_HOME%\bin\tini.jar BuildDependency
      -f slush
      -o slush.tbin
      -l
      -d %TINI_HOME%\bin\tini.db
      -x %TINI_HOME%\bin\owapi_dep.txt
      -p %TINI_HOME%\bin\owapi_dependencies_TINI.jar
      -add OneWireContainer01;OneWireContainer10 -debug
```

What we are doing is including the whole slush subdirectory by using the -f slush command line switch. This is much easier than worrying about what intermediate files the Java compiler creates. We need to execute this batch file on the directory that contains the slush directory (not in the slush directory) since we are specifying the whole slush directory with the -f slush commandline directive.

For the remainder of this book, most TINI programs will be compiled in a separate directory (as we are doing here) of the same name as the main class name. In the directory we will have a src and a bin directory. The Java source files will reside in the src directory and we will direct javac to put the class files into the bin directory. We will also have TINIConvertor or BuildDependency place the tbin or tini files in the bin directory. This will greatly help with running class files through BuildDepencency as we can convert the entire bin directory and not have to specify multiple files in complex builds.

Compile Slush:

```
C:\> build
...
Converting to flash format. (59119 bytes)
Segment start address: 70100, length: 59119, CRC: 70bc
Flash file size: 59126
Finished with build.
```

We can then load this version of slush onto TINI and test it out.

```
TINI /> owr
Adapter: TINIExternalAdapter
DS1920 - 700000004B8F1010
Device type: 18 - 1C00000002795818
Device type: 12 - CB00000017006112
DS1990A - 21000007997D9F01
Adapter: TINIInternalAdapter
Device type: 89 - 9F5E70005C8D1089
```

You may be wondering why we only included `OneWireContainer01` and `OneWireContainer10` when there are more devices connected to TINI. The primary reason is that if we add the other containers then we will seriously exceed the 64kbyte limit. Why's that? Take a peek in the file `\opt\tini\bin\owapi_dep.txt` and see why. This file tells `BuildDependency` where to find all of the classes that are needed by each container type. Look at line 20 where `OneWireContainer18` is defined (CONT_ROOT is defined as "com.dalsemi.onewire.container") so this line means that `OneWireConatiner18` includes the following classes:

```
com.dalsemi.onewire.container.OneWireContainer18
com.dalsemi.onewire.container.MemoryBank
com.dalsemi.onewire.container.MemoryBankNV
com.dalsemi.onewire.container.MemoryBankNVCRC
com.dalsemi.onewire.container.MemoryBankScratch
com.dalsemi.onewire.container.MemoryBankScratchCRC
com.dalsemi.onewire.container.MemoryBankScratchEx
com.dalsemi.onewire.container.MemoryBankScratchSHA
com.dalsemi.onewire.container.PagedMemoryBank
com.dalsemi.onewire.container.ScratchPad
com.dalsemi.onewire.container.SHAiButton
```

The other containers are similarly defined. If we include several of these into our version of slush (using the –add option), then suddenly we are adding a lot of classes.

Other Tools to Make Life Simpler

Utilities

Using DOS batch files

On our Windows 98 computers, these commands for BuildDependency are too long to type in a DOS command window. DOS seems to limit any single command we type to 127 characters. To get around this, we need to create a batch file (like build.bat) and enter the command in there. There doesn't seem to be a limit to the command length in a batch file. Then all we need to do is execute the build.bat file, which also saves in typing when we need to rerun BuildDependency.

Here is a batch file that we find quite handy. This can easily be tailored to compile each new application. It will also FTP your .tini file to TINI stick if the compile completes successfully. Note that you will need to specify the hostname of your TINI either in the batch file (set TINI=name) or on the command line or have the DOS environment variable MYTINI set (set MYTINI=whatever). This batch file is well commented, so we will not discuss it in detail here.

Listing 7-3: Build.bat

```
@echo off
:: Build TINI and 1-Wire programs and optionally ftp the file to your TINI
::
:: Fill in PROG as the name of the program to compile
::      ex: SET PROG=Thermometer
:: Add "-add" and class names to the BuildDependency list as neeed
::      Seperate muiltiple classes with a semicolon (;)
::      ex: SET ARGS=-add OneWireContainer10
:: Add your TINI host name. The first command line parameter will override
::      this setting if provided. If not set and no parameter then the
::      environment variable MYTINI will be used. If none of these are
::      specified then the file will NOT be ftp'ed anywhere
::      ex: SET HOST=TINI01
:: If you get an "Out of environment space" error from DOS then add
::      SHELL=C:\COMMAND.COM C:\ /E:2048 /P
::      to your config.sys and reboot.

SET ·PROG=Thermometer
SET ARGS=-add Thermometers
SET TINI=

:: — No need to mess with whats below this line —

:: Check to see if any environment variables are set, complain as needed.

IF "%TINI_HOME%"=="" GOTO notini
IF "%OW_HOME%"=="" GOTO noow
IF "%CLASSPATH%"=="" GOTO noclass
GOTO begin

:notini
ECHO Environment variable "TINI_HOME" is not set.
GOTO end
```

233

```
:noow
ECHO Environment variable "OW_HOME" is not set.
GOTO end

:noclass
ECHO Environment variable "CLASSPATH" is not set.
ECHO You may have trouble running this program"

:: Good so far. Look for a bin directory, create as needed.

:begin
Echo Looking for bin directory
IF EXIST bin GOTO next
mkdir bin

:: OK, lets compile. Look for errors on the way, bail if any.

:next
Echo Building %PROG%

echo javac ...
javac -bootclasspath %TINI_HOME%\bin\tiniclasses.jar -d bin
src\%PROG%.java

IF ERRORLEVEL 1 GOTO end

echo TINIConvertor ...
java -classpath %TINI_HOME%\bin\tini.jar;. BuildDependency -p
%TINI_HOME%\bin\owapi_dependencies_TINI.jar -f bin -x
%TINI_HOME%\bin\owapi_dep.txt -o bin\%PROG%.tini -d
%TINI_HOME%\bin\tini.db %ARGS%

IF ERRORLEVEL 1 GOTO end

:: Lets send the .tini file to the TINI
:: Use %1 as first coice. Then look for %TINI% then %MYTINI%
:: Give up if none of these

IF NOT "%1"=="" SET TINI=%1
IF "%TINI%"=="" SET TINI=%MYTINI%
IF "%TINI%"=="" GOTO end

:: Make a temp file "ftptotini"
echo sending %PROG%.tini to %TINI% ...
echo open %TINI%> ftptotini
echo root>> ftptotini
echo tini>> ftptotini
echo send bin/%PROG%.tini>> ftptotini
echo quit>> ftptotini
:: send file using ftp script
```

```
ftp -s:ftptotini
:: clean up
del ftptotini

:end

echo .
echo Done!
```

We have found the following tools to be quite helpful when developing Java applications in general and for TINI.

Using FTP

We have used FTP to copy files from our computer to our TINI. In the development of our programs we use FTP repeatedly for copying the same file. Here is a simple way to automate this FTP step. If you are using FTP under Windows, FTP is able to take a script file

```
C:\> ftp -s:script.ftp
```

where the script file contains the things you would normally type at the FTP prompt. This is what this script.ftp file looks like. You should personalize it to include the IP address of your TINI and the filename of the program you are developing.

```
open 192.168.1.85
root
tini
send TiniWebStat.tini
quit
```

If you are using FTP from Unix or Linux, this is a little different. Use lftp instead, as this also deals nicely with script files, just a little differently than the Windows version of FTP:

```
% lftp -f script.lftp
```

where this script file contains the things you would normally type at the lftp prompt. This is what this script.lftp file looks like. Again, as with FTP, you should personalize it to include the IP address of your TINI and the filename of the program you are developing.

```
open 192.168.1.85
user root tini
put TiniWebStat.tini
quit
```

Alternately, you can specify everything on the command line:

```
lftp -e "put bin/TiniWebStat.tini;quit" -u root,tini 192.168.1.85
```

With either of these, FTP or lftp, you can add any other FTP command you need to get the job done, like `cd` to change directory or even use `get` to retrieve files from

TINI and `rm` or `delete` to delete files from TINI. Note that if you use both Windows and Linux, FTP and lftp don't have exactly the same command set.

Using the DOS command window

When you are using Windows as your development environment you will be using a DOS[16] command window quite a bit. You can make this a little easier to use. First, you should put an icon on your desktop that is a link to command.com. Using Windows Explorer, find command.com (it's in `c:\windows\`). Right click on command.com and select "copy." Then right click on your desktop and select "Paste Shortcut." You can double click on this icon to open a DOS command window. This opens a DOS window with the initial directory as c:\windows by default. You can change this to be your TINI development directory and assign a batch file to this DOS command window shortcut. Right-click on the icon we just put on your desktop and select properties and then pick the "Program" tab. Here you can enter the working directory and assign a batch file to be run whenever that DOS windows is opened. The batch file is run first and then the working directory is set. You can leave the working directory blank and use the batch file to change to the appropriate directory if you like, but as we tend to change this with each project, it's simpler to change the DOS Prompt Properties.

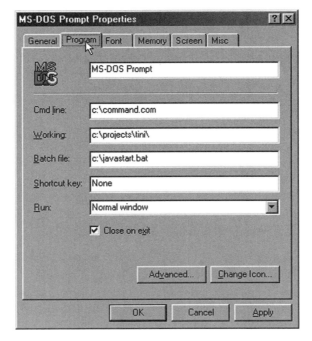

Figure 7-18: Assigning a batch file to a DOS window

---

[16] *The EasyDOS Internet Guide to DOS* – http://www.easydos.com/

Here is what I use for a batch file (`javastart.bat` in the example)

```
doskey
mode con: lines=43
ls
```

`doskey` lets you use the up/down arrow keys to view previous commands and it keeps a short command history. The `mod con: lines=43` sets the DOS window to 43 lines of text.

GNUmake

We have not been using make or any other program development tool so far because we want you to see the CLASSPATH and command line options to the Java compiler and run time system so you can get comfortable with all of the options you need to use to develop TINI and 1-Wire applications. For the rest of the book, we will only show the CLASSPATH or command line options when they are significant. We will probably be using a batch file as mentioned above or make (as in GNUmake).

Linux

If you don't have it installed on Linux, you can get it from the GNUmake web page[17]. Follow the Link for the make RPM. Download the RPM to a temporary directory and install.

```
% rpm -install make-3.79.1-7-i386.html
```

Windows

For Windows 95/98/NT/2000/XP, you will need to get Karl M. Syring's "GNU utilities for Win32"[18]. This is a set of GNU tools that have been ported to the Windows environment. You can install the whole package or just pull the individual make program (and any others that you may want, like ls) out of the archive and stick them someplace that's on your PATH (we use `c:/opt/bin`). Download the `UnxUtils.zip` files and save to a temporary folder. Using your favorite zip/unzip utility, extract the directory hierarchy in the temporary folder. Create a bin folder in the opt folder; this is where we will add our assorted utilities. If you already have a preferred folder for adding utilities, use that. Unzipping the `UnxUtil.zip` file will create a folder hierarchy similar to a Unix hierarchy for GNU tools. Using Windows Explorer, change to the `usr\local\wbin` folder that was created when you extracted the zip file. Find the `make.exe` file and copy it to your `c:\opt\bin folder`. Make sure this `c:\opt\bin\` is added to your PATH environment variable in your `autoexec.bat` file using the same method we added to it in the previous paragraphs. If you are not familiar with GNU make, the complete GNU tool manuals can be found at the web site "Documentation of the GNU Project"[19].

---

[17] GNUmake – http://www.gnu.org/gnulist/production/make.html

[18] GNU utilities for Win32 – http://www.weihenstephan.de/~syring/win32/UnxUtils.htm

[19] Documentation of the GNU Project – http://www.gnu.org/manual/

Here is a makefile that is the equivalent of the DOS batch file presented above. It does essentially the same thing. You need to modify the first three definitions in the makefile. This makefile will work on both Windows and Linux operating systems. You can certainly modify this makefile for more or less complex operation. You will need to consult the make manual[20] for details on what you can do with make.

Listing 7-4: Makefile

```
# A Generic GNUmake file for either WINDOWS/DOS or Linux.
#
# GNUmake allows for Linux style directory separators "/" or Windows style "\"
# Use Linux for compatability

# GNUmake allows for Linux style directory separators "/" or Windows style "\"
# Use Linux for compatability

# Build TINI and 1-Wire programs and optionally ftp the file to your TINI
#
# Fill in PROG as the name of the program to compile
#      ex: PROG=Thermometer
# Add "-add" and class names to the BuildDependency list as neeed
#      Seperate muiltiple classes with a semicolon (;) to work on
#      Windows or a colon (:) to cork on both Windows and Linux
#      ex: ARGS=-add OneWireContainer10
# Add your TINI host name. The first command line parameter will override
#      this setting if provided. If not set and no parameter then the
#      environment variable MYTINI will be used. If none of these are
#      specified then the file will NOT be ftp'ed anywhere
#      ex: SET HOST=TINI01
# If you get an "Out of environment space" error from DOS then add
#      SHELL=C:\COMMAND.COM C:\ /E:2048 /P
#      to your config.sys and reboot.

# SET THESE
PROG=Thermometer
TINI=
ARGS=-add Thermometers

# Now tell me where all of the various components are. Note that Windows is
# not case sensitive BUT Linux is. If you plan to use this for BOTH platforms
# then watch the case. This also assumes that these APIs and JARs are installed
# in the same place on both systems (ie: /opt/... )

# Needs the environment variable OW_HOME to point to the 1-Wire
# install Directory
```

---

[20] GNUmake manual – http://www.gnu.org/manual/make-3.79.1/make.html

```
#       DOS ex:    SET OW_HOME=c:\opt\onewire
#       Bash ex:   OW_HOME=/opt/onewire; export OW_HOME
# and the environment variable TINI_HOME to point to the TINI API
#       install directory
#       DOS ex:    SET TINI_HOME=c:\opt\tini
#       Bash ex:   TINI_HOME=/opt/tini; export TINI_HOME

javax_comm = /opt/jdk/lib/comm.jar
one_wire_lib = $(OW_HOME)/lib/OneWireAPI.jar
tini_classes = $(TINI_HOME)/bin/tiniclasses.jar
tini_tools = $(TINI_HOME)/bin/tini.jar
tini_one_wire_lib = $(TINI_HOME)/bin/owapi_dependencies_TINI.jar
tini_db = $(TINI_HOME)/bin/tini.db
build_x = $(TINI_HOME)/bin/owapi_dep.txt
build_p = $(TINI_HOME)/bin/owapi_dependencies_TINI.jar


# Your CLASSPATH must include
$(tini_tools);$(javax_comm);$(one_wire_lib);.


# You don't need to modify ANYTHING below this line. At least I don't
think so.


# Here we compose the CLASSPATH (CP) for javac and java.
# This varies depending on the operating system.
# There ought to be a better way to do this.

ifdef COMSPEC
        # Then we are on a WIN machine
        platform = "Windows"
        T1 = $(tini_classes);$(tini_one_wire_lib);$(tini_tools);.
        C1 = $(javax_comm);$(one_wire_lib);.
        CP = SET
CLASSPATH=$(tini_tools);$(javax_comm);$(one_wire_lib);.
        CLASSES_T = $(subst /,\,$(T1))
        CLASSES   = $(subst /,\,$(C1))
else
        # We are on a Linux machine
          platform = "Linux"
        CLASSES_T =
$(tini_classes):$(tini_tools):$(tini_one_wire_lib):.
        CLASSES = $(javax_comm):$(one_wire_lib):.
        CP = CLASSPATH=$(tini_tools):$(javax_comm):$(one_wire_lib):.
endif


# Make ALL
all:
        -mkdir bin
        @echo Building $(PROG)
        @echo javac ...
```

```
        @javac -classpath $(CLASSES_T) -d bin src/$(PROG).java
        @echo BuildDependency ...
        @java -cp $(tini_tools) BuildDependency -p $(build_p) -x
$(build_x) \
        -d $(tini_db) -f bin  -o bin/$(PROG).tini $(ARGS)

        @echo sending $(PROG).tini to $(TINI) ...

ifdef COMSPEC
        @echo open $(TINI)> ftptotini
        @echo root>> ftptotini
        @echo tini>> ftptotini
        @echo send bin/$(PROG).tini>> ftptotini
        @echo quit>> ftptotini      @ftp -s:ftptotini
        del ftptotini
else
        @lftp -e "put bin/$(PROG).tini;quit" -u root,tini $(TINI)
endif
        @echo Done!


info:
        @echo PROG      = $(PROG)
        @echo ARGS      = $(ARGS)
        @echo TINI      = $(TINI)
        @echo MYTINI    = $(MYTINI)
        @echo OW_HOME   = $(OW_HOME)
        @echo TINI_HOME = $(TINI_HOME)
        @echo CLASSPATH = $(CLASSPATH)
```

JEdit

jEdit[21] is a very nice editor for Java. It's not absolutely necessary, since Windows Notepad and Linux's vi do just fine. However, jEdit is a programmer's text editor and so it makes writing Java significantly easier. It is released under the GNU General Public License. jEdit requires Java 2 (or Java 1.1 with Swing 1.1). It has an easy-to-use interface that resembles that of many other Windows and MacOS text editors, is extremely customizable, and has an extensive feature set that includes, among other things:

- Syntax highlighting

- Auto indent with support for intelligent indentation

- Search and replace with support for regular expressions, and searching in multiple files

---

[21] jEdit – http://jedit.sourceforge.net/

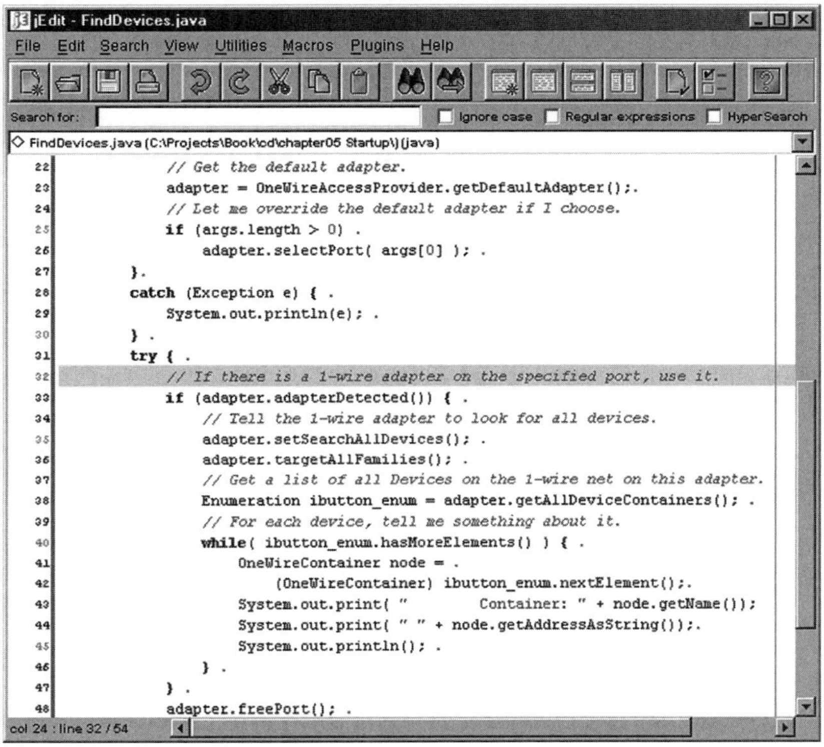

Figure 7-19: jEdit

- Bracket matching
- Multiple clipboards
- Split-window operation
- Word wrap
- Macro recording
- Support for plugins, which extend the editor's functionality

Other TINI Software

A number of people have developed some nice software for running on TINI or for use in developing programs for TINI. Here is a short list of some of these.

TiniHttpServer

TiniHttpServer[22] by Smart Software Consulting is a multi-threaded HTTP server for TINI that supports Java Servlets. TiniHttpServer turns your TINI into a web server with server-side programming capabilities. TiniHttpServer is ready to serve up your Java applets, HTML documents, and other files directly from your TINI. Included with it are eight demonstration servlets. TiniHttpServer is free and licensed under the GNU General Public License. Full source code is available.

TiniInstaller

TiniInstaller[23], also by Smart Software Consulting, is a user-friendly graphical user interface that simplifies the installation and configuration of software on your TINI. TiniInstaller offers a number of simplifying features:

- During the installation process, allows you to specify the file containing the TINI OS firmware (typically, tini.tbin).

- Performs diagnostics on your javax.comm installation and reports any problems using informative and helpful messages.

- Allows you to specify your TINI's network configuration in an easy-to-use GUI.

- Installs a complete working image into your TINI's RAM. This image, also called a TINI Package File, is a snapshot taken from an existing (and working) TINI's memory. This guarantees that your TINI will have the exact same file system and heap as a working TINI.

- Ensures that the version of installed firmware matches the version required by the TINI Package File.

- Streamlines the installation process by installing the TINI Package file included in TiniInstaller's jar file (if present).

TINIAnt

TiniAnt[24] (pronounced "tiny ant" or "teeny ant") is an extension to Ant that simplifies building applications for the TINI. Ant is a *portable* project management tool for Java projects, replacing system-specific build scripts and makefiles. You write a build description in XML, and Ant does the rest, generally speeding things up since it rarely needs to invoke additional instances of the Java Virtual Machine. You can learn more about Ant on the Jakarta Site Ant[25] page.

---

[22] TiniHttServer – http://www.smartsc.com/tini/TiniHttpServer/docs/index.html
[23] TiniInstaller – http://www.smartsc.com/tini/TiniInstaller/index.html
[24] TiniAnt – http://www.ad1440.net/~kelly/sw/tiniant/index.html
[25] Jakarta site, Ant page – http://jakarta.apache.org/ant/index.html

Conclusion

In this chapter we have shown you the various software programs and applications that you can use to program your TINI microcontroller. You should be very familiar with the needed tools before you start off developing your own applications. We highly recommend a good editor as it will certainly make your work simpler. jEdit is a very good choice.

For the rest of the book, we will only show the CLASSPATH or command line options when they are significant, so you should thoroughly understand all of the needed classes for both compiling and running the various programs and tools. The batch file that we used to compile the programs will, however, be included in the companion CD.

References

1. *Request For Comment Editor,*
   http://www.rfc-editor.org/

2. *Introducing TINI: Tiny InterNet Interface,*
   http://www.iButton.com/TINI/

3. *Your view of the Java universe,*
   http://www.jguru.com/

4. *The Tiny InterNet Interface FAQ,*
   http://www.jguru.com/faq/home.jsp?topic=TINI

5. *TINI Community Contributions,*
   http://www.ibutton.com/TINI/developers/community.html

6. *GNU's Not Unix,*
   http://www.gnu.org/

8

Enhancing TINI

In Chapter 6 we discussed the hardware perspective of the TINI stick, but TINI and its associated socket board were designed with flexibility and expansion in mind. In this chapter we will discuss a number of additions for TINI; some are part of the Dallas Semiconductor E10/E20 socket board but most are additional circuitry and are intended to demonstrate how you can add new peripherals to your TINI. For each new device, we will give detailed schematics and a Java program to demonstrate the capabilities of that device.

Adding 512 kbytes on the SIMM

TINI is currently available from Dallas Semiconductor in two versions depending on the amount of SRAM included on the stick: one version with 512 kbytes of SRAM (DSTINI1-512) and the other version with 1 Mbyte (two 512 kbyte chips) of SRAM (DSTINI1-1MG). Early in TINI's development, Dallas Semiconductor was only shipping the 512 kbyte version but is now shipping both.

The amount of memory that the TINI stick knows is available for use was determined by a software memory probe at boot time in the TINI API previous to version 1.02. In API 1.02, the amount of memory available is determined by examining the contents of the DS2502 1-Wire chip (1024 bits of write-once memory) on the TINI stick. This was implemented to avoid some of the possible errors that occur with a software probe[1]. It is possible to add memory to your TINI stick if you purchased a 512-kbyte version, but you will need to reprogram the DS2502 for the API to recognize that additional memory. This is not a simple effort, as the DS2502 needs a 12-volt program voltage to perform the EPROM write and this is not available on the TINI stick. You must remove the DS2502 and connect it to a 1-Wire bus that can deliver a

---

[1] Much valuable information on the internal details of TINI is released by the Dallas Semiconductor engineers using the TINI Discussion Mailing List – http://lists.dalsemi.com/ mailman/listinfo/tini

12-volt program pulse. If you are purchasing a new TINI, it is much more cost-effective to purchase a TINI with the full 1 Mbyte of memory than to purchase a 512-kbyte version and add another 512 kbyte on your own.

Figure 8-1:
Photo of second SRAM location

In the event that you decide to add memory to the TINI stick, the possible memories that are pin-for-pin compatible with the layout of the TINI stick are shown in Table 8-1.

Table 8-1: SRAM part numbers

Symbol	Part Number	Description	Manufacturer
U5	HM628512BLTT5[1]	512Kbyte SRAM	Hitachi Semiconductor
	M5M5408BTP-55L[2]		Mitsubishi Semiconductor
	K6T4008C1C[3]		Samsung Semiconductor

[1] HM628512BLTT5 – http://www.halsp.hitachi.com/products/pdf/msmtd031d5.pdf
[2] M5M5408BTP-55L – http://www.mitsubishichips.com/data/datasheets/memory/mempdf/ds/d99024.pdf
[3] K6T4008C1C – http://www.usa.samsungsemi.com/Memory/SRAM/Asynchronous_Low_Power/4M_bit/K6T4008C1C/K6T4008C1C.pdf

Note that each of these memory chips is available in several speeds and several package styles. TINI uses the 55-ns memory in the 32-lead TSOP (thin small outline package).

Use the `df` command to find out the amount of free memory after booting. A number less than 512,000 indicates one memory chip (or lots of stuff in the file system) and a number between 512,000 and 1,024,000 indicates two memory chips (1 megabyte). The exact amount of free RAM will vary depending on what you have stored on your file system. You can use the TINIOS class for your programs to determine the amount of free memory.

Listing 8-1: FreeMem.java

```
import com.dalsemi.system.*;
import com.dalsemi.tininet.*;
// Class FreeMem tells us how much FreeMemory TINI has available
class FreeMem {
    public static void main(String[] args) {
```

```
        String hn = TININet.getHostname();
        int ram   = TINIOS.getFreeRAM();
        System.out.println( "Node " + hn + " has " + ram + " free RAM." );
    }
}
```

Compile this and convert it to a TINI file with the following commands:

```
C:\> javac -bootclasspath %TINI_HOME%\bin\tiniclasses.jar
           -d bin src\FreeMem.java
C:\> java   -classpath %TINI_HOME%\bin\tini.jar;. BuildDependency
           -p %TINI_HOME%\bin\owapi_dependencies_TINI.jar
           -f bin
           -x %TINI_HOME%\bin\owapi_dep.txt
           -o bin\FreeMem.tini
           -d %TINI_HOME%\bin\tini.db
```

Try this out on a 1-megabyte TINI (and with a relatively empty file system):

```
TINI /> java FreeMem.tini
Node TINI has 710528 free RAM.
TINI />
```

The amount of memory TINI has installed is stored on the DS2502. If the data in page 0 of the DS2502 is corrupted, TINI tries to figure out the amount of available memory using a software probe. If you add memory it will be wrong until you corrupt the DS2502. Be careful as this is where the TINI MAC address is stored. [2] [3] The following program dumps the contents of the DS2505 in hex and ASCII so we can see what's there:

Listing 8-2: UniDump.java

```
import java.util.*;
import com.dalsemi.onewire.*;
import com.dalsemi.onewire.adapter.*;
import com.dalsemi.onewire.container.*;
import com.dalsemi.onewire.utils.*;

// Class UniDump - Tells us all about whats stored in the TINI
// UniquieWare 1-wire chip
class UniDump {

    public static void dump( byte[] data, int width)
    {
        int i=0;
        boolean done=false;
```

---

[2] DS2502 Data sheet – http://pdfserv.maxim-ic.com/arpdf/DS2502.pdf

[3] DS2502-UNW data sheet from Dalsemi – http://pdfserv.maxim-ic.com/arpdf/
DS2502-UNW-DS2506S-UNW.pdf

```
        int w = width;
        int pad=0;

        do {
            if ((i+width)>(data.length-1)) {
                done=true;
                w=data.length-i;
                pad=(width-w)*3;
            }
            System.out.print( ByteUtils.toHexString(data,i,w) );
            for (int j=0; j<pad; j++) System.out.print( " " );
            System.out.print( "     " );
            System.out.println( ByteUtils.toAsciiString(data, i,w) );

            i+=width;
        } while (!done);
    }

    public static void main(String[] args)
    {
        try {
            DSPortAdapter adapter = OneWireAccessProvider.getAdapter(
            "TINIInternalAdapter", "default" );
            System.out.println( "Adapter: " + adapter.getAdapterName() );
            System.out.println( "Port: " + adapter.getPortName() );

            if (adapter.adapterDetected()) {
                System.out.println( "Searching for all 2502 devices" );
                System.out.println( "(0x89 family code devices)" );
                adapter.setSearchAllDevices();
                adapter.targetFamily( 0x89 );

                Enumeration ibutton_enum = adapter.getAllDeviceContainers();
                while( ibutton_enum.hasMoreElements() ) {
                    OneWireContainer node =
                        (OneWireContainer) ibutton_enum.nextElement();
                    System.out.print( "Found Container " + node.getName() );
                    System.out.println( "at address "
                        + node.getAddressAsString() );
                    System.out.println( "" );

                    for (Enumeration banks=node.getMemoryBanks();
                            banks.hasMoreElements(); ) {
                        //
                        Object memobj = banks.nextElement();
                        MemoryBank mem = (MemoryBank)memobj;
                        PagedMemoryBank pmb = (PagedMemoryBank)memobj;

                        System.out.println( "Has "
```

```
                           + pmb.getNumberPages() + " pages of "
                           + pmb.getPageLength() + " bytes each" );

                   int pages = pmb.getNumberPages();

                   System.out.println( "Bank: "
                       + mem.getBankDescription() );
                   System.out.print( "size is "
                       + mem.getSize() );
                   System.out.print( ", start address is "
                       + mem.getStartPhysicalAddress() );
                   System.out.println("");

                   if (mem.isWriteOnce()) {
                       System.out.print( "write protected" );
                   }
                   if (mem.isReadWrite()) {
                       System.out.print( ", read/write" );
                   }
                   if (mem.isNonVolatile()) {
                       System.out.print( ", non volatile" );
                   }
                   if (mem.isReadOnly()) {
                       System.out.print( ", read only" );
                   }
                   if (mem.needsPowerDelivery()) {
                       System.out.print( ", needs power delivery" );
                   }
                   if (mem.needsProgramPulse()) {
                       System.out.print( ", needs program pulse" );
                   }
                   System.out.println( "" );

                   byte[] buff2=new byte[pmb.getPageLength()];
                   for (int i=0; i<pages; i++) {
                       pmb.readPageCRC( i, false, buff2, 0 );
                       dump( buff2, 16 );
                       System.out.println( "" );
                   }
               }
           }
       }
       adapter.freePort();
   }
   catch (Exception e) {
       System.out.println(e);
       }
   }
}
```

This program uses two methods from the `ByteUtils` class (found in Appendix B on the CD-ROM) to print out the byte array in hex and ASCII. To compile this, you need to add `-add OneWireCOntainer09` to the `BuildDependency` options:

```
C:\> cd src
C:\> javac -bootclasspath %TINI_HOME%\bin\tiniclasses.jar
            -d ..\bin UniDump.java
C:\> cd ..
C:\> java    -classpath %TINI_HOME%\bin\tini.jar;. BuildDependency
            -p %TINI_HOME%\bin\owapi_dependencies_TINI.jar
            -f bin
            -x %TINI_HOME%\bin\owapi_dep.txt
            -o bin\UniDump.tini
            -d %TINI_HOME%\bin\tini.db
            -add OneWireContainer09
```

Notice that we change the working directory to the directory where the Java source is located, so that javac can find the static methods in `ByteUtils.java` and compile that as well. We direct javac to place the class files in a separate directory (bin). We then run `BuildDependency` and tell it to convert the entire bin directory. We do this so we don't need to tell `BuildDependency` which files in that directory we want to convert (we want them all). We will use this technique throughout the book.

The output of this program (on a 1-Mb TINI) looks like this:

```
TINI /> java UniDump.tini
Adapter: TINIInternalAdapter
Port: default
Searching for all 2502 devices
(0x89 family code devices)
Found Container DS1982at address 0A5E70005D54B589

Has 4 pages of 32 bytes each
Bank: Main Memory
size is 128, start address is 0
write protected, non volatile, needs program pulse

0A 29 11 00 00 6D 8B 00 35 60 00 5B 9E FF FF FF     .)...m..5`.[....
FF FF FF FF FF FF FF FF FF FF FF FF FF FF FF FF     ................

1D 01 23 44 53 20 54 49 4E 49 20 4D 6F 64 65 6C     ..#DS TINI Model
20 33 39 30 20 52 65 76 20 44 20 44 53 54 F3 3C      390 Rev D DST.<

1D 49 4E 49 31 2D 31 4D 47 02 04 86 3E 36 3A 03     .INI1-1MG...>6:.
01 02 04 03 00 00 08 05 01 00 06 01 01 07 65 37     ..............e7

02 01 00 AF AF FF FF FF FF FF FF FF FF FF FF FF     ................
FF FF FF FF FF FF FF FF FF FF FF FF FF FF FF FF     ................
```

```
Has 1 pages of 8 bytes each
Bank: Write protect pages and Page redirection
size is 8, start address is 0
write protected, non volatile, needs program pulse

EE FF FF FF FF FF FF 00                                 . . . . . . . .

TINI />
```

In case you are curious what's here, in the first line of hex, the 6D 8B 00 35 60 00 (in bold in the UniDump output above) is the MAC address of this particular TINI. Compare this to the output of an earlier release of the TINI stick with 512 kbytes of memory. Not a lot of information was kept in the DS2502 (just the MAC address, also in bold, below).

```
0A 29 11 00 00 16 55 00 35 60 00 F9 C6 FF FF FF        .).....U.5`......
FF FF FF FF FF FF FF FF FF FF FF FF FF FF FF FF        ................

FF FF FF FF FF FF FF FF FF FF FF FF FF FF FF FF        ................
FF FF FF FF FF FF FF FF FF FF FF FF FF FF FF FF        ................

FF FF FF FF FF FF FF FF FF FF FF FF FF FF FF FF        ................
FF FF FF FF FF FF FF FF FF FF FF FF FF FF FF FF        ................

FF FF FF FF FF FF FF FF FF FF FF FF FF FF FF FF        ................
FF FF FF FF FF FF FF FF FF FF FF FF FF FF FF FF        ................
```

Adding 512 kbytes Flash Memory

The TINI stick has 512 kbytes of flash EEPROM that is used for storing the Java Virtual Machine and Slush. TINI uses an Advanced Micro Devices AM29F040B[4] 512-kbyte flash EEPROM. If you examine the memory map again, you will see that TINI can address 1 Mbyte of flash EEPROM. If you are using the E10/E20 socket board or you have constructed your own, you can add flash off stick. One of the biggest advantages of using a second flash chip is to allow for an alternate operating system. Notice in the section of the TINI socket board schematic shown below that the flash memory control logic is configured so that either the on-stick or the off-stick flash can be addressed first. If you change these solder-jumpers to a switch, you now have switch-selectable boot control. Notice that the flash EEPROM on the TINI stick is enabled with the /XCE0 line and the flash EEPROM on the TINI socketboard is enabled with the /RCE0.

---

[4] AM29F040B – http://www.amd.com/products/nvd/techdocs/21445.pdf

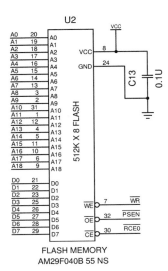

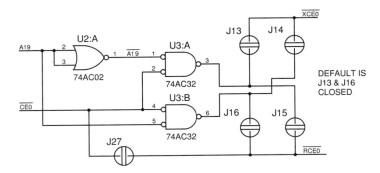

Figure 8-2:
EEPROM connections

FLASH MEMORY
AM29F040B 55 NS

If your socket board does not have provision for a second flash chip, then the /CE0 line is routed back onto the TINI stick as /XCE0. If you do have provision for a second flash then these two lines are controlled by the flash control with solder jumpers. These jumpers either bypass the flash control directly when J27 is shorted or determine which of the two flash chips is first addressed (/XCE0). The on-stick flash is first when J13 and J16 are shorted (as a pair) and the off-stick flash is first when J14 and J15 are shorted. Note that an unpopulated E10/E20 socketboard uses another solder jumper (J27) to bypass the flash control altogether.

Figure 8-3: Flash memory control

If you solder on the components for the flash control, then you can change these solder jumpers to select which flash your TINI uses to boot from. You can replace these solder jumpers with switches so you can select which flash ROM is the boot flash quicker then messing with solder jumpers.

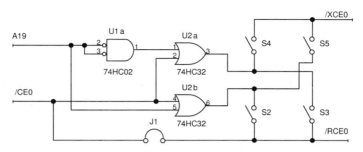

Figure 8-4: Flash memory switches

Adding a SIMM Connector

The current TINI stick is based on the common 72-pin SIMM (single inline memory module) standard. An early version of the TINI was based on a 68-pin SIMM but this was changed to take advantage of the more common 72-pin connectors that are popular for personal computer memory modules. The 72-pin SIMM socket is available in many configurations, depending on how you need to mount your TINI (for mounting the TINI stick perpendicular or parallel to the socket board). The TINI stick form factor conforms to the JEDEC JEP95 MO-116[5] standard specification, more or less. The TINI SIMM fits in a standard 72-pin SIM socket, including the key (the notch near pin 1) but the overall card height seems to be nonstandard. Molex[6] makes a number of 72-pin SIMM connectors as shown in Table 8-2.

Table 8-2: SIMM styles

1.27mm (.050") SIMM Socket – Left Polarization, Vertical, Metal Latch	78962
1.27mm (.050") SIMM Socket – Right Polarization, Vertical, Metal Latch	78962r
1.27mm (.050") SIMM Socket – Left Polarization, Low Profile (22.5°), Metal Latch	78964
1.27mm (.050") SIMM Socket – Left Polarization, Right Angle, Metal Latch	78968
1.27mm (.050") SIMM Socket – Left Polarization, Right Angle, Plastic Latch	78968l
1.27mm (.050") SIMM Socket – Right Polarization, Right Angle, Metal Latch, Surface Mount	78968m
1.27mm (.050") SIMM Socket – Right Polarization, Right Angle, Plastic Latch	78968p
1.27mm (.050") SIMM Socket – Right Polarization, Right Angle, Metal Latch	78968r
1.27mm (.050") SIMM Socket – Left Polarization, Right Angle, Metal Latch, Surface Mount	78968s
1.27mm (.050") SIMM Socket – Left Polarization, Low Profile (40°), Metal Latch	78976

[5] JEDEC MO-116 is part of JEP95, JEDEC Registered and Standard Outlines for Solid State and Related Products, http://www.jedec.org/, requires registration for access to free Standards.

[6] Molex – http://www.molex.com/

The E10/E20 sockets support a second SIMM connector for expansion boards. Adding a second SIMM connector is almost as simple as unclogging the soldered through-holes on the socket board and soldering in a second connector.

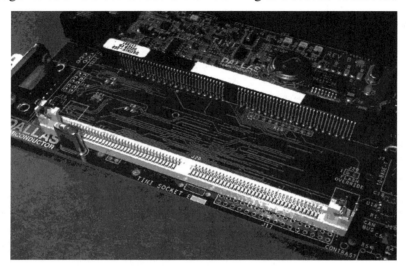

Figure 8-5: SIMM connector

So, what to do with a second SIMM socket? There are two current expansion boards on the market at the moment:

- **SIMMSerial** – The Systronix_SIMMSerial[7] is a TINI-pinout compatible, 72-pin SIMM module with dual hardware UARTS (16C552) compatible with the current TINI firmware. Each RS232 can be wired as DCE or DTE. One RS232 can be used as IrDA. The module works with any TINI system with an available SIMM72 socket.

- **protoModule** – The TINI protoModule[8] allows for further expansion of the TINI stick. The board is simply a 0.1" center grid of through holes on a 72-pin SIMM. This allows a developer to design a variety of circuitry on one or more protoModules and then plug them into a TINI socketboard equipped with a 72-pin SIMM connector for test and debug. ProtoModules can be used with a variety of boards such as the Dallas Semiconductor E10/E20, the Systronix STEP board and the Vinculum NEXUS board.

---

[7] Systronix SIMMSerial – http://www.systronix.com/expansion/exp_simm.htm
[8] Vinculum protoModule – http://www.vinculum.com/1005.php

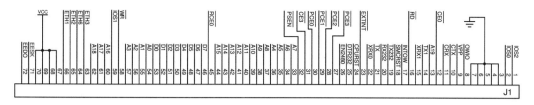

Figure 8-6: SIMM pinout

Adding Memory-mapped Devices

The rest of this chapter is devoted to adding memory-mapped devices to your TINI for user interaction. We will discuss adding other devices such as serial ports, I²C devices and other things in later parts of this book. We will be adding:

- Liquid crystal display

- 4-digit, 7-segment LED display

- Buttons for command input

- Keypad for text/numeric input

When we implement all of these devices, we will use a common address decoder and data bus buffer. The buttons and keypad also share some common interrupt logic as well. A simple block diagram of what we are adding is shown in Figure 8-7 to help give the big picture on how these components connect. We will start with the data bus buffer and the address decoder first, since the four input or display components use these. All of these components can be successfully implemented on solderless breadboards, soldered protoboards or any of the prototype systems for TINI that have been previously mentioned (such as the TINI protoModule or the TINI Nexus, both from Vinculum).

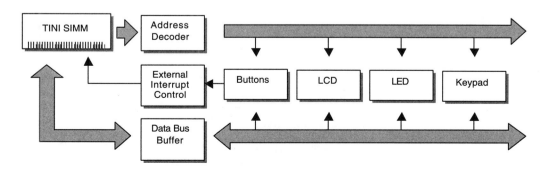

Figure 8-7: A block diagram of memory-mapped devices

Adding data bus buffer

As mentioned in the TINI datasheet[9], "The address bus, data bus and strobe lines are subject to strict loading limitations. Exceeding these limits can cause erratic system operation with on-board as well as off-board resources. Be sure to buffer any signals that will be heavily loaded off-board." So, to avoid adding excessive capacitive loading on the data bus, we add a simple 74ACT245, octal bi-directional transceiver. By connecting the /RD line from TINI to the 245's T/R, TINI will control the direction of the transceiver appropriately. The schematic in Figure 8-8 shows how this is connected to TINI.

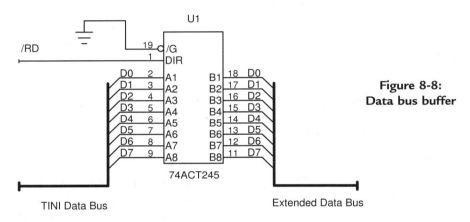

Figure 8-8: Data bus buffer

The address decoder

Since we are adding several devices to TINI, we need to assign them each a place in the TINI address space. The TINI socketboard does not come with a general-purpose address decoder. Shown here (Figure 8-9) is a simple address decoder for a liquid crystal display.

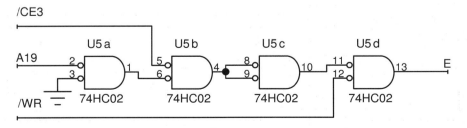

Figure 8-9: Address decoder

---

[9] DSTINI1 – TINI Verification Module – http://www.ibutton.com/TINI/dstini2.pdf

This is essentially the logical AND of /CE3, A19 and /WR; the LCD enable (E) is high when Chip Enable 3 (CE3) is low, when the write (/WR) line is low and when address line A19 is high.

This scheme for address decoding works fine for the LCD on the TINI socket board but has several drawbacks: it does not allow for any flexibility (it's wired for A19 and /CE3), it does not allow for additional peripherals to be added without additional address decoding and, worse, it takes up a large block of address space since it only decodes on address A19 (valid address to talk with the LCD will range from 0x00380000 to 0x003FFFFF). We will be implementing a more traditional address decoding scheme for our peripherals using a 74ALS138, 1-of-8 decoder/ demultiplexer. We will show how to modify the address decoder we use to be compatible with the TINI LCD class as well as how to configure the TINI class to be compatible with this address decoder in the section on the LCD display. The schematic in Figure 8-10 shows the address decoder we will be using that allows us to control eight peripherals (the blocks labeled "Buttons," "LCD," "LED" and "Keypad" will be discussed in detail shortly).

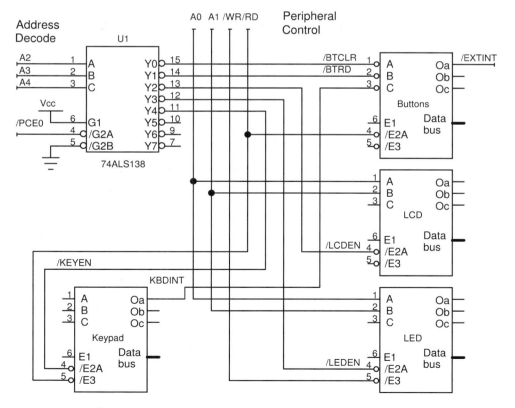

Figure 8-10: Memory-mapped address decoder schematic

With this address decoder we use Peripheral Chip Enable 0 (/PCE0) and address lines A2, A3, and A4. We will also be using address lines A1 and A2 to either address specific portions of the device, as is the case in the LED display, or to enable certain modes of the device, as is the case of the LCD display. You can very easily use a different Peripheral Chip Enable line or different address lines to put these devices anywhere else in the TINI

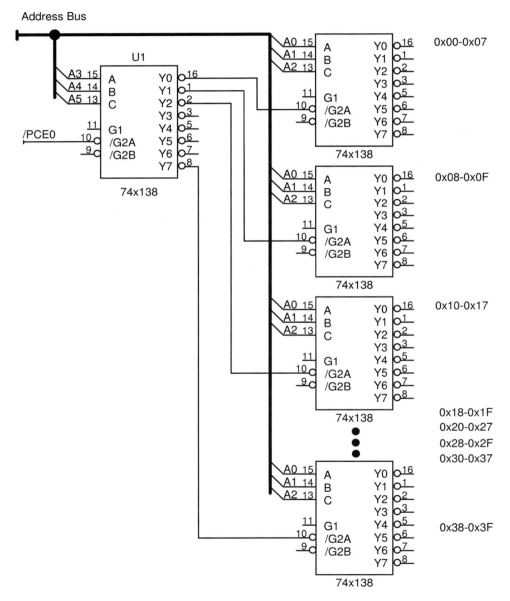

Figure 8-11: Expanded address decoder for addressing more devices

memory space that you desire. In Table 8-3 we list how the address decoder maps these devices into TINI address space. Remember from the TINI memory map (in Chapter 6, Table 6-3) that PCE0 selects addresses in the range 0x0800000-0x08FFFFF. We are not decoding on address lines A5-A19 so if we needed to add more address decoding we would need to build a larger address decoder, as shown in Figure 8-11 (in the table, x means this address line is not decoded, so the level of this address line is irrelevant in the decoding scheme).

Table 8-3: Address decoder addresses

Decode Line	Device	A19->A0	Address (HEX)
Y0	Button Clear	xxxx xxxx xxxx xxx0 00xx	00800000
Y1	Button Read enable	xxxx xxxx xxxx xxx0 01xx	00800004
Y2	LCD display enable	xxxx xxxx xxxx xxx0 10xx	00800008
Y3	LED display enable	xxxx xxxx xxxx xxx0 11xx	0080000C
Y4	Keypad read enable	xxxx xxxx xxxx xxx1 00xx	00800010
Y5		xxxx xxxx xxxx xxx1 01xx	00800014
Y6		xxxx xxxx xxxx xxx1 10xx	00800018
Y7		xxxx xxxx xxxx xxx1 11xx	0080001C

We will gain software access to these devices through the `com.dalsemi.system.dataport` class. This class allows byte-wide reads and writes to memory-mapped I/O devices. Here is a quick summary of what is needed:

We need to import the proper class:

```
import com.dalsemi.system.*;
```

then create a new `DataPort` for the particular address:

```
DataPort myDevice =  new DataPort(0x0080000C);
```

We then configure the `DataPort` for the proper access. TINI provides a method for user applications to set the number of machine cycles needed in order to execute a bus read or write. This allows TINI access to both fast and slow peripherals without additional logic. Often memory-mapped peripherals have slow access times, so it may not be possible to access external devices at full speed. This timing is controlled by the selection of *stretch* cycles. A stretch of 0 will result in two machine cycles for a data bus read or write. A stretch of 7 will result in twelve machine cycles for a data bus read or write. Your software can dynamically change the stretch value depending on the particular memory or peripheral being accessed.

```
myDevice.setStretchCycles(DataPort.STRETCH10);
```

We can read from or write to the device as needed:

```
myDevice.write( 0x00 );
int i = myDevice.read();
```

Table 8-4: Stretch cycles

Stretch	Memory Bus Cycles	Number of clocks	Time (ns)*
STRETCH0	2	1	54
STRETCH1	3	2	108
2	4	4	217
3	5	6	325
7	9	8	434
8	10	10	542
9	11	12	651
10	12	14	759

* Remember that external oscillator frequency = 18.432 MHz.

Refer to Chapter 6 for more details on the TINI memory map with respect to CE and PCE.

Adding an LCD display

A liquid crystal display (LCD) is a simple and cheap device to use for your TINI to provide an output for the user. There are many parallel interface LCDs on the market these days that adhere to a data standard of sorts. This standard seems to follow the data formats and pinouts of displays based on the Hitachi HD44780[10] controller chip. You can find LCDs in a variety of sizes, all based on the number of characters displayed and the size of the array: 1x16, 1x20, 1x40, 2x20, 2x40, and 4x20 are common but a number of other sizes can be found as well.

We will connect an LCD to the TINI stick as a memory-mapped device. This involves connecting the data bus lines from TINI to the LCD and implementing some sort of enable for the LCD. This enable will let the LCD know when data should be read from the data bus, and whether that data is a command or information to be displayed. We will be using the address decoder shown in Figure 8-10 for this, although there are many ways this address decoding can be implemented. Simply purchasing a serial LCD and connecting that to a serial port is also an option (but we won't be discussing that here).

The TINI class `LCDPort` can be used to communicate with a HD44780-based display, but it is somewhat limited in its implementation. You can use the address decoder shown in Figure 8-9 and this will work nicely with the `LCDport` that is part of the TINI API. [11] [12] The `LCDport` class uses the address that is decoded by the decoder

[11] TINI LCD Example – http://www.vinculum.com/LCD_Servlet_Example.php

[12] How To Connect a LCD To Your TINI – http://www.dreamfabric.com/tini/LCD/howtoconnectLCD.html

[10] The Hitachi web site doesn't seem to have the HD44780 data sheet but various other places do. Try http://www.acfr.usyd.edu.au/teaching/4th-year/mech4710-uP/material/ref/Hitachi/HD44780U.pdf or http://www.electronic-engineering.ch/microchip/datasheets/lcd/hd44780.pdf

shown in Figure 8-9 by default, but the base address can be changed as needed if you choose to implement a different address decoder (like we do, as shown in Figure 8-10). The TINI LCDport class will not let you change which address line you use to select the LCD mode (in this case it's fixed on A3). The sample program below will display "Hello World" if you have connected your LCD using the address decoder from either of the two listed references. Note that this uses address line A19 and chip select /CE3 to put the LCD at address 0x00380000 in memory, using A3 to select between command mode and data mode. Listing 8-3 is written to work with the address decoder shown in Figure 8-9 and the default settings of the LCDport class.

Listing 8-3: dsLCDporttest.java

```java
import com.dalsemi.comm.*;
import com.dalsemi.system.*;

// Class dsLDPporttest tests out the dalsemi LCDport class
public class dsLCDporttest
{
    public static void main(String[] args)
    {
        // Configure display to 8bits, 2 lines
        LCDPort.sendControl(0x38);
        // Turn display on, cursor off
        LCDPort.sendControl(0x0C);
        // Clear the display
        LCDPort.sendControl(1);
        // Start at 00
        LCDPort.setAddress(0x00);

        String message = "Hello World";
        byte[] databytes = message.getBytes();

        for (int i = 0; i < databytes.length; i++)
        {
            LCDPort.sendData(databytes[i]);
        }
    }
}
```

Compile this program:

```
C:\> javac  -bootclasspath %TINI_HOME%\bin\tiniclasses.jar
            -d bin src\dsLCDporttest.java
C:\> java   -classpath %TINI_HOME%\bin\tini.jar;. BuildDependency
            -p %TINI_HOME%\bin\owapi_dependencies_TINI.jar
            -f bin
            -x %TINI_HOME%\bin\owapi_dep.txt
            -o bin\dsLCDporttest.tini
            -d %TINI_HOME%\bin\tini.db
```

You can place this LCD elsewhere in memory by changing the LCD port address using the `com.dalsemi.system.TINIOS.setLCDAddress()` method but, as we mentioned already, there is no method that allows us to select a different address line to select the LCD data/command mode and the Dallas Semiconductor classes make no provision for enabling the LCD mode that would allow us to read data back from it.

To add flexibility and take advantage of all of the LCD's features, we offer an alternative schematic for connecting the LCD using the address decoder shown in Figure 8-10. We will connect the TINI address bus lines A0 and A1 to the LCD to control the LCD's modes. This allows us to read from the display (things like cursor position or status) as well as write to it and also to control whether we are writing text for display or sending commands (like "clear screen" and "home cursor"). We will use address line A0 to control the LCD R/W pin, which puts the LCD in either read (high signal) or write (low signal) mode. Read mode is the mode in which the LCD will send data back to us, and write mode is the mode in which we will send data to it. Address line A1 is used to control the LCD RS (register select) pin to control whether the LCD interprets data on the data bus as instructions (signal is low for select mode) or as text data to display (signal is high for register mode). Figure 8-12 shows how we will connect our address decoder to an LCD.

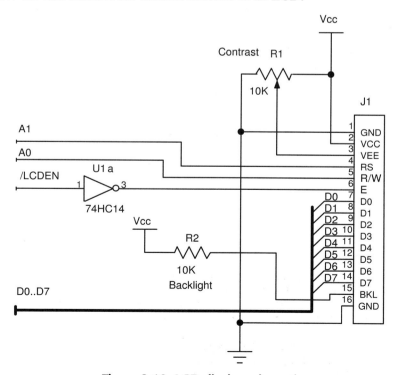

Figure 8-12: LCD display schematic

Examining the schematic, there are a few noteworthy things. Some displays may have fewer than 16 pins. If your display does not have a backlight LED, then you may have a 14-pin connector. Some LCDs only accept data in nibbles (4 bits) so you will have fewer data lines. We found that this circuit didn't need a contrast adjustment so we simply tied pin 3 on the LCD to V_{cc}. In all cases, consult the data sheet for your LCD to determine the function and order of the connector pins.

Listing 8-4 is a simple program, LCDhello, that demonstrates accessing the LCD directly using the DataPort class to give us full control over the LCD. Note that we can change the chip select from /PCE0 to any other unused chip select and change the address lines to put the LCD elsewhere in memory as needed. In contrast to our previous example, the LCD now resides in a completely different place in memory. The LCD now lives at address 0x00800008 as decoded by the address decoder (Figure 8-10) and is in command mode and ready for writing when A0 and A1 are low. When A1 is high, then the address for the LCD for writing data is 0x0080000A.

Listing 8-4: LCDhello.java

```java
// Class LCDhello demonstrates how to simply communicate with an LCD
import com.dalsemi.system.*;

public class LCDhello
{
    public static void main(String[] args)
    {
        DataPort data    = new DataPort( 0x0080000A );
        DataPort command = new DataPort( 0x00800008 );
        data.setStretchCycles(DataPort.STRETCH10);
        command.setStretchCycles(DataPort.STRETCH10);

        String message="The Quick Brown Fox Jumps Over The Lazy Sleeping Dog.";

        try {
            // set display mode
            command.write(0x38);
            TINIOS.sleepProcess( 150 );
            // clear display
            command.write(0x01);
            TINIOS.sleepProcess( 5 );
            // turn on display, cursor
            command.write(0x0F);
            TINIOS.sleepProcess( 10 );

            byte[] databytes = message.getBytes();
            for (int i = 0; i < databytes.length; i++)
            {
                data.write(databytes[i]);
```

```
        }
    }
    catch(IllegalAddressException e) {
        System.out.println( e );
    }
  }
}
```

Taking apart the above Java program a bit, we can see that two DataPorts are created, one for sending data and one for sending commands. These are the addresses that are defined by the address lines used by the address decoder and the data/command enable for the LCD (with this simple program we have not yet used the read mode).

```
DataPort data = new DataPort( 0x0080000A );
DataPort command = new DataPort( 0x00800008 );
```

Also notice that we have set the StretchCycles to STRETCH10. You can try changing the values of this to see what happens. With lower values we didn't get consistent operation and at the lowest values the LCD does not seem to respond at all, since the commands to the LCD are changing too fast for it to process them.

```
data.setStretchCycles(DataPort.STRETCH10);
command.setStretchCycles(DataPort.STRETCH10);
```

After each of the writes to the command dataport, you will notice a sleepProcess. This is because these commands require a little longer time than the StretchCycles provides for. Consult the Hitachi data sheets and previously mentioned references for detailed timing information and the commands that these displays understand.

```
command.write(0x38);
TINIOS.sleepProcess( 150 );
```

Finally, we send our text to the display. You will notice that the dataport write() method takes bytes so we first need to convert our message into an array of bytes, and then each byte is written to the dataport sequentially.

```
byte[] databytes = message.getBytes();
for (int i = 0; i < databytes.length; i++)
{
    data.write(databytes[i]);
}
```

Compile this program the usual way:

```
C:\> javac -bootclasspath %TINI_HOME%\bin\tiniclasses.jar
           -d bin src\LCDhello.java
C:\> java  -classpath %TINI_HOME%\bin\tini.jar;. BuildDependency
           -p %TINI_HOME%\bin\owapi_dependencies_TINI.jar
           -f bin
           -x %TINI_HOME%\bin\owapi_dep.txt
           -o bin\LCDhello.tini
           -d %TINI_HOME%\bin\tini.db
```

There are two other features of the LCD that we can take advantage of: The LCD allows us to define eight custom characters for displaying, and we can also read the cursor position, the LCD display contents, and the LCD display status. To read the LCD status, we set the R/W line (A0) for read (high) and the R/S line (A1) for instructions (low). To read the LCD contents we need to set the R/W line (A0) for read (high) and the R/S line (A1) for data (high). So the dataport address for reading the status is 0x00800009 and the dataport address for reading data is 0x0080000B. You will see this in the program (Listing 8-7: myLCD.java).

Each custom character is defined as a sequence of bytes, each bit representing horizontal lines of pixels that are on (1) or off (0). The figure shows two examples of how these custom characters are defined. This data is sent to the LCD by first sending the LCD a command to select the internal LCD memory address and then writing a sequence of data to the LCD for it to interpret as a custom font. Figure 8-13 shows an example character definition.

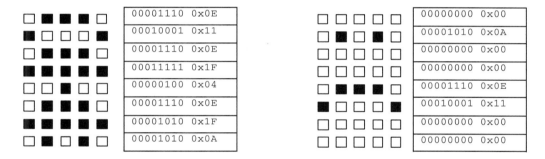

Figure 8-13: LCD character definition

The following program defines the class LCDfont. This class will be used in our final LCD class and lets us treat each custom font as an object.

Listing 8-5: LCDFont.java

```java
// Class LCDFont implements a user defined font set for a LCD display
public class LCDfont {

    public int fontdata [];
    public int fontcode;

    // Some interesting font characters
    public static int SMILEY []  = { 0x00,0x0A,0x00,0x00,0x11,0x0E,0x00,0x00 };
    public static int MAN []      = { 0x0E,0x11,0x0E,0x14,0x1F,0x04,0x0A,0x0A };
    public static int WOMAN []    = { 0x0E,0x11,0x0E,0x1F,0x04,0x0E,0x1F,0x0A };
    public static int DEGREE []   = { 0x07,0x05,0x07,0x00,0x00,0x00,0x00,0x00 };
```

```java
    public static int FROWNY []   = { 0x00,0x0A,0x00,0x00,0x0E,0x11,0x00,0x00 };
    public static int DOWNARROW []= { 0x00,0x04,0x04,0x15,0x0E,0x04,0x00,0x00 };
    public static int UPARROW []  = { 0x00,0x04,0x0E,0x15,0x04,0x04,0x00,0x00 };
    public static int INVADER []  = { 0x04,0x0E,0x1F,0x15,0x1F,0x0E,0x0A,0x15 };

    public LCDfont( int f1, int f2, int f3, int f4,
                    int f5, int f6, int f7, int f8 ) {

        fontdata = new int [8];
        fontcode = 0;

        fontdata[0] = f1;
        fontdata[1] = f2;
        fontdata[2] = f3;
        fontdata[3] = f4;
        fontdata[4] = f5;
        fontdata[5] = f6;
        fontdata[6] = f7;
        fontdata[7] = f8;
    }

    public LCDfont () {
        // The default is a simple smiley :)
        this(0x00,0x0A,0x00,0x00,0x11,0x0E,0x00,0x00);
    }

    public LCDfont( int data[] ) {
        fontdata = new int[8];
        fontdata = data;
        fontcode = 0;
    }

    public void setCode( int code ) {
        fontcode = code;
    }

    public String toString() {
        return ( "" + (char) fontcode );
    }
}
```

Our final class, LCDport, uses the classes LCDfont and
com.dalsemi.system.dataport to construct a full-featured class for driving your
LCD and taking advantage of all of its features.

Listing 8-6: LCDport.java

```java
import com.dalsemi.system.*;

// Class LCDport implements an alternative class to com.dalsemi.com.LCDport
// with additional funtionality (like reading back data, status, defining
```

```
// fonts, etc
public class LCDport
{
    public static final int DISPLAY_CLEAR     = 0x01;
    public static final int DISPLAY_HOME      = 0x02;

    public static final int ENTRY_MODE        = 0x04;
    public static final int CURSOR_INC         = 0x02;
    public static final int CURSOR_DEC         = 0x00;
    public static final int SHIFT              = 0x01;

    public static final int DISPLAY_MODE      = 0x08;
    public static final int DISPLAY_ON         = 0x04;
    public static final int DISPLAY_OFF        = 0x00;
    public static final int CURSOR_ON          = 0x02;
    public static final int CURSOR_OFF         = 0x00;
    public static final int CURSOR_BLINK       = 0x01;
    public static final int CURSOR_NOBLINK     = 0x00;

    public static final int SHIFT_MODE        = 0x10;
    public static final int CURSOR_MOVE        = 0x00;
    public static final int DISPLAY_SHIFT      = 0x08;
    public static final int SHIFT_LEFT         = 0x00;
    public static final int SHIFT_RIGHT        = 0x04;

    public static final int FUNCTION_SET      = 0x20;
    public static final int DATA_4bit          = 0x00;
    public static final int DATA_8bit          = 0x10;
    public static final int LINES_1            = 0x00;
    public static final int LINES_2            = 0x08;
    public static final int FONT_5x7           = 0x00;
    public static final int FONT_5x10          = 0x04;

    public static final int CHARACTER_ADDRESS = 0x80;

    public static final int DATA_ADDRESS      = 0x40;

    public static final int BUSY_FLAG         = 0x80;
    public static final int ADDRESS_PART      = 0x7F;

    DataPort dataport;
    DataPort cmdport;
    DataPort readport;
    DataPort statport;

    public LCDport(int cmd_addr, int data_addr, int stat_addr, int read_addr) {
        cmdport  = new DataPort( cmd_addr );
        cmdport.setStretchCycles(DataPort.STRETCH10);
        dataport = new DataPort( data_addr );
        dataport.setStretchCycles(DataPort.STRETCH10);
```

```
        statport = new DataPort( stat_addr );
        statport.setStretchCycles(DataPort.STRETCH10);
        readport = new DataPort( read_addr );
        readport.setStretchCycles(DataPort.STRETCH10);
    }

    public void init() {
        // set display mode
        this.set(FUNCTION_SET + DATA_8bit + LINES_2 + FONT_5x7);
        // Wait for it. These waits are IMPORTANT, if you don't
        // then you will be sending commands while its not ready
        TINIOS.sleepProcess( 150 );
        // clear the display
        this.set(DISPLAY_CLEAR);
        TINIOS.sleepProcess( 5 );
        // turn on the display and cursor
        this.set(DISPLAY_MODE + DISPLAY_ON + CURSOR_ON +
                    CURSOR_BLINK);
        TINIOS.sleepProcess( 10 );
    }

    public void set( int value ) {
        try {
            cmdport.write( value );
        }
        catch(IllegalAddressException e)   {
            System.out.println( "Error in SET" );
            System.out.println( e );
        }
    }

    public void write( String message ) {

        byte[] databytes = message.getBytes();

        try {
            for (int i = 0; i < databytes.length; i++)
            {
                dataport.write(databytes[i]);
            }
        }
        catch(IllegalAddressException e)   {
            System.out.println( "Error in WRITE" );
            System.out.println( e );
        }
    }

    public void write( int address, String message ) {
```

```
            this.set( CHARACTER_ADDRESS + address );
            byte[] databytes = message.getBytes();

            try {
                for (int i = 0; i < databytes.length; i++)
                {
                    dataport.write(databytes[i]);
                }
            }
            catch(IllegalAddressException e)  {
                System.out.println( "Error in WRITE" );
                System.out.println( e );
            }
        }

    public String read(int n)
    {
        byte[] d = new byte [20*4];

        // read n bytes from whatever the current address is
        // return as a String
        try {
            // Wait for display to get into output mode
            readport.setStretchCycles(DataPort.STRETCH10);
            for(int i = 0; i < n; i++) {
                d[i] = (byte)readport.read();
            }
        }
        catch (IllegalAddressException e)  {
            System.out.println( "Error in WRITE" );
            System.out.println( e );
        }
        // This does not translate special characters
        String s = new String(d);
        return(s);
    }

    public void defineFont( int code, LCDfont font ) {
        // code defines the ASCI code for this character.
        int address = (code)*8;

        this.set( DATA_ADDRESS + address );
        font.setCode( code );

        try {
            for (int i = 0; i < font.fontdata.length; i++)
            {
                dataport.write(font.fontdata[i]);
            }
        }
```

```
                catch(IllegalAddressException e)   {
                    System.out.println( "Error in WRITE" );
                    System.out.println( e );
                }
        }

        public byte getAddress() {
            int i = 0;
            try {
                i = statport.read();
            }
            catch(IllegalAddressException e)   {
                System.out.println( e );
            }
            return( (byte)(i & ADDRESS_PART) );
        }

        public boolean isBusy() {
            int i = 0;
            try {
                i = statport.read();
            }
            catch(IllegalAddressException e)   {
                System.out.println( e );
            }
            return( (i & BUSY_FLAG)>0 ? true : false );
        }
}
```

Most of the functions of this class are fairly straightforward.

- `LCDport( int, int, int, int )`, the constructor, takes four parameters: the addresses for each of the different modes (command, sending text, status, read text)

- `init()` initializes the display to a known state.

- `set( int )` sends commands to the LCD.

- `write( string )` sends a character string to the LCD for display.

- `write( int, string )` sends a character string to the LCD for display, starting at the specified display address.

- `read( int )` returns the specified number of characters from the LCD as a character string.

- `defineFont( int, Font )` sends a `Font` object to the LCD as the specified character (0..7). The font needs to be defined using the `LCDFont( int array )` method.

- `getAddress()` returns the current LCD cursor address.

- isBusy() returns a boolean indicating if the LCD is busy or ready (true for busy).

Let's take this LCDport class out for a test drive. We will create a new class, myLCD, that will use both LCDport and LCDfont.

Listing 8-7: myLCD.java

```
import com.dalsemi.comm.*;
import com.dalsemi.system.*;

// Class myLCD demonstrates the methods in our LCDport class
public class myLCD
{
    public static void main(String[] args)
    {
        LCDport mylcd =
            new LCDport(0x00800008, 0x0080000A, 0x00800009, 0x0080000B);

        // define some custom fonts
        LCDfont man        = new LCDfont(LCDfont.MAN);
        LCDfont woman      = new LCDfont(LCDfont.WOMAN);
        LCDfont smiley     = new LCDfont(LCDfont.SMILEY);
        LCDfont frowny     = new LCDfont(LCDfont.FROWNY);
        LCDfont invader    = new LCDfont(LCDfont.INVADER);
        LCDfont degree     = new LCDfont(LCDfont.DEGREE);
        LCDfont uparrow    = new LCDfont(LCDfont.UPARROW);
        LCDfont downarrow  = new LCDfont(LCDfont.DOWNARROW);

        // initialize it, check the status
        mylcd.init();
        System.out.println( "Busy? " + mylcd.isBusy() );

        // home the cursor
        mylcd.set(LCDport.DISPLAY_HOME);

        // Send the custom fonts to the display memory
        mylcd.defineFont( 0, invader );
        mylcd.defineFont( 1, man );
        mylcd.defineFont( 2, woman );
        mylcd.defineFont( 3, smiley );

        // Try writibng, assumes a 4x20 display.
        // Addresses will be different for other sizes
        mylcd.write( 0x00, "Line 1" );
        // get the current display address, should be 6
        System.out.println( "Address is " + mylcd.getAddress() );
        // Send some special characters
        mylcd.write( 0x40, "Line 2" + invader + man + woman + smiley);
```

```
        // write some more.
        mylcd.write( 0x14, "Line 3" );
        mylcd.write( 0x54, "Line 4" );
        mylcd.write( 0x61, "The End" );

        // Lets rtead back alll of the text we sent to the display.
        String stuff;
        System.out.println( "Reading back data");
        mylcd.set( LCDport.CHARACTER_ADDRESS + 0x00 );
        stuff = mylcd.read( 20 );
        System.out.println( "["+stuff+"] " + stuff.length() );

        mylcd.set( LCDport.CHARACTER_ADDRESS + 0x40 );
        stuff = mylcd.read( 20 );
        System.out.println( "["+stuff+"] " + stuff.length() );

        mylcd.set( LCDport.CHARACTER_ADDRESS + 0x14 );
        stuff = mylcd.read( 20 );
        System.out.println( "["+stuff+"] " + stuff.length() );

        mylcd.set( LCDport.CHARACTER_ADDRESS + 0x54 );
        stuff = mylcd.read( 20 );
        System.out.println( "["+stuff+"] " + stuff.length() );

        // done!
    }
}
```

Note that writing custom characters to the display requires no special action on our part. Instead we use the `toString` method (implied) of the `LCDfont` class to return `fontcode`, a number that corresponds to the character code for that custom character. If we tried

```
System.out.println( invader );
```

Java would call the `toString` method for the invader object (the `toString()` method of the `LCDFont` class) which would return the character code we assigned to the `invader` object in the line:

```
mylcd.defineFont( 0, invader );
```

Compile this program:

```
C:\> cd src
C:\> javac -bootclasspath %TINI_HOME%\bin\tiniclasses.jar
            -d ..\bin myLCD.java
C:\> cd ..
C:\> java   -classpath %TINI_HOME%\bin\tini.jar;. BuildDependency
            -p %TINI_HOME%\bin\owapi_dependencies_TINI.jar
            -f bin
            -x %TINI_HOME%\bin\owapi_dep.txt
            -o bin\myLCD.tini
            -d %TINI_HOME%\bin\tini.db
```

This is what a 4x20 LCD looks like after running this program.

Figure 8-14: LCD example

Remember, LCD displays will vary depending on the controller chip and the size of the LCD display. Be sure to get and read the data sheets. Also, be aware of the way your display addresses are arranged (the 4x20 is treated as two 2x40 lines).

Adding buttons

The LCD is a nice way for your TINI to display test messages, but what about a way to capture external events to trigger TINI software routines? In other words, how do we get input based on some external events? We can do this using the TINI external interrupt. The TINI stick has an /EXTINT line and the TINI API includes several classes for dealing with and managing these external interrupts.

Figure 8-15 shows the external interrupt logic on the TINI E10/E20 socket board. This allows for two serial port interrupts and two auxiliary interrupts to control the TINI CPU /EXTINT line. To trigger an interrupt we need to take the /EXTINT line low. The TINI API class `com.dalsemi.system.ExternalInterrupt` and `ExternalInterruptEvent` are used for accessing the external interrupt and interrupt events.

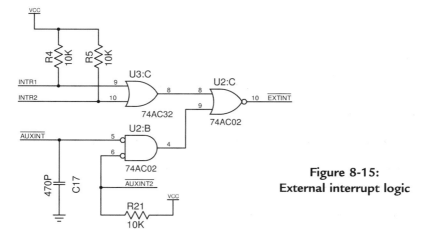

**Figure 8-15:
External interrupt logic**

We can trigger external interrupts by attaching a simple pushbutton to the /EXTINT line so that when the button is pressed it connects the /EXTINT line momentarily to ground. Something along the lines of that shown in Figure 8-16 will do nicely.

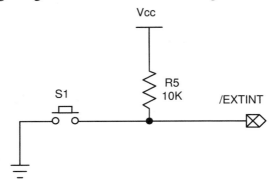

Figure 8-16: A button to trigger an external interrupt

The 10K resistor is a pull-up on the /EXTINT line. It holds this line at V_{cc} until someone (or some event) presses the button. When the button is closed it connects ground to the /EXTINT line and this triggers an interrupt on the TINI stick. If we have implemented an `ExternalInterruptEvent` then we can start a Java class executing with a button press. Note that this is a button and not a switch. TINI can be configured so the ExternalInterruptEvent is either falling-edge triggered or low-level triggered. The default is level triggering. If you use level triggering with a switch then TINI will be repeatedly sending interrupts while the switch is closed, leaving very little of the CPU to service the interrupt. Your interrupt should be short durations to avoid this.

Listing 8-8: ExtIntDemo.java

```java
import java.util.TooManyListenersException;
import com.dalsemi.system.*;

// Class ExtIntDemo provides a simple deonstration of implementing an
// ExternalInterruptEventListener
class ExtIntDemo implements ExternalInterruptEventListener
{
    int interruptions;

    public void init() throws TooManyListenersException
    {
        ExternalInterrupt myInterrupt = new ExternalInterrupt();
        myInterrupt.addEventListener(this);
        try {
            myInterrupt.setTrigger( true, this );
        }
```

```
        catch (ExternalInterruptException e) {
            System.out.println( e );
        }
    }

    public void externalInterruptEvent(ExternalInterruptEvent ev)
    {
        System.out.println("Interruptions = " + ++interruptions );
        if (interruptions > 25) { System.exit(0); }
    }

    public static void main(String[] args) throws
            TooManyListenersException
    {
        ExtIntDemo interrupt = new ExtIntDemo();
        interrupt.init();

        while (true) {
            // do nothing
        }
    }
}
```

Compile this program:

```
C:\> javac -bootclasspath %TINI_HOME%\bin\tiniclasses.jar
           -d bin src\ExtIntDemo.java
C:\> java   -classpath %TINI_HOME%\bin\tini.jar;. BuildDependency
           -p %TINI_HOME%\bin\owapi_dependencies_TINI.jar
           -f bin
           -x %TINI_HOME%\bin\owapi_dep.txt
           -o bin\ExtIntDemo.tini
           -d %TINI_HOME%\bin\tini.db
```

Run this on your TINI. Note the triggering in the line

```
        myInterrupt.setTrigger( true, this );
```

Try changing this to false and see how the program reacts to button presses. Notice that we are not doing any switch debouncing here. You can add that to your circuits as needed but for this example we can be content to ignore any switch bounce as being too short of a duration to register multiple interrupts, but that's not always the case. Changing the triggering can help make this program a little more sensitive to keybounce. Appendix C (on the CD-ROM) provides a number of possible debounce circuits.

To complicate this a little more, you can then connect multiple buttons or switches by combining their signals as shown in Figure 8-17. It's worth noting that when the ExternalInterruptEvent is executing, TINI will be ignoring (not queuing) any additional external interrupts that occur. If this is a bad thing, you will need to keep the ExternalInterruptEvent method you implement as simple as possible so it can be executing quickly.

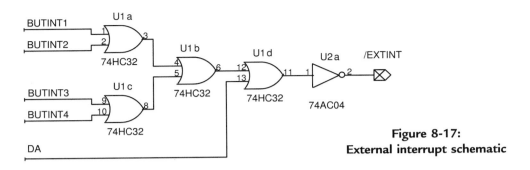

Figure 8-17:
External interrupt schematic

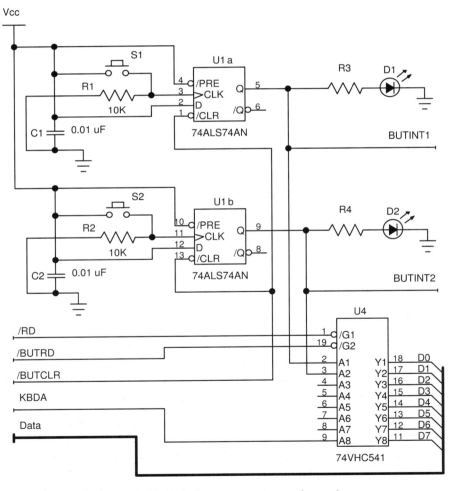

Figure 8-18: Switch state memory schematic

But if we want to add more than one button, how will we know which button was pressed? We only have one external interrupt line on the TINI stick, so we need a way to save the state of each button so we can query them after an interrupt is caught. The circuit in Figure 8-18 shows a 74ATC74, dual D-type flip-flop configured to store the on state of either button that's pressed. We use a 75HC541, octal buffer, enabled by one of our chip selects from the address decoder to connect the stored button states to the data bus, and another chip select to clear the stored state after our interrupt service method has determined which of the buttons caused the external interrupt.

Now we can support multiple buttons and know which button was pressed after we catch the interrupt. We can add additional 74ATC74 devices for more buttons as needed. The schematic also shows a keypad data available line (KBDA) connected to the data bus buffer. We will use it to determine if an interrupt was caused by the keypad in the next section.

The `Button` class, below, provides methods for accessing the button state and clearing them.

Listing 8-9: Button.java

```java
import com.dalsemi.system.*;

// Class Button provides methods for accessing push buttons
class Button  {

    DataPort clearButtons;
    DataPort readButtons;

    public Button( int clearaddr, int buttonaddr ) {
        clearButtons = new DataPort( clearaddr );
        clearButtons.setStretchCycles(DataPort.STRETCH10);
        readButtons  = new DataPort( buttonaddr );
        readButtons.setStretchCycles(DataPort.STRETCH10);
    }

    public int read() {
        int d=0;

        try {
            d = readButtons.read();
        }
        catch (IllegalAddressException e)  {
            System.out.println( "Error in reading switches" );
            System.out.println( e );
        }
        return( d );
    }
}
```

```
public void clear() {

    try {
        clearButtons.write( 0x00 );
    }
    catch (IllegalAddressException e)   {
        System.out.println( "Error in reading switches" );
        System.out.println( e );
    }
}

public boolean isButton1() {
    int s = this.read();
    return( (s & 0x01)>0 ? true : false );
}

public boolean isButton2() {
    int s = this.read();
    return( (s & 0x02)>0 ? true : false );
}

public boolean isButton3() {
    int s = this.read();
    return( (s & 0x04)>0 ? true : false );
}

public boolean isButton4() {
    int s = this.read();
    return( (s & 0x08)>0 ? true : false );
}
}
```

This is a summary of the methods in this class:

- `Button( int, int)` is the constructor for this class, taking two parameters, the address of the clear dataport and the address of the read dataport.

- `read()` returns an integer that contains the state of buttons.

- `clear()` clears the button states.

- `isButton1(), isButton2(), isButton3(), isButton4()` all return Boolean values of the individual button states.

The simple program below demonstrates the `Button` class and shows how to check the button status by simple polling. If any button (or several) is pressed, the program prints the result of a dataport read.

Listing 8-10: pollButton.java

```java
import com.dalsemi.system.*;

// Class pollButtons demonstrates how to poll the status of the buttons
public class pollButton {

    public static void main(String[] args)  {

        int state = 0;
        int i=0;
        Button mybutton = new Button(0x00800000, 0x00800004 );
        mybutton.clear();

        while (i<200) {
            state = mybutton.read();
            if (state > 0) {
                if (mybutton.isButton1()) {
                    System.out.println( "Button: 1" );
                }
                if (mybutton.isButton2()) {
                    System.out.println( "Button: 2" );
                }
                if (mybutton.isButton3()) {
                    System.out.println( "Button: 3" );
                }
                if (mybutton.isButton4()) {
                    System.out.println( "Button: 4" );
                }
            }
            mybutton.clear();
            TINIOS.sleepProcess(50);
            i++;
        }
    }
}
```

Compile this program:

```
C:\> cd src
C:\> javac -bootclasspath %TINI_HOME%\bin\tiniclasses.jar
         -d ..\bin pollButton.java
C:\> cd ..
C:\> java  -classpath %TINI_HOME%\bin\tini.jar;. BuildDependency
         -p %TINI_HOME%\bin\owapi_dependencies_TINI.jar
         -f bin
         -x %TINI_HOME%\bin\owapi_dep.txt
         -o bin\pollButton.tini
         -d %TINI_HOME%\bin\tini.db
```

This works well when we don't require the program to know about the button presses in a timely manner. A busy CPU may not get around to servicing this often enough for reasonable response time. We should use the `ExternalInterrupt` when we need better response. We will implement that in the next section with the keypad.

Adding a keypad

We can implement a numeric keypad using the previously mentioned buttons and interrupt events. But it will get a bit tedious to trap a large number of buttons and also store which was pressed. To simplify things a bit, we will use a keypad encoder. There are several on the market for 16 and 20 key keypads. Fairchild Semiconductor makes the MM74C922 and MM74C923[13], and e-lab makes the EDE1144[14] keypad encoder integrated circuits. Figure 8-19 shows a typical keypad implementation based on a MM74C922.

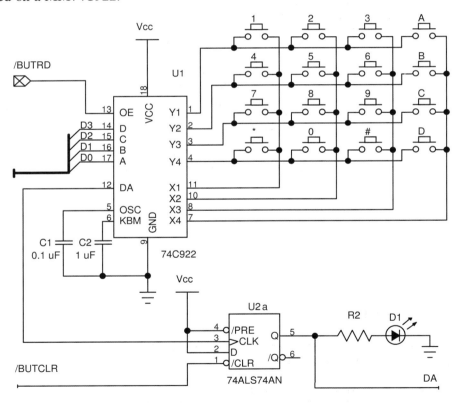

Figure 8-19: Keypad schematic

[13] MM74C922/923 Data Sheet – http://www.fairchildsemi.com/pf/MM/MM74C922.html
[14] EDE1144 Data Sheet – http://www.elabinc.com/ede1144.pdf

We can monitor our keypad by polling the DataPort or we can attach the DataAvailable output from the IC to the /EXTINT pin on TINI (through an inverter since the DataAvailable line is active high). The schematic for the buttons in the previous section shows this DataAvailable (KBDA) line is connected to the 74VHC541 buffer and the external interrupt logic along with the push buttons. In this way, we can capture events from the keypad or the pushbuttons. If you only needed to use the keypad, without the push buttons, then there would be no need to implement the 74LS74 D flip flops to store the state of the buttons, as the only external interrupt would be from the keypad data available signal, and probably no need to use a circuit like Figure 8-17 to combine multiple interrupt sources.

Be careful of the keypad pin-out. These encoder ICs need matrix switch keypads that are arranged in rows and columns, where a single button push will connect the row pin with the column pin for that key. Shown is the pin-out for one particular keypad. There appears to be quite a bit of variation between keypad pinouts.

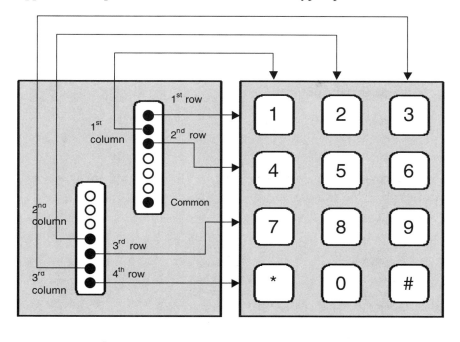

Back View   Front View

Figure 8-20: Keypad pinout

The following class, Keypad, can be used to access a keypad implemented according to the schematic. You can use this by either polling or implementing an ExternalInterruptEvent listener.

Listing 8-11: Keypad.java

```java
import com.dalsemi.system.*;

// CLass Keypad defines methods for acceing a numeric keypad
class Keypad  {

    DataPort keypad;

    public Keypad( int addr ) {
        keypad = new DataPort( addr );
        keypad.setStretchCycles(DataPort.STRETCH10);
    }

    // read raw key info from keypad
    public int readRaw() {
        int d=0;

        try {
            d = keypad.read();
        }
        catch (IllegalAddressException e)  {
            System.out.println( "Error in reading keypad" );
            System.out.println( e );
        }
        // mask off upper 4 bits
        return( (d & 0x0F ) );
    }

    // read keypad and returs the symbol for the appropriate key
    public char readKey() {
        int d = readRaw();
        char k = ' ';
        switch(d) {
                case 0x00 :     k='1';    break;
                case 0x01 :     k='2';    break;
                case 0x02 :     k='3';    break;
                case 0x03 :     k=' ';    break;
                case 0x04 :     k='4';    break;
                case 0x05 :     k='5';    break;
                case 0x06 :     k='6';    break;
                case 0x07 :     k=' ';    break;
                case 0x08 :     k='7';    break;
                case 0x09 :     k='8';    break;
                case 0x0A :     k='9';    break;
                case 0x0B :     k=' ';    break;
                case 0x0C :     k='*';    break;
                case 0x0D :     k='0';    break;
                case 0x0E :     k='#';    break;
```

```
            case 0x0F :     k=' ';    break;
            default:     break;
        }
        return( k );
    }

}
```

- `Keypad( int addr )` is the constructor. It takes one parameter, the address of the keypad dataport.

- `readRaw()` returns an integer representing the key position on the keypad. This starts with 0 and counts up through the rows sequentially.

- `ReadKey()` maps the key position number into a specific character. This method returns a character of the key. You could modify this method for specific keypad meanings, possibly returning bytes, strings or even objects rather than simple characters.

We can read this keypad in a manner similar to how we read the buttons, by polling.

Listing 8-12: pollKeypad.java

```java
import com.dalsemi.system.*;

// Class pollKeypad demonstrates how (not very well) to poll the keypad
public class pollKeypad {

    public static void main(String[] args)
    {
        char key = ' ';
        int now = 0, last=0, i=0;

        Keypad mykeypad = new Keypad(0x00800010 );

        while (i<200) {
            now = mykeypad.readRaw();
            key = mykeypad.readKey();
            if (now!=last) {
                System.out.println( "Key: " + Integer.toHexString(now)
                    + ", keypad " + key );
            }
            last=now;
            TINIOS.sleepProcess(50);
            i++;
        }
    }
}
```

Compile this program:

```
C:\> cd src
C:\> javac -bootclasspath %TINI_HOME%\bin\tiniclasses.jar
            -d ..\bin pollKeypad.java
C:\> cd ..
C:\> java  -classpath %TINI_HOME%\bin\tini.jar;. BuildDependency
            -p %TINI_HOME%\bin\owapi_dependencies_TINI.jar
            -f bin
            -x %TINI_HOME%\bin\owapi_dep.txt
            -o bin\pollKeypad.tini
            -d %TINI_HOME%\bin\tini.db
```

Unfortunately, the keypad encoder has no provision for clearing its output after we have read which key was pressed, so this works well only if we never expect the user to press the same key twice in a row. To overcome this minor limitation, we can implement the ExternalInterruptEventListener as we did for a single button earlier.

Listing 8-13: myKeypad.java

```java
import java.util.TooManyListenersException;
import com.dalsemi.system.*;

// Class myKeypad demonstrates reading the keypad and buttons
// using an ExternalInterruptEventListener
class myKeypad implements ExternalInterruptEventListener {

    int i;
    Keypad mykeypad = new Keypad(0x00800010 );
    Button mybutton = new Button(0x00800000, 0x00800004 );

    public void init() throws TooManyListenersException
    {

        // This is the signal to which we will add an event listener
        ExternalInterrupt myInterrupt = new ExternalInterrupt();
        // Add the event listener
        myInterrupt.addEventListener(this);

        mybutton.clear();
    }

    public void externalInterruptEvent(ExternalInterruptEvent ev)
    {
        int state = 0;

        System.out.println( "Interrupt Caught: " + ++i );
        state = mybutton.read();
```

```
        // We can catch multiple simultaneous presses
        if (mybutton.isButton1()) {
            System.out.println( "Keypad:  " + mykeypad.readKey() );
        }
        if (mybutton.isButton2()) {
            System.out.println( "Button: 2" );
        }
        if (mybutton.isButton3()) {
            System.out.println( "Button: 3" );
        }
        if (mybutton.isButton4()) {
            System.out.println( "Button: 4" );
        }
        mybutton.clear();

        if (i > 9) { System.exit(0); }
    }

    public static void main(String[] args) throws TooManyListenersException
    {
        myKeypad interrupt = new myKeypad();
        interrupt.init();

        while (true) {
            // do nothing
        }
    }
}
```

Compile this program:

```
C:\> cd src
C:\> javac -bootclasspath %TINI_HOME%\bin\tiniclasses.jar
           -d ..\bin myKeypad.java
C:\> cd ..
C:\> java  -classpath %TINI_HOME%\bin\tini.jar;. BuildDependency
           -p %TINI_HOME%\bin\owapi_dependencies_TINI.jar
           -f bin
           -x %TINI_HOME%\bin\owapi_dep.txt
           -o bin\myKeypad.tini
           -d %TINI_HOME%\bin\tini.db
```

The output of this program looks like this (after some random button and keypad pressing):

```
TINI /> java myKeypad.tini
Interrupt Caught: 1
Keypad:   5
Interrupt Caught: 2
Keypad:   9
Interrupt Caught: 3
```

```
Keypad:   0
Interrupt Caught: 4
Keypad:   5
Button:   2
Button:   3
Interrupt Caught: 5
Keypad:   2
Button:   2
Button:   3
Interrupt Caught: 6
Button:   2
Button:   3
Interrupt Caught: 7
Keypad:   7
Interrupt Caught: 8
Keypad:   5
Interrupt Caught: 9
Keypad:   6
Interrupt Caught: 10
Keypad:   9
TINI />
```

Much better. We can now identify which button was pressed, and which key on the keypad was pressed, and deal with multiple presses of the same key and also simultaneous presses of several buttons.

Add an LED display

For our last memory-mapped device we will implement an LED display. If the liquid crystal display was not good enough for you, let's try implementing a four-digit 7-segment LED display for variety. There are a number of multiple-digit, 7-segment, LED display driver chips available. Fairchild Semiconductor makes the MM74C911 and MM74C912[15] and e-labs make the EDE707.[16] Both of these work with common anode or common cathode 7-segment LED displays. Again, we will be using one of the chip selects from our address decoder to enable the LED driver. The schematic (Figure 8-21) shows the circuit we will be using. Note that the LED driver needs the 2N3904 transistors to drive the common anode LED displays. The circuit will be slightly different for common cathode LEDs.

The class provided here, LEDport, supports sending messages to a four character array of 7-segment LED displays. Each of the four characters of the display are then selected by using the address lines A0 and A1; the class implements this as four consecutive dataports starting with the base address as determined by our chip select logic.

---

[15] MM74C911/912 data sheet – http://www.fairchildsemi.com/pf/MM/MM74C911.html
[16] EDE707data sheet – http://www.elabinc.com/ede707.pdf

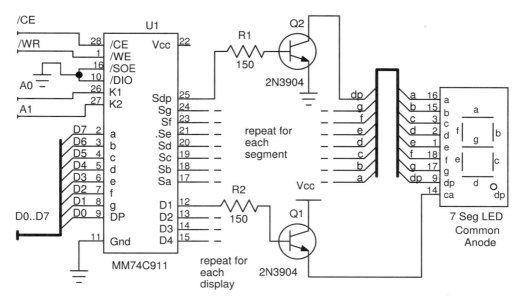

Figure 8-21: LED display schematic

Because we are only using seven segments, not all ASCII characters are possible. We can display all numbers and a reasonable representation for these letters and symbols:

- AbCcdEFGHhIiJLnOoPrStUuYZ

- :?.[]|-_

This means you need to use peculiar case and spell certain words oddly (or not at all). Some examples of this oddness are: tHE HErE tHAt tini Hello hi HI dALLAS StAtUS AlArm Error StOP HALt HELP rESEt rESTArt rEbOOt UP dn LEFT rIGHt UnDEr OvEr. But you can see that it is still possible to get the message across to the user.

Listing 8-14: LEDport.java

```java
import com.dalsemi.system.*;

// Class LEDport defines a set of methods for accessing an LED
display.
public class LEDport
{
    DataPort led0;
    DataPort led1;
    DataPort led2;
    DataPort led3;
```

```
int timedelay = 150;
int flashcount = 4;

public LEDport( int baseaddr )
{
    // the LED driver datasheet says that address to write enable
    // time
    // is 50 ns and the write enable width is 250 ns
    led0 =  new DataPort( baseaddr );
    led0.setStretchCycles(DataPort.STRETCH10);
    led1 =  new DataPort( baseaddr+1 );
    led1.setStretchCycles(DataPort.STRETCH10);
    led2 =  new DataPort( baseaddr+2 );
    led2.setStretchCycles(DataPort.STRETCH10);
    led3 =  new DataPort( baseaddr+3 );
    led3.setStretchCycles(DataPort.STRETCH10);
}

public void init()
{
    clear();
}

public void clear()
{
    try {
        led0.write( 0x00 );
        led1.write( 0x00 );
        led2.write( 0x00 );
        led3.write( 0x00 );
    }
    catch(IllegalAddressException e)   {
        System.out.println( "Error in INIT" );
        System.out.println( e );
    }
}

public void setDigit( int digit, int value )
{
    try {
        switch (digit) {
            case 0:     led0.write( value );
                        break;
            case 1:     led1.write( value );
                        break;
            case 2:     led2.write( value );
                        break;
            case 3:     led3.write( value );
                        break;
            default:    break;
```

```
        }
    }
    catch(IllegalAddressException e)  {
        System.out.println( "Error in SET" );
        System.out.println( e );
    }
}

public int toSegment( char c)
{
    // convert ASCII characters (as in INT into 7 Segments representation
    return ( toSegment((int)c) );
}

public int toSegment( int x )
{
    int i=0;
    // We map SOME letters into an equivalent form (different case).
    // You can add more as you like.
    switch (x) {
        case ((int) '0'): i=0x3F; break;
        case ((int) '1'): i=0x06; break;
        case ((int) '2'): i=0x58; break;
        case ((int) '3'): i=0x4F; break;
        case ((int) '4'): i=0x66; break;
        case ((int) '5'): i=0x6D; break;
        case ((int) '6'): i=0x7D; break;
        case ((int) '7'): i=0x07; break;
        case ((int) '8'): i=0x7F; break;
        case ((int) '9'): i=0x6F; break;
        case ((int) 'A'):
        case ((int) 'a'): i=0x77; break;
        case ((int) 'B'):
        case ((int) 'b'): i=0x7C; break;
        case ((int) 'C'): i=0x39; break;
        case ((int) 'c'): i=0x58; break;
        case ((int) 'D'):
        case ((int) 'd'): i=0x5E; break;
        case ((int) 'E'):
        case ((int) 'e'): i=0x79; break;
        case ((int) 'F'):
        case ((int) 'f'): i=0x71; break;
        case ((int) 'G'):
        case ((int) 'g'): i=0x7D; break;
        case ((int) 'H'): i=0x76; break;
        case ((int) 'h'): i=0x74; break;
        case ((int) 'I'): i=0x06; break;
        case ((int) 'i'): i=0x04; break;
        case ((int) 'J'):
        case ((int) 'j'): i=0x1E; break;
```

```
                case ((int) 'L'): i=0x38; break;
                case ((int) 'l'): i=0x06; break;
                case ((int) 'N'):
                case ((int) 'n'): i=0x54; break;
                case ((int) 'O'): i=0x3F; break;
                case ((int) 'o'): i=0x5C; break;
                case ((int) 'P'):
                case ((int) 'p'): i=0x73; break;
                case ((int) 'R'):
                case ((int) 'r'): i=0x50; break;
                case ((int) 'S'):
                case ((int) 's'): i=0x6D; break;
                case ((int) 'T'):
                case ((int) 't'): i=0x78; break;
                case ((int) 'U'): i=0x3E; break;
                case ((int) 'u'): i=0x1C; break;
                case ((int) 'Y'):
                case ((int) 'y'): i=0x66; break;
                case ((int) 'Z'):
                case ((int) 'z'): i=0x5B; break;
                case ((int) '?'): i=0x53; break;
                case ((int) '.'): i=0x80; break;
                case ((int) '['): i=0x39; break;
                case ((int) ']'): i=0x0F; break;
                case ((int) '-'): i=0x40; break;
                case ((int) '_'): i=0x08; break;
                case ((int) '|'): i=0x30; break;
                case ((int) ' '): i=0x00; break;
                case ((int) ':'): i=0x09; break;
                default:
                    // other characters get mapped into a ? sort of thing
                    i = 0x53;
                    System.out.println( "Bad character: " + x);
                    break;
            }
        return( i );
    }


    // Format the string for the LED display, look for "." and set
    // this as
    // the decimal point then convert all characters to 7seg
    // representation.
    public byte[] format( String text )
    {
        String message = new String( text );
        byte[] databytes = message.getBytes();

        // scan data looking for "."
        for(int i=0; i<databytes.length; i++) {
            if (databytes[i]=='.') {
```

```
                    // put the decimal on previous character
                    databytes[i-1] = (byte) (databytes[i-1] | 0x80);
                    // now delete it by shifting all characters left by 1
                    for (int j=i; j<databytes.length-1; j++) {
                        databytes[j] = databytes[j+1];
                    }
                    // slap a space on the end
                    databytes[databytes.length-1]=(char)' ';
                }
                // convert it to a segment
                databytes[i] = (byte) toSegment(databytes[i]);
        }
        return( databytes );
}


// Make a long text message scoll across the 4 character display.
// pad the left with 4 spaces for it to scroll onto the display.
// pad the right with 4 spaces for it to scroll off the display.
public void scrollMessage( String text )
{
    byte[] databytes = format( text );

    // Now scroll the message
    for(int i=0; i<databytes.length-3; i++) {
        for(int j=0;j<4;j++) {
            if ((i+j)>databytes.length-1) {
                this.setDigit(j, 0x00);
            }
            else {
                this.setDigit(j, databytes[i+j]);
            }
        }
    TINIOS.sleepProcess(timedelay);
    }
}

// Flash a short message on the display to get attention
public void flashMessage( String text )
{
    byte[] databytes = format( text );

    for( int x=0; x<flashcount; x++) {
        // Now flash the first 4 characters
        for(int i=0; i<4; i++) {

            if (i>databytes.length-1) {
                this.setDigit(i, 0x00);
            }
            else {
                this.setDigit(i, databytes[i]);
```

```
                }
            }
            TINIOS.sleepProcess(timedelay);
            clear();
            TINIOS.sleepProcess(timedelay);
        }
    }

    public void setDelay( int delay)
    {
        timedelay = delay;
    }

    public void setFlashCount( int count )
    {
        flashcount = count;
    }
}
```

Here is a summary of the methods in this class:

- `LEDport( int )` is the constructor. It takes one parameter, the base address of the dataport.

- `init()` initializes the LED display.

- `clear()` clears the display (no digits on).

- `setDigit( int, int )` sets a digit (0..3) to a particular value. The value is the character that has been encoded as an integer to turn on the proper segments.

- `toSegment( char )` takes a character and returns an integer that represents the proper segments on the 7-segment display.

- `toSegment ( int )` takes integer (ASCII value) and returns an integer that represents the proper segments on the 7-segment display

- `format( String )` takes a character string and returns an array of bytes that have been properly encoded for display.

- `scrollMessage( String )` takes a character string and scrolls it across the LED display from right to left.

- `flashMessage( String )` takes a character string and flashes it on the LED display.

- `setDelay( int )` sets the delay amount in ms that the scrollMessage will delay between each character or the time between flashes, depending on which method is used.

- `setFlashCount( int )` sets the number of times to flash a message using the flashMessage() method.

The 7-segment encoding is quite simple. You select the segment you want turned on for a particular character. This character then requires those segments to be on, or a logic 1. These binary segments are then ordered: dp, g, f, e, d, c, b, a, according to the diagram in Figure 8-22. For example, "C" requires segments a, d, e and f. This is 00111001 in binary or 39 hex. Writing a 0x39 to the LED dataport for one of the characters will display a "C" on that LED.

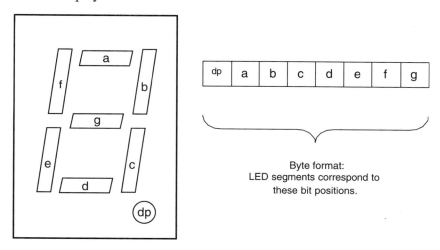

Figure 8-22: 7-segment encoding

The following program demonstrates the capabilities of the LEDport class and this LED display circuit.

Listing 8-15: myLED.java

```
import com.dalsemi.comm.*;
import com.dalsemi.system.*;

// Class myLED demonstrates the methods in our LEDport class
public class myLED
{
    public static void main(String[] args)
    {
        final LEDport myled = new LEDport(0x0080000C);

        myled.init();
        // milliseconds to wait bewteen scroll steps and flashes
        myled.setDelay( 150 );
        // our version of "hello world"
        myled.scrollMessage( "    HELLO tini    " );
        // number of times to flash
```

```
        myled.setFlashCount( 4 );
        myled.flashMessage( "ThIS" );
        myled.flashMessage( " IS " );
        myled.flashMessage( "CooL" );
    }
}
```

Compile this program:

```
C:\> cd src
C:\> javac  -bootclasspath %TINI_HOME%\bin\tiniclasses.jar
            -d ..\bin myLED.java
C:\> cd ..
C:\> java   -classpath %TINI_HOME%\bin\tini.jar;. BuildDependency
            -p %TINI_HOME%\bin\owapi_dependencies_TINI.jar
            -f bin
            -x %TINI_HOME%\bin\owapi_dep.txt
            -o bin\myLED.tini
            -d %TINI_HOME%\bin\tini.db
```

Summary

In this chapter we discussed adding components and interfacing user input/output devices to TINI. There are certainly many other types of displays or I/O devices that you may wish to add. We hope that this chapter has provided you with the tools necessary to add these devices. In following chapters we will be discussing some of the other features of the Dallas Semiconductor E10/20 socketboards, such as the serial ports, parallel I/O, CAN, and I²C interface.

References

1. *Computer/Microcontroller Interfacing,*
   http://www.ffldusoe.edu/faculty/Denenberg/courses/GK415/Computer-Microcontroller_Interfacing.htm

2. *Beyond Logic,*
   http://www.beyondlogic.org/

3. *L.O.S.A - List of Stamp Applications,*
   http://www.hth.com/losa/

4. *How to use Intelligent LCDs,*
   http://www.epemag.wimborne.co.uk/resources.htm

5. *The Extended Concise LCD Data Sheet,*
   http://www.electronic-engineering.ch/microchip/datasheets/lcd/the_lcd_data_sheet.pdf

6. *How to Control a HD44780-based Character-LCD,*
   http://home.iae.nl/users/pouweha/lcd/lcd.shtml

## CHAPTER 9

TINI Serial and Parallel I/O

The TINI microcontroller is equipped for many forms of I/O. The simpler two of these are the serial and parallel ports. The TINI CPU can directly support two serial ports and many others can be added as memory-mapped peripherals. TINI's parallel I/O ports are simply 8-bit wide, memory-mapped I/O busses for general-purpose control. We will examine each of these two I/O devices in detail and provide some example circuits and programs.

Serial Ports

Some have called the RS-232/EIA-232 serial port the most popular interface standard in the world[1]. It was first introduced in 1962 and has been widely used throughout the industry on computers, computer terminals, and many different types of devices from modems to multimeters. It was developed for single-ended data transmission at relatively slow data rates (20 kbps) over short distances (typically up to 50 feet) but is often used for faster data rates and much longer cable lengths.

Almost all personal computers currently made have at least one serial port. The serial port converts data from internal parallel data to a serial data stream and changes the electrical representation of the data so it can be transmitted over distance without data loss. The serial port is defined by the RS-232-C (RS for Recommended Standard) or the EIA-232-D (EIA for Electronics Industry Association) specifications. The RS specification is now obsolete but still widely used. The TINI microcontroller has two serial ports on the SIMM and more can be added as memory-mapped devices. We have already used the primary serial port in earlier chapters for communicating with TINI to load and configure the firmware.

---

[1] Data Transmission Circuits – http://www.national.com/appinfo/interface/0,1801,128,00.html

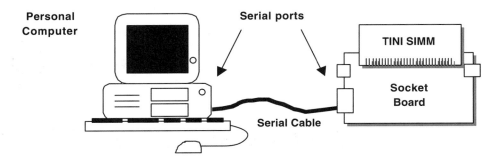

Figure 9-1: Connecting to the TINI serial port

A few serial port details

You don't have to fully understand the details of RS-232-C to use a serial port, but a familiarization with the basics makes working with the TINI serial ports much simpler and certainly helps if you run into any problems along the way.

The UART

The UART (Universal Asynchronous Receiver/Transmitter) is the integrated circuit that controls the serial port. It basically does everything for the computer in the way of managing the transmission and receipt of data. Specifically, the UART:

- converts bytes from parallel data to a serial data stream when transmitting data.

- converts the received serial data stream back into parallel data for the computer when receiving data.

- deals with the parity bit on both outgoing and incoming transmissions.

- manages the serial port flow control lines.

- Some UARTS also provide buffering (like 16 bytes or so).

The UART works with parallel-to-serial (and flow control) signals at the same voltage levels as the computer or device; in the case of TINI this is 5 volts. A serial line driver, discussed in a few paragraphs, will then shift these voltages to serial line voltages.

Flow control, parity, stop bits, data format

The serial port is said to be asynchronous, meaning that there is no clock transmitted with the data to identify to the receiving end when each bit should be valid. A transmitted sequence of all 1's or all 0's would be hard for the receiver to identify the individual bits (or just how many bits there are, for that matter) without some sort of timing information. Since this timing information is not in the data stream, the UART provides this. The transmitting UART frames each byte sent by placing a start bit at the beginning of the serial data and a stop bit at the end. The receiving UART listens to the serial line for a start bit and when it detects one it starts a clock running. It uses this clock to determine the amount of time needed for each bit in the serial data stream. In this way, asynchronous data is actually synchronized as it is received. In serial transmission of data by RS-232/EIA-232 ports the low-order bit is always sent first.

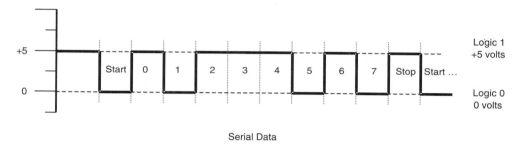

Figure 9-2: Serial data

The transmitting and receiving UARTs also need a way to communicate with each other so that the transmitter does not send too much data for the receiver, and the receiver can tell the transmitter if it's ready for more data or not. This flow control prevents data from being lost. Flow control can be implemented in either hardware or software.

Software flow control for serial ports is called XON/XOFF. With XON/XOFF flow control, the receiving device tells the computer when to pause by sending it an XOFF character (control-S) and when to resume transmission by sending the computer the XON character (control-Q). The advantage of using software flow control is that you can implement a serial port with only three wires (transmit, receive, common).

Hardware flow control is accomplished by using additional wires for signaling between the transmitting device and the receiving device. Hardware flow control is managed by the UART. It controls four additional lines for this (but some devices will only implement two of these lines):

- RTS - Ready To Send
- CTS - Clear To Send
- DSR - Data Set Ready
- DTR - Data Terminal Ready

Here is how this works. When a computer wants to stop the flow of data on the serial line, it negates the RTS line. Negated RTS (–12 volts) means "request NOT to send" or stop sending data. When the computer is ready for more bytes it asserts RTS (back to +12 volts) and the flow of data resumes. Flow control signals are always sent in a direction opposite to the flow of data that is being controlled. Serial devices (not computers) work the same way but they send the stop signal to the computer via the CTS pin. This is called RTS/CTS flow control.

In addition to RTS/CTS flow control; a device can implement DTR/DSR control. The normal use of DTR and DSR like this: A device asserting DTR (+12 volts) says that it is powered on and ready to communicate (data terminal is ready). Some modems interpret the DTR signal from the computer as a "hang up" signal (hang up when DTR is negative) but not always. In fact some devices require that DTR be high before they will communicate. Readers should note that in the case of TINI and Serial0, taking the DTR line to a non-HIGH (0 or negative) will cause a hardware reset.

Characters are normally transmitted serially as either 7 or 8 bits of data. An additional parity bit may (or may not) be appended to this, resulting in a byte length of 7, 8 or 9 bits. The parity may be set to odd, even, or none. With odd parity, the parity bit is determined so that the number of 1's in a byte, including the parity bit, is odd. If a byte gets corrupted in transmission by a bit being flipped, the result is an invalid byte of even parity (the wrong parity). Even parity works the same way but with all valid bytes including the parity bit having an even number of 1's. The UART will detect a parity error and this allows the software application to detect (if the software is properly written) the errors and request retransmission of the appropriate information. Figure 9-2 shows 8 data bits, no parity, 1 stop bit. This is often abbreviated as 8N1. It is important that you know what format your serial device and computer is expecting and set the software settings for them both to the same parameters.

Serial line voltages

Before these serial signals are transmitted on the serial cable the voltages are increased to between 3 and 25 volts, but between 10–12 volts is common (we will use 10 or 12 volts throughout this book but remember that this really means 3–25). Serial port data is considered valid for a logic "1" if the voltage is between –3 and –25 volts and a logic "0" is valid between +3 and +25 volts. Both positive and minus voltages are needed for data transmission. The serial port voltages are bipolar, which means that both positive and negative voltage relative to ground are used. For the transmit and receive lines, +12 volts represents a logical "0" and –12 volts represents a logical "1" (which is often called reverse logic since typically a logic "1" is represented by the positive or higher voltage). The flow control lines will be +12 volts when asserted and –12 volts when negated. This needs to be converted to –12 to +12 volts for the serial port using a serial line driver. There are many serial line drivers on the market. Common ones include the MAX232[2], the National Semiconductor DS14C232[3], and the Dallas Semiconductor DS232[4].

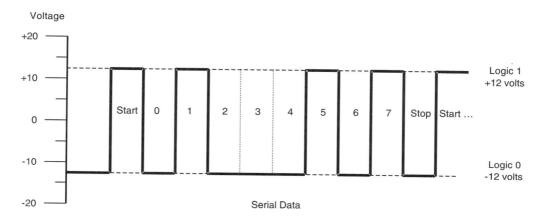

Figure 9-3: Serial line voltages

Figure 9-3 shows an example of a serial line communication, the same data as shown in Figure 9-2, but notice that the serial line voltages are not only shifted from 0–5 volts to −12 to +12 volts, but the logic is also inverted. The serial port line driver does this. The MAX232 and many other serial line drivers include an internal charge pump so that the device will work on a single 5-volt supply voltage. If this is the case, it is not uncommon for the serial line driver to only output ±10 volts. This voltage is often fine for most serial devices but we have encountered a few that need ±12 volts to work properly. The devices referenced provide two TTL to RS-232 voltage level shifters (for transmitting lines) and two RS-232 to TTL/CMOS level shifters (for receiving lines). This is suitable for use with two serial ports that do not use hand-shaking or a single serial port that simply uses RTS/CTS flow control. There are many other line drivers that are suitable for shifting all data and handshake lines on a serial port. We will use one of these in a few pages to implement a memory-mapped serial port on TINI.

[2] MAX232 Datasheet – http://pdfserv.maxim-ic.com/arpdf/MAX220-MAX249.pdf
[3] DS14C232 Datasheet – http://www.national.com/pf/DS/DS14C232.html
[4] DS232 – http://pdfserv.maxim-ic.com/arpdf/DS232A.pdf

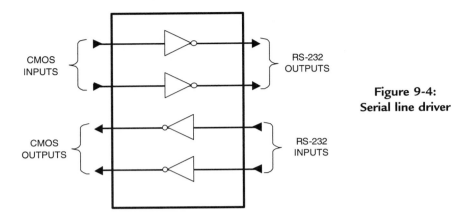

Figure 9-4:
Serial line driver

Cables and connectors

The next things we need to worry about with wiring up a serial port is the connector and cable. There are two different types of serial devices and so there are two different wiring configurations of the serial port. In addition there are several common physical connectors for the serial port, resulting in a variety of possible cable/connector wiring patterns.

If the device transmitting and receiving serial data is a computer or a computer terminal, then these devices are called data terminal equipment (DTE). If the serial device is some other type of device (like a modem or a printer), then these are called data communication equipment (DCE).

The RS-232 standard defines how a DTE is connected to a DCE. The cable between the DTE and the DCE should be straight-through wiring (simply connect pin1 to pin1, pin2 to pin2, and so on). The main signals and their direction of flow are shown in Figure 9-5 and described below. It is important to note that a signal that is an output from a DTE (a computer) is an input to a device (a DCE) and vice versa. This means that you can *never* tell from the signal name alone whether it is an input or an output from a particular piece of equipment.

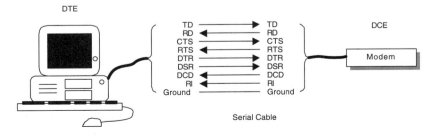

Figure 9-5: Serial data lines

- TD – Transmit data. This is the serial encoded data sent from a DTE to a DCE device.

- RD – Receive data. This is the serial encoded data received by a DTE from a DCE device.

- DCD – Data Carrier Detect. This is set true by the DCE when it detects the data carrier signal on the telephone line (for modems; it may have other meanings for other devices or it may be ignored). Active high.

- DTR – Data Terminal Ready. This should be set true by a DTE whenever it is powered on and ready to communicate. It can be read by the DCE to determine that the DTE is ready. Active high.

- DSR – Data Set Ready. This should be set true by DCE whenever it is powered on and ready. It can be read by the DTE to determine if the DCE is ready. Active high.

- RTS – Ready To Send. This is set true by the DTE when it wishes to transmit data. Active high.

- CTS – Clear To Send. This is set true by DCE to notify the DTE that it can transmit data. Active high.

- RI – Ring Indicator. This line informs the DTE that the DCE wants to start a connection (for a modem; it may be ignored by other devices or always high). Active high.

Part of the confusion that is common with serial ports occurs when you have two computers (both DTE) or two devices (both DCE) connected together with a serial cable (or, instead of being a DCE device, some serial communication devices might be configured as DTE). Then you need to be careful that the transmit line from one is connected to the receive line on the other. To solve this, some devices can be configured as either DTE or DCE. If the device configuration cannot be changed, then you need to perform the signal crossover in the cable. In either case (DCE to DCE or DTE to DTE), you need a crossover cable or an adapter. This crossover is typically called a "null modem" cable or "null modem" connector.

The most common RS-232 connectors are the D9 and D25 connector as shown in Figure 9-6. It is common (but not a rule) to find the female connector on the DCE and the male connector on the DTE. If you are going to be working with serial devices you need a collection of adapters, cable, and a null modem adapter. You can purchase most of these ready made or you can wire your own connectors and cables using the pinout information given in Figures 9-6 through 9-10.

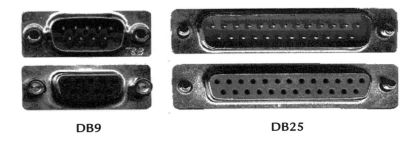

DB9   DB25

Figure 9-6: D9 and D25 male (top) and female (bottom) connectors

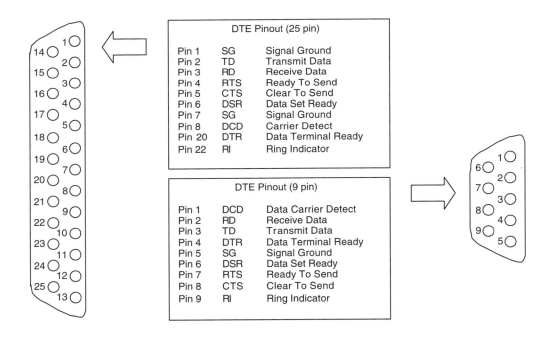

Figure 9-7: D9 and D25 pinouts

Technically, the DCE pinout is the same as the DTE pinout, knowing that the TD output (transmitted data) from the DTE connects to the TD input of the DCE. Often the DCE pinout is relabeled so that the TD line from the DTE connects to the RD line of DCE. Care should be given to making serial port connection diagrams.

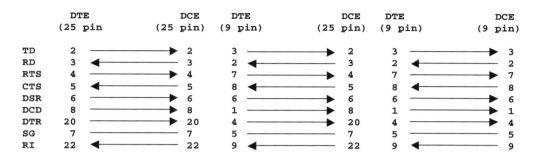

Figure 9-8: DTE–DCE cables (straight-through wired)

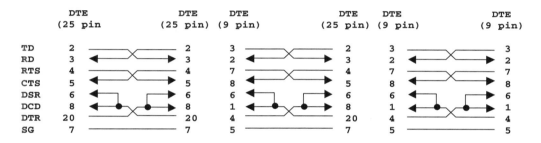

Figure 9-9: DTE-to-DTE cables (null modem cables or adapters)

In many devices software flow control is required and the device does not implement any sort of hardware handshaking. In these cases it is possible to simplify the serial cable to three wires—TD, RD and signal ground. The remaining lines can be ignored, or looped back within the connector as shown in Figure 9-10.

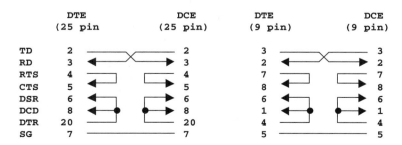

Figure 9-10: Minimum serial cables

An alternative to these D9 and D25 connectors and the need for a null modem in some circumstances and not others is one reason we are particularly fond of "The Yost Serial Device Wiring Standard"[5] using RJ-45 connectors and CAT5 cables. Essentially,

The RS-232 specification lists the maximum cable length to be 50 feet for 20,000 bits/second data rates. For lower data rates, like 2400 bits/second, this can be extended to 400 feet using telephone wire (untwisted pair) and in excess of 2000 feet using CAT-5 cable.

onto each serial port of every piece of equipment that you use you put on an appropriately wired adapter from DB-25 or DB-9 to RJ-45. Now every serial port has the same kind of connector regardless of its function (DTE or DCE). The benefits are that now every serial port transmits and receives data and has its control lines on the same pins so you only need one cable configuration; essentially all cables are in a null-modem-like configuration. In addition, you only need to keep one kind of cable (CAT5) and connector (RJ45) and crimping tool on hand. You can use a colored CAT5 cable to keep your serial cables distinctly different from your network cables.

Table 9-1: RJ45 serial connector pinout

DB-9	DB-25	Signal	Function	Wire Color	DTE RJ45	DCE RJ45
8	5	CTS	Clear To Send	Blue	1	8
1	8	DCD	Data Carrier Detect	Orange	2	7
2	3	RD	Received Data	Black	3	6
5	7	SG	Signal Ground	Red	4	5
5	7	SG	Signal Ground	Green	5	4
3	2	TD	Transmitted Data	Yellow	6	3
4	20	DTR	Data Terminal Ready	Brown	7	2
7	4	RTS	Request To Send	White	8	1
6	6	DSR	Data Set Ready	–	–	
9	22	RI	Ring Indicator	–	–	

Wire DSR to DTR in the RJ45 connector to support the use of the DSR line when needed.

Figure 9-11: RJ45 serial adapter

[5] Yost Serial Device Wiring Standard – http://www.yost.com/computers/RJ45-serial/index.html

Cables for the Yost Serial standard are simply a reversed-order wiring on each end. Whatever color order you use on one end to connect to pins 1–8 on the RJ45, use the opposite order on the opposite end (in other words, you are *always* using a crossover style cable).

TINI serial ports

The TINI provides direct support for up to four serial ports: serial0–serial3. The DS80C390 has two built-in UARTs for control of serial0 and serial1. TINI also supports communication with a 16550 UART. The details and capabilities of these serial ports are listed in Table 9-2.

Table 9-2: TINI serial ports

Serial Port	Details	CMOS Interface	RS232 Interface (± 10 volts)
serial0	Software flow control but no hardware flow control Used by serial server Configured as DCE UART internal to CPU Baud rates of 300, 600, 1200, 2400, 4800, 9600, 19200, 38400, 57600, 115200 Supports 7 or 8 data bits, 1 stop bit, Odd, Even or No parity (or 2 stop bits with 7 data bits) E10 socketboard supports use of D9 and a nonstandard RJ11 connector	TD: pin 21 RD: pin 22	TD: pin 19 RD: pin 20
serial1	Software flow control but no hardware flow control Disables External 1-Wire when used UART internal to CPU External Level Shifter required Baud rates of 2400, 4800, 9600, 19200, 38400, 57600, 115200 (300, 600, 1200 not supported) Supports 7 or 8 data bits, 1 stop bit, Odd, Even or No parity (or 2 stop bits with 7 data bits) User configured as either DCE or DTE E10 socketboard provides connection to header pins	TD: pin 14 RD: pin 15	
serial2	Hardware flow control but no software flow control External UART and Level Shifter required Baud rates of 300, 600, 1200, 2400, 4800, 9600, 19200, 38400, 57600, 115200 Supports 5, 6, 7 or 8 data bits, 1, 1/5 or 2 stop bits, Odd, Even or No parity	Configured as a memory mapped device	Uses an external level shifter
serial3	Hardware flow control but no software flow control External UART and Level Shifter required Baud rates of 300, 600, 1200, 2400, 4800, 9600, 19200, 38400, 57600, 115200 Supports 5, 6, 7 or 8 data bits, 1, 1/5 or 2 stop bits, Odd, Even or No parity	Configured as a memory mapped device	Uses an external level shifter

Both serial0 and serial1 are driven by the UART that is integrated in the 80C390 CPU on TINI. Figure 9-12 shows the connections of serial0 and serial1 to the TINI CPU and the TINI SIMM (Figure 9-13).

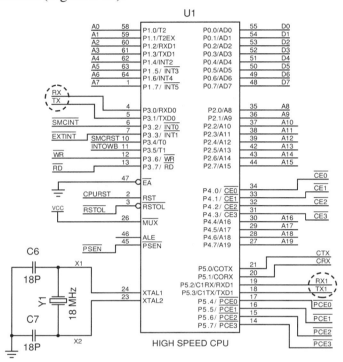

Figure 9-12: Serial0 and serial1 Ports on CPU

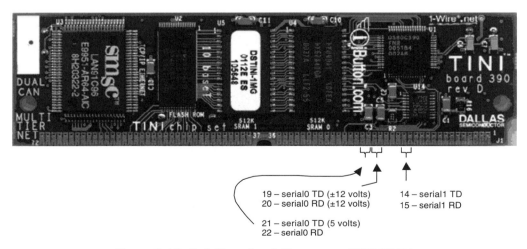

19 – serial0 TD (±12 volts)
20 – serial0 RD (±12 volts)
21 – serial0 TD (5 volts)
22 – serial0 RD

14 – serial1 TD
15 – serial1 RD

Figure 9-13: Serial0 and serial1 ports on TINI SIMM

Serial0

We have already used serial0, the primary serial port, for connecting to TINI with JavaKit. Note that on the Dallas Semiconductor E10 and E20 sockets, this port is configured as a DCE serial port. This means that to connect TINI to your computer you need a simple serial cable, not a null modem cable. But if you are going to connect another DCE device to this port, then you need a null modem adapter or null modem cable. If you examine the TINI schematic, you will notice that the serial0 level shifters are included on the TINI stick (U14). This puts the complete serial port on the stick except for the connector (serial1, 2 and 3 all require additional hardware to do the level shifting). Also you will notice that this level shifter only deals with three signals: TX232 (transmitted data), RX232 (received data) and DTR232. The DTR232 is used as an external hardware reset for TINI. When this line goes high it causes TINI to perform a power-on reset. This DTR232 can be disabled if you use the E10 or E20 socketboard by removing the J1 solder jumper.

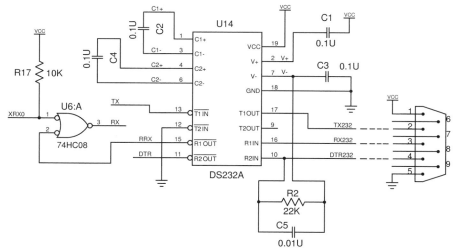

Figure 9-14: Serial0 (serial port on TINI SIMM)

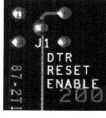 

Jumper in position   Jumper removed

Figure 9-15: Serial0 DTR reset jumper

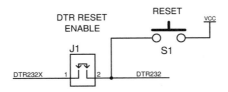

Figure 9-16: Serial0 reset jumper schematic

Removing this jumper will prevent devices that use the DTR line from resetting your TINI. It will also prevent you from resetting your TINI using the RESET button in JavaKit. If you do remove this jumper, it's a good idea to wire a switch back in so you can reset TINI easily if you need to.

Serial server

Recall from Chapter 6 that TINI is running a server that listens for incoming terminal connections (like JavaKit, Hyperterm or minicom) to serial0. If you are using serial0 for connection to a device other than a computer, you will want to disable the boot messages and the serial server (or your serial device will be getting these messages and may become confused). The slush command `stopserver -s` is used to shutdown the server. It accepts an optional argument, `-d`, that will suppress all of the console messages the next time the TINI is booted.

You can also start or stop the serial server by editing the `/etc/.startup` file on TINI. Remember that the `/etc/.startup` file contains instructions for the Slush command shell that are read at boot time. The default contents of this file are as follows:

```
########
#Autogen'd slush startup file
setenv FTPServer enable
setenv TelnetServer enable
setenv SerialServer enable
##
#Add user calls to setenv here:
##
initializeNetwork
########
#Add other user additions here:
```

By changing the line:

```
setenv SerialServer enable
```

to

```
setenv SerialServer disable
```

or simply deleting that line, you will prevent the serial server from being started when TINI is rebooted.

Serial1

Serial1 is similar to serial0 in that the UART is part of the 80C390 CPU. It does not have a serial line driver on the TINI SIMM. Serial1 is primarily for driving the TINI external 1-Wire adapter (U8) but can be used as a standard serial port as well, with the addition of a line driver. If you are planning on using this to communicate with another serial device that does not have a line driver, then you can wire these directly. If you need to talk with standard serial devices (that need ± 10 volts on the serial line) then you need to connect a line driver to this to get the proper voltages. The line driver you pick can be any of the commonly available ones. In the case of serial1, you only need to drive one CMOS-to-±12 volt line and one ±12-volt-to-CMOS line, so a very simple line driver is all that's needed, such as a DS232A or a MAX233 (which has the added benefit of not needing external capacitors for the charge pump).

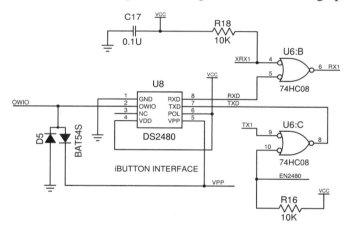

Figure 9-17: Serial1 (and 1-Wire interface)

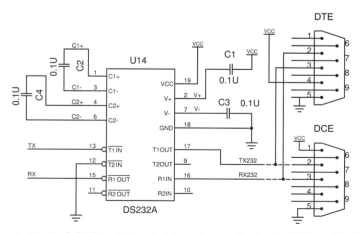

Figure 9-18: Serial1 line driver (wiring shown for both DTE and DCE)

If you use serial1 for a serial port, you need to disable the external 1-Wire port. To do that, you need to put a 1KΩ pull-down resistor on the EN2480 line and you need to include the following line in your program:

```
TINIOS.enableSerialPort1( false );
```

If you don't do both of these, you are likely to get 1-Wire data on the serial port and this will corrupt your data.

Serial2, 3

If you need more serial ports, then you can implement them on the Dallas Semiconductor socketboard or an external board as memory-mapped devices. The TINI API provides direct support for two additional memory-mapped UARTs (16550 compatible) with the added benefit of supporting full hardware flow control. Figure 9-19 below shows a dual UART and one of the two line drivers (they are both basically the same).

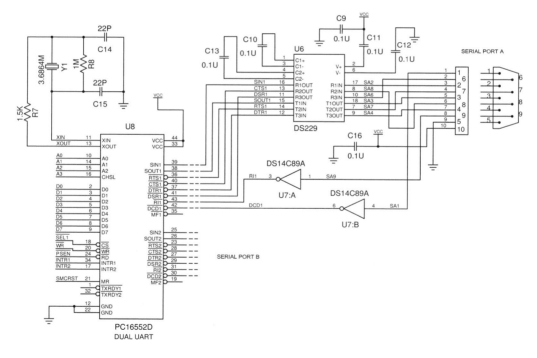

Figure 9-19: Serial2,3 port driver

The Dallas Semiconductor implementation uses a DS229 line driver for most of the serial port data and signal lines. A DS14C98 receiver is used to shift the incoming flow control lines to CMOS logic levels (we need three CMOS-to-±12 volt drivers and five ±12-volt-to-CMOS receivers). Alternatively, a different RS-232 line driver, like a MAX235, would support all of the needed data and flow control lines.

The 74AC138 on the TINI E10/E20 socketboard partially decodes the address bus and places the serial ports in memory as follows:

- serial2: 0x380020 – 0x380027

- serial3: 0x380028 – 0x38002F

Notice that the UART uses address line A3 to determine if we are communicating with serial2 or serial3 and that the UART uses an 8-byte block in memory as decoded by A0–A2.

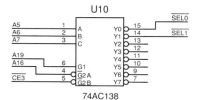

Figure 9-20:
Serial2 and serial3 address decode

For adding single serial ports or for use on protoboards, we can use the National Semiconductor single UART PC16550DN in a DIP package. With this it is possible to implement a serial port with full hardware flow control. The address is decoded using a 74AC138 decoder.

If you want the serial port to occupy some other address space, then you need to modify the address decoder appropriately and then use the method

`com.dalsemi.system.TINIOS.setExternalSerialPortAddress( newaddress );`

to change the addresses. You must enable these external serial ports with the method

`com.dalsemi.system.TINIOS.setExteranlSerialPortEnable( port, true );`

Serial communication software (API)

Let's try out the various serial ports and see how they behave and what the differences are to the TINI API. There are essentially three classes we are concerned with when programming the TINI serial ports.

- The obvious class is the `javax.comm.SerialPort` class that we used in Chapter 3 to communicate with the PC's serial port.

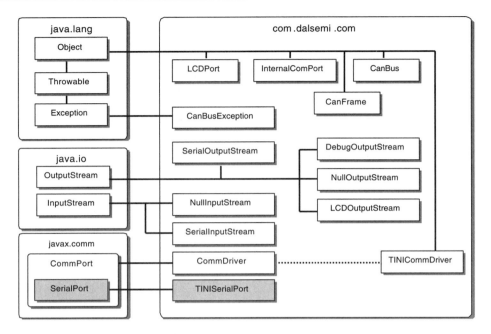

Figure 9-21: com.dalsemi.com

- If you need more direct control over the TINI serial ports, you can use the `com.dalsemi.comm.TINISerialPort` class but you will give up portability. Your programs must be recompiled to run on a PC and may not work if you have used any methods specific to TINI.

- In addition to the `javax.comm.SerialPort` class, you need to be able to select and configure various options that are specific to TINI's serial ports. You will find a collection of methods in the `com.dalsemi.system.TINIOS` class. The methods that you will probably be most interested in are:

    - `enableSerialPort1( boolean )` – This method enables serial1 (and in doing that it disables the external TINI 1-Wire bus). The state of serial1 is preserved in TINI memory; this method only needs to be executed once after the firmware is loaded or the heap has been cleared.

    - `setExternalSerialPortAddress( portnumber, address )` – The method sets the address for the external serial ports, serial2 and serial3. You only need to use this method if you install serial2 or serial3 at a location other than the default address. The address is preserved in TINI memory, so this method only needs to be executed once after the firmware is loaded or the heap has been cleared.

- `setExternalSerialPortEnable( portnumber, boolean )` – Call this method to enable or disable serial2 or serial3. The state of these ports is preserved in TINI memory until the heap is cleared.
- `setExternalSerialPortSearchEnable( bootlean )` – This method tells the TINI firmware to look for serial2 and serial3 at boot time. The state of this setting is preserved in TINI memory until the heap is cleared.
- `setRTSCTSFlowControlEnable( portnumber, boolean )` – This method enables hardware flow control on the specified serial port. TINI only supports hardware flow control on one serial port at a time.
- `setSerialBootMessageState( boolean )` – The method enables or disables boot messages to serial0. The state of these ports is preserved in TINI memory until the heap is cleared.
- `getExternalSerialPortAddress( portnumber )` – Returns the memory map address of the specified serial port.
- `getExternalSerialPortEnable( portnumber )` – Returns a boolean value indicating if the specified serial port is enabled.
- `getExternalSerialPortSearchEnable( portnumber )` – This method returns a boolean value indicating if the firmware will search for the specified serial port on boot.
- `getRTSCTSFlowControlEnable( portnumber )` – Returns a boolean value that indicates if hardware flow control is enabled on the specified port.

These are straightforward as to their function. The TINI API provides some additional detail on each of these methods. Remember that before you can use serial1 you must call this method:

```
TINIOS.enableSerialPort1( true );
```

And before you can use serial2 or serial3 you need to enable them and set their address if you have placed them at some other address in memory than the default (0x380020 – 0x38002F)

```
TINIOS.setExternalSerialPortAddress( 2, 0x3800020 );
TINIOS.setSerialPortEnable( 2, true );
```

A serial example

Serial0

To test serial0 we will start by using the same `SerialLoopTest.java` program that we used in Chapter 3, without modification. Put your loopback plug on serial0, the same as you used on your PC's serial port. Remember to use a cable that *does not* connect DTR or you will need to remove the solder jumper on J1 on the bottom of your TINI socket board. If you are using a Dallas Semiconductor socketboard and you leave the J1 jumper connected and your serial cable has the DTR line wired, your

TINI will reboot (and then hang as the DTR line is pulled low) as soon as you connect the loopback plug. Compile SerialLoopTest.java for TINI and FTP `SerialLoopTest.tini` to your TINI. The program takes one command line parameter, the name of the serial port to test. The `SerialLoopTest.java` is listed below for your convenience, but refer to Chapter 3 for a more detailed discussion.

Listing 9-1: SerialLoopTest.java

```java
import java.io.*;
import java.util.*;
import javax.comm.*;
import com.dalsemi.system.*;
import com.dalsemi.comm.*;

public class SerialLoopTest implements Runnable,
SerialPortEventListener {

    static CommPortIdentifier portId;
    static Enumeration portList;

    static InputStream inputStream;
    static OutputStream outputStream;

    static SerialPort serialPort;
    Thread readThread;

    static String message2send = "Hello Port!";

    static String messagereceived;

    static byte[] inbuf = new byte[20];
    int i = 0;
    static String portname;

    public static void main(String[] args) {

        // check out the command line args
        if (args.length < 1) {
            System.out.println( "Specify a port! (COM1 or /dev/ttyS0
            or something)." );
              return;
        } else {
            portname = args[0];
            System.out.println( "Testing port: " + portname );
        }

        try {
            // Get the ID of this port
            portId = CommPortIdentifier.getPortIdentifier(portname);
```

```
        // Is it a serial port?
        if (portId.getPortType() != CommPortIdentifier.PORT_SERIAL) {
            System.out.println( "Port is not a serial port");
            return;
        }
    }
    catch(NoSuchPortException e) {
        System.out.println("No Such Port!");
        return;
    }
    catch (Exception e) { System.out.println(e); }
    SerialLoopTest tester = new SerialLoopTest();
}

public SerialLoopTest() {
    try {
        serialPort = (SerialPort) portId.open("SimpleReadApp", 2000);
    }
    catch(PortInUseException e) {
        System.out.println("Port In Use.");
        return;
    }
    catch (Exception e) {
        System.out.println(e);
        return;
    }

    try {
        inputStream = serialPort.getInputStream();
        outputStream = serialPort.getOutputStream();
    }
    catch (IOException e) { System.out.println(e); }

    try {
        serialPort.addEventListener(this);
    }
    catch (TooManyListenersException e) { System.out.println(e); }

    // Turn on some notifiers so we can catch them with an event listener.
    serialPort.notifyOnDataAvailable(true);
    serialPort.notifyOnCTS(true);
    serialPort.notifyOnDSR(true);

    // We don't really need to set the port parameters for a loop back test
    // but if you did, this is how you would.
    try {
        serialPort.setSerialPortParams(19200,
            SerialPort.DATABITS_8,
            SerialPort.STOPBITS_1,
            SerialPort.PARITY_NONE);
```

```
        serialPort.setFlowControlMode(SerialPort.FLOWCONTROL_NONE);
    }
    catch (UnsupportedCommOperationException e) {
        System.out.println(e);
    }

    readThread = new Thread(this);
    readThread.start();
}

public void run() {
    // send characters out the port
    try {
        outputStream.write( message2send.getBytes() );
    }
    catch (IOException e){ System.out.println(e); }

    System.out.println("Flipping RTS...");
    serialPort.setRTS( ! serialPort.isRTS() );

    System.out.println("Flipping DTR...");
    serialPort.setDTR( ! serialPort.isDTR() );
    try { Thread.sleep(1000); } catch (Exception e) { }

    serialPort.removeEventListener();
    serialPort.close();

    System.out.print( i + " bytes read from port " + portname + ". " );
    if (i<1) {
        System.out.println( "Maybe something is not working." );
    }
    else { System.out.println();   }
}

public void serialEvent(SerialPortEvent event) {
    // determine whuch event has happened
    switch(event.getEventType()) {
    case SerialPortEvent.BI:
    case SerialPortEvent.OE:
    case SerialPortEvent.FE:
    case SerialPortEvent.PE:
        System.out.println("Some status line changed.");
        break;
    case SerialPortEvent.CD:
        System.out.println("Status line CD changed.");
        break;
    case SerialPortEvent.CTS:
        System.out.println("Status line CTS changed.");
        break;
    case SerialPortEvent.DSR:
```

```
                   System.out.println("Status line DSR changed.");
                   break;
             case SerialPortEvent.RI:
                   System.out.println("Status line RI changed.");
                   break;
             case SerialPortEvent.OUTPUT_BUFFER_EMPTY:
                   System.out.println("Buffer Empty");
                   break;
             case SerialPortEvent.DATA_AVAILABLE:
                   byte[] readBuffer = new byte[20];
                   try {
                       while (inputStream.available() > 0) {
                             int numBytes = inputStream.read(readBuffer);
                             i += numBytes;
                             messagereceived = new String(readBuffer);
                             System.out.println("Read: " + messagereceived);
                       }
                   }
                   catch (IOException e) { System.out.println(e); }
                   break;
          }
      }
}
```

Compile the program:

```
C:\> javac -bootclasspath %TINI_HOME%\bin\tiniclasses.jar
            -d bin src\SerialLoopTest.java
C:\> java   -classpath c:\opt\tini1.02d\bin\tini.jar;. BuildDependency
            -p %TINI_HOME%\bin\owapi_dependencies_TINI.jar
            -f bin
            -x %TINI_HOME%\bin\owapi_dep.txt
            -o bin\SerialLoopTest.tini
            -d %TINI_HOME%\bin\tini.db
```

Run the program on TINI and observe the results:

```
TINI />java SerialLoopTest.tini serial0
Testing port: serial0
[ Sat Jan 01 00:00:00 GMT 2000 ]  Message from System: Serial server stopped.
Flipping RTS...
Flipping DTR...
Read: Hello Port!
11 bytes read from port serial0.
TINI />
[ Sat Jan 01 00:00:00 GMT 2000 ]  Message from System: Serial server started.
```

Notice the output. When we access serial0, the TINI OS automatically stops the serial server and then restarts it when we are done. Also notice that we didn't receive the RTS and DTR events as we did in Chapter 3. This is simply because serial0 does not support hardware flow control.

Let's try a real example where we send meaningful characters to a serial device and read back meaningful characters. We will be reading data from a digital multimeter. This program is not much more complicated, but it does show more of the methods for controlling the serial port. The meter expects us to talk to it at 2400 baud using 7 data bits, 2 stop bits and no parity (we know this because we looked in the manual for the meter). To have the meter take a measurement and send back the data we first send it a "D". The meter then replies back with 14 bytes of ASCII information (which is more or less what is on the meter display). Also, because the meter is configured as a DCE and so is serial0, we will need a null modem adapter.

Listing 9-2: MeterReader.java

```java
import java.io.*;
import java.util.*;
import javax.comm.*;
import com.dalsemi.system.*;
import com.dalsemi.comm.*;

public class MeterReader {

    static CommPortIdentifier portId;
    static SerialPort serialPort;
    static String portname;

    //static Enumeration portList;

    static InputStream inputStream;
    static OutputStream outputStream;

    static String message2send = "D\r";
    static String messagereceived;

    public static void main(String[] args) {

        // check out the command line args
        if (args.length < 1) {
            System.out.println( "Specify a port! (COM1, /dev/ttyS0 or something)." );
            return;
        } else {
            portname = args[0];
            System.out.println( "MeterReader. Using " + portname );
        }

        int times=1; // number of readings to take
        if (args.length>1 ) {
            times = (byte) Integer.valueOf(args[1]).intValue();
        }
```

```
// Is this a valid Serial port?
try {
    // Get the ID of this port
    portId = CommPortIdentifier.getPortIdentifier(portname);
    // Is it a serial port?
    if (portId.getPortType() != CommPortIdentifier.PORT_SERIAL) {
        System.out.println( "Port is not a serial port");
        return;
    }
}
catch(NoSuchPortException e)
{
    System.out.println("No Such Port!");
    return;
}
catch (Exception e) { System.out.println(e); }

// Open the port, set parameters
System.out.println( "Configuring port..." );
try {
    serialPort = (SerialPort) portId.open("MeterReader", 1000);

    serialPort.setSerialPortParams(2400,
        SerialPort.DATABITS_7,
        SerialPort.STOPBITS_2,
        SerialPort.PARITY_NONE);
    serialPort.setFlowControlMode(SerialPort.FLOWCONTROL_NONE);
}
catch(PortInUseException e) {
    System.out.println("Port In Use.");
    return;
}
catch (UnsupportedCommOperationException e) {
    System.out.println("Port option unsupported.");
}
catch (Exception e) {
    System.out.println(e);
    return;
}

// Set input & output streams
try {
    inputStream = serialPort.getInputStream();
    outputStream = serialPort.getOutputStream();
}
catch (IOException e) { System.out.println(e); }

System.out.println( "Reading ..." );
byte[] readBuffer = new byte[20];
int numBytes = 0;

for( int i = 1; i<=times; i++ ) {
```

```
                    // Send the command text
                    try {
                        outputStream.write( message2send.getBytes() );
                        Thread.sleep(500);

                        numBytes = inputStream.read(readBuffer);

                        messagereceived = new String(readBuffer);
                        System.out.println( "Meter:(" + numBytes + ") " +
                            messagereceived);
                    }
                    catch (IOException e) { System.out.println(e); }
                    catch (Exception e) { System.out.println(e); }
                }

            serialPort.close();

        }
}
```

Notice that we need to set the serial port to the proper parameters (baud rate, databits, stopbits, and parity). While some devices are fairly tolerant of miss-set stop bits, the receiving UART will not be able to synchronize with the serial data if the baud rate is improperly set.

```
serialPort = (SerialPort) portId.open("MeterReader", 1000);

serialPort.setSerialPortParams(2400,
    SerialPort.DATABITS_7,
    SerialPort.STOPBITS_2,
    SerialPort.PARITY_NONE);
serialPort.setFlowControlMode(SerialPort.FLOWCONTROL_NONE);
```

The program loops for the specified number of readings, each time sending a "D" to the meter and then reading back the reply from the meter.

```
for( int i = 1; i<=times; i++ ) {
    // Send the command text
    try {
        outputStream.write( message2send.getBytes() );
        Thread.sleep(500);

        numBytes = inputStream.read(readBuffer);

        messagereceived = new String(readBuffer);
        System.out.println( "Meter:(" + numBytes + ") " + messagereceived);
    }
    catch (IOException e) { System.out.println(e); }
    catch (Exception e) { System.out.println(e); }
}
```

Compile the program:

```
C:\> javac -bootclasspath %TINI_HOME%\bin\tiniclasses.jar
           -d bin src\MeterReader.java
C:\> java  -classpath c:\opt\tini1.02d\bin\tini.jar;. BuildDependency
           -p %TINI_HOME%\bin\owapi_dependencies_TINI.jar
           -f bin
           -x %TINI_HOME%\bin\owapi_dep.txt
           -o bin\MeterReader.tini
           -d %TINI_HOME%\bin\tini.db
```

then FTP it to your TINI. In this case we need to stop the serial server before we run the program. If we don't, then it won't work (when the program sends the first "D" to the meter, the TINI OS sees outgoing data so it stops the serial server but then that "D" is lost so the meter never replies with data and our program waits forever). The program takes two command line parameters: the name of the serial port that the meter is connected to and the number of readings to take. Run the program.

```
TINI /> downserver -s
Warning:  This will disconnect users on specified servers.

OK to proceed? (Y/N): y
[ Sat Jan 01 00:00:00 GMT 2000 ]  Message from System: Serial server
stopped.

TINI /> java MeterReader.tini serial0 5
MeterReader. Using serial0
Configuring port...
Reading ...
Meter:(14) DC  05.09   V
Meter:(14) DC  05.10   V
Meter:(14) DC  05.10   V
Meter:(14) DC  05.09   V
Meter:(14) DC  05.09   V

TINI /> startserver -s
[ Sat Jan 01 00:00:00 GMT 2000 ]  Message from System: Serial server
started.
```

The program took five readings of 14 bytes each. In this case we were reading a DC voltage of 5.09 volts (the output of the TINI power supply). Notice we restarted the serial server when we were done.

Serial1

We can run the same two examples on serial1 that we just tested on serial0. To do this we must first add a line driver to serial1, add the optional 1K resistor between the EN2480 pin on the TINI stick and ground to disable the 1-Wire driver, and add a "fake" DTR signal to the serial1 connector. This particular meter (as with many serial devices) expects to see the DTR line high before it will communicate with a computer. So we need to connect pin 4 of the serial1 to Vdd (basically we are saying to any serial device that TINI is always ready to communicate). For the serial line level shifter we used a MAX232 but just about any serial level shifter should do. We chose this one because it does not require external capacitors for the charge pump (to provide ±10 volts).

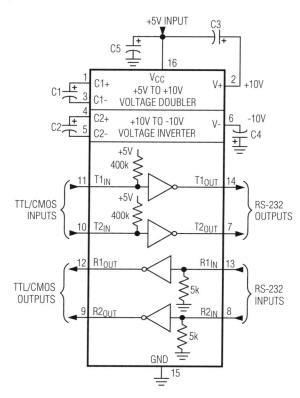

Figure 9-22: MAX232

You should be able to rerun both `SerialLoopTest.tini` and `MeterReader.tini` on serial1 with the exact same results. You will not need to worry about stopping the serial server for this port but you must enable serial1 first. Since the same CPU pins control both the external 1-Wire bus and the serial1 port, we will need to indicate to TINI that we want to use the serial port and not the 1-Wire bus. You can do this by adding the following line to both programs (someplace in the program before actually trying to open the serial port):

```
TINIOS.enableSerialPort1( true );
```

Before you modify the programs to enable serial1, try running either program on TINI and specifying serial1 just for fun. You should see the exception

```
java.io.IOException: Could not write to serial port.
```

Since the state of the serial1 port enable is preserved in TINI memory, we can write a separate program that enables and disables serial1 (and even serial2 and serial3 if we need them) so that our original program does not have to be modified. Why would we want to do this? Without these TINI specific additions to enable serial1 (and we will need similar ones for serial2 and serial3) our programs so far have been 100% non-TINI specific. The `MeterReader.java` and `SerialLoopTest.java` program will run on a PC just as well as on TINI by telling it to read from COM1 (Windows) or \dev\ttyS0 (Linux).

Here is a program that runs on TINI that changes the serial1, serial2 and serial3 settings in TINI memory so that you don't need to modify your programs to enable these ports.

Listing 9-3: serialports.java

```java
import java.io.*;
import java.util.*;
import javax.comm.*;

import com.dalsemi.comm.*;
import com.dalsemi.system.*;
import com.dalsemi.onewire.*;
import com.dalsemi.onewire.adapter.*;

public class serialports {

    static CommPortIdentifier portId;
    static SerialPort serialPort;
    static DSPortAdapter myPortAdapter = null;


    // Tell me the command line options
    public static void usage() {
        System.out.println( "serialports -enable [123] -disable [123] " );
        System.out.println( "                      -search -nosearch -query" );
    }


    // Query the serial ports, report what we find
    public static void query() {
        boolean isonewire = false;
        // The only way to check if serial1 enabled is to open it and
        // catch an exception if there is one.
        System.out.print( "serial1: " );
                try {
                    myPortAdapter =
```

```
                    OneWireAccessProvider.getAdapter("TINIExternalAdapter",
                        "serial1");
                    myPortAdapter.freePort();
                    System.out.println( "enabled for 1-wire communication" );
                    isonewire=true;
                }
                catch (Exception e) {
                    System.out.println( "disabled for 1-wire communication" );
                    isonewire=false;
                }
        if (!isonewire) {
            System.out.print( "           " );
                try {
                    portId = CommPortIdentifier.getPortIdentifier("serial1");
                    serialPort = (SerialPort) portId.open("port enabler", 1000);
                    serialPort.close();
                    System.out.println( "enabled for serial communication" );
                }
                catch (Exception e) {
                    System.out.println( "disabled for serial communication" );
                }
        }

        // Checking serial2 and 3 is easy
        System.out.println( "serial2: "
            + (TINIOS.getExternalSerialPortEnable(2) ? "enabled" : "disabled")
            + ", address 0x"
            + Integer.toHexString(TINIOS.getExternalSerialPortAddress(2)) );
        System.out.println( "serial3: "
            + (TINIOS.getExternalSerialPortEnable(3) ? "enabled" : "disabled")
            + ", address 0x"
            +
            Integer.toHexString(TINIOS.getExternalSerialPortAddress(3)) );
        System.out.println( "Search for ports on boot "
            + (TINIOS.getExternalSerialPortSearchEnable() ? "enabled" : "disabled" ) );
    }


    // set if TINI should search for ports on boot or not
    public static void searchOnBoot( boolean search ) {
        System.out.println( "search on boot " + (search ? "enabled" :
                    "disabled") );
        TINIOS.setExternalSerialPortSearchEnable(search);
    }


    // enable/disable serial ports.
    public static void enableSerial( char port, boolean state ) {
```

```
    switch (port) {
        case '1':
            System.out.println( (state ? "enabling" : "disabling") + " serial1");
            TINIOS.enableSerialPort1( state );
            break;
        case '2':
            System.out.println( (state ? "enabling" : "disabling") + " serial2");
            TINIOS.setExternalSerialPortEnable(2,state);
            break;
        case '3':
            System.out.println( (state ? "enabling" : "disabling") + " serial3");
            TINIOS.setExternalSerialPortEnable(3,state);
            break;
        default:
            System.err.println("invalid port" + port);
            break;
    }
}


public static void main(String[] args) {

    String arg;
    char flag;
    String ports_on="", ports_off="";
    int i=0;

    // Check out all of the comamnd line args and process each as we
    // find them.

    while (i < args.length && args[i].startsWith("-")) {
        arg = args[i++];

        if (arg.startsWith("-s")) {                 // s for search
            searchOnBoot(true);
        }
        else if (arg.startsWith("-n")) {            // n for nosearch
            searchOnBoot(false);
        }
        else if (arg.startsWith("-q")) {            // q for query
            query();
        }
        else if (arg.startsWith("-e")) {            // e for enable
            if (i < args.length) {
                // the the port numbers if any
                ports_on = args[i++];
                for (int j = 0; j < ports_on.length(); j++) {
                    flag = ports_on.charAt(j);
                    enableSerial( flag, true );
```

```
                              }
                          }
                          else {
                              System.err.println("-enable requires a port");
                          }
                      }
                      else if (arg.startsWith("-d")) {        // d for disable
                          if (i < args.length) {
                              // the the port numbers if any
                              ports_off = args[i++];
                              for (int j = 0; j < ports_off.length(); j++) {
                                  flag = ports_off.charAt(j);
                                  enableSerial( flag, false );
                              }
                          }
                          else {
                              System.err.println("-enable requires a port");
                          }
                      }
                      else {
                          System.out.println( "Don't understand " + arg );
                      }
                  }

              }
          }
```

This TINI utility program takes several possible parameters:

`-e [1][2][3]` to enable any of the serial ports 1, 2 or 3 (or any combination).

`-d [1][2][3]` to disable any of the serial ports 1, 2, or 3 (or any combination of ports).

`-s` to tell TINI to search for serial2 and 3 on boot.

`-n` to tell TINI *not* to search for serial2 and 3 on boot.

`-query` to query the current settings.

As you study the program, you will see that `main()` method simply parses the command line and calls the appropriate methods depending on what is specified. There are four helper methods: `usage()`, `query()`, `searchOnBoot( boolean state )`, and `enableSerial( char port, Boolean state )`. The `usage()` method simply reports the command line options if you don't provide any. The `query()` method reports back what TINI thinks the current serial port settings are. The `searchOnBoot( boolean state )` method either enables or disables searching for serial2 and 3 on boot. The `enableSerial( char port, Boolean state )` method enables or disables the specified serial port. All of this is straightforward use of the methods in the `com.dalsemi.system.TINIOS` class with the exception of how we determine if serial1 is enabled or not. The `com.dalsemi.system.TINIOS` class, does not provide a method for querying the status of serial1 but we know that if it is not enabled we get an exception when we try to open it. Actually there are two ways to get an exception: opening serial1 for 1-Wire communication when it is enabled for serial communication, or opening and accessing it as a serial port when it is disabled for 1-Wire communication. The method first tries to open serial1 as a 1-Wire port adapter. If we succeed, we know serial is not enabled as a serial port. If that method does cause an exception, then we know serial1 is enabled for serial port communication.

Compile this program:

```
C:\> javac -bootclasspath %TINI_HOME%\bin\tiniclasses.jar
           -d bin src\serialports.java
C:\> java   -classpath c:\opt\tini1.02d\bin\tini.jar;. BuildDependency
           -p %TINI_HOME%\bin\owapi_dependencies_TINI.jar
           -f bin
           -x %TINI_HOME%\bin\owapi_dep.txt
           -o bin\serialports.tini
           -d %TINI_HOME%\bin\tini.db
```

So now we are ready to test out serial1. Put the loopback plug on serial1 and try the `SerialLoopTest.tini` and `MeterReader.tini` programs.

```
TINI /> java SerialLoopTest.tini serial1
Testing port: serial1
java.io.IOException: Could not write to serial port
Flipping RTS...
Flipping DTR...
0 bytes read from port serial1. Maybe something is not working.
TINI />
```

See, it didn't work. We didn't enable serial1 for serial port communications. Run the `serialport.tini` program to enable serial1 and try again.

```
TINI /> java serialports.tini -e 1
enabling serial1
TINI /> java serialports.tini -q
serial1: disabled for 1-wire communication
         enabled for serial communication
serial2: disabled, address 0x380028
serial3: disabled, address 0x380020
Search for ports on boot enabled
TINI />
```

With the serial port now enabled we should be successful running both `SerialLooptest.tini` and `MeterReader.tini` and telling them to read from serial1.

```
TINI /> java SerialLoopTest.tini serial1
Testing port: serial1
Flipping RTS...
Flipping DTR...
```

```
Read: Hello Port!
11 bytes read from port serial1.
TINI />
```

```
TINI /> java MeterReader.tini serial1 5
MeterReader. Using serial1
Configuring port...
Reading ...
Meter:(14) DC   05.03    V
Meter:(14) DC   05.03    V
Meter:(14) DC   05.03    V
Meter:(14) DC   05.02    V
Meter:(14) DC   05.03    V
TINI />
```

No surprises: the same results as with accessing serial0, and the best part is that we didn't need to modify our original program to use serial1.

Serial2 and serial3

We can run the same two examples on serial2 and serial3 that we just tested on serial0. To do this you must implement the full serial port hardware as shown in the schematic in Figures 9-19 and 9-20 (the UART and line drivers).

You should be able to rerun both `SerialLoopTest.tini` and `MeterReader.tini` on serial2 and serial3 with the exact same results. But again, just as with serial1, we need to indicate to TINI that we are interested in using the serial port2 or 3 this time. Not only must we enable these serial ports but we have found that we need to reboot TINI after doing so, so that the TINI firmware can find and initialize them. Run `serialports.tini` to enable them.

```
TINI /> java serialports.tini -e 23 -q
enabling serial2
enabling serial3
serial1: disabled for 1-wire communication
         enabled for serial communication
serial2: enabled, address 0x380028
serial3: enabled, address 0x380020
Search for ports on boot enabled
TINI />
```

Now reboot TINI. If you do this with JavaKit running and TINI serial0 connected to your PC, you should see some new information in the boot test that goes whizzing by. Before installing the serial2 and serial3 ports, your boot test probably looked something like this:

```
—> TINI Boot <—
TINI OS 1.02d
API Version 800C
Copyright (C) 1999 - 2001 Dallas Semiconductor Corporation
18000000
```

```
Running POR Code
Memory POR Routines
000020
0080,0100,0180,0200,0280,0300,0380,0400,0480,0500,0580,0600,Transient
blocks freed: 0626, size: 01FDC0
CPersistant blocks freed: 0000, size: 000000
KM_Init Passed
Ethernet MAC Address Part Found
TTS Revision: 179 , Date: 11/05/01 5:16p
Thread_Init Passed
External Serial Port Init
External serial ports not enabled
Memory Available: 06D3C0
Creating Task:
0100
01
Loading application at 0x070100
Creating Task:
0200
02
Application load complete
```

The interesting lines are in bold text, telling us that the serial ports (meaning serial2 and serial3) are not enabled. If you enable them but don't implement them in hardware, or your hardware is not working properly, then you might see something like this:

```
. . .
TTS Revision: 179 , Date: 11/05/01 5:16p
Thread_Init Passed
External Serial Port Init
Port serial2 NOT detected
Port serial3 NOT detected
Memory Available: 0F3620
Creating Task:
. . .
```

This is telling us that while TINI was trying to initialize serial2 and serial3, it couldn't find them. Either they are not connected or not working properly. Once the hardware is working properly you will see this sort of message in that part of the boot sequence:

```
. . .
TTS Revision: 179 , Date: 11/05/01 5:16p
Thread_Init Passed
External Serial Port Init
Port serial2 detected
Port serial3 detected
Memory Available: 06D3C0
Creating Task:
. . .
```

If you have gotten to this point, then serial2 and serial3 should be working just fine. You can run both `SerialLoopTest.tini` and `MeterReader.tini` on serial2 and serial3 with the exact same results as with serial0 and serial1.

A parting word on serial ports

It is possible to change the speed of the serial port by directly changing the clock divisor the UART uses. Why would you want to do this? In Chapter 12 on controller area networks, we will find that we cannot achieve CAN bus speeds greater than 125 kbps because the TINI CPU oscillator of 18.432 MHz doesn't divide nicely and leaves us with an unacceptable percent error (for the CAN bus). If we switch the TINI CPU to a 18.0 MHz oscillator, then we get very nice CAN bus speeds (with no error) at speeds of 500 kbps and 1 Mbps but this unfortunately changes the speed of the internal TINI UART as well (the external UART has its own oscillator so that remains unchanged). By changing the oscillator from 18.432 MHz to 18 MHz we are slowing TINI by 2.3% (and remember that the TINI clock will be 2.3% slower so all time and time-related methods will be 2.3% off). The 16550 UART has a number of programmable registers for adjusting various things and controlling the UART operation. The serial port baud rate is controlled by a divisor that divides the UART clock down. The divisor is determined by:

$$divisor = \frac{frequency}{baud\ rate \cdot 16}$$

If we leave the divisor alone but change the TINI clock, we can find the actual baud rate using this new clock speed (it's 2.3% slower):

$$baud\ rate = \frac{frequency}{divisor \cdot 16}$$

Table 9-3: Baud rates after changing clock

Desired baudrate (bps)	Divisor	Actual baudrate using 18.0 MHz clock (bps)
300	3840	293
600	1920	586
1200	960	1172
2400	480	2344
4800	240	4687
9600	120	9375
19200	60	18750
38400	30	37500
57600	20	56250
115200	10	112500

Again, this error is 2.3%, which is within the 5% allowed in RS-232 specification. If we are interested in reducing the error brought on by changing the CPU clock, then we can program the UART with a new divisor to account for this slower clock using this method:

```
TINISerialPort.setDivisor( int );
```

Table 9-4 shows the new divisor and the error. There is still some error as the 18-MHz clock we use is not evenly divisible by the baud rates we want. It is worth noting that we can't reduce the error for the higher speeds but with all baud rates below 38400 there is less than 1% error.

Table 9-4: UART baud rate divisor after changing clock

Desired baudrate (bps)	Divisor	Actual baudrate	Error (%) (bps)
300	3750	300	0
600	1875	600	0
1200	937	1200	0
2400	469	2399	0.05
4800	234	4808	0.02
9600	117	9615	0.1
19200	59	19067	0.7
38400	29	38793	1
57600	20	56250	2.3
115200	10	112500	2.3

I think we can conclude that if you do need the faster speeds for a CAN bus and you change the CPU oscillator to 18 MHz, it's probably not worth changing the UART baud rate divisor (unless, of course, you select an oscillator that is significantly faster or slower than 18.432 MHz—then you will need to change the serial port baud rate divisor).

Parallel Ports

The TINI stick and socketboard also support parallel I/O. This is not the traditional parallel port that you would find on a personal computer such as that meant for a printer, but simply parallel data lines for input and output to other digital devices. The E10 socketboard has direct support for 16 inputs and 16 outputs. These parallel I/O lines provide digital control lines to you for whatever purpose you can dream up. With these you can control external logic, light-emitting diodes, and relays, and read the status of switches and simple sensors. Review how we a added memory-mapped device in Chapter 8. That's exactly how the E10 socketboard implements parallel I/O.

We can add multiple banks of parallel inputs, outputs or bi-directional I/O depending on our needs. These parallel I/O lines can be constructed from a wide variety of logic circuits depending on the application, and they can be configured to control a still wider variety of devices.

TINI parallel ports

If you examine the TINI socketboard Rev C schematic[6], page 4, you notice that there are two major sections to the parallel I/O: the port control logic (address decoders and selectors) and the I/O buffers/drivers.

Port control

The port control logic performs the address decoding and selects the appropriate buffer/driver for either writing data to a parallel device or reading data from a parallel device. The address decoders place the E10 parallel I/O at 0x380000 and 0x3800001 in the TINI memory map. Both locations are available for reading and writing, but both read and write use different drivers/buffers (not the same as 16 bi-directional I/O lines). When writing data, the /WR line enables U4:B, which in turn enables either /ENWR0 or /ENWR1. /ENWR0 enables U12 and /ENWR1 enables U16. When reading parallel data, the /WR line enables U4:B, which in turn enables either /ENWR0 or /ENWR1. /ENWR0 enables U12 and /ENWR1 enables U16.

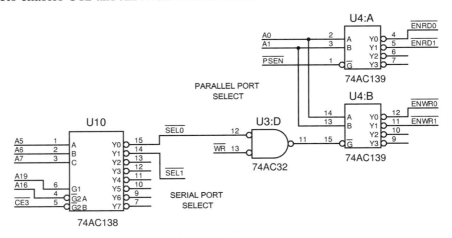

Figure 9-23: Parallel port control

Parallel I/O buffers/drivers

The chips U12, U14, U16, and U17 are the input buffers and output drivers for the I/O ports.

---

[6] TINI Socket Rev C schematic – http://www.ibutton.com/TINI/hardware/index.html

- U12, U16 use a 74HC574 (octal D-type flip-flip)[7] to provide 16 tristate, latched, outline lines. U12 does not have pull-ups (these eight outputs will float when not driven) and U16 does (these eight outputs will go high when not driven by the flip-flop).

- U14, U17 use a 74HC541 (octal buffer/line driver)[8] to provide 16 latched inputs. All 16 input lines have pull-ups, so they will be high when there is no input signal.

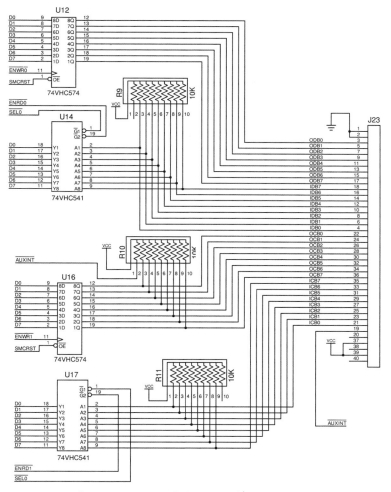

Figure 9-24: Parallel port buffers/drivers

---

[7] 74HC574 datasheet – http://www.fairchildsemi.com/ds/MM/MM74HC574.pdf
[8] 74HC541 datasheet – http://www.fairchildsemi.com/pf/MM/MM74HC541.html

Parallel communication software (API)

All of the parallel I/O communication is done through the TINI `DataPort` class. With this class, we can read and write to any address in the TINI memory map.

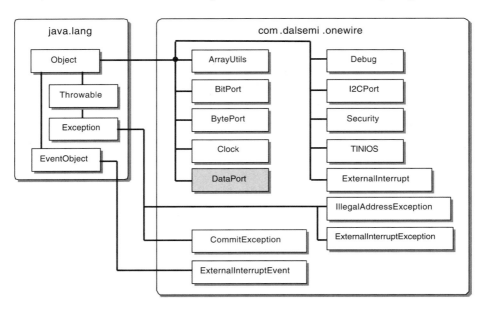

Figure 9-25: com.dalsemi.system

To access the parallel I/O, we must do four things: 1 – Create a new `DataPort` at a specific address. 2 – Set it as sequential or FIFO. 3 – Set the stretch cycles as needed. Finally, we will read or write data as needed. These are the methods to use:

- `DataPort( int address )` – Create a new `DataPort` beginning at the specified address in memory. The `DataPort` created can be used for reading and writing (provided the hardware is properly connected to enable either reading or writing or both).

- `setFIFOMode( bloolean )` – Each `DataPort` can be configured for accessing sequential memory locations or as a FIFO. With sequential access, the `read(byte array[], int start, int length)` or `write(byte array[], int start, int length)` methods will automatically increment the DataPort address to the next location. The address is set back to the beginning with the next read() or write(). With FIFO access, reads and writes do not increment the address.

- `getFIFOMode()` – This method returns true if FIFO mode is set and false if it is not.

- `setStretchCycles( byte stretch )` – Stretch cycles allow the application to set the number of machine cycles needed in order to execute a bus read or write. This allows access to both fast and slow peripherals without additional logic. Some memory-mapped peripherals have slow access times, so it may not be possible to access these external devices at full speed. A STRETCH0 will result in two memory bus cycles for a read or write. A STRETCH10 will result in twelve machine cycles for a data bus read or write.

- `read()` – This method reads and returns a single byte from the DataPort. Note that the value returned is really of the type int. Since we are reading a single byte, it doesn't matter if we have FIFO mode set or not.

- `read( byte array[], int start, int length )` – This method reads data from the `DataPort` and places it into an array. It returns the number of bytes read. This method puts the read data into the array starting with the specified offset and reads the number of bytes as specified by the length parameter. This reads from a single `DataPort` address if FIFOMode is true or it sequentially increases the `DataPort` address for each byte read if FIFOMode is false. The next read or write starts at the beginning address for this `DataPort`.

- `write( int data )` – The write() method writes a single byte to the `DataPort`. Since we are writing a single byte, it doesn't matter if we have FIFO mode set or not.

- `write(byte array[], int start, int length)` – This method writes data to the `DataPort` from an array. It starts writing data from the array starting with the specified offset and writes the number of bytes as specified by the length parameter. This writes to a single `DataPort` address if FIFOMode is true or it sequentially increases the `DataPort` address for each byte written if FIFOMode is false. The next read or write starts at the beginning address for this `DataPort`.

A word of caution when working with bytes. Java does unexpected things with bytes since it thinks it is working with signed numbers. If you perform any mathematical or bitwise operation on a primitive data type smaller than an int (like a char, byte, or short) then Java automatically promotes them to an int before performing the operation. The operation will be performed on the resulting int value and the resulting value will then be an int. This is why we need to cast the result back to a byte when we are done. The following program shows how this can get us into unexpected trouble:

Listing 9-4: byteExample.java

```java
public class byteExample {

    public static void main(String[] args)    {
```

```
        byte b=0;
        int i=0;

        b=0x01;
        System.out.println( ".......... b= 0x" + ByteUtils.toHexString(b) );
        b=(byte)(b<<7);
        System.out.println( "b=(b<<7),   b= 0x" + ByteUtils.toHexString(b) );
        b=(byte)(b>>7);
        System.out.println( "b=(b>>7),   b= 0x" + ByteUtils.toHexString(b) );
        System.out.println( );

        b=0x01;
        System.out.println( ".......... b= 0x" + ByteUtils.toHexString(b) );
        b=(byte)(b<<7);
        System.out.println( "b=(b<<7),   b= 0x" + ByteUtils.toHexString(b) );
        b=(byte)(b>>>7);
        System.out.println( "b=(b>>>7),  b= 0x" + ByteUtils.toHexString(b) );
        System.out.println( );

        i=0x01;
        System.out.println( ".......... i= 0x" + Integer.toHexString(i) );
        i=(i<<31);
        System.out.println( "i=(i<<31),  i= 0x" + Integer.toHexString(i) );
        i=(i>>>31);
        System.out.println( "i=(i>>>31), i= 0x" + Integer.toHexString(i) );
        System.out.println( );

        b=0x01;
        System.out.println( ".......... b= 0x" + ByteUtils.toHexString(b) );
        i=(b<<7);
        System.out.println( "i=(b<<7),   i= 0x" + Integer.toHexString(i) );
        i=(i>>7);
        System.out.println( "i=(i>>7),   i= 0x" + Integer.toHexString(i) );
        b=(byte)i;
        System.out.println( "b=(byte)i,  b= 0x" + ByteUtils.toHexString(b) );

    }
}
```

Compile this program:

```
C:\> cd src
C:\> javac -bootclasspath %TINI_HOME%\bin\tiniclasses.jar
          -d ..\bin byteExample.java
C:\> cd ..
C:\> java  -classpath c:\opt\tini1.02d\bin\tini.jar;. BuildDependency
          -p %TINI_HOME%\bin\owapi_dependencies_TINI.jar
          -f bin
          -x %TINI_HOME%\bin\owapi_dep.txt
          -o bin\byteExample.tini
          -d %TINI_HOME%\bin\tini.db
```

Now run this program on either your PC or on a TINI and observe the results.

```
TINI /> java byteExample.tini
........... b= 0x01
b=(b<<7),   b= 0x80
b=(b>>7),   b= 0xFF

........... b= 0x01
b=(b<<7),   b= 0x80
b=(b>>>7),  b= 0xFF

........... i= 0x1
i=(i<<31),  i= 0x80000000
i=(i>>>31), i= 0x1

........... b= 0x01
i=(b<<7),   i= 0x80
i=(i>>7),   i= 0x1
b=(byte)i,  b= 0x01
```

Notice that we need to explicitly cast the result of the left shift (<<) and right shift (>>) back to a byte. If we don't, we will get a compile time error message "possible loss of precision." In the first part of this example we shift a 1 bit from the least significant position to the most significant position and back again. You might think this works as expected since we shifted the 1 into the most significant bit position indicating that this is a negative number, so when we shift right again Java keeps this as a negative number. Another obvious choice would be to use the shift right with 0 extension operator (>>>) as in the second part of this example. But this doesn't work any better as you can see, because Java promotes the value of b to an int and we cast this back to a byte for both the left shift and the right shift. The shift right with 0 extension is actually working, but it is working on an int so the 8th bit of the int becomes the most significant bit of our byte when we cast it back to a byte, and that's still a 1. Part 3 of this example shows how the right shift with 0 extension works on an integer. Part 4 of this example shows the proper way to work with bytes, keeping the intermediate results of the byte operations as an int and then casting this back to a byte when we are done.

A simple parallel device example

Let's build a simple parallel communication example, connect it to TINI and write some Java code to talk to it (both inputs and outputs). You can follow the parallel schematics presented previously (like what's on the E10 and E20 socketboards) or you can implement this on a prototype board with a few simplifications. A simplified address decoder is shown in Figure 9-26. This is used to select the inputs and outputs and place them in the TINI memory map at 0x0800000 (0x0800000–0x0800003, actually).

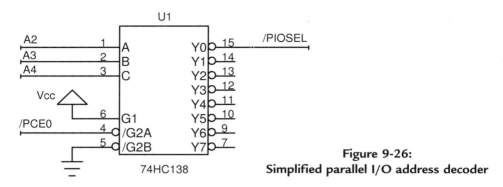

Figure 9-26:
Simplified parallel I/O address decoder

We are only working with one set of input buffers for this example (although you can implement as many as you like and connect them to different addresses on the address decoder). We are using a 74VHC541 octal line driver for these inputs. This is enabled by both the chip select and the TINI /RD line as we are putting these inputs and the outputs at the same location in memory.

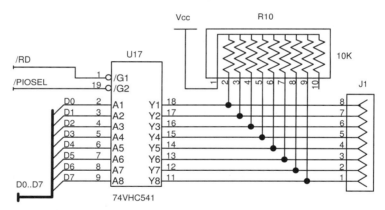

Figure 9-27: Input buffer

For the output latches we will use a 74VHC574 octal d-type flip-flop to hold the state on the output lines after we have written to them. For both the inputs and the outputs we will use pull-ups on all of the input and output lines, but you can just as easily change these to pull-downs as needed by your application (just change it on the resistor networks to ground).

What you connect to the input and output is up to you. You can read the position of switches for inputs and can control LEDs for some simple output. See Appendix C for examples of general-purpose circuits. In the case of this example, we will be connecting the output latches directly to the input buffers so we can easily see what's working and what's not. It's not the most exciting example but it shows that the hardware and DataPorts are working.

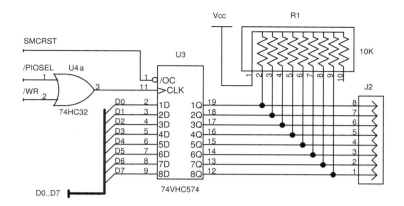

Figure 9-28: Output latches

Listing 9-5: ParallelIO.java

```java
import com.dalsemi.system.*;

public class ParallelIO {

    public static void main(String[] args)  {

        int d=0;
        byte b=0;

        // Configure the dataport
        DataPort pio = new DataPort( 0x00800000 );
        pio.setStretchCycles(DataPort.STRETCH2);
        pio.setFIFOMode(false);

        if (args.length>=1) {
            // Get the command line integer
            d=Integer.decode(args[0]).intValue();
            b=(byte)d;
            // tell me whats going on
            System.out.println( "Write " + ByteUtils.toBinaryString(b)
                                + " 0x" + ByteUtils.toHexString(b) );

            // write the bit pattern to the output port
            try {
                pio.write( d );
            }
            catch( Exception e) {
                System.out.println( "error in read" );
            }
```

```
        }

        // read the bit pattern on the input port
        try {
            d=pio.read( );
            b=(byte)d;
            System.out.println( "Read  " + ByteUtils.toBinaryString(b)
                                + " 0x" + ByteUtils.toHexString(b) );
        }
        catch( Exception e) {
            System.out.println( "error in read" );
        }


    }
}
```

This program is very simple and straightforward. Notice that we are doing simple single-byte reads and writes. The methods for printing bytes in hex and binary are included in the ByteUtils class (in appendix B).

Compile this program, and convert it to a .tini file

```
C:\> javac -bootclasspath %TINI_HOME%\bin\tiniclasses.jar
         -d bin src\ParallelIO.java
C:\> java  -classpath c:\opt\tini1.02d\bin\tini.jar;. BuildDependency
         -p %TINI_HOME%\bin\owapi_dependencies_TINI.jar
         -f bin
         -x %TINI_HOME%\bin\owapi_dep.txt
         -o bin\ParallelIO.tini
         -d %TINI_HOME%\bin\tini.db
```

Then FTP the .tini file to your TINI. When you run this program with no command line parameters it will read the value input buffers. You can optionally specify a single value on the command line (decimal or hex) that will be written to the output latches before the program reads from the inputs. Here is an example of the output from this program:

```
TINI /> java ParallelIO.tini 0x55
Write 01010101 0x55
Read  01010101 0x55
TINI /> java ParallelIO.tini
Read  01010101 0x55
TINI /> java ParallelIO.tini 0xAA
Write 10101010 0xAA
Read  10101010 0xAA
TINI /> java ParallelIO.tini
Read  10101010 0xAA
TINI /> java ParallelIO.tini 0xFF
Write 11111111 0xFF
Read  11111111 0xFF
TINI /> java ParallelIO.tini
```

```
Read   11111111 0xFF
TINI /> java ParallelIO.tini 0x00
Write 00000000 0x00
Read   00000000 0x00
```

Notice that whatever value is written to the outputs is read on the inputs. If no value is written to the outputs, then the previous value is still read (that's what the output latches do). While this is a very simple circuit and program, there are many applications for simple parallel I/O lines control. These outputs could be connected to LEDs to indicate status or to relays to control appliances. The inputs could be connected to optical-isolators so you can sense switch positions or detect voltages. There are lots of possibilities.

Another example

In the previous example we read and wrote single bytes from and to the parallel I/O lines. This works well for simple device control but is somewhat slow if you are using the parallel lines for data communication with some external device. Where data speed is more important, we would want to use array reads and writes. You would also want to place the address decoder for these parallel I/O lines in the CE memory space (somewhere in /CE3, probably, but not overlapping the Ethernet controller or the real-time clock) because accesses to CE devices are faster than accesses to PCE devices. PCE device access is slower because the CPU is copying data from CE memory space (internal memory) to PCE space. The following program illustrates the differences in reading from CE space and PCE space. We are not reading any particular data, just demonstrating the differences in the speeds of array reads.

Listing 9-6: pspeed.java

```java
import com.dalsemi.system.*;

public class pspeed {

    public static void testPortBlock(int port)   {

        int d=0;

        DataPort pio = new DataPort( port );
        pio.setStretchCycles(DataPort.STRETCH0);
        pio.setFIFOMode(false);

        int    bytes=65100;
        long   start=0, stop=0;
        float time;
        byte[] data = new byte[bytes];
```

```
        try {
            System.out.println( "Testing 0x" + Integer.toHexString(port) );
            start = System.currentTimeMillis();

            d=pio.read(data,0,bytes );

            stop = System.currentTimeMillis();
            time = ((float)(stop-start));
            System.out.println( bytes + " bytes in " + time/1000 + " seconds or "
                                + bytes/time*1000 + " Bytes/Sec" );
        }
        catch( Exception e) {
            System.out.println( "error in read" );
        }

    }

    public static void testPortSequence(int port)   {

        int d=0;

        DataPort pio = new DataPort( port );
        pio.setStretchCycles(DataPort.STRETCH0);
        pio.setFIFOMode(false);

        int    bytes=4096;
        long   start=0, stop=0;
        float  time;

        try {
            System.out.println( "Testing 0x" + Integer.toHexString(port) );
            start = System.currentTimeMillis();
            for(int i=0; i<=bytes; i++) {
                d=pio.read();
            }
            stop = System.currentTimeMillis();
            time = ((float)(stop-start));
            System.out.println( bytes + " bytes in " + time/1000 + " seconds or "
                                + bytes/time*1000 + " Bytes/Sec" );
        }
        catch( Exception e) {
            System.out.println( "error in read" );
        }

    }

    public static void main(String[] args)   {
        System.out.println( "DataPort Speed Test" );
        System.out.println( "Block reads" );
        System.out.println( "————" );
```

```
        testPortBlock( 0x00300000 );
        testPortBlock( 0x00800000 );
        System.out.println( "Sequential reads" );
        System.out.println( "——————" );
        testPortSequence( 0x00300000 );
        testPortSequence( 0x00800000 );
    }
}
```

This class declares two methods: `testPortBlock(int port)` reads a single large block of data from a specified address, and `testPortSequence(int port)` reads single bytes from a specified address. We will invoke each of these methods on a chunk of memory in both CE and PCE space. Since we are simply measuring the read speed, it doesn't really matter what the exact section of memory is or if there is a real hardware device mapped to that section of memory or not.

Compile this program:

```
C:\> javac -bootclasspath %TINI_HOME%\bin\tiniclasses.jar
            -d bin src\pspeed.java
C:\> java   -classpath c:\opt\tini1.02d\bin\tini.jar;. BuildDependency
            -p %TINI_HOME%\bin\owapi_dependencies_TINI.jar
            -f bin
            -x %TINI_HOME%\bin\owapi_dep.txt
            -o bin\pspeed.tini
            -d %TINI_HOME%\bin\tini.db
```

FTP the .tini file to your TINI and run it. The output of this is:

```
TINI /> java pspeed.tini
DataPort Speed Test
Block reads
———— —
Testing 0x300000
65100 bytes in 0.1099999994 seconds or 591818.18 Bytes/Sec
Testing 0x800000
65100 bytes in 0.400000005 seconds or 162750.0 Bytes/Sec
Sequential reads
————————
Testing 0x300000
4096 bytes in 5.4699997 seconds or 748.8117 Bytes/Sec
Testing 0x800000
4096 bytes in 5.4499998 seconds or 751.55963 Bytes/Sec
```

Notice that accessing memory by block reads is about three times faster from CE space than from PCE space and that reading blocks of data rather than single bytes is 200–800 times faster. If you are simply controlling the parallel I/O lines for occasionally sensing a status change or turning a device on or off then it doesn't matter much. But if you are interfacing a device that sends a large amount of data, like an analog-to-digital converter, then the speed of using block reads is essential.

Other ways of handling parallel I/O

We have shown here how to implement memory-mapped parallel I/O drivers. In Chapter 11 we discuss the I²C capability of TINI and there we implement I²C devices that are capable of adding 8-bit and 16-bit parallel I/O lines.

Summary

In this chapter we have discussed the details of TINI serial ports and parallel I/O. These two interfaces will enable you to connect many devices to your TINI for control and automation tasks.

References

1. *Interfacing the standard parallel port, Craig Peacock,*
    http://www.beyondlogic.org/spp/parallel.htm

2. *Interfacing the standard serial port, Craig Peacock,*
    http://www.beyondlogic.org/serial/serial.htm (part 1 & 2)
    http://www.beyondlogic.org/serial/serial1.htm (part 3 & 4)

3. *Serial HOWTO, v2.15 November 2001, David S.Lawyer,*
    http://www.ibiblio.org/mdw/HOWTO/Serial-HOWTO.html

4. *ePanorama – WiringRS-232 to RJ-45 connector,*
    http://www.epanorama.net/documents/lan/rs232_rj45.html

5. *ePanorama – Common RS-232 cable wirings,*
    http://www.epanorama.net/documents/pc/rs232cables.html

6. *Fairchild datasheets,*
    http://www.fairchildsemi.com/

CHAPTER **10**

1-Wire Basics for TINI

The 1-Wire Net, sometimes known as a MicroLAN, is a low-cost network for communicating digitally over twisted-pair cable with 1-Wire components. A 1-Wire network system consists of three main elements: a bus master (such as a TINI microcontroller or a microprocessor) with controlling software, the wiring and associated connectors, and the 1-Wire devices. In this chapter we discuss the details of the 1-Wire network and how to communicate with a variety of 1-Wire devices using the 1-Wire Java API from both the TINI microcontroller and from a personal computer through a serial or parallel port.

What Is the 1-Wire Bus?

1-Wire is a bus technology developed by Dallas Semiconductor to be used for communicating with the myriad of electronic components produced by Dallas Semiconductor. We're going to talk more about these devices later but, to summarize, they're things like temperature sensors, switches, potentiometers, A/D converters, memories, battery monitors and identification devices. The 1-Wire bus itself gets its name from the fact that it consists only of one signal line and a ground. In order to communicate information over such a minimal bus, all the devices on the bus are *smart*. They have their own internal circuitry to handle things like timing, communications, and maintaining their state with respect to who is supposed to be talking and who is supposed to be listening. Many 1-Wire devices don't require external power—instead, they steal power parasitically from the bus.

When a number of 1-Wire devices are networked to a 1-Wire bus master controller such as a PC or a TINI, you have what Dallas Semiconductor calls a Micro Local Area Network, or MicroLAN. The recommended media used for interconnecting such a network is simple category 5 twisted pair for long runs or telephone cable for short runs.

How the 1-Wire Bus Works

The details of how to communicate with sophisticated remote electronics through just one signal wire and one ground aren't trivial. In this section, we examine exactly how it's done. Before burrowing into the details of 1-Wire, it helps to stand back and take a broad look at some of the salient features. We'll start by listing and describing some of the most important of these:

The 1-Wire bus is a master/slave environment.

A single intelligent master device such as a PC or a TINI acts as a bus controller, initiating all bus communications, while one or more external Dallas Semiconductor 1-Wire devices on the bus act as slaves. While there can be multiple slaves, there can be only one master. Communication always starts with the master talking, then the slaves responding. But, as is often the case with the use of the word "always," there are exceptions. In some cases, certain types of slaves can post interrupts on the bus.

1-Wire devices are self timed.

Each of the slave devices on the bus has its own independent internal 4-MHz clock. It uses that clock to keep track of read/write timeslots on the 1-Wire bus, and to identify a bus reset.

There are two sorts of timing associated with the 1-Wire bus: that associated with a reset, and that associated with data.

Both make use of the fact that individual slave devices are independently monitoring the passage of time and can keep track of the state of the bus on their own.

Each 1-Wire device has a unique 64-bit ID code.

This ID consists of an 8-bit family code byte, a 48-bit unique serial number, and an 8-bit CRC, or cyclic redundancy check, byte. The 8-bit family code establishes what type of device it is. The 48-bit serial number is a number guaranteed to be unique to the individual device you have, within a family. So while you may have many devices with the same family code, none ever has the same serial number, and hence, never has the same 64-bit ID code. The CRC, or cyclic redundancy check, byte represents the value of a specific logical operation on the preceding 56 bits. After the master reads the 64-bit ID code, it can re-compute the value of the CRC based on the first 56 bits and compare it to the CRC that it received embedded in the 64-bit ID code. If they match, that's an indication that the data received was error free.

1-Wire devices are individually selectable.

The 64-bit ID code can be used to select individual devices on the 1-Wire bus, deselecting all others.

1-Wire devices respond to a series of commands.

These commands are typically 8 bits. A family of commands is common to all 1-Wire devices. These commands tend to relate to different methods of selecting and identifying the devices. Beyond that, some devices have additional commands specific to device function.

The bus master can figure out what devices are present on the bus.

There are some ingenious algorithms that are part of the 1-Wire bus protocol that enable the bus master to identify what's on the bus, through a smart process of elimination.

The 1-Wire bus is open collector.

This means that the bus is actively pulled low by the master or slave devices, but never actively driven high. Instead, the electronics responsible for pulling the bus low are simply turned off, allowing the bus to passively be pulled high through a pull-up resistor. This eliminates the possibility of something on the bus actively driving the bus high while something else is actively pulling the bus low. With the open collector configuration, bus conflicts such as this result in a harmless "wired and."

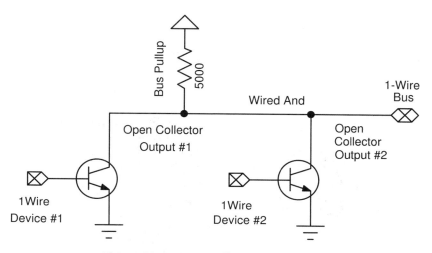

Figure 10-1: Open collector, 5K pull-up

The 1-Wire bus is a 5V bus.

The 1-Wire bus has logic high value (a "one") of 2.2 volts or greater and a logic low value (a "zero") of 0.8 volts or less.

The TINI has a direct 1-Wire port on it.

The TINI also has a Java API that supports high-level communication with 1-Wire devices. Details of how the individual bits are put on the bus and how the master identifys what's on the bus are made completely transparent to the user.

A PC RS232 Com port or printer port can control the 1-Wire bus.

Dallas Semiconductor offers a variety of electronic components that act as adapters between the RS232, parallel, and USB ports on a PC and 1-Wire bus, allowing you to use your PC as the bus master. There is also a Java API that supports high-level communication with 1-Wire devices. Once again, details of how the individual bits are put on the bus and how the master identifys what's on the bus are made completely transparent to the user.

Figure 10-2: Miscellaneous port adaptors

There are special 1-Wire devices known as iButtons.

iButtons are 1-Wire devices that have been packaged in a special container known as a MicroCan.

Figure 10-3: Front and back photo of iButton

The MicroCan provides a very rugged, simple, two-contact, container for the 1-Wire electronics inside it, and a whole host of products allow you to mount, connect, and access iButtons. iButtons are designed to be a competing technology to bar codes, smart cards, RF tags, and similar identification/authorization type products. There are iButtons that provide authentication, and they can be worn on a ring, key chain, or a watchband. There are iButtons that have nonvolatile RAM, and they can be mounted on the outside of a piece of equipment. When the equipment calibration/ maintenance is done, one can use a simple probe to download the time/date/ maintenance record to the iButton.

MicroCans come in two sizes, the F3 and F5. Both are 17.35 mm in diameter. The F3 is 3.1 mm thick and the F5 is 5.89 mm thick.

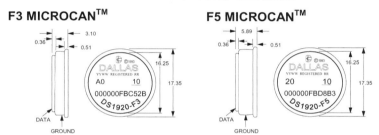

Figure 10-4: Dimensions of a MicroCan

There's also a fascinating iButton known as a Thermochron. It automatically measures temperatures at intervals set up by the user and stores them in internal memory. If you have perishable materials and you want to monitor the temperature they experience during shipment, you can put one of these in the shipping crate. After shipment, you can plug it into a PC using one of the myriad of products designed to connect to iButtons, and download the complete temperature profile seen by the iButton during the trip.

In discussing 1-Wire devices, we will occasionally make use of iButtons because they are very easy to handle.

With that as background on 1-Wire technology, let's start looking at the micro details of how it all works. We'll start by taking a detailed look at the 1-Wire bus and its associated timing.

The 1-Wire Bus Protocol

There are two types of timing associated with the bus: reset and data. Let's examine the reset[1].

---

[1] Consult the Dallas/Maxim Semiconductor 1-Wire Devices data sheets – http://para.maxim-ic.com/1Wire.asp

1-Wire Reset Details

A reset halts whatever is taking place on the bus and prepares devices for the beginning of a new communication cycle. A reset begins when the master pulls the bus low for a period greater than 480 μs. There is no upper limit as to how long the bus master can hold the bus low during a reset. The slave devices, upon seeing the bus go low, use their internal clock to time how long the bus is being held low. If the period exceeds 480 μs, they know the master has issued a reset. The slaves wait until the master releases the bus, by letting it be pulled high by the 5K pull-up resistor that needs to be present somewhere on the bus. Upon seeing the bus go high, the slaves then use their internal timer once again to count out a delay that can be anywhere from 15–60 μs, and then they issue a "presence pulse," by pulling the bus low for a period of time that can be anywhere from 60–240 μs. At the completion of this process, the slave devices know that they have been reset and to await a further command. They now listen to the bus. The master, on the other hand, knows whether or not there are any 1-Wire devices connected to the net by virtue of the presence pulse. The master doesn't necessarily know what type or how many devices are on the net, but if it sees a presence pulse, it knows there is at least one device. It's much easier to understand this with a picture.

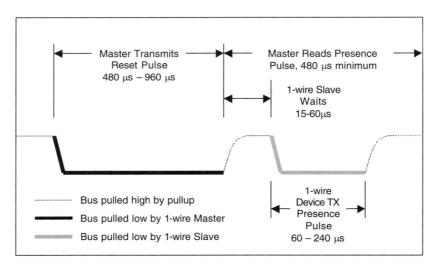

Figure 10-5: Reset timing diagram and textual flow

1-Wire Data Communication Details

The other type of communication on the 1-Wire bus is data communications, the reading and writing of individual bits. While the process isn't exactly simple, it can be understood if you go through it carefully and review it a couple of times.

Data transfer on the 1-Wire bus occurs in time slots, which are predetermined windows of time. As we've said, communication always begins with an action on the part of the bus master, and consistent with this, time slots begin when the master pulls the bus low. What differentiates this from the reset is that the duration is much shorter. 1-Wire slave devices then keep track of whether or not they should be listening or responding, and the time since the last falling edge on the bus. If the master wants to write a 1 to the bus, it will pull the bus low for a period not to exceed 15 μs and then the master releases the bus so that it can be pulled high by the pull-up resistor for the remainder of the timeslot, which can be between 60 μs and 120 μs wide. If the master wants to write a 0 to the bus, it pulls the bus low and holds it for the entire timeslot, and then releases it, letting it be pulled high.

If the bus master is writing to the bus, then the 1-Wire slave devices are reading from the bus. Reading by the 1-Wire slaves devices is accomplished by sampling the bus at a time at least 15 μs after the master pulls the bus low.

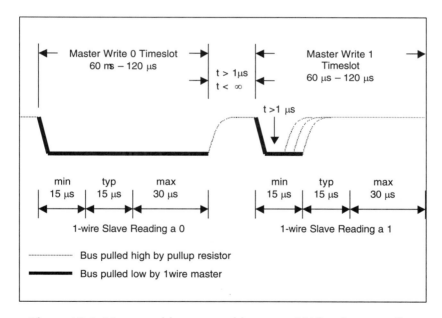

Figure 10-6: Master writing one, writing zero, 1-Wire slaves reading

How does the master read from the 1-Wire bus and the 1-Wire slave devices write to the bus? Once again, communication on the 1-Wire bus is initiated by the bus master, who pulls the bus low and holds it low for a period not to exceed 15 μs. The 1-Wire slave devices, who are now writing to the bus, will meter out a 15-μs delay from the time they saw the master pull the bus low, and then place their data on the bus. This means that if they want to write a 1, they allow the bus to be pulled high. If they want to write a 0, they pull the bus low. They hold this value until the end of the timeslot and then release the bus. The bus master waits at least 1 µs and then samples the value from the bus. This is also much easier to understand with a picture.

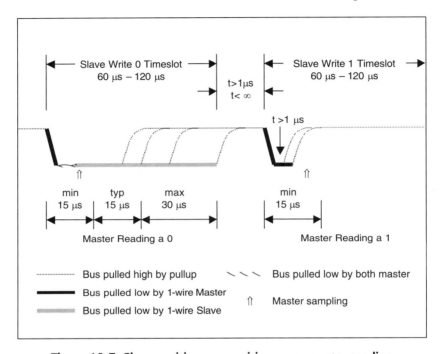

Figure 10-7: Slaves writing one, writing zero, master reading

This description begs two important questions:

    1) How do the 1-Wire slave devices know they are supposed to be reading or writing?

    2) What happens if more than one device is on the bus, trying to write data?

The answer to 1) has to do with the fact that 1-Wire devices have circuitry built into them that monitors time and implements the 1-Wire bus protocol. In effect, each device is independently keeping track of what's going on. When the master issues a reset, all devices are put into a known state and from that point on they follow a strict, predefined protocol that keeps everybody on the same page in terms of who is supposed to be talking and who is supposed to be listening.

With respect to question 2) there are cases when more than one device puts data on the bus at the same time. This generally occurs when the master is trying to find out what devices are on the bus. During that phase, the master hasn't had the opportunity to select an individual device, so all are talking at once. Since all the devices on the bus are open collector, with a pull-up, the result is a "wired AND" of the data of all the devices that are trying to talk. The 1-Wire bus protocol specifies the algorithms that allow the master to iteratively, through a process of elimination, identify all the devices on the bus, even in an environment where more than one device is talking at once.

1-Wire Bus Commands

Having seen the timing details for the 1-Wire bus, let's now examine the data content during communications. We've made note of the fact that 1-Wire devices are individually selectable, can respond to commands, and that there are some commands that are common to most devices. We're going to take a look at some of these common commands now.

The commands that are common to most devices are known as the ROM commands, because they deal with reading the device's 64-bit ID ROM. These four commands are the Read ROM, Search ROM, Match ROM, and Skip ROM. Each is an 8-bit command, meaning that in order to invoke this command, the bus master writes the 8-bit command to the 1-Wire bus.

Table 10-1: ROM command and values

Rom Command	Command Value (Hex)
Read Rom	33
Search Rom	F0
Match Rom	55
Skip Rom	CC

The best way to learn this stuff is to go through a real example, with a real device. We'll use the simplest device of all: the DS2401 Silicon Serial Number.

We noted earlier that 1-Wire devices all have a unique 64-bit ID consisting of an 8-bit family code byte, a 48-bit unique serial number, and an 8-bit CRC byte. This ID code is used to select the device, which, once selected, responds to commands and normally performs some sensing or actuating function and responds with data. The DS2401 is nothing more than the 64-bit ID. It has no other function. It's the most basic of 1-Wire devices, and is literally a silicon serial number. It comes in a variety of packages, but always utilizes just one signal and one ground connection.

Let's see how this device works by looking at the DS2401 command flow chart, like those provided by Dallas Semiconductor in their data sheets[2]. The DS2401 command flow charts discuss only the Read ROM command and the Search ROM command. This is because the device is so simple it only needs two of the four commands that are commonly shared by all 1-Wire devices and no function-specific commands. This will make more sense as we delve into it a little deeper.

---

[2] DS2401 Silicon Serial Number, Data sheet – http://pdfserv.maxim-ic.com/arpdf/DS2401.pdf

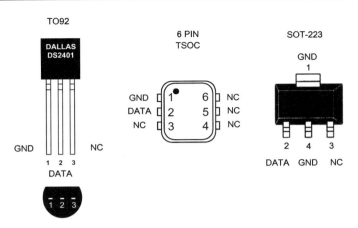

Figure 10-8: DS2401 package styles, pin-outs

As shown in the flow chart (Figure 10-9), the process begins with the bus master issuing a reset by pulling the bus low for a period > 480 µs, and then releasing the bus to be pulled high. When the DS2401 sees the reset pulse, it waits at least 15 µs but less than 60 µs, then responds with a presence pulse, which is at least 60 µs but less than 240 µs. After this sequence of events, the 1-Wire bus protocol specifies that the 1-Wire slave devices are all waiting for an 8-bit command. In the case of the DS2401, there are only two commands that we can give it: Read ROM (0x0F) and Search ROM (0xF0).

The Read ROM command

The Read ROM command can be represented on the bus by either 33h or 0Fh. The reason there are two different bytes representing the same command has to do with maintaining backward compatibility with earlier devices like the DS2400 (which is an earlier version of the DS2401 and is no longer available).

The Read ROM command only works if there is one device on the bus. When the master issues the read ROM command, the DS2401 slave will respond with its 64-bit ID. That ends the process. The only function of the DS2401 is to supply that unique ID code. The Read ROM command also works with all other 1-Wire devices in the same fashion. When issued to them, while they are alone on the bus, they will respond with their 64-bit ID code. What happens when there is more than one device on the bus and a Read ROM is issued? They all respond with their 64-bit ID code at the same time. Since the bus is open collector, the output of all the devices is ANDed together, and the master has no idea of what the ID code really is. It thinks there is *one* device on the bus.

To find out the ID code of a device when there are multiple devices on the bus, the master needs to issue a Search ROM command.

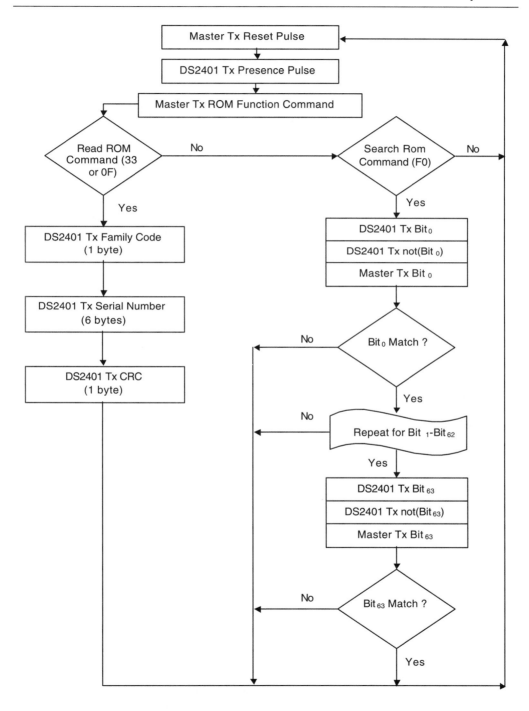

Figure 10-9: DS2401 command flow chart

The Search ROM command

The Search ROM command, represented by F0h on the bus, is used when there are multiple devices on the bus. When the bus master issues a Search ROM command, that tells all the 1-Wire slave devices to prepare for an algorithm involving the process of elimination. It goes like this:

1) All the 1-Wire slave devices put the least significant bit (bit_0) of their 64-bit ID code on the bus all at once.

2) Then, the very next data time slot, they put the opposite of their least significant bit ($Nbit_0$) on the bus, all at once.

3) Then, in the next data time slot, the bus master writes a bit. Those devices that match the bit written by the master remain active, those that don't are effectively deselected and no longer participate. They remain deselected until a reset pulse is issued.

Since the bus is open collector, when the different devices try to write a 1 and a 0 at the same time, the result is a wired AND. This means that the only way the bus can be pulled high by the pull-up resistor is if ALL devices on the bus are trying to write a 1. If any device is trying to write a 0, the bus is pulled low. With this in mind, there are four possibilities as the result of the 1-Wire slaves writing bit_n and $Nbit_n$. In the discussion below, bit_n is the nth bit of the 64-bit ID code, starting with 0 and going up to 63, and $Nbit_n$ is the opposite of that bit. The values of bit_n and $Nbit_n$ are what the bus master will see—that is, the wired AND result of numerous devices talking at once and putting different data on the bus.

Case 1: $bit_n=0$, $Nbit_n=0$

This can only happen if two or more devices are trying to write different values to the bus at the same time. This tells the bus master that, at this bit position, there is an address conflict that indirectly tells the bus master that there are at least two devices remaining on the bus at this point in the process.

Case 2, and Case 3: $bit_n=0$, $Nbit_n=1$ or $bit_n=1$, $Nbit_n=0$

This can only happen if all the devices on the bus are trying to write the same data at the same time. This tells the bus master that the value for this bit_n is equal to the value on the bus, but it does not give the master any insight as to how many devices are on the bus.

Case 4: $bit_n=1$, $Nbit_n=1$

The only way this can happen is if there are NO devices responding on the bus.

The bus master performs the sequence of two reads and a write, from bit_0 on up to bit_{63} and after each case, makes note of the bit position of any conflicts. Conflicts correspond to case 1, above. It also uses this conflict information to decide whether or not to write a 1 or a 0. The bus master always writes a bit after the two reads, and in conflict situations (case 1) , this always has the effect of removing the conflict devices whose bit_n did not match the bit written. Upon reaching bit_{63}, the master knows the 64-bit ID code of one of the devices. By repeating the entire 64-bit process (64 cycles of reading two bits and writing one bit) again and again until all of the conflicted bit positions have been resolved, all devices will be identified.

So, if on bit_n, it is determined that there is no conflict, (Case 2) then all devices that are active on the bus agree on the value of bit_n in their 64-bit ID code. So we know their value of bit_n. We say active, because within any 64-bit cycle, some devices may have been deselected. If there was a conflict, (case 1) and it's the first time we've encountered this conflict, the master will write a 0 and remember this position. 1-Wire slaves that have $bit_n = 1$ in their 64-bit ID code are removed from this 64-bit cycle. The master will dedicate a later 64-bit cycle to resolving the conflict in this bit position by returning and writing a 1, thereby deselecting the devices that previously remained active and selecting the devices that didn't. You can think of each bit in the 64-bit ID code as *being branch points in a binary tree*. The Search ROM process is an iterative process of traversing and mapping the entire tree.

Each of these 64 -bit cycles begins with a reset pulse from the bus master, followed by a presence pulse from all 1-Wire slaves, at the same time. The master then reissues the Search ROM command. All of the devices write bit_0 and $Nbit_0$ at the same time, but after that point, the master uses its one bit write to take different paths through the branches of the binary tree by selecting/deselecting different groups of devices. Old bit conflicts are resolved, new bit conflicts are remembered and later resolved on a subsequent pass. Each complete pass identifies an additional device's ID code. The bus master makes as many passes as there are devices on the bus. So, if there are 12 (for example) 1-Wire slave devices on the bus, this method identifies all of their unique 64-bit ID codes in exactly 12 64-bit search ROM passes.

The bus master can also insert a measure of optimization in the Search ROM command. For instance, if it's only interested in identifying the DS2401 devices on the 1-Wire bus, it can use that fact to speed up the process and limit its search to just DS2402 Silicon Serial Numbers. The first eight bits of the ROM ID for any 1-Wire device will be its family code. That will be the same for all 2401 devices. So, when performing the search ROM command, the bus master can use the family code byte during the first 8 cycles of the 64-cycle Search ROM process and not even pay attention to the values of bit_n and $Nbit_n$ being written. By doing so, all other non-DS2401 devices are eliminated from consideration right off the bat. The only devices on the bus remaining when the ninth ROM bit is being processed will be DS2401 devices. To use our binary tree analogy, any branches that would have occurred during the first eight bits aren't going to be explored. In 1-Wire jargon, this is "targeting the family."

The Read ROM and Search ROM commands are found in all 1-Wire slave devices. Additional ROM commands found in most 1-Wire devices are Match ROM and Skip ROM.

Match ROM

The Match ROM command is represented by 55h. It is used to select individual 1-Wire devices once their 64-bit ID code is known. A common situation in which this might be used is when there are numerous devices on the bus, all of their device ID codes are known (having been previously found with a Search ROM command and remembered by the application), and the bus master wants to communicate with one of them. Here, the bus master issues a reset, waits for the presence pulse, issues the Match ROM command, then writes the 64-bit ID code of the device it is interested in. By issuing the Match ROM command, the bus master is telling all of the devices on the bus to listen to (read) the next 64 bits. Any device that does not match the 64-bit ID code will be deselected and will do nothing else but wait for the next reset pulse from the bus master. The one device that matches the 64-bit ID code (there can be only one, since they are all unique) will now be put into a state in which is it is waiting for additional commands that are specific to its function.

A more common situation is the case where there are multiple devices on the bus, but the bus master isn't maintaining their ID codes in memory. It simply knows that one of them is of a specific type it wants to communicate with—a thermometer, for example—on a bus with several other types of devices such as switches and A/D converters. In this situation, the bus master issues a reset, waits for the presence pulses, issues the Search ROM, and determines the device IDs for everything on the bus. The first 8 bits of the device ID is the family code, which differentiates the thermometer from the switches and the A/D converters. The bus master takes the device ID for the thermometer, issues a reset, waits for the presence pulse, issues a Match ROM, writes the thermometer's device ID, and then writes thermometer-specific commands to the bus and retrieves the desired temperature data.

Skip ROM

The Skip ROM command is represented by CCh. It's used when you know there is only one device on the bus, you know what it is, and you want to select it without going through the process of giving it the 64-bit ID code. To communicate with a 1-Wire device in this fashion, the bus master issues a reset pulse, waits for the presence pulse, and then issues the Skip ROM command. Then, the one device on the bus is selected and awaiting further device-specific commands.

We mentioned earlier that the only two functions that the DS2401 Silicon Serial Number uses are the Read ROM and Search ROM command. We've also mentioned that the Match ROM and Skip ROM are common to all 1-Wire devices. That contradiction is easily explained. Match ROM and Skip ROM aren't relevant to the DS2401 because the DS2401 doesn't have any other functions beyond merely responding with its 64-bit ID code. Both Match ROM and Skip ROM are functions that involve selecting a device with the purpose of issuing further commands. The DS2401 ignores Match ROM and Skip ROM.

In addition to Read ROM, Search ROM, Match ROM, and Skip ROM, some 1-Wire devices have additional ROM commands that allow more options when it comes to selecting them. An example is the Alarm Search ROM found in the DS1920 thermometer iButton. It functions much like a Search ROM, with the exception that only thermometer iButtons that have experienced a temperature alarm will actually respond.

Memory commands

We've mentioned that the Match ROM command and the Skip ROM command select individual 1-Wire devices and put them in a state where they are ready to read additional commands from the 1-Wire bus. These additional, function-specific commands are frequently referred to as Memory commands on the Dallas Semiconductor data sheets. We're not going to go into them in detail here. Instead, we'll discuss them when we cover some of the 1-Wire devices in more detail. For the time being, just be aware that there are additional commands known as memory commands that work generally the same way as the ROM commands.

Cyclic Redundancy Check (CRC)

The CRC, or cyclic redundancy check, is a method of verifying the integrity of data transfers. This verification comes in the form of a CRC byte, which is the result of a logical operation on a stream of bits. In 1-Wire devices there are two different CRC types. One CRC is an 8-bit type and is stored in the most significant byte of the 64-bit ROM. The other CRC is a 16-bit type. While the CRC8 is used in a number of places in 1-Wire data transfers, a good example of it can be found in the 64-bit ID code that every 1-Wire device has. The last 8 bits of this ID code is a CRC8 byte. That byte is computed using the first 56 bits of the ROM ID according to the following formula:

$$CRC8 = X^8 + X^5 + X^4 + 1$$

The CRC16 is generated according to the standardized CRC16-polynomial. A CRC16 is used for fast verification of a data transfer when writing memory devices. That byte is computed according to the following formula:

$$CRC16 = X^{16} + X^{15} + X^2 + 1$$

A picture can be used to put this in to more meaningful terms. Consider the following diagram for a CRC8.

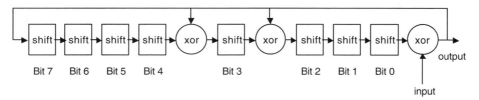

Figure 10-10: The CRC shift register

For the CRC8, the process starts with the 8-bit CRC "shift register" initialized to all zeros. (Although we are calling it a shift register, it's important to remember that it's really an algorithm being implemented in software by the bus master. We're simply using the shift register to visualize the process.) Once the shift register is initialized to all zeros, the bus master takes the ROM ID, one bit at a time, starting with the least significant bit and working up, and inserts it into the CRC shift register.

1) The current input bit and the previous value of the least significant shift register bit, Bit 0, are subjected to a logical exclusive or (XOR). XOR is another way of saying, "one or the other, but not both." If both are zero, the output is zero. If both are one, the output is zero. If one is zero and the other is one, the output is one. The result of this XOR is the feedback bit that gets fed back into several other registers.

2) Bits 1, 2, 5, 6, and 7 get the value of their higher-order neighbor (bits 2, 3, 6, 7, and 8 respectively) shifted into them unmodified.

3) Bit 3 gets the value of the feedback bit XOR bit 4.

4) Bit 4 gets the value of the feedback bit XOR bit 5.

5) Bit 8 takes on the value of the feedback bit.

Then, another input bit is taken from the ROM ID and put into this algorithm. Once 56 bits have been taken from the ROM ID and put into the shift register computation, the value of the 8-bit CRC shift register should equal the CRC byte. If you continue to perform the shifting algorithm on the remaining 8-bits of the ROM ID—that is, shift in the CRC byte into the CRC register—the contents should go to zero.

Pictures and explanations are good, but sometimes an example is even better. Below is a worked out example using an actual ROM ID from a DS1920 thermometer iButton.

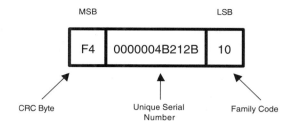

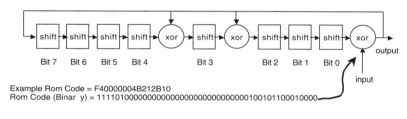

Figure 10-11: CRC example, ROM ID, ID breakout, first 8 register cycles

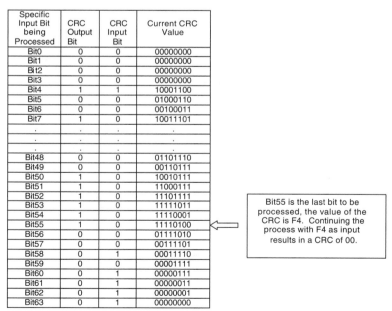

Specific Input Bit being Processed	CRC Output Bit	CRC Input Bit	Current CRC Value
Bit0	0	0	00000000
Bit1	0	0	00000000
Bit2	0	0	00000000
Bit3	0	0	00000000
Bit4	1	1	10001100
Bit5	0	0	01000110
Bit6	0	0	00100011
Bit7	1	0	10011101
.	.	.	.
.	.	.	.
.	.	.	.
Bit48	0	0	01101110
Bit49	0	0	00110111
Bit50	1	0	10010111
Bit51	1	0	11000111
Bit52	1	0	11101111
Bit53	1	0	11111011
Bit54	1	0	11110001
Bit55	1	0	11110100
Bit56	0	0	01111010
Bit57	0	0	00111101
Bit58	0	1	00011110
Bit59	0	0	00001111
Bit60	0	1	00000111
Bit61	0	1	00000011
Bit62	0	1	00000001
Bit63	0	1	00000000

Bit55 is the last bit to be processed, the value of the CRC is F4. Continuing the process with F4 as input results in a CRC of 00.

Figure 10-12: CRC example, table with all 64 cycles

Now that we've looked at what the CRC is and how it works, there are a couple of additional points. The cyclic redundancy check is fundamentally the responsibility of the bus master. While the 1-Wire slave devices may send CRC bytes along with their data, the bus master doesn't actually have to pay any attention to them or act upon them. The CRC is merely a capability that allows the bus master to determine whether or not the data transfer was good, but the existence of this capability doesn't imply automatic error checking. The bus master has to first use the CRC byte to identify a communication problem, and then act on that problem by repeating the communication. Neither of those actions is mandatory or automatic.

Although the example we've looked at focuses on the ROM ID, many other data transfers from the 1-Wire devices also incorporate CRC8 or CRC16 bytes. The specific data sheets for each of the 1-Wire devices explain where and when they get sent.

One last comment about CRC. If you are wondering how you would go about writing programs that verified the accuracy of CRC bytes, the 1-Wire Java class libraries have CRC classes in them that provide objects and methods for handling CRC checking.

We took a look at the DS2401 Silicon Serial Number in our discussion about the Read ROM and Search ROM commands. Now, let's take a look at some other common 1-Wire devices: the DS2405 Addressable Switch and the DS1920 Temperature iButton.

1-Wire Device Example: the DS2405 Addressable Switch

This is one of the most useful 1-Wire devices, and it lends itself well to a whole range of applications with respect to Internet-enabled devices. The DS2405, as its name implies, is a 1-Wire, selectable switch. It has an output, which can be thought of as a switchable pin, a 1-Wire bus pin, and a ground. It comes in a variety of packages similar to the DS2401.

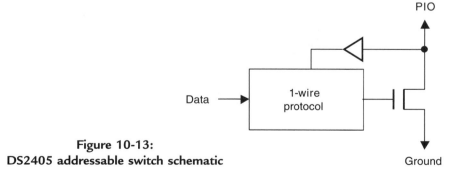

Figure 10-13:
DS2405 addressable switch schematic

Table 10-2: DS2405 electrical characteristics

Parameter	Symbol	Min	Typ	Max	Units	Notes
Logic 1	V_{IH}	2.2		$V_{CC}+0.3$	V	1, 4, 5
Logic 0	V_{IL}	-0.3		0.8	V	1,7
Output Logic Low @4mA	V_{OL}			0.4	V	1
Output Logic High	V_{OH}		V_{PULLUP}	6.0	V	1,2
Input Load Current(Data Pin)	I_L		5		mA	3
Nput Resistance (PIO pin)	I_R	10			MW	6

1. All voltages referenced to ground.
2. V_{pullup} is the external pullup voltage.
3. Input load is to ground.
4. V_{IH} is a function of the external pullup resistor and the V_{CC} supply.
5. V_{IH} for the PIO pin should always be greater than or equal to V_{pullup}-0.3 volts.
6. Input resistance is to ground.
7. Under certain low voltage conditions V_{ILMAX} may have to be reduced to as much as 0.5 volts to always guarentee a presence pulse

The switch pin can be used to pull a node (PIO on the pinout above) to ground, sinking up to 4 mA in the process. Since the device doesn't connect to a positive supply, it can't drive the node high; it is either pulling the node low or off, and allowed to be pulled high. You can give the circuit controlled by the PIO pin its own positive supply that acts as that pullup. You can also query the DS2405 to find out whether or not it is pulling the node low. Thus, it can be used to control LEDs, trigger logic, read and control the state of relays, etc.

DS2405 Addressable Switch ROM commands

The DS2405 has the standard four ROM commands that we've learned about: Read ROM, Search ROM, Match ROM, and Skip ROM. It also has an additional ROM command, Active Only Search ROM.

Table 10-3: Table of DS2405 ROM commands

Rom Command	Command Value (Hex)
Read Rom	33
Search Rom	F0
Match Rom	55
Skip Rom	CC
Active Only Search Rom	EC

The DS2405 Match ROM command

The Match ROM command has characteristics for the DS2405 that are a little different from what we saw earlier. The procedure is very similar: the bus master issues a rest pulse, waits for a presence pulse, then issues a 64-bit ROM ID, and the device that matches it is then selected. But in the case of the DS2405, after a device receives its 64th bit and is selected, it toggles the state of the PIO output node. This is the mechanism by which one turns the DS2405 on and off: by selecting it. Once selected with a Match ROM command, it will output the state of its switch (on or off) during every subsequent data time slot initiated by the bus master until a reset is issued. This means that if the DS2405 is currently pulling the PIO pin to ground, it will respond to every timeslot following the Match ROM with a logic 0. If the PIO node is being pulled high, it will respond with a logic 1.

The DS2405 Search ROM command

As with the Match ROM command, the Search ROM command also has characteristics for the DS2405 that are a little different from what we saw earlier. The process proceeds as a standard Search ROM, but at the end of a 64-bit cycle in which a DS2405 1-Wire switch has been identified, any subsequent data time slots after this prompt the DS2405 to output its state to the bus. This means that if the PIO pin on the DS2405 is currently being pulled to ground, it will respond to every time slot following the match ROM with a logic 0. If the PIO node is being pulled high, it will respond with a logic 1. It will do this until it sees a reset. The Search ROM process *does not* affect the state of the switch. It will not toggle as the result of a Search ROM command.

The Active Only Search ROM command

The Active Only Search ROM command adds an additional level of selection to the standard Search ROM process. As we saw earlier, the Search ROM command is a method by which the bus master can iteratively identify all 1-Wire devices on the bus. All 1-Wire devices will respond to it. We also mentioned the concept of targeting the device family. That consists of performing a Search ROM command and automatically using a device's family code as the first 8 bits the bus master writes to the bus during the process, independent of the bit$_n$ and Nbin$_n$ values being written by the 1-Wire devices. This eliminates identifying 1-Wire device ROM ID codes for devices that the bus master is not currently interested in. The Active Only Search ROM command adds an additional level of selection up front. When an Active Only Search ROM command is issued, the only devices that will respond to it are 1-Wire switch devices that presently have their internal switch control signals set to true, or logic 1, meaning the switch is actively trying to pull the PIO pin low. Additionally, after an Active Only Search ROM command is issued and the 64th bit cycle has been completed identifying one DS2405 ROM ID, that device will now output a logic 0 on the bus during every subsequent data time slot.

There's a lot of significance in the differences between the Search ROM and the Active Only Search ROM for the DS2405. After bus master has completed a 64-bit Search ROM cycle, finding a DS2405, that DS2405 will output what it sees on the PIO pin. After the bus master has completed a 64-bit Active Only Search ROM command, finding a DS2405 with its internal switch control signal set to true, it will output a logic 0 to the bus during data time slots until reset. The significance is this: the Search ROM command can be used to determine the actual PIO pin voltage values for DS2405s on the bus, while the Active Only Search ROM can be used to identify the switches that have a switch control signal set to true, thereby *thinking* they are pulling the PIO pin low. But just because the internal switch control signal is set to true, this doesn't necessarily mean the PIO pin is *able* to pull that node low. Or, the internal switch control signal could be set to false, thereby letting the PIO pin float to a logic 1, but something else could be pulling that node low outside the DS2405.

The DS2405 PIO pin and the DS2405 internal switch control signal don't necessarily have to agree, and by providing a difference in functionality between the Active Only Search ROM and the Search ROM, the bus master has a way of identifying not only how the switches are set, but how they are actually behaving.

Table 10-4: DS2405 review table

Setting of the Internal Latch	Value on the PIO Pin of the Switch	Returned Value of the Sensed Level of the PIO Pin	Comments
false (let PIO pin float)	Logic Low	false	The DS2405 is not driving the PIO pin low, but something external to it is driving it low.
true (drive PIO pin low)	Logic Low	false	The DS2405 is driving the PIO pin low.
false (let PIO pin float)	Logic High	true	The DS2405 is not driving the PIO pin low but something external to it has pulled it high.
true (drive PIO pin low)	Logic HIgh	true	The DS2405 is driving the PIO pin low, but something external to it is overdriving the PIO pin high.

1-Wire Device Example: the DS1920 Thermometer iButton

The DS1920[3] is a selectable 1-Wire thermometer in a rugged iButton container. It has 0.5 °C accuracy and is useful from –55 °C to 100 °C.

The DS1920 provides an accurate temperature measurement, requires no complicated calibration, and only uses one signal and one ground. It uses a proprietary scheme involving the temperature dependence of oscillators to measure a temperature-related count and places that value into an internal memory that is referred to as scratch-pad memory. This memory also supports the storage of alarm values, which the DS1920 compares the current temperature against. All of this smart circuitry is powered parasitically from the 1-Wire bus.

Figure 10-14:
Picture of a DS1920 iButton

Table 10-5: Memory in the DS1920 iButton

Byte Number	Scratchpad	EEPROM
0	Temperature LSB	
1	Temperture MSB	
2	High Alarm (TH) or User Byte 1	High Alarm (TH) or User Byte 1
3	Low Alarm (TL) or User Byte 2	Low Alarm (TL) or User Byte 2
4	Reserved	
5	Reserved	
6	Count Remain	
7	Count / Deg C	
8	CRC	

Bytes zero and one correspond to the result of a temperature conversion performed on the raw measurement data in bytes six and seven. Bytes two and three are the only writable locations and can be used as temporary storage by the user. They also serve the purpose of being the registers in which you will load any alarm values that you want to enter. Scratchpad byte two is the value of the high temperature alarm point while scratchpad byte three is the value of the low temperature alarm point. Any temperature falling outside those bounds will result in the device being active during a Alarm Search Only ROM command, provided that another reading isn't performed in the interim that clears the alarm condition. To ensure the alarm values remain active over time, you write them to the scratchpad and then copy them to the nonvolatile EEPROM memory. The purpose of the EEPROM is to provide a

---

[3] DS1920 Temperature iButton data sheet – http://pdfserv.maxim-ic.com/arpdf/DS1920.pdf

nonvolatile place for the alarm values to be stored during times when the device isn't powered. During these times the scratchpad no longer retains its values. When the device is powered back up, the EEPROM locations automatically are placed back into the scratchpad memory. Scratchpad bytes four and five are labeled as reserved and are not used. Byte nine is a CRC byte, representing a cyclic redundancy check performed on the previous eight bytes.

The DS1920 draws as much as 1 mA during a temperature measurement, and this requires what Dallas Semiconductor refers to as a "strong pullup." The normal pullup value for the 1-Wire bus is about 5k ohms and that won't supply the necessary current for the DS1920. Normally, this won't be a problem, because in order to interface to the DS1920 one normally uses a Dallas Semiconductor bus adapter that already takes this sort of thing into account. But you'll need to be aware of this if you make your own interface circuitry to the DS1920.

DS1920 ROM commands

The DS1920 has the standard four ROM commands that we know about: Read ROM, Search ROM, Match ROM and Skip ROM. These function exactly as described for the DS2401. There is one additional ROM command known as the Alarm Search Command.

The DS1920 Alarm Search command

The Alarm Search command is exactly like the Search ROM command, except that it only applies to thermometer devices, meaning only devices with the thermometer family code, and only those thermometers that experienced an alarm at their last temperature measurement, will respond. When the bus master tells the thermometer iButton to measure temperature, the iButton also compares the result to any alarm values that it has stored away in memory. If it experiences an alarm, it remembers this and knows to participate in any subsequent Alarm Search command.

Table 10-6: DS1920 iButton ROM command table

Rom Command	Command Value (Hex)
Read Rom	33
Search Rom	F0
Match Rom	55
Skip Rom	CC
Alarm Search	EC

The other DS1920 commands: memory and temperature conversion

The DS1920 has additional commands, four of which are referred to as memory functions, while one is called a temperature conversion function. Whereas ROM functions all tend to be aimed at selecting a device, or identifying a device, these other commands have to do with making the device do something once selected. We're not going to go into them in tremendous detail here, because the best way to learn about them is from the Dallas Semiconductor data sheets, but we'll briefly review them. These commands are: Write Scratchpad, Read Scratchpad, Copy Scratchpad, Convert Temperature, and Recall EEPROM.

Table 10-7: DS1920 iButton additional command table

Memory and Control Functions	Command Value (Hex)
Write Scratchpad	4E
Read Scratchpad	BE
Copy Scratchpad	48
Convert Temperature	44
Recall	B8

DS1920 Write Scratchpad command

The Write Scratchpad command is issued by the bus master before writing two bytes of data into the scratchpad memory. It tells the DS1920 to read the next 16 data time slots. This memory gets put into scratchpad bytes two and three. The bus master can issue a reset during this write process, which terminates it and leaves the contents of the scratchpad in an unknown state.

DS1920 Read Scratchpad command

The Read Scratchpad command is issued by the bus master when it wants to read the nine bytes of data in the DS1920 scratchpad memory. The master can stop the read process at any time by issuing a reset.

DS1920 Copy Scratchpad command

The Copy Scratchpad command moves the values in scratchpad bytes two and three into nonvolatile EEPROM. These two locations can be thought of as storage for the alarm values. The alarm registers are scratchpad bytes two and three. The EEPROM memory programming requires the use of the strong pullup, which the bus master must enable immediately after this command is issued and hold for 10 ms.

DS1920 Convert Temperature command

The Convert Temperature command causes a temperature measurement to be performed. This command also requires that the strong pullup be enabled immediately after the command is issued by the bus master and held for 0.5 sec. The raw result of the process is stored in scratchpad locations seven and eight, while the value of the temperature computed from it is stored in bytes zero and one. The conversion between the 16-bit temperature value and an actual Celsius number is shown in Table 10-8.

Table 10-8: DS1920 iButton hex to temperature table

Temperature (Deg C)	Digital Output (Binary)	Digital Output (Hex)
100	00000000 11001000	00C8
25	00000000 00110010	0032
0.5	00000000 00000001	0001
0	00000000 00000000	0000
-0.5	11111111 11111111	FFFF
-25	11111111 11001110	FFCE
-55	11111111 10010010	FF92

DS1920 Recall EEPROM command

This command places the two bytes of data stored in the EEPROM into bytes two and three in scratchpad memory. This happens automatically every time the device is powered up, but also on demand through the use of this command.

There are a number of temperature-related 1-Wire devices, such as the DS1820 1-Wire thermometer. It makes use of the same commands as the DS1920 with the addition of some features related to how the device is powered up.

Table 10-9 lists the names and family codes of a variety of common 1-Wire devices.

Table 10-9: 1-Wire devices and their family codes

1-Wire Device or iButton	Description	Family Code (Hex)
DS2401, DS1990A	1-Wire Address Only	01
DS1425, DS1991	Secure Memory Device	02
DS2404, DS1994	4K NVRAM memory, Clock, Timer, Alarms	04
DS2405	Single Addressable Switch	05
DS1993	4K NVRAM memory	06
DS1992	1K NVRAM memory	08
DS2502, DS1982	1K EPROM memory	09
DS1995	16K NVRAM memory	0A
DS2505, DS1985	16K EPROM memory	0B
DS1996	64K NVRAM memory	0C
DS2506, DS1986	64K EPROM memory	0F
DS18S20, DS1820, DS1920	Temperature and Alarm Trips	10
DS2406, DS2407	1K EPROM memory, Dual Switch	12
DS2503, DS1983	4K EPROM memory	13
DS1971	256 bit EEPROM memory and OTP register	14
DS1954	Java Powered Cryptographic iButton	16
DS1963S	4K NVRAM memory and SHA-1 engine	18
DS1963L	4K NVRAM memory with Write Cycle Counters	1A
DS2423	4K NVRAM memory with External Counters	1B
DS2409	Dual Switch, Coupler	1F

DS2450	Quad A/D	20
DS1921	Thermocron Temperature Logger	21
DS1973	4K EEPROM memory	23
DS2438	Temperature, A/D	26
DS18B20	Adjustable Resolution Temperature	28
DS2890	Single Channel Digital Potentiometer	2C
DS2890	Temperature, Current, A/D	30
DS2423, DS1961S	1K EEPROM memory with SHA-1 engine	33

Connecting a PC to the 1-Wire Bus

We've discussed some of the 1-Wire devices that are interesting for web-enabled devices, but our overall goal is to be able to access these devices with a computer and, ultimately, the Internet. In this section, we look at the process of accessing 1-Wire devices with a personal computer.

Dallas Semiconductor offers a host of products that make the PC-to-1-Wire interface easy to accomplish. But the sheer variety of products they offer can obscure how easy it really is. Let's take a high-level look at what we're trying to do, then examine the details.

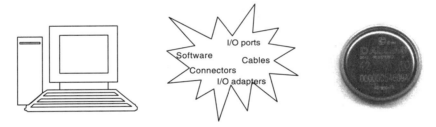

Figure 10-15: Bridging the gap between computer and devices

We have a PC, and we're trying to connect it up to 1-Wire devices which may be iButtons, surface mount or through-hole packaged devices. To bridge the gap, we're going to need the following: software to drive the bus, I/O ports on the computer for communication to the bus, a method of adapting the I/O port to the bus, cables, and a method of connecting cables to our devices. This is how we'll accomplish this:

Software to control the PC I/O ports

> Java API supplied by Dallas Semiconductor

> TMEX Touch Memory Exchange Software supplied by Dallas Semiconductor

PC I/O ports

> RS232 COM ports

The parallel or printer port

The Universal Serial Bus, or USB, port

Adapters to go from the PC I/O ports to the 1-Wire bus

DS1411, DS1413 COM port to iButton adapters

DS1410E Parallel Port to iButton adapter

DS9097U-09 COM port to RJ11 adapter

DS2480B 1-Wire line driver

DS2490 USB to 1-Wire bridge chip

Cables between the adapters and the 1-Wire devices

Category 5 telephone cable, with RJ11 modular connectors

DS1420X pre-made cables

Connectors to attach the cables to printed circuit boards with 1-Wire electronics

RJ11 modular plugs

DS9094 iButton clip, DS9098 iButton retainer

DS9092R iButton port

DS1401 front panel iButton holder

We'll start by examining the physical and electrical interfaces, and then end with a discussion of the Java 1-Wire API and some examples.

Communication ports on the PC

There are three ports on the PC that we can use to connect to a 1-Wire bus: RS232 COM ports, the parallel port, and the Universal Serial Bus or USB port. Dallas Semiconductor makes a variety of products that can be used as translators/adapters. These products provide mechanical connections to the bus, and contain electronics that help translate your computer's output into the 1-Wire protocol. Let's take a look at them all, starting with the serial, or RS232, port.

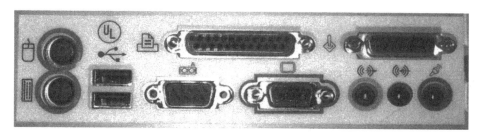

Figure 10-16: Ports

The RS232 or serial (COM) ports

Most, if not all, PCs have traditional RS232 serial ports often referred to as COM ports. They usually have a male DB-9 connector as shown in Figure 10-17.

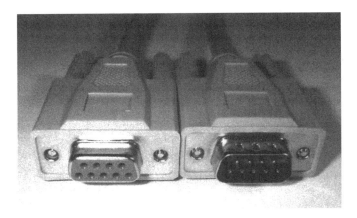

Figure 10-17: Male, female DB-9, pinout

To connect the 1-Wire bus to this, you need a female DB-9 connector. Dallas Semiconductor makes several adapters that connect to a male DB-9 connector and provide a connection to either an iButton directly, an iButton cable, or an RJ11 (telephone modular plug) and category 5 1-Wire cable.

The DS1413 Passive Serial iButton holder

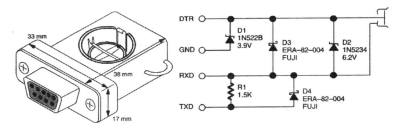

Figure 10-18: DS1413 images and schematic

This port adapter, the most basic and least expensive, has a metal retaining clip for holding an iButton device. You plug the iButton device into the retaining clip and plug the adapter into your COM port and run software that communicates in the 1-Wire protocol. There are cables that can plug into the iButton retaining clip that allow you to use this as a generic 1-Wire adapter. But that basic design of the DS1413 has limitations.

What it does

1. It performs the mechanical adaptation between the male DB-9 COM port and either an iButton or an iButton cable.

2. It performs voltage level conversions between the 12V RS232 provided by the COM port and the 5V needed by the 1-Wire bus.

What it does *not* do

1. It has no active electronics inside it, so it doesn't actually format data coming from the COM port into the 1-Wire protocol for you. The data coming from the COM port into the DS1413 must already have the correct timing. This makes the controlling software somewhat more complicated.

2. The Dallas Semiconductor Java 1-Wire API doesn't support it directly—rather, it supports it indirectly, by using a driver supplied in the Dallas Semiconductor TMEX software.

3. The datasheet makes note of the fact that it does not support what is called a strong 5V pull-up. Certain devices need a pull-up on the bus beyond what is normally supplied by the 5K resistor. The DS1411 has no provision to supply that. Having said that, We've found that it seems to work with thermometer iButtons in terms of making a temperature measurement, but not for writing to the EEPROMS, even though they both require the strong pull-up.

4. It doesn't have a provision for supplying the 12V signals required for programming EPROM devices.

The limitations of the DS1413 are significant for our applications, so we won't really be discussing it further in this book. It's designed for use in special-purpose applications where cost is an issue. We're mentioning it here because you need to understand the differences between it and the DS1411, which is basically the same device without the limitations described above. Be aware that it *looks* exactly like a DS1411, with the exception of a tiny little sticker label. If you have both, it's best to keep them separate.

The DS1411 Serial Port iButton holder

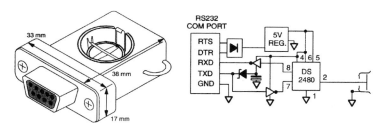

Figure 10-19: DS1411 images and schematic

This port adaptor is more sophisticated than the DS1413 mentioned above. Notice on the schematic that there is a DS2480 device embedded within it. The DS2480, or serial 1-Wire line driver, is an integrated circuit that takes byte-based commands and data from the COM port and generates all the necessary 1-Wire timing (the time slots) for you. This frees up the computer and software from having to deal it. Both the Dallas Semiconductor TMEX software and their 1-Wire Java API support the DS1411, which means that you can communicate with it through software that's entirely Java-based, or communicate with it using Java that uses a TMEX driver. The DS1411 translates the voltage levels and has a strong pull-up, allowing it to be used with thermometer devices and devices with EEPROM that you want to write to. It does not support the 12V 1-Wire programming voltage required for EPROM devices.

This is a very useful device, especially when you are just getting started, because of its versatility and ease of use. You can plug a DS1920 thermometer iButton into it, plug it into the COM port, and start working on software, confident that you don't have any cabling or connections or soldering problems, etc. As with the DS1413, it can also accept iButton cables.

The DS9097U Universal 1-Wire COM Port adapter

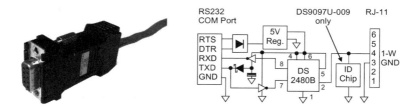

Figure 10-20: DS9097U images and schematic

This port adapter doesn't accept an iButton device or an iButton cable; it accepts an RJ-11 modular plug. This makes it really useful, because you can use telephone cabling instead of the special iButton cables. The DS9097U uses the DS2480 serial 1-Wire line driver just like the DS1411, so it takes bytes from the COM port and translates them into 1-Wire time slots. Also like the DS1411, it can be used with the 1-Wire Java API alone, or a combination of the Java API and the TMEX 1-Wire drivers. The DS9097U also supports the strong pull-up so you can use with it with EEPROM devices and temperature 1-Wire devices/iButtons. It does not support the 12V signals required for EPROM programming though.

DS9097U comes in three flavors, one with an embedded DS2502 ID chip embedded within it, another with the embedded DS2502 and 12V supply for programming EPROMs and one version without the DS2502. The presence of the DS2502 ID chip provides a way to identify a particular adapter to a particular COM port in an environment when there might be numerous adapters being used. This can also be useful for simple software setup experiments because you can plug it into the COM port and test 1-Wire operation without having to hook anything else up to it: it already has a 1-Wire device inside it that will respond.

Table 10-10: DS9097U varieties

DS9097U-009	Active 1-Wire adapter with Ds2502 EPROM
DS9097U-E25	Active 1-Wire adapter with Ds2502 EPROM and 12 volt supply
DS9097U-S09	Active 1-Wire adapter without Ds2502 EPROM

The DS2480 Serial 1-Wire line driver chip

We've noted that two of the COM port adapters have a chip embedded within them. Let's take a moment and examine that device.

The DS2480B[4] is a serial-port-to-1-Wire interface chip that supports both the regular and overdrive speeds of the 1-wire bus. It connects directly to UARTs and 5V RS232 systems. The DS2480B contains internal timers that relieve the host of the burden of generating the time-critical 1-Wire communication waveforms. The DS2480B can be set to communicate at four different data rates, including 115.2 kbps, 57.6 kbps and 19.2 kbps with 9.6 kbps being the power-on default. The various control functions of the DS2480B are optimized for MicroLAN 1-Wire networks and support the special needs of all current 1-Wire devices including the crypto iButton, EPROM-based add-only memories, EEPROM devices and 1-Wire thermometers. The DS2480B is the integrated circuit inside the 9097U and DS1411 serial port adapters. The DS2480B is controlled by a variety of commands but we won't discuss programming the DS2480 directly. Rather, we will discuss using the 1-Wire API and allowing it to handle all of the low-level commands to the DS2480B.

The parallel or printer port

The parallel port, often called the printer port, can also be used to interface with the 1-Wire bus. The printer port uses a DB-25 male connector on the PC. Dallas Semiconductor makes a device for connecting to the printer port, the DS1410E.

---

[4] DS2480B 1-Wire Line Driver with Load Sensor data sheet – http://pdfserv.maxim-ic.com/ arpdf/DS2480B.pdf

Figure 10-21: DB-25 male, female, pinout

The DS1410E parallel port adapter

The DS1410E is a port adapter that has a female DB-25 connector on one side and a male DB-25 connector on the other side. It connects between the parallel port on a computer and the printer cable, and can co-exist with the printer. In the center of this adapter are two iButton retaining clips. You can connect either iButtons or iButton cables into these retaining clips. The intended purpose of the DS1410E is a little different than our previous discussions. It is primarily intended for applications such as software authorization. An iButton like the DS1994 (clock plus memory) can be supplied as an authorization kit with commercial software that is otherwise unrelated to 1-Wire. The timer in the iButton can be preprogrammed to meter out a specified number of days and the memory in the iButton can hold software authorization codes that match those in the software.

Figure 10-22:
Parallel port iButton holder

This isn't our application, but that's why they make the DS1410E. We're interested in this because it provides one more way to access the 1-Wire bus. The DS1410E supports the strong pull-up required by temperature and EEPROM devices, and it contains active circuitry inside it that manages the timing and some electrical details dealing with the fact that it's sharing the same bus with the printer. The Dallas

Semiconductor 1-Wire Java API supports the DS1410E indirectly by making use of low-level drivers in the TMEX software package.

PC universal serial bus, or USB

The universal serial bus, USB, is found on most computers these days. At the time of this writing, Dallas Semiconductor doesn't offer any ready-made USB port adapter. They do, however, offer the DS2490, an integrated circuit that performs USB protocol to 1-Wire bus protocol conversion.

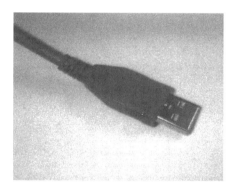

Figure 10-23:
USB port connectors and pinout

Let's take a brief look at the DS2490 USB-to-1-Wire adapter bridge chip.

Figure 10-24:
DS2490 chip and pinout table

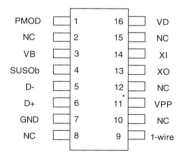

Pin	Name		Pin	Name
1	PMOD		16	VD
2	NC		15	NC
3	VB		14	XI
4	SUSOb		13	XO
5	D-		12	NC
6	D+		11	VPP
7	GND		10	NC
8	NC		9	1-wire

The DS2490 supports capabilities that allow access to all 1-Wire devices:

1. It supports the 12V programming voltage required to program EPROM 1-Wire devices.

2. It supports the 5V strong pull-up required by thermometer and EEPROM 1-Wire devices.

3. It handles all the protocol conversion.

This capability comes with requirements though. The DS2490 can't handle all this with power from the USB bus, so for some of that it requires an additional power supply. To handle some of the timing, it must have an external time-base attached to it in the form of a 12-MHz clock. Given the popularity of the USB bus, a ready-made adapter will be most likely available in the future.

We've talked about the various ports on the PC, and various adapters that connect those ports to the bus. Now let's take a very brief look at what's available to connect between the adapters and a circuit board with 1-Wire electronics on it: cables and connectors.

Cables and connectors

For short 1-Wire runs (less than 10 feet) and very simple 1-Wire networks, four-wire telephone cable will work acceptably. A disadvantage of phone cable (not twisted pair) is that it lacks the noise rejection properties of twisted pair-cables. For that reason, category 5 twisted-pair cable (used for 100base-T networks) is recommended for most 1-Wire applications. This is connected to a bus adapter and to circuit boards, usually using an RJ11 modular phone jack and plug.

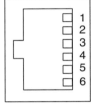

1 Blue   - Regulated +5VDC (<50ma)
2 Yellow - Power return
3 Green - 1-wire HOT
4 Red   - 1-wire return
5 Black   - No connection
6 White - Unregulated + supply (<500ma)

Figure 10-25: Cat 5 cable connecting to modular plug, with pinout

Pre-made iButton cables

During our discussion of port adapters, we mentioned that some of them have iButton retaining clips as their 1-Wire interface (DS1411, DS1413, DS1410E) and we mentioned something called iButton cables. These are the DS1402X MicroLAN cables. They come in a variety of lengths and a variety of different flavors. Some of the more relevant ones are shown below. The significance of these is that some have an RJ11 plug on one end and an iButton interface on the other, so they can be plugged into the iButton retaining clips in the port adapters that are meant for iButtons.

DS1402BB   **DS1402BR**

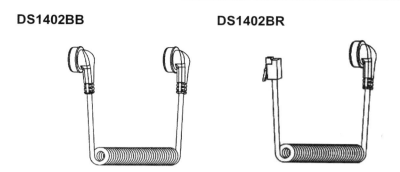

Figure 10-26. Pre-made iButton cables

DS9098 iButton receptacle. This is a metal iButton receptacle that can be soldered onto a PC board. It can also be used to hold iButton cables.

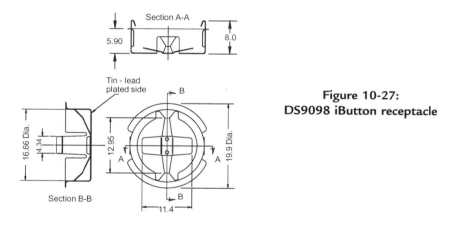

Figure 10-27:
DS9098 iButton receptacle

DS9094 iButton retaining clip. This is a plastic and metal surface-mount or through-hole iButton holder that can be soldered onto a circuit board.

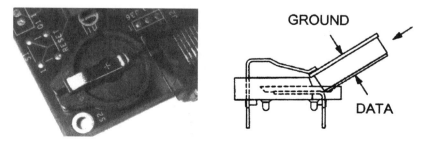

Figure 10-28: DS9094 iButton retaining clip

DS9092R iButton port. This is basically an empty iButton container with little tabs on it that you can solder to. In effect, you can solder wires to this and make your own iButton cable, or your own iButton-like devices.

**Figure 10-29:
DS9092R iButton port**

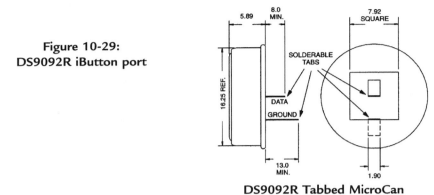

DS9092R Tabbed MicroCan

DS1401 iButton front panel holder. This is a strip with four or 24 iButton holders all interconnected on a 1-Wire bus. You can put an iButton cable into one of them and put iButtons in the others. It's a way of mating an iButton cable to multiple devices.

DS1401-04

Figure 10-30: DS1401 iButton front panel holder

The 1-Wire Java API

Throughout the previous discussion we've made mention of the 1-Wire Java API. In this section we will be looking at this API and a number of examples of how to use it.

The 1-Wire Java API, TMEX drivers, and these mysterious things called port adapters

Before we go into the details of what's inside the Java API, we need to talk a little about how the API talks to the 1-Wire bus. The API itself is actually one piece of a very interrelated, three-piece puzzle.

1. The Java API provides high-level control over the MicroLAN and the 1-Wire devices found on it. It can be used alone to drive the 1-Wire bus provided you

are using a port adapter based on a DS2480 Serial 1-Wire line driver. The DS2480 takes timing-independent, byte-based commands from the serial port and formats them into proper 1-Wire timing. The Java API relies on that formatting from either the DS2480 or an additional low-level device driver. Examples of port adapters that contain the DS2480 are the DS1411 and the DS9097U-09.

2. The Touch Memory Exchange, or TMEX, software provides a standalone Windows-based utility for examining devices on a 1-Wire net connected to a personal computer. There are three drivers that come as part of the TMEX software: IB10E32.DLL, IB97E32.DLL, and the IB97U32.DLL. These drivers provide the TMEX Windows-based utility with their interface with the 1-Wire bus. They also can be used by the Java API to provide low-level access to the 1-Wire bus. Which driver Java uses depends on which port adapter you're using.

   • IB10E32.DLL provides low-level control over the PC parallel printer port, normally referred to as LPT1, and subsequent communication with the 1-Wire bus through the use of a DS1410E parallel port adapter.

   • IB97E32.DLL provides low-level control over the PC serial ports, such as COM1, and subsequent communication with the 1-Wire bus through the use of serial port adapters such as the DS1413 and DS9097E. Note, these two port adapters do *not* contain active circuitry in the form of the DS2480 serial line driver chip. They are passive, and this driver is intended to work with that in mind.

   • IB97U32.DLL provides low-level control over the PC serial ports, such as COM1, and subsequent communication with the 1-Wire bus through the use of serial port adapters such as the DS1411 and DS9097U-09. These port adapters have the DS2480 serial line driver chip in them, taking care of the timeslot generation, and this driver takes this into account. If this driver is installed on your machine, the Java API will use it when trying to communicate with DS2480-based devices. If it is not installed, it will fall back to driving the serial port itself.

3. The port adapters themselves provide the electromechanical interface to the communication ports on the PC. As we've noted above, some have active circuitry in them in the form of the DS2480 that generates timing. These devices, the DS1411 and DS9097U-09, don't need the TMEX drivers and can be used with the Java API alone. Other devices, such as the DS1413, DS9097E, and DS1410E, don't have the DS2480 and need the help of a native driver.

Below is a chart that summarizes the port adapters and the drivers that support them.

Table 10-11: Port adapter, driver summary

Hardware Port Adapter Driver Name	Supported by TMEX Port Adapter (Adapter Name)	Supported Directly By 1-Wire API	Comments
DS1410E	Yes {DS1410E}, IB10E32.DLL	No	Java programs using the 1-Wire API must use the TMEX driver {DS1410E}
DS1411	Yes {DS9097U}, IB97U32.DLL	Yes, DS9097U	Java Programs using the 1-Wire API can use either the TMEX driver or the API's own driver.
DS1413	Yes {DS9097E}, IB97E32.DLL	No	Java programs using the 1-Wire API must use the TMEX driver {DS9097E}
DS9097U	Yes {DS9097U}, IB97U32.DLL	Yes, DS9097U	Java Programs using the 1-Wire API can use either the TMEX driver or the API's own driver.

So, how your software deals with low-level communications to the 1-Wire bus is actually a function of the port adapter that you are using and what you have installed on your computer. Here we have to bring up a word of caution: discussions of how the 1-Wire bus is being controlled often involve the phrase "port adapter" in different contexts with slightly different meanings. Sometimes "port adapter" means a piece of hardware that you connect on your computer and then connect the 1-Wire bus to. Other times, it means a Java software object in a program. We'll try to put things in the proper perspective as we go and will touch upon this issue again, as needed, as we go through examples later. Now, let's look at the 1-Wire Java API. We'll start with a summary of the packages and classes.

Example: finding all 1-Wire devices on a specific port

The first example we'll start with is a Java program that communicates with the 1-Wire bus and retrieves the 64-bit ROM ID of all the devices it finds on the bus. Let's take a high-level look at how we'll do it.

1. Read the port adapter to be used on the PC and the communication port it is to be connected to as command line arguments.

2. Create a port adapter object, using the `DSPortAdapter` class, and the `OneWire AccessProvider` class.

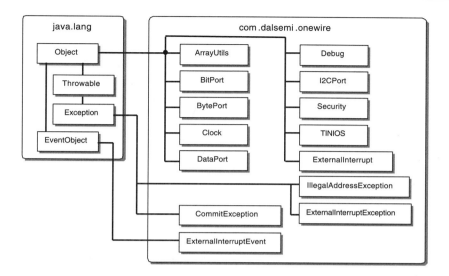

Figure 10-31: 1-Wire API packages and classes

3. Create an `Enumeration` of device *containers,* each an instance of the `OneWireContainer` class.

4. Loop over each element in the enumeration and for each element, create a `OneWireContainer` object.

5. Use methods in the `OneWireContainer` class to grab the ROM ID and device description. Print them.

6. Done!

Looking at this flow, four classes are interesting: `DSPortAdapter`, `OneWireAccessProvider`, `Enumeration`, and `OneWireDeviceContainer`. These classes are going to be a large part of many of our programs. Let's talk about each one, and then we'll look at the program and see it run.

The DSPortAdapter class

The `DSPortAdapter` class is an abstract class found in the Java 1-Wire API. As an abstract class, it can only be subclassed and can't be instantiated. For instance, you can't do the following:

```
DSPortAdapter myAdapter = new DSPortAdapter();
```

You'll get a compiler error. You can however, declare `DSPortAdapter` objects in the following manner:

```
DSPortAdapter myAdapter = null;
```

Then, you can get access to the DSPortAdapter derivatives by using the OneWireAccessProvider class in the following manner:

myAdapter = OneWireAccessProvider.getPortAdapter(adapter_name, port_name);

The DSPortAdapter class has a few abstract methods—that is, methods that are not implemented and need to be implemented somewhere else—and many methods that are implemented. Some of the most useful ones are listed below. There are many others, and some that are similar to these, but take different arguments. Refer to the actual API documentation for the complete list.

Port and Port Adapter Related Methods

- public abstract boolean **adapterDetected()**
- public abstract String **getAdapterName()**
- public abstract Enumeration **getPortNames()**
- public abstract String **getPortName()**
- public abstract boolean **selectPort(** String port_name **)**
- public abstract void **freePort()**

Device Container Related Methods

- public Enumeration **getAllDeviceContainers()**
- public OneWireContainer **getFirstDeviceContainer()**
- public OneWireContainer **getNextDeviceContainer()**
- public OneWireContainer **getDeviceContainer(** String **)**

Search Related Methods

- public abstract boolean **findFirstDevice()**
- public abstract boolean **findNextDevice()**
- public String **getAddressAsString()**

Device Family Related Methods

- public void **targetAllFamilies()**
- public void **targetFamily(** int family **)**

The OneWireAccessProvider class

The OneWireAccessProvider class provides the object creation for the abstract DSPortAdapter class. It also provides several useful methods.

- public static Enumeration **enumerateAllAdapters()**

- public static DSPortAdapter **getAdapter(** String adapter, String port **)**
- public static DSPortAdapter **getDefaultAdapter()**

The Enumeration class

The Enumeration class isn't strictly a 1-Wire thing, it's also a Java thing. Instances of the Enumeration class represent a series of objects that can be sequenced through. Two useful methods:

- public boolean **hasMoreElements()**
- public Object **nextElement()**

The OneWireContainer class

Instances of the OneWireContainer class, OneWireContainer objects, represent specific devices on the 1-Wire bus. They can be thought of as encapsulating the specific port adapter being used, the 1-Wire device network address, and the methods used for dealing with the 1-Wire device. There are methods in this class that are applicable to any device.

- public String **getName()**
- public String **getDescription()**
- public String **getAddressAsString()**
- public boolean **isPresent()**

The OneWireContainer class has numerous subclasses, such as the OneWireContainer10 class that deals specifically with 1-Wire devices that have a family code (the first 8 bits of the ROM ID) of 10h. Devices in this family are all thermometer devices. The OneWireContainer10 class extends the OneWireContainer class and adds many methods that are specifically related to temperature measurement.

We've seen a general description of a program that will take in two command line parameters, the adapter name and the port name, and return the ROM ID codes of any 1-Wire devices on the bus as well as a description of those devices. We've just looked at the 1-Wire API classes that will be used in the program. Let's now go through the program. First, we'll present the entire program, then go though it line by line.

Listing 10-1: ROM_ID.java

```
import com.dalsemi.onewire.*;
import com.dalsemi.onewire.adapter.*;
import com.dalsemi.onewire.container.*;
import java.io.*;
```

```
import java.util.*;

public  class ROM_ID {
    public static void main (String[] args) {

        String       adapter_name = "";
        String       port_name    = "";
        DSPortAdapter myPortAdapter = null;

          // Fetch the command line parameters if given
          // adapter_name should be like {DS9097U} or DS9097U or
              TINIExternalAdapter
              if (args.length>0) { adapter_name = args[0]; }
          // port_name should be like COM1, LPT1, /dev/ttyS0, or serial1
              if (args.length>1) { port_name = args[1]; }

          // Guess at defaults if the user didn't specify
          // Each operating system & platform is a little different.
          if (adapter_name.length()<1) {
              if (System.getProperty("os.name").indexOf("slush")!=-1) {
                  adapter_name = "TINIExternalAdapter";
              }
              if (System.getProperty("os.name").indexOf("Linux")!=-1) {
                  adapter_name = "DS9097U";
              }
              if (System.getProperty("os.name").indexOf("Windows")!=-1) {
                  adapter_name = "{DS9097U}";
              }
          }
          if (port_name.length()<1) {
              if (System.getProperty("os.name").indexOf("slush")!=-1) {
                  port_name = "serial1";
              }
              if (System.getProperty("os.name").indexOf("Linux")!=-1) {
                  port_name = "/dev/ttyS0";
              }
              if (System.getProperty("os.name").indexOf("Windows")!=-1) {
                  port_name = "COM1";
              }
          }

        System.out.println( "Looking for " + adapter_name + " on " + port_name );

        try {
            myPortAdapter =
                  OneWireAccessProvider.getAdapter(adapter_name, port_name);
              System.out.println( "Found it!" );
        }
        catch (Exception e) {
          System.out.println(e);
```

```
            System.exit(0);
         }

      myPortAdapter.targetAllFamilies();

      try {
         myPortAdapter.beginExclusive(true);

         Enumeration myContainers = myPortAdapter.getAllDeviceContainers();

         while (myContainers.hasMoreElements()) {
            OneWireContainer singleContainer =
               (OneWireContainer)myContainers.nextElement();

            System.out.println("\nROM ID:   " +
               singleContainer.getAddressAsString());

            System.out.println("Device Name: " + singleContainer.getName());
            System.out.println("Alternate Name:  " +
               singleContainer.getAlternateNames());

            System.out.println("Description: \n" +
               singleContainer.getDescription() + "\n");
         }
      }
       catch (Exception e) {
         System.out.println(e);
         System.exit(0);
      }
   }
}
```

First, we need to import the necessary libraries, and declare our class and the `main()` method.

```
import com.dalsemi.onewire.*;
import com.dalsemi.onewire.adapter.*;
import com.dalsemi.onewire.container.*;
import java.io.*;
import java.util.*;

public  class ROM_ID {
   public static void main (String[] args) {
```

Next, we are going to declare some objects. `Adapter_name` and `port_name` are String objects that will represent the software port adapter we are using and the PC communication port we plan to connect to the 1-Wire bus, respectively. The `DSPortAdapter`, `myPortAdapter`, will be the object that represents our port adapter.

```
      String         adapter_name = null;
```

```
String          port_name    = null;
DSPortAdapter myPortAdapter = null;
```

The command line arguments are placed into our String objects. If no command line
parameters are specified, then this block selects acceptable values and also shows the
syntax. If you specify a PortAdapter name enclosed in curly braces then those are
supported by the TMEX software; those not are those supported by the Java 1-Wire
API directly. Note that there is no version of the native 1-wire PortAdapter for Linux
so we need to use the Java 1-Wire API.

```
if (args.length>0) { adapter_name = args[0]; }
  // port_name should be like COM1, LPT1, /dev/ttyS0, or serial1
if (args.length>1) { port_name = args[1]; }
  if (adapter_name.length()<1) {
      if (System.getProperty("os.name").indexOf("slush")!=-1) {
          adapter_name = "TINIExternalAdapter";
      }
      if (System.getProperty("os.name").indexOf("Linux")!=-1) {
          adapter_name = "DS9097U";
      }
      if (System.getProperty("os.name").indexOf("Windows")!=-1) {
          adapter_name = "{DS9097U}";
      }
  }
  if (port_name.length()<1) {
      if (System.getProperty("os.name").indexOf("slush")!=-1) {
          port_name = "serial1";
      }
      if (System.getProperty("os.name").indexOf("Linux")!=-1) {
          port_name = "/dev/ttyS0";
      }
      if (System.getProperty("os.name").indexOf("Windows")!=-1) {
          port_name = "COM1";
      }
  }
  System.out.println( "Looking for " + adapter_name + " on " + port_name );
```

Next, we need to set our `DSPortAdapter` object, my`PortAdapter`, to the
`DSPortAdapter` returned by the `OneWireAccessProvider.getAdapter()` method. It
takes our strings as arguments. Since this method throws the `OneWireIOException`
and the `OneWireException`, we must either catch or specify these. We will catch
these exceptions by enclosing this in a try/catch block.

```
try {
    myPortAdapter = OneWireAccessProvider.getAdapter(adapter_name,
                        port_name);
} catch (Exception e) {
```

```
        System.out.println(e);
        System.exit(0);
}
```

We are interested in any 1-Wire device, so we must establish the fact that our search ROM process should look for all device families. This is done with the `targetAllFamilies()` method of the `DSPortAdapter` class.

```
        myPortAdapter.targetAllFamilies();
```

The next section of code starts with the beginExclusive() method of the `DSportAdapter` class. This establishes the fact that the current program thread will get exclusive use of the 1-Wire bus to communicate with an iButton or 1-Wire Device. Following this, we create an Enumeration object, myContainers, and initialize it to contain all of the device container objects that can be found on the 1-Wire bus. These objects are found using the `getAllDeviceContainers()` method of the `DSPortAdapter` class. This method, and the `beginExclusive()` method both throw exceptions that must be caught or specified. We will catch them by putting them inside a try/catch block. Since the `myContainers` Enumeration is used throughout the rest of the program, the rest of the program must also be included in the same try/catch block, since they are only valid inside the block in which they were created.

```
        try {
            myPortAdapter.beginExclusive(true);
            Enumeration myContainers = myPortAdapter.getAllDeviceContainers();
```

Next, we will loop through the Enumeration, once for each element, and create a single `OneWireContainer` object for each element. Then, we will use a series of methods to get at specific information about the `OneWireContainer` object. Since each `OneWireContainer` object basically represents a single 1-Wire device on the bus, that equates to getting information about the individual devices on the bus.

```
            while (myContainers.hasMoreElements()) {
                OneWireContainer singleContainer =
                    (OneWireContainer)myContainers.nextElement();

                System.out.println("\nROM ID:   " +
                    singleContainer.getAddressAsString());

                System.out.println("Device Name: " +
                    singleContainer.getName());
                System.out.println("Alternate Name: " +
                    singleContainer.getAlternateNames());

                System.out.println("Description: \n" +
                    singleContainer.getDescription() + "\n");
        }
```

Finally, we take care of any exceptions by catching them, printing them out, and exiting the program.

```
    } catch (Exception e) {
        System.out.println(e);
        System.exit(0);
    }
  }
}
```

Earlier, we discussed the various Dallas Semiconductor components used to connect PC communications ports to the 1-Wire bus, such as the DS1410E, DS1413, and the DS9097U. We also mentioned that the Java API supports some of these directly, and some through the use of drivers found in the TMEX software (IB10E32.DLL, IB97E32.DLL, and IB97U32.DLL). In this program demo, we have all the drivers installed and the Java 1-Wire API. We're going to communicate to the 1-Wire bus through the parallel port (LPT1) and the serial port (COM1). You may have different port names on your computer, but these are the ones that will be most commonly used. We also have on hand a DS1410E to connect the 1-Wire bus to the parallel port, and DS1411, DS1413, and some variety of DS9097U serial port adapters connect the COM1 serial port to the 1-Wire bus. Let's start by querying the DS1410E connected to the LPT1 port. This device has spots for two iButtons, both of which are currently empty. The software "port adapter name" for this is the {DS1410E}. The curly brackets ({ }) around the portAdapter name tells the 1-Wire API to use the TMEX native 1-Wire driver and the lack of curly braces means to the Java API 1-Wire drivers.

> *Note:* We don't show the compile command-line options (like CLASSPATH, etc.) here because they might be confusing if you don't put your files in the same folder names that we did. If you use the CDROM, the build.bat will compile the code for you.

```
C:\> javac src\ROM_ID.java -d bin
C:\> cd bin
C:\> java  ROM_ID {DS1410E} LPT1

ROM ID:  280000001B2BB881
Device Name: DS1990A
Alternate Name: DS2401
Description:
64 bit unique serial number
```

The DS1410E contains a DS1990A 64-bit silicon serial number embedded within it, and our search has picked up that device. Suppose we were to put a temperature iButton into one of the DS1410E iButton clips and run the program:

```
C:\> java  ROM_ID {DS1410E} LPT1

ROM ID:  F40000004B212B10
```

```
Device Name: DS1920
Alternate Name: DS1820
Description:
Digital thermometer measures temperatures from -55C to 100C in typi-
cally 0.2 seconds. +/- 0.5C Accuracy between 0C and 70C. 0.5C standard
resolution, higher resolution through interpolation.Contains high and
low temperature set points for generation of alarm.
ROM ID:  280000001B2BB881
Device Name: DS1990A
Alternate Name: DS2401
Description:
64 bit unique serial number
```

It has now found the iButton placed in the DS1410E. Let's move on and try using a DS1411 serial port adapter in COM1. It can hold one iButton. Let's put a different temperature iButton in it and try running the program. The DS1411 can be interfaced with the TMEX driver or the driver found in the 1-Wire API. Let's try the TMEX driver first; the syntax for that port adapter is {DS9097U}.

`C:\> ` **`java ROM_ID {DS9097U} COM1`**

```
ROM ID:  EF0000004B224210
Device Name: DS1920
Alternate Name: DS1820
Description:
Digital thermometer measures temperatures from -55C to 100C in typi-
cally 0.2 seconds. +/- 0.5C Accuracy between 0C and 70C. 0.5C standard
resolution, higher resolution through interpolation.Contains high and
low temperature set points forgeneration of alarm.
ROM ID:  8B00000293A1C009
Device Name: DS1982
Alternate Name: DS2502
Description:
1024 bit Electrically Programmable Read Only Memory (EPROM) parti-
tioned into four 256 bit pages.Each memory page can be permanently
write-protected to prevent tampering. Architecture allows software to
patch data by supersending a used page in favor of a newly programmed
page.
```

The temperature iButton was found, as well as a DS1982 EPROM device. The EPROM is embedded in the DS1411 to act as a user-programmable data space. Let's try running it using the Java 1-Wire API driver. The syntax for specifying that port adapter is DS9097U.

`C:\> ` **`java ROM_ID DS9097U COM1`**

```
ROM ID:  EF0000004B224210
Device Name: DS1920
Alternate Name: DS1820
Description:
```

```
Digital thermometer measures temperatures from -55C to 100C in typi-
cally 0.2 seconds. +/- 0.5C Accuracy between 0C and 70C. 0.5C standard
resolution, higher resolution through interpolation.Contains high and
low temperature set points forgeneration of alarm.

ROM ID:  8B00000293A1C009
Device Name: DS1982
Alternate Name: DS2502
Description:
1024 bit Electrically Programmable Read Only Memory (EPROM) parti-
tioned into four 256 bit pages.Each memory page can be permanently
write-protected to prevent tampering. Architecture allows software to
patch data by supersending a used page in favor of a newly programmed
page.
```

Once again, it found the iButton and the embedded memory. Let's try using the DS1413 serial port adapter. The syntax for referring to its software port adapter is {DS9097E}. We'll put the same temperature iButton that we used in the DS1411 into it.

```
C:\> java ROM_ID {DS9097E} COM1

ROM ID:   EF0000004B224210
Device Name: DS1920
Alternate Name: DS1820
Description:
Digital thermometer measures temperatures from -55C to 100C in typi-
cally 0.2 seconds. +/- 0.5C Accuracy between 0C and 70C. 0.5C standard
resolution, higher resolution through interpolation.Contains high and
low temperature set points forgeneration of alarm.
```

The temperature iButton was found without any other devices. The DS1413 doesn't contain any embedded 1-Wire devices in it for ID or memory storage. For the sake of argument, what do you think would happen if we tried to use the wrong software port adapter name when trying to communicate with it? Let's try…

```
C:\> java ROM_ID {DS9097U} COM1
com.dalsemi.onewire.OneWireException: 1-Wire Net not available
```

It didn't work. When we specify the {DS9097U} port adapter name, we're telling the Java program to use the TMEX driver and look for a port adapter on COM1 that uses a DS2480 serial line driver for communication. That means it looks for a DS9097U or a DS1411.

Before we leave this example program, let's try one more thing. We have a DS9097U Universal COM Port Adapter, and a small circuit board with four DS2406 1-Wire switches on it. Connecting the two, we have a 6" piece of telephone wire. The DS9097U port adapter can be accessed with the port adapter name of {DS9097U}, using the TMEX driver, or DS9097U, using the Java 1-Wire API. Let's use the Java 1-Wire version.

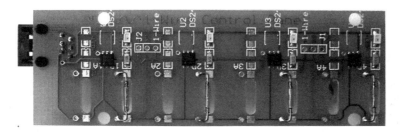

Figure 10-32: Photo of Dallas Semiconductor LED board with DS9097U COM port adapter

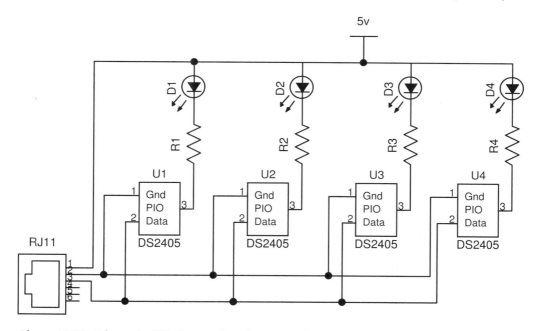

Figure 10-33: Schematic of Dallas Semiconductor LED board with DS9097U COM port adapter

```
C:\> java ROM_ID DS9097U COM1
```

```
ROM ID:  9E00000017844012
Device Name: DS2406
Alternate Name: Dual Addressable Switch, DS2407
Description:
1-Wire Dual Addressable Switch. PIO pin channel A sink capability of
typical 50mA at 0.4V with soft turn-on; optional channel B typical 10
mA at 0.4V. 1024 bits of Electrically Programmable Read Only Memory
(EPROM) partitioned into four 256 bit pages. 7 bytes of user-program-
mable status memory to control the device.
```

```
ROM ID:   7F00000017841A12
Device Name: DS2406
Alternate Name: Dual Addressable Switch, DS2407
Description:
1-Wire Dual Addressable Switch. PIO pin channel A sink capability of
typical 50mA at 0.4V with soft turn-on; optional channel B typical 10
mA at 0.4V. 1024 bits of Electrically Programmable Read Only Memory
(EPROM) partitioned into four 256 bit pages. 7 bytes of user-program-
mable status memory to control the device.

ROM ID:   0200000017461E12
Device Name: DS2406
Alternate Name: Dual Addressable Switch, DS2407
Description:
1-Wire Dual Addressable Switch. PIO pin channel A sink capability of
typical 50mA at 0.4V with soft turn-on; optional channel B typical 10
mA at 0.4V. 1024 bits of Electrically Programmable Read Only Memory
(EPROM) partitioned into four 256 bit pages. 7 bytes of user-program-
mable status memory to control the device.

ROM ID:   9200000017473B12
Device Name: DS2406
Alternate Name: Dual Addressable Switch, DS2407
Description:
1-Wire Dual Addressable Switch. PIO pin channel A sink capability of
typical 50mA at 0.4V with soft turn-on; optional channel B typical 10
mA at 0.4V. 1024 bits of Electrically Programmable Read Only Memory
(EPROM) partitioned into four 256 bit pages. 7 bytes of user-program-
mable status memory to control the device.

ROM ID:   D1000001B934D509
Device Name: DS1982
Alternate Name: DS2502
Description:
1024 bit Electrically Programmable Read Only Memory (EPROM) parti-
tioned into four 256 bit pages.Each memory page can be permanently
write-protected to prevent tampering. Architecture allows software to
patch data by supersending a used page in favor of a newly programmed
page.
```

It found four DS2406 devices and a DS1982 EPROM memory device. The four DS2406 devices correspond to the devices on the little circuit board and the DS1892 is embedded in the DS9097U itself.

Example: Finding devices by family on a specific port

What if, instead of finding all 1-Wire devices on a specified port, I only wanted to find devices corresponding to a particular device family? The solution to this is simple. In the previous program, we have the line:

```
myPortAdapter.targetAllFamilies();
```

Replace it with

```
myPortAdapter.targetFamily(familyInteger);
```

where `familyInteger` is an integer representing the family code of the devices we are interested in finding. In the previous example run, we used a DS9097U on COM1 that was connected to a little circuit board that had four switches on it. We saw the four switches in the program output, but we also saw a DS2502 EPROM that was embedded in the DS9097U for identification purposes. What if we were only interested in the switches? The ROM ID code of each switch begins with 12h. That is, 12 hex is in the least-significant 8 bits of the ROM ID code, which when printed out, are to the right. Let's make the following change:

```
myPortAdapter.targetFamily(0x12);
```

By preceding our number with 0x, we are telling Java that the number is in hex. We could also use the line:

```
myPortAdapter.targetFamily(18);
```

`C:\> `**`java ROM_ID DS9097U COM1`**

```
ROM ID:   9E00000017844012
Device Name: DS2406
Alternate Name: Dual Addressable Switch, DS2407
Description:
1-Wire Dual Addressable Switch. PIO pin channel A sink capability of
typical 50mA at 0.4V with soft turn-on; optional channel B typical 10
mA at 0.4V. 1024 bits of Electrically Programmable Read Only Memory
(EPROM) partitioned into four 256 bit pages. 7 bytes of user-program-
mable status memory to control the device.

ROM ID:   7F00000017841A12
Device Name: DS2406
Alternate Name: Dual Addressable Switch, DS2407
Description:
1-Wire Dual Addressable Switch. PIO pin channel A sink capability of
typical 50mA at 0.4V with soft turn-on; optional channel B typical 10
mA at 0.4V. 1024 bits of Electrically Programmable Read Only Memory
(EPROM) partitioned into four 256 bit pages. 7 bytes of user-program-
mable status memory to control the device.

ROM ID:   0200000017461E12
Device Name: DS2406
Alternate Name: Dual Addressable Switch, DS2407
Description:
1-Wire Dual Addressable Switch. PIO pin channel A sink capability of
typical 50mA at 0.4V with soft turn-on; optional channel B typical 10
mA at 0.4V. 1024 bits of Electrically Programmable Read Only Memory
(EPROM) partitioned into four 256 bit pages. 7 bytes of user-program-
mable status memory to control the device.
```

```
ROM ID:   9200000017473B12
Device Name: DS2406
Alternate Name: Dual Addressable Switch, DS2407
Description:
1-Wire Dual Addressable Switch. PIO pin channel A sink capability of
typical 50mA at 0.4V with soft turn-on; optional channel B typical 10
mA at 0.4V. 1024 bits of Electrically Programmable Read Only Memory
(EPROM) partitioned into four 256 bit pages. 7 bytes of user-program-
mable status memory to control the device.
```

By using the `targetFamily()` method, we have found only the DS2407 switch devices.

Example: Identifying all software port adapters present

In our previous example, we entered the name of the adapter type and communication port we wanted to use. What if we didn't want to enter this information? What if, instead, we wanted to look to see which port adapters were currently supported on the computer? What if you didn't happen to know the syntax of the text string used for the adapter name? The following simple example shows how to obtain a list of all the software port adapters installed on a computer. We'll show the program in its entirety first, and then go through it bit by bit.

Listing 10-2: PortAdapters.java

```java
import com.dalsemi.onewire.*;
import com.dalsemi.onewire.adapter.*;
import java.io.*;
import java.util.*;

public  class PortAdapters {

    public static void main (String[] args) {
        DSPortAdapter singleAdapter = null;
        Enumeration myAdapters = null;
        Enumeration myPorts = null;

        myAdapters = OneWireAccessProvider.enumerateAllAdapters();
        while (myAdapters.hasMoreElements()) {
            singleAdapter = (DSPortAdapter)myAdapters.nextElement();
            System.out.print("PortAdapter = " +singleAdapter.getAdapterName());

            myPorts = singleAdapter.getPortNames();
              System.out.print( "; CommPorts = " );
            while (myPorts.hasMoreElements()) {
                System.out.print(myPorts.nextElement() + " " );
            }
            System.out.println();
        }
    }
}
```

The first section imports the necessary class libraries.

```
import com.dalsemi.onewire.*;
import com.dalsemi.onewire.adapter.*;

import java.io.*;
import java.util.*;
```

The next section is the class declaration, the `main()` method declaration, and two object declarations. We establish an Enumeration object that contains all of the `DSPortAdapter` objects, and a single `DSPortadapter` object that is used in an iterative loop to represent a single member of the Enumeration.

```
public  class PortAdapters {
    public static void main (String[] args) {
        DSPortAdapter singleAdapter = null;
        Enumeration myAdapters = null;
        Enumeration myPorts = null;
```

Having declared the Enumeration `myAdapters`, we're now going to set it to the return values of the `OneWireAccessProvider.enumerateAllAdapters()` method. That method returns an enumeration of `DSPortAdapter` objects, one for each software port adapter found. Then, we loop through the entire Enumeration, once for each object in the Enumeration. Each time, we set the value of `singleAdapter` to the next element in the Enumeration of `DSPortAdapters`. We then use the `getAdapterName()` method of the `DSPortadapter` class to return a string value representing the name of the software adapter represented by that object.

```
        myAdapters = OneWireAccessProvider.enumerateAllAdapters();
        while (myAdapters.hasMoreElements()) {
            singleAdapter = (DSPortAdapter)myAdapters.nextElement();
            System.out.print("PortAdapter = " +singleAdapter.getAdapterName());

            myPorts = singleAdapter.getPortNames();
              System.out.print( "; CommPorts = " );
            while (myPorts.hasMoreElements()) {
                System.out.print(myPorts.nextElement() + " " );
            }
            System.out.println();
        }
    }
```

The system this program is being demonstrated on has the TMEX software loaded, as well as the Java 1-Wire API.

```
C:\> java PortAdapters
PortAdapter = {DS9097E}; CommPorts = COM0 COM1 COM2 COM3 COM4 COM5
COM6 COM7 COM
8 COM9 COM10 COM11 COM12 COM13 COM14 COM15
PortAdapter = {DS1410E}; CommPorts = LPT0 LPT1 LPT2 LPT3 LPT4 LPT5
LPT6 LPT7 LPT
```

```
8 LPT9 LPT10 LPT11 LPT12 LPT13 LPT14 LPT15
PortAdapter = {DS9097U}; CommPorts = COM0 COM1 COM2 COM3 COM4 COM5
COM6 COM7 COM
8 COM9 COM10 COM11 COM12 COM13 COM14 COM15
PortAdapter = DS9097U; CommPorts = COM1 COM2 COM3 COM4
```

And on Linux

```
PortAdapter = DS9097U; CommPorts = /dev/ttyS0 /dev/ttyS1 /dev/ttyS2 /
dev/ttyS3
```

The first three entries are software port adapter names coming from the TMEX software. The last one comes from the Java 1-Wire API.

Example: Finding the default adapter

The `OneWireAccessProvider` class has a `getDefaultAdapter()` method. This method has an order of precedence:

1. If the TMEX software is installed, it sees what that package has installed as its default, and tries to use that—i.e., either the {DS1410E}, {DS9097E}, or the {DS909U} as the adapter name.

2. If the TMEX software is not installed, it tries to use the DS9097U as the adapter name.

It then tries to establish communications over the bus with a compatible hardware port adapter. If it doesn't sense one, it throws an exception. If it does find one, it returns the port adapter name. There is only one default adapter in the TMEX software, and it can be set with the "1-Wire Net Port Selection" utility (`SetPer32.exe`), that comes with the TMEX software.

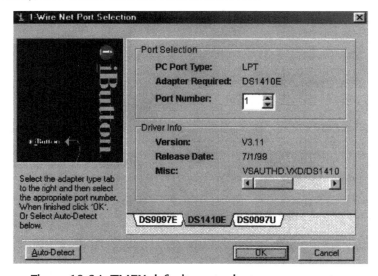

Figure 10-34: TMEX default port adapter screen capture

As the image shows, the default adapter on the demo machine is the DS1410E, which translates to a port adapter name of {DS1410E}. The following is a simple program that uses the `getDefaultAdapter()` method to see what the default software adapter is and whether or not its corresponding hardware adapter is present on the bus. It returns the name of the adapter if it is present and prints an exception if it is not.

Listing 10-3: DefaultAdapter.java

```java
import com.dalsemi.onewire.*;
import com.dalsemi.onewire.adapter.*;
import java.io.*;
import java.util.*;

public  class DefaultAdapter {

    public static void main (String[] args) {
        DSPortAdapter myDefaultAdapter = null;
         Enumeration myPorts = null;

        try {
            myDefaultAdapter =

(DSPortAdapter)OneWireAccessProvider.getDefaultAdapter();
            System.out.println(myDefaultAdapter.getAdapterName());

            myPorts = myDefaultAdapter.getPortNames();
            while (myPorts.hasMoreElements()) {
                System.out.println(myPorts.nextElement());
            }

        } catch(Exception e) {
            System.out.println(e);
        }
    }

}
```

```
C:\> java DefaultAdapter
{DS1410E}LPT0
LPT1
LPT2
LPT3
LPT4
LPT5
LPT6
LPT7
LPT8
LPT9
LPT10
```

```
LPT11
LPT12
LPT13
LPT14
LPT15
```

In reality, we only have an LPT0 port on the machine where we ran this, but the program still found LPT1 through LPT15. The `getPortNames()` method actually retrieves a list of the platform-appropriate port names for this port adapter. It doesn't, however, guarantee that your machine actually has all of those ports. If we remove the DS1410E from the parallel port on the computer and re-run this:

```
C:\>java DefaultAdapter
com.dalsemi.onewire.OneWireException: 1-Wire Net not available
```

Example: Finding all 1-Wire devices on any port

So far, we've presented programs that accept a user-specified port adapter name and port and identify 1-Wire devices on that bus, and we've presented programs that examine what port adapters are supported by the software currently loaded on the system and what the default port adapter might be. An interesting combination of all these concepts would be a program that looked at all port adapters for all devices and printed out information on all 1-Wire devices it finds. It turns out that one of the example programs distributed with the Java 1-Wire API does exactly that. The program is freely distributed by Dallas Semiconductor and is already commented fairly well, so we will only show its use here. The program is called `FindiButtonsConsole.java`. In preparation for running it, we've placed the DS1410E back on the LPT1 parallel printer port with a temperature iButton in it (DS1920). We've also placed a DS1413 on COM1 with another temperature iButton in it.

```
C:\>java FindiButtonsConsole

FindiButtonsConsole Java console application: Version 2.00

Adapter/Port    iButton Type and ID        Description
--------------------------------------------------------------
{DS9097E}/COM1  DS1920   EF0000004B224210   Digital thermometer measu...
{DS1410E}/LPT1  DS1920   F40000004B212B10   Digital thermometer measu...
{DS1410E}/LPT1  DS1990A  280000001B2BB881   64 bit unique serial numb...
```

An interesting thing happens if we replace the DS1413 iButton COM port adapter with a DS1411, and put the same temperature iButton in it:

```
C:\>java FindiButtonsConsole

FindiButtonsConsole Java console application: Version 2.00

Adapter/Port    iButton Type and ID        Description
--------------------------------------------------------------
```

```
{DS1410E}/LPT1   DS1920   F40000004B212B10   Digital thermometer measu...
{DS1410E}/LPT1   DS1990A  280000001B2BB881   64 bit unique serial numb...
{DS9097U}/COM1   DS1920   EF0000004B224210   Digital thermometer measu...
{DS9097U}/COM1   DS1982   8B00000293A1C009   1024 bit Electrically Pro...
DS9097U/COM1     DS1920   EF0000004B224210   Digital thermometer measu...
DS9097U/COM1     DS1982   8B00000293A1C009   1024 bit Electrically Pro...
```

Notice how it finds the temperature iButton (DS1920) and the 1024 bit EPROM (DS1982) in the DS1411 port adapter? Notice how it finds them twice? This happens because this program examines all the various software port adapter names supported by the system and then looks at each to see if a compatible hardware adapter is present. Since Java supports the DS1411 COM port adapter indirectly through the use of a driver supplied with the TMEX software, and directly through a driver in the Java 1-Wire API itself, it is listed twice as both avenues are explored by this program.

Example: Controlling the DS2405 addressable switch

So far our examples have dealt with basic concepts involving the PC ports, the software port adapters that support communications over them, and the hardware port adapters that work with the software to drive the 1-Wire bus. Now, we're going to shift gears and concentrate more on 1-Wire devices that we want to control. The following examples assume that we are relying solely on the DS9097U port adapter in the Java 1-Wire API. We will make use of both the DS1411 COM port adapter, for use with iButtons, and the DS9097U-09 Universal COM Port Adapter, for use with non-iButton type devices. We are going to start by looking at a program to turn on an LED using a DS2405 Addressable Switch[5].

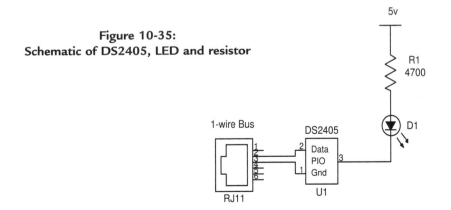

Figure 10-35:
Schematic of DS2405, LED and resistor

---

[5] DS2405 Addressable Switch data sheet – http://pdfserv.maxim-ic.com/arpdf/DS2405.pdf

We'll start by making a Java class that takes a parameter that turns an LED on or off. Then we'll present a program that acts as an HTTP server and allows you to control the LED with a web browser. Let's take a high-level look at the 1-Wire API as it relates to the DS2405.

The OneWireContainer05 class

The `OneWireContainer05` class represents devices in the 05(hex) family, which are single addressable switches. There are numerous methods completely documented in the 1-Wire API Javadocs, but the methods we'll be using, for review, are:

- `public String getAddressAsString()`

- `public byte[] readDevice()`

- `public boolean getLatchState(int channel, byte[] state)`

- `public void setLevel(int channel, byte[] state)`

- `public void writeDevice(byte[] state)`

- `public void setLatchState(int channel, boolean latchState, boolean doSmart, byte[] state)`

An important consideration when using the DS2405 is that it has an internal latch that holds the value of what we set the switch to do, and a level sensor so we can determine what the switch is really doing. This allows you to use the DS2405 as a simple sensor, and it also allows you to check for faults such as the output shorted to power or ground. However, the polarity of the internal latch and the level sensor are opposite. By setting the internal latch to true, we are telling the DS2405 to make the PIO pin logic zero. By setting the latch to false, we are telling the DS2405 to let the PIO pin float (since there's no positive voltage supply on the DS2405, it can't drive the PIO pin high). But if the PIO pin is at logic level zero, and we sense its level, the level will come back false. If its value is above a threshold of 2.2 volts, it will come back true. To reiterate the point: setting the latch and reading the level have what can be considered opposite polarities.

Our Switch class will consist of the following:

1. an overloaded constructor which can take no arguments, the port adapter and port, or the specific ROM ID of an individual device and port adapter and port names.

2. `turnOn()` and `turnOff()` methods, which take no arguments and do exactly as their name implies, turn our switch on and off. In this context, we're assuming that the DS2405 is controlling a small LED being pulled high by a resistor, as shown in Figure 10-35.

3. a `main()` method that takes a command line parameter of "on" or "off" and adjusts the switch accordingly.

The program is presented in its entirety below, then explained piece by piece.

Listing 10-4: Switch.java

```
import java.util.*;
import com.dalsemi.onewire.*;
import com.dalsemi.onewire.adapter.*;
import com.dalsemi.onewire.container.*;

public class Switch {

    DSPortAdapter adapter;
    String ROM_ID;
    byte[] state;
    boolean latchState;
    boolean level;
     static int speed=0;

     // Use container types rather then specific container numbers
    SwitchContainer container;
     OneWireContainer owc;

    public Switch() {
       try {
            // get the default adapter
          adapter = (DSPortAdapter)OneWireAccessProvider.getDefaultAdapter();
             Init("");
       }
         catch(Exception e) {
            System.out.println(e);
         }
    }

    public Switch( String PAadapt, String Port) {
       try {
           adapter=(DSPortAdapter)OneWireAccessProvider.getAdapter(PAadapt,Port);
             Init("");
       }
         catch(Exception e) {
            System.out.println(e);
         }
    }

    public Switch( String ROM, String PAadapt, String Port) {
        try {
           adapter=(DSPortAdapter)OneWireAccessProvider.getAdapter(PAadapt,Port);
             Init(ROM);
```

```
        }
      catch(Exception e) {
          System.out.println(e);
      }
  }


  public void Init(String ROM) {
       // Get both DS2405 and DS2406 devices since they both are switches
       byte[] targetfamlies = { 0x05, 0x12 };

     try {
           adapter.beginExclusive(true);
           adapter.reset();
        adapter.targetFamily(targetfamlies);

           if (ROM.length()<1) {
               owc = adapter.getFirstDeviceContainer();
           }
           else
           {
               container = (OneWireContainer12)adapter.getDeviceContainer(ROM);
           }

           // cast it to a switchContainer
               container = (SwitchContainer)owc;
           // get its ROM_ID
               ROM_ID = owc.getAddressAsString();
           // shouldn't the container object know the adapter object?
               owc.setupContainer(adapter, ROM_ID);
               state = container.readDevice();
               latchState = container.getLatchState(0, state);
               level = container.getLevel(0, state);

           adapter.setSpeed(speed);
       }
      catch(Exception e) {
          System.out.println(e);
      }
  }


  public void turnOn() {
      try {
          state = container.readDevice();
          latchState = container.getLatchState(0, state);
          level = container.getLevel(0, state);
          if ((level == true) && (latchState == false)) {
              container.setLatchState(0, true, false, state);
              container.writeDevice(state);
```

```
        }
    }
     catch (Exception e) {
         System.out.println(e);
     }
}

public void turnOff() {
    try {
        state = container.readDevice();
        latchState = container.getLatchState(0, state);
        level = container.getLevel(0, state);
        if ((level == false) && (latchState == true)) {
           container.setLatchState(0, false, false, state);
           container.writeDevice(state);
        }
    }
     catch (Exception e) {
         System.out.println(e);
     }
}

public void toggle() {
    try {
        state = container.readDevice();
        level = container.getLevel(0, state);
          // since the level is the opposite of the latchstate,
          // set the new latchstate to the existing level
        container.setLatchState(0, level, false, state);
          container.writeDevice(state);
    }
     catch (Exception e) {
         System.out.println(e);
     }
}

public void blink() {
     for( int i=0; i<10; i++ ) {
        try {
        state = container.readDevice();
        level = container.getLevel(0, state);
             // since the level is the opposite of the latchstate,
             // set the new latchstate to the existing level
        container.setLatchState(0, true, false, state);
             container.writeDevice(state);
        container.setLatchState(0, false, false, state);
             container.writeDevice(state);
        }
         catch (Exception e) {
             System.out.println(e);
```

```
                }
            }
    }

    public void update() {
        try {
            state = container.readDevice();
            latchState = container.getLatchState(0, state);
            level = container.getLevel(0, state);
        } catch (Exception e) {}
    }

    public static void main(String args[]) {

        String inputCommand = (args.length>0) ? args[0] : "flip";
        speed = Integer.valueOf((args.length>1) ? args[1] : "0" ).intValue();

        Switch blinker = new Switch();

        if (inputCommand.equalsIgnoreCase("on")) {
                System.out.println( "Turn on switch." );
            blinker.turnOn();
        } else if (inputCommand.equalsIgnoreCase("off")) {
                System.out.println( "Turn off switch." );
            blinker.turnOff();
        } else if (inputCommand.equalsIgnoreCase("blink")) {
                System.out.println( "Blinking." );
                blinker.blink();
          } else if (inputCommand.equalsIgnoreCase("flip")) {
                System.out.println( "Toggling switch." );
                blinker.toggle();
          } else {
                System.out.println( "Invalid option. " );
                System.exit(0);
        }

        System.out.println("Device ROM ID: " + blinker.ROM_ID);
        System.out.println("Device Latch State: " + blinker.latchState);
        System.out.println("Device Level: " + blinker.level);
    }
}
```

The program begins with the normal import statements and class declaration. We follow that by declaring all of our data members. These are the data items that each switch object contains. The member called adapter is the DSPortAdapter object we're using to communicate with the 1-Wire bus, as in DS9097U or {DS9097U}, etc. ROM_ID is the device-unique ID code. The byte array called state is actually an array with only a single element of type byte that contains information necessary for the device to maintain its state. The boolean flag latchState is the setting of the device's internal latch as of the last time the state byte was read, while level is the last sensed value of the PIO pin as of the last time the state byte was read. The `OneWireContainer05` object called `container` is the object we're using to represent, or encapsulate, our switch.

```
import java.util.*;
import com.dalsemi.onewire.*;
import com.dalsemi.onewire.adapter.*;
import com.dalsemi.onewire.container.*;

public class Switch {
    DSPortAdapter adapter;
    String ROM_ID;
    byte[] state;
    boolean latchState;
    boolean level;
    OneWireContainer05 container;
    static int speed=0;
```

The first constructor takes no arguments. It attempts to use the default port adapter and then call the `Init()` method that attempts to find the first DS2405 on the 1-Wire bus to be identified. We use the `Init()` method call in the constructor because this block of code is common for all of the constructors. Most of this is creating the data members that were previously declared, but a couple of the actions are responsible for other functions. The `targetFamily(targetfamlies)` is actually telling the 1-Wire bus that we are going to limit the underlying 1-Wire bus searches (Search ROM passes) to devices with a family code of 0x05 and 0x12 (these are both switch family codes). Note that the byte array targetfamlies is defined as `{ 0x05, 0x12 }`. You can place as many families in this array as you want. The `setupContainer()` method provides the container object with the adapter we're communicating over and the ROM_ID of the device we're communicating with. Since several of the methods throw exceptions, we enclose them in a try/catch block.

```
    public Switch() {
        try {
            // get the default adapter
            adapter = (DSPortAdapter)OneWireAccessProvider.getDefaultAdapter();
            Init("");
        }
          catch(Exception e) {
            System.out.println(e);
          }
    }

    public void Init(String ROM) {
        // Get both DS2405 and DS2406 devices since they both are switches
        byte[] targetfamlies = { 0x05, 0x12 };
```

```
      try {
          adapter.beginExclusive(true);
          adapter.reset();
        adapter.targetFamily(targetfamlies);

          if (ROM.length()<1) {
              owc = adapter.getFirstDeviceContainer();
          }
          else
          {
              container = (OneWireContainer12)adapter.getDeviceContainer(ROM);
          }

          // cast it to a switchContainer
              container = (SwitchContainer)owc;
          // get its ROM_ID
              ROM_ID = owc.getAddressAsString();
          // shouldn't the container object know the adapter object?
              owc.setupContainer(adapter, ROM_ID);
              state = container.readDevice();
              latchState = container.getLatchState(0, state);
              level = container.getLevel(0, state);

          adapter.setSpeed(speed);
      }
        catch(Exception e) {
            System.out.println(e);
        }
    }
```

The second constructor is almost identical to the first, except this one takes a specific port adapter and port as arguments, as opposed to using the defaults.

```
public Switch( String PAadapt, String Port) {
    try {

        adapter=(DSPortAdapter)OneWireAccessProvider.getAdapter(PAadapt,Port);
        Init("");
    }
        catch(Exception e) {
            System.out.println(e);
        }
}
```

The third and final constructor allows you to specify all the specifics: port adapter, port name, and the ROM ID of the device you are interested in.

```
public Switch( String ROM, String PAadapt, String Port) {
    try {

        adapter=(DSPortAdapter)OneWireAccessProvider.getAdapter(PAadapt,Port);
        Init(ROM);
```

```
        }
      catch(Exception e) {
          System.out.println(e);
    }
  }
```

The `turnOn()` method illustrates how to communicate with the DS2405. To use any of the methods, such as `getLatchState`, or `getLevel`, you have to know the state of the device, determined by using the `readDevice()` method. The state byte array returned by that method can then be supplied to the other methods that parse it.

```
    public void turnOn() {
        try {
            this.state = (this.container).readDevice();
```

The `latchState` and `level` are determined by the `getLatchState` and `getLevel` methods. The "0" in each one of them corresponds to the channel number. These methods are designed to be compatible with other switch devices, such as the DS2407 that has two switches, and hence two channels inside it. The DS2405 only has one channel and the channel number will always be 0 for it.

```
this.latchState = (this.container).getLatchState(0, this.state);
this.level = (this.container).getLevel(0, state);
```

Before turning the switch on, we actually check to see that it is off. If it is off, we then set the latch state to true, indicating that we want it to drive the PIO pin to logic zero, thereby turning on our LED. Doing this involves using the `setLatchState()` method to write our changes to the state array, then sending that array to the device with the `writeDevice()` method. Again, the `setLatchState()` method is designed to be compatible with other switch devices that have more capabilities. The third argument is the `doSmart` flag. It refers to a capability (smart sensing) that the DS2405 does not have and will always be false for the DS2405.

```
            if ((this.level == true) && (this.latchState == false)) {
                (this.container).setLatchState(0, true, false, this.state);
                (this.container).writeDevice(this.state);
            }
        } catch (Exception e) {System.out.println(e);}
    }
```

The `turnOff()` method proceeds in the same fashion as the turnOn() method.

```
    public void turnOff() {
        try {
            this.state = (this.container).readDevice();
            this.latchState = (this.container).getLatchState(0, this.state);
            this.level = (this.container).getLevel(0, this.state);
            if ((this.level == false) && (this.latchState == true)) {
                (this.container).setLatchState(0, false, false, this.state);
                (this.container).writeDevice(this.state);
            }
```

```
    } catch (Exception e) {System.out.println(e);}
}
```

The `update()` method reads the device state and then supplies that to the `getLatchState()` and `getLevel()` methods so that the `latchState` and `level` data members can be updated. This is useful for looking at activity on the output of the switch that might be caused by a source other than our program.

```
public void update() {
    try {
        this.state = (this.container).readDevice();
        this.latchState = (this.container).getLatchState(0, this.state);
        this.level = (this.container).getLevel(0, this.state);
    } catch (Exception e) {}
}
```

The `main()` method is straightforward. It creates a `switch` object called `blinker`, using the version of the constructor that takes no arguments, then looks at the command line. If we entered an "on," it turns the switch on. If we enter an "off," it turns the switch off. If we didn't enter anything then it calls the `toggle()` method to invert the state of the switch. If we entered blink then it turns the switch on and off ten times. Also note that, using the second argument, it is possible to set the speed of the 1-Wire communication. It then prints out the ROM ID, latch state, and level.

```
public static void main(String args[]) {

    String inputCommand = (args.length>0) ? args[0] : "flip";
      speed = Integer.valueOf( (args.length>1) ? args[1] : "0" ).intValue();

    Switch blinker = new Switch();

    if (inputCommand.equalsIgnoreCase("on")) {
        System.out.println( "Turn on switch." );
      blinker.turnOn();
    } else if (inputCommand.equalsIgnoreCase("off")) {
        System.out.println( "Turn off switch." );
        blinker.turnOff();
    } else if (inputCommand.equalsIgnoreCase("blink")) {
        System.out.println( "Blinking." );
        blinker.blink();
    } else if (inputCommand.equalsIgnoreCase("flip")) {
        System.out.println( "Toggling switch." );
        blinker.toggle();
    } else {
        System.out.println( "Invalid option. " );
        System.exit(0);
    }

    System.out.println("Device ROM ID: " + blinker.ROM_ID);
    System.out.println("Device Latch State: " + blinker.latchState);
```

```
        System.out.println("Device Level: " + blinker.level);
    }
}
```

The following sample output was performed with a DS9097U attached to COM1, which was attached to a small circuit board with the DS2405, an LED, and resistor via a cat 5 1-Wire bus cable.

```
C:\> java Switch on
Device ROM ID: 9A0000000C152305
Device Latch State: true
Device Level: false

C:\> java Switch off
Device ROM ID: 9A0000000C152305
Device Latch State: false
Device Level: true
```

You will have to take our word for it that the light did, in fact, turn on and then turn off. It really did, honest.

Example: Measuring temperature with a DS1920 temperature iButton

Let's now go through a similar exercise making a Java class that will return the temperature measured from a DS1920 temperature iButton. As with the switch example, we'll make a simple, reusable class that provides a basic thermometer object, with methods that return the current temperature. We'll start by looking at the relevant class in the 1-Wire API, the `OneWireContainer10` class.

The OneWireContainer10 class

The `OneWireContainer10` class represents and encapsulates devices with a family code of 10h. These are thermometer devices such as the DS1820 and DS1820. We're not going to list all of the methods here, as they can be completely explored in the Javadocs that come with the API, but we will look at some of the more important methods. Some of the methods come from classes that we've already seen, but we're going to list them here for review.

Class OneWireAccessProvider

- `public static DSPortAdapter` **getDefaultAdapter()**
- `public static DSPortAdapter` **getAdapter(** String port_adapter, String port **)**

Class DSPortAdapter

- `public abstract boolean` **beginExclusive(** boolean blocking **)**
- `public abstract int` **reset( )**

- public OneWireContainer **getFirstDeviceContainer()**
- public abstract void **endExclusive()**
- public void **targetFamily(** int family **)**

Class OneWireContainer10

- public String **getAddressAsString()**
- public byte[] **readDevice()**
- public void **doTemperatureConvert(** byte[] state **)**
- public double **getTemperature(** byte[] state **)**
- public static double **convertToFahrenheit(** double celciusT **)**
- public void **writeDevice(** byte[] state **)**

Our thermometer class will consist of the following:

1. An overloaded constructor, `thermometer()`, that can take anywhere from zero to three arguments, depending on how specific you want to be when creating the object.

2. A `measureT()` method that causes the DS1920 thermometer iButton to make a measurement and place the temperature in both Celsius and Fahrenheit into the object's data members.

3. A `main()` method that provides us with a way of testing our class. We'll use it to create a couple of thermometer objects, on different computer I/O ports, and print the results.

The complete program is presented below, then presented in dissected and explained fashion, followed by a sample run of the program.

Listing 10-5: Thermometer.java

```
import com.dalsemi.onewire.*;
import com.dalsemi.onewire.adapter.*;
import com.dalsemi.onewire.container.*;
import java.io.*;

public class Thermometer {

    // also get ALL thermometers not just container 10

    DSPortAdapter adapter;
    OneWireContainer10 container;

    byte[] state;
    String ROM_ID;
    double degC;
    double degF;
```

```java
public Thermometer() {
    try {
        adapter = (DSPortAdapter)OneWireAccessProvider.getDefaultAdapter();
        Init("");
    } catch (Exception e) {
        System.out.println("problem in constructor");
        System.out.println(e);
    }
}


public Thermometer( String PAadapt, String Port) {
    try {
        adapter = (DSPortAdapter)OneWireAccessProvider.getAdapter(PAadapt,Port);
        Init("");
    } catch (Exception e) {
        System.out.println("problem in constructor");
        System.out.println(e);
    }
}

public Thermometer( String ROM, String PAadapt, String Port) {
    try {
        adapter = (DSPortAdapter)OneWireAccessProvider.getAdapter(PAadapt, Port);
        Init(ROM);
    } catch (Exception e) {
        System.out.println("problem in constructor");
        System.out.println(e);
    }
}

public void Init(String ROM) {

    try {
        adapter.beginExclusive(true);
        adapter.reset();
        adapter.targetFamily(0x10);

        // If we specified a specific device, get it else get the first one
        if (ROM.length()<1) {
            container =
              (OneWireContainer10)adapter.getFirstDeviceContainer();
        }
        else {
            container =
              (OneWireContainer10)adapter.getDeviceContainer(ROM);
        }

        // cast the generic container into a TemperatureContainer
        ROM_ID= container.getAddressAsString();
```

```
                state = container.readDevice();
                container.doTemperatureConvert(state);
                degC = container.getTemperature(state);
                degF = container.convertToFahrenheit(degC);
                adapter.endExclusive();
            } catch (Exception e) {
                System.out.println("problem in constructor");
                System.out.println(e);
            }
        }

    public void measureT() {
        try {
            adapter.beginExclusive(true);
            adapter.reset();
            state = container.readDevice();
            container.doTemperatureConvert(state);
            degC = container.getTemperature(state);
            degF = container.convertToFahrenheit(degC);
            container.writeDevice(state);
            adapter.endExclusive();
        } catch(Exception e) {
            System.out.println("problem in measure");
            System.out.println(e);
        }
    }

    public static void main (String[] args) {
        Thermometer myTherm;

        // port_name should be like:   COM1, LPT1, /dev/ttyS0, or serial1
        // portAdapter should be like: {DS1410E}, DS9097U, TINIExternalAdapter
        if (args.length==2) {
            myTherm = new Thermometer( args[0], args[1] );
        }
        else {
            myTherm = new Thermometer();
        }

        // Read the temp sensor
        myTherm.measureT();

        // Display what we know (temoerature) in C and F
        System.out.println("The device ROM ID: " + myTherm.ROM_ID);
        System.out.println("The measured temperature: " + myTherm.degC
                    + " Deg C" + ", or " + myTherm.degF + " Deg F");

    }
}
```

Our Java program starts with the class declaration and the declaration of object data members, or instance variables. There is a port adapter that represents the communication interface, a `OneWireContainer10` object, that represents the individual device, and an 8-element array of bytes called `state` that holds the current information on the raw sensor data before it's been parsed into an actual temperature reading. A string containing the ROM_ID and two doubles, each holding the last measured temperature is also present.

```
public  class Thermometer {

    DSPortAdapter adapter;
    OneWireContainer10 container;
    byte[] state;
    String ROM_ID;
    double degC;
    double degF;
```

Next, there is the first of three constructors. As with the Switch program, each constructor calls the `Init()` method, which takes care of all the things that are common to each constructor. It attempts to use the default port adapter and attempts to find the first 1-Wire device with a family code of 10h to be identified. Most of this is creating the data members that were previously declared, but a couple of the actions are responsible for other functions. The `targetFamily(10)` is actually telling the 1-Wire bus that we're going to limit the underlying 1-Wire bus searches (Search ROM passes) to devices with a family code of 10h. The `beginExclusive()` method and the `reset()` method prepares the 1-Wire bus and prevent other possible 1-Wire threads from interrupting the current communication. This seems to be particularly important when communicating via the DS1410E parallel port adapter. When using the COM port adapters, it doesn't seem as important. After completing those methods, we create objects that were declared earlier, in a similar fashion to our switch example. First, we read the state array from the device with `readDevice()`, then we pass that array to a temperature conversion method, `doTemperatureConvert()`. After the conversion is complete, we can read the actual temperature using the `getTemperature()` method. That temperature is in Celsius, and can be converted to Fahrenheit with the `convertToFarhenheit()` method. Lastly, we release the 1-Wire bus from the exclusive control with the `endExclusive()` method. Those steps form the pattern for all of our temperature measurement. Since several of the methods throw exceptions, we enclosed the code in a try/catch block.

```
    public Thermometer() {
        try {
            adapter = (DSPortAdapter)OneWireAccessProvider.getDefaultAdapter();
            Init("");
        } catch (Exception e) {
```

```
            System.out.println("problem in constructor");
            System.out.println(e);
      }
  }

  public void Init(String ROM) {

      try {
        adapter.beginExclusive(true);
        adapter.reset();
        adapter.targetFamily(0x10);

          // If we specified a specific device, get it else get the first one
          if (ROM.length()<1) {
              container =
                (OneWireContainer10)adapter.getFirstDeviceContainer();
          }
          else {
              container =
                (OneWireContainer10)adapter.getDeviceContainer(ROM);
          }

          // cast the generic container into a TemperatureContainer
        ROM_ID= container.getAddressAsString();
        state = container.readDevice();
        container.doTemperatureConvert(state);
        degC = container.getTemperature(state);
        degF = container.convertToFahrenheit(degC);
        adapter.endExclusive();
      } catch (Exception e) {
        System.out.println("problem in constructor");
        System.out.println(e);
      }
  }
```

The second constructor is similar to the first, except that it accepts a specific port adapter name and port as arguments.

```
  public Thermometer( String PAadapt, String Port) {
      try {
        adapter = (DSPortAdapter)OneWireAccessProvider.getAdapter(PAadapt,Port);
        Init("");
      } catch (Exception e) {
        System.out.println("problem in constructor");
        System.out.println(e);
      }
  }
```

The third and final constructor takes the port adapter, port name, and ROM ID of a specific device as arguments.

```
public Thermometer( String ROM, String PAadapt, String Port) {
   try {
      adapter =
      (DSPortAdapter)OneWireAccessProvider.getAdapter(PAadapt, Port);
      Init(ROM);
   } catch (Exception e) {
      System.out.println("problem in constructor");
      System.out.println(e);
   }
}
```

Each of our constructors performs a temperature measurement that initializes the data members. Subsequent temperature measurements require a repeat of the temperature measurement process. That's what the measureT() method does. It grabs exclusive control of the 1-Wire bus, reads the state, converts it to a temperature, gets the temperature, converts it to Fahrenheit, returns control. Any time we need an updated temperature, we simply invoke this method and read the temperatures from the instance variables, degC and degF.

```
public void measureT() {
   try {
      adapter.beginExclusive(true);
      adapter.reset();
      state = container.readDevice();
      container.doTemperatureConvert(state);
      degC = container.getTemperature(state);
      degF = container.convertToFahrenheit(degC);
      container.writeDevice(state);
      adapter.endExclusive();
   } catch(Exception e) {
      System.out.println("problem in measure");
      System.out.println(e);
   }
}
```

The main() method tests our thermometer class. The first thing it does is examine the command line arguments. If there are two arguments, then it assumes we specified a PortAdapter and CommPort to access and it calls that constructor. If we didn't supply any arguments, then it uses the constructor that gets the default PortAdapter.

```
public static void main (String[] args) {
   Thermometer myTherm;

   // port_name should be like:  COM1, LPT1, /dev/ttyS0, or serial1
   // portAdapter should be like: {DS1410E}, DS9097U, TINIExternalAdapter
   if (args.length==2) {
      myTherm = new Thermometer( args[0], args[1] );
   }
   else {
      myTherm = new Thermometer();
```

```
        }

        // Read the temp sensor
        myTherm.measureT();

        // Display what we know (temoerature) in C and F
        System.out.println("The device ROM ID: " + myTherm.ROM_ID);
        System.out.println("The measured temperature: " + myTherm.degC
                + " Deg C"+ ", or " + myTherm.degF + " Deg F");
    }
}
```

This sample program doesn't make use of all the features of the DS1920 temperature iButton, by any stretch of the imagination, but it illustrates the highlights of how to talk to the device using the `OneWireContainer10` class. A sample run is below.

Note: We don't show the compile command-line options (like `CLASSPATH`, etc.) here because they might be confusing if you don't put your files in the same folder names that we did. If you use the CDROM, the build.bat will compile the code for you.

```
C:\> java Thermometer
The device ROM ID: D40000004B996410
The measured temperature: 24.0 Deg C, or 75.2 Deg F

The device ROM ID: 700000004B8F1010
The measured temperature: 24.5 Deg C, or 76.1 Deg F

C:\> java Thermometer DS9097U COM1
The device ROM ID: D40000004B996410
The measured temperature: 21.5 Deg C, or 70.7 Deg F
```

The arguments are just a little different for Linux:

```
$ java Thermometer DS9097U /dev/ttyS0
The device ROM ID: D40000004B996410
The measured temperature: 22.0 Deg C, or 71.6 Deg F
```

The preceding sections have discussed how the 1-Wire bus works, how to interface a PC to the 1-Wire bus, and how to use the Java 1-Wire API to communicate with 1-Wire devices. The next section is going to examine how to use TINI to communicate with the 1-Wire bus.

How TINI Communicates with the 1-Wire Bus

Our discussion of how the PC communicates with the 1-Wire bus involved a lot of talk about the different ports on the PC, hardware adapters that connected the 1-Wire bus to those ports, and the various different software drivers used by Java to communicate with the hardware adapters. Life is much simpler when discussing TINI. TINI comes with a 1-Wire bus that's ready for you to connect to, and it has an associated Java API that contains classes that allow you to communicate with that bus. This API, the TINI API, is closely related to, and sometimes draws upon, the 1-Wire API.

There are actually two 1-Wire buses on TINI—an external 1-Wire bus and an internal 1-Wire bus. Let's take a close look at each one, and then look at some examples.

The TINI external 1-Wire bus

The method by which TINI interfaces with the external 1-Wire bus is straightforward. Pins 18 and 19 on the 80C390 microprocessor communicate directly with a DS2480 serial 1-Wire line driver. The DS2480 outputs a signal, OWIO, which is routed to pin 8 on the TINI edge card connector. That signal, OWIO, is a 1-Wire bus. That's all there is to it. The TINI E10/20 socketboard has an RJ11 modular jack on it for the external 1-Wire bus. You plug a category-5 1-Wire cable into the jack and you are ready to go. Also on the socketboard is an iButton connector (S2) and a jumper that can be used to connect the bus to power or ground.

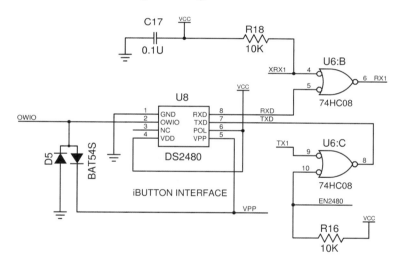

Figure 10-36: Schematic highlights of the DS2480 portion

**Figure 10-37:
The modular jack and iButton clip**

The TINI internal 1-Wire bus

The TINI stick has an internal 1-Wire bus, used for communication on the board itself. It talks to U11, which is a DS2502 memory and Ethernet address chip. It also controls the CPU status LED. The schematic shows that it also talks to an EEPROM, labeled U9. The TINI board rev E has silk-screening for the device, showing where it would be, but the board itself doesn't appear to have traces for it. The internal 1-Wire bus can be controlled through software just like the external one and it is routed off the TINI board via pin 17 on the edge card connector. On the socketboard it connects to a jumper, J4, and J11, which is a diagnostic port.

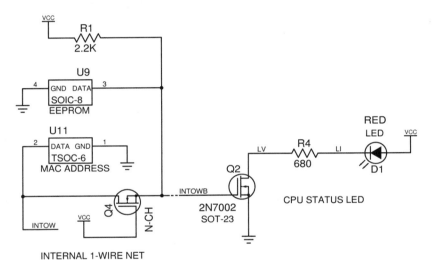

Figure 10-38: Portions of the schematic showing the internal 1-Wire bus

TINI port adapter objects

In our discussion of how to use a PC to communicate with the 1-Wire bus, we had numerous choices as to what type of communication port to use, what type pf electrical hardware adapter to use to connect that to the 1-Wire bus, and what type of software driver to use with Java to communicate with the 1-Wire bus. With TINI, as we have said, things are a little different. The software port adapter for the external 1-Wire bus on TINI is called the TINIExternalAdapter, and its port name is serial1. Both of these are fixed. If we are going to use the external 1-Wire bus on TINI, those are what we will use and we don't have to deal with choices or options and think about compatibility. The situation is similar with the TINI internal 1-Wire bus. Its port adapter name is TINIInternalAdapter and its port is called default. These are also both fixed.

The TINI API

We've taken a brief look at how the TINI board talks to the 1-Wire bus. Now let's look at how to use the TINI API to talk to the 1-Wire bus. In general, most 1-Wire programs that work on the PC will work on TINI. There are just a few things you have to keep in mind when compiling them. Let's start with a series of examples dealing with the port adapters.

Example: A Java program for TINI that identifies port adapters

In our discussion above, we made note of the fact that the port adapters for the internal and external 1-Wire buses on TINI are known and fixed. It is still a good first exercise to see for ourselves the names of these ports. We can run the same program (`PortAdapters.java`) on our TINI stick to see these names. Don't forget to pass the `PortAdapter.class` file through TINIConvertor to create `PortAdapters.tini`:

Let's take a look at the program actually running on a TINI.

```
C:\> javac -bootclasspath %TINI_HOME%2d\bin\tiniclasses.jar
           -d bin src\PortAdapters.java
C:\> java  -classpath %TINI_HOME%\bin\tini.jar;. BuildDependency
           -p %TINI_HOME%\bin\owapi_dependencies_TINI.jar
           -f bin
           -x %TINI_HOME%\bin\owapi_dep.txt
           -o bin\PortAdapters.tini
           -d %TINI_HOME%\bin\tini.db
```

FTP PortAdapters.tini to your TINI, and then run the program:

```
TINI /> java PortAdapters.tini
PortAdapter = TINIExternalAdapter; CommPorts = serial1
PortAdapter = TINIInternalAdapter; CommPorts = default

TINI />
```

There's nothing surprising about the results of this program, or how it works, but since port adapter objects are the foundation for communication with the 1-Wire bus, it's important to understand them. With that in mind, we're going to continue to look at a few simple programs that illustrate how to set up communications with the TINI 1-Wire buses. The first illustrates the default port adapter on TINI.

Example: Determining the default port on TINI

Even though our external and internal 1-Wire buses on TINI have fixed port adapters and ports, there is still a default port adapter. Again, we can use a previously written program to illustrate this. Compile `DefaultAdapter.java` and run it on your TINI stick to see these names. Don't forget to pass the `.class` file through BuildDependency to create the `.tini` file.

```
C:\> javac -bootclasspath %TINI_HOME%2d\bin\tiniclasses.jar
             -d bin src\DefaultAdapter.java
C:\> java    -classpath %TINI_HOME%\bin\tini.jar;. BuildDependency
             -p %TINI_HOME%\bin\owapi_dependencies_TINI.jar
             -f bin
             -x %TINI_HOME%\bin\owapi_dep.txt
             -o bin\PortAdapters.tini
             -d %TINI_HOME%\bin\tini.db
```

FTP PortAdapters.tini to your TINI, and then run the program:

```
TINI /> java DefaultAdapter.tini
TINIExternalAdapter
serial1
TINI />
```

What this tells us is that the default port for TINI is the TINIExternalAdapter, on port serial1, which is on the external 1-Wire bus. Next, let's take a look at a simple program that looks at the 1-Wire bus on TINI and determines the ROM ID for every 1-Wire device present.

Example: Determining the ROM ID for all 1-Wire devices attached to TINI

We've already looked at a similar program for doing this on the PC, and we could actually use that program here just as well, but we're going to review this a little because it provides us an example of the different ways of declaring and creating DSPortAdapter objects for TINI. If you like, you can pass the ROM_ID.class through TINIConvertor. Or better yet, BuildDependency and –add all of the OneWireContainer types (ie: OneWireContainer10 or Thermometers to get all temperature sensors) that you know you have connected. Then try running ROM_ID on your TINI. You will need to properly specify the PortAdapter and CommPort for TINI.

```
TINI /> java ROM_ID.tini TINIExternalAdapter serial1
or
TINI /> java ROM_ID.tini TINIInternalAdapter default
```

This clearly shows how you can write Java programs that use the 1-Wire API that will compile and run on both your PC and TINI with no modification. You can simplify your Java quite a bit if you only intend to run your programs on a TINI. This will also help save valuable memory space for other functions. A specialized version of ROM_ID (called TINIROM_ID) program is presented below in its entirety, then explained. Also a sample output is shown.

Listing 10-8: TINIROM_ID.java

```
import com.dalsemi.onewire.*;
import com.dalsemi.onewire.adapter.*;
import com.dalsemi.onewire.container.*;
```

```
import java.io.*;
import java.util.*;

public  class TINIROM_ID {
    public static void main (String[] args) {
        DSPortAdapter singleAdapter = null;
        OneWireContainer singleContainer = null;
        String singlePort = null;
        Enumeration myAdapters = null;
        Enumeration myPorts = null;
        Enumeration myContainers = null;
        myAdapters = OneWireAccessProvider.enumerateAllAdapters();
        while (myAdapters.hasMoreElements()) {
            singleAdapter = (DSPortAdapter)myAdapters.nextElement();
            System.out.println("Adapter Name: " + singleAdapter.getAdapterName());
            myPorts = singleAdapter.getPortNames();
            while (myPorts.hasMoreElements()) {
                singlePort = (String)myPorts.nextElement();
                System.out.println("Port Name: " + singlePort);
                try {
                    singleAdapter.selectPort(singlePort);
                    singleAdapter.targetAllFamilies();
                    myContainers = singleAdapter.getAllDeviceContainers();
                    while (myContainers.hasMoreElements()) {
                        singleContainer =
                            (OneWireContainer)myContainers.nextElement();
                        System.out.println("ROM ID:   " +
                            singleContainer.getAddressAsString());
                    }
                    singleAdapter.freePort();
                } catch (Exception e) {}
            }

            System.out.println();
        }
    }
}
```

Our program begins with the usual import statements, class declaration, and `main()` method declaration. We declare a number of objects: a `DSPortAdapter`, a `OneWireContainer`, and three Enumerations. We're going to grab an Enumeration of all the adapters present, then grab an Enumeration of all ports on the adapter, then grab an Enumeration of all device containers present on that adapter/port pair.

```
import com.dalsemi.onewire.*;
import com.dalsemi.onewire.adapter.*;
import com.dalsemi.onewire.container.*;
import java.io.*;
import java.util.*;
```

```
public  class TINIROM_ID {
   public static void main (String[] args) {
       DSPortAdapter singleAdapter = null;
       OneWireContainer singleContainer = null;
       String singlePort = null;
       Enumeration myAdapters = null;
       Enumeration myPorts = null;
       Enumeration myContainers = null;
```

Here, we're creating the Enumeration of port adapters, and iterating over each element in that Enumeration. For each one, we print out its name.

```
myAdapters = OneWireAccessProvider.enumerateAllAdapters();
while (myAdapters.hasMoreElements()) {
    singleAdapter = (DSPortAdapter)myAdapters.nextElement();
    System.out.println("Adapter Name: " +
    singleAdapter.getAdapterName());
```

Here, we're creating the Enumeration of port names relevant to the particular port adapter in question. We iterate over this Enumeration and print out the name for each.

```
myPorts = singleAdapter.getPortNames();
while (myPorts.hasMoreElements()) {
    singlePort = (String)myPorts.nextElement();
    System.out.println("Port Name: " + singlePort);
```

Now, we select the given port, tell the 1-Wire bus that any search ROM should include all device families, and create an Enumeration of device containers corresponding to all the devices found on the bus. For each device container, we access its ROM ID and print it.

```
        try {
            singleAdapter.selectPort(singlePort);
            singleAdapter.targetAllFamilies();
            myContainers = singleAdapter.getAllDeviceContainers();
            while (myContainers.hasMoreElements()) {
                singleContainer = (OneWireContainer)myContainers.nextElement();
                System.out.println("ROM ID:   " +
                    singleContainer.getAddressAsString());
            }
            singleAdapter.freePort();
        } catch (Exception e) {}
    }

    System.out.println();
    }
  }
}
```

A sample run of this program on TINI looks like this:

```
C:\> javac -bootclasspath %TINI_HOME%\bin\tiniclasses.jar
        -d bin src\TINIROM_ID.java
```

424

```
C:\> java   -classpath %TINI_HOME%\bin\tini.jar;. BuildDependency
            -p %TINI_HOME%\bin\owapi_dependencies_TINI.jar
            -f bin
            -x %TINI_HOME%\bin\owapi_dep.txt
            -o bin\TINIROM_ID.tini
            -d %TINI_HOME%\bin\tini.db
```

FTP the ROM_ID.tini to your TINI, and then run the program:

```
TINI /> java TINIROM_ID.tini
Adapter Name: TINIExternalAdapter
Port Name: serial1
ROM ID:   EF0000004B224210
ROM ID:   9A0000000C152305

Adapter Name: TINIInternalAdapter
Port Name: default
ROM ID:   D45E70005C8FAA89


TINI />
```

The program above can be compiled and run unmodified on a PC. There's nothing TINI-specific about it. Our next example is a modified version of this that *is* TINI-specific. Its purpose is to show us how to access the TINIExternalPortAdapter and TINIInternalPortAdapter objects.

Example: Another way of determining the ROM ID for all 1-Wire devices attached to TINI

The program below performs the same function on TINI as our previous example, but uses TINI-specific objects. We start with the program intact, then dissect it, and show a sample run of the program.

Listing 10-9: TINIROM_ID2.java

```java
import com.dalsemi.onewire.*;
import com.dalsemi.onewire.adapter.*;
import com.dalsemi.onewire.container.*;
import java.io.*;
import java.util.*;

public  class TINIROM_ID2 {
    public static void main (String[] args) {
        DSPortAdapter myTINIExternal = null;
        DSPortAdapter myTINIInternal = null;
        OneWireContainer singleContainer = null;
        Enumeration myContainers = null;
        try {
```

```
            myTINIExternal =
                OneWireAccessProvider.getAdapter("TINIExternalAdapter",
                                            "serial1");
            myTINIExternal.targetAllFamilies();
            myContainers = myTINIExternal.getAllDeviceContainers();
            System.out.println("Adapter: " +
                            myTINIExternal.getAdapterName());
            System.out.println("Port: " + myTINIExternal.getPortName());
            while (myContainers.hasMoreElements()) {
                singleContainer =
                    (OneWireContainer)myContainers.nextElement();
                System.out.println("ROM ID:  " +
                    singleContainer.getAddressAsString());
            }
            System.out.println();
            myTINIInternal =
                OneWireAccessProvider.getAdapter("TINIInternalAdapter",
                                "default");
            myTINIInternal.targetAllFamilies();
            myContainers = myTINIInternal.getAllDeviceContainers();
            System.out.println("Adapter: " +
                            myTINIInternal.getAdapterName());
            System.out.println("Port: " + myTINIInternal.getPortName());
            while (myContainers.hasMoreElements()) {
                singleContainer =
                    (OneWireContainer)myContainers.nextElement();
                System.out.println("ROM ID:   " +
                                singleContainer.getAddressAsString());
            }
        } catch (Exception e) {
            System.out.println(e);
            System.exit(0);
        }
        System.out.println();
    }
}
```

We start with the normal import statements, class declaration, and `main()` method declaration. We also declare some objects: `DSPortAdapter` objects representing our TINI external and internal 1-Wire buses, a single `OneWireContainer` object and an Enumeration of containers. We're going to create each one of the port adapters, then create an Enumeration of device containers representing the devices found on each one.

```
import com.dalsemi.onewire.*;
import com.dalsemi.onewire.adapter.*;
import com.dalsemi.onewire.container.*;
import java.io.*;
```

```
import java.util.*;

public  class TINIROM_ID2 {
    public static void main (String[] args) {
        DSPortAdapter myTINIExternal = null;
        DSPortAdapter myTINIInternal = null;
        OneWireContainer singleContainer = null;
        Enumeration myContainers = null;
```

Here we are creating our `DSPortAdapter` object representing the TINI external 1-Wire bus. In contrast to the previous program, we are now specifying the port adapter and port names. We're then telling the 1-Wire bus to include all device families in any search ROM process. As before, we then create an Enumeration of all device containers found and print out all the ROM ID for the corresponding devices.

```
do search the bus for all device families
        try {
            myTINIExternal =
                OneWireAccessProvider.getAdapter("TINIExternalAdapter",
                                                    "serial1");
            myTINIExternal.targetAllFamilies();
            myContainers = myTINIExternal.getAllDeviceContainers();
            System.out.println("Adapter: " + myTINIExternal.getAdapterName());
            System.out.println("Port: " + myTINIExternal.getPortName());
            while (myContainers.hasMoreElements()) {
                singleContainer =
                    (OneWireContainer)myContainers.nextElement();
                System.out.println("ROM ID:   " +
                    singleContainer.getAddressAsString());
            }
            System.out.println();
```

Now, we repeat the process for the TINI internal 1-Wire bus.

```
            myTINIInternal =
                OneWireAccessProvider.getAdapter("TINIInternalAdapter",
                                                    "default");
            myTINIInternal.targetAllFamilies();
            myContainers = myTINIInternal.getAllDeviceContainers();
            System.out.println("Adapter:   " +
                myTINIInternal.getAdapterName());
            System.out.println("Port: " + myTINIInternal.getPortName());
            while (myContainers.hasMoreElements()) {
                singleContainer =
                    (OneWireContainer)myContainers.nextElement();
                System.out.println("ROM ID:   " +
                    singleContainer.getAddressAsString());
            }
        } catch (Exception e) {
```

```
            System.out.println(e);
            System.exit(0);
        }
        System.out.println();
    }
}
```

When executed on a TINI, the program produces the following output:

```
C:\> javac -bootclasspath %TINI_HOME%\bin\tiniclasses.jar
            -d bin src\TINIROM_ID2.java
C:\> java   -classpath %TINI_HOME%\bin\tini.jar;. BuildDependency
            -p %TINI_HOME%\bin\owapi_dependencies_TINI.jar
            -f bin
            -x %TINI_HOME%\bin\owapi_dep.txt
            -o bin\TINIROM_ID.tini
            -d %TINI_HOME%\bin\tini.db
```

FTP the ROM_ID.tini to your TINI, and then run the program:

```
TINI /> java ROM_ID2.tini
Adapter: TINIExternalAdapter
Port: serial1
ROM ID:   EF0000004B224210
ROM ID:   9A0000000C152305

Adapter: TINIInternalAdapter
Port: default
ROM ID:   D45E70005C8FAA89
```

This is the same result as before, just a different way of getting to it. It's important to note that this program will only work on TINI because it uses TINI specific objects. Additionally, since the TINIExternalAdapter and TINIInternalAdapter only have one port each, we don't need to go through the process of selecting the port as we did before.

Our last example of this takes it a step further.

Example: Yet another way of determining the ROM ID for all 1-Wire devices attached to TINI

Below is one more example of how to do the same thing.

Listing 10-10: TINIROM_ID3.java

```
import com.dalsemi.onewire.*;
import com.dalsemi.onewire.adapter.*;
import com.dalsemi.onewire.container.*;
import java.io.*;
import java.util.*;
```

```
public  class TINIROM_ID3 {
    public static void main (String[] args) {
        DSPortAdapter myTINIExternal = null;
        DSPortAdapter myTINIInternal = null;
        OneWireContainer singleContainer = null;
        Enumeration myContainers = null;
        try {
            myTINIExternal = new TINIExternalAdapter();
            myTINIExternal.targetAllFamilies();
            myContainers = myTINIExternal.getAllDeviceContainers();
            System.out.println("Adapter: " +
                myTINIExternal.getAdapterName());
            while (myContainers.hasMoreElements()) {
                singleContainer =
                    (OneWireContainer)myContainers.nextElement();
                System.out.println("ROM ID:  " +
                    singleContainer.getAddressAsString());
            }
            System.out.println();
            myTINIInternal = new TINIInternalAdapter();
            myTINIInternal.targetAllFamilies();
            myContainers = myTINIInternal.getAllDeviceContainers();
            System.out.println("Adapter: " +
                myTINIInternal.getAdapterName());
            while (myContainers.hasMoreElements()) {
                singleContainer =
                    (OneWireContainer)myContainers.nextElement();
                System.out.println("ROM ID:  " +
                    singleContainer.getAddressAsString());
            }
        } catch (Exception e) {
            System.out.println(e);
            System.exit(0);
        }
        System.out.println();
    }
}
```

The only thing that differs in this program is the manner in which we create the
DSPortAdapter objects. This time, instead of using OneWireAccessProvider
methods to create our object for us, we are going to use the following:

```
        myTINIExternal = new TINIExternalAdapter();

        myTINIInternal = new TINIInternalAdapter();
```

These constructors directly create TINIExternalAdapter and TINIInternalAdapter
objects that are subclasses of the DSPortAdapter class. The only other difference is with
respect to the ports. In the previous example, we specified a port for each adapter, which
had the effect of selecting a port. That allowed us to use the getPortName() method. In

this example, we haven't specified or "selected" a port, and therefore aren't able to retrieve port names in the same fashion.

While this discussion has focused on some differences between how the 1-Wire bus is accessed on TINI vs. the PC, most programs that run on the PC can be run on TINI without changes. The key is compilation. Our next examples illustrate this.

Example: Controlling a DS2405 addressable switch from TINI

Previously, we made a self-contained Java class called *switch* that we accessed from the PC. This same class can be compiled and loaded onto TINI in the form of a .tini file and executed under Slush. We don't have to modify the source code, but we do have to take a few things into consideration during compilation. These things were discussed in detail in Chapter 7 but we will review them here. The following is a listing of the commands used to compile the program for TINI. Carriage returns have been inserted into some of the command lines for readability. These commands are stored in a .bat file and executed as a script.

```
C:\> javac-d bin src\Switch.java
C:\> java -classpath %TINI_HOME%\bin\tini.jar;. BuildDependency
     -p %TINI_HOME%\bin\owapi_dependencies_TINI.jar
     -f bin
     -x %TINI_HOME%\bin\owapi_dep.txt
     -o bin\Switch.tini
     -d %TINI_HOME%\bin\tini.db
     -add OneWireContainer05
```

Let's take the same small circuit board, featuring an LED and a 2504 addressable switch, used in our previous switch example, and attach it to the 1-Wire bus on TINI. When this program is loaded onto a TINI module via FTP and executed via a Telnet session on TINI under the Slush operating system, the following results:

```
TINI /> java Switch.tini on
Device ROM ID: 9A0000000C152305
Device Latch State: true
Device Level: false
TINI /> java Switch.tini off
Device ROM ID: 9A0000000C152305
Device Latch State: false
Device Level: true
```

The program functions exactly as before.

Example: Using a temperature iButton with TINI

Previously we saw how a temperature iButton could be accessed on a PC. That same program can be used on a TINI module. Our iButton is placed on a small circuit board using an iButton clip and the board is connected to a TINI socket with cat 5 cable and RJ11 connectors. When we previously used the Thermometer.java example, we were illustrating the use of the parallel port and the COM ports on the PC. As we previously mentioned, we can pass two parameters to the program to indicate which PortAdapter and which CommPort to use. If no parameters are given, then the program uses the default PortAdapter and the default CommPort. As we saw from running the DefaultAdapter program, the default TINI 1-Wire portAdapter is `TINIExternalAdapter` and the default communication port is `serial1`. We can compile `Thermometer.java`, run the class file through BuildDependency and then run `Thermometer.tini` on our TINI stick with results similar to those from the previous run.

Don't forget that this program needs to be converted to a TINI program, a .tini file, using the methodology outlined above. The commands used are:

```
C:\> javac -d bin src\Thermometer.java
C:\> java -classpath %TINI_HOME%\bin\tini.jar;. BuildDependency
     -p %TINI_HOME%\bin\owapi_dependencies_TINI_001.jar
     -f bin
     -x %TINI_HOME%\bin\owapi_dep.txt
     -o bin\Thermometer.tini
     -d %TINI_HOME%\bin\tini.db
     -add OneWireContainer10

TINI /> java Thermometer.tini
The devices ROM ID: EF0000004B224210
The measured temperature: 23.5 Deg C, or 74.3 Deg F
TINI />
```

Summary

This chapter has given you a good introduction to the 1-Wire bus and writing Java programs to talk to 1-Wire devices. We will be using what we have learned in this chapter in the remaining sections of this book, so if there are parts that were not clear, go back and reread them. If necessary, consult the following references and the data sheets for the specific 1-Wire devices you need to communicate with.

References

1. *Tech Brief1: 1-Wire Net Design Guide*,
   http://www.maxim-ic.com/1st_pages/tb1.htm

2. *Understanding and Using Cyclic Redundancy Checks with Dallas Semiconductor iButton Products*,
   http://pdfserv.maxim-ic.com/arpdf/AppNotes/app27.pdf

3. *Reading and Writing iButtons via Serial Interfaces*,
   http://pdfserv.maxim-ic.com/arpdf/AppNotes/app74.pdf

4. *Dallas Semiconductor / Maxim Semiconductor 1-wire devices*,
   http://dbserv.maxim-ic.com/1-Wire.cfm

## CHAPTER 11

The I²C Bus

Philips developed the I²C (Inter-IC) bus in the early 1980s for mass-produced items such as televisions and audio equipment. The I²C bus is a bidirectional, two-wire serial bus that provides a communication link between multiple integrated circuits (ICs) in a system. I²C has become a generally accepted industry standard for embedded applications and has been adopted by many IC manufacturers. All devices that are compatible with the I²C bus include an on-chip interface that allows them to communicate directly with each other on the bus. The I²C bus supports three data transfer speeds: standard, fast-mode, and high-speed mode. All data transfer speeds modes are backward compatible. Each device on the I²C bus has a unique address and can operate as either a transmitter or receiver depending on its function.

What Is the I²C bus?

I²C, or Inter Integrated Circuit, is a bus protocol developed by Philips Semiconductor for communication between integrated circuits. A document describing the complete bus protocol standard is freely available for download from the Philips website[1], but the protocol itself is patented and the integrated circuits that make use of it are subject to a sort of licensing agreement with Philips. I²C is primarily used in embedded applications where a microcontroller communicates with and controls a variety of peripheral devices. Digital potentiometers, EEPROMS, A/D converters, phase-locked loop synthesizers, microcontrollers and audio/video products are all good examples of products that use I²C. Some of the most salient features of the bus are found in the following list:

- The I²C bus consists of two signals: the serial clock (SCL) and a serial data line (SDA).

- The bus is bidirectional and makes use of pull-up resistors. I²C devices either pull the bus to logic low, or allow the bus pull-up to pull it high.

---

[1] Philips Semiconductors I²C-bus – http://www.us.semiconductors.philips.com/i2c/

- The bus has three speed modes, a standard mode (<100 kHz), a fast mode (100 kHz – 400 kHz) and a high-speed mode (400 kHz – 3.4 MHz).

- Data transfer is based on 8-bit words.

- Every device on the bus has a unique address, which is either 7 bits or 10 bits wide.

- The bus is based on a master/slave device relationship. Devices can be one or the other or switch back and forth. The bus can have more than one master and features a process called "arbitration" to resolve conflicts when multiple devices try to control the bus at once.

- The number of devices on the I²C bus is limited by the capacitance of the bus, which must be less than 400 pF.

The I²C Bus in More Detail

We've outlined the general characteristics of the I²C bus, so let's take a look at how it all works in more detail.

The master/slave concept in I²C

In the Dallas Semiconductor 1-Wire bus protocol, there can be only one master on the bus, and every other device is a slave. In I²C, things are more complicated. Devices can be masters sometimes, slaves sometimes, and sometimes there can be multiple masters trying to control the bus at the same time. The best way to delve into this is to introduce some basic terminology from the I²C specification. It is important to note that these definitions relate to the I²C bus, and if we use the same words in the context of discussing a different bus protocol, they have slightly different meanings.

Table 11-1: Definition of some basic I²C terms

Term	Description
Transmitter	The device which sends data to the bus.
Receiver	The device which receives data from the bus.
Master	The device which initiates a transfer, generates clock signals, and terminates a transfer.
Slave	The device addressed by the master.
Multi-master	More than one master can attempt to control the bus at the same time without corrupting the message.
Arbitration	Procedure to ensure that, if more than one master simultaneously tries to control the bus, only one is allowed to do so and the winning message is not corrupted.
Synchronization	Procedure to synchronize the clock signals of two or more devices.

Source: The I²C Bus Specification, Version 2.1, page 7.

The most interesting feature is the multimaster concept in which several I²C devices may try to be a master at the same time. The I²C protocol handles this through "synchronization" and "arbitration." Synchronization is the process by which masters all use the same clock. It relies on the fact that the clock line (SCL) is pulled high by a pull-up resistor. The result is that the SCL line value is the wired-AND of all the SCL connections from the various I²C devices on the bus. Masters generate their own clock during data transfers. If two or more masters attempt a data transfer at the same time, they will all attempt to put their own clock on the SCL line. Each "would-be" master generating a clock is going to try to pull the clock line low for a period of time (the low period) and then let the bus be pulled high for a period of time (the high period). They each have internal timers metering out these periods of time. Different devices may have slightly different times for the low periods and high periods. The first clock to go from high to low "resets" the clock-generating circuitry of all the other "would-be" masters and starts them all counting out their low period. The device with the longest period will still be holding the SCL line low when all the other devices have released it to go high. That device will determine the low period of the SCL line.

When the last device releases the SCL line and it goes from low to high, all the devices now start counting out their high period. The first device to pull the SCL line from high to low causes the entire process to be repeated. The resulting waveform on the SCL line is what is called the synchronized clock. It has a low period equal to the longest low period of all the "would-be" masters and a high period equal to the shortest high period of all the "would-be" masters.

The process of arbitration is very similar. The synchronization process has not determined which device is the master—it has only determined which device has defined a clock they can all agree upon. The SDA (serial data) line is also a wired-AND, this time of all the individual SDA values. As each would-be master is participating in generating the clock, it is also putting data (in the form of individual bits) on the SDA line. If one device puts out a logic 1 while another device outputs a logic 0, the logic 1 is eliminated by the wired AND. Any device whose bit is eliminated by a wired AND loses the arbitration and will not become the master during this data transfer. So the last device to put out a logic 1 on the SDA line wins the arbitration and takes command of the bus, which means it completes the data transfer that's already been started.

The I²C data format

There are a number of different elements that make up the bit format on the I²C bus. These are:

- The start condition
- The address

- The read/write bit
- The acknowledge or not acknowledge bit
- The data
- The stop condition

The start condition

The start condition indicates the beginning of communication by a master. It occurs when the master pulls the data line (SDA) from high to low while the clock is high. The start condition always comes from the master.

The address

The address consists of a series of bits (7 bits in the examples we'll discuss) and each bit must be valid before the rising edge of the clock and be held valid until after the falling edge of the clock. The address bits always come from the master.

The read/write bit

The read/write bit occurs immediately after the address bits. Like the address bits, it must be valid before the clock goes high and held valid until the clock goes low. The read/write bit always comes from the master.

Table 11-2: Table showing meaning of the read/write bit

Mode	Read/Write Bit Value
Read	1
Write	0

The acknowledge bit

The acknowledge bit is used by both the master and slave to indicate continued responses to communication. Like the address and R/W bits, it must "overlap" the clock. Its exact use will be illustrated in more detail when we take a detailed look at the communications between master and slave. Both the master and slaves can produce an acknowledge bit.

Data bits

Data occurs in 8-bit chunks and after each chunk an acknowledge bit is issued. Data must overlap clock in the same fashion as the address, R/W and acknowledge bits.

The stop condition

The stop condition ends the communication and indicates that the bus is free. To generate a stop condition, the master lets the bus be pulled high while the clock is high. The stop condition is always generated by the master.

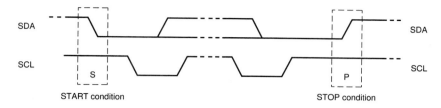

START and STOP conditions

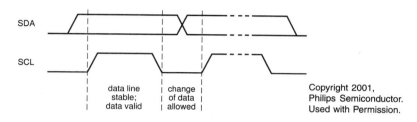

Copyright 2001,
Philips Semiconductor.
Used with Permission.

Bit transfer on the I²C-bus

Figure 11-1: Diagram showing start, stop, and data with respect to clock

The data format for basic I²C communication using 7-bit addressing comes in three very similar configurations, corresponding to three possible actions:

- *Master writing to slave.* The process of the bus master writing to a receiving slave device proceeds as follows:

  a) The master issues a start condition.

  b) The master writes the 7-bit address to the bus.

  c) The master issues 1-bit R/W indicator (0 for write).

  d) The slave issues an acknowledge bit (logic 1).

  e) The master issues 8-bit data chunks, each followed by a 1-bit acknowledge from the slave.

  f) This continues until the master issues a stop condition.

- *Master reading from slave.* The process of the bus master reading from the slave proceeds much like that of writing to the slave.

  a) The master issues a start condition.

  b) The master writes the 7-bit address to the bus.

  c) The master issues a read/write bit (1 for read).

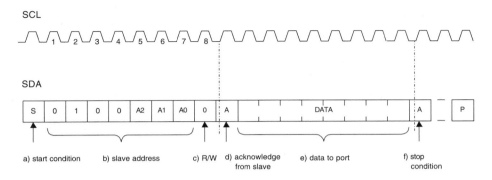

Figure 11-2: I²C Write

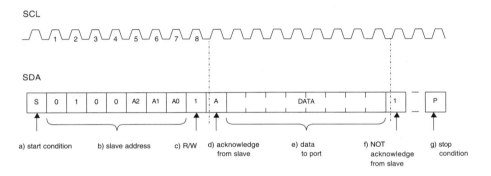

Figure 11-3: I²C Read

d) The slave issues an acknowledge bit (logic 1).

e) The slave outputs 8-bit data chunks, each of which is acknowledged by the master with an acknowledge bit (logic 1).

f) When the master is done reading, it will output a "not acknowledge" (logic 0).

g) Followed by the stop condition.

- *Master doing one, then doing the other.* When the master both reads from and writes to a slave, the result is what is referred to as the combined format. Like the name implies, it's basically a combination of the two previous examples. If we were to first write, then read, our process would be:

  a) Master issues a start condition.

  b) Master writes the 7-bit address, followed by a read/write bit (0 for write).

  c) The slave issues an acknowledge bit (logic 1).

d) Master writes 8-bit chunks, and after each chunk, the slave issues an acknowledge bit (logic 1).

e) When the master is done writing, and now wants to read, it reissues the start condition, reissues the address, and asserts the read bit (logic 1).

f) The slave will respond with an acknowledge bit (logic 1) followed by 8-bit data chunks. After each 8 bits of data, the master will issue an acknowledge bit (logic 1). When the master is done reading, it will issue a "not acknowledge" (logic 0) and a stop condition.

A few words about addressing

We have mentioned earlier that devices on the bus have a unique address. This has a somewhat different meaning than the "addresses" discussed in the section on the 1-Wire bus protocol. An I²C product such as the SAA1064[2], which is an I²C compatible seven-segment LED display driver, has a 7-bit address, 5 bits of which are the same for all SAA1064 devices and 2 of which are user configurable. Thus, there are 5 fixed and two programmable bits, respectively. Since two are programmable, you can have 2^2 or four SAA1064 devices on a single I²C bus. Other device types may have more or less fixed and programmable address bits (still adding up to seven). On the SAA1064, the 2 configurable bits are controlled by assigning a voltage to an external pin.

A typical I²C bus configuration

The most basic type of bus configuration for I²C is shown in Figure 11-4.

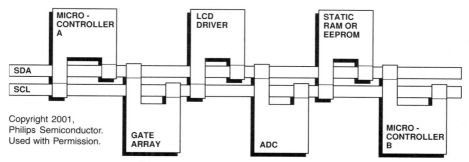

Example of an I²C-bus configuration using two microcontrollers

Figure 11-4: Drawing illustrating the basic I²C bus configuration

---

[2] SAA1064 Data Sheet – http://www.semiconductors.philips.com/pip/saa1064t

Extensions to the basic concept

The I²C protocol has many more features and extensions than described here, such as faster speeds, 10-bit addressing, and multivoltage pull-up configurations. We're not going to elaborate on them here. The best source for the complete story on I²C is the Philips I²C specification available on the Philips web site.

How TINI Does I²C

This next section examines how TINI communicates with devices over the I²C bus. We'll talk first about the hardware involved and then discuss the I2Cport class in the TINI API.

TINI and I²C: Hardware

There are a couple of ways in which TINI can generate the I²C data (SDA) and clock (SCL) signals. The primary way is through the direct use of two specific pins on one of the microcontroller data ports. But TINI is also capable of generating I²C signals through memory-mapped I/O, where one bit of a specific memory location is used to generate SDA, and one bit from another memory location is used to generate SCL.

Direct use of microcontroller port pins for I²C

The simplest way to access I²C with TINI is through the use of Port #5, bit0 and bit1. These are often referred to as P5.0 and P5.1. These pins don't always use the I²C protocol. In fact, they are actually designed to communicate using the CAN bus protocol. But, when used in conjunction with the I2Cport class found in the TINI API, they act as an I²C bus. These correspond to pins 21 and 20 on the TINI microcontroller and pins 10 (labeled CTX) and 11 (labeled CRX) on the TINI edge card connector. The CAN ports, such as Port 5 on the microcontroller, already have weak pull-ups built into them, so when using them to communicate I²C we haven't found the need to put pull-ups on the SDA and SCL lines. If you experiment with TINI and I²C and you find that the bus isn't being pulled high, your application may benefit from a stronger pull-up on the bus (20kΩ resistors to Vcc will do nicely).

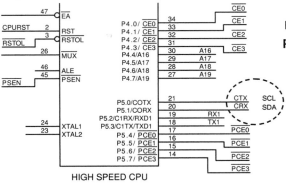

Figure 11-5: Drawing highlighting port 5 on the TINI microcontroller

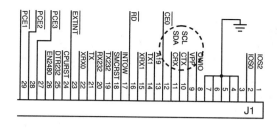

Figure 11-6:
Drawing of edge card connector

Memory-mapped driver for I²C

Another way to access I²C with TINI is through a memory-mapped driver. The circuit in the figure below shows the necessary hardware for this. The circuit uses a 74ACT138 address decoder to select the logic chips when the CPU is reading or writing I²C information. This is connected in the exact same manner as the address decoder we used in Chapter 8 for connecting other memory-mapped devices. The 74ACT244 input buffer is only enabled on data reads and the 74ACT753 latch is wired so it is enabled on data writes. These two chips are connected so that we have a bidirectional data flow between the data bus and the I²C bus and so that the input buffer reads the data on the outputs of the latch. This is necessary so we can make this a bi-directional bus and we can read data from I²C slave devices.

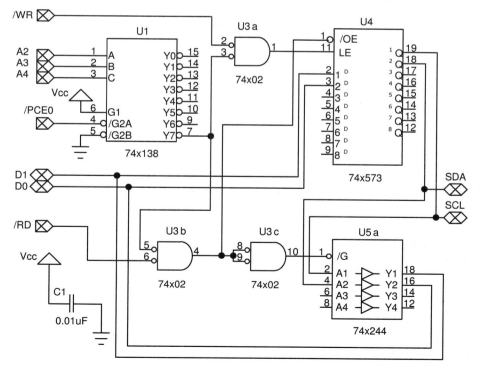

Figure 11-7: Memory-mapped I²C driver

TINI and I²C: Software

The TINI API contains a java class, `I2CPort`, which can be used to generate the proper I²C signals. The `I2CPort` class has an overloaded constructor which provides for two ways of constructing `I2CPort` objects. These correspond to the two ways of generating I²C signals with TINI: directly using P5.0 and P5.1 or through memory-mapped I/O. For direct use of P5.0 and P5.1 the I2Cport constructor takes no arguments. For memory-mapped I²C drivers, the constructor requires that you pass the address of the address decoder and a mask that tells the API which data line is to drive the SCL line and which data line is to drive the SDA line. Below is a list of the methods that we will use to talk I²C on TINI.

- `public void` **`setAddress`**`(byte address)`
- `public void` **`setClockDelay`**`(byte delay)`
- `public int` **`write`**`(byte[] dataArray, int offset, int length)`
- `public int` **`read`**`(byte[] dataArray, int offset, int length)`

`setAddress()`

The `setAddress()` method accepts a byte representing the address of the I²C device we are communicating with. It's important to note that the address we provide is the 7-bit device address *right justified*. So, the 7 bits of our address make up the 7 least significant digits of this byte, and the most significant bit is a 0. This is somewhat different than the address byte that actually gets sent out on the I²C bus. That byte will be *left justified* (dropping the most significant bit which is 0) and the least significant bit will be the read/write bit. The conversion between the 7-bit address we provide the `setAddress()` method and the actual address byte sent on the I²C bus is done for us by the `I2CPort` class.

`setClockDelay()`

The `setClockDelay()` method is used to modify the frequency of the SCL line. It accepts a byte as an argument, representing an additional increment of delay between all edges. When using the P5.0 and P5.1 pins for access to I²C, our frequency is said to vary between 2.5 kbits/sec and 250 kbits/second. The documentation accompanying the API notes that each increment of clock delay byte adds .109 μsec between the clock edges. So a larger value as an argument to the `setClockDelay()` method leads to a slower clock, and vice versa. Dallas Semiconductor, in their TINI news group, has provided the following relationship between the clock period and the clock delay argument:

$$\text{SCL period} = (1\mu s + .109\mu s * \text{clock delay})*4$$

Experimentally, we've noticed that the relationship is more like this:

$$\text{SCL period} = \text{clock delay}*1.25 \ \mu s + 5 \ \mu s$$

This was derived from testing clock delay values of 2, 4, 8, 12, 14, 24, and 127. It should also be noted that the value in our test circuit (presented at the end of this section) worked for all of those values. The discrepancy between the clock period that we see and what TINI should be producing according to the documentation may have to do with the specifics of our setup.

write()

The `write()` method writes an array of bytes to the slave device currently being addressed. It takes the byte array as an argument, along with an offset and a length. The offset indicates where in the array you wish to begin the write and the length indicates how many bytes after the offset you wish to write. It's important to note that when constructing the array, you should not put the address byte into the array. The addressing is handled by the `setAddress()` method. The method returns a 0 if it received an acknowledge from the slave and a –1 if it didn't.

read()

The `read()` method behaves very much like the `write()` method. It reads data from the currently addressed slave and places it into an array. It takes the byte array as an argument, along with an offset and a length. The offset indicates where in the array you wish to begin placing the data and the length indicates how many bytes after the offset you wish to put there. The TINI 1.02 API notes that the method returns the number of bytes read on success, or –1 if it fails to receive an acknowledge from the slave. This appears to be a typo in the Javadocs. It actually returns 0 on success, like the `write()` method.

The process of connecting TINI to an I²C device and communicating is best illustrated with an example. For our example, we're going to connect an I²C-compatible 7-segment LED driver to TINI. We'll make a generic Java class that allows us to display digits, then use that class with one of our earlier example classes, `Thermometer`, to create a standalone TINI digital thermometer. This and all of the examples in this chapter will use the microprocessor ports pins for I²C communication. If you wish to use memory-mapped I²C then you simply need to use an alternate form of the constructor. Here are the two different forms of constructors:

- For Microcontroller Port driven I²C, use the following constructor:
  ```
  LEDPort = new I2CPort();
  ```
  This simply creates and returns a new I2CPort.

- For memory-mapped I²C following the schematic shown above, use the following constructor:
  ```
  LEDPort = new I2CPort(0x0080001C, (byte)0x1, 0x0080001C,
  (byte)0x2 );
  ```

This creates and returns a new I2CPort based on a memory-mapped driver. The address decoder is wired to decode the line driver and latch at 0x80001C in TINI memory and designates data lines D0 to drive SCL and D1 to drive SDA.

Example: Using TINI and I²C to drive a 7-segment LED display

We've chosen this as an example because it's easy to do, while illustrating all of the features key to understanding the TINI to I²C communication link. This example also shows an alternative way to implement an LED display from what we discussed in Chapter 8. We'll start with a quick discussion of the I²C-compatible 7-segment LED driver, the Philips SAA1064.

The SAA1064 is available in a 24-pin DIP package. It provides two 8-bit busses that can each handle one or two 7-segment LED displays. If they each are handling two displays, they are to be multiplexed. For simplicity, we're going to make a nonmultiplexed display in which each 8-bit bus drives a single 7-segment display. You can build the 4-digit display by following the schematic provided in the SAA1064 datasheet. The device pinout and descriptions of the pins are shown in Figure 11-8.

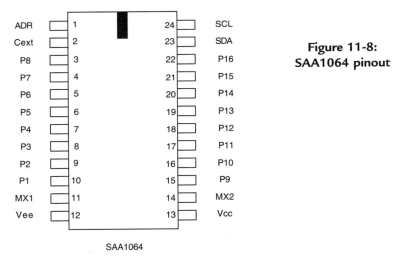

Figure 11-8: SAA1064 pinout

SAA1064

SAA1064 Data Sheet, dated feb 1991, page 4

ADR (pin 1) – This pin is used to configure the programmable address bits of each device. The two least significant bits of the 7-bit address of the SAA1064 are determined by the voltage applied to the ADR pin.

Table 11-3: Table of ADR values

ADR Pin Value	A1	A0
V_{ee} to $(3/16)V_{cc}$	0	0
$(5/16)V_{cc}$ to $(7/16)$ V_{cc}	0	1
$(9/16)V_{cc}$ to $(11/16)$ V_{cc}	1	0
$(13/16)V_{cc}$ to V_{cc}	1	1

Note: 7 Bit Slave Address = 0 1 1 1 0 A1 A0
Source: Excerpt from SAA1064 Data Sheet,
dated Feb 1991, page 9

C_{EXT} (**pin 2**) – This pin can be used to control the frequency at which we multiplex between two pairs of 7-segment displays. We won't be using this feature and will simply ground this pin.

P8-P1 (pins 3-10) – These pins are the data bus for one of the two data ports on the device. They each drive one segment of the 7-segment displays. They are designed to *sink* current, so the 7-segment displays need to be *common anode*. P9 is the MSB, P1 is the LSB.

MX1 (pin 11), MX2(pin 14) – These output pins can be used to power the anode of the LED displays, or to control transistors used to power them. They are switching outputs that switch at the frequency of the multiplexing oscillator. We will not be using them and will leave them unconnected.

Vee (pin 12) – This is the chip ground.

Vcc (pin 13) – This is the chip power. We will set it to 5V, but it has a maximum of 18V.

P9-P16 (pins 15-22) – These pins are the data bus for the second of the two data ports on the device. They each will drive one segment of the 7-segment displays. They are designed to *sink* current, so the 7-segment displays need to be *common anode*. P16 is the MSB, P9 is the LSB.

SDA (pins 23) – This is the I²C data line.

SCL (pins 24) – This is the I²C clock line.

We will connect each of the two data buses on the SAA1064 to a single common anode 7-segment display. Then we will connect the SDA line to TINI pin 11 (CRX) and the SCL line to TINI pin 10 (CTX). Since there are weak pull-ups in the TINI microcontroller on those pins, we're not going to put additional pull-ups on these lines. The schematic for this is shown in Figure 11-9.

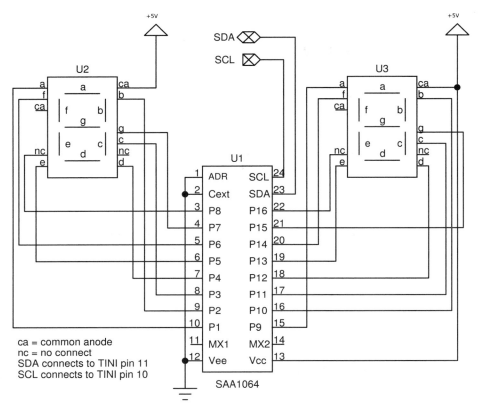

Figure 11-9: Schematic of the I²C LED

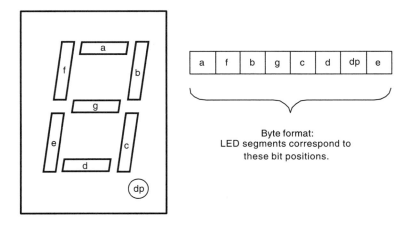

Figure 11-10: LED segments

For reference, a table and figure showing the mapping between bits on the data bus and the character that is displayed by those bits is also presented.

Table 11-4: Data bits to character displayed

Display Character	Output Bus (bits)	Output Bus (hex)
0	11101101	ED
1	00101000	28
2	10110101	B5
3	10111100	BC
4	01111000	78
5	11011100	DC
6	11011101	DD
7	10101000	A8
8	11111101	FD
9	11111100	FC
U	01101101	6D
F	11010001	D1

The next thing we need to consider is how to talk to the SAA1064.

SAA1064 data format

The process of displaying digits with the SAA1064 LED display driver is simple: you send it an array of data containing the commands and data. The array is seven bytes long, and the format is illustrated in the chart shown in Table 11-5.

Table 11-5: Chart showing SAA1064 data format

Data Byte	Byte Purpose	Byte Contents
1	Slave Address	0 1 1 1 0 A1 A0 Read/Write
2	Instruction Byte	0 0 0 0 0 SC SB SA
3	Control Byte	X C6 C5 C4 C3 C2 C1 C0
4	Digit 1 Data	D7 D6 D5 D6 D3 D2 D1 D0
5	Digit 2 Data	D7 D6 D5 D6 D3 D2 D1 D0
6	Digit 3 Data	D7 D6 D5 D6 D3 D2 D1 D0
7	Digit 4 Data	D7 D6 D5 D6 D3 D2 D1 D0

A1, A0 = configurable address bits.
SC, SB, SA = subaddress bits that are set to 0 for our purposes.
X = don't care (set to 0).
C6 – C0 are further explained in the text.
Source: Excerpt from the SAA1064 Data Sheet, dated Feb 1991, page 5.

The slave address

The slave address is seven bits long, with the most significant five bits fixed at 01110. The remaining two bits are programmable, based on the value of the ADR pin. We will tie our ADR pin low, which means the least significant two bits of our 7-bit address will be 00. Our 7-bit address makes up the "upper" seven bits of the first 8-bit byte in the data array that we send to the SAA1064. The eighth bit, the least significant bit of that byte, is the read/write bit. Since our data array will be written to the SAA1064, the read/write bit will be set to 0. Our slave address is 0111000, and the first data byte in our data array is 01110000, or 0x70.

The instruction byte

The instruction byte contains three subaddress bits, SC, SB, SA, which can be used to control where in the SAA1064 our data array gets written. We're not going to be making use of this feature, and all of our subaddressing bits are going to be set to zero. The second byte in the data array that we're going to send to the SAA1064 becomes 00000000.

The control byte

The control byte consists of an unused bit, which is the most significant bit of this byte, and seven control bits. The meaning of the seven control bits is shown below. Our control byte will be 0x26, or 00100110, which, from the table below, means that we are in static mode as opposed to multiplexed, sinking a current of 3 mA in each segment of the display.

Table 11-6: Chart showing SAA1064 control bytes

Bit Within Control Byte	Bit Meaning
C0	0 = static mode, constant display of digits 1 & 2
	1 = dynamic mode, digits 1 & 3 alternating with 2 & 4
C1	0 = digits 1 & 3 blanked
	1 = digits 1 & 3 not blanked
C2	0 = digits 2 & 4 blanked
	1 = digits 2 & 4 not blanked
C3	0 = normal operation
	1 = test mode, all segments lit
C4	0 = add no current
	1 = add 3 mA to the segment drive
C5	0 = add no current
	1 = add 6 mA to the segment drive
C6	0 = add no current
	1 = add 12 mA to the segment drive

Source: Excerpt from SAA1064 Datasheet, dated Feb. 1991, page 6.

Data bytes

The four data bytes each represent one of the four possible 7-segment LED displays that we can control with the SAA1064. Since we aren't using it in the dynamic, or multiplexed, mode, we are only concerned with two of the digits. In the static, two-digit mode, we only need to be concerned with the contents of the first two bytes. The last two bytes we set to 0x00. The coding that relates how the individual bits map into illuminated segments is specific to the individual design. Our encoding is illustrated in Table 11-4.

With that as background, if we wanted to display the number "38" on our system, we would write the following data array to the device: 0x70, 0x00, 0x26, 0xBC, 0xFD, 0x00, 0x00. Let's take a look at a generic Java class called `Digits` that takes in an integer and displays it on an SAA1064 controlled by TINI. We'll present the whole program, then study it in detail. It should be noted that making I²C work with TINI is actually quite simple, but it requires attention to detail. The `I2Cport` class handles some of the low-level details for us, which is a good thing. But it also means that the device address and the data array that we send the device have two different contexts. There's the address and data array that we use in our Java program, and then there's the address byte and the data array that gets transmitted on the I2C bus itself. They're not the same.

Our `Digits` class is designed to take in a two-digit number and display it on two 7-segment LED displays. If the number is less than 0, it displays "UF" for "underflow" and if the number is more than 99, it displays "OF" for "overflow." The class has a method to display a byte, and a method to turn the digits off. It has a `main()` method that acts as a test, displaying all of the digits.

Listing 11-1: Digits.java

```java
import com.dalsemi.system.*;
import java.io.*;

public class Digits {

    private static byte LETTER_U = (byte) 0x6D;
    private static byte LETTER_F = (byte) 0xD1;
    private static byte LETTER_O = (byte) 0xED;
    private static byte BLANK = 0x00;

    byte[] data = new byte[6];
    I2CPort LEDPort;

    public Digits() {
        LEDPort = new I2CPort();
        LEDPort.setAddress((byte)0x38);
```

```
        LEDPort.setClockDelay((byte)0x7F);
    data[0] = 0x00;        // instruction byte
    data[1] = 0x26;        // control byte
    data[2] = 0x00;        // digit 1 data
    data[3] = 0x00;        // digit 2 data
    data[4] = 0x00;        // digit 3 data
    data[5] = 0x00;        // digit 4 data
}


public byte getBits(byte displayChar) {
    switch (displayChar) {
        case 1: return (byte)(0x28);
        case 2: return (byte)(0xB5);
        case 3: return (byte)(0xBC);
        case 4: return (byte)(0x78);
        case 5: return (byte)(0xDC);
        case 6: return (byte)(0xDD);
        case 7: return (byte)(0xA8);
        case 8: return (byte)(0xFD);
        case 9: return (byte)(0xFC);
        case 0: return (byte)(0xED);
        default: return (byte)(0);
    }
}

public void setValue(byte displayValue) {
    byte char1, char2;
    int i;
    if (displayValue < 0) {
            // Underflow (UF)
        char1 = LETTER_U;
        char2 = LETTER_F;
    }
      else if (displayValue > 99) {
            // Overflow (OF)
        char1 = LETTER_O;
        char2 = LETTER_F;
    }
      else {
        char2 = getBits((byte)(displayValue%10));
        char1 = getBits((byte)(((displayValue-(displayValue%10))/10)));
    }
    this.data[2] = char1;
    this.data[3] = char2;
    try {
        i = this.LEDPort.write(data, 0, 6);
            System.out.print( "Stat: " + i );
    } catch (Exception e) {System.out.println(e);}
}
```

```
public void turnOff() {
    int i;
    this.data[2] = BLANK;
    this.data[3] = BLANK;
    try {
        i = this.LEDPort.write(data, 0, 6);
    } catch (Exception e) {System.out.println(e);}
}

public static void main(String[] args) {
    Digits displayChars = new Digits();

    for (int i=-5; i<105; i++) {
        System.out.print( "N: " + i + " " );
        displayChars.setValue((byte)i);
        try {
            Thread.sleep(500);
        } catch(Exception e){}
    }
    displayChars.turnOff();
}
}
```

The program begins with a couple of import statements, gaining access to the necessary Java class libraries.

```
import com.dalsemi.system.*;
import java.io.*;
```

Shown below is our class and data member declarations. The byte array data is only six bytes long. In our discussion of the SAA1064 we noted that the data array that gets sent to the device is seven bytes long. The difference comes from the fact that, in the I2Cport class, we don't have to explicitly put the address byte in the data array. Instead, we use the setAddress() method to set the address, and the class handles the details of putting the address into the data array. LEDPort is a I2CPort object that will give us access to the I2CPort methods.

```
public class Digits {

    private static byte LETTER_U = (byte) 0x6D;
    private static byte LETTER_F = (byte) 0xD1;
    private static byte LETTER_O = (byte) 0xED;
    private static byte BLANK = 0x00;

    byte[] data = new byte[6];
    I2CPort LEDPort;
```

Following is our constructor. It creates an I2CPort object, sets its device address, the clock delay, and initializes its data array. Here, we run into one source of confusion: the address. The actual device address is seven bits, and in our case it will be

0111000. The data field called `slaveAddress` in the `I2CPort` class, which is set by the `setAddress()` method, is a byte. Our 7-bit address is *right justified.* That is, they give it a leading zero, turning 0111000 into 00111000, or 0x38. When that address actually gets written out on the bus, it won't appear as 0x38. The I2CPort class extracts the actual 7-bit address from the byte, *left justifies* it, and makes the least significant bit the read/write bit, which in our case (writing), will be a 0. So, on the I²C bus itself, the address byte will turn out to be 01110000, or 0x70. With respect to the clock delay, the value of 0x7F represents the slowest possible clock. Theoretically, the clock can vary between 2.5 kbits/sec and 250 kbits/sec. When measured with a scope, this example had a clock speed of 6 kbits/sec. In practice, with this example, this value hasn't proven to be critical. Experimentally, any value larger than 1 worked.

```
public Digits() {
    LEDPort = new I2CPort();
    LEDPort.setAddress((byte)0x38);
    LEDPort.setClockDelay((byte)0x7F);
    data[0] = 0x00;       // instruction byte
    data[1] = 0x26;       // control byte
    data[2] = 0x00;       // digit 1 data
    data[3] = 0x00;       // digit 2 data
    data[4] = 0x00;       // digit 3 data
    data[5] = 0x00;       // digit 4 data
}
```

The `getBits()` method takes a single digit between 0 and 9 and returns the 7-segment encoding for that digit. A bit value of "1" means that segment "a" will be illuminated. Refer to Table 11-4.

```
public byte getBits(byte displayChar) {
    switch (displayChar) {
        case 1: return (byte)(0x28);
        case 2: return (byte)(0xB5);
        case 3: return (byte)(0xBC);
        case 4: return (byte)(0x78);
        case 5: return (byte)(0xDC);
        case 6: return (byte)(0xDD);
        case 7: return (byte)(0xA8);
        case 8: return (byte)(0xFD);
        case 9: return (byte)(0xFC);
        case 0: return (byte)(0xED);
        default: return (byte)(0);
    }
}
```

The `setValue()` method takes in a byte that represents the 2-digit number we want to display, extracts the two digits from it, gets the bit encoding from the `getBits()`

method, and writes the data to the SAA1064 using the `write()` method of the `I2CPort` class. If the number is less than zero, it puts "UF" into the variables that will be displayed. If it's greater than 99, it puts "OF" into them. If between the two, it converts a number into two digits.

```
public void setValue(byte displayValue) {
    byte char1, char2;
    int i;
    if (displayValue < 0) {
        // Underflow (UF)
      char1 = LETTER_U;
      char2 = LETTER_F;
    }
      else if (displayValue > 99) {
        // Overflow (OF)
      char1 = LETTER_O;
      char2 = LETTER_F;
    }
      else {
        char2 = getBits((byte)(displayValue%10));
        char1 = getBits((byte)(((displayValue-(displayValue%10))/10)));
    }
```

We've established what characters to display, so we place them into the third and fourth byte positions in the data array. The data array is passed to the `write()` method with an offset of 0 and a length of six. The 0 offset indicates start with the 0 element in the array. The method returns an integer: 0 if the write functioned properly, and –1 if there was no Acknowledge bit sent from the slave.

```
    this.data[2] = char1;
    this.data[3] = char2;
    try {
        i = this.LEDPort.write(data, 0, 6);
          System.out.print( "Stat: " + i );
    } catch (Exception e) {System.out.println(e);}
}
```

The `turnOff()` method turns off all segments in both displays. We do this by setting all bits to 0 in both data bytes. Note that we're not telling them to write the digit 0, we're telling the SAA1064 to put 0s on all 8 bits of both data buses.

```
public void turnOff() {
    int i;
    this.data[2] = BLANK;
    this.data[3] = BLANK;
    try {
        i = this.LEDPort.write(data, 0, 6);
    } catch (Exception e) {System.out.println(e);}
}
```

The `main()` method tests the functionality of the `Digit` class. It simply counts up from –5 to 100. In doing so, it exercises all segments in both digits and tests for the correct encoding of all the numbers plus the "UF" (underflow) and "OF" (overflow) cases.

```java
public static void main(String[] args) {
    Digits displayChars = new Digits();
    for (int i=-5; i<101; i++) {
        displayChars.setValue((byte)i);
        try {
            Thread.sleep(500);
        } catch(Exception e){}
    }
    displayChars.turnOff();
}
}
```

If you compile this into `Digits.tini`, then you will need to send it to TINI using FTP and execute it under the Slush operating system. If you compile it into `Digits.tbin`, then you would load it into TINI with JavaKit. This program provides no output to the screen, unless there is an exception. The commands used to compile this program into a `.tini` file are shown below.

```
C:\> javac -bootclasspath %TINI_HOME%\bin\tiniclasses.jar
    -classpath %TINI_HOME%\bin\owapi_dependencies_TINI.jar;.
    -d bin   src\Digits.java
C:\> java -classpath %TINI_HOME%\bin\tini.jar;. BuildDependency
    -p %TINI_HOME%\bin\owapi_dependencies_TINI_001.jar
    -f bin
    -x %TINI_HOME%\bin\owapi_dep.txt
    -o bin
    -d %TINI_HOME%\bin\tini.db
```

Figure 11-11:
LED display in action

Chapter 7 as well as the thermometer example at the end of Chapter 10 has a discussion of what some of these options mean. Command options have been shown on separate lines for readability. In practice, they need to be on the same line.

Example: A TINI digital thermometer

The Digits class can be used in conjunction with the Thermometer class from an earlier example to make a simple thermometer that uses TINI, a DS1920 temperature iButton or a DS1820 1-Wire thermometer, and the SAA1064 display driver. Simply implement the previous example, and connect a thermometer iButton or 1-Wire device to TINI via the 1-Wire bus. We'll call the new class LEDTherm.

Listing 11-2: LEDTherm.java

```java
import java.io.*;
public  class LEDTherm {
    public static void main (String[] args) {
        Thermometer therm = new Thermometer();
        Digits LEDs = new Digits();
        while (true) {
        try {
            therm.measureT();
            LEDs.setValue((byte)(therm.degF));
            Thread.sleep(1000);
            } catch(Exception e)  {System.out.println(e);}
        }
    }
}
```

```
C:\> cd src
C:\> javac -bootclasspath %TINI_HOME%\bin\tiniclasses.jar
    -classpath %TINI_HOME%\bin\owapi_dependencies_TINI.jar;.
    -d ..\bin  Digits.java
C:\> cd ..
C:\> java -classpath %TINI_HOME%\bin\tini.jar;. BuildDependency
    -p %TINI_HOME%\bin\owapi_dependencies_TINI_001.jar
    -f bin
    -x %TINI_HOME%\bin\owapi_dep.txt
    -o bin
    -d %TINI_HOME%\bin\tini.db
```

When you run the program on your TINI you can watch the LED digits display the temperature.

Example: Extending TINI's parallel I/O

In the previous two examples we were writing to an I²C device. We could read back a status byte from the SA1064 LED driver, but this is not particularly interesting. This status byte contains a single 1-bit field that indicates that there was a power failure since the last time you read the status byte. A more interesting example is using a Philips PCF8574[3], remote 8-bit I/O expander, for adding 8-bit parallel I/O to your TINI.

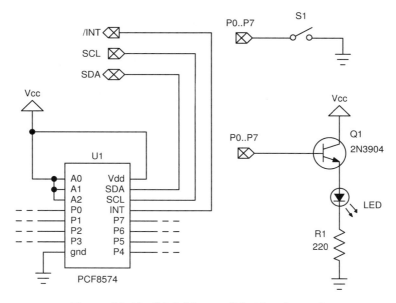

Figure 11-12: I²C 8-bit parallel I/O schematic

Listing 11-3: Parallel_IO.java

You can connect the switches and LEDs to any of the pins that you like. For the example Java program listed here, switches are connected to P0–P3 and LEDs are connected to P4–P7.

```java
import com.dalsemi.system.*;
import java.io.*;

public class Parallel_IO {

    byte[] data = new byte[1];
    I2CPort PioPort;

    public Parallel_IO() {
        PioPort = new I2CPort();
        PioPort.setAddress((byte)0x27);
        PioPort.setClockDelay((byte)0x7F);
         data[0] = 0x00;
    }

     private static char[] hexChars =
         { '0','1','2','3','4','5','6','7','8','9','A','B','C','D','E','F' };
```

---

[3] PCF8574 datasheet – http://www.semiconductors.philips.com/pip/pcf8574p

```java
public static String toHex( byte data )
{
    StringBuffer output = new StringBuffer();
    int firstNibble, secondNibble;

        firstNibble = ( data >> 4 ) & 0x0F;
        secondNibble = data & 0x0F;
        output.append( hexChars[ firstNibble ] );
        output.append( hexChars[ secondNibble ] );

    return output.toString();
}

public void Blinky() {
    int stat=0;

    for (int i=1; i<10; i++) {
      System.out.print( "Write: " + i );

      try {
            data[0] = (byte)(0x1A);
            stat = PioPort.write( data, 0, 1);
            System.out.print( " [ " + toHex(data[0]) + " " + stat + " ]" );
        TINIOS.sleepProcess(250);

            data[0] = (byte)(0x2A);
            stat = PioPort.write( data, 0, 1);
            System.out.print( " [ " + toHex(data[0]) + " " + stat + " ]" );
        TINIOS.sleepProcess(250);

            data[0] = (byte)(0x4A);
            stat = PioPort.write( data, 0, 1);
            System.out.print( " [ " + toHex(data[0]) + " " + stat + " ]" );
        TINIOS.sleepProcess(250);

            System.out.println();
      }
        catch(Exception e){
            System.out.println( "Error in I2C write..." );
            System.out.println( e );
        }
    }


    for (int i=1; i<10; i++ ) {
        System.out.println( i );

        try {
            data[0] = (byte)(0x00);
```

```
                System.out.print( "read: " + i );
                stat = PioPort.read( data, 0,1 );
                System.out.println( " [ " + toHex(data[0]) + " " + stat + " ]" );
                TINIOS.sleepProcess(250);

            }
            catch(Exception e) {
                System.out.println( "Error in I2C read..." );
                System.out.println( e );
            }
        }

    }

    public static void main(String[] args) {
        Parallel_IO myPio = new Parallel_IO();
          myPio.Blinky();
    }
}
```

As with previous programs, the first few lines declare a data buffer for storing the data to be sent to, or received from, the I²C device, in this case a single byte. We have also created a single constructor that creates a new I2CPort object and assigns the address and clock delay.

```
import com.dalsemi.system.*;
import java.io.*;

public class Parallel_IO {

    byte[] data = new byte[1];
    I2CPort PioPort;

    public Parallel_IO() {
        PioPort = new I2CPort();
        PioPort.setAddress((byte)0x27);
        PioPort.setClockDelay((byte)0x7F);
         data[0] = 0x00;
    }
```

We also have a toHex() method for displaying the contents read from, or written to, the I²C device. This is entirely for our convenience, so we don't have to read decimal and determine if the output is proper. Then we have the bulk of the class in the blinky() method.

```
            try {
                data[0] = (byte)(0x1A);
                stat = PioPort.write( data, 0, 1);
                System.out.print( " [ " + toHex(data[0]) + " " + stat + " ]" );
                TINIOS.sleepProcess(250);
```

```
            . . .
         System.out.println();
      }
      catch(Exception e){
         System.out.println( "Error in I2C write..." );
         System.out.println( e );
      }


   for (int i=1; i<10; i++ ) {
      System.out.println( i );

      try {
         data[0] = (byte)(0x00);
         System.out.print( "read: " + i );
         stat = PioPort.read( data, 0,1 );
         System.out.println( " [ " + toHex(data[0]) + " " + stat + " ]" );
         TINIOS.sleepProcess(250);

      }
      catch(Exception e) {
         System.out.println( "Error in I2C read..." );
         System.out.println( e );
      }
   }
```

The `blinky()` method does two things. First it writes various bytes to the PCF8574 to turn on and off some of the LEDs. Then it reads from the PCF8574 and displays the results of the various switch settings. We have liberally filled this program with lots of print statements so we can see what's happening along the way.

Compile the program and run it on TINI and watch the results.

```
C:\> javac -bootclasspath %TINI_HOME%\bin\tiniclasses.jar
   -classpath %TINI_HOME%\bin\owapi_dependencies_TINI.jar;.
   -d bin   src\Parallel_IO.java
C:\> java -classpath %TINI_HOME%\bin\tini.jar;. BuildDependency
   -p %TINI_HOME%\bin\owapi_dependencies_TINI_001.jar
   -f bin
   -x %TINI_HOME%\bin\owapi_dep.txt
   -o bin
   -d %TINI_HOME%\bin\tini.db
```

This next example is a slight extension of the last one. Instead of reading or writing from the same device, we will be reading inputs from one PC8574 and writing outputs to a second one. This will also demonstrate connecting several devices to an I²C bus at the same time. We will be using the first remote 8-bit I/O expander to read the position of eight push buttons and then writing this value to the second I/O expander to turn on or off eight LEDs. We will also use the interrupt feature of the first PCF8574 to trigger an external interrupt on a TINI stick when any of the buttons is pressed.

Listing 11-04: InOut.java

```java
import java.util.TooManyListenersException;
import com.dalsemi.system.*;
import java.io.*;

class InOut implements ExternalInterruptEventListener {

    int i;
    byte[] data = new byte[1];

    I2CPort PioPort_I;
    I2CPort PioPort_O;

    private static char[] hexChars =
        { '0','1','2','3','4','5','6','7','8','9','A','B','C','D','E','F' };

    public static String toHex( int data )
    {
        StringBuffer output = new StringBuffer();
        int firstNibble, secondNibble;

            firstNibble = ( data >> 4 ) & 0x0F;
            secondNibble = data & 0x0F;
            output.append( hexChars[ firstNibble ] );
            output.append( hexChars[ secondNibble ] );
        return output.toString();
    }

    public void init() throws TooManyListenersException
    {
        int stat=0;

        // This is the signal to which we will add an event listener
        ExternalInterrupt myInterrupt = new ExternalInterrupt();
        // Add the event listener
        myInterrupt.addEventListener(this);

        // Set this to EDGE triggering
        try {
            myInterrupt.setTrigger( true, this );
        }
        catch (Exception e){
            System.out.println( e );
        }
```

```
    // Set the addresses and clock delay
    PioPort_I = new I2CPort();
    PioPort_I.setAddress((byte)0x21);
    PioPort_I.setClockDelay((byte)0x7F);

    PioPort_O = new I2CPort();
    PioPort_O.setAddress((byte)0x22);
    PioPort_O.setClockDelay((byte)0x7F);

    // Set all outputs low
    try {
        data[0] = (byte)(0x00);
        stat = PioPort_I.write( data, 0,1 );
        stat = PioPort_O.write( data, 0, 1);
    }
    catch (Exception e) {
        System.out.println( e );
    }

}

public void externalInterruptEvent(ExternalInterruptEvent ev)
{
    int stat = 0;

    System.out.println( "Interrupt Caught: " + ++i );

    try {
        // Fetch the Input states
        data[0] = (byte)(0x00);
        stat = PioPort_I.read( data, 0,1 );
        System.out.println( "Read [ " + toHex(data[0]) + " " + stat + " ]" );

        // Write the states to the Outputs on the other device
        stat = PioPort_O.write( data, 0, 1);
        System.out.println( "Write [ " + toHex(data[0]) + " " + stat + " ]" );

        // Reset inputs
        data[0] = (byte)0x00;
        stat = PioPort_I.write( data, 0,1 );
        System.out.println( "Reset [ " + toHex(data[0]) + " " + stat + " ]" );
    }
    catch (Exception e) {
        System.out.println( e );
    }

    // Die after 10 pushes
    if (i > 9) { System.exit(0); }
}
```

```
public static void main(String[] args) throws TooManyListenersException
{
    // Start up the InterruptListender
    InOut interrupt = new InOut();
    // Initialize everything
    interrupt.init();

    // Hang out for awhile
    while (true) {
        // do nothing
    }
}
}
```

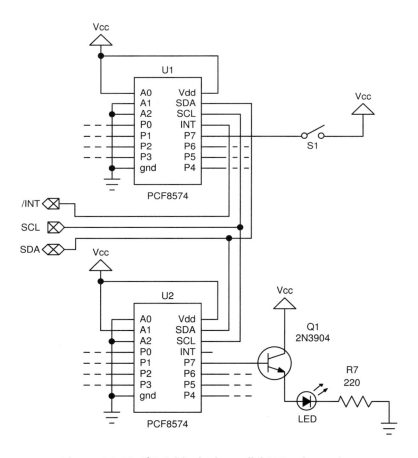

Figure 11-13: I²C 8-bit dual parallel I/O schematic

The program for this schematic is a slight modification of the previous, combined with what we learned in Chapter 8 for setting up an ExternalInterruptEventListener. We will spend much less time going through this program, as it's very much like the program from Chapter 8, ExtInt.java.

We have created the init() method to create the ExternalInterrupt object and set the EventListener. We also needed to set the interrupt triggering to "edge triggering" so we can catch which button was pressed when we trigger an interrupt. Edge triggering will trigger an interrupt every time the button changes state. This is in contrast to "level triggering," the other form of interrupt trigger, where the ExternalInterruptEventListener is called continually until the button is released. In this method we also create two I2CPort objects, one for each of the I²C devices, and we initialize them to all bits off.

```
public void init() throws TooManyListenersException
{
    int stat=0;

    // This is the signal to which we will add an event listener
    ExternalInterrupt myInterrupt = new ExternalInterrupt();
    // Add the event listener
    myInterrupt.addEventListener(this);

    // Set this to EDGE triggering
    try {
        myInterrupt.setTrigger( true, this );
    }
    catch (Exception e){
        System.out.println( e );
    }

    // Set the addresses and clock delay
    PioPort_I = new I2CPort();
    PioPort_I.setAddress((byte)0x21);
    PioPort_I.setClockDelay((byte)0x7F);

    PioPort_O = new I2CPort();
    PioPort_O.setAddress((byte)0x22);
    PioPort_O.setClockDelay((byte)0x7F);

    // Set all outputs low
    try {
        data[0] = (byte)(0x00);
        stat = PioPort_I.write( data, 0,1 );
        stat = PioPort_O.write( data, 0, 1);
    }
    catch (Exception e) {
        System.out.println( e );
```

```
        }
    }
```

The last thing before our main starts the whole thing running is the
externalInterruptEvent() method. Each time the first PCF8574 fires an interrupt,
this method is called. In this method we read the byte from the input device and write
this to the output device to turn on or off the corresponding LEDs to match the
buttons pushed. As with the previous example, this program is quite verbose so we
can see what is going on in case the LEDs don't work as expected.

```java
public void externalInterruptEvent(ExternalInterruptEvent ev)
{
    int stat = 0;

    System.out.println( "Interrupt Caught: " + ++i );

    try {
        // Fetch the Input states
        data[0] = (byte)(0x00);
        stat = PioPort_I.read( data, 0,1 );
        System.out.println( "Read [ " + toHex(data[0]) + " " +
            stat + " ]" );

        // Write the states to the Outputs on the other device
        stat = PioPort_O.write( data, 0, 1);
        System.out.println( "Write [ " + toHex(data[0]) + " " +
            stat + " ]" );

        // Reset inputs
        data[0] = (byte)0x00;
        stat = PioPort_I.write( data, 0,1 );
        System.out.println( "Reset [ " + toHex(data[0]) + " " +
            stat + " ]" );
    }
    catch (Exception e) {
        System.out.println( e );
    }

    // Die after 10 pushes
    if (i > 9) { System.exit(0); }
}
```

To compile this:

```
C:\> javac -bootclasspath %TINI_HOME%\bin\tiniclasses.jar
    -classpath %TINI_HOME%\bin\owapi_dependencies_TINI.jar;.
    -d bin   src\InOut.java
C:\> java -classpath %TINI_HOME%\bin\tini.jar;. BuildDependency
    -p %TINI_HOME%\bin\owapi_dependencies_TINI_001.jar
    -f bin
    -x %TINI_HOME%\bin\owapi_dep.txt
```

```
-o bin
-d %TINI_HOME%\bin\tini.db
```

After you compile this and FTP it to your TINI, give it a test run. If you see lots of -1s printed in the output, this is probably because there is something not quite right with the way you have connected your I²C bus or devices, so check the schematics again. While it's hard to show the LEDs lighting, the screen output looks like this:

```
Interrupt Caught: 1
Read [ 01 0 ]
Write [ 01 0 ]
Reset [ 00 0 ]
Interrupt Caught: 2
Read [ 00 0 ]
Write [ 00 0 ]
Reset [ 00 0 ]
...
Interrupt Caught: 6
Read [ 81 0 ]
Write [ 81 0 ]
Reset [ 00 0 ]
Interrupt Caught: 7
Read [ 00 0 ]
Write [ 00 0 ]
Reset [ 00 0 ]
...
Interrupt Caught: 10
Read [ 80 0 ]
Write [ 80 0 ]
Reset [ 00 0 ]
```

Here you can see that we press the first button (01), then both the first and last button (81 is button 8 and button 1), then just the last button (80). Notice that each interrupt is followed with another that reads 00. This is the button release (it's changing state on the device and so it triggers another interrupt).

All of the examples in this chapter have used the microprocessor port driver for I²C communication. If you wish to use memory-mapped I²C then you simply need to use an alternate form of the constructor given in the discussion of the API. The rest of the example programs do not need any further modification.

Summary

The section has provided a very brief look at the I²C bus protocol and how to use it with TINI. There are a number of aspects of I²C and TINI that we have not attempted to cover here. The Dallas Semiconductor TINI archives are a rich source of information, in a question-and-answer format, for those interested in more information. Additionally, the Philips web site provides the complete I²C specification, free of charge.

References

1. *Philips Semiconductors, About the I²C-bus,*
   http://www-us.semiconductors.philips.com/i2c/facts/

2. *Philips Semiconductors, I²C Bus Specification,*
   http://www-us.semiconductors.philips.com/acrobat/various/
   I2C_BUS_SPECIFICATION_3.pdf

3. *I²C FAQ,*
   http://perso.club-internet.fr/mbouget/i2c-faq.html

4. *The I²C-bus and how to use it (including specification),*
   http://www.semiconductors.philips.com/acrobat/various/
   I2C_BUS_SPECIFICATION_1995.pdf

## CHAPTER 12

Controller Area Network

The TINI microcontroller and the TINI API support dual Controller Area Network (CAN) interfaces. CAN is a popular network for communicating between sensors and controllers in automotive and industrial applications. In this chapter we will discuss some of the details in the CAN specification and get you started using TINI as both a CAN controller and a CAN sensor interface.

What Is the CAN Bus?

General overview

The Controller Area Network (CAN) is a serial bus system that was developed in the late 1980s for automotive applications by Robert Bosch GmbH, Germany. CAN was developed to support distributed control systems in automobiles and has also been implemented fairly widely in industrial control systems as well.

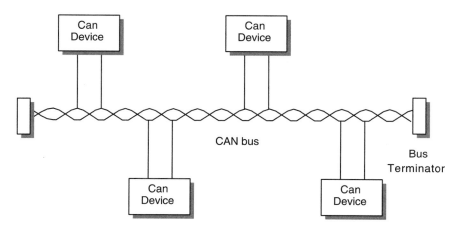

Figure 12-1: A CAN bus

CAN uses bit-serial transmission at rates up to 1 megabit/second in twisted-pair cabling. Messages are passed between nodes on a CAN bus using a message identifier. CAN is similar to I²C, which was discussed in the previous chapter, with a few significant differences. The primary differences are the signaling and the method of identifying devices and data. CAN uses differential signaling on two wires rather than the clock and data lines that I²C uses. With CAN the data has the identification, where in I²C the devices have the identification. This identifier does not indicate the transmitting or receiving device but rather identifies the content of the message (for instance, temperature or shaft position). All nodes on a CAN bus receive all of the messages and check the message identifier to determine if that particular message is of interest. The identifier also determines the message priority. Lower numerical values have a higher priority on the CAN bus.

The CAN specification is available from the Bosch CAN Literature[1] web page. Additionally, CAN has been standardized by the International Standards Organization in ISO 11989 (Controller area network for high-speed communication) and ISO 11519 (Low-speed controller area network). The Bosch CAN specification only defines the Data Link and Physical Layers (using the OSI reference model). Additional layers are defined in one of several higher-level protocols that use CAN for the Data Link layer. A few of these higher-layer protocols will be mentioned soon. The details of CAN are essentially transmission media independent, but the ISO specifications have defined the Physical layer, including cabling and connectors.

CAN versions

The Bosch CAN specification has been revised over the years from version 1.0 to the current version of 2.0. Version 1.0 and 1.2 defined CAN with an 11-bit message identification. Version 2.0 has allowed an 18-bit message ID extension allowing for an effective 29-bit message ID. To keep new CAN devices compatible with older implementations, the CAN 2.0 specification is defined in two parts, 2.0A and 2.0B. In CAN 2.0A, the message format is consistent with older versions of CAN that use only an 11-bit message ID. In CAN 2.0B the 18-bit message ID extension is allowed. CAN 2.0B can then be implemented in either the *passive* or *active* mode. In the passive mode, the CAN controller will transmit only messages with 11-bit message IDs and will receive message frames with the standard 11-bit and the extended 29-bit ID. In this way it can be compatible with both older and newer CAN devices. In the active mode the CAN controller receives and transmits messages with both 11-bit and 29-bit message IDs. CAN version 1.0, 1.2 and 2.0A are called "standard CAN" because they all use an 11-bit message ID. CAN 2.0 B is called "Extended CAN" as it uses the extended 29-bit message ID.

---

[1] CAN Literature – http://www.can.bosch.com/content/Literature.html

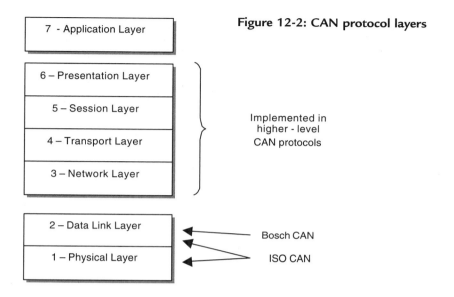

Figure 12-2: CAN protocol layers

The CAN Bus in More Detail

As mentioned already, CAN messages contain a message identifier to indicate the contents of the message rather than using device addresses. This makes the CAN bus a *multimaster* bus, that uses *multicast* communication. As a multimaster bus, any device can determine that the bus is available for transmission of a message. If several devices start transmitting at the same time, then the message priority is used to determine which device gets to complete transmission. CAN is also a multicast form of communication because the messages are transmitted on the bus to all devices. Any device on the bus may determine that the message it received is of interest and act on that message. The benefit of being both multimaster and multicast is that new devices can be added to the bus without reconfiguring any of the existing devices. The diagram below shows multiple devices using a common CAN bus to send messages. Only the devices that are interested in the data they receive (determined by the message identifier) need to actually process and act on the message.

Now let's examine some of the details on how the CAN bus is implemented.

Bus states

The CAN bus has two states, one representing a logical 1, called the recessive state, and the other representing a logical 0, called the dominant state. When the bus is idle (no message traffic) the bus is in the recessive state. A device communicating on the bus will pull the bus to the dominant state.

Dominant = Logic 0
Recessive = Logic 1

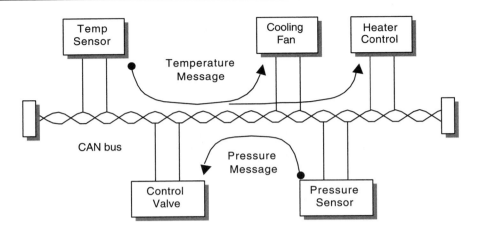

Figure 12-3: CAN bus messages

CAN controllers are connected to the CAN bus through a transceiver. The Bosch CAN specification does not specify a bus media but common implementations include twisted-pair and optical media. The diagram below shows a typical connection to a twisted-pair cable. In this case the CAN controller is our TINI microcontroller and the CAN transceiver is the Philips PCA82C250 (or compatible). The CAN transceiver puts the data on the twisted pair using differential voltage (balanced line) signaling for noise immunity.

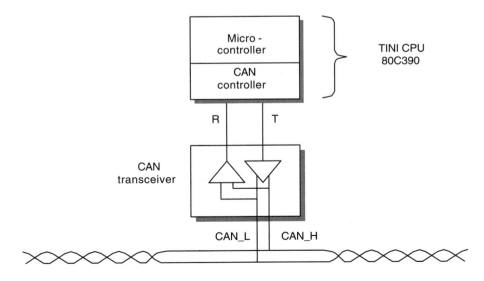

Figure 12-4: CAN bus signaling

Like I²C devices, CAN devices are connected to the CAN bus in a wired-AND configuration. This means that it is possible for multiple devices to change the bus state to a dominant state without adverse effects. Exactly which device and how to handle multiple devices acting as masters will be discussed in the section on arbitration.

In the case of twisted-pair bus wiring, the transceiver converts the microcontroller CAN-transmit and CAN-receive signals into differential voltages. A typical CAN transceiver for twisted pair will hold the CAN_L (CAN Low) and CAN_H (CAN High) lines at 2.5 volts in the recessive state. To signal a dominant state on the CAN bus, the transceiver will pull CAN_H to 3.5 volts and CAN_L to 1.5 volts (note that CAN_H is higher than CAN_L, hence the names high and low) as shown in the following diagram.

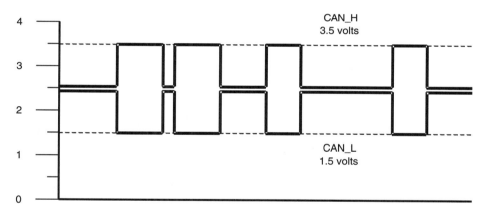

Figure 12-5: Differential signaling

The receiving transceiver will invert CAN_L and add that to the CAN_H signal to recover the CAN signal. In doing this, any noise induced on the line will be cancelled out.

Message coding

CAN bus signals are encoded on twisted-pair wiring using non-return-to-zero (NRZ) bit encoding. NRZ encoding is a two-level signaling mechanism used to transmit data. Using NRZ encoding, one bit of data is transmitted per clock cycle. The significance of NRZ is more easily seen when compared to return-to-zero (RZ) encoding. With RZ encoding, the signal returns to the low state after each bit is transmitted. With NRZ encoding it does not. If two or more high value bits are transmitted, the voltage stays at the level.

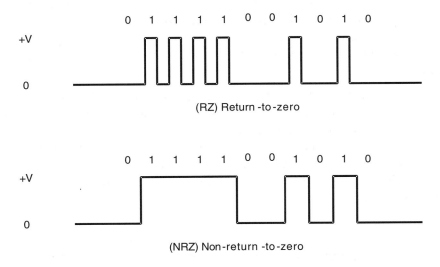

Figure 12-6: NRZ bit encoding

Frames

Now that we know how signals are put on the CAN bus, let's examine how data packets are sent on the bus. The data packets are called "frames" on a CAN network. A frame is the message that is transmitted between nodes. It contains a message identification, necessary protocol information, data, a header and footer. The CAN specification allows for several types of frames for different purposes.

- Data Frame – Data sent from the transmitting device to one or more receiving devices.

- Remote Frame – A request for a specific type of data.

- Error Frame – Sent when any unit detects an error on the CAN bus.

- Overload Frame – Used by a device to delay further frames so it can have additional time to process the data it has received.

- Interframe space – Used to separate data or remote frames.

In addition to these types of frames, two formats are possible depending on the CAN version being used: Standard CAN format following the Bosch 2.0A specification and Extended CAN format following the Bosch 2.0B specification.

We will examine the data frame in detail. If you need more information on the other frame types you should consult the Bosch CAN specification. The following diagram shows the various fields and bits in a CAN 2.0A standard data frame.

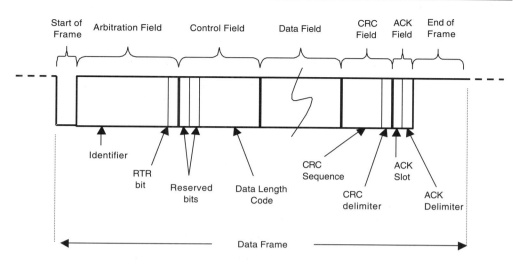

Figure 12-7: Standard data frame

Before a CAN node can start transmission of a data frame, it watches the bus for completion of any existing CAN frames. Once the bus is idle any node can begin transmission. The fields of a standard data frame are:

- Start Of Frame – The start of a frame is indicated when any node pulls the bus (low) dominant (logic "0") for 1 bit time (the duration of a bit time is explained later).

- Arbitration Field – The arbitration field is a 12-bit field consisting of an 11-bit Identifier and a single Remote Transmission Request bit (RTR bit).

   o Identifier – Is the message identifier, transmitted most significant bit first. The 7 most significant bits cannot be all recessive (logic 1).

   o RTR bit – Is dominant in a data frame and recessive in a remote frame.

- Control Field – The control field is six bits.

   o Reserved bits – The first two bits are reserved for future expansion. Set to the dominant state.

   o Data Length Code – The last four bits form a binary number (MSB is transmitted first) that indicates the number of bytes in the data field. Can have the value of 0 through 8.

- Data Field – These are the bytes of data to be transmitted. There can be 0 through 8 bytes, each transmitted most significant bit first.

- CRC Field – The Cyclic Redundancy Check field includes the CRC sequence and the CRC delimiter bit.

  - CRC Sequence – The CRC sequence is a 15-bit CRC code. The CRC polynomial used is $X^{15} + X^{14} + X^{10} + X^8 + X^7 + X^4 + X^3 + 1$
    The CRC sequence includes all bits including the Start of Frame bit, the arbitration field, the control field and through the end of the data field.

  - CRC delimiter – The CRC delimiter is a recessive (logic 1) bit.

- ACK field – The Acknowledge (ACK) field is two bits that include an acknowledge slot and an acknowledge delimiter. During these two bits the transmitter sends two recessive bits. Any receiving device that has correctly received the frame will overwrite this bit with a dominant bit.

  - ACK slot – The ACK slot is the time slot for other devices to acknowledge the receipt of the frame by writing a dominant bit.

  - ACK delimiter – The ACK delimiter is a recessive bit. Note that by having the CRC delimiter and the AC delimiter be recessive, the ACK slot will always be surrounded by recessive bits.

- End Of Frame – The end of the frame is marked with seven recessive bits.

A CAN node transmits a data frame to any and all interested receivers whenever necessary by simply transmitting a message on the bus. This can be either some prearranged event, like the closure of a switch contact, or periodically based on some internal timer. Alternately, a receiving node can specifically request a data frame of a particular type be sent out on the bus by issuing a Remote Frame with the message identifier that matches the data frame that it is interested in.

A remote frame is formatted like a data frame but with three differences:

- The RTR bit is recessive to indicate this is a remote frame, not a data frame.

- There is NO data field.

- The data length code in the control field is ignored (it may not be set to 0, it may be the length of the data frame that is being requested).

Extended CAN Version 2.0B adds an 18-bit extension on the message identifier while maintaining 100% backward compatibility with standard CAN (CAN 2.0A and previous versions). Recall that there are two types of CAN 2.0A controllers:

- Ones that can transmit and receive only version 2.0A messages (11-bit message ID) and will issue an error on receiving a 2.0B message format.

- Ones that can transmit and receive 2.0A messages (11-bit message ID) and will acknowledge 20.B messages (29-bit message ID) and ignore them.

So, it is possible for CAN 20.B controllers to work on a 2.0A CAN bus but there is a possibility that the reverse will not work depending on the capability of the 2.0A devices.

The differences between the standard format and the extended format are entirely in the arbitration field of a data frame (and remote frame). The following diagram shows the various fields and bits in a CAN 2.0B extended data frame.

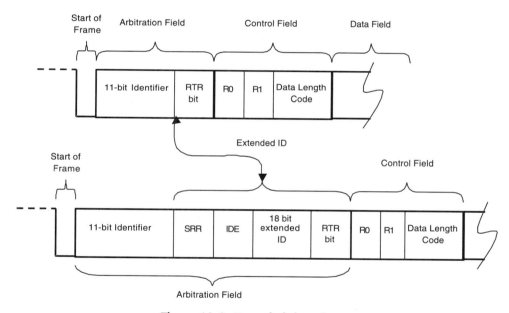

Figure 12-8: Extended data frame

With the extended CAN frame message ID, essentially 20 bits are inserted after the 11-bit message ID in the arbitration field. Notice that the first two bits of the control field in standard CAN format were reserved and set to the dominant state. Extended CAN uses these reserved bits to indicate that this message is using an extended ID frame format. The new bits introduced for the extended format are:

- SRR bit – Substitute Remote Request bit. This bit is set to recessive (logic 1).

- IDE bit – Extended Identification bit. This bit is set to recessive.

- 18-bit extended identification – These are the additional 18 bits that make up the 29-bit message identifier in the extended format.

What this means is that if a receiving CAN node notices what it thinks are the two reserved bits to be recessive, then it knows that this frame is really an extended frame (so those bits then become the SRR and IDE bits). Also note that with the SRR (R0) and IDE (R1) bits set to recessive, standard format frames are given priority over extended format frames. We will discuss message priority in the next section.

CAN devices can also transmit error frames when errors are detected, overload frames when a receiver requires additional time, or an interspace frame to separate sequential data or remote frames. Details of these frames can be found in the Bosch CAN specification.

Priority and arbitration

When two or more CAN devices attempt to transmit at the same time, the collision will be detected and resolved using Carrier Sense Multiple Access with Arbitration on Message Priority (CSMA/AMP) protocol. What this means is that the message with the highest priority will be transmitted while all messages of a lower priority will stop. The priority of a message is determined by the message ID; lower numbers have a higher priority. Here is how this works. Recall that all CAN devices are connected to the bus in a wired-AND configuration and that the recessive state of the CAN bus is a logic 1. Each node will transmit its 11-bit identifier on the bus, one bit at a time starting with the most significant bit. While transmitting, the CAN node will monitor the bus state to determine if it has successfully driven the bus to the proper value. If one device is trying to write a logical 1 (recessive) while another is trying to write a logical 0 (dominant) then the dominant state will have priority. The device(s) writing the logical 1 will abort transmission until the bus goes idle again. This will continue on each bit until the device with the lowest ID (the highest priority) is the only device left transmitting on the bus.

For example, consider three CAN devices each trying to transmit messages:

- Device 1 – address 433 (decimal or 00110110001 binary)
- Device 2 – address 154 (00010011010)
- Device 3 – address 187 (00010111011)

Assuming all three see the bus is idle and begin transmitting at the same time, this is how the arbitration works out.

All three devices will drive the bus to a dominant state for the start-of-frame (SOF) and the two most significant bits of each message identifier. Each device will monitor the bus and determine success. When they write bit 8 of the message ID, the device writing message ID 433 will notice that the bus is in the dominant state when it was trying to let it be recessive, so it will assume a collision and give up for now. The remaining devices will continue writing bits until bit 5, then the device writing message ID 187 will notice a collision and abort transmission. This leaves the device

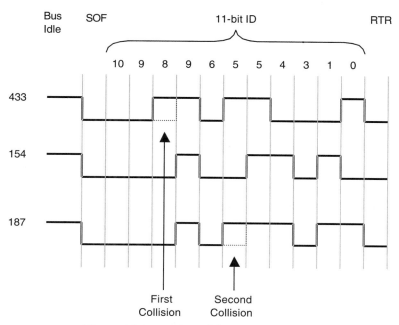

Figure 12-9. Device arbitration example.

writing message ID 154 remaining. It will continue writing bits on the bus until complete or an error is detected. Notice that this method of arbitration will always cause the lowest numerical value message ID to have priority. This same method of bit-wise arbitration and prioritization applies to the 18-bit extension in the extended format as well.

Error detection and handling

CAN devices implement multiple error-detection schemes. As previously mentioned, message frames contain a CRC value for verifying the validity of the data received. If a receiver determines an error as a result of examining a frame and its CRC, then it does not acknowledge receipt of the message. If no device acknowledges a message frame, then the transmitter knows that there was an error in transmission.

Each transmitter also performs a frame check while transmitting a message. If a transmitter detects a dominant bus state for any of these bits, then the transmitter aborts and generates a frame error:

- CRC delimiter
- Acknowledge delimiter
- End of frame
- Interframe space

Each transmitter also performs bit monitoring except when checking the arbitration field. If it detects the wrong bit on the bus (different from what it was trying to transmit) then it aborts transmission and generates an error frame. After generating an error frame, a CAN device tries to transmit the message frame again.

Synchronization and bit stuffing

With CAN, the data transmission is synchronous. Each node has its own internal clock (oscillator) but it needs to synchronize itself with the data on the bus. Each node is hard synchronized at the beginning of each message by the falling edge of the start-of-frame bit. Additionally, each CAN node is resynchronized on each recessive-dominant falling edge in a message. Bit stuffing allows for the CAN devices on a bus to resynchronize with the data in the event that the data being transmitted contains long consecutive runs of the same value. What happens is that a CAN transmitter will detect five consecutive bits of any single value and insert one bit of the opposite polarity. The CAN receiver will do the opposite; whenever it sees five consecutive bits of the same value it will remove the next bit from the message frame. Bit stuffing ensures that there are enough recessive-dominant falling edges in the data stream to keep the other nodes on the bus in synchronization.

Bit timing

The *bit rate* of data transmission on the CAN bus is the number of bits per second that are transmitted. The nominal *bit time* is the time required to put one bit on the bus (1/bit rate). A CAN controller can have this *bit time* programmed to various times for different bitrates. The CAN specification partitions this *bit time* into four time segments. Each of these time segments is an integer number of *time quanta* long (the exact number varies depending on the bitrate). A *time quantum* is a unit of time that is derived from the transmitter clock frequency (the CAN controller CPU oscillator). A *time quantum* is some fraction of the transmitter clock as determined by a *bit rate prescaler*. Each bit has a minimum of eight time quanta and a maximum of 25. The four segments of a *bit time* are shown below:

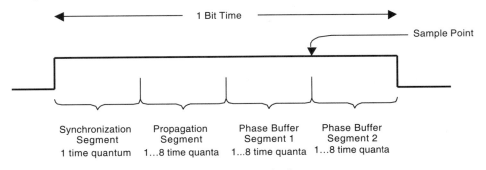

Figure 12-10: Bit time

- Synchronization Segment – This is the time required to synchronize each node to the bus. This segment is always 1 *time quantum*.

- Propagation Segment – This is the part of a bit that is used to compensate for the physical delay on the network. This segment can vary from 1 to 8 *time quanta*.

- Phase Buffer Segment 1 – This is used to compensate for edge phase errors before the sample point. This part of the bit time can vary from 1 to 8 *time quanta*.

- Phase Buffer Segment 2 – This is used to compensate for edge phase errors after the sample point. This part of the bit time can vary from 1 to 8 *time quanta*. Phase Buffer Segment 2 is less than or equal to Phase Buffer Segment 1.

The *sample point* between the phase buffer segments is the point in time when the CAN node samples the bus and interprets the value of that particular bit.

The *bit time* and therefore the *bit rate* is determined by programming the width of the *time quantum* and the number of *time quanta* in the various segments.

It may be necessary to resynchronize the CAN receiver clock based on a recessive to dominant falling edge. To do this, the *phase buffer segment 1* may be lengthened or the *phase buffer segment 2* may be shortened. The amount of shortening or lengthening is called the *resynchronization jump width* and is programmable and must be greater than 0 and less than or equal to the smaller of either 4 *time quanta* or *Phase Buffer Segment 1*.

All of this gets a bit confusing, so perhaps an example will help. Actually, we need an example as we will need to figure out these segment values when programming TINI. We will use some information specific to TINI and we will revisit this topic again when we start programming. The TINI microcontroller has an 18.432-MHz clock. This is the clock that the CAN controller that is built into the Dallas Semiconductor's 80C360 CPU uses. Let's assume we are interested in transmitting data on the CAN bus at 125,000 bits/second. How long is a *time quantum* and how many *time quanta* would we need to program the various segments to?

First we find the desired *bit rate*:

bit time = 1/*bit rate* = 1/125000 bps (bits per second) = 8 µs (microseconds)

Then we find the *clock time* of the CPU:

clock time = 1/*clock frequency* = 1/18.432 MHz = 0.05425 µs

Since the *time quantum* is an integer multiple of the *clock time,* we need to find some *bit rate prescaler* to give us a reasonable value. We could pick a *time quantum* equal to the *clock time* but we would need 147 *time quanta* to make up a bit and that wouldn't do at all since a *bit time* has a maximum of 25 *time quanta*. The idea in picking a reasonable *bit rate prescaler* is in finding one that results in a *bit time* that is between 8 and 25 *time quanta* in length. Let's pick 7 (I know that will work, but you can try others if you like).

> *bit rate prescaler = 7*

Then we compute a *time quantum*:

> *time quantum = bit rate prescaler / clock = 7 / 18.432 MHz = 0.379 µs*

Once we have a *time quantum*, we need to figure out how many of them are needed to make a *bit time*:

> *N time quanta = bit time / time quanta = 8 µs / 0.379 µs = 21.108*

But since we need to use integer multiples of *time quanta*, we will need 21 *time quanta* to make a bit. That is good as it is ≥ 8 and ≤ 25 and that's what we need. Now we allocate these 21 *time quanta* using the requirements of the *bit time*:

> Synchronization is always 1 *time quantum*.
> Propagation Segment can vary from 1 to 8 *time quanta*.
> Phase Buffer Segment 1 can vary from 1 to 8 *time quanta*.
> Phase Buffer Segment 2 can vary from 1 to 8 *time quant*a and is < Phase Buffer Segment 1.

Let's pick these, although there are a number of possibilities that all add up to 21 that will work:

> Synchronization = 1
> Propagation Segment = 5
> Phase Buffer Segment 1 = 8
> Phase Buffer Segment 2 = 7

The exact allocation of *time quanta* to the various segments may vary a bit. In reality, on TINI the Synchronization, Propagation Segment and Phase Buffer Segment 1 are treated as a single unit that can vary from 2 to 16.

All that's left is to pick a *synchronization jump width*. This is not calculated, just picked; 1 or 2 is a good number. It needs to be ≥ 1 and $\leq$ the smaller of (4, *Phase Buffer Segment 1*).

So, how good are these numbers? Let's find the error.

> *Actual bit time = 21 time quanta x 0.379 µs = 7.959 µs (we needed 8 µs)*

> *Actual bit rate = 1 / Actual bit time = 1/ 7.959 µs = 125,644 bits/second.*

$$Bit\ rate\ error\ = (Actual\ Bit\ Rate - Desired\ Bit\ Rate) / Desired\ Bit\ Rate$$
$$= (125644 - 125000)/125000 = 0.5\%$$

OK, 0.5% error, not bad. Actually that's the limit as the CAN specification lists that this needs to be within 0.5% tolerance.

You can work through other transmission speeds using a similar methodology. Note that with some clock speeds you cannot get less than 0.5% error so you will need to use some other speed or use a different clock. This is the case with TINI. With its 18.432-MHz clock, you cannot get 1-Mbit CAN communication. The Bosch document "The Configuration of the CAN Bit Timing"[2] may also prove to be helpful.

Physical layers and media

That about does it for the inner workings of CAN. One last topic we need to examine is the hardware needed for a proper CAN bus implementation. We will do this with a simple CAN bus like the one shown here, where we will be using TINI as a CAN sensor (transmitter) and as a CAN actuator (receiver).

The Bosch specification does not include any physical layer details like the media, connectors, pinout, etc. It is possible to implement the CAN protocol on a variety of media like twisted-pair wires, optical fiber or even power lines. The ISO specification does provide details for implementing CAN on twisted pair.

The number of devices on a CAN network is theoretically unlimited (remember, that message ID is an ID on the data, not the device, so multiple nodes can be sending messages using the same message ID, which will not limit the network size). The real limit, however, is the signal drive capability of the transmitter, which limits the practical number of nodes to around 30–90 depending on the devices.

The CAN network cable length is dependent on the data rate and the media; 1 Mbit/ second is guaranteed by the CAN specification if you are using twisted-pair cabling (like CAT 3 or better network cable) under 40 meters in length. Some typical CAN bus maximum lengths are listed in Table 12-1.

Table 12-1: CAN bus length

Data Rate	Maximum Length
1 Mbps	40 meters
500 Kbps	100 meters
250 Kbps	200 meters
125 Kbps	500 meters
10 Kbps	6 kilometers

[2] The Configuration of the CAN Bit Timing – http://www.can.bosch.com/docu/ CiA99Paper.pdf

The ISO specification also specified terminating resistors of 120 Ω on each end of the CAN bus to cut down on reflections, which can increase the error rate on the bus, but these are often unnecessary at low data rates (< 125 kbps).

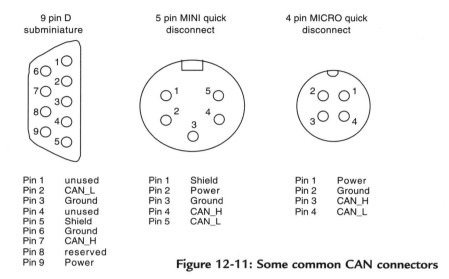

9 pin D subminiature		5 pin MINI quick disconnect		4 pin MICRO quick disconnect	
Pin 1	unused	Pin 1	Shield	Pin 1	Power
Pin 2	CAN_L	Pin 2	Power	Pin 2	Ground
Pin 3	Ground	Pin 3	Ground	Pin 3	CAN_H
Pin 4	unused	Pin 4	CAN_H	Pin 4	CAN_L
Pin 5	Shield	Pin 5	CAN_L		
Pin 6	Ground				
Pin 7	CAN_H				
Pin 8	reserved				
Pin 9	Power				

Figure 12-11: Some common CAN connectors

There is no standard for the CAN connector. Each higher layer protocol (we talk about them in the next section) defines its own. Some common connectors include the 9-pin D-subminiature connector (like what is common on PC serial ports), the 5-pin mini quick disconnect, the 4-pin micro quick disconnect (or quick change) and screw-terminals.

Higher-layer protocols

So far we have only talked about the lower-layer details of CAN. For CAN to be used in any complex applications, it is necessary to work with one of a number of higher-layer protocol details such as:

- Message ID assignment

- Network management

- Message ID meaning

- Method of exchanging data (assigning meaning to data)

While we won't go into any detail on higher-layer protocols, as the TINI API does not implement any, there are a few popular protocols based on CAN, listed in Table 12-2.

Table 12-2: Higher-layer protocols

SDS	SDS = Smart Distributed System. Developed by Honeywell for industrial automation systems. http://content.honeywell.com/sensing/prodinfo/sds/
DeviceNet	Developed by Allen Bradley for industrial control devices. Now the responsibility of the OpenDeviceNetVendors Association (ODVA). http://www.odva.org/
CAL	CAL = CAN Application Layer. CAL is an application-independent standard application layer developed by the CAN-in-Automation (CiA) users group. http://www.can-cia.de/
CANOpen	CANopen uses the CAN protocol for communication but builds on this by adding standardized communication mechanisms and device functionality. http://www.can-cia.de/

How TINI Does CAN

The TINI hardware and TINI API effectively implement CAN 2.0B. In fact the TINI CPU, the 80C390, has two on-board CAN controllers, allowing the possibility for TINI to be used on two separate CAN networks or as a smart bridge connecting two CAN networks.

First we will look at how the TINI CPU supports CAN, and then we will discuss the necessary hardware to support CAN on the TINI stick. We'll examine the TINI API and the CAN classes before we end this chapter with a few examples.

80C390 CAN controllers

The DS80C390[3] microcontroller incorporates two CAN controllers that are compliant with the CAN 2.0B specification. These CAN controllers support both 11-bit standard or 29-bit extended message identifiers and support 15 message centers for each controller. Global controls and status registers in each CAN unit allow the microcontroller to evaluate error messages, generate interrupts, locate and validate new data, establish the CAN Bus timing, establish identification mask bits, and verify the source of individual messages. The specifics of the CAN controller are discussed in the *DS80C390 datasheet* and the *DS80C390 User's Guide Supplement*[4].

---

[3] 80C390 Datasheet – http://pdfserv.maxim-ic.com/arpdf/DS80C390.pdf

[4] 90C390 User's Guide Supplement – http://pdfserv.maxim-ic.com/arpdf/Design/80c390_userguide.pdf

Message centers

Each CAN controller evaluates CAN bus activity and determines if an incoming message should be loaded into one of the 15 message centers. A message center is an internal SRAM segment that is used for storing incoming and outgoing CAN message frames. All CAN data is sent and received through one of these message centers.

The first 14 of the 15 message centers are programmable in either transmit or receive modes. All message centers support media arbitration fields for incoming message verification. Acceptance of an incoming message is determined by comparing the message ID field to an arbitration value assigned to each message center. If the bits match the arbitration value, then the message is placed in the message center. If the bits don't match or there is an error, then the message is simply discarded. Each message center also supports an optional bit-masking feature that restricts arbitration to specific bits. Each incoming message is tested to the arbitration value (and subject to the bit mask if enabled) in each message center in sequence, 1-15. The first message center that passes the test will receive the message. Message centers 1-14 use a common bit mask and unique arbitration values.

Each message center can establish direction, identification mode (standard or extended), data field size, data status, automatic remote frame request and acknowledgment, and perform masked or nonmasked identification acceptance testing. The first 14 message centers can support four different operations:

- Transmitting a data message
- Receiving a data message
- Transmitting a remote frame
- Receiving a remote framer request

The 15th message center is receive only. It has a buffered FIFO arrangement so that up to two messages can be received without being lost. The first message received by message center 15 is stored in the message center. If the next message is received before the previous message has been read by the microcontroller then the second message received is buffered. Once the first message received is read, then the second message is automatically moved to the message center. Message center 15 also has its own bit mask rather than using the global bit mask.

TINI CAN hardware

The two CAN controllers on the TINI stick are called CAN0 and CAN1. They are identical except they use different pins on the CPU chip.

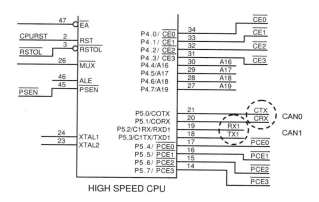

Figure 12-12: The CAN ports on the 80C390 CPU

CAN0

CAN0 uses pins 20 (CAN0 receive) and 21 (CAN0 transmit) of the 80C390 and pins 10 (CAN0 transmit) and 11 (CAN0 receive) of the TINI SIMM connector. The Dallas Semiconductor E10 and E20 socketboards have areas for the CAN transceiver, terminator and connector header.

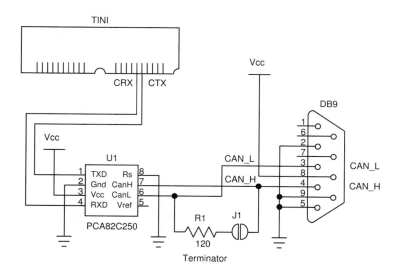

Figure 12-13: CAN0

You will need a CAN transceiver for each of CAN0 and CAN1 if you intend to use both CAN ports. Dallas Semiconductor specifies the Philips PCA82C250 CAN controller[5] interface. Texas Instruments offers the Unitrode UC5350 Can Transceiver[6] and has declared it "pin compatible with PCA82C250 and DeviceNet, SDS." The schematic (Figure 12-13) shows an optional CAN bus terminator (a 120Ω resistor) that can be included on the bus with a jumper.

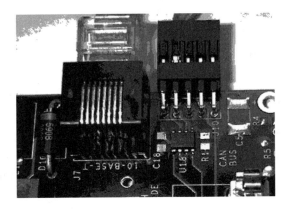

Figure 12-14:
CAN0 on socketboard

CAN1

CAN1 uses pins 18 (CAN1 transmit) and 19 (CAN1 receive) of the 80C390 and pins 14 (CAN1 transmit) and 15 (CAN1 receive) of the TINI SIMM connector. CAN1 shares the same CPU pins as serial1 and the 1-Wire port. To use CAN1 you will need to disable the 1-Wire port by tying the EN2480 pin on the SIMM (pin 26 on the 72 pin SIM) to ground.

Figure 12-15:
CAN1 on Protoboard

---

[5] PCA82C250 datasheet – http://www.semiconductors.philips.com/pip/PCA82C250U/N4
[6] UC5350 datasheet – http://focus.ti.com/docs/prod/folders/print/uc5350.html

The CAN classes

Dallas Semiconductor provides several classes in the TINI API for low-level configuration of the CAN controllers and access to CAN message frame data. The three classes of interest are: `com.dalsemi.comm.CanBus`, `com.dalsemi.comm.CanFrame` and `com.dalsemi.comm.CanBusException`. Shown here is a diagram of the `com.dalsemi.comm` package.

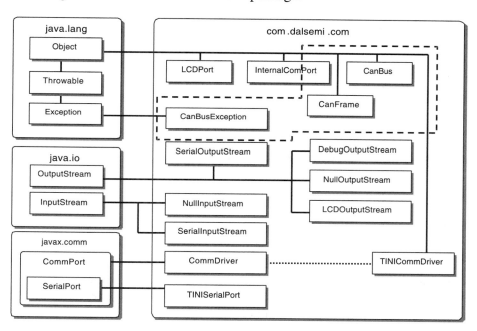

Figure 12-16: CAN API

CanBus

The `com.dalsemi.comm.CanBus` class provides methods for configuring the CAN controllers, sending and receiving CAN messages, and configuration of the CAN message centers. Some of the classes we will need to use:

CanFrame

Data frames are sent and received as `CanFrame` class. Instances of this class contain all of the components of a CAN frame (message ID and data) as well as an indication of the ID length (extended or standard), the data length (number of bytes), which message center received the frame and if this is a Remote Frame Request or a Data Frame.

CanBusException

All `CanBus` operations throw a `CanBusException`. Typically this is an error on the bus (like no Acknowledgement received) or an error in configuring the CanBus.

Here is a rough outline of a CAN program operation:

- Select and reset the CAN controller
- Set the CAN controller operating parameters
- Enable the CAN controller
- Configure the message centers
- Create frame objects
- Stuff data into frames
- Send frames
- Listen for incoming frames
- Read frame data and take action
- Loop
- Close CAN controller

Another word on bit timing

TINI allows for direct access to the CAN controller time segments. The *synchronization segment* is always 1 *time quantum* so this is not programmable; TINI combines the *propagation segment* and the *phase buffer 1 segment* and calls this TSEG1 (time segment 1) and leaves *phase buffer 2 segment* programmable as TSEG2. This means that the CAN baud rate is:

$$baud\ rate = \frac{18.432MHz}{baud\ rate\ prescaler \cdot (1 + TSEG1 + TSEG2)}$$

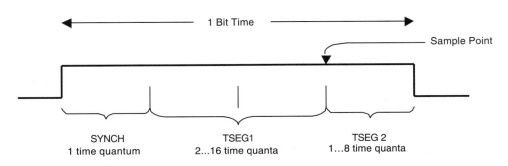

Figure 12-17: Bit timing

To set TINI to a particular baud rate (let's say 50 kbps) you would use the following methods:

```
setBaudRatePrescaler(41);
setTSEG1(5);
setTSEG2(3);
setSynchronizationJumpWidth(1);
```

Some of the convenient possible baud rates are shown in Table 12-3.

Table 12-3: TINI CAN Baud Rates

Baud Rate (bits per second)	Prescaler	Time Quanta μ(s)	TSEG1	TSEG2	Actual Baud Rate (bits per second)	Baud Rate Error (%)
10,000 bps	123	6.673	9	5	9,990	0.1%
20,000	71	3.851	5	7	19,969	0.15%
50,000	41	2.224	3	5	49,951	0.1%
125,000	7	0.3798	13	7	125,387	0.3%
250,000	4	0.217	9	8	256,000	2.4%
500,000	2	0.108	11	6	512,000	2.4%
1,000,000	1	0.0542	11	6	1,024,000	2.4%
			11	7	970,010	2.9%

Notice that at the common baud rates above 125,000 bits per second, the error is greater than 0.5%. This means that this will not work with standard CAN devices at these speeds. If you are only using TINI CAN devices (like multiple TINI modules talking using CAN) then you can use any baud rate that you like, including 512,000 bits per second. To get TINI CAN to run at standard speeds greater than 125,000 kbps, you will need to change the TINI crystal oscillator. 18.0 MHz is common and is also convenient for these speeds, as shown in Table 12-4.

Table 12-4: Modified TINI CAN baud rates

Baud Rate (bits per second)	Prescaler	Time Quanta μ(s)	TSEG1	TSEG2	Actual Baud Rate (bits per second)	Baud Rate Error (%)
125,000	8	0.444	11	6	125,000	0
500,000	4	0.222	11	6	250,000	0
1,000,000	1	0.055	11	6	1,000,000	0

Notice that an 18.0-MHz clock is very convenient for CAN timing. By keeping the sum of all the bit time segments equal to 18, then the actual baud rates are simply the inverse of the baudrate prescaler, which reduces the error from the clock to zero:

$$baud\ rate = \frac{18.432MHz}{baud\ rate\ prescaler \cdot (1+TSEG1+TSEG2)} = \frac{1MHz}{baud\ rate\ prescaler}$$

However, changing the TINI clock to a clock that is 2.3% slower will change other things in TINI that use the crystal oscillator, like the serial ports and the sleep times. You will need to compensate for this.

A CAN bus monitor

This is a very simple demonstration on communicating using a CAN bus. We simply connect two TINIs as CAN devices using a short length of twisted-pair wire. We will be running a simple CAN activity monitor on one TINI and a simple CAN message sender on the other. This is just to get our feet wet with the TINI CAN API. The program is well commented, so there is not much need to explain it line by line. But there are a few things that are worth noting:

- The CAN bus controller needs to be configured before the `enableController()` method is invoked. Any changes to the CAN controller (like timing parameters) after it has been enabled will be ignored.

- The CAN message ID global mask needs to be set (`set11BitGlobalIDMask` or `set28BitGlobalIDMask`) and enabled (`setMessageCenterMessageIDMaskEnable`) for each message center *or* each CAN message center you wish to use needs to be configured to use an arbitration ID (`set29BitMessageCenterArbitrationID` or `set11BitMessageCenterArbitrationID`).

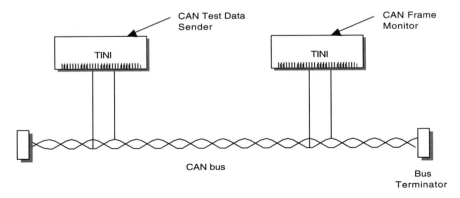

Figure 12-18: A TINI CAN network

Listing 12-1: CanBusViewer[7]

```java
import com.dalsemi.comm.*;
import com.dalsemi.system.*;

public class CanBusViewer {

    static CanBus myCanBus;
    static int KILL_ID=0x666;

    // utility method for making the output look nice
    static String justifytext( String str, int dir, int width ) {
        String padding = "                    ";
        if (dir<0) { // left
            str = str + padding.substring( 0,width );
        }
        if (dir>0) { // right
            str = padding.substring( 0,width-str.length() ) + str;
        }
        return( str.substring(0,width) );
    }


    static void main( String args[] )
    {
        System.out.println( "CAN Bus Viewer" );
        System.out.println( "Configuring CANBUS0 for receiving." );
        try {

            // Create a new CanBus object
            myCanBus = new CanBus( CanBus.CANBUS0 );

            // Set up the CANBUS speed (125 Kbps)
            myCanBus.setBaudRatePrescaler( 7 );
            myCanBus.setTSEG1( 13 );
            myCanBus.setTSEG2( 7 );
            myCanBus.setSynchronizationJumpWidth( 1 );

            myCanBus.enableController();

            System.out.println( "Enabling Message Center 1." );
            myCanBus.setMessageCenterRXMode( 1 );
            myCanBus.setMessageCenterRXMode( 2 );
            myCanBus.setMessageCenterRXMode( 3 );
            myCanBus.setMessageCenterRXMode( 4 );

            System.out.println( "Setting up filtering.");
```

---

[7] The ByteUtils class used in the program is provided in Appendix B. The class provides a number of methods that are handy for dealing with bytes. Here we use the toHexString() method.

```
                // filtering
                myCanBus.setMessageCenterMessageIDMaskEnable( 1, false );
                myCanBus.setMessageCenterMessageIDMaskEnable( 2, false );
                myCanBus.setMessageCenterMessageIDMaskEnable( 3, true );
                myCanBus.setMessageCenterMessageIDMaskEnable( 4, true );

                // Look for all addresses
                myCanBus.set11BitGlobalIDMask(0xFFFFFFFF);
                myCanBus.set29BitGlobalIDMask(0xFFFFFFFF);

                // need this so that MC1 will look for 29 bit addresses
                myCanBus.set11BitMessageCenterArbitrationID( 1, 0x00 );
                myCanBus.set11BitMessageCenterArbitrationID( 2, 0x222 );
                myCanBus.set29BitMessageCenterArbitrationID( 3, 0x01432520 );
                myCanBus.set11BitMessageCenterArbitrationID( 4, 0x00 );

                // Enable Message Centers
                myCanBus.enableMessageCenter( 1 );
                myCanBus.enableMessageCenter( 2 );
                myCanBus.enableMessageCenter( 3 );
                myCanBus.enableMessageCenter( 4 );

        }
        catch( Exception e ) {
            System.out.println( e );
        }

        System.out.println( "Monitoring CANBUS0" );
        CanFrame myFrame = new CanFrame();

        byte[] data = new byte[8];
        boolean done=false;              // loop till done
        int loops=0;                     // loops done so far
        int maxloops=20;                 // max loops allowed

        while( !done) {
            loops++;

            try {
                myCanBus.receive( myFrame );
            }
            catch (Exception e) {
                System.out.println( e );
            }

            if (myFrame.getID()==0) {
                loops--;
                continue;
            }

            System.out.print( "Frame " );
            System.out.print( justifytext( Integer.toString(loops)+"," , 1, 3 ) );
```

```
                System.out.print( " ID 0x" );
                System.out.print(
                        justifytext(Integer.toHexString(myFrame.getID())+",",-1,8));
                if (myFrame.getExtendedID()) {
                    System.out.print( " extended" );
                } else {
                    System.out.print( " standard" );
                }
                System.out.print( ", MC " + myFrame.getMessageCenter() );
                if (myFrame.getRemoteFrameRequest() ) {
                    System.out.print( ", Remote Frame Request" );
                }
                System.out.print( " " );

                if (myFrame.getID()==KILL_ID) {
                    System.out.print( ", kill frame" );
                    done=true;
                }
                else {
                    System.out.print( ", " + myFrame.getLength() );
                    System.out.print( " bytes: " );
                    System.out.print( ByteUtils.toHexString( myFrame.getData(),
                                        0, myFrame.getLength(), ' ' ));
                }

                System.out.println( );

                if (loops>=maxloops) done=true;
            }

            try {
                myCanBus.close();
            }
            catch( Exception e ) {
                System.out.println( "Error in closing..." );
                System.out.println( e );
            }

            System.exit(0);
        }
}
```

You can compile and run `CanBusViewer.tini` on the TINI controller that will be the receiver for our simple CAN test (it doesn't matter which of the two TINIs).

Notice how to set the CAN speed for this device:

```
myCanBus.setBaudRatePrescaler( 7 );
myCanBus.setTSEG1( 13 );
myCanBus.setTSEG2( 7 );
myCanBus.setSynchronizationJumpWidth( 1 );
```

The device that is sending frames will need to use the same settings. To change the speed at which your CAN bus monitor (and any TINI CAN device) communicates, you will need to set these values as a set. Refer to Table 12-3 for different baud rates (the Synchronization Jump Width will be 1 for all of these speeds). After the baud rate is set we can enable the CAN controller:

```
myCanBus.enableController();
```

We enable the global masks to let the CAN processor accept all 11-bit and all 29-bit message IDs:

```
myCanBus.set11BitGlobalIDMask(0xFFFF);
myCanBus.set29BitGlobalIDMask(0xFFFFFFFF);
```

We then configure four message centers for receiving frames. First, each is set in the receive (RX) mode. Then different filters are configured. Finally, each message center is enabled. All changes in the arbitration ID and mask enable must be done when the message center is not enabled.

Here message center 1 is configured so that an incoming frame ID must be an 11-bit ID frame and match an arbitration ID of 0x00. Message masking is disabled so the frame ID must match the arbitration ID.

```
myCanBus.setMessageCenterRXMode( 1 );
myCanBus.setMessageCenterMessageIDMaskEnable( 1, false );
myCanBus.set11BitMessageCenterArbitrationID( 1, 0x00 );
myCanBus.enableMessageCenter( 1 );
```

Here message center 2 is configured so that an incoming frame ID must be an 11-bit ID frame and match an arbitration ID 0x22.

```
myCanBus.setMessageCenterRXMode( 2 );
myCanBus.setMessageCenterMessageIDMaskEnable( 2, false );
myCanBus.set11BitMessageCenterArbitrationID( 2, 0x222 );
myCanBus.enableMessageCenter( 2 );
```

Here message center 3 is configured so that an incoming frame ID must be a 29-bit ID frame and match the arbitration ID of 0x01432520. But, since masking is enabled and the global mask is set to 0xFFFFFFFF (match all bits), then this message center will receive all 29-bit ID frames (regardless of the arbitration ID).

```
myCanBus.setMessageCenterRXMode( 3 );
myCanBus.setMessageCenterMessageIDMaskEnable( 3, true );
myCanBus.set29BitMessageCenterArbitrationID( 3, 0x01432520 );
myCanBus.enableMessageCenter( 3 );
```

Here message center 4 is configured so that an incoming frame ID must be an 11-bit ID frame and match the arbitration ID of 0x000. But, since masking is enabled and the global mask is set to 0x0FFF (match all bits), then this message center will receive all 29-bit ID frames (regardless of the arbitration ID).

```
myCanBus.setMessageCenterRXMode( 4 );
myCanBus.setMessageCenterMessageIDMaskEnable( 4, true );
myCanBus.set11BitMessageCenterArbitrationID( 4, 0x00 );
myCanBus.enableMessageCenter( 4 );
```

Incoming frames are processed in a loop. Each frame is received with:

```
myCanBus.receive( myFrame );
```

We then take apart the frame using various methods in the `CanFrame` class and display this information so we can see what is going on.

Compile CanBusViewer.java:

```
C:\> cd src
C:\> javac -bootclasspath %TINI_HOME%\bin\tiniclasses.jar -d ..\bin
CanBusViewer.java
C:\> cd ..
C:\> java -classpath %TINI_HOME%\bin\tini.jar;. BuildDependency
     -p %TINI_HOME%\bin\owapi_dependencies_TINI.jar
     -f bin
     -x %TINI_HOME%\bin\owapi_dep.txt
     -o bin\CanBusViewer.tini
     -d %TINI_HOME%\bin\tini.db
```

Once this program is up and running on TINI, then next we need to send data out to the CAN bus. We will use the next simple program to do just that. The data sent is nothing meaningful (except that the first byte indicates the number of the frame, so we can see which frames made it to the CAN monitor program), and we use a number of different methods for sending CAN frames so we can see how they work and what the differences are.

The program is rather obvious in what it does, but there are a few things here we should also note.

- We try 10 methods or variations on methods from the `com.dalsemi.comm.CanBus` class to send frames on the CAN bus. Some will be successful and some will not. You should carefully examine the program and the program output so that you see which CAN frames were generated with which methods.

- Each test is in its own try/catch block so we can see the error messages from each attempt and all 10 tests will be executed even if previous methods throw an exception.

Listing 12-2: CanSendTest

```
import com.dalsemi.comm.*;
import com.dalsemi.system.*;
```

```
public class CanSendTest {

    // We store our CAN messages is the data array
    static CanBus myCanBus;
    static CanFrame myFrame1 = new CanFrame();
    static int delay = 100;

    static void main( String args[] )
    {
        System.out.println( "CAN SendTest" );
        try {
            // Create a new CanBus object
            myCanBus = new CanBus( CanBus.CANBUS0 );

            // Set up the CANBUS speed (125 Kbps)
            myCanBus.setBaudRatePrescaler( 7 );
            myCanBus.setTSEG1( 13 );
            myCanBus.setTSEG2( 7 );
            myCanBus.setSynchronizationJumpWidth( 1 );
            myCanBus.setTransmitQueueLimit(1);
            myCanBus.enableController();

            // Set up messagecenter 1
            myCanBus.setMessageCenterTXMode( 1 );
            myCanBus.enableMessageCenter( 1 );
        }
        catch( Exception e ) {
            System.out.println( e );
        }

        // just some data for a frame to send
        byte[] data= { 0x00,0x03,0x01,0x04,0x01,0x05,0x09,0x02 };

        try {
            System.out.println( " 1: sendDataFrame, standard, ID 0x0432" );
            data[0] = (byte) 0x01;
            myCanBus.sendDataFrame( 0x0432, false, data );
        }
        catch( Exception e ) { System.out.println( e ); }
        TINIOS.sleepProcess( delay );

        try {
            System.out.println( " 2: sendDataFrame, extended, ID 0x01432520" );
            data[0] = (byte) 0x02;
            myCanBus.sendDataFrame( 0x01432520, true, data );
        }
        catch( Exception e ) { System.out.println( e ); }
        TINIOS.sleepProcess( delay );
```

```
try {
    System.out.println( " 3: sendFrame, standard, ID 0x0543" );
    data[0] = (byte) 0x03;
    myFrame1.setData( data );
    myFrame1.setLength( 8 );
    myFrame1.setID( 0x0543 );
    myFrame1.setMessageCenter( 1 );
    myFrame1.setRemoteFrameRequest( false );
    myFrame1.setExtendedID( false );
    myCanBus.sendFrame( myFrame1 );
}
catch( Exception e ) { System.out.println( e ); }
TINIOS.sleepProcess( delay );

try {
    System.out.println( " 4: sendFrame, standard, fewer bytes, ID 0x0543" );
    data[0] = (byte) 0x04;
    myFrame1.setData( data );
    myFrame1.setLength( 4 );
    myCanBus.sendFrame( myFrame1 );
}
catch( Exception e ) { System.out.println( e ); }
TINIOS.sleepProcess( delay );

try {
    System.out.println( " 5: sendFrame, extended, ID 0x01543210" );
    data[0] = (byte) 0x05;
    myFrame1.setData( data );
    myFrame1.setLength( 8 );
    myFrame1.setID( 0x01543210 );
    myFrame1.setExtendedID( true );
    myCanBus.sendFrame( myFrame1 );
}
catch( Exception e ) { System.out.println( e ); }
TINIOS.sleepProcess( delay );

try {
    System.out.println( " 6: sendRemoteFrameRequest, standard, ID 0x123" );
    data[0] = (byte) 0x06;
    myCanBus.sendRemoteFrameRequest( 0x0123, false, data );
}
catch( Exception e ) { System.out.println( e ); }
TINIOS.sleepProcess( delay );

try {
    System.out.println( " 7: sendFrame, RTR, standard, ID 0x0543" );
    data[0] = (byte) 0x07;
    myFrame1.setData( data );
    myFrame1.setLength( 8 );
    myFrame1.setID( 0x0543 );
```

```
                myFrame1.setMessageCenter( 1 );
                myFrame1.setRemoteFrameRequest( true );
                myFrame1.setExtendedID( false );
                myCanBus.sendFrame( myFrame1 );
        }
        catch( Exception e ) { System.out.println( e ); }
        TINIOS.sleepProcess( delay );

        try {
                System.out.println( " 8: sendDataFrame, standard, ID 0x0432" );
                data[0] = (byte) 0x08;
                myCanBus.sendDataFrame( 0x0432, false, data );
        }
        catch( Exception e ) { System.out.println( e ); }
        TINIOS.sleepProcess( delay );

        try {
                System.out.println( " 9: autoAnswerRemoteFrameRequest,
                            standard, ID 0x0111" );
                data[0] = (byte) 0x09;
                myCanBus.autoAnswerRemoteFrameRequest( 1, 0x0111, data );
        }
        catch( Exception e ) { System.out.println( e ); }
        TINIOS.sleepProcess( delay );

        try {
                System.out.println( "10: sendDataFrame, standard, ID 0x0222" );
                data[0] = (byte) 0x10;
                myCanBus.sendDataFrame( 0x0222, false, data );
        }
        catch( Exception e ) { System.out.println( e ); }
        TINIOS.sleepProcess( delay );


        try {
                myCanBus.close();
        }
        catch( Exception e ) { System.out.println( e ); }

        System.exit(0);
    }

}
```

Compile this program:

```
C:\> cd src
C:\> javac -bootclasspath %TINI_HOME%\bin\tiniclasses.jar -d ..\bin
CanSendTest.java
C:\> cd ..
```

```
C:\> java -classpath %TINI_HOME%\bin\tini.jar;. BuildDependency
     -p %TINI_HOME%\bin\owapi_dependencies_TINI.jar
     -f bin
     -x %TINI_HOME%\bin\owapi_dep.txt
     -o bin\CanSendTest.tini
     -d %TINI_HOME%\bin\tini.db
```

FTP `CanSendTest.tini` to your other TINI in our simple CAN network and run it. Examine the output of these two programs (remember to start running `CanBusViewer.tini` before you start running `CanSendTest.tini` or you might miss a few frames). In this case there are a few differences between the versions of the TINI API.

This is the output of CanSendTest running TINI API 1.02d

```
TINI1 /> java CanSendTest.tini
CAN SendTest
 1: sendDataFrame, standard, ID 0x0432
 2: sendDataFrame, extended, ID 0x01432520
 3: sendFrame, standard, ID 0x0543
 4: sendFrame, standard, fewer bytes, ID 0x0543
 5: sendFrame, extended, ID 0x01543210
 6: sendRemoteFrameRequest, standard, ID 0x123
    com.dalsemi.comm.CanBusException: failed in send -920933632
 7: sendFrame, RTR, standard, ID 0x0543
    com.dalsemi.comm.CanBusException: failed in send -920933888
 8: sendDataFrame, standard, ID 0x0432
 9: autoAnswerRemoteFrameRequest, standard, ID 0x0111
    com.dalsemi.comm.CanBusException: Don't use
    CanBus:autoAnswerRemoteFrameRequest()
10: sendDataFrame, standard, ID 0x0222
```

Note at this point that we got an exception when using the following methods:

```
myCanBus.autoAnswerRemoteFrameRequest( 1, 0x0111, data );

myCanBus.sendRemoteFrameRequest( 0x0123, false, data );

myFrame1.setRemoteFrameRequest( true );
myCanBus.sendFrame( myFrame1 );
```

Apparently these methods (anything to do with Remove Frame Requests) have not been implemented in this version of the API.

Now let's look at what the CanBusViewer.tini program received:

```
TINI2 /> java CanBusViewer.tini
CAN Bus Viewer
Configuring CANBUS0 for receiving.
Enabling Message Center 1.
Setting up filtering.
```

```
Monitoring CANBUS0
Frame  1, ID 0x432,     standard, MC 4 , 8 bytes: 01 03 01 04 01 05 09 02
Frame  2, ID 0x1432520, extended, MC 3 , 8 bytes: 02 03 01 04 01 05 09 02
Frame  3, ID 0x543,     standard, MC 4 , 8 bytes: 03 03 01 04 01 05 09 02
Frame  4, ID 0x543,     standard, MC 4 , 4 bytes: 04 03 01 04
Frame  5, ID 0x1543210, extended, MC 3 , 8 bytes: 05 03 01 04 01 05 09 02
Frame  6, ID 0x432,     standard, MC 4 , 8 bytes: 08 03 01 04 01 05 09 02
Frame  7, ID 0x222,     standard, MC 2 , 8 bytes: 10 03 01 04 01 05 09 02
```

Isn't that interesting! Our CAN test program sent 10 frames but our CAN monitor only received 7 CAN frames. This is where the first byte in the data field comes in handy. That byte corresponds to the number of the frame that was sent so we can see which methods worked and which didn't. To get the most benefit from this example, you should examine the output of the CanSenTest program and compare this with the output of the CanBusViewer program. Then go and find the section of code that generated each frame in the CanSendTest program. Each frame was sent with a slightly different method or different frame ID, so you can see how they appear on the CAN bus and how the message centers filter the frames.

It is also worth noting two errors you are likely to see and what they mean (particularly if you are NOT sending extended ID message frames and you are NOT sending remote frame requests).

- If the receiver is not listening (as in there are no receivers) or the CAN bus is not connected properly, you will get an exception indicating there was NO_ACKNOWLEDGEMENT

  ```
  com.dalsemi.comm.CanBusException: Send Failed: No Ack
  ```

- If the CAN transceiver is not connected properly to TINI or is not powered then you will see an exception indicating that the CAN controller noticed that the CAN bus was in a state other than what it expected:

  ```
  com.dalsemi.comm.CanBusException: Send Failed: Bit Zero
  ```

Another CAN example

In this example, we will send real (meaningful) data across the CAN bus. We will be connecting 1-Wire devices (a temp sensor and a switch) to each TINI so we need to use CAN0 on both modules (recall that CAN1 uses the same CPU and SIMM pins as the 1-Wire bus so we can't access 1-Wire and CAN1 at the same time).

See Figure 12-19. What we will do is connect a 1-Wire thermometer (DS1820) to one TINI and send that temperature in a CAN message to another TINI. On that other TINI we will examine the temperature, compare it to some limit value and turn on or off a 1-Wire switch (a DS2406) that controls some external device (in this case an LED, but it could be all sorts of meaningful things).

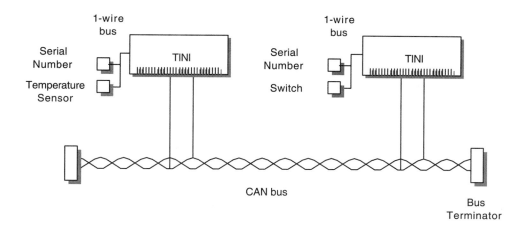

Figure 12-19: TINI CAN sensor and actuator

A common circuit was used for both TINIs, containing a DS2401 (silicon serial number), a DS1820 (thermometer) and a DS2406 (switch) connected to an LED. This is the same board that was used in the 1-Wire chapter. By using the same board on both TINIs we could send data either direction.

Figure 12-20: TINI CAN Sensor and Actuator 1-Wire devices

A schematic for this is shown below.

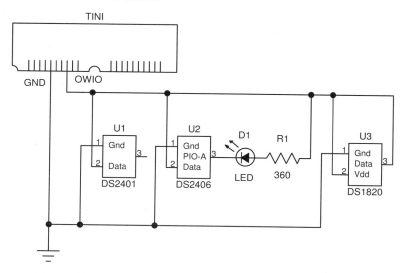

Figure 12-21: TINI CAN Sensor and Actuator schematic

The original thought behind this was that we could send temperature frames from TINI1 to TINI2 and we would use the serial numbers on each TINI as a means of identification using Remote Frame Requests. Lacking a functioning API for successful Remote Frame Requests, we abandon that idea but continued on with sending temperature in a data frame.

Listed below are both the sending (CanTempSensor) and receiving (CanTempControl) programs. They are very similar to the previous two programs with the addition of the 1-Wire classes Switch and Thermometer that were introduced in Chapter 10 and a helper library called ByteUtils[8] for converting various data types to byte arrays and back again so we can send them over a CAN network in data frames.

Listing 12-3: CanTempSensor

```
import com.dalsemi.comm.*;
import com.dalsemi.system.*;

public class CanTempSensor {

    static CanBus myCanBus;
    static boolean gotone = false;
```

---

[8] The ByteUtils class used in the program is provided in Appendix B, on the CD-ROM.

```
static CanFrame myFrame = new CanFrame();
static CanFrame myKillFrame = new CanFrame();

static int TEMP_ID    = 0x432;
static int SWITCH_ID  = 0x123;
static int KILL_ID    = 0x666;

static byte[] buffer = { 0,0,0,0,0,0,0,0 };

static TemperatureFrame myTempFrame;
static SerialNumberFrame mySerialNumberFrame;

static void main( String args[] )
{
    System.out.println( "CanTempSensor" );

    try {
        // Create a new CanBus object
        myCanBus = new CanBus( CanBus.CANBUS0 );
        myCanBus.resetController();

        // Set up the CANBUS speed (125 Kbps)
        myCanBus.setBaudRatePrescaler( 7 );
        myCanBus.setTSEG1( 13 );
        myCanBus.setTSEG2( 7 );
        myCanBus.setSynchronizationJumpWidth( 1 );

        // Connect the CabBus controller to the CanBus
        myCanBus.enableController();

        // Set up messagecenter 1
        //myCanBus.setMessageCenterRXMode( 1 );
        myCanBus.setMessageCenterTXMode( 10 );

        //  No filtering
        //myCanBus.setMessageCenterMessageIDMaskEnable( 1, true );
        //myCanBus.setMessageCenterMessageIDMaskEnable( 10, true );
        // Look for all addresses
        myCanBus.set11BitGlobalIDMask(0xFFFFFFFF);

        //Enable the MC
        //myCanBus.enableMessageCenter( 1 );
        myCanBus.enableMessageCenter( 10 );

    }
    catch( Exception e ) {
        System.out.println( "Error in configuring CANBus" );
        System.out.println( e );
    }
```

```
System.out.println( "Finding 1-wire devices..." );

// Configure a TemperatureFrame using a DS 1820 temp sensor
myTempFrame = new TemperatureFrame( TEMP_ID );
System.out.println( "Temp sensor: " + myTempFrame.temperature.ROM_ID );

// Snooze for 5 secs to give the receiver time to get started
TINIOS.sleepProcess( 3000 );

// Send 10 frames on the canbus

for( int i=0; i<10; i++ ){
    System.out.print( "Sending frame " + i + ": " );

    // read temp and stuff into frame
    myTempFrame.updateTemperature();
    System.out.println( myTempFrame.temperature.degC + " C");

    try {
        // Send the frame out to the bus
        //myCanBus.sendFrame( myTempFrame );
        myCanBus.sendDataFrame( TEMP_ID, false, myTempFrame.data );

    }
    catch (Exception e) { System.out.println( e ); }

    TINIOS.sleepProcess( 2000 );

}

try {
    // Send out a kill frame
    System.out.println( "Sending Kill Frame" );
    myKillFrame.setID( KILL_ID );
    myCanBus.sendFrame( myKillFrame );

    myCanBus.close();
}
catch( Exception e ) { System.out.println( e ); }

System.exit(0);
    }

}
```

Compile this:

```
C:\> cd src
C:\> javac -bootclasspath %TINI_HOME%\bin\tiniclasses.jar -d ..\bin
CanTempSensor.java
```

```
C:\> cd ..
C:\> java -classpath %TINI_HOME%\bin\tini.jar;. BuildDependency
     -p %TINI_HOME%\bin\owapi_dependencies_TINI.jar
     -f bin
     -x %TINI_HOME%\bin\owapi_dep.txt
     -o bin\CanTempSensor.tini
     -d %TINI_HOME%\bin\tini.db
```

Listing 12-4: CanTempMonitor

```java
import com.dalsemi.comm.*;
import com.dalsemi.system.*;

public class CanTempControl {

    static CanBus myCanBus;
    static CanFrame myFrame = new CanFrame();
    static CanFrame myKillFrame = new CanFrame();

    static int TEMP_ID    = 0x432;
    static int SWITCH_ID  = 0x123;
    static int KILL_ID    = 0x666;

    static byte[] buffer = { 0,0,0,0,0,0,0,0 };

    static TemperatureFrame myTempFrame;
    static SerialNumberFrame mySerialNumberFrame;

    static void main( String args[] )
    {
        System.out.println( "CanTempControl" );

        try {
            // Create a new CanBus object
            myCanBus = new CanBus( CanBus.CANBUS0 );

            // Set up the CANBUS speed (125 Kbps)
            myCanBus.setBaudRatePrescaler( 7 );
            myCanBus.setTSEG1( 13 );
            myCanBus.setTSEG2( 7 );
            myCanBus.setSynchronizationJumpWidth( 1 );

            // Connect the CabBus controller to the CanBus
            myCanBus.enableController();

            // Set up messagecenter 1
            myCanBus.setMessageCenterRXMode( 1 );
            //myCanBus.setMessageCenterTXMode( 10 );
```

```
        //   No filtering
        myCanBus.setMessageCenterMessageIDMaskEnable( 1, true );

        // Look for all addresses
        myCanBus.set11BitGlobalIDMask(0xFFFFFFFF);

        //Enable the MC
        myCanBus.enableMessageCenter( 1 );

}
catch( Exception e ) {
    System.out.println( "Error in configuring CANBus" );
    System.out.println( e );
}

System.out.println( "Finding 1-wire devices..." );

// Configure a TemperatureFrame using a DS 1820 temp sensor
Switch mySwitch = new Switch();
System.out.println( "Switch:         " + mySwitch.ROM_ID );
mySwitch.turnOff();

myTempFrame = new TemperatureFrame();

// Send 10 frames on the canbus
System.out.println( "Listening..." );

boolean done=false;
int n=0;
while(done==false){

    try {
        // Check for incomming frames
        myCanBus.receive(myFrame);
    }
    catch (Exception e) { System.out.println( e ); }

        if (myFrame.getID()==TEMP_ID) {
            System.out.print( "Received frame " + n++ + ": " );
            myTempFrame.setData( myFrame.getData() );
            System.out.print( myTempFrame.getTemperature() +
                        " deg C" );
            if ( myTempFrame.getTemperature()>= 30.0 ) {
                mySwitch.turnOn();
                System.out.print( "  switch ON" );
            }
            else {
                mySwitch.turnOff();
            }
            System.out.println();
```

```
                } else
                if (myFrame.getID()==KILL_ID) {
                    System.out.println( "Received a KillFrame, exiting..." );
                    done = true;
                }

            TINIOS.sleepProcess( 2000 );

        }

        try {
            myCanBus.close();
            mySwitch.turnOff();
        }
        catch (Exception e) { System.out.println( e ); }

        System.exit(0);
    }


}
```

Compile this:

```
C:\> cd src
C:\> javac -bootclasspath %TINI_HOME%\bin\tiniclasses.jar
    -d ..\bin CanTempControl.java
C:\> cd ..
C:\> java -classpath %TINI_HOME%\bin\tini.jar;. BuildDependency
    -p %TINI_HOME%\bin\owapi_dependencies_TINI.jar
    -f bin
    -x %TINI_HOME%\bin\owapi_dep.txt
    -o bin\CanTempControl.tini
    -d %TINI_HOME%\bin\tini.db
```

Notice that we have also defined a message frame called a KillFrame. This is an empty data frame that has the message ID of 0x666. The CanTempSensor sends this frame when it is done. When the CanTempControl program, sees this frame, it knows to perform an orderly exit.

FTP these two programs to your TINIs in your CAN network. Run the CanTempControl.tini first and then start CanTempSensor.tini on the other TINI. The output of each is shown below.

```
TINI1 /> java CanTempSensor.tini
CanTempSensor
Finding 1-wire devices...
Temp sensor:    700000004B8F1010
Sending frame 0: 27.5 C
Sending frame 1: 27.5 C
Sending frame 2: 29.0 C
Sending frame 3: 31.0 C
```

```
Sending frame 4: 31.5 C
Sending frame 5: 29.5 C
Sending frame 6: 28.5 C
Sending frame 7: 29.5 C
Sending frame 8: 30.5 C
Sending frame 9: 30.0 C
Sending Kill Frame

TINI2 /> java CanTempControl.tini
CanTempControl
Finding 1-wire devices...
Switch:         CB00000017006112
Listening...
Received frame 0: 27.5 deg C
Received frame 1: 27.5 deg C
Received frame 2: 29.0 deg C
Received frame 3: 31.0 deg C    switch ON
Received frame 4: 31.5 deg C    switch ON
Received frame 5: 29.5 deg C
Received frame 6: 28.5 deg C
Received frame 7: 29.5 deg C
Received frame 8: 30.5 deg C    switch ON
Received frame 9: 30.0 deg C    switch ON
Received a KillFrame, exiting...
```

You can also watch the LED on the `CanTempControl` end and see that it does indeed turn on and off depending on the value of the temperature received. We added a 2-second delay between the sent data frames so there is enough time to actually cause a temperature change.

Summary

In this chapter we have discussed the details of the Controller Area Network. We have seen how to configure TINI to talk and listen to CAN data frames and we have implemented a CAN sensor device (`CanTempSensor`) and a CAN actuator (`CanTempControl`). To be compatible with most available CAN sensors, you will need to implement some of the higher-layer protocol that these devices use.

References

1. *A list of devices that use CAN,*
   http://www.omegas.co.uk/CAN/devices.htm

2. *MicroCAN Project,*
   http://www.emicros.com/microcan/

3. *CAN links,*
   http://www.chipcenter.com/circuitcellar/september99/C99r7.htm

4. *CAN monitor*,
   http://www.precisielandbouw.nl/project/tini/CanMonitor.html

5. *CAN Products List*,
   http://www.synergetic.com/catalog/can/

6. *Caraca*,
   http://caraca.sourceforge.net/

7. *CAN Specification*,
   http://www.infineon.com/us/micro/can/can2spec.pdf

8. *CAN Protocol Introduction*,
   http://www.infineon.com/cmc_upload/migrated_files/document_files/
   Application_Notes/CANPRES.pdf

9. *Controller Area Network Basics*,
   http://www.microchip.com/Download/appnote/category/analog/can/
   00713a.pdf

10. *On-line Training Class – Introduction to CAN, Controller Area Network*,
    http://www.esacademy.com/faq/classes/CANIntro/

11. *Home Automation Posts Concerning CAN*,
    http://ha.ro.nu/hypermail/index.html#51

12. *The CAN Protocol*,
    http://www.kvaser.com/can/protocol/index.htm

13. *CAN-based Higher Layer Protocols and Profiles*,
    http://www.ixxat.de/deutsch/knowhow/artikel/pdf/icc97.pdf

14. *Motorola Semiconductor Application Note, AN1798*
    CAN Bit Timing Requirements,
    http://e-www.motorola.com/brdata/PDFDB/docs/AN1798.pdf

## CHAPTER 13

Connecting TINI to an IP Network

In this chapter, we will examine various aspects of TCP/IP networking with TINI, with a special emphasis on using a modem to connect TINI to the Internet via PPP. We'll begin with a very basic discussion on how to construct an IP network consisting of a TINI and a PC, then work our way up to using TINI with a modem. We will do examples in which a TINI dials out to an ISP, and behaves as a PPP client on the Internet, as well as examples in which we use a PC to dial into a TINI, with the TINI acting as a PPP server. Throughout this chapter, we will be assuming that the primary Java application running on TINI is slush. If you aren't familiar with basic networking concepts, now would be a good time to review Chapter 2. Reviewing the discussion of RS232 in Chapter 9 may also be helpful.

The ipconfig Command

The first step in putting a TINI stick on an IP network is to configure it with an IP address. The IP address, and a variety of other network parameters, are set up using the slush command, *ipconfig*. Let's take a look at the command, and its command line parameters.

The command is issued: `ipconfig <options>` where the options are as follows.

`-a XX.XX.XX.XX`

Sets the IP address of your TINI stick. You must use the **-a** option with the **-m** option, which sets the subnet mask. For example,

        `ipconfig -a 192.168.0.5 -m 255.255.255.0`

`-n domain_name`

Allows you to set the domain name of the network on which this stick will reside, for example,

```
ipconfig -n stick.net.
```

-m XX.XX.XX.XX

Sets the subnet mask. This must be used with the -a option, for example,

```
ipconfig -a 192.168.0.5 -m 255.255.255.0
```

-g XX.XX.XX.XX

Sets the IP address of the gateway on your TINI network. A gateway, in this context, is a machine with two network interfaces capable of performing IP forwarding or routing between the two interfaces. For example, one network interface on the gateway could be connected to a local network (containing several TINI sticks) and the other could be attached to the Internet. The gateway, in this case, would forward data from your local TINI network to the Internet. Data destined for an address not on the local network is sent to the gateway, which is sent out to the Internet. The gateway IP address must be on the same subnet as the TINI's IP address. For instance, if we stick with the example above, and our TINI has an IP address of 192.168.0.5 with a subnet mask of 255.255.255.0, our gateway must be on the 192.168.0.X subnet. Thus, we could make our gateway, 192.168.0.3

```
ipconfig -g 192.168.0.3
```

This tells our stick that, on its local network, the machine at 192.168.0.3 is the device acting as gateway.

-p XX.XX.XX.XX

Sets the IP address of the primary dynamic name service (DNS) that your TINI will use. The DNS translates textual domain names into IP addresses. For instance, if you attempt to run the command *ftp dalsemi.com* on TINI, there must be a *DNS query* performed that will translate dalsemi.com into an IP address.

```
ipconfig -p 192.168.20.80
```

This tells our stick that the machine at 192.168.20.80 is its primary DNS server. Note that it could only *get* to this machine if there were a gateway on the local network that provided access to the network on which 192.168.20.80 resides.

-s XX.XX.XX.XX

Sets the IP address of the secondary dynamic name system (DNS) that your TINI will use. If the primary DNS does not respond to a query, the secondary DNS will be queried.

```
ipconfig -p 192.168.20.88
```

-t `dns_timeout`

Sets the timeout, in milliseconds, for DNS queries. A value of 5000 translates into 5 seconds, and establishes that TINI will wait 5 seconds after making a DNS query before timing out, and giving up in the query. A value of 0 establishes a *backoff and retry* protocol, that makes a second attempt after 2 seconds, then waits 4 seconds and tries again, then waits 8 seconds and tries again, then tries after 16 more seconds, before it gives up. For example,

```
ipconfig -t 5000
```

-d

Tells TINI to use dynamic host configuration protocol (DHCP) to obtain a temporary, server assigned, IP address.

```
ipconfig -d
```

-r

Tells TINI to release the temporary, server assigned, IP address obtained via dynamic host configuration protocol, and the -d option.

```
ipconfig -r
```

-x

Shows all of the current IP settings.

```
ipconfig -x
```

-h `XX.XX.XX.XX`

Sets the IP address of the mail host for use with the *sendmail* slush command. This must be an address on the local network, or an address that can be reached via a gateway on the network. For example,

```
ipconfig -h 192.168.0.12
```

-c

Commits the current network settings to flash memory. The network settings are stored in the heap, which is in RAM. The RAM is nonvolatile, so your settings are still stored on power down. However, there are times when you may want to clear the heap, which can clear your network settings. Committing them to flash memory allows you clear the heap and have TINI restore your settings on reboot. If, upon reboot, you have settings in flash and on the heap that are different, the settings in flash are written over those in the heap. You can only use the -c option once, and then you have to erase bank 7 of the flash before you can use it again. That is, once you've written settings to the flash, they have to be erased before you can write different settings. You do this by reloading `tini.tbin` and `slush.tbin`.

```
ipconfig -C
```

-D

De-commits the settings previously committed to flash by the -c option. If you commit your settings to flash, they will be restored at boot time, overwriting whatever settings you may have previously had on the heap. If you no longer want those settings restored at boot time, you use the -D option. After using -D, your settings will stored on the heap, and the values stored in flash will be ignored. Any previously committed data in flash remains there, so you still have to erase the settings in flash if you want to use the -c option again.

```
ipconfig -D
```

-f

Don't prompt for confirmation. Many of the ipconfig options will cause the FTP and Telnet servers to be shut down and restarted. In these cases, there will be a prompt asking you if this is OK. The -f option suppresses this prompt.

You must have admin privileges to use the ipconfig command, and as noted above, it will often shut down the FTP and Telnet servers and restart them.

Other relevant network commands

In addition to the ipconfig command, there are a variety of other slush commands that are network related that we will make use of in this chapter. These are netstat, downserver, startserver, arp, hostname, nslookup, ping, ppp, sendmail, and ftp. Refer to Table 7-4 for more details on these commands.

A simple TINI network

Let's take what we've learned about the ipconfig command and construct a simple TINI network. We will connect a TINI stick to a PC running Windows 98[1], via Ethernet.

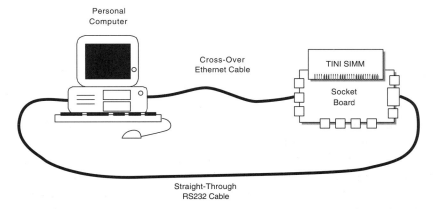

Figure 13-1: A simple TINI IP network

---

[1] Windows, Windows 98, Windows 2000, Windows XP, and Windows NT are registered trademarks of Microsoft Corp.

In the network shown above, we have several elements.

1. A TINI stick, in a socketboard that provides an RJ45 connector to the Ethernet port, an RS232 DB-9 connector to serial0, and a DTR jumper that is closed.

2. A serial cable, DB9 female on one end and male on the other. This cable must be a straight-through cable, as we're connecting a DCE to a DTE.

3. An Ethernet cable. This cable must be a crossover cable.

4. A PC. In this example, we're going to be running Windows 98. The PC could be running Linux, Windows 2000, NT, etc. The PC must have an Ethernet network interface card.

We'll assume that JavaKit has been installed on the PC. The next thing to do with the PC is to assign an IP address to its Ethernet interface. We'll use 192.168.0.2, with a netmask of 255.255.255.0. To set this up on Windows 98, go to the *Control Panel*, click on *Network*.

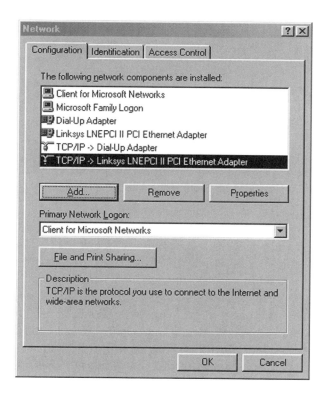

Figure 13-2:
Configuring the network settings on your PC dial-up adapter

In our specific case, we have a Linksys[2] LNEPCI II PCI Ethernet Adapter. You might have a different product, but that doesn't matter. It's listed twice under the installed components. Select the one that references TCP/IP, as shown (by left clicking), and then left click on *Properties*. Left click on the IP address tab. Fill in the data as shown.

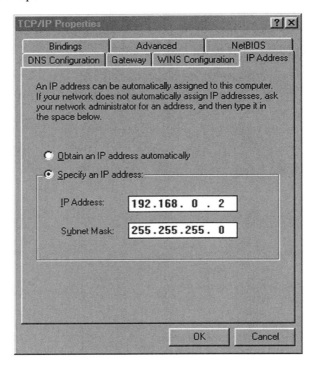

Figure 13-3: Setting the TCP/IP properties

Right click on OK, twice to get rid of both pop-up windows. That's how to set up the IP address of the Ethernet network address card. The process is similar for Windows systems other than Windows98. WindowsNT users need to select the "Network" control panel, click on the "Protocols" tab, and double-click on the "TCP/IP protocol" to view its properties. Then click on the "IP Address" tab in the properties window and set the IP address and subnet mask. Windows 2000 users need to click on the "Start" button, "Settings," then "Network and Dial-Up Connections." Then double-click on "Internet Protocol (TCP/IP)" to view its properties and set the IP address and subnet mask. WindowsXP users need to click on "Control Panel," then double-click on "Network Connections," then double-click on "Local Area Connection." In the "General" tab, click on "Internet Protocol (TCP/IP)," then click on "Properties" and

---

[2] LNEPCI II is a registered trademark of the Linksys Corp.

set the IP address and subnet mask. Our PC will be at 192.168.0.2. Let's put our TINI at 192.168.0.5, and give it a host name of drosera[3]. To get our PC to recognize our TINI by it's host name, we need to create a HOSTS file in the WINDOWS directory. There is a sample file called HOSTS.SAM in the WINDOWS directory. It can be edited in Notepad (or any other ASCII editor that you like) and the comments in the header of the file will explain the format. Our file will look like this:

```
#
#Win98 HOSTS file for the
#simple TINI network.
127.0.0.1      localhost
192.168.0.5    drosera
```

Save this file as HOSTS (drop the .sam file extension) in the Windows directory. The process is similar for Windows systems other than Windows98. For WindowsNT/2000/XP Pro, the HOSTS file needs to be placed in c:\winnt\system32\drivers\etc. For WindowsXP Home, the HOSTS file needs to be placed in c:\WINDOWS\system32\drivers\etc. This file isn't necessary for our network to work. It merely allows us to refer to our TINI by its hostname on the PC as opposed to an IP address. Now that we have the PC set up, we need to assign an IP address to the TINI stick. Plug the serial cable into the PC and into the TINI socketboard and run JavaKit. Reset the TINI, and type E to execute slush.

Login as root. We know the IP address we want, and the subnet mask, so we can run the ipconfig command.

```
ipconfig -a 192.168.0.5 -m 255.255.255.0
```

That's all there is to it. The servers in TINI are restarted and, provided we have our Ethernet cable in place, we can ping and FTP from TINI to the PC, referring to it as 192.168.0.2. From the PC, we can Telnet, ping, and FTP to TINI, referring to it as either drosera or 192.168.0.5.

A slightly more elaborate TINI network

Suppose we have a bunch of TINI sticks that we want to network together with a PC via Ethernet?

To make this network, we need to use an Ethernet hub, which is a device that connects multiple Ethernet devices into a star network configuration. **Each of our TINI sticks and the PC must connect to the hub via a straight-through cable as opposed to the crossover cable that we used in the previous section.** Assign each of the TINI sticks a different IP address on the 192.168.0.xxx subnet, and give them each a host name. Put the host name in the HOSTS file that we created in the previous section. One by one, take each TINI stick and connect it to the PC via the

---

[3] Drosera is the scientific name for the Sundew, a carnivorous plant.

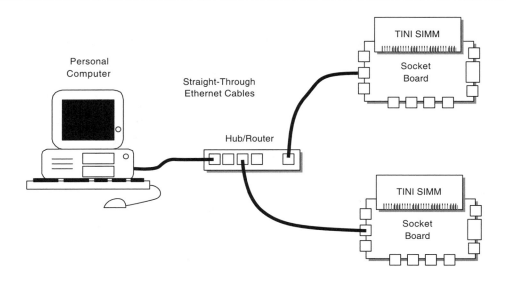

Figure 13-4: Multiple TINIs with a PC on an Ethernet hub

straight-through serial cable, run JavaKit, and assign the IP address with ipconfig. We now have a network of TINIs. They can refer to each other and the PC by IP address, and the PC can refer to them by host name, or IP address. If the PC had a second network interface to the Internet, we could configure it to act as a gateway. We could then go back to each TINI stick and use the ipconfig command to assign the IP address of the PC as the gateway for each TINI. We're going to forego the discussion of how to configure a PC to act as a gateway to the Internet in this fashion, in favor of discussing how to connect a TINI to an Internet gateway via a modem.

The TINI networking classes

Before we leave this section it's worth noting that, in Chapter 7, we took a detailed look at the Java API for TINI, including the networking classes. These classes give us all the tools necessary to serve http requests, perform DNS requests, receive dynamically assigned IP addresses through DHCP, implement ping, and among other things, communicate via PPP. Refer to Chapter 7, Figure 7-16, for more details on the TINI networking classes. PPP, the point-to-point protocol, is our next topic.

Using PPP

In this section, we will look at how to communicate with a TINI stick via PPP. We're going to do this by connecting a modem to TINI serial0, then executing a Java application under Slush that communicates with the modem and forms a PPP connection between the TINI and another modem-connected computer. The second computer could be an Internet Service Provider (ISP) *called by* the TINI, in which case the TINI would be acting as a PPP client on the Internet. The Telnet and FTP servers running on the stick will now be visible to the Internet, and applications running on the TINI stick can serve web data directly to the Internet, making the TINI stick truly web enabled. Alternatively, the second computer could be a laptop or desktop PC that *calls* the TINI stick. Here, we're not putting the stick on the Internet, but rather, we're treating it as a PPP server and logging into it remotely.

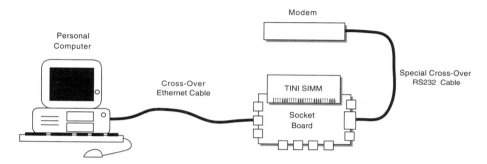

Figure 13-5: Our configuration for testing TINI as a PPP client

We will consider both cases in detail, first by making our own PPP client and PPP server programs, and then by using the optional slush command ppp. We'll start by taking a look at how the TINI API does PPP.

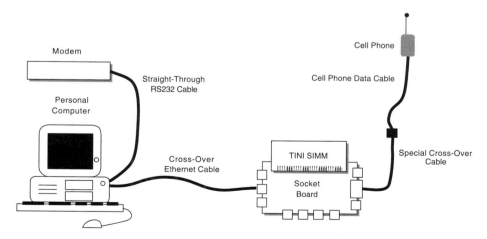

Figure 13-6: Our configuration for testing TINI as a PPP server

How TINI does PPP

The TINI API handles PPP connections via the PPP, PPPEventListener, and PPPEvent classes in the com.dalsemi.tininet.ppp package. The PPP acts as a layer between the IP network layer and the physical interface. To communicate via PPP, an application must create a PPP object and pass a serial port object to it, telling it which port to use for communication. Table 13-1 illustrates some of the PPP methods (the ones we'll be making use of). The TINI API has more complete information.

Table 13-1: The PPP Related methods used in our upcoming examples

Method in the PPP class	Purpose of method
setAuthenticate(boolean var)	In the case of establishing a server, when true, the calling party will be required to authenticate with a username and password.
setLocalAddress(byte[] ip)	Sets the local IP address.
setRemoteAddress(byte[] ip)	Sets the remote IP address.
addEventListener (PPPEventListener el)	Add the PPPEventListener to the specified PPP object.
setDefaultInterface(boolean var)	Establishes PPP as the default interface if argument is true.
setACCM(int num)	Gets the Asynchronous Control Character Map (ACCM).
setPassive(boolean var)	Establishes whether a STOPPED event is generated when Line Control Protocol negotiations time out. True means no stopped event is generated.
open()	Opens a PPP connection.
up()	Called when the serial port is ready for PPP data.
addInterface(string str)	Adds the PPP interface to the interface table under the name specified.
getPeerID()	During authentication, retrieves the username input by the calling party.
getPeerPassword()	During authentication, retrieves the password input by the calling party.
down()	Called when the serial port is no longer ready for PPP data.
close()	Closes the PPP connection.

The application must also listen for PPPEvents, via a PPPEventListener. The PPPEventListener class is an interface that we need to provide an implementation for. The TINI API for PPPEventListener describes its functionality in terms of a finite state machine (FSM). That is, during PPP operation, there are a fixed number of internal *states* that our PPPEventListener can be in. As changes occur in the PPP connection, PPPEvents are generated, and we move from state to state based on what state we're in and what event we see. There are six states in our FSM. These states, for the most part, map directly into the five events that our event listener is responsible for handling.

Table 13-2: The five possible PPPEvents

Event	Cause
STARTING	Generated when a `open()` is called.
AUTHENTICATION_REQUEST	Generated when `up()` is called with `setAuthenticate(true)`.
UP	Generated when `up()` is called with `setAuthenticate(false)`, or, when `authenticate(true)` is called.
STOPPED	Generated when there has been a link negotiation error, a remote termination, or `authenticate(false)` has been called.
CLOSED	Generated when the `close()` method is called.

The six states of the PPPEventListener FSM

INIT

We move to this state upon creation of a PPP object, i.e. `pppObject = new ppp();`

START

We move to the START state when the owner of our PPP object calls the `open()` method. During this state, the event listener must call the `up()` method and provide, as an argument, the serial port we wish to use for our PPP connection.

AUTH

We move from the START state to the AUTH state after the owner of the PPP object calls the `up()` method. During this state, the event listener must perform authentication on a user name and password. This state is only part of the PPP connection process if user authentication is required. Authentication is established as part of the connection process by calling the `setAuthenticate()` method with an argument of true. We will see examples both with and without authenticate in this fashion. Authentication is accomplished by calling the `getPeerID()` and `getPeerPassword()` method, then comparing the returned values to those values stored in the password file. If the values match, the `authenticate()` method is called with an argument of false. It's the `authenticate()` method that will determine which state we go to next.

STOPPED

To get to the STOPPED state, something such as a link negotiation error, remote termination, or an authentication failure has occurred. During this state, the event listener must call the `close()` method and print out any diagnostic messages that are desired.

UP

We get to the UP state when authentication has succeeded (`authenticate(true)` was called). During this state, the event listener is responsible for calling the `addInterface()` method, with the interface name to be added as an argument. If authentication wasn't required, we get here from the START state.

CLOSED

We get to the CLOSED state when a `close()` method is called. During this state, the event listener is responsible for calling the `down()` and `removeInterface()` methods.

This state machine is best understood by looking at it graphically.

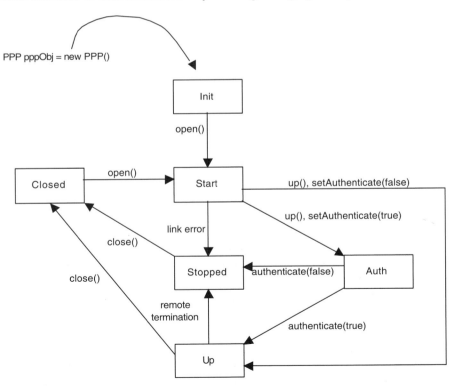

Figure 13-7: The PPPEventListener Finite State Machine

So, putting it all together, the various methods in the PPP class cause events to be generated. The `PPPEventListener` listens for these events, and uses them as a basis for defining what state our PPP connection is in. The response to an event will involve invoking additional PPP methods, which in turn, may cause an event, causing us to change state. The state we're currently in is a function of the most recent event that occurred, and that event was a function of the previous state we were in. The finite state machine allows us to envision this fairly complicated process in a simple way. The best way to learn about this is with some example code, but before we can move on to that, we have to address the somewhat troublesome subject of cables and modems.

The physical interface (cabling and modems)

Sometimes the devil is in the details, and in the case of TINI PPP connectivity, the devil has a lot of places to hide. One such place is the physical interface: the modem and modem cable.

Cables

One way or another, to connect a modem to a TINI stick you're going to have to use some kind of RS232-style cable. Some key things to keep in mind:

- Both the TINI serial0 and the modem have RS232 ports that behave as data communications equipment (DCE), so you have to use a cross-over cable (otherwise known as a null modem cable). This is in contrast to the type of modem cable you use between a PC and a modem, and between a PC and TINI when using JavaKit. Since the PC acts as data terminal equipment (DTE) in these instances, the cable needs to be straight-through.

- Modems may require signals that the TINI doesn't support. Specifically, the TINI stick only uses TX and RX on serial0. Many modems require a logic "1" on DTR and RTS. Without this, you may get outright failure or very erratic behavior from the modem.

- *The DTR signal can reset the TINI stick if you connect it.* So if you tie the DTR to logic "1" to make the modem work, you need to keep that logic "1" from the TINI stick's DTR line by removing the DTR jumper, or by not connecting it all the way through to the TINI DB9 connector.

Figure 13-8a shows a cable we made by cutting a straight-through RS232 cable in half, splicing in a 9V battery, and reconnecting it to be cross-over. This is not an elegant solution, but it works well for experimentation. No matter how you choose to construct it, it will need to implement the functionality shown. Chapter 9 has additional information on RS232.

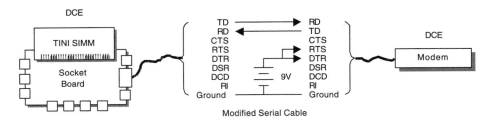

Figure 13-8a: A special crossover modem cable for use with a TINI

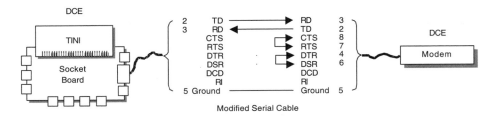

Figure 13-8b: Another special crossover modem cable for use with a TINI

Figure 13-8b shows a different version of a special cross-over cable. This one connects the modem signal on the CTS line to the RTS pin and the modem signal on the DSR to the DTR pin. This type of connector works if your modem sends traditional status signals on the CTS and DSR lines. This may not work if you are using a wireless modem or a wireless device with a built-in modem. You will need to do a little experimentation. This cable worked well with the external modems we used, but it did not work with the cell phone that we were using as a modem.

Modem AT commands/HyperTerminal

Modem control is handled by sending the modem a series of commands through the serial cable. For many years Hayes was the standard in modems. As the number of modem manufacturers grew, most manufacturers adhered to a somewhat loosely defined standard set of commands that was originally determined by Hayes. These are now called the *AT commands*. Below is a table of commonly used AT commands and their meaning.

Table 3-3: Some Basic AT commands

AT Command	Meaning
A	Answer incoming call.
DTnnnnnnnnnn	Dial the phone number with tone dialing

&D0	DTR assumed on. Useful if your modem needs to see a DTR, and you can't supply it from the computer.
E0	Disable echoing of commands (E1 = enable).
&F	Load factory profile.
&K0	Disable flow control.
Ln, where n = 0-3	Set speaker volume (0=lowest).
Mn where n=0-3	Speaker always off, speaker on until carrier detected, speaker always on, speaker on only during answering.
Q0	Enable responses to computer (Q1 = disable).
V1	Enable verbose responses (V0=terse, numeric responses).
X0	Report OK, CONNECT, RING, NO CARRIER, ERROR, and NO ANSWER.
X1	Report all X0 messages, plus CONNECT speed.
X2	Report all X1 messages, plus NO DIALTONE.
X3	Report all X2 messages, plus BUSY.
X4	Report all messages.

The syntax associated with AT commands can be summarized as follows:

- Commands from the table are preceded by "AT" and followed by a carriage return "\r".

- Multiple commands can be strung together on one line, up to forty characters. The downside of this is that if something goes wrong and the command line is rejected, you won't know which command caused the problem. That's why it's common to see one or two commands per line.

There are a great many more AT commands than those shown above. If you're not familiar with AT commands, the best way to learn about them is to experiment. Windows environments have a terminal-emulating program called HyperTerminal that allows you to issue commands directly to your modem. The following discussion assumes that you have a modem attached to your PC via a COM port. Click on the HyperTerminal icon to run it (HyperTerminal can usually be found in the Windows menus in Programs...Accessories... Communications...HyperTerminal). A popup window will appear asking you for a *connection name*. Put in anything you want, and click OK.

Figure 13-9:
Starting HyperTerminal

Another popup window will appear. Select the COM port that your modem is connected to.

Figure 13-10:
Selecting the COM port
in HyperTerminal

In the next window that pops up, configure the port as shown.

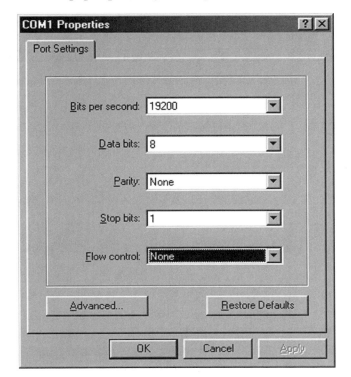

Figure 13-11: Configuring the COM port for HyperTerminal

You can now type AT commands directly to your modem and watch the result. This can be useful in debugging modem problems. You can take the modem that you plan to connect to the TINI, connect it to your PC via a straight-through cable, and then use HyperTerminal to test the series of AT commands that you plan to use when it's connected to the TINI stick. This way you eliminate as many problems with the modem as possible before you connect it to the TINI stick. If you are using Linux, minicom can be used to try your modem commands as well.

Once you have a set of AT commands that works well with your modem (such as the set of commands with which you will dial into an ISP), you can see if the modem works the same way when connected to the TINI stick. To help with this step, we wrote up a simple `Modem` class and test program, ModemDialTest.

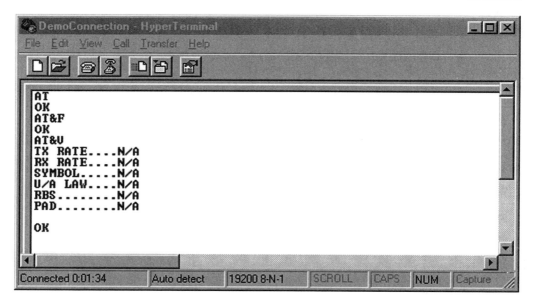

Figure 13-12: AT commands in HyperTerminal

Getting TINI to talk to a modem: The Modem class

In the previous section we discussed ways of testing modem dialing strings using a terminal emulator on a PC. Now we're going to connect the modem to a TINI stick through our special cross-over cable (Figure 13-8) and send it AT commands. We will use three classes: `Modem`, `ModemATTest`, and `ModemDialTest`. The `Modem` class contains utilities for opening a serial port, sending AT commands to a modem and printing out the response, calling an ISP and waiting for the CONNECT response, and answering an incoming call. We'll present the program in its entirety first, then go through it in detail `ModemATTest`, `ModemDialTest` are programs that test our `Modem` class.

Listing 13-1: Modem.java

```java
import java.io.*;
import javax.comm.*;

public class Modem  {

  SerialPort serialPort = null;

  public boolean openSerialPort(String port) {
    boolean flag = true;
    try {
```

```
      CommPortIdentifier portId = CommPortIdentifier.getPortIdentifier(port);
      serialPort = (SerialPort)portId.open("ppp0", 0);
      serialPort.setSerialPortParams(19200,
                                  SerialPort.DATABITS_8,
                                  SerialPort.STOPBITS_1,
                                  SerialPort.PARITY_NONE);
      serialPort.setFlowControlMode(serialPort.FLOWCONTROL_NONE);
    } catch(Exception e) {
      System.out.println(e);
      System.out.println("We failed to open the port");
      flag = false;
    }
    return flag;
  }

  public String sendCommand(String command) {
    String modemResponse = "";
    try {
      InputStream inputStream = serialPort.getInputStream();
      OutputStream outputStream = serialPort.getOutputStream();
      System.out.println("Sending: " + command);
      System.out.println("Receiving: ");
      outputStream.write((command+'\r').getBytes());
      Thread.sleep(500);
      int bytesToGet = inputStream.available();
      if (bytesToGet > 0) {
        byte[] readBuffer = new byte[bytesToGet];
        int bytesToPrint = inputStream.read(readBuffer, 0, bytesToGet);
        modemResponse = new String(readBuffer, 0, bytesToPrint);
        System.out.println(modemResponse);
      }
    } catch(Exception e) {}
    return modemResponse;
  }

  public boolean dial(String[] atCommands) {
    String atCommand = "";
    String modemMessage;
    int bytesToGet;
    int n=0;
    boolean flag = true;
    try {
      InputStream inputStream = serialPort.getInputStream();
      for (int i=0; i<atCommands.length; i++) {
        sendCommand(atCommands[i]);
      }
      boolean notConnected = true;
      modemMessage = "";
      while ((n<180) && (notConnected)) {
        try {Thread.sleep(500);} catch(Exception e) {}
```

```
      bytesToGet = inputStream.available();
      if (bytesToGet > 0) {
        byte[] readBuffer = new byte[bytesToGet];
        int bytesToPrint = inputStream.read(readBuffer, 0, bytesToGet);
        modemMessage = modemMessage + (new String(readBuffer, 0,
                            bytesToPrint));
        if (modemMessage.indexOf("CONNECT") != -1) {
          notConnected = false;
          System.out.println(modemMessage);
        }
      }
      n++;
    }
  } catch (IOException e) {
    System.out.println(e);
    flag = false;
  }
  return flag;
}

public boolean answer() {
  String atCommand = null;
  String modemMessage;
  boolean flag = true;
  int n=0;
  int m=0;
  int bytesToGet=0;
  try {
    InputStream inputStream = serialPort.getInputStream();
    atCommand = "AT";
    sendCommand(atCommand);
    modemMessage = "";
    System.out.println("Wait for 3 rings");
    while (n<3) {
      bytesToGet = inputStream.available();
      if (bytesToGet > 0) {
        byte[] readBuffer = new byte[bytesToGet];
        int bytesToPrint = inputStream.read(readBuffer, 0, bytesToGet);
        modemMessage = modemMessage + (new String(readBuffer, 0,
                            bytesToPrint));
        if (modemMessage.indexOf("RING") != -1) {
          n++;
          System.out.println(modemMessage);
          modemMessage = "";
        }
      }
    }
    atCommand = "ATA";
    sendCommand(atCommand);
    boolean notConnected = true;
```

```
      modemMessage = "";
      System.out.println("Wait for CONNECT");
      while ((m<180) & (notConnected)) {
         try {Thread.sleep(500);} catch(Exception e) {}
         bytesToGet = inputStream.available();
         if (bytesToGet > 0) {
           byte[] readBuffer = new byte[bytesToGet];
           int bytesToPrint = inputStream.read(readBuffer, 0, bytesToGet);
           modemMessage = modemMessage + (new String(readBuffer, 0,
                               bytesToPrint));
           if (modemMessage.indexOf("CONNECT") != -1) {
             notConnected = false;
             System.out.println(modemMessage);
           }
         }
         m++;
      }
    } catch (IOException e) {
      System.out.println(e);
      flag = false;
    }
    return flag;
  }
}
```

We start out by importing the necessary Java class libraries. No TINI specific libraries are used in the Modem class. We also make our class declaration, and declare our member variable serialPort.

```
import java.io.*;
import javax.comm.*;

public class Modem  {
  SerialPort serialPort = null;
```

The openSerialPort() method takes the name of the port we wish to open as an argument and returns a Boolean representing whether this operation succeeded. Note that we set the port for 8 databits, 1 stop bit, no parity bit, and no flow control. Since we will be using this later for establishing PPP connections, we supplied "ppp0" as the application name assigned to the port in the open() method.

```
  public boolean openSerialPort(String port) {
    boolean flag = true;
    try {
        CommPortIdentifier portId = CommPortIdentifier.getPortIdentifier(port);
        serialPort = (SerialPort)portId.open("ppp0", 0);
        serialPort.setSerialPortParams(19200,
                              SerialPort.DATABITS_8,
                              SerialPort.STOPBITS_1,
                              SerialPort.PARITY_NONE);
```

```
            serialPort.setFlowControlMode(serialPort.FLOWCONTROL_NONE);
      } catch(Exception e) {
         System.out.println(e);
         System.out.println("We failed to open the port");
         flag = false;
      }
      return flag;
   }
```

The `sendCommand()` method takes a string representing an AT command and sends it to the port, then prints and returns the response. One thing to note here is that before we send the AT command to the port, we append a carriage return "\r" to the string. This is required syntax and by placing it here it keeps us from having to deal with it later. The half-second delay we introduce next may or may not be necessary, depending on your modem. Without it, we found that we sometimes didn't read the entire response back from the modem, as if we tried to read it before the modem was ready. The `sendCommand()` method is fairly generic.

```
   public String sendCommand(String command) {
      String modemResponse = "";
      try {
         InputStream inputStream = serialPort.getInputStream();
         OutputStream outputStream = serialPort.getOutputStream();
         System.out.println("Sending: " + command);
         System.out.println("Receiving: ");
         outputStream.write((command+'\r').getBytes());
         Thread.sleep(500);
         int bytesToGet = inputStream.available();
         if (bytesToGet > 0) {
            byte[] readBuffer = new byte[bytesToGet];
            int bytesToPrint = inputStream.read(readBuffer, 0, bytesToGet);
            modemResponse = new String(readBuffer, 0, bytesToPrint);
            System.out.println(modemResponse);
         }
      } catch(Exception e) {}
      return modemResponse;
   }
```

The `dial()` method takes as its argument an array of strings representing the series of AT commands required to connect to an ISP. It uses the `sendCommand()` method to send the AT commands, then waits for the word *CONNECT* to be in the response after it has sent the last AT command in the sequence. It returns true if we succeed in connecting, false if something goes wrong. The method will wait 90 seconds for the *CONNECT*, then it will give up. The timeout is implemented in half-second increments, by looping 180 times. The method prints out the *CONNECT* if it receives it.

```
   public boolean dial(String[] atCommands) {
      String atCommand = "";
      String modemMessage;
```

```
      int bytesToGet;
      int n=0;
      boolean flag = true;
      try {
        InputStream inputStream = serialPort.getInputStream();
        for (int i=0; i<atCommands.length; i++) {
          sendCommand(atCommands[i]);
        }
        boolean notConnected = true;
        modemMessage = "";
        while ((n<180) && (notConnected)) {
          try {Thread.sleep(500);} catch(Exception e) {}
          bytesToGet = inputStream.available();
          if (bytesToGet > 0) {
            byte[] readBuffer = new byte[bytesToGet];
            int bytesToPrint = inputStream.read(readBuffer, 0, bytesToGet);
            modemMessage = modemMessage + (new String(readBuffer, 0,
                              bytesToPrint));
            if (modemMessage.indexOf("CONNECT") != -1) {
              notConnected = false;
              System.out.println(modemMessage);
            }
          }
          n++;
        }
      } catch (IOException e) {
        System.out.println(e);
        flag = false;
      }
      return flag;
  }
```

The `answer()` method waits for an incoming call by looking for the *RING* response from the modem three times. When it sees it, it uses the `sendCommand()` method to instruct the modem to answer via the ATA command. Then it waits 90 seconds for the *CONNECT* to appear before giving up. The issue of answering an incoming call and then forming a connection has proven to be the most problematic of this entire chapter. It can take a lot of modem experimentation to get this to work; from modem to modem, the required trick seems to vary.

```
public boolean answer() {
      String atCommand = null;
      String modemMessage;
      boolean flag = true;
      int n=0;
      int m=0;
      int bytesToGet=0;
      try {
        InputStream inputStream = serialPort.getInputStream();
        atCommand = "AT";
```

```
        sendCommand(atCommand);
        modemMessage = "";
        System.out.println("Wait for 3 rings");
        while (n<3) {
          bytesToGet = inputStream.available();
          if (bytesToGet > 0) {
            byte[] readBuffer = new byte[bytesToGet];
            int bytesToPrint = inputStream.read(readBuffer, 0, bytesToGet);
            modemMessage = modemMessage + (new String(readBuffer, 0,
                                  bytesToPrint));
            if (modemMessage.indexOf("RING") != -1) {
              n++;
              System.out.println(modemMessage);
              modemMessage = "";
            }
          }
        }
        atCommand = "ATA";
        sendCommand(atCommand);
        boolean notConnected = true;
        modemMessage = "";
        System.out.println("Wait for CONNECT");
        while ((m<180) && (notConnected)) {
          try {Thread.sleep(500);} catch(Exception e) {}
          bytesToGet = inputStream.available();
          if (bytesToGet > 0) {
            byte[] readBuffer = new byte[bytesToGet];
            int bytesToPrint = inputStream.read(readBuffer, 0, bytesToGet);
            modemMessage = modemMessage + (new String(readBuffer, 0,
                                  bytesToPrint));
            if (modemMessage.indexOf("CONNECT") != -1) {
              notConnected = false;
              System.out.println(modemMessage);
            }
          }
          m++;
        }
      } catch (IOException e) {
        System.out.println(e);
        flag = false;
      }
      return flag;
    }
}
```

Our first goal with the Modem class is to see that we can get a TINI stick to send AT commands to a modem. We'll test this out by using the Modem class to send AT commands to an external modem from a TINI via our special cross-over cable (Figure 13-8). The programs we will use are ModemATTest and ModemDialTest. They use the Modem class. Let's take a look at ModemATTest.

Testing the Modem class: The ModemATTest

The `ModemATTest` class uses the `Modem` class to send AT commands to a modem. It takes the serial port to open as the first command line argument, then AT commands after that.

Listing 13-2: ModemATTest.java

```
import java.io.*;
import javax.comm.*;

public class ModemATTest  {

    public static void main(String[] args) {
      Modem external = new Modem();
      external.openSerialPort(args[0]);
      for (int i=1; i<args.length; i++) {
        external.sendCommand(args[i]);
      }
    }
}
```

For this example, we're using a TINI connected to a PC via Ethernet, and we've connected the TINI to an external modem via the specially made cross-over cable. To compile the program, create a separate `src` folder and place the `ModemATTest.java` in it, as well as `Modem.java`. Make a `bin` folder in the same directory. Then type the following:

```
C:\> cd src
C:\> javac -bootclasspath %TINI_HOME%\bin\tiniclasses.jar
          -d ..\bin ModemATTest.java
C:\> cd ..
C:\> java -classpath %TINI_HOME%\bin\tini.jar;. BuildDependency
          -p %TINI_HOME%\bin\owapi_dependencies_TINI.jar
          -f bin
          -x %TINI_HOME%\bin\owapi_dep.txt
          -o bin\ModemATTest.tini
          -d %TINI_HOME%\bin\tini.db
```

As we've done in previous examples, some of the command line arguments for the java command have been shown on a separate line. Everything after *java* should be entered on the same line. Transfer the `.tini` file to your TINI stick via FTP, and via Telnet attempt the following:

```
TINI /> java ModemATTest.tini serial0 AT ATM1L0 ATE0 AT ATE1 AT

Sending: AT
Receiving:
AT
OK
```

```
Sending: ATM1L0
Receiving:
ATM1L0
OK

Sending: ATE0
Receiving:
ATE0
OK

Sending: AT
Receiving:

OK

Sending: ATE1
Receiving:

OK

Sending: AT
Receiving:
AT
OK
```

What did we just do? Entering AT by itself does nothing, but will inspire the modem to respond with an OK. Entering M1L0 tells the speaker to stay on until the carrier is detected and makes the volume low. The commands E0 and E1 allow you to turn off or turn on the echoing of commands in the response. If this didn't work, you may want to double check the cable or connect the modem to the PC with a straight-through cable and try the same command sequences in a terminal emulator (since this program is not TINI specific and does not use any TINI classes it will run fine on your PC from either Windows or Linux—just remember to specify the proper serial port for your operating system). If it did work, then we're ready to move on to the next step.

A Modem Dialing Test: The ModemDialTest class

The `ModemDialTest` class uses the `dial()` method of the Modem class to dial out to an ISP. It exits after receiving the *CONNECT* message from the modem. You need to put the phone number of your own ISP where you see 5555555555. The program takes as arguments the serial port you plan on using for the connection, and a series of strings representing the AT commands in your dialing string. The program is very similar to our previous example, ModemATTest, with the addition of code that waits for the *CONNECT*.

Listing 13-3: ModemDialTest.java

```
import java.io.*;
import javax.comm.*;

public class ModemDialTest  {

    public static void main(String[] args) {
      Modem external = new Modem();
      String[] dialString=new String[(args.length)-1];
      external.openSerialPort(args[0]);
      for (int i=0;i<(args.length)-1; i++) {
        dialString[i]=args[i+1];
      }
      external.dial(dialString);
    }
}
```

We're still using a TINI connected to a PC via Ethernet, and we've connected the TINI to an external modem via the specially made crossover cable. To compile the program, create a separate folder and place the `ModemDialTest.java` in it, as well as `Modem.java`. Make a `bin` folder in the same directory. Then type the following:

```
C:\> cd src
C:\> javac -bootclasspath %TINI_HOME%\bin\tiniclasses.jar
            -d ..\bin ModemDialTest.java
C:\> cd ..
C:\> java -classpath %TINI_HOME%\bin\tini.jar;. BuildDependency
      -p %TINI_HOME%\bin\owapi_dependencies_TINI.jar
      -f bin
      -x %TINI_HOME%\bin\owapi_dep.txt
      -o bin\ModemDialTest.tini
      -d %TINI_HOME%\bin\tini.db
```

As we've done in previous examples, some of the command line arguments for the java command have been shown on a separate line. Everything after *java* should be entered on the same line. Transfer the `.tini` file to your TINI stick via FTP, and via Telnet attempt the following:

```
TINI /> java ModemDialTest.tini serial0 AT ATM1L0 ATDT5555555555
Sending: AT
Receiving:

Sending: ATM1L0
Receiving:
AT
OK
ATM1L0
OK
```

```
Sending: ATDT5555555555
Receiving:
ATDT5555555555

CONNECT 48000

PROTOCOL:LAPM
```

Once again, for the example, we've pasted over the actual phone number we used with the 5555555555. You need to put the phone number of your ISP in your dialing string on the command line. If this worked, and you get results similar to the above in that the *CONNECT* was received, then we're ready to move on to considering the PPP client connection. If this *didn't* work, you need to determine whether it's a problem with the AT commands you're sending to the modem, or something related to the cable, etc. The AT command string can be debugged by putting the modem back on the PC and trying the same commands in a terminal emulator. If they don't work, consider commands such as &F (restore factory defaults), &K0 (disable flow control), X4(provide all responses), and E0 (turn off command echoing). If the command string works on PC but not on the TINI, then you need to double check the cable.

Example: Dialing out to an ISP (TINI as a PPP Client)

In the previous sections, we looked at ways of getting the TINI stick talking with a modem. Now it's time to focus our attention on actually implementing a PPP connection on a TINI. We'll start this by making a PPP client program. In this context, a client means that we'll be *dialing out* to an ISP and receiving a server assigned IP address from them. It is important to note that the ISP is going to want us to supply a username and password, and that the TINI PPP API supports only Password Authentication Protocol (PAP) for this. Your ISP will have to support PAP, or this won't work. In our earlier discussion of the PPP API, we noted that to handle PPP connections, we have to provide an implementation of the PPPEventListener. This will be the bulk of our PPP client program.

The PPPClient class

To make the TINI stick act as a PPP client, dialing out to an ISP to establish a PPP connection, we will make a program that dials out to the ISP, creates a PPP object, and implements the PPPEventListener. This class is called PPPClient. We'll show it in its entirety below, and then work our way through it.

Listing 13-4: PPPClient.java

```
import java.io.*;
import javax.comm.*;
import com.dalsemi.tininet.ppp.*;
```

```
public class PPPClient implements PPPEventListener {

    static SerialPort serialPort = null;
    static PPP ppp;


    public void pppEvent (PPPEvent e) {

      switch(e.getEventType()) {
        case PPPEvent.STARTING:
            System.out.println("PPP sent the STARTING event!");
            ppp.up(serialPort);
        break;

        case PPPEvent.UP:
            System.out.println("PPP sent the UP event!");
            ppp.addInterface("ppp0");
        break;

        case PPPEvent.AUTHENTICATION_REQUEST:
            //We don't have to do anything here, because
            //We're dialing out TO a server.
        break;

        case PPPEvent.STOPPED:
            System.out.println("Calling ppp.close()" );
            ppp.close();
        break;

        case PPPEvent.CLOSED:
            System.out.println("PPP sent the CLOSED event!");
            ppp.down();
            ppp.removeEventListener(this);
            serialPort.close();
            System.exit(0);
        break;

        default:
            System.out.println( "Some other ppp event happened" );
        break;
    }

  }


  public static void main(String[] args) {
    String[] dialString=new String[(args.length)-2];
    for (int i=0;i<(args.length)-2; i++) {
      dialString[i]=args[i+2];
    }
```

```
Modem external = new Modem();
external.openSerialPort("serial0");
serialPort = external.serialPort;
PPPClient ourListener = new PPPClient();
ppp = new PPP();
byte[] localAddress = new byte[] {0, 0, 0, 0};
byte[] remoteAddress = new byte[] {0, 0, 0, 0};
try {
  ppp.addEventListener(ourListener);
  ppp.setLocalAddress(localAddress);
  ppp.setRemoteAddress(remoteAddress);
  ppp.setACCM(0x00000000);
  ppp.setAuthenticate(false);
  ppp.setUsername(args[0]);
  ppp.setPassword(args[1]);
  ppp.setDefaultInterface(true);
} catch(Exception e) {
  System.out.println(e);
  System.out.println("The ppp methods failed");
  serialPort.close();
  System.exit(0);
}
if (external.dial(dialString)) {
  ppp.open();
} else {
  System.out.println("The dialer failed!");
  serialPort.close();
  System.exit(0);
}

while(true) {
  //run forever...
}
}
}
```

We start by importing the necessary java classes. We now are using classes specific to TINI: com.dalsemi.tininet.ppp.* We declare our class, and our member variables. We only have two variables, a `SerialPort` object and a `PPP` object.

```
import java.io.*;
import javax.comm.*;
import com.dalsemi.tininet.ppp.*;

public class PPPClient implements PPPEventListener {

    static SerialPort serialPort = null;
    static PPP ppp;
```

The `pppEvent()` method is required for the implementation of `pppEventListener`. It takes a `PPPEvent` as an argument. The method itself consists simply of a switch statement that implements the PPP finite state machine that we discussed earlier in this chapter. Each possible `PPPEvent` is handled by a case in the switch statement, and each of these corresponds to a state in our FSM. Note that we don't do anything in the AUTHENTICATION_REQUEST state because as a client, we're not going to be requesting authentication. The PPP server we're calling will request it of us. So we don't need to worry about this case.

```
public void pppEvent (PPPEvent e) {

    switch(e.getEventType()) {
      case PPPEvent.STARTING:
          System.out.println("PPP sent the STARTING event!");
          ppp.up(serialPort);
      break;

      case PPPEvent.UP:
          System.out.println("PPP sent the UP event!");
          ppp.addInterface("ppp0");
      break;

      case PPPEvent.AUTHENTICATION_REQUEST:
          //We don't have to do anything here, because
          //We're dialing out TO a server.
      break;

      case PPPEvent.STOPPED:
          System.out.println("Calling ppp.close()" );
          ppp.close();
      break;

      case PPPEvent.CLOSED:
          System.out.println("PPP sent the CLOSED event!");
          ppp.down();
          ppp.removeEventListener(this);
          serialPort.close();
          System.exit(0);
      break;

      default:
          System.out.println( "Some other ppp event happened" );
      break;
    }

}
```

The only other method in this class is the `main()` method. Our program takes the username, password, and AT command strings as arguments. We start by creating a

`Modem` object and a `serialPort` object. Then we create a PPPClient object, to act as a `pppEventListener`.

```
public static void main(String[] args) {
    String[] dialString=new String[(args.length)-2];
    for (int i=0;i<(args.length)-2; i++) {
     dialString[i]=args[i+2];
    }
    Modem external = new Modem();
    external.openSerialPort("serial0");
    serialPort = external.serialPort;
    PPPClient ourListener = new PPPClient();
```

When we create the PPP object, the `pppEventListener` FSM is in the INIT state. We create two byte arrays that hold the local and remote IP addresses. The remote machine we are calling will provide those addresses.

```
ppp = new PPP();
byte[] localAddress = new byte[] {0, 0, 0, 0};
byte[] remoteAddress = new byte[] {0, 0, 0, 0};
```

This next section sets up parameters required to form a PPP connection. We add the event listener, and supply the username and password (stored in the first two command line arguments). These are the username and password used to login to the account we are dialing. We set authentication to false, meaning we don't require the ISP to supply a username and password. It also means that we won't go to the AUTHENTICATION_REQUEST state. Finally, we set the default interface to true, which means that our PPP interface will be the default IP interface on TINI.

```
try {
   ppp.addEventListener(ourListener);
   ppp.setLocalAddress(localAddress);
   ppp.setRemoteAddress(remoteAddress);
   ppp.setACCM(0x00000000);
   ppp.setAuthenticate(false);
   ppp.setUsername(args[0]);
   ppp.setPassword(args[1]);
   ppp.setDefaultInterface(true);
} catch(Exception e) {
   System.out.println(e);
   System.out.println("The ppp methods failed");
   serialPort.close();
   System.exit(0);
}
```

Having set up the PPP parameters, we send the dial string of AT commands to the modem and wait for it to succeed. If it fails, we print some stuff, close the port, and exit. It if succeeds, we call the `open()` method and that will send us out of the INIT state in the `pppEventListener` FSM and starts the whole PPP connection process rolling.

```
        if (external.dial(dialString)) {
          ppp.open();
        } else {
          System.out.println("The dialer failed!");
          serialPort.close();
          System.exit(0);
        }

        while(true) {
          //run forever...
        }
    }
```

Once the connection is established, this program loops forever. If you're in a Telnet window, simply form a connection right over the top of this or close that Telnet window and open another one. In this new Telnet window, you can now access the Internet with FTP and ping. We've found that ping is sometimes unsuccessful in finding its IP target, when FTP works. You can run applications under Slush that communicate with the Internet and they will use the interface established by PPPClient. To stop PPPClient, you need to use the kill command. Let's try running it.

Again, use a TINI connected to a PC via Ethernet. Connect the TINI to a modem via the specially made cross-over cable. To compile the program, create a separate folder and place PPPClient.java in it, as well as Modem.java. Make a bin folder in the same directory. Then type the following:

```
C:\> cd src
C:\> javac -bootclasspath %TINI_HOME%\bin\tiniclasses.jar
          -d ..\bin PPPClient.java
C:\> cd ..
C:\> java -classpath %TINI_HOME%\bin\tini.jar;. BuildDependency
          -p %TINI_HOME%\bin\owapi_dependencies_TINI.jar
          -f bin
          -x %TINI_HOME%\bin\owapi_dep.txt
          -o bin\PPPClient.tini
          -d %TINI_HOME%\bin\tini.db
```

As we've done in previous examples, some of the command line arguments for the java command have been shown on a separate line. Everything after *java* should be entered on the same line. Transfer the .tini file to your TINI stick via FTP, and via Telnet attempt the following as the root user:

```
TINI /> downserver -s
Warning:  This will disconnect users on specified servers.

OK to proceed? (Y/N): y
[ Wed Feb 20 00:13:05 GMT 2002 ]  Message from System: Serial server
stopped.
```

```
TINI /> java PPPClient.tini <username> <password> AT ATM1L0
ATDT5555555555
Dialing ...
Sending: AT
Receiving:

Sending: ATM1L0
Receiving:
AT
OK
ATM1L0
OK

Sending: ATDT5555555555
Receiving:
ATDT5555555555

CONNECT 48000

PROTOCOL:LAPM

PPP sent the STARTING event!
PPP sent the UP event!
```

Once you see the notice about the UP event, you have a connection. You can log in to the TINI stick with another Telnet session and try the following:

```
TINI /> ps
3 processes
1: Java GC (Owner root)
2: init (Owner root)
31: PPPClient.tini (Owner root)

TINI /> ipconfig -x
Interface 0 is active.
Name         : eth0
Type         : Ethernet
IP Address   : 192.168.0.5
Subnet Mask  : 255.255.255.0
Gateway      : 0.0.0.0

Interface 1 is active.
Name         : lo
Type         : Local Loopback
IP Address   : 127.0.0.1
Subnet Mask  : 255.0.0.0
Gateway      : 0.0.0.0

Interface 2 is active.
Name         : ppp0 (default)
```

```
Type          : Point-to-Point Protocol
IP Address    : xxx.xxx.xx.xxx
Subnet Mask   : 255.255.255.0
Gateway       : 0.0.0.0

Interface 3 is not active.
TINI />
```

There are several things to note about what we've just done. To start with, we need to be the root user to do this, and we always need to start by shutting down the serial server with the `downserver -s` command, or, disable the server by modifying the `etc/.startup` file, with the line `setenv SerialServer disable`. In the examples shown above, we've removed the real phone numbers, usernames, passwords, and IP addresses used. You need to use your own phone number, username, and password. (The username and password required by your ISP, not the ones you use on TINI.) Upon executing `ipconfig -x` you will see that a new interface is now active and is the default. It's ppp0, the interface we just added. The IP address shown for that (X'd out in this case) will actually be the IP address given to you by your ISP. You can go further with the ipconfig command and input a DNS IP address (provided by your ISP), and a mail host for the sendmail command (also provided by your ISP). To stop the PPPClient, you will have to use the kill command, and kill the PPPClient process.

What if things didn't work for you? There are a number of things that can go wrong. You should power cycle the modem before running the program, make sure that any processes from previous PPPClient attempts are killed, always shut down the serial server (or disable it), and make sure your ISP supports PAP. You may also want to double check to see that the connection preferences of your ISP wants (data bits, parity, stop bits, flow control) match those being set in the program. With respect to compilation and TINIconvertor, always use a separate directory in which the only java files are `PPPClient.java` and `Modem.java`. Beyond this, if you've tested the dialing string with the previous examples but the PPP still doesn't work, consider browsing the TINI archives on the web. There is a wealth of information about PPP out there. If everything above worked, but when you did the `ipconfig -x` you did NOT see the ppp0 interface, try the last resort: clear the heap, reload the TINI firmware (`tini.tbin`, `slush.tbin`) and try again.

Example: Dialing into TINI from a PC (TINI as a PPP Server)

The previous example discussed how to make the TINI behave as a PPP client, where by *client* we mean *dialing out* to an ISP. Now, we're going to make the TINI behave as a PPP server, where by server we mean *answering* a call placed by a PC *dialing into* the TINI. We are going to connect a cell phone acting as a modem to the TINI, then call the cell phone modem using our PC with a second modem and the house phone line. This proceeds very much like the previous example, but getting the modem to answer and form a connection can be finicky. So, we'll start by testing the process of answering an incoming call before messing with PPP. We used a Motorola, StarTAC[4], model ST7868W, and its associated data connectivity kit (a package of stuff that allows you to use it as a modem). When connecting the cell phone to the TINI, we needed to put the specially modified crossover cable between the TINI and the cell phone data connectivity cable. Note that of the two cables shown in Figure 13-8a and 13-8b, only the one that had the fixed voltage spliced into it (13-8a) worked properly with the cell phone. Your cell phone may be different.

A Modem Call Answering Test: The ModemAnswerTest class

The `ModemAnswerTest` class uses the `answer()` method from the Modem class to answer an incoming call. It exits immediately upon receiving the incoming call.

Listing 13-5: ModemAnswerTest.java

```java
import java.io.*;
import javax.comm.*;

public class ModemAnswerTest   {

    public static void main(String[] args) {
        Modem external = new Modem();
        external.openSerialPort(args[0]);
        external.answer();
    }
}
```

The program takes a single command line argument, the name of the serial port you wish to use. It can be run on a PC or a TINI. We'll try this out using a cell phone and its associated data connectivity kit, which consists of a special serial cable that has a female DB9 connector on one end and a special connector on the other that mates with the phone. **The trick: the phone we used needs to be put into the *Incoming Data Only* mode before it will answer under AT command control.** The *Incoming Data Only* mode is selected under *Phone Options/Data Setup* selector from the keypad of the phone. The Data Setup choice will only show up in the menu if the special data connectivity cable is attached, and plugged into a computer. In the case of TINI, if we plug the data connectivity cable into our special cable, the phone instantly realizes the cable is connected. Then, from the keypad, you can select Phone Options, and Data Setup will be one of the choices. You can then change it to *Incoming Data Only*. If you connect the cell phone to a PC, however, the Data Setup option may only appear in the menu after you send the modem an AT command. The

---

[4] StarTAC is a registered trademark of the Motorola Corp.

difference has to do with the special cable we're using when we connect it to a TINI. Other phones will most likely have their own quirks.

Let's connect the phone to a TINI, using the special crossover cable that we made for TINI and the data connectivity cable for the cell phone. Then, we'll dial the cell phone number from the modem in our PC. The object of this exercise is to see whether or not we can get the cell phone to see an incoming call, answer it, and see a *CONNECT* response from the modem.

To compile the program, create a separate folder and place ModemAnswerTest.java in it, as well as Modem.java. Make a bin folder in the same directory. Then type the following:

```
C:\> cd src
C:\> javac -bootclasspath %TINI_HOME%\bin\tiniclasses.jar
         -d ..\bin ModemAnswerTest.java
C:\> cd ..
C:\> java -classpath %TINI_HOME%\bin\tini.jar;. BuildDependency
         -p %TINI_HOME%\bin\owapi_dependencies_TINI.jar
         -f bin
         -x %TINI_HOME%\bin\owapi_dep.txt
         -o bin\ModemAnswerTest.tini
         -d %TINI_HOME%\bin\tini.db
```

As we've done in previous examples, some of the command line arguments for the Java command have been shown on a separate line. Everything after *java* should be entered on the same line. Transfer the .tini file to your TINI stick via FTP, and via Telnet attempt the following as the root user. Once you run the program on the TINI, immediately bring up a Windows Dialup window and call the cell phone.

```
TINI /> downserver -s
Warning:  This will disconnect users on specified servers.

OK to proceed? (Y/N): y
[ Wed Feb 13 02:46:11 GMT 2002 ]  Message from System: Serial server
stopped.

TINI /> java ModemAnswerTest.tini serial0
Sending: AT
Receiving:
AT
OK

Wait for 3 rings

RING

RING
```

```
RING

Sending: ATA
Receiving:
ATA
Wait for CONNECT

CONNECT

TINI />
```

It worked. When we dialed out from the PC, the cell phone saw the incoming call, answered it on the third ring, and waited for the *CONNECT*, then exited. We used the same dial-up setting that we used when we call our ISP: 8 data bits, No parity, 1 stop bit, no flow control. It should be noted that this is somewhat specific to this exact exercise. If you are using a different cell phone, or perhaps an external modem instead of a cell phone, your experience may be a bit different and there might be different or additional AT commands that you may need to do to get your phone or modem to answer and spot the *CONNECT*. Consult the documentation on your phone, and check out the Internet—specifically, the TINI archives. You may also want to search the Internet for information on your specific phone or modem.

Once you get this step to work, you're ready to add PPP connectivity to this.

The PPPServer class

To make the TINI stick act as a PPP server, waiting for an incoming call and establishing a PPP connection, we will make a program that answers incoming calls, creates a PPP object, and implements the PPPEventListener. This class is called PPPServer. We'll show it in its entirety below, and then work our way through it. It's very similar to our previous example, PPPClient.

Listing 13-6: PPPServer.java

```java
import java.io.*;
import javax.comm.*;
import com.dalsemi.tininet.ppp.*;

public class PPPServer implements PPPEventListener {
    static SerialPort serialPort = null;
    static PPP ppp;

    public void pppEvent (PPPEvent e) {
      switch(e.getEventType()) {
        case PPPEvent.STARTING:
          System.out.println("PPP sent the STARTING event!");
          ppp.up(serialPort);
        break;
```

```
      case PPPEvent.UP:
         System.out.println("PPP sent the UP event!");
         ppp.addInterface("ppp0");
      break;

      case PPPEvent.AUTHENTICATION_REQUEST:
         //We don't have to do anything here, because
         //We're dialing out TO a server.
      break;

      case PPPEvent.STOPPED:
         System.out.println("PPP sent the STOPPED event!");
         ppp.close();
      break;

      case PPPEvent.CLOSED:
         System.out.println("PPP sent the CLOSED event!");
         ppp.down();
         ppp.removeEventListener(this);
         serialPort.close();
         System.exit(0);
      break;

      default:
      break;
   }
}

public static void main(String[] args) {
  Modem external = new Modem();
  external.openSerialPort("serial0");
  serialPort = external.serialPort;
  PPPServer ourListener = new PPPServer();
  ppp = new PPP();
  byte[] localAddress = new byte[] {(byte)192, (byte)168, (byte)10, (byte)9};
  byte[] remoteAddress = new byte[] {(byte)192, (byte)168, (byte)10, (byte)12};
  try {
     ppp.close();
     ppp.addEventListener(ourListener);
     ppp.setLocalAddress(localAddress);
     ppp.setRemoteAddress(remoteAddress);
     ppp.setACCM(0x00000000);
     ppp.setAuthenticate(false);
     ppp.setDefaultInterface(true);
  } catch(Exception e) {
     System.out.println(e);
     System.out.println("The ppp methods failed");
     serialPort.close();
     System.exit(0);
  }
```

```
      if (external.answer()) {
        ppp.open();
      } else {
        System.out.println("The dialer failed!");
        serialPort.close();
        System.exit(0);
      }
      while(true) {
        //run forever...
      }
    }
  }
}
```

We first import the necessary libraries, one of which is TINI specific. We also declare our class, and declare two member variables, serialPort and ppp.

```
import java.io.*;
import javax.comm.*;
import com.dalsemi.tininet.ppp.*;

public class PPPServer implements PPPEventListener {
    static SerialPort serialPort = null;
    static PPP ppp;
```

Next, we have the pppEvent() method, which is required for imlementation of the PPPEventListener. There is no difference between this and the version we used in PPPClient. It takes a pppEvent() as an argument. The method itself consists simply of a switch statement that implements the PPP finite state machine that we discussed earlier in this chapter. Each possible pppEvent() is handled by a case in the switch statement, and each of these corresponds to a state in our FSM. Note, again, that we don't do anything in the AUTHENTICATION_REQUEST state. As a server, this means that whoever calls in gets logged in without any kind of username or password authentication! This isn't good, and we're going to fix this in the next example, but for now we're keeping it simple.

```
    public void pppEvent (PPPEvent e) {
      switch(e.getEventType()) {
        case PPPEvent.STARTING:
          System.out.println("PPP sent the STARTING event!");
          ppp.up(serialPort);
        break;

        case PPPEvent.UP:
          System.out.println("PPP sent the UP event!");
          ppp.addInterface("ppp0");
        break;

        case PPPEvent.AUTHENTICATION_REQUEST:
          //We don't have to do anything here, because
          //We're dialing out TO a server.
```

```
      break;

      case PPPEvent.STOPPED:
         System.out.println("PPP sent the STOPPED event!");
         ppp.close();
      break;

      case PPPEvent.CLOSED:
         System.out.println("PPP sent the CLOSED event!");
         ppp.down();
         ppp.removeEventListener(this);
         serialPort.close();
         System.exit(0);
      break;

      default:
      break;
   }
}
```

Finally, we have our `main()` method. It takes no arguments. We start by creating a `Modem` object, opening a serial port, and creating our event listener.

```
public static void main(String[] args) {
   Modem external = new Modem();
   external.openSerialPort("serial0");
   serialPort = external.serialPort;
   PPPServer ourListener = new PPPServer();
```

Next, we create our PPP object, which starts the PPP connection process. We now have to set values for the local and remote IP address for their respective PPP interfaces because we are now the server, and the client calling in will be expecting us to assign one. We made up these numbers. If you choose to insert different ones, make sure they are on a different network than any other interfaces your TINI or PC may have.

```
   ppp = new PPP();
   byte[] localAddress = new byte[] {(byte)192, (byte)168, (byte)10, (byte)9};
   byte[] remoteAddress = new byte[] {(byte)192, (byte)168, (byte)10, (byte)12};
```

We now add our event listener, set up a bunch of PPP connection parameters, and set PPP as our default interface. We also leave the `setAuthenticate()` method set to false, because we aren't doing any authentication on the client calling in.

```
   try {
      ppp.addEventListener(ourListener);
      ppp.setLocalAddress(localAddress);
      ppp.setRemoteAddress(remoteAddress);
      ppp.setACCM(0x00000000);
      ppp.setAuthenticate(false);
```

```
            ppp.setDefaultInterface(true);
        } catch(Exception e) {
          System.out.println(e);
          System.out.println("The ppp methods failed");
          serialPort.close();
          System.exit(0);
        }
```

We call the answer method from the `Modem` class. It will wait for three rings, answer the call, then wait for the *CONNECT*. If the *CONNECT* comes, it will call the `open()` method, which starts us moving through the PPP FSM.

```
        if (external.answer()) {
          ppp.open();
        } else {
          System.out.println("The dialer failed!");
          serialPort.close();
          System.exit(0);
        }
        while(true) {
          //run forever...
        }
      }
    }
```

Once the connection is established, this program loops forever. If you're in a Telnet window, simply form a connection right over the top of this or close that Telnet window and open another one. In this new Telnet window, you can now access the client with ftp and ping. You can run applications under Slush that communicate with the client and they will use the IP interface established by PPPServer. To stop PPPServer, you will need to use the kill command. Let's try running it.

Again, use a TINI connected to a PC via Ethernet. Connect the TINI to a modem (a cell phone in our case) via the specially made crossover cable and the cell phone's data connectivity cable. To compile the program, create a separate folder and place `PPPServer.java` in it, as well as `Modem.java`. Make a bin folder in the same directory. Then type the following:

```
C:\> cd src
C:\> javac -bootclasspath %TINI_HOME%\bin\tiniclasses.jar
          -d ..\bin PPPServer.java
C:\> cd ..
C:\> java -classpath %TINI_HOME%\bin\tini.jar;. BuildDependency
     -p %TINI_HOME%\bin\owapi_dependencies_TINI.jar
     -f bin
     -x %TINI_HOME%\bin\owapi_dep.txt
     -o bin\PPPServer.tini
     -d %TINI_HOME%\bin\tini.db
```

As we've done in previous examples, some of the command line arguments for the java command have been shown on a separate line. Everything after `java` should be entered on the same line. Transfer the .tini file to your TINI stick via FTP, and via telnet attempt the following as the root user:

```
TINI /> downserver -s
Warning:  This will disconnect users on specified servers.

OK to proceed? (Y/N): y
[ Wed Feb 13 03:56:21 GMT 2002 ]  Message from System: Serial server
stopped.

TINI /> java PPPServer.tini
Sending: AT
Receiving:
AT
OK

Wait for 3 rings

RING

RING

RING

Sending: ATA
Receiving:
ATA
Wait for CONNECT

CONNECT

PPP sent the STARTING event!
PPP sent the UP event!
```

Then, log into the same TINI via telnet either right on top of the current process, or in a different window. Run `ipconfig -x`:

```
TINI /> ipconfig -x
Interface 0 is active.
Name          : eth0
Type          : Ethernet
IP Address    : 192.168.0.5
Subnet Mask   : 255.255.255.0
Gateway       : 0.0.0.0

Interface 1 is active.
Name          : lo
Type          : Local Loopback
```

```
IP Address    : 127.0.0.1
Subnet Mask   : 255.0.0.0
Gateway       : 0.0.0.0

Interface 2 is active.
Name          : ppp0 (default)
Type          : Point-to-Point Protocol
IP Address    : 198.168.10.9
Subnet Mask   : 255.255.255.0
Gateway       : 0.0.0.0

Interface 3 is not active.
```

It worked! You have a PPP connection with the PC, the TINI on 192.168.10.9 and the PC on 192.168.10.12. You can now log into the TINI using Telnet and FTP by referring to it as 192.168.10.9 and you will connect over the PPP interface, and if you refer to the TINI as 192.168.0.5, you will connect over the Ethernet interface.

The same comments we made about `PPPClient` apply here. We need to be the root user to do this, and we always need to start by shutting down the serial server with the `downserver -s` command, or, disable the server by modifying the etc/.startup file, with the line `setenv SerialServer disable`. To stop the `PPPServer`, you will have to use the kill command, and kill the `PPPServer` process.

And if things didn't work for you? There are a number of things that can go wrong. You should power cycle the modem before running the program, make sure that any processes from previous `PPPClient` or `PPPServer` attempts are killed, and always shut down the serial server (or disable it). You may also want to double check to see that the connection preferences of your PC dial up adapter (data bits, parity, stop bits, flow control) match those being set in the program. With respect to compilation and TINIconvertor, always use a separate directory in which the only java files are PPPServer.java and Modem.java. Beyond this, if you've tested the modem answering process with the previous examples, but the PPP still doesn't work, consider browsing the TINI archives on the web. There is a wealth of information about PPP out there. If everything above worked, but when you did the `ipconfig -x` you did *not* see the ppp0 interface, try the last resort: clear the heap, reload the TINI firmware (tini.tbin, slush.tbin) and try again.

Example: Dialing into TINI from a PC (With Authentication)

The previous example involved making a TINI act as a PPP server that can be called and logged into remotely from a PC. For simplicity, we omitted user authentication. Anybody can call into TINI and start up a PPP connection. That's a great big weakness. So, we're going to redo the example adding user authentication. There are really only two changes to the program. We have to add some code that takes a user name and a password from the client requesting a connection and compare them against the data stored in the TINI password file. We need to then execute this code when the AUTHENTICATION_REQUEST event occurs (that is, during the AUTH state). Last, we need to add the `setAuthenticate(true)` method to `main()`. We're going to present the whole program below, then look at the portions that differ from the previous example.

Listing 13-7: PPPServerWA.java

```java
import java.io.*;
import javax.comm.*;
import com.dalsemi.tininet.ppp.*;

public class PPPServerWA implements PPPEventListener {
    static SerialPort serialPort = null;
    static PPP ppp;

    public void pppEvent (PPPEvent e) {
      switch(e.getEventType()) {
        case PPPEvent.STARTING:
           System.out.println("PPP sent the STARTING event!");
           ppp.up(serialPort);
        break;

        case PPPEvent.UP:
          System.out.println("PPP sent the UP event!");
          ppp.addInterface("ppp0");
        break;

        case PPPEvent.AUTHENTICATION_REQUEST:
          System.out.println("PPP sent the AUTHENTICATION_REQUEST event!");
          String userName = ppp.getPeerID();
          String password = ppp.getPeerPassword();
          if (validateLogin(userName, password)) {
            ppp.authenticate(true);
            System.out.println("Login Validation has succeeded");
          } else {
            ppp.authenticate(false);
            System.out.println("Login Validation has failed");
          }
        break;

        case PPPEvent.STOPPED:
          System.out.println("PPP sent the STOPPED event!");
          ppp.close();
        break;

        case PPPEvent.CLOSED:
          System.out.println("PPP sent the CLOSED event!");
          ppp.down();
```

```
                ppp.removeEventListener(this);
                serialPort.close();
                System.exit(0);
            break;

            default:
            break;
        }
    }

    public boolean validateLogin(String user, String passwd) {
        String inputLine;
        boolean flag=true;
        byte[] hashFromFile = new byte[20];
        ParsePasswdLine pwl = new ParsePasswdLine();
        try {
            BufferedReader passwdFileLines = new BufferedReader(
                                        new FileReader("/etc/passwd"));
            while ((inputLine = passwdFileLines.readLine()) != null) {
                pwl.parse(inputLine);
                if ( (pwl.userName).equals(user) ) {
                    hashFromFile = pwl.passwdHash;
                    byte[] testHash = com.dalsemi.system.Security
                                .hashMessage((user + ":" + passwd).getBytes());
                    for (int i=0; i<20;i++) {
                        if (testHash[i]!=hashFromFile[i]) {
                            return false;
                        }
                    }
                    return true;
                }
            }
        }
        catch (Exception e) {
            System.out.println(e);
            return false;
        }
        return false;
    }


    public static void main(String[] args) {
        Modem external = new Modem();
        external.openSerialPort("serial0");
        serialPort = external.serialPort;
        PPPServerWA ourListener = new PPPServerWA();
        ppp = new PPP();
        byte[] localAddress = new byte[] {(byte)192,(byte)168,(byte)10,(byte)9};
        byte[] remoteAddress = new byte[]{(byte)192,(byte)168,(byte)10,(byte)12};
        try {
```

```
            ppp.close();
            ppp.addEventListener(ourListener);
            ppp.setLocalAddress(localAddress);
            ppp.setRemoteAddress(remoteAddress);
            ppp.setACCM(0x00000000);
            ppp.setAuthenticate(true);
            ppp.setDefaultInterface(true);
            ppp.setPassive(true);
        } catch(Exception e) {
          System.out.println(e);
          System.out.println("The ppp methods failed");
          serialPort.close();
          System.exit(0);
        }
        if (external.answer()) {
          ppp.open();
        } else {
          System.out.println("The answer has failed!");
          serialPort.close();
          System.exit(0);
        }
        while(true) {
          //run forever...
        }
    }
}
```

The first change we see is in the AUTHENTICATION_REQUEST case. We use the `getPeerID()` and the `getPeerPassword()` methods to grab the username and password entered by the client requesting a PPP connection. Then we pass those to a method called `validateLogin()`. If that method returns true, we use the `authenticate(true)` method to move us into the UP state. Else, we use `authenticate(false)` to move to the STOPPED state.

```
      case PPPEvent.AUTHENTICATION_REQUEST:
        System.out.println("PPP sent the AUTHENTICATION_REQUEST event!");
        String userName = ppp.getPeerID();
        String password = ppp.getPeerPassword();
        if (validateLogin(userName, password)) {
          ppp.authenticate(true);
          System.out.println("Login Validation has succeeded");
        } else {
          ppp.authenticate(false);
          System.out.println("Login Validation has failed");
        }
      break;
```

The `validateLogin()` method takes the username/password and compares it to what is found in the TINI password file. We make use of a utility class, `ParsePasswordLine`, which is stored in a separate file in the same directory. The

`ParsePasswordLine` class has two member variables, the user name and the 20 bit hash associated with that user name. We read in the contents of the password file, line by line, and as we do, we parse the line and separate out the username and 20 bit hash (via the `ParsePasswordLine` class). If the client's user name matches a name in the file, we create a string consisting of the username, a colon, and the password the client entered. We compute the SHA-1 hash of that string. We compare that hash, with the hash retrieved from the password file, byte for byte. If they match, the client gets logged.

```java
public boolean validateLogin(String user, String passwd) {
  String inputLine;
  boolean flag=true;
  byte[] hashFromFile = new byte[20];
  ParsePasswdLine pwl = new ParsePasswdLine();
  try {
    BufferedReader passwdFileLines = new BufferedReader(
                                 new FileReader("/etc/passwd"));
    while ((inputLine = passwdFileLines.readLine()) != null) {
      pwl.parse(inputLine);
      if ( (pwl.userName).equals(user) ) {
        hashFromFile = pwl.passwdHash;
        byte[] testHash = com.dalsemi.system.Security
                    .hashMessage((user + ":" + passwd).getBytes());
        for (int i=0; i<20;i++) {
          if (testHash[i]!=hashFromFile[i]) {
            return false;
          }
        }
        return true;
      }
    }
  }
  catch (Exception e) {
    System.out.println(e);
    return false;
  }
  return false;
}
```

The `ParsePasswordLine` class has one method, `parse()`, which takes a string and grabs the first two colon separated fields. The second field is treated as hex bytes, and put into a byte array.

```java
import java.io.*;
import com.dalsemi.system.*;
public class ParsePasswdLine  {
  String userName;
  byte[] passwdHash = new byte[20];
```

```
public void parse(String passwdLine) {
    int firstField = passwdLine.indexOf(':', 0);
    int secondField = passwdLine.indexOf(':', firstField+1);
    userName = passwdLine.substring(0, firstField);
    String passwdHashStr = passwdLine.substring(firstField+1, secondField);
    int n=0;
    int i=0;
    String str = "";
    while (n<39) {
      str = passwdHashStr.substring(n,n+2);
      passwdHash[i] = (byte)Short.parseShort(str, 16);
      i++;
      n=n+2;
    }
  }
}
```

Like the previous example, use a TINI connected to a PC via Ethernet. Connect the TINI to a modem (a cell phone in our case) via the specially made crossover cable and the cell phone's data connectivity cable. To compile the program, create a separate folder and place PPPserverWA.java in it, as well as Modem.java, and ParsePasswordLine.java. Make a bin folder in the same directory. Then type the following:

```
C:\> cd src
C:\> javac -bootclasspath %TINI_HOME%\bin\tiniclasses.jar
          -d ..\bin PPPServerWA.java
C:\> cd ..
C:\> java -classpath %TINI_HOME%\bin\tini.jar;. BuildDependency
          -p %TINI_HOME%\bin\owapi_dependencies_TINI.jar
          -f bin
          -x %TINI_HOME%\bin\owapi_dep.txt
          -o bin\PPPServerWA.tini
          -d %TINI_HOME%\bin\tini.db
```

As we've done in previous examples, some of the command line arguments for the java command have been shown on a separate line. Everything after *java* should be entered on the same line. Transfer the .tini file to your TINI stick via FTP, and via telnet attempt the following as the root user:

```
TINI /> downserver -s
Warning:  This will disconnect users on specified servers.

OK to proceed? (Y/N): y
[ Wed Feb 13 08:52:58 GMT 2002 ]  Message from System: Serial server
stopped.

TINI /> java PPPServerWA.tini
Sending: AT
Receiving:
```

```
AT
OK

Wait for 3 rings

RING

RING

RING

Sending: ATA
Receiving:
ATA
Wait for CONNECT

CONNECT

PPP sent the STARTING event!
PPP sent the AUTHENTICATION_REQUEST event!
Login Validation has succeeded
PPP sent the UP event!
```

Then, log into the same TINI via Telnet either right on top of the current process, or in a different window. Run `ipconfig -x`:

```
TINI /> ipconfig -x
Interface 0 is active.
Name         : eth0
Type         : Ethernet
IP Address   : 192.168.0.5
Subnet Mask  : 255.255.255.0
Gateway      : 0.0.0.0

Interface 1 is active.
Name         : lo
Type         : Local Loopback
IP Address   : 127.0.0.1
Subnet Mask  : 255.0.0.0
Gateway      : 0.0.0.0

Interface 2 is active.
Name         : ppp0 (default)
Type         : Point-to-Point Protocol
IP Address   : 192.168.10.9
Subnet Mask  : 255.255.255.0
Gateway      : 0.0.0.0

Interface 3 is not active.
```

Success! As in the previous example, we now have a PPP connection between the TINI stick and a PC, with the stick acting as a server. This time, the PPP process checked to see if we entered a valid user name and password when dialing in form the PC. If this didn't work for you, refer to comments at the end of the previous example.

Rebuilding Slush to include PPP

The Optional Slush Command ppp

In the TINI software distribution, `tini1_102b.tgz` (or whichever version you're using), there is a file called `OptionalSlushCommandsSrc.jar`. If you unzip that file, you will find that it contains many files, among them, `PPPCommand.java`. It will unzip into a directory structure based on .\com\dalsemi\slush\command. The mechanics of taking an optional slush command like this and building it into slush is a topic that was discussed in Chapter 7. What we're going to discuss here is what the PPPCommand class does for us, and what we have to do to make it work.

The PPPCommand class inserts a command called ppp into slush. The ppp command has the following options:

-a `XX.XX.XX.XX`

Sets the IP address of the TINI stick ppp interface. This gets used when you are using the ppp command to set up the stick as a PPP server, waiting for an incoming call from another computer. The IP address of the remote computer's PPP interface will be set with the -r option. You will also be using the -x and -s options with this.

-c

This closes the PPP connection. In our previous examples, we started the PPPClient or PPPServer application and it ran until you killed it. But, if you establish a ppp connection with the ppp command in slush, you can close the connection cleanly by typing `ppp -c`. This only works if you started the connection with the ppp command in slush. If you form the PPP connection using one of the previous examples, and you use `ppp -c`, nothing happens.

-p `password`

This sets the login password in cases when you are using the TINI stick as a PPP client, dialing into a PPP server. It gets used in conjunction with the -x, -d, and -u options. For instance if you have a dialup account at an ISP and you are trying to form a connection to it with a TINI stick, you would use this option and enter the account login password that you use with the ISP.

-r `XX.XX.XX.XX`

Sets the IP address of the remote ppp interface in cases when you are using the ppp command to set up the stick as a PPP server, waiting for an incoming call from another computer. The IP address of the TINI stick's PPP interface will be set with the –a option. You will also be using the –x and –s options with this.

-u username

This sets the login username in cases when you are using the TINI stick as a PPP client, dialing into a PPP server. It gets used in conjunction with the –x, –d, and –p options. For instance if you have a dialup account at an ISP and you are trying to form a connection to it with a TINI stick, you would use this option and enter the account login ID that you use with the ISP.

-s

This is the start server option. You use this when you want the TINI to act as a PPP server and await an incoming phone call from another computer. You use it in conjunction with the –x, –a, and –r options.

-d

This is the dial up a server option. You use this when you want the TINI to act as a PPP client and call a PPP server such as an ISP. You use it in conjunction with the –x, –p, and –u options.

-x serial_port_number

This defines which serial port you want to use for the PPP connection. This gets used whenever you are forming a PPP connection. Oddly, it doesn't seem to be documented.

Usage Examples

Suppose you want to form a PPP connection with an ISP. You have a login account with a name (rosie) and a password (dalmation). You want to use serial0.

```
ppp -x 0 -d -u rosie -p dalmation
```

The –x 0 is for serial0, the –d for dialup, the –u and –p for username and password.

Suppose you want to form a PPP connection with your laptop. You want to use serial0. You will type the following on TINI:

```
ppp -x 0 -s -a 207.168.0.5 -r 130.130.132.10
```

The –x 0 is for serial0, the –s for start server, the –a and –r are the IP addresses of the PPP interfaces on the TINI and the laptop, respectively. If the TINI has an IP address defined for the Ethernet interface, the PPP interface should have an IP address on a different network. The same is true for the laptop. For instance, if you TINI eth0 at 192.168.0.5, and the laptop eth0 at 192.168.0.2, you can't put their ppp IP addresses on the 192.168.0.x network. You get the ppp.UP event, and the interface will be present, but nothing can communicate. You can, however, put them at 192.168.10.x such as 192.168.10.9 and 192.168.10.12, respectively. If both are stand alone, with no other interfaces, you can pretty much use any numbers you want. The command, above, will be entered on the TINI. The TINI will wait for an incoming call from the laptop. On the laptop, it will be just like you are calling an ISP. (You have to have a userID and password setup on TINI, because authentication will be performed.)

The PPPCommand.java code

The PPPCommmand.java code provides an implementation for the *Slushcommand* and *PPPEventListener* interfaces. The code can be broken down into roughly three categories.

1. Code that implements the *SlushCommand* interface for the command *ppp* and its command line parameters.

2. Code that implements the `PPPEventListener`, implementing the FSM that we discussed earlier.

3. Misc utility methods.

   - `closePPP()`
   - `closeSerialPort()`
   - `openSerialPort()`
   - `createIPFromString()`
   - `waitForCall()`
   - `waitFor()`
   - `ATCommand()`
   - `login()`
   - an inner class called `ModemCommand()`

We're not going to dive into the details of the code itself, beyond identifying some slight modifications we had to make in our experiments to get it to work. There are four changes you have to make in order to use the ppp command.

1. Early in the PPPCommand.java file there is an inner class called `ModemCommand`. A `ModemCommand` object called `dialSequence` is later created. You must modify this to contain the phone number of your ISP. We also found that it's helpful to increase the timeout value from 30 to 60.

2. In the `execute()` method, where the program decides whether or not to call a server, you must add the line `ppp.setDefaultInterface(true);` right after the line `ppp.setPassword(password);`

3. In the `waitForCall()` method, after the first `waitFor("RING", null, 0);` line, add two more just like it.

4. In the `waitForCall()` method, in the line

    ```
    if (!atCommand(new ModemCommand("ATA\r", "CONNECT", 25)))
    ```

    change the timeout value of 25, to 120.

With those changes, rebuild Slush to include the `PPPCommand` class, so the command ppp is implemented. Detailed instructions for this are in Chapter 7.

TINI as a PPP client using the Slush command ppp

We're now going to assume that you've succeeded in making the changes to Slush described in the previous section, and that you've succeeded at getting the PPPClient program to work on a TINI. So we know we've got a cable that works with your modem, and dialing strings that work, etc. Connect a modem to TINI serial0, Telnet into the TINI via Ethernet, and do the following commands. Be sure to substitute your username and password, where you see the words username and password in the results below. (These are the username and password required by your ISP)

```
TINI /> downserver -s
Warning:  This will disconnect users on specified servers.

OK to proceed? (Y/N): y
[ Wed Feb 13 09:12:01 GMT 2002 ]  Message from System: Serial server
stopped.

TINI /> ppp -d -x 0 -u username -p password
PPP connection established

TINI /> ipconfig -x
Interface 0 is active.
Name         : eth0
Type         : Ethernet
IP Address   : 192.168.0.5
Subnet Mask  : 255.255.255.0
Gateway      : 0.0.0.0

Interface 1 is active.
Name         : lo
Type         : Local Loopback
IP Address   : 127.0.0.1
Subnet Mask  : 255.0.0.0
Gateway      : 0.0.0.0
```

```
Interface 2 is active.
Name          : ppp0 (default)
Type          : Point-to-Point Protocol
IP Address    : xxx.xxx.xx.xxx
Subnet Mask   : 255.255.255.0
Gateway       : 0.0.0.0

Interface 3 is not active.

TINI /> ppp -c
PPP connection closed
```

It pays to use a modem that has a speaker, because that will give you some feedback as to where you are in the dialing process. There can be a long pause (~1 minute) between issuing the command and getting the *PPP connection established* message. Where you see xxx.xxx.xx.xxx in the results, your server assigned IP address will appear. The ppp -c command is used to shut down the PPP connection. We only showed this here because you need to shut down the connection before we open it again, which is what we're going to do in the next section.

TINI as a PPP server using the slush command ppp

We're now going to assume that you've succeeded in making the changes to slush described in the previous section, and that you've succeeded at getting the PPPServer program to work on a TINI. So we know we've got a cable that works with your modem, and dialing strings that work, etc. Connect a modem (such as the cell phone) to TINI serial0, Telnet into the TINI via Ethernet as root, and do the following commands. Then, from a PC connected to a second modem, call the modem connected to the TINI. Enter a username and password valid for the TINI you are using.

```
TINI /> ppp -s -x 0 -a 192.168.10.9 -r 192.168.10.12
PPP connection established

TINI /> ipconfig -x
Interface 0 is active.
Name          : eth0
Type          : Ethernet
IP Address    : 192.168.0.5
Subnet Mask   : 255.255.255.0
Gateway       : 0.0.0.0
Interface 1 is active.
Name          : lo
Type          : Local Loopback
IP Address    : 127.0.0.1
Subnet Mask   : 255.0.0.0
Gateway       : 0.0.0.0
Interface 2 is active.
```

```
Name          : ppp0 (default)
Type          : Point-to-Point Protocol
IP Address    : 192.168.10.9
Subnet Mask   : 255.255.255.0
Gateway       : 0.0.0.0
Interface 3 is not active.
```

We now have a PPP connection between the TINI and the PC. You can Telnet and FTP over either the Ethernet interface and/or PPP interface. Applications running under Slush can use either also. You don't have to use the IP addresses shown, just make sure the Ethernet addresses and the PPP addresses are on different networks.

Summary

This chapter has examined TINI IP networking, with an emphasis on PPP. We looked at the `ipconfig` command in detail, and examined how TINI does PPP. Ways of making TINI behave as a PPP client to the Internet or a PPP server to a PC were presented. Examples included standalone applications, as well as implementing the optional `ppp` command in slush. The `ppp` command is a convenient, more sophisticated way of achieving PPP connectivity than some of the simpler examples shown. But the process of getting the cable, modem, and PPP software to work together can be difficult, and it pays to take an incremental approach:

1. Learn how to use AT commands with your modem by connecting it to a PC (via a straight-through cable) and talking to it with a terminal emulator.

2. Learn how to get a TINI to properly talk to a modem by using the proven AT commands and a specially made crossover cable. Be mindful that DTR resets the TINI, but may be needed by the modem (as well as RTS).

3. Try dialing out to an ISP, with TINI acting as a PPP client. Remember, the ISP must support PAP (Password Authentication Protocol).

4. Try dialing into TINI from a PC, with TINI acting as a PPP server. This requires two modems and two phone lines. We used a cell phone, with a special accessory cable that allows it to be used as an RS232 modem. Remember, cell phones and modem may have varied requirements with respect to *answering* calls.

5. Implement the optional command ppp, by making the modifications described in this chapter, and then following the instructions in Chapter 7 on modifying Slush.

Common problems include the cable (not crossover, not providing DTR and RTS to the modem), failure to shut down the serial server before starting PPP, failure to get rid of old processes/connections before starting up new ones, mixing up java files during compilation (keep everybody separate), and having an incorrect modem setup. If you run across something that defies explanation, *specifically*, the case when you receive the UP event but the ppp0 interface never shows up after an ipconfig: clear the heap, goto JavaKit and fill the flash full of 0's, and reload the firmware. Last but not least, always be watching the TINI message archives. If you're having trouble, someone else has probably had the same problem and fixed it.

References

1. Modem AT commands fall under TIA/EIA/IS707-A.3. Wireless enhancements to the command set are covered by ITU-T recommendation V.250. For more AT command information, visit www.modem.com. For information about cell phones as modems, visit http://www.shorecom.com/wirelessly.html

CHAPTER 14

A Few Final Thoughts

Recent advances in computers and networking technology have spurred tremendous interest in the development of computer-controlled devices, smart appliances, and so called web-enabled devices: electronic devices that communicate directly with the Internet. We hope this book has helped jump start you on the development of your own web-enabled devices using commercially available electronics.

Using a generic, Java-programmable network interface with a wide variety of interface busses, you can now make just about any device a network device. In this chapter we will briefly comment on the future of TINI and some of the many possibilities for connecting devices using TINI as the network controller.

The Future of TINI

During the early development of this book, Maxim Integrated Products Inc.[1] purchased Dallas Semiconductor. Before this purchase, Dallas had big plans for future versions of TINI. All indications are that these plans will continue to develop into new TINI products. Look for continued improvements to TINI in the coming months and years. By the time you read this book Dallas Semiconductor will have released the TINI software version 1.1, which will include several significant improvements.

- Dynamic class loading.
- Object serialization.
- Reflection.
- IPv6.
- Prioritized processes and threads.

---

[1] Maxim – http://www.maxim-ic.com/

- Stack traces.
- Support for mountable file systems.

Dallas Semiconductor has also announced[2] and released a preliminary datasheet for the DS80C400[3] Network Microcontroller that is expected to replace the 80C390 microcontroller on a future TINI version. The 80C400 will be an integrated CPU, 1-wire interface and 10/100 Ethernet interface. It will support the following features:

- Flat 16-MB address space.
- CAN 2.0B controller.
- Three full-duplex serial ports.
- Eight bidirectional 8-bit ports.
- Support for IPv4 and IPv6.
- Clock rates up to 50 MHz.
- 16 total interrupt sources with 6 external interrupts.
- Programmable IrDA clock.
- Advanced power management.

Dallas Semiconductor is clearly on the right road to reducing the chip count of the TINI chipset for reduced cost, size and power on future versions of TINI.

Connecting Your Device

There are many visions of the networked future, with everything connected to and controllable through the Internet. Some fanciful visions include refrigerators that will track your home food inventory and automatically reorder your groceries as you consume them. Other visionaries dream of the days when all of your home appliances (like your dishwasher and clothes washer) will be networked and will automatically send email to the proper service technician when *the appliance* determines that it needs maintenance.

While these (and other visions) are certainly possible, the value of these services seems questionable, particularly after considering the added cost to add a network capability to a low-cost appliance and the added cost of providing a network connection and the monthly monitoring service.

---

[2] Dallas Semiconductor Re-Engineers Its Microcontrollers For Network Computing, March 20, 2001 – http://dbserv.maxim-ic.com/view_press_release.cfm?release_id=284

[3] 80C400 product datasheet (preview) – http://www.dalsemi.com/TINI/ds80c400.pdf

Why internet-enable anything?

While the need to network *everything* seems questionable, there is plenty of reason for connecting *certain* devices to either a LAN or the Internet. One of the more compelling reasons is that an embedded controller no longer needs a display or hardware user interface. A standard web browser can become the standard user interface (everyone has one of those, right?) for your device. The user requires no new software to monitor and interact with your hardware and you can reduce the cost of your design by eliminating the need for user interface hardware (keyboard, display, etc). Another benefit is that the Internet provides a way for you to collect operational data about your device and learn how and when your customers use it and what features they use or don't use. This also provides a way for you to add features or correct problems in the software remotely.

So, why use the Internet? Why not use one of the many other available network technologies? First and foremost, the Internet (and Ethernet) has become very common and so connectivity (routers, hubs, network interface cards, cables) is cheaper than with most proprietary communications schemes. Most office buildings have full network connectivity (even if it's just a LAN) and many houses are now being fully wired for Ethernet. This existing network can now be the basis of home or office automation and monitoring tasks previously done with other wired networks. Worldwide connectivity via the Internet is everywhere (almost). By taking advantage of this, you can monitor and upgrade your devices over great distances almost as easily as if they were in the same room. The Internet also provides an easy means for distributing some of the processing load to other computers. By using a standard network and a TINI (which provides access to this network almost for free), you might monitor a collection of weather or environmental sensors, for example, distributed all over the world. While TINI is well suited for the task of monitoring sensors and reporting data over the network, a networked TINI could then retrieve additional weather-related information from publicly accessible weather servers. Additionally, data that may be too computationally intensive, such as the time of sunrise or the phase of the moon, could be calculated and retrieved from a computer on the network that is more suited to the task.

Possibilities

Throughout this book we have discussed and demonstrated the many interfaces available to you for controlling hardware and reading sensors—from I²C, CAN, 1-Wire, parallel IO, and serial ports.

We have also discussed and demonstrated the many ways TINI offers to connect to your LAN and the Internet: 10 base-T, RS-232 serial connection, and PPP connections.

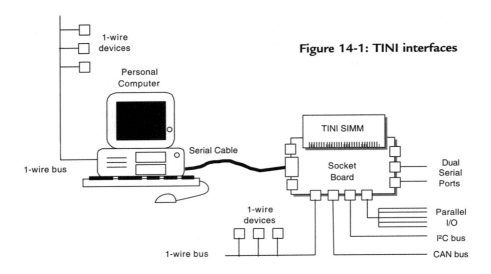

Figure 14-1: TINI interfaces

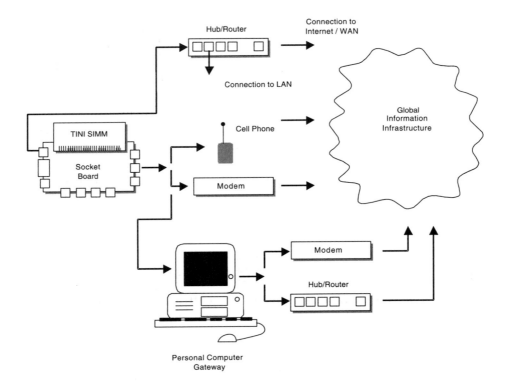

Figure 14-2: TINI network connections

Using TINI as the base of your next embedded hardware design provides you with all of the tools to network enable *just about anything* (sensible or not). Here are just of few of the limitless possibilities of devices you can embed with TINI to make a remote networked device:

- Instrumentation and laboratory processes.

- Remote monitoring of manufacturing facilities, office buildings.

- Home or office alarm systems.

- Monitoring of distributed events (weather stations, remote seismic stations, environmental monitoring).

- Even networking your coffee pot (as silly as this may seem at first, this is little more than a scaled-back implementation of remote monitoring and control of things like manufacturing processes).

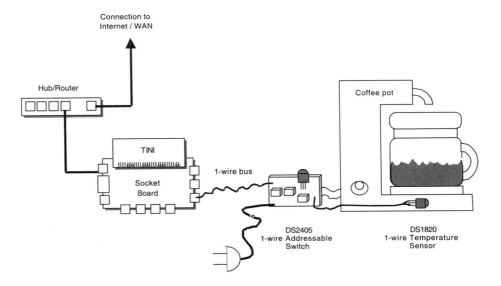

Figure 14-3: TINI networked coffee pot

What's Been Done with TINI

A number of talented developers have produced a very interesting and varied array of applications using TINI. Here is a sampling of some of the hardware and software development using TINI.

TINI Ethernet MP3 Player[4]

The MP3elf is an Ethernet-connected MP3 player that receives an MP3 stream from a local area network server and delivers it to amplified speakers or a hi-fi system. The MP3elf hardware is based on the STA013 MP3 decoder chip (from STMicroelectronics) and a TINI single-board Java computer.

TINI CAN Monitor[5]

TINI is used in a prototype system that is able to establish an on-line connection between agricultural equipment with CAN sensors (that senses monitor equipment operating conditions) and a TCP/IP-based network for data analysis.

Servertec Web Server for TINI[6]

The Servertec Internet Server is a Web Server designed to run on TINI. Using this server, developers can easily create web-based applications that interact with a wide range of devices to control lighting, heating/cooling units, door entry, refrigeration, medical testers, monetary transactions, appliances and vending machines.

X10 Libraries for TINI[7]

Jesse Peterson has developed a Java library that can control both the CM11A and CM17A X10 controllers. This allows you to control X10-enabled devices from Java programs running on TINI.

TINI WAP Server[8]

The lightweight server allows any WAP-enabled PDA or cell phone to be served with WML and WMLScript based applications from a TINI embedded device. This server includes full image support to send WBMP and PNG graphics to the wireless browser.

TINI Beer Keg[9]

The device demonstrates the use of TINI for remote monitoring the status of an office beer keg (temperature and volume remaining).

---

[4] TINI Ethernet MP3 Player — http://mp3elf.net/
[5] TINI CAN Monitor — http://www.precisielandbouw.nl/project/tini/CanMonitor.html
[6] Servertec Web Server for TINI — http://www.servertec.com/products/tini_iws/tini_iws.html
[7] X10 Libraries for TINI — http://www.jpeterson.com/rnd/
[8] TINI WAP server — http://www.sysgen.co.uk/Products/TINIwap/tiniwap.html
[9] TINI Beer Keg — http://www.dolske.net/hacks/beer/

TINI Drink machine[10]

TINI monitors the drink machine in the Rochester Institute of Technology Computer Science building. This uses 1-Wire devices that include switches and a temperature sensor for each slot.

Toasty[11]

TINI is the heart of a true Internet appliance, a toaster that collects weather forecasts and burns that forecast onto a piece of bread.

* * * * * * * * * * * * * *

In the early 90s, when most people were just becoming aware of the Internet, there were a few university labs experimenting with connecting hardware to the Internet. The *webcam* was born. Nowadays, just about everybody has an Internet connection at home, and at work, our photocopiers, laser printers, and lab instruments are all IP addressable on a LAN. Web browsers are an integral part of how we access information. Do *you* have some project idea that you would like to put on the Internet? Are *you* ready to build the better Internet mousetrap? We hope this book will give you a good start, by introducing how to build Internet-enabled devices via an inexpensive, ready-made, Java-powered microcontroller.

References

1. Warren Webb,
   Ethernet Invades Embedded Space,
   EDN, September 11, 1998, pg 71-80

2. Warren Webb,
   Embed The Web for Fun and Profit,
   EDN, March 18, 1999, pg 57-68

3. Warren Webb,
   Designing Web Appliances on a Shoestring,
   EDN, April 13, 2000, pg 89-96

4. NS Manju Nath,
   Low-Cost Techniques bring Internet Connectivity to Embedded Devices,
   EDN, November 11, 1999, pg 159-166

5. Dan Strassberg,
   www.your_instrument.com,
   EDN, September 2, 1999, 101-108

---

[10] TINI Drink Machine — http://www.csh.rit.edu/projects/drink/
[11] Toasty — http://www.dancing-man.com/robin/webhome/report2.htm

6. Richard A Quinnell,
   Web Servers in Embedded Systems Enhance User Interaction,
   EDN, April 10, 1997

7. Nicholas Cravotta,
   Managing Internet Enabled Devices,
   EDN, September 20, 1001, pg 48-60

8. Bill Travis,
   Sensors Smarten Up,
   EDN, March 8, 1999, pg 76-86.

Index